Ritual, Caste, and Religion in Colonial South India

Neue Hallesche Berichte

Quellen und Studien zur Geschichte und Gegenwart Südindiens

Im Auftrag der Franckeschen Stiftungen zu Halle
herausgegeben von
Michael Bergunder und Daniel Cyranka

Band 9

Ritual, Caste, and Religion in Colonial South India

Edited by Michael Bergunder, Heiko Frese, and Ulrike Schröder

Verlag der Franckeschen Stiftungen zu Halle 2010
Harrassowitz Verlag in Kommission

Bibliografische Information der Deutschen Nationalbibliothek:
Die Deutsche Nationalbibliothek verzeichnet diese Publikation in der Deutschen Nationalbibliografie; detaillierte bibliografische Daten sind im Internet über http://dnb.d-nb.de abrufbar.
Bibliographic information published by the Deutsche Nationalbibliothek:
The Deutsche Nationalbibliothek lists this publication in the Deutsche Nationalbibliografie; detailed bibliographic data are available in the internet at http://dnb.d-nb.de

ISSN 2190-7331
ISBN 978-3-447-06377-7

Satz: Ellen Weinel
Index: Sara Heinrich
Umschlag: Daniel Cyranka
Druck: dmv druck-medienverlag GmbH, Halle-Queis

Contents

Caste

The Telugu context

Appendices

Introduction[1]

This book focuses on colonial South India, a field of research that has been neglected in the past. Taking an interdisciplinary approach, it centres on the interrelated concepts of 'ritual', 'caste', and 'religion', which had a deep impact on cultural and religious change in colonial South Indian society. These concepts were embedded in wider-ranging discourses, often mirroring social conflicts and challenging political and religious authority. They provided, thus, dynamic resources for the negotiation of social, cultural and religious identities within colonial society. There is a particular focus on the analysis of printed media, which became established as a form of communication at the time, in English and in South Indian vernacular languages, and how they contributed to the transformation of identities.

This volume is divided into two parts. The first deals with studies of Tamil sources, the second with those of Telugu. It should be kept in mind, however, that there was an extensive discursive interaction across language borders, which can be seen in the caste-related articles, and that the Tamil and Telugu contexts both came under the same colonial administrative structure of the Madras Presidency. Andreas Nehring's article, on performance and performativity in the colonial discourse in South India, opens the Tamil section and, due to its span of theoretical reflections, provides a helpful introduction to the book as a whole. His reflections connect with the history of Saiva Siddhanta, which serves to introduce a section of articles related to this topic. Nehring begins with thoughts on culture, cultural turn, and postcolonial studies. He presents theoretical deliberations on representation and performance, which he illustrates and contextualizes with regard to the encounter between Saiva Siddhanta leaders and protestant missionaries in the first decade of the twentieth century. Nehring interprets the ritualized quotations of Bible

[1] This book project has its origin in a conference on "Ritual, Caste, and Colonial Discourse in South India", hosted by two research projects financed by the German Research Foundation (Deutsche Forschungsgemeinschaft – DFG): The SFB 619 A6, "The Discourse of Non-Brahmanical Rituals and Their Transformation Within the South Indian History of Religions Since the 18th Century", and the DFG-Project "Religion, Caste, and Nation: Discourses of Identity and Power in Telugu Journals of the Late 19th and Early 20th Century". The Symposium took place in Heidelberg in September 2008. We thank all those involved for making this conference possible and for the success it turned out to be.

verses in Saiva Siddhanta writings as a 'performance' that subverts hegemonic discourse.

Michael Bergunder follows with a contribution on J. M. Nallasvami Pillai, the most influential voice of Saiva Siddhanta in the late nineteenth and early twentieth century. He traces Nallasvami's particular way of argumentation, with an examination of one of his programmatic essays, and locates his views within the debates on Hinduism in colonial India of the time. Bergunder argues that framing the South Indian Saiva Siddhanta revival within the perspective of the later emerging Tamil nationalism has ignored its aspect of religious universalism, and he relates this argument to reflections on agency and the appropriation of Indian traditions within the colonial discourse.

Maraimalai Adigal, one of the key figures of the Tamil Saivite revivalist movement, stands in the centre of the article by Ravi Vaitheespara. Inspired and influenced by certain strands of European and missionary orientalist discourses, Maraimalai reimagined and renegotiated the notion of caste and caste hierarchy by authoring a counter narrative, which reclaimed caste as a Tamil creation. Vaitheespara sketches the political and socio-cultural developments of Maraimalai's time. He argues that Maraimalai's understanding and deployment of Saivism and Saiva Siddhanta signals a new understanding of Saiva practices as 'religion', and that the major thrust of his writings on caste was to fight and argue against its actual discriminatory practice in the contemporary Tamil context.

Peter Schalk analyses the thoughts and actions of Arumuga Navalar, one of the leading figures of Saiva Siddhanta among the Vellalars in nineteenth-century Jaffna, who connected concepts of Saiva Siddhanta with those of class, caste and ethnicity. Schalk takes a critical look at the different historiographical representations of Arumuga in the literature. He argues, against the established narrative, that Arumuga was trying to defend and sustain a continuous tradition of Saivism, based on the Agamas, against the attacks of Christians and against the rise of alternative elites among Tamil speakers, which he did by employing ritual formalism and traditionalism as indicators of orthodoxy and orthopraxis.

Though almost every article in this book deals, in some measure, with ritual and caste, there are contributions that are more explicit in their engagement with these themes. For this reason, within the Tamil section, there are parts that come under the heading 'ritual' and 'caste', though this is, to some extent, an arbitrary arrangement, as these themes are closely interrelated. The section on rituals begins with the impact of the Anglican Mission in South India. Robert Caldwell's book on 'The Tinnevelly Shanars', written in 1849, is the theme around which Ulrike

Schröder's reflections revolve. By elaborating on the various contexts of this often misunderstood or ignored work, its contents, the local (Tamil) circumstances which led to its emergence, the ideological missionary frames, and, not least, the global colonial settings and processes, the author identifies the discourses in which Caldwell's work participates. Through this, Schröder interprets the missionary agency at the time and the impact it had on the identity formation of the Nadars / Shanars, as well as on the comparative study of religion in the nineteenth century.

Through the writings of Grace Stephens, the Anglo-Indian superintendent of the Methodist Episcopal Zenana Mission from 1886–1919, Mary Hancock takes a look at the key topics of domesticity and femininity, associated with discourses on the zenana, in Methodist writing during the period between 1870 and 1920. She focuses on the material aspects of Christian subject formation and suggests that conversion be considered a process comprising material exchanges and embodied performances. These rely on, reproduce and rework codes of gender, race and class – this offers an important supplement to scholarship on the linguistic dimensions of conversion.

Torsten Tschacher writes about the changing ways of representing and imagining ritual among Tamil-speaking Muslims settled throughout Southeast Asia. His main sources of study are newspapers – he says that normative texts did not vanish, but they were complemented by a new vision of ritual, one that seems partly to be connected to this new type of media. Through poetry, participation in rituals was imagined, and individuals started playing a more important role in statements about them. The creation of public spheres probably also contributed to the representation of ritual, which witnessed a certain standardization of the parameters of ritual.

The section on caste begins with new material on a well-known topos. The agraharam, traditionally the exclusive living space of Brahmans in rural areas, is the theme of Chris Fuller's and Haripriya Narasimhan's article. They reflect on the transformation of social space and Brahman status in the Tamil context during colonial times and thereafter, and connect their insights with fieldwork carried out in Tippirajapuram, an agraharam close to the town of Kumbakonam.

By means of a close reading of the *Tami<u>l</u>a<u>n</u>*, a Tamil newspaper from the Madras area, Gnanasigamony Aloysius describes the vicissitudes of subaltern self-identification during the first third of the twentieth century. The contents of the journal reveal how subaltern groups in Tamilnadu tried to re-identify themselves both conceptually and concretely, in order to bring about a minimal congruence between power and the culture they represented, as Aloysius states. The targets of their efforts were, naturally enough, the Brahmans, who represented the other pole of an imagined power scale. Aloysius draws a detailed picture of the successes and dilemmas of this process of identification, connecting it with various historical developments and political discourses.

In the article 'More Kshatriya than Thou', A. R. Venkatachalapathy traces and discusses an ideological conflict between two castes in early twentieth-century Tamilnadu. The Nadars and Vanniyars, though not physical neighbors, began to dispute each other's status in the emerging public sphere of the early twentieth century, with the help of the print media. Venkatachalapathy's main sources are journals, published at that time, especially *Vaṉṉikula mittiraṉ* and *Kṣattiriya mittiraṉ* from the Madras region. Relating this debate to various colonial contexts, the paper interprets it as closely connected to the extensive organization of systematic knowledge about the colonized by the British.

Caste, identity and journalism build a bridge to the Telugu part of this volume. Three divergent yet related articles shed light on the northern part of the Madras Presidency; they recall accounts about identities and social reform in colonial Andhra, and trace discourses of power in the contexts of the sources used. Heiko Frese describes a Telugu-English journal from the nineteenth century and takes a closer look at statements of identity given therein. *Satya saṃvardhani* was a bilingual monthly, published over a period of ten years in Rajahmundry during the last quarter of the nineteenth century. Inspired and guided by Kandukuri Viresalingam, one of the leading intellectuals in the northern Madras Presidency of the late nineteenth century, it offered advice in religious and social matters. In this journal, written by Brahmans for Brahmans, clearly identifiable as pro-social reform, Brahman identities were challenged and negotiated in a new way, made possible by reform movements. Frese, who embeds his concept of identity in the philosophy of Laclau and Mouffe, attempts to reconstruct concepts of caste based on a study of its indigenous historical representation.

An anthology of essays by Kasibhatta Brahmayya Sastri (1863–1940), an orthodox Brahman scholar from coastal Andhra Pradesh, is the main source of Vakulabharanam Rajagopal's article on anti-reform discourse in Andhra. In this collection, *Upanyāsa payōnidhi*, Sastri gives his opinion on a number of topics concerning social reform, social reform movements and religion, positioning himself firmly among the traditionalists. Rajagopal arranges and classifies Sastri's views and ideas under a number of headings, reflecting on the cultural setting which influenced and was influenced by Sastri's work, and then connects this with a discussion on several aspects of nationalism.

It is the 'career' of a text in its cultural contexts that Velcheru Narayana Rao traces in his article about the *Sumati śatakamu*. Analysing its inner structures, its historical origins and its colonial reinterpretation, Narayana Rao shows how a guide to success in worldly life for upper-caste men became a general moral treatise, due to epistemological shifts in the colonial discourse. Using the *Sumati śatakamu* as an example, he demonstrates the effects of these epistemological shifts in the concepts of texts and authors in South India. In his concluding remarks, he suggests that legends about authors and texts cannot be dismissed as unhistorical, but that – in contrast to colonial practice and thinking – they are valuable sources in understanding the nature of an indigenous text-culture. This last chapter closes the book but, to the extent that Rao points beyond the self-imposed topical borders of this volume, it opens up possible new areas of concern and study. A variety of footholds then appears, from whence one could start another scholarly endeavour.

Note on transliteration

For ease of reading, in most cases where a word or term in a South Asian language is well-known in English – for example, Brahman – diacritical marks have not been used. Some words, less well-known in English and variously constructed in different South Asian languages, have also been transcribed without diacritics. When first mentioned, however, the ways of transcribing these words with diacritics in the different South Asian languages are provided. In order to facilitate reading, italics are not used. There remain in a few places, though, words that are rendered from the outset with diacritical marks and these are mostly italicised.

Andreas Nehring

Performing the revival: Performance and performativity in a colonial discourse in South India

One of the central theoretical concerns of colonial discourse theory, for a long time, has been the problem of representation and the political implications of representing the colonized in anthropology, Indology, literature and even art. Another line of theoretical reflection is related to the areas of anti-colonial resistance, counter-discourses, pre-colonial knowledge, knowledge subjugated in the dominant discourse, agency of the colonized, subaltern consciousness etc. In both fields of concern, the question of subjectivity or position of the subject is at stake. For further theoretical interventions into the field of colonial discourse – historically oriented as well as concerned with the present – the question of how these subject-positions are constructed seems relevant. While, during the 1960s and 70s, the focus of academic concern was predominantly on the social aspects of colonial encounter, postcolonial studies, since the 1980s, have shifted the emphasis of critique to a deconstruction of colonial knowledge and its underlying assumptions. The focus of attention has been moved from social aspects to the question of culture.[1]

The widely discussed 'Cultural Turns'[2] have furthermore led to a deferral in the validation of culture, from a constraint of culture as a predominantly mental affair and a moment of representation to an estimation of culture as a dynamic product and force of human activity and social practices. It can be argued that an anti-essentialist characterization of culture, as undertaken in various fields of cultural studies today, is a result of one of the major innovative theoretical shifts that took place in the late 1980s. "Cultures", James Clifford has maintained, "do not hold still for their portraits. Attempts to make them do so always involve simplification and exclusion, selection of a temporal focus ..."[3] This widespread analytical conviction has informed a variety of postcolonial attempts to analyse the colonial encounter as hybrid, unbounded, as 'in-between' spaces and the like. There is, nevertheless, a theoretical as well as practical problem in this emphasis on the fluidity of culture in postcolonial contexts. The estimation of culture as fluid seems best to serve the postmodern theorizers

[1] Thomas 1994.
[2] Bachman-Medick 2006.
[3] Clifford 1986: 10.

of western academia, but it rarely matches with the self-estimation of those who have been forced to establish new or transformed identity-positions in a colonial or postcolonial context. The essentialization of cultural identity as original, divinely created, national, racial, and the like, is widespread not only among fundamentalist but among a wide range of cultural agents in all postcolonial contexts. Therefore, hybridity or fluidity as analytical tools for those who analyse colonial encounters, to my mind, seem to be insufficient. How are colonial as well as postcolonial identities formed? What are the means to convincingly formulate identity-positions? I would like to argue that performance studies and theories of performativity have contributed to highlight the practical dimensions of producing culturally valid experience and meaning. Therefore, they could play an eminent role in analysing various colonial discourses.

Contesting the language of representation

Postcolonial studies have been at the forefront in pointing critically at the connection between the representation of the 'other' and power; or, to put it differently, they have attempted to deconstruct the politics of representation. Although Edward Said's *Orientalism* is often considered to be the key document of this critical theoretical move, at about the same time, similar critical shifts or turns in various fields of cultural and historical studies took place. The writing culture debate,[4] Hayden White's *Metahistory*,[5] Jacques Derrida's critique of western logocentrism, Richard Rorty's reflections on the *Mirror of Nature*[6], and several other theoretical interventions coming up around 1980, have been concerned with the problem of representation and in a way have questioned the assumption that language, speech and written texts are referring to the world 'out there'.

Words do not only name, describe, and judge; they also produce, constitute or create reality. Edward Said has called this relationship of reality and text, "the worldliness of a text". The question arises, how do words like Orientalist texts constitute the reality they describe? How do they function? Said has reflected on this question in his theoretical essay, *The World, the Text and the Critic*, in which he pointed out that every text is a text-in-the-world. All texts according to Said are worldly, "even when they appear to deny it, they are nevertheless part of the social world,

---

[4] Clifford and Marcus 1986; Marcus and Fischer 1986.

[5] White 1973.

[6] Rorty 1987.

human life, and of course the historical moments in which they are located and interpreted."[7]

Said's understanding of the worldliness of the text and his conceptualisation of Orientalism as a discursive formation, therefore, is an attempt to read texts in relation to an extra-textual, socially, and historically determined reality, which provides texts with a certain authority to function. Texts carry traces of the context in which they are written. They exceed by far that which is immediately visible and obvious in their words as signs.[8] The role of the critic is to "speak truth to power" by laying open these historically and socially determined discursive layers that inform a certain predication. Literary criticism, according to Said, implies a scrutinizing of stereotyped terms and words and their usage that contribute to form reality. If discursive formations shape the Orientalist and colonial speech, and if the Orientalist textual representations exercise a certain power on the colonized, the generative power of speech as such has to be analysed.

The 'contact zone'

Postcolonial theoretical interventions, by connecting anti-essentialist theoretical shifts with the question of power, differed largely from the classical paradigm of anticolonialism by challenging the unacknowledged essentialist assumptions of the latter regarding history, origin, race, subjectivity, culture, and even caste and language. The debate between postcolonial and anticolonial approaches, time and again, circulates around questions related to power and agency. Epistemologically the problem arises, whether postcolonial studies, by emphasising the epistemic force of colonial representation of the other, are at all able to recognize counterforce and resurgent movements.

Edward Said has consistently been criticized for presenting Orientalism as a single, monolithic formation of knowledge in which power is assigned only to the West; and thereby Europe, in a way, is essentialized as the central dominant force of all discourses, even in postcolonial criticism. Laura Ann Stoler and Frederic Cooper have accused postcolonial studies of adopting a "Manichaean conception"[9] of colonialism by giving Europe and the West a dominant and separated position in the study of the colonial period. Stoler and Cooper claim that Europe has been trans-

---

[7] Said 1997: 11.
[8] Compare also Ma Castro Varela and Dhawan 2005: 46.
[9] Cooper and Stoler 1997: 3.

formed as well in the colonial encounter and that postcolonial studies should not be limited to the effects of colonialism in the colony.

Mary Louise Pratt has introduced the term 'contact zone' for an analysis of travel accounts in colonial contexts; a term which helps to describe the space in which the interactions and processes of exchange in intercultural colonial encounters are to be located.[10] Pratt's intention is to reject the idea that these encounters are predominantly shaped by Western conquest and dominance. Contact zones are places of compromise, resistance, hybridity, adaptations, acculturation and imitation, and the term denotes a change in cultural studies from a chronologically structured discourse of identity that searches for roots to one that is structured in terms of space.

Dialogue in South India?

The assumption that power only runs from the Western metropolitan centre to the colonial periphery has also been questioned in historical studies on South India.

The historian Eugene Irschick, in a conscious bid to differ from Said's arguments, has termed the dispute between colonial authority and Tamil interests as a 'dialogue'. His book, *Dialogue and History*, published in 1994, is a striking example of an attempt to interpret the formation of a new Tamil identity during the 19th century as a product of dialogical processes, which were shaped by several agents from inside India as well as from abroad.[11] Irschick describes the changes in the rural society in the Chingleput District near Madras (Chennai) as a result of the joint project of British colonial officials and native inhabitants. Both Englishmen and the dominant South Indian groups in the society worked together in the construction of the 'Hindu-Past', which was presented as an internally very well ordered one in order to serve as a model for future cultural policy. Irschick's model of a colonial dialogue ensues from the idea that such a dialogue is possible, even if the dialogue partners have differing status in society and unequal access to power. He, therefore, questions the thesis that the political dominance of the British meant, at the same time, a sovereign power over representation. He suggests instead "that changed significations are the heteroglot and dialogic production of all members of any historical situation, though not always in equal measure".[12] By repudiating the authorship of the discourse, Irschick's approach elabo-

[10] Pratt 1992.
[11] Irschick 1994.
[12] Irschick 1994: 8.

rates the discursive order of the cross-cultural encounter in a more consistent manner than Said's.

> The argument here focuses less on the willed or repressive aspect of a colonial state as part of the construction of knowledge than on the dialogic, heteroglot productive process through which culture is formed.[13]

Cultural change is, therefore, not induced by colonial power alone, but by the indigenous as well as by the dominant participants of colonial dialogue. The heteroglot aspects of this dialogue are contained in every form of meaning and institution, and Irschick emphasizes, therefore, that it is impossible to reconstruct the pure origins of these meanings and institutions, irrespective of the fact whether they are 'British' or 'Tamil' in origin. In contrast to Ronald Inden, to whom the western representation of India appears as a closed discourse, Irschick adheres to the position of not 'essentializing' the different dialogue positions. The results of this dialogue – in this respect, Irschick as a historian comes closer to the post-colonial deconstructions of Orientalism as expressed by Homi Bhabha – are 'hybrid', that is, authorship cannot be fixed beyond doubt. However, in the case of Irschick, a problem has to be pointed out: does not the rejection of the question of authorship justify, at the same time, colonial authority? If there are no identifiable 'natural speakers' in the colonial encounter, be it traditional Indian society or concrete colonial interests, and if colonialism cannot simply be understood as the destroyer of indigenous culture, then we are left with only the creative process of inter-cultural dialogue in our analysis of the colonial discourse. This also means that even the criticism of colonialism can only be related to discursive structures.

I agree with Irschick's historiographic attempts to locate what he calls a 'dialogue' within a discursive formation which is deeply shaped by colonial power structures. As long as we talk of dialogue, encounter, exchange, and so on, we implicitly make use of concepts such as agency, subject-position, identity and the like. The insistence, however, of colonized groups on a subject-position or on self-identity as a counter-position to a colonizing centre is, as Gayatri Spivak has emphasised, not an easy claim. Her seminal essay, *Can the subaltern speak?*, is not only a critique of western conceptions of political representation, but also a caution against uncritical claims of subaltern subject-positions, untouched by dominant hegemonic power.[14] Not unlike Homi Bhabha, Spivak has emphasized that it would be a simplified view of these processes to

[13] Irschick 1994: 10.
[14] Spivak 1988.

differentiate radically the dominating forces and the subalterns as active and passive discourse partners respectively.

In his book on colonialism and the making of modern India, *Castes of Mind*, the South Asia historian, Nicholas Dirks, has been raising this question concerning the centre of power, which he specifies as a question of agency and a subject-position. I would like to follow Dirks, in the sense that to interpret the exertion of colonial power as a dialogue, like Eugene Irschick has attempted, hides the actual transaction of this power. Dirks interprets culture principally as an effect of power and insists "that contemporary assumptions about cultural difference have been largely produced out of the long history of colonial domination".[15] But how, then, is power exercised in the colonial encounter or, if you like, 'dialogue'. Since these "contemporary assumptions about cultural difference" Dirks is talking about are the manifestations of a discursive representation of what is central and what is marginal, some critics of the colonial discourse argue that the effect of this discursive production is that all counter-narratives are constantly entering the dominant culture. It was Edward Said who alluded to this aporia in his book on the Palestinian struggle, *After the Last Sky*:

> We can read ourselves against other people's pattern, but since it is not ours ... we emerge as its effects, its errata, its counternarratives. Whenever we try to narrate ourselves, we appear as dislocations in their discourse.[16]

And Dipesh Chakrabarty, in his well known essay *Provincializing Europe*, argued that all histories of African or Asian countries have the tendency to be nothing but variations of a European master-narrative.[17]

Saiva Siddhanta Samaj

How, then, if we do not consider this 'narration of oneself' as an encounter or dialogue in the sense of equal communication and mutual exchange, can such a reading of oneself "against other people's pattern" be interpreted. I suggest that some of the most prominent recent reflections on performance and performativity can shed a different light on single incidents as well as on religious, political and social movements in colonial India.

As an example, I take the Saiva Siddhanta Samaj (Tam. caiva cittānta-c camājam) and the publication *The Light of Truth or Siddhanta Deepika*

[15] Dirks 2001: 313.
[16] Said 1986: 140.
[17] Chacrabarthy 1992.

(referred to here on as *Siddhanta Deepika*). I will only focus on a small aspect in the history of the Saiva Siddhanta Samaj, namely the encounter with protestant missionaries in the first decade of the 20th century.

J. M. Nallasvami Pillai (Tam. je. em. nallacāmi-p piḷḷai, 1864–1920), the publisher of *Siddhanta Deepika*, a journal appearing since 1897, which has taken upon itself the publishing of Tamil and Sanskrit texts in the vernacular and in English translation, sketches the motivation to publish the magazine in its first issue:

> We have considered it a shame that we should be coached in our Veda and Vedanta by German Professions on the banks of the Rhine and the Ouse, and that an American from a far off country should be the first translator of the foremost work in Tamil philosophy and that an old Oxford Professor should sit pouring over the Tamil 'Word', and render it into English verse. All these facts redound greatly to the glory of the European, who could forget for the time being his narrow bit of native land, and his own selfish wants and go out to distant lands and to remote antiquities, in search of the diggings of the past and bay living laborious days, live to finish the task he had set to himself, in a thoroughly universal and truly Christian spirit. Noble examples these! May we follow![18]

Nallasvami, a Tamil Vellalar (Tam. veḷḷāḷar), is regarded as one of the spiritual leaders of the Saiva Siddhanta movement, and his son, J. N. Ramanathan, was one of the outstanding representatives of Saivism and a patron of Tamil culture in the 'Justice Party'. The significance of Nallasvami to the Saiva Siddhanta Samaj has been compared to that of Vivekananda for Advaita Vedanta. In 1897, on the 'commemoration day' of Queen Victoria's coronation, he began to publish the monthly magazine *Siddhanta Deepika,* with the intention:

> To transplant in the Indian soil some of those activities in the field of Indian religion and literature and history which are carried on in far off countries by Western Savants, and to stimulate indigenous talent to work and achieve a moderate share of success in these departments.[19]

Besides the publication of classical Tamil texts in the English language, *Siddhanta Deepika* consists of reports of conferences of the Saiva Siddhanta Samaj and essays by Europeans and Tamils on Tamil literature and Saivism. Nallasvami himself, who was considered an outstanding non-Brahman scholar in the Tamil movement, wrote extensively about Saiva Siddhanta (Tam. caiva cittāntam, Skt. śaiva siddhānta) and he taught on various occasions about the relationship of Saiva Siddhanta and Advaita Vedanta.[20] From 1905 onwards, he was involved in the organisa-

---

[18] *Siddhanta Deepika* 1 (1897/1898) 14.

[19] *Siddhanta Deepika* 1 (1897/1898) 14.

[20] Nallaswami Pillai 1911/1984. Cf. also M. Bergunder 'Saiva Siddhanta as a Universal Religion' in this volume: 30–88.

tion of annual conferences with the intention to unite the already existing Saiva organizations into a larger structure.[21] The Saiva Siddhanta Samaj was founded at the conference in December 1906 and in 1911, and the *Siddhanta Deepika* became the official organ of the Saiva Siddhanta Samaj. The essential aspects of the missionary work of the Saiva Siddhanta Samaj were laid down during this conference and recommended as a strategy for the individual local sabhas during the 1910 conference in Ramnad:

1. The publication of Siddhanta works and classical writings in Tamil;
2. Courses and lectures on Saiva Siddhanta during the year;
3. Social service for the downtrodden castes;
4. Improvements in temple administration, especially the opening of temples to the members of the lower castes.

R. S. Subramanyam gave a lecture entitled *The Work Before Us*, in which he proposed these points. He advised the conference to emulate the missionary work of the Bible-Societies. Yet, another important event was the talk given by Swami Vedachalam Pillai (Tam. cuvāmi vētācalam piḷḷai, 1876–1950) at the conference. Vedachalam was a co-founder of the Saiva Siddhanta Samaj, but had distanced himself from the conference in 1910 for political reasons. In a speech on the "social aspects of Saiva Siddhanta", he levelled similar criticisms against the ethical implications of Hindu idealism, especially the Advaita Vedanta, as often made by the western Orientalists, including the missionaries. Against this, Saivism was presented as a religion in which equality of all castes and social justice had been realized. Vedachalam, who, since 1911, referred to himself as Maraimalai Adigal (Tam. maṟaimalai aṭikaḷ), is regarded as a noted Tamil anti-Brahman reformer, who stood for the purity of the Tamil language and culture. He propounded a theory that the Vellalars were the original representatives of Tamil *iṉam*.

The Saiva Siddhanta Samaj regarded the Swaraj movement with reservations, because it was chiefly dominated by North Indian Brahmans. To be sure, the Dravidian movement had, in 1910, not yet been consolidated into a political entity, but even people like Vedachalam were, from the very outset, critically opposed to the Swaraj movement because of its Sanskrit domination. It was only in 1916 that the 'Justice Party' was formed, which stressed, in its manifesto, the loyalty of the non-Brahmans to the Crown and refused the 'Home-Rule' politics of Annie Beasant, the president of the neo-Vedantic Theosophical Society.

The above elucidated dialogic or hybrid moment in the colonial discourse in Tamilnadu becomes especially explicit in the reception of

[21] Balasubramaniam 1965: 98.

Christianity by the Saiva Siddhanta Samaj. Nallasvami had expressed positive sentiments towards Christianity at an annual Saiva Siddhanta Samaj conference in Tiruchirapally, when some Christian missionaries, who participated, expressed their gratitude for the invitation:

> The missionaries are people, who teach the truth according to their own conscience and are prepared to accept it where and when it encounters them ... We are especially grateful to them, because it is they who have initiated this revival of Siddhānta. If it were not for them, we would hardly have come together ...[22]

One German missionary from Leipzig, Hilko Wiardo Schomerus, published a report of this conference. He does not contradict Nallasvami's assessment. He even sees in Saiva Siddhanta a comrade for the Christian mission. His résumé of the conference, along with the annotations of the publisher of *Siddhanta Deepika,* not only illustrates the mutual interpretation of Christian mission and Saiva Siddhanta, but also shows how, in the light of post-colonial discourse analysis, the discursive conditions of Orientalist power can likewise result in the subversion of the dominance structures of representative authority. Schomerus writes:

> Several speakers quoted passages from the Bible which were almost every time received with applause, especially the beautiful verses from Hebrews XII about chastisement. So much are the Indians impressed by the sublimity of the Bible that they use it as a Pramāṇam, an observation I have often made. They endeavour to revive their religion in opposition to Christianity, but one sees they try to do it with the aid of thoughts and ideas derived from Christianity, which, of course, they will disclaim, but which is nevertheless a fact, and with a high esteem towards Christianity. Particularly the leaders are strongly influenced by Christian Mysticism, as I had occasion to learn from talks with them, and from their writings.[23]

To this estimation of a Lutheran missionary, V. V. Ramana Sastrin, the editor of *Siddhanta Deepika,* gives the following comment:

> The Hindus have, as Orientals, the greatest esteem for the Christian Holy Bible, because it is an oriental book in matter and manner, in spirit and in truth. They use the Holy Bible as an accessory in the interpretation of their own scriptures, solely to guide the present-day missionaries of the Christian faith in understanding the sense of the Holy Bible aright. The contention of the Hindus is that the Holy Bible is an exceedingly weighty document, but that it is being grossly misinterpreted by the Westerners. Consequently, what the Hindus do, is calculated more to open the eyes of the Christian missionaries, brought up in the schools of European materialism and commercialism, to the real truths enshrined in this

---

[22] Schomerus 1910.

[23] *Siddhanta Deepika* 11 (1910/1911) 228.

Holy Bible, than to help themselves. The greatest problem now is, how best to teach the Holy Bible to the West.[24]

The discourse in which the Gospel was supposed to have been brought closer to the Indians neither silenced individual dissenting voices, nor did it initiate a spate of conversions. Nallasvami's claim of a Gospel from the East and the eastern interpretation of Christ as the door to *śiva-darśanam* placed the missionary project of conversion, in view of its approximation to Bhakti, in a hopeless situation.

One could, in the words of Homi Bhabha, describe this association with Bhakti, which at first glance seems to reveal the intercultural nature of the Gospel, as 'mimikry', as a 'subversive mimesis', which exposes the ambivalence and the limitations of the Orientalist discourse. Bhabha launches his post-colonial criticism with the observation that the colonial power-discourse was interrupted time and again by native voices, which created for themselves a free space in their own language within the limits of the discourse. Bhabha's reading of the post-colonial texts reveals the voice of the colonial subjects that is always present in these texts, but which is brought to life only through a deconstructive reading of the text. He rejects Said's insistence that the post-colonial discourse was dominated one-sidedly by Europeans and tries to show the breaks and framework of the discursive authority in the various colonial texts. For this purpose, he refers to Michael Bachtin's model of linguistic hybridity that expresses a basic ability of the language to be identical and at the same time to be different, and to utter in the same statement two different social languages. Homi Bhabha interprets Bachtin's model of linguistic hybridity as a subversion of the monologic authority of the language and applies it to the colonial situation. Hybridity describes a situation in which the western representational monologues of the Orientalist discourse undermine the effects of colonial authority by expressing in the words of the natives something other than that intended. Colonial authority, according to Bhabha, does not mean suppression of the voice of the natives, but it is from the very beginning ambiguous. Bhabha sees in it a possible opportunity for the subversion of the colonial discourse.

Hybridity is the sign of the productivity of colonial power, its shifting forces and fixities: It is the name for the strategic reversal of the process of domination through disavowal (that is, the production of discriminatory identities that secure the 'pure' and original identity of authority). Hybridity is the revaluation of the assumption of colonial identity through repetition of discriminatory identity

---

[24] *Siddhanta Deepika*, 11 (1910/1911) 228.

effects. It displays the necessary deformation and displacement of all sites of discrimination and domination.[25]

The report that Schomerus gives on his encounter with members of the Saiva Siddhanta Samaj, is an attempt to understand the Tamil Saivites, but more importantly it reveals the authoritative claim of the European to be able to represent Indian religiosity and changes that have been initiated by the Samaj.

Then followed another Tamil paper on Guru-worship ... After him, a Brahmin read a paper on the esoteric meaning of the four paths, Śariyai, Kiriyai, Yogam and Jñānam. Unfortunately the preface was so long, that on the theme proper almost nothing was said. Nevertheless I take the liberty to delineate here in short the doctrine of the Siddhānta on the four paths.[26]

The very same report of Schomerus does, however, also reveal a difference, by showing that the Tamils have accepted in toto the representational forms of the European, in order to articulate something totally different from what was intended by the Europeans.

After the recess, the Secretary of the Conference delivered a lecture in elegant, finely-sounding Tamil on the Śivaliṅgam. He tried to explain the whole of idolatry symbolically. Even Kant's theory of the origin of the world had to submit to be used for that purpose, although Kant's name was not mentioned.[27]

Bhabha sees in the mimicking of European representational structures by the colonial subjects, which are never the copy of the European originals, a permanent interruption of the 'Master Discourse' that reveals the ambivalences of the Orientalist texts.

The Bible as the basis of the missionary claim of discursive dominance is taken away from the Europeans and made into a book from the East, which thus also justifies its hermeneutic legitimization against the West. The associative-strategy of the missionaries, which seeks to make the Siddhanta an instrument of the missionary work in Tamilnadu, was not rejected in toto, rather, its intentions were taken seriously and used against the work of the missionaries themselves.

---

[25] Bhabha 1994: 112.

[26] *Siddhanta Deepika* 11 (1910/1911) 26. H. W. Schomerus' book on Saiva Siddhanta (Schomerus 1912) was nevertheless considered to be "the most valuable and systematic treatise on Saiva Philosophy in the German language and the author has gone fully into the metaphysics and mysticism of the Philosophy". Balasubramaniam 1965: 51.

[27] *Siddhanta Deepika* 11 (1910/1911) 25.

Mimicry as performance

The assumption that words have power has informed Edward Said's criticism of Orientalism. Words and symbolic acts, under certain circumstances, have the power to create non-symbolic facts by mere execution. The central critical point of Said's intervention has been that he interpreted Orientalism not as a representational field that could be exploited by colonial power but as a field that exerted power by itself. Speaking is doing something.

Only recently, Thomas Blom Hansen has suggested studying the political role of Shiv Sena in Maharashtra, not in terms of its ideological background but in terms of its performance in society.[28] Blom Hansen is convinced that the performative approach to the role of Shiv Sena as a political organisation is fruitful because of two connotations that the term performative carries. Similar to Judith Butler, referred to later, he suggests that the term has, on the one hand, the meaning of dramatic action and, on the other, non-referentiality.[29] The whole debate about performance and performativity focuses on these two aspects. On the one hand, there is a concept of performance, as used in theatre or performance art, which refers predominantly to the act of playing or the moment of staging. On the other hand, there is a concept of performativity that is rooted in theoretical reflections on speech-acts. Culturalistic approaches to performance, as represented by Marvin Carlson,[30] Shoshana Felman,[31] Judith Butler, Sybille Krämer,[32] Erika Fischer-Lichte[33] and some others, try to bring together these two aspects and intend to describe the interface between performance and performativity.[34] Both aspects, I would argue, are present in various colonial discourses and the interface can be exemplarily seen as reflected in the annual conventions of the Saiva Siddhanta Samaj.

There is hardly any other basic conviction that has been more influential on the philosophical reflections on language than the one that assumes a connection between language and action; a connection which has been expounded first and foremost by John Longshaw Austin in his famous 1955 William James Lectures *How to do Things with Words*.[35] Austin, in the first of his lectures, differentiated between 'constative' and 'perfor-

28 Hansen 2004: 19–36.
29 Hansen 2004: 23.
30 Carlson 1996.
31 Felman 1983.
32 Krämer 2004.
33 Fischer-Lichte 2004.
34 Cf. Bublitz and Butler 2002: 21 ff.
35 Austin 1979.

mative' utterances. He proposed that while there are constative expressions that say something about the reality and can be validated as right or wrong, there are other predications that do not describe, report, or claim something, but do something.[36] Austin has used, as is well known, some ritual expressions as examples for his discovery of performative speech-acts: the baptism of a ship and the entailment of a watch. With the predication of "I baptize this ship ..." or "I entail this watch to ..." a certain act is performed.

Like all actions, a speech-act can fail if something goes wrong. Speech-acts depend on certain conditions in which they take place, on the authority of the performer, on the proper execution, and so on. Predications are always predications in a context. Austin, therefore, in a later lecture, dropped the differentiation between constative and performative expressions, since he realized that even constative expressions are subject to the conditions of success. All meaningful predications according to Austin's later conviction, therefore, are actions. Language has a communicative dimension and has to be seen as a predominantly social activity.

Pierre Bourdieu has taken up Austin's reflections on speech-acts and has emphasized the importance of the non-lingual context for the success of all predications. Bourdieu has criticized all language philosophy that neglects the social and cultural conditions under which utterances are produced. According to him, the power, position, authorization or legitimacy of the speaker in a certain situation is central for the performative success of any utterance. Speech-acts are institutionalized rituals and, as such, expressions of symbolic power, which are effective because of an authority which is itself outside of language.[37] Following Bourdieu's argument in the interpretation of colonial discourses, various Orientalist predications on other cultures by Europeans, such as racist devaluations, romantic admirations, critical editions of classical texts in Sanskrit or Tamil, as well as ethnological researches on society and caste in India, are significant not by themselves but by the authority of certain European institutions that legitimise them. If we would, specifically, apply Bourdieu's argument to an interpretation of the meetings and publications of the Saiva Siddhanta Samaj, the question would arise, as to who had been authorized and through which institutions to perform meetings and publish speeches that led to the formation of Neo-Saivite movement in Tamilnadu. Can the performative power of language in a colonial context be interpreted as a representation or incorporation of a non-verbal force? How, then, is power attributed to a non-Brahman Vellalar group of Saivites in Tamilnadu? Is the invocation of Queen Victoria and the inau-

[36] Austin 1979: 37 ff.

[37] Bourdieu 1990: 52 ff.

guration of the magazine *Siddhanta Deepika* an attempt to secure this extra-lingual legitimation? For a critical reading of *Siddhanta Deepika* and the success of the Saivite movement in a colonial context, the challenge is to highlight why language not only represents power, but executes power by itself.

Austin's disciple, John R. Searle, even more than Austin himself, emphasized the institutional character of language, which he considered as a standardized product of conventions, rules and regulations. The success of a speech-act, according to Searle, depends on the congruence with these conventions. All usage of language that is regarded as inauthentic – like quotations, theatre recitations, lyrics – Austin had disqualified as parasitic and not normal and, therefore, irrelevant for the understanding of performative speech-acts. How then do we interpret the performance of Bible-quotations by Saivite Hindus during their annual meetings?

For a critical analysis of colonial discourses, it is of eminent importance that this differentiation of language as authentic and parasitic has been criticized by Jacques Derrida, who has accused Austin and Searle of overlooking the iterability of language. Language functions by repetition. Derrida holds that structured language is only possible because of its inherent quotationability. Language includes the echoes of former predications or speech-acts. Quotationability or iterability is a necessary presupposition of any performative predication, since it can only be successful if it is recognizable as a repetition that is in conformity with a model. In other words, performative speech-acts are only successful if they are in some ways identifiable as quotation.

Derrida nevertheless cautions that the iterability of speech-acts should not be confused with mere repetition of the same. Iterability, as Derrida has emphasized, implies alteration, since every quotation is a repetition of former predications in a new context. Due to the contextuality of any meaning, every predication necessarily is a deferral of meaning, or as Derrida puts it, it is différant.[38]

Judith Butler has taken up Derrida's idea that the meaning of signs cannot directly be connected to the context of its usage since a sign is predominantly defined by its iterability, its ability to be repeated. What makes Butler's thoughts so interesting for the analysis of colonial discourses is that she has related this observation to the question of power. Butler is interested in challenging hegemonic discourses and hegemonic constructions of reality.

The challenge for the study of a movement in a colonial context, as for example reform-Hindu movements like the Saiva Siddhanta Samaj or

[38] Derrida 1988: 311.

Ramakrishna Movement or any other, is to dispute the very premises that have conventionally governed its politics. One needs to interrogate the manner in which certain concepts come to be seen as foundational to such movements and have come to acquire a hegemonic status in their new context. How does Tamil Saivism articulate itself? For Butler, one of the aims of radical political intervention is to challenge and critique the very terms in which political debates are expressed. We are reminded here of the long and ongoing debate about the antiquity of Tamil culture in which Nallasvami played a key role.[39] We can follow the deferral of concepts of origin, developed in western ethnographic and romantic views on culture in the 19th century, straight down to Tamilnadu.[40]

If speech, as predication of a discursive formation, has the power to change the world, it is only possible since the discourse has a history that not only precedes the present usages of language but informs them.[41] "[W]hen words engage actions or constitute themselves a kind of action, they do this not because they reflect the power of an individual's will or intention, but because they draw upon and reengage conventions which have gained their power precisely through *a sedimented iterability*."[42] Butler argues for an iterative model of the subject, relying upon Derridean citationality as her primary theoretical tool:

> In the first instance, performativity must be understood not as a singular deliberate act, but, rather, as the reiterative and citational practice by which discourse produces the effects that it names.[43]

The sedimented iterability, according to Butler, is closely connected to what she calls materialization. There is a constitutional link or an undissolvable entanglement between discourse and matter. Performative speech acts, in this sense, are quotations of conventions and discourses that have sedimented in historical processes. In a sense, they are comparable to rituals or ceremonial acts.

What is striking about the annual conventions of the Saiva Siddhanta Samaj, and of course of many other religious, cultural or political organizations in the late 19th century, is that in many ways they adopted European modes of expression and rituals that determined these meetings. If performativity can be explained in terms of a logic of iterability, as Butler intends,[44] and if predications gain their power through the historicity of

---

[39] See, for example, Kanakasabhai 1904; Raja 1909.

[40] Cf. Iyengar 1925; Savariroyan 1907.

[41] Butler 1997: 310 ff. This point has been emphasized by Sybille Krämer to whom I will refer. Krämer 2001: 252.

[42] Butler 1995: 134.

[43] Butler 1993.

[44] Butler 1998: 208.

conventions, then, the concept of performativity can help to highlight how power is effective in colonial discourses.

However, if performativity would just be a continuation of conventional speech-acts, it would be a continuous and conservative affirmation of already existing structures. Therefore, the question remains as to how change is possible and how hegemonic power can be broken or at least changed by discourses.[45] In the concluding part of her book, *Excitable Speech: A Politics of the Performative*, Butler asks whether a certain performative power results from the repetition of conventional rituals in non-conventional forms:

> I would insist that the speech act as a rite of institution, is one whose contexts are never fully determined in advance, and that the possibility for the speech act to take on a non-ordinary meaning, to function in contexts where it has not belonged, is precisely the political promise of the performative, one that positions the performative at the center of a politics of hegemony, one that offers an unanticipated political future for deconstructive thinking.[46]

The staging or performance of citational rituals, like the quotations of Bible-verses in the annual meetings of the Saiva Siddhanta Samaj, subverts the hegemonic evangelical missionary discourse by repetition and quotation. Whatever materializes in the colonial discourse, be it related to the question of identity or to alterity, is not the reflection of an ideal or universal concept but a sedimentation of repetitive predications. The performative approach, in my understanding, can contribute to explain the various religious, cultural and political identity-positionings that we are investigating in the colonial contact zones of South Asia.

Bibliography

Austin, John L. 1979. *Zur Theorie der Sprechakte.* (How to do things with words. <ger.>) Stuttgart: Reclam.

Bachman-Medick, Doris. 2006. *Cultural Turns. Neuorientierungen in den Kulturwissenschaften.* Hamburg: Rowohlt.

Balasubramaniam, K. M. 1965. *The Life of J. M. Nallaswami Pillai.* Tiruchirapalli: J. M. Somasundaram Pillai.

Bhabha, Homi. 1994. *The Location of Culture.* London: Routledge.

Bourdieu, Pierre. 1990. *Was heißt sprechen? Die Ökonomie des sprachlichen Tausches.* Wien: Braumüller.

Bublitz, Hannelore. 2002. *Judith Butler zur Einführung.* Hamburg: Junius.

Butler, Judith. 1993. *Bodies That Matter.* London: Routledge.

---

[45] Krämer 2001: 252.
[46] Butler 1998: 228.

——. 1995. 'For a Careful Reading', in: Benhabib, Seyla et al., eds. *Feminist Contentions. A Philosophical Exchange*. London: Routledge.

——. 1997. *Körper von Gewicht: Die diskursiven Grenzen des Geschlechts*. Frankfurt a. M.: Suhrkamp.

——. 1998. *Hass spricht: Zur Politik des Performativen*. Berlin: Berlin-Verlag.

Carlson, Marvin. 1996. *Performance. A Critical Introduction*. London: Routledge.

Chakrabarthy, Dipesh. 1992. 'Provincializing Europe: Postcoloniality and the Critique of History', in: *Cultural Studies* 6: 337–357.

Clifford, James and Marcus, George, eds. 1986. *Writing Culture: The Poetics and Politics of Ethnography*. Berkeley: University of California Press.

Cooper, Frederick and Stoler, Laura Ann, eds. 1997. *Tensions of Empire: Colonial Cultures in a Bourgeois World*. Berkeley: University of California Press.

Derrida, Jacques. 1988. 'Signatur, Ereignis, Kontext', in: Jacques Derrida, *Randgänge der Philosophie*. Wien: Passagen-Verlag, 291–314.

Dirks, Nicholas B. 2001. *Castes of Mind*. Princeton: Princeton University Press.

do Mar Castro Varela, Maria and Dhawan, Nikita. 2005. *Postkoloniale Theorie: Eine kritische Einführung*. Bielefeld: Transcript.

Felman, Shoshana.1983. *The Literary Speech Act: Don Juan with J. L. Austin or Seduction in Two Languages*. Ithaca-New York: Cornell University Press.

Fischer-Lichte, Erika. 2004. *Ästhetik des Performativen*. Frankfurt a. M.: Suhrkamp.

Hansen, Thomas Blom. 2004. 'Politics as Permanent Performance: The Production of Political Authority in the Locality', in: John Zavos, Andrew Wyatt and Vernon Hewitt, eds. *The Politics of Cultural Mobilization in India*. New Delhi: Oxford University Press.

Irschick, Eugene. 1994. *Dialogue and History: Constructing South India, 1795–1895*. Berkeley: University of California Press.

Kanakasabhai, V. 1904. *The Tamils Eighteen Hundred Years Ago*. Madras: Higginbotham.

Krämer, Sybille. 2001. *Sprache, Sprechakt, Kommunikation: Sprachtheoretische Positionen des 20. Jahrhunderts*. Frankfurt a. M.: Suhrkamp.

——. ed. 2004. *Performativität und Medialität*. München: Fink.

Marcus, George and Fischer, Michael, eds. 1986. *Anthropology as Cultural Critique. An Experimental Moment in the Social Sciences*. Chicago-London: University of Chicago Press.

Nallaswami Pillai, J. M. 1911/1984. *Studies in Saiva Siddhanta*. Madras: South India Saiva Siddhanta Works Pub. Society.

Pratt, Mary Louise. 1992. *Imperial Eyes. Travel Writing and Transculturation*. London: Routledge.

Raja, E. S. W. Senath. 1909. 'Glimpses of Ancient Dravidians', *Tamilian Antiquary* 1,5: 1–21.

Rorty, Richard. 1987. *Der Spiegel der Natur: Eine Kritik der Philosophie*. Frankfurt a. M.: Suhrkamp.

Said, Edward.1986. *After the Last Sky: Palestinian Lives*. New York: Pantheon Books.

——. 1997. *Die Welt, der Text und der Kritiker*. (The World, the Text, and the Critic. <ger.>) Frankfurt a. M.: S. Fischer.

Savariroyan, D. 1907. 'The Bharata Land or Dravidian India', *Tamilian Antiquary* 1,1: 1–28.

Schomerus, Hilko Wiardo. 1910. 'The Saiva Siddhanta Conference at Trichinopoly', *Siddhanta Deepika* 11,7, July: 27–28.

——. 1912. *Der Çaiva-Siddhānta. Eine Mystik Indiens.* Leipzig: J. C. Hinrichs.

Sesha Iyengar, T. R. 1925. *Dravidian India.* Calcutta: Asian Educational Service 1986.

Spivak, Gayatri. 1988. 'Can the Subaltern speak? Speculations on Widow Sacrifice', in: G. Nelson and L. Grossberg, eds. *Marxism and the Interpretation of Culture.* Basingstoke: Macmillan Education, 271–313.

Thomas, Nicholas. 1994. *Colonialism's Culture: Anthropology, Travel and Government.* Princeton: Princeton University Press.

White, Hayden. 1973. Metahistory: *The Historical Imagination in Nineteenth-Century Europe.* Baltimore: John Hopkins University Press.

Michael Bergunder

Saiva Siddhanta as a universal religion: J. M. Nallasvami Pillai (1864–1920) and Hinduism in colonial South India

J. M. Nallasvami Pillai (Tam. je. em. nallacāmi-p piḷḷai) is a household name in the history of Tamil culture and religion.[1] Arguably, he was the most influential propagator of Saiva Siddhanta (Tam. caiva cittāntam, Skt. śaiva siddhānta) in late 19th and early 20th-century India, and the main coordinator of a vast network of regional Saiva Siddhanta organizations all over South India and Ceylon. These had a considerable impact on cultural and religious debates in South India, which we know, for instance, from contemporary missionary reports.[2] Nallasvami was a typical representative of the English educated Vellalar (Tam. veḷḷāḷar) elite in colonial South India. He earned a law degree in 1886. From 1887–1893, he worked as a lawyer in Madurai and then became District Munsiff in different places of the Madras Presidency, a position he maintained for nearly 20 years. From 1912 onwards, he worked again as a lawyer in Madurai.[3] He was a prolific writer and conference speaker, translator of Tamil classics into English, and the main editor of the journal *The Light of Truth or Siddhanta Deepika* (referred to here on as *Siddhanta Deepika*), the central mouthpiece of the Saiva Siddhanta revival.

However, in sharp contrast to Nallasvami's undisputed importance stands his treatment in scholarly research, where he has been widely neglected.[4] One reason for this could be that he does not fit into the established scholarly narrative of Tamil Saivism in colonial South India. Gene Irschick set the tone. On the one hand, he emphasized that many non-Brahman Hindus in the Justice Party favoured Saiva Siddhanta; and he declared Nallasvami to be the leading propagator of Saivism as *the* 'Dravidian religion'. To prove further the close link to the Dravidian movement, he did not forget to mention that Nallasvami's son, J. N. Ramanathan, was "a prominent exponent of Tamil interests in the Justice

[1] The English transliteration of 'nallacāmi' varies; common are also the versions 'J. M. Nallaswamy Pillai' and 'J. M. Nallaswami Pillai'.

[2] See Nehring 2003: 335–341.

[3] See Vaitheespara 1999: 158–178.

[4] The small monograph of Balasubramaniam is not a scholarly biography (Balasubramaniam 1965). The best scholarly summary of Nallasvami's life and work is in Vaitheespara 1999: 158–178.

Party".[5] Yet, on the other hand, in Irschick's judgement, Nallasvami failed in his attempt to promote the Dravidian case:

> He had hoped through his work to unite non-Brahmans, but as he told a Justice Party conference in 1918, Saiva Siddhanta did not have the same force in mobilizing non-Brahman opinion as the Justice Party did.[6]

Other scholars have followed this path of interpretation. S. Kailasapathy acknowledges that Nallasvami's journal, *Siddhanta Deepika*, had "served for many years as the rallying forum for non-Brahmin Saiva protagonists".[7] Nevertheless, he also certifies that Nallasvami did not go along with the core convictions of other Tamil Saiva revivalists, since "Nallasvami Pillai was not anti-Sanskrit like Vedachalam", alias Maraimalai Adigal (Tam. maṟaimalai aṭikaḷ, 1876–1950), the leading figure of the Pure Tamil movement (taṉittamiḻ iyakkam). These circles would have considered him "too moderate".[8] Similarly, Vaitheespara observes a lack of clarity in Nallasvami's work:

> There was much ambiguity in Nallaswamy Pillai's revivalist efforts. Though he worked with great passion for the revivalism of Saiva Siddhanta and Tamil, his revivalist efforts were not characterized by the pronounced anti-Aryan or anti-Brahman ideology that was typical of many Dravidian ideologues. ... he did not wish to alienate the Tamil Brahmins.[9]

Hence, Nallasvami is seen as someone who was inconsistent in his views on Tamil revivalism and, in addition, there are certain doubts about the coherence of his views. This perspective regards the revival of Tamil Saivism and Saiva Siddhanta, in the 19th and early 20th century, as a mere precursor of the later Tamil nationalist and Dravidian movement. However, these developments only took on a clear shape as late as 1916, when the Justice Party was founded and, at least according to common historiography, the Pure Tamil movement was established.[10] Reading the whole Tamil Saiva renaissance, which started much earlier in the 19th century, against the background of these later developments makes it difficult to do justice to its complex and different identity positionings. The discursive context of prominent thinkers and activists, like Nallasvami, is measured by its contribution to later developments and not in its

[5] Irschick 1969: 292, see also Ryerson 1988: 61.

[6] Irschick 1969: 292–293.

[7] Kailasapathy 1979: 27.

[8] Kailasapathy 1979: 27, 45 note 13. Cf. also Sumathi Ramaswamy, who also says Nallasvami represents a "'moderate' Shaivism" (Ramaswamy 1997:30).

[9] Vaitheespara 1999: 159 note 103, 175.

[10] See Irschick 1969: 44–54; Vaitheespara has shown that there is no historical evidence to show that the Pure Tamil movement formally started in 1916, as later claimed (see Vaitheespara 1999: 462–480).

own right. Moreover, the later developments propose a dichotomy of identities (for instance, Brahman / Non-Brahman, Dravidian / Non-Dravidian) as an analytical starting point, which was itself the product of the colonial discourse. This needs to be historicized, but not reified through its application to earlier contexts.[11]

In any case, freeing the view of Nallasvami from preconceived notions proves to be very fruitful. It opens up the space to see that his understanding of Saivism was neither "moderate" nor incoherent, but in its own way quite radical; claiming no less than Saiva Siddhanta as a universal religion, far superior to the heavily criticized Advaita Vedanta oriented Neo-Hinduism. As Nallasvami's positions are widely unknown, a close reading of his most programmatic essay will be undertaken first of all, in order to trace his specific way of argumentation and analyse the sources he refers to. Next, Nallasvami's concept of Saiva Siddhanta as a universal religion will be located within the then contemporary debates on Hinduism in colonial India. This is followed by a closer look into the broader historical context of South Indian Saivism in the late 19th and early 20th century. The relationship between the South Indian Saiva Siddhanta revival, led by Nallasvami, and the emergent Tamil nationalism will be discussed; it will be asked whether universalist concepts, in 19th-century Tamil Saivism, existed before Nallasvami. In conclusion, some broader theoretical implications, raised by a universalist interpretation of Saiva Siddhanta, will be addressed.

'The Saiva Religion and Saiva Advaita Siddhanta Philosophy' (1909)

In 1909, the first issue of the journal *Siddhanta Deepika* published an article of Nallasvami with the programmatic title 'The Saiva Religion and Saiva Advaita Siddhanta Philosophy'. This article summarizes Nallasvami's ideas on Saiva Siddhanta in a comprehensive way and can be taken as a guide to his thought. The argument of the text is highly sophisticated and not easy to summarize. Nallasvami argued in at least three directions. Firstly, he tried to elaborate how "Modern Śaivism"[12], i. e. "Śaivism of the South"[13] or Saiva Siddhanta, stands in relation to the Sanskrit tradition; secondly, how it is related and superior to other Indian philosophies, especially Advaita Vedanta; finally, he defended Saivism against the Western critique of Hinduism, and conceptualized it as a universal religion in its own right.

---

[11] See Bergunder 2004; Srinivasan 2006.

[12] Nallasvami Pillai 1911m: 274.

[13] Nallasvami Pillai 1911m: 315.

Nallasvami started his discourse with reference to Max Müller, who had suggested that behind the six systems of philosophy stood an older ancient Indian tradition, a "National or Popular Philosophy"[14]. Saivism and Vaishnavism, as "the two popular Hindu religions of modern India",[15] are the direct heirs of this old philosophical tradition. Comparing them, Saivism is described as the religion of the "majority of Hindus"[16] and it represents, particularly, the "old traditional and parent religion of the days of the Vēdas and Upanishats, Āgamas or Tantras, and Itihāsas and Purāṇas, and bases its authority on these ancient revealed books and histories. It claims God Śiva to be the author of the Vēdas and Āgamas."[17]

Nallasvami then went on to explain this historical claim in greater detail, starting with a discussion of passages from the Rigveda (Skt. ṛgveda) on Rudra. He interpreted Rudra's (i. e., implicitly, Siva's) peculiar position there as if Rudra was already considered a supreme god.[18] He quoted directly from the Vedic texts, and his argument was not explicitly based on any Indian or Oricntalist authority. For certain etymological proofs, he referred to Sayana (Skt. sāyaṇa), the famous 14th-century commentator, whose views were also widely adopted by Western Orientalists in the 19th century.[19] Nallasvami made the case that core elements of Saivite cosmology could already be found in the Rigveda, quoting the first four verses from the creation hymn in X,129.[20] Though he did not mention it, he used a well-known translation by Monier Monier-Williams (1819–1899) with slight alterations, which suggests that he might have compared it to the original Sanskrit.[21] This method of using English Orientalist translations of Sanskrit classics, is characteristic of Nallasvami in all of his writings. The hymn deals with the "One" that existed before the universe, and Nallasvami laid special emphasis on the phrase "in the beginning there was neither sat nor asat"[22] as pointing to the core of later Saivite cosmology. When the hymn speaks

---

[14] See Müller 1899a: xviii. The book received a lengthy review in Siddhanta Deepika by V. V. Ramana Sastrin, see *Siddhanta Deepika* 3 (1899/1900) 59–81.

[15] Nallasvami Pillai 1911m: 273.

[16] Nallasvami Pillai 1911m: 273.

[17] Nallasvami Pillai 1911m: 274.

[18] For Rudra's position in the Vedas see Gonda 1978: 85–89.

[19] For a good overview of the contemporary Orientalist discussion of Sayana, see Griffith 1973: vii–x.

[20] For a modern indological interpretation of Rigveda X.129 see, for instance, Mehlig 1987: 67–76.

[21] Monier-Williams 1875: 22; Monier-Williams 1883: 13.

[22] Nallasvami Pillai 1911m: 277. Instead of "sat (being) nor asat (non-being)", Monier-Williams translated it into the more poetical "naught nor aught" (Monier-Williams 1883: 13). Nallasvami probably changed to the original "sat / asat" because of the central usage of these terms in the Saiva Siddhanta.

of "desire" as the "primal germ" that brings the universe into being, he identified this desire with the concept of icchā-śakti (Tam. iccā catti) in Saiva Siddhanta, where it was the main original cause of cosmological evolution.[23] It seems likely that Nallasvami, in his interpretation of Rigveda X.129, not only relied on the translation of Monier-Williams but also on his interpretation. Monier-Williams also suggested that this hymn was the "first dim outline of the later philosophical theories, both Sānkhyan and Vedāntic", and that the "idea of the female principle as necessary to the act of creation" is already "vaguely implied" in the mentioning of "desire".[24]

In his final discussion on the Rigveda, Nallasvami pointed to a well-known two-birds metaphor: "Two birds, inseparable friends, cling to the same tree. One of them eats the sweet fruits, the other 'Anya' looks without eating."[25] He highlighted the frequent quotation of the verse in the Atharvaveda and the later Svetasvatara (Skt. śvetāśvatara) Upanishad, the Katha (Skt. kaṭha) Upanishad, and the Mundaka (Skt. muṇḍaka) Upanishad. He characterized it as "the chief stronghold of Indian Theism against Idealism [i. e., Advaita Vedanta]"[26], which probably refers to Srikantha's or Ramanuja's interpretation of the two birds as showing the difference between the individual soul and the supreme soul; but Nallasvami did not explain it further.[27]

To further prove his point that theistic Saivism is rooted in the Vedas, he took a look at the Yajurveda in a similar way to the Rigveda. In the Yajurveda, he saw "the position of Rudra ... more established as Paśupati ... and as The One without a second"[28], and it contained already "the words Pati, Paśu and Pāśam"[29], the core terms of later Saiva Siddhanta. In the Tamil Saiva tradition, Siva is often referred to as the destroyer of the

---

[23] See Schomerus 1912: 68–69. In the Sanskrit original, "kāma" stands for "desire".

[24] Monier-Williams 1883: 14, see also 183; see also Monier-Williams 1875: 502.

[25] Rigveda I.164,20 (Nallasvami Pillai 1911m: 277). Nallasvami quoted from the translation of Max Müller, see Müller 1884: 38 (Mundaka Upanishad III.1,1), 251 (Svetasvatara Upanishad IV.9,6), but Nallasvami did not acknowledge his source. Moreover, 'Anya' was added by him and shows again that the translation was checked with the Sanskrit original. For an interpretation of Rigveda I.164 see Mehlig 1987: 56–67.

[26] Nallasvami Pillai 1911m: 277. See Atharvaveda IX.9,20 and Katha Upanishad III.1 (which is not a direct parallel, but given as a cross reference in Müller's translation, see Müller 1884: 12, 38 note 1).

[27] The two birds are mentioned in Srikantha's commentary of the Vedanta Sutras on several occasions, see Sastry 1897–1906: 2:73 (I.2.4.), 2:98 (I.3.1.), 3:159 (III.2.5.). For Ramanuja, see the translation of Ramanujas commentary of the Vedanta Sutras by Thibaut, which Nallasvami knew fairly well (Thibaut 1904: 98). However, in this translation, the verse is not given special attention; though see Monier-Williams, who gave it more prominence in his discussion on Ramanuja (Monier-Williams 1883: 120).

[28] Nallasvami Pillai 1911m: 277.

[29] Nallasvami Pillai 1911m: 280.

three cities (Skt. tripura, Tam. muppuram) of demons.[30] Nallasvami quoted from Tirumantiram, where the three cities are metaphorically explained as the three impurities (Tam. mummalam), which is a central theme in Tamil Saiva Siddhanta.[31] Nallasvami showed that this narrative goes back to a story of the destruction of three cities (Skt. tripurasamhāra) in the Yajurveda, which again provided for him a link to the Vedas.[32]

Nallasvami proceeded to the Upanishads. The development from the Vedas to the Upanishads resulted, in his view, in a further deepening of the belief in one God and the spiritualisation of rituals:

> the worship of the many Gods was being given up in favour of the one God, and the efficacy of sacrifices in general were being doubted, and a more spiritual form of worship was being substituted in its place.[33]

He referred to the Kena Upanishad, where he saw the beginning of this development. He quoted a lengthy passage,[34] where Uma (Tam. / Skt. umā), commonly identified as the wife of Siva, points to her "Lord", the "One Supreme Brahma" which, for Nallasvami, is identical with Siva. However, his main interest was in the Svetasvatara Upanishad belonging to the Yajurveda (Taittīriya), which he considered one of the founding texts of Saiva Siddhanta:

> The Śvetāśvatara Upanishat, the greatest authority of the Śaiva School, repeats the text of the Yajur Veda 'Eka Eva Rudrō Nadvitīyāya Taste',[35] and the philosophy of Advaita Siddhānta is fully expounded in this Upanishat. This Advaita is neither the Śāṅkhya nor the Yōga, neither Dvaita nor Advaita, as ordinarily understood. Hence, Oriental Scholars like Monier Williams, Professor Macdonnel [sic] and Garbe regard this Upanishat as the oldest representative of the ancient eclectic school of Hindu philosophy. With this book they couple the Bhagavat Gītā.[36]

---

30 For references in the Tamil Saiva literature, see e. g., Pope 1900: 175, 178; Peterson 1989: 34–35, 68, 116–117, 122, 128, 154, 169, 173, 181, 255, 288, 292, 303–304.

31 He quoted Tirumantiram Nr. 343, probably in his own translation. Nallasvami had published a translation of the First Tantra of Tirumantiram in Siddhanta Deepika, which was only finished in volume 13. See also Schomerus 1912: 101–179.

32 He referred to Taittiriya Samhita (Skt. taittirīya saṃhitā) vi.2.3. (see, for instance, the translation in Keith 1914: 504). Nallasvami directly quoted a longer passage where he gave both the original Sanskrit text and an English translation. As this is unique for him, one might assume he got the passage and translation from a pandit and not from the literature.

33 Nallasvami Pillai 1911m: 281.

34 Nallasvami Pillai 1911m: 281–282; the translation is from Max Müller, see Müller 1879: 149–151 (3.1–12, 4.1) (There are slight but unimportant modifications in Nallasvami's quotation).

35 Nallasvami probably referred to Yajurveda 1.8.6 and Svetasvatara Upanishad 3.2. (see also Nallasvami Pillai 1911l: 245). Max Müller translated: "For there is one Rudra only, they do not allow a second" (Müller 1884: 244).

36 Nallasvami Pillai 1911m: 283.

Nallasvami's main interest lay in the peculiar concept of God as a person in this Upanishad. He illustrated the notion of a personal God in the Svetasvatara Upanishad by long quotations,[37] and he emphasized that Max Müller compared the concept of a personal God in the Svetasvatara Upanishad to the Christian counterpart.[38] Although God is called "without qualities" (Skt. nirguṇa) in the Svetasvatara Upanishad, Nallasvami insisted that it does not mean he is impersonal, as taught by Sankara. He interpreted "without qualities" from the background of Saiva Siddhanta philosophy, where this does not mean that God is without any quality but only without the three qualities of matter (Skt. sattva, raja, tamas).[39]

Here, Nallasvami did not follow Müller's monistic interpretation of the Svetasvatara Upanishad,[40] but referred to other leading contemporary indologists, who were of the opinion that there existed an old eclecticism in the Indian tradition. He quoted Arthur Anthony MacDonell (1841–1930):

> Of the eclectic movement combining Śāṅkhya, Yōga and Vēdānta doctrines, the oldest representative is the Śvētāśvatara Upanishat, more famous is the Bhagavat Gītā.[41]

He also referred to Monier-Williams and Richard Garbe (1857–1927) as having the same opinion.[42] Nallasvami, thus, found a way to legitimize his argument with contemporary indological research. In a similar way, Neo-Hinduism backed up its claim of Advaita Vedanta as the central philosophy of Hinduism.[43]

Nallasvami continued his journey through the Sanskrit tradition and discussed the Puranas as the "earliest interpreters of the Vēda and the Upanishats"[44]. He claimed that not only the oldest Purana (i. e. the Vāyu-Purāṇa) but also the largest number of all Puranas was Saivite. He treated

---

[37] The translation is from Max Müller; see Müller 1884: 263–265. The quotations were taken from Svetasvatara Upanishad in the following order: 6.11, 6.19, 6.7 (here, Nallasvami gives a paraphrase of the verse and does not quote Müller), 6.14.

[38] The general reference probably refers to the following statement of Max Müller: "... the nearest approach to our own ideas of a personal God" (Müller 1884: xxxvi).

[39] See also Schomerus 1912: 59–60. The quote "without qualities" is from Svetasvatara Upanishad 6.11.

[40] See Müller 1884: xxxvi–xlii.

[41] Nallasvami Pillai 1911m: 283 note. With slight variations in spelling and the omission of one word, the quote is taken from Macdonell 1900: 282.

[42] See also Nallasvami Pillai 1911h: 118, where Nallasvami rightly pointed out that the idea of an eclectic school came first from Monier-Williams. However, he did not give specific references from Garbe or Monier-Williams, though they could have easily been found – see, for example, Monier-Williams 1875: 134–154 (where he explicitly coins the phrase "eclectic school"); Garbe 1897: 23–24 (Garbe speaks of an "eclectic movement").

[43] See King 1999.

[44] Nallasvami Pillai 1911m: 287.

the Mahabharata in similar fashion. He saw Saivism as the "only worship universal" and as the worship of the "superior castes" in the time of the Mahabharata.[45] The Mahabharata showed Rudra or Siva in "the beneficent and apparently terrible forms, as the Creator, Protector, and Destroyer"[46], and Nallasvami illustrated this by quoting a longer passage from the Mahabharata.[47] Nallasvami viewed this threefold aspect of Siva, as creator, protector and destroyer, also as a basic principle of Saiva Siddhanta. He referred to Sivagnana Botham (Tam. civañāṉa pōtam, Skt. śivajñāna bodha),[48] and he cited portions from Srikantha's commentary of the Vedanta Sutras, where the trembling of the universe is seen as part of God's (Skt. parameśvara) command over it. As will be seen later, the commentary of the less known Srikantha (Skt. śrīkaṇṭha) became one of Nallasvami's traditional authorities. As this ambivalence of Siva was constantly criticized by Western researchers and Christian missionaries,[49] Nallasvami also took some pains to prove that the Christian tradition also knew a "fierce" and "terrible" picture of God, and curiously quoted from an English Sunday School book that taught the "consuming fire and the love that passeth knowledge are two different sides of the same God"[50].

It is noteworthy that Nallasvami, when referring to the Mahabharata, did not enter into any deeper discussion of the Bhagavadgita. Nevertheless, he stated, throughout the text, that the Bhagavadgita "epitomizes the philosophy of the Śvētāśvatara Upanishat"[51]; but its content is nowhere discussed in detail. As the Bhagavadgita had become a central text for Neo-Hinduism in the late 19th century,[52] it was apparently of strategic importance for Nallasvami to claim the text for the Saiva tradition. On the other hand, this was not without difficulties, not only because of its Vaishnava context, but even more because the "Tamil reader knows

[45] Nallasvami Pillai 1911m: 288.
[46] Nallasvami Pillai 1911m: 288.
[47] See Nallasvami Pillai 1911m: 288. The passage is the last portion of section 160 of the Anusasana Parva (vv. 7458–7501). Apparently, he used John Muir's translation, which can be found in Muir 1873: 197–205 (including the original Sanskrit text). Muir provided the whole section 160 without any special comment towards Siva, which makes one ask why Nallasvami chose his passage. Perhaps this passage was reprinted in another book relating specifically to Siva, but it was not possible to trace a probable source.
[48] See Nallasvami Pillai 1911m: 289; Nallasvami Pillai 1984: 6 (to Sivagnana Botham 1).
[49] See, for instance, Dubois 1906: 627–628.
[50] Nallasvami Pillai 1911m: 289–290. The passage is, with slight alterations, taken from M. 1879: 79. Nallasvami quoted two different passages from this book (M. 1879: 46–47, 78–79).
[51] Nallasvami Pillai 1911m: 291.
[52] See Bergunder 2006.

nothing about it [the Bhagavadgita]",[53] as he pointed out in the introduction to his Sivagnana Botham translation from 1895. It seems that, at one point, Nallasvami had tried to engage deeper in a discussion on the content of the Bhagavadgita. In his translation of Tiruvarutpayan (Tam. tiruvaruṭpayaṉ) from 1896, which had already been partially published in the Neo-Hindu journal *Brahmavadin*, he annotated his English translation with cross-references to the Bhagavadgita to show "the great resemblance ... in language and thought between the two"[54]. However, in his later texts, he never came back to a detailed analysis of the Bhagavadgita. He consigned it, with his overall claim on the text, as belonging to the old "eclectic school of Hindu Philosophy"[55].

Next to the Mahabharata, Nallasvami discussed the Vaishnava Ramayana and tried to show that the "worship of Śiva and Śiva-Liṅga was Universal [at that time] as shown by the establishment of the temple at Rāmeśvaram", where the Stalapurana said that Rama and Sita worshipped the Linga upon successfully returning from Lanka.[56]

His passage through the classical Sanskrit tradition culminated in a rereading of the Vedanta Sutras and a strong rejection of Sankara's commentary on them. Following a typical structure of argumentation, he first referred to the German indologist George Thibaut (1848–1914), who had translated Sankara's and Ramanuja's commentaries of the Vedanta Sutras for the "Sacred Books of the East".[57] Thibaut expressed the opinion that the Vedanta Sutras did not teach a distinction between brahman and God (Skt. īśvara), nor the unreality of the world, as Sankara proposed.[58] Nallasvami pointed out that, lately, even Max Müller had conceded to this interpretation.[59] Regarding the Sanskrit tradition, Nallasvami claimed that Sankara's commentary was not the oldest one, but the much lesser known commentary of Srikantha, which provided a theistic and Saivite interpretation of the Vedanta Sutras. So, Nallasvami made his case that both contemporary indological research and the old Sanskrit tradition supported his views. For Nallasvami, Srikantha's commentary was "the accepted authority by the Southern Śaiva School"[60] and, being the oldest and the most appropriate interpretation of the Vedanta Sutras, it provided the firm link between the Vedanta tradition and Saivism.

---

[53] Nallasvami Pillai 1984: vii. For the popularization of the Bhagavadgita in the 19th and early 20th century see also Bergunder 2006.

[54] Nallasvami Pillai 1896: iii.

[55] Nallasvami Pillai 1911m: 291.

[56] Nallasvami Pillai 1911m: 291–292.

[57] See Thibaut 1890/1896; Thibaut 1904.

[58] Thibaut 1890/1896: I. c. The passage is quoted in Nallasvami Pillai 1911m: 292.

[59] See Nallasvami Pillai 1911m: 293.

[60] Nallasvami Pillai 1911m: 292.

After establishing this historical argument, Nallasvami turned to the exposition of the central doctrines of Saiva Siddhanta. His strong reliance on Srikantha, as the historical link between the Sanskrit tradition and Tamil Saiva Siddhanta, made it necessary to present the central teachings of Saiva Siddhanta as being nearly identical with Srikantha's system, which is called Sivadvaita (Skt. śivādvaita). He pointed affirmatively to Srikantha's equation of the supreme brahman with Siva, and his illustration of the relationship between God and the soul with that of soul and body. He downplayed a "slight difference" in the notion of advaita, as it was apparently difficult to reconcile Srikantha's conception of identity, which sees the soul as a transformation (Skt. parināma) of Siva, with the elaborate and central argument in Saiva Siddhanta about the eternal and separate existence of God, soul, and matter.[61] Nallasvami marked a significant difference at this point, so it is somewhat surprising that he went on to repeatedly claim that the concepts of advaita of Srikantha and of Saiva Siddhanta are more or less the same.[62]

Nallasvami's exposition of Saiva Siddhanta teachings tried to avoid being too technical. He also paid little attention to ritualistic aspects and declared that Saiva Siddhanta did not support external ritualism, though it was based on the ritual-oriented Agamas (Skt. āgama, Tam. *ākamam*). The Saivite who entered the temple offers "his self as sacrifice; and the self-sacrifice thus becomes the centre of Hindu and Śaivite Philosophy, on which the whole process of salvation depends"[63]. This he called "Arpaṇa [offering] or Śivārpaṇa", and he saw a parallel to it in the Bhagavadgita.[64] His main strategy of argument was to show that the real understanding of advaita is not that of Sankara, but is to be found in the Sivadvaita of Srikantha and Saiva Siddhanta. He was mainly concentrating on topics that were also central to Neo-Hinduism and Theosophy, to

---

[61] See Nallasvami Pillai 1911l: 266–267. See also Suryanarayana Sastri 1930: 24–25. For the notion of the soul and its relation to God in Tamil Saiva Siddhanta, see Schomerus 1912: 180–208.

[62] The difference between Saiva Siddhanta and Sivadvaita is not easy to establish, but they are far reaching, and include fundamental issues: 1. In Sivadvaita, the non-intelligent world is the result of the transformation of Lord Siva and of the same kind as the soul; 2. Srikantha does not anywhere mention anavamala, the basic principle of matter encasing the soul in Saiva Siddhanta; 3. For Srikantha, past karma could not cease to exist in the present life of a person (Skt. jīvanmukti) even after he has attained salvation; 4. Srikantha is legitimizing his teachings with reference to revelation alone (Skt. śruti) and does not hold reasoning in high esteem. (See Suryanarayana Sastri 1930: 22–27.)

[63] Nallasvami Pillai 1911m: 296.

[64] The reference is to the Bhagavadgita 18,57, see Nallasvami Pillai 1911m: 296. However, the Sanskrit original of the Bhagavadgita does not know arpaṇa and the reference remains unclear in its meaning. Perhaps Nallasvami referred to a certain interpretation of the verse, which he read somewhere, but I have not yet been able to trace a possible source.

show how Saiva Siddhanta could treat and explain them better. Parallel to this, he repeatedly developed the argument that the concept of God and the human being in Saiva Siddhanta was, in many ways, similar to that of Christianity, as it was different to Advaita Vedanta.

Nallasvami made clear that Siva in Saiva Siddhanta is identical with the supreme brahman of Vedanta. Siva is without a specific gender and not part of any trimurti. Siva cannot "be born as a man through the womb of the women" and has, therefore, no avataras (Skt. avatāra); still, that did not prevent Siva from "appearing as Guru and Saviour in the form of a man, out of His Great Love and feeling for the sin and sorrow of mankind".[65] In this context, he explicitly mentioned the Theosophist Subba Row in order to give him credit for having made clear that God cannot have avataras.[66]

Nallasvami reiterated that God is nirguna and that nirguna does not mean "impersonal"[67]. God is both nirguna and personal, in the same way as he "neither has form nor is formless".[68] Consequently, Nallasvami also explicitly rejected the notion that saguna (Skt. saguṇa) means "personal", as it is commonly interpreted in Advaita Vedanta. Hence, God is both immanent and transcendent, and Nallasvami brought this into a threefold terminology that characterized God as "being", "light" and "love":

> As Pure Being, the absolute, God is unknowable; and as Light and Love He links himself to Man; and it is possible to Man to approach Him through Love.[69]

This threefold terminology was explained through the concepts of saccidananda (Skt. saccidānanda) and somaskanda (Skt. somāskanda). The use of the term saccidananda is especially noteworthy. In Tamil Saiva Siddhanta the threefold compound (Skt. sat-cit-ānanda), as a technical term, was not unknown, but apparently not often used, although its respective components played a central role in describing Siva's supreme status, especially as sat and cit.[70] On the other hand, saccidananda was firmly established in Vedanta philosophy and, accordingly, Srikantha's commentary on the Vedanta Sutras began with a reference to Siva as saccidananda and mentioned it on several other occasions. However, even in Srikantha's commentary, saccidananda remains a formula that is

---

[65] Nallasvami Pillai 1911m: 299.

[66] Apparently, he referred to Subba Row 1994: 57–68. In this passage, Subba Row interpreted the Vaishnava belief in avataras from a Theosophical perspective that certainly has no room for a personal God in the sense that Nallasvami propagated.

[67] See Nallasvami Pillai 1911m: 297.

[68] Nallasvami Pillai 1911m: 298.

[69] Nallasvami Pillai 1911m: 301.

[70] See Schomerus 1912: 49–62; Murtti 1998: 103. It is noteworthy that Schomerus does not give any reference from the Tamil sources as to where the term saccidananda occurs.

neither explained nor explicitly introduced as a central concept.[71] This makes it most likely that Nallasvami's application of the term was a reaction to its prominent and widespread use by contemporary Neo-Hindu thinkers, like Vivekananda and his Tamil Brahman disciples.[72] Nallasvami claimed saccidananda for Saiva Siddhanta and provided it with a theistic interpretation. It is obvious that Nallasvami gave the term a meaning which was completely different from Advaita Vedanta and its reception in Neo-Hinduism, especially when he equated it with somaskanda. Somaskanda (Skt. sa-umā-skanda) is a classical image of Siva together with his wife Uma – which Nallasvami pointed out originally means light –, and his son Skanda (Tam. murukaṉ). Somaskanda was widely used as the main processional deity in Tamil Saiva temples. As its prominence goes back to medieval times, it was often subject to reinterpretation,[73] but its equation with saccidananda is rather far-fetched. However, as both saccidananda and somaskanda are three-part conceptions of the supreme god, occasionally, this equation already occurred in the Tamil Saiva tradition, for instance through the 17th-century prolific Tamil poet Kumarakuruparar.[74]

In any case, the threefold terminology "being", "light" and "love" is probably Nallasvami's own, and it might have been inspired by seeking an expression that was compatible to the Christian understanding of God. He pointed out that the liberal Anglican theologian Brooke Foss Westcott (1825–1901) understood the Christian trinity as "Spirit, Light, and Love"[75] in the same way.

Light and Love were, for Nallasvami, the immanent aspects of God, his central Sakti, the "Mother of the Universe"[76], but categorically different from Māyā. Nallasvami emphasized the peculiar concept of Maya (Skt. māyā, Tam. māyai) in Saiva Siddhanta, which he equated with the

---

[71] In the version of the commentary that was published by Nallasvami in Siddhanta Deepika, it is detectable in only four places and, on each occasion, as an unexplained formula (see Sastry 1897–1906: 1:193, 1:220, 2:4, 2:193; see also Chaudhury 2004: 32).

[72] See, for example, Vivekananda 1959: I.365; II.194, III.37, 336, 453; IV.334; V.385, 432–433; VIII.11–12. For a Tamil Brahman disciple of Vivekananda see, for example, Aiyar 1946: 297–298.

[73] See Younger 1995: 76 note 25; Smith 1996: 203–206; Ghose 1996: 11–54; Ekambaranathan 2000.

[74] Ghose 1996: 125. For Kumarakurupara see Zvelebil 1975: 229–230.

[75] Nallasvami Pillai 1911m: 301, see also Nallasvami Pillai 1911o: 355. Perhaps Nallasvami collected the phrase from Westcott's correspondence with Lady Welby-Gregory (1837–1912) on the Gospel of John and Christian mysticism (see Westcott 1903: II.72, 78). The exact phrase in the other writings of Westcott could not be traced, though similar expression can be found in his exegetical works on John's Gospel.

[76] Nallasvami Pillai 1911m: 302.

Western notion of "matter" as the "'object' of Western philosophy",[77] and which he described in positive terms, probably to make a clear distinction from its usage in Neo-Hindu circles. To make his point, Nallasvami referred to Sivagnana Siddhiyar (Tam. civañāṉacittiyār) and quoted long passages from it.[78] For the reader unfamiliar with Saiva Siddhanta philosophy, his description at this point might sound technical, but this was probably unintentional, since much of the complicated philosophical context in which the Maya concept is embedded in Saiva Siddhanta is left out. Nallasvami concentrated fully on a twofold argument. Firstly, Maya has to be seen positively. Maya and its products have to be understood in the context of cosmological evolution, through the interplay of thirty-six elements (Skt. tattvas), and Maya also comprises higher spiritual spheres (Skt. śuddha māyā).[79] Maya is different from God and soul, but plays a positive role in the way to liberation and is not the cause of the soul's blindness. It is external to the soul, and acts as a perceptive tool for the soul that enables it to wish, to know and to act,[80] and thus helps it search for the way to liberation. However, liberation itself can only be provided by God directly. This specific aspect of Maya was central for Nallasvami:

According to the Pūrvapakshin [opponent], Māyā is the cloud that hides the light of the Sun. But the Siddhāntin answers ... Māyā acts as the lamp-light ... in darkness. But when the sun [i. e. God] rises, all darkness and night vanish and there is no need of any lamp, however powerful ...[81]

Secondly, it is not the external world, or Maya, which hinders the soul in realizing its spiritual destiny, but another principle, which is peculiar to Saiva Siddhanta, and which is called Āṉava Mala. Āṉava Mala forms a close bond with the soul and instigates ignorance (Skt. avidya):

Understand well, that Māyā causes Ichcha [wish], Jñana [knowledge] and Kriyā [action] to arise in the Jīvas [souls], but Āṉava causes the same to disappear.[82]

---

[77] Nallasvami Pillai 1911m: 303.

[78] See Nallasvami Pillai 1911m: 303–305. The argument is based mainly on Sivagnana Siddhiyar II, 80–85. The English quotes are from Nallasvami's own translation (Nallasvami Pillai 1897–1902: 3:237). His definition of Maya came from Sivagnana Siddhiyar II, 53 (Nallasvami Pillai 1897–1902: 3:203, see also Schomerus 1981: 153–154, and Schomerus 1912: 131).

[79] See Nallasvami Pillai 1911m: 304.

[80] See Sivagnana Siddhiyar II, 81, see Nallasvami Pillai 1897–1902: 3:237; Schomerus 1981: I.184–185.

[81] Nallasvami Pillai 1911m: 304–305. The quotation paraphrases Sivagnana Siddhiyar II, 82–83, see Nallasvami Pillai 1897–1902: 3:237; Schomerus 1981: 185.

[82] Nallasvami Pillai 1911m: 304. This is an English translation from Sivagnana Siddhiyar II, 81, see Nallasvami Pillai 1897–1902: 3:237; Schomerus 1981: 184–185. Note that the original Tamil text has "uyir" for "Jīva". Nallasvami's use of "Jīva", which is not a core technical term in Saiva Siddhanta, hints at his intention to make a broader appeal.

Nallasvami focused on the principal difference between Maya and Āṉava Mala, but he did not discuss the aspect in Saiva Siddhanta where Maya, together with Āṉava Mala, belong to the same third material principle or substance that exists besides God (Skt. Śiva / pati) and the soul (Skt. paśu). This third principle is called Mala or Pāśa in Sanskrit, and consists of three different "impurities" (Āṉava Mala, Maya[-mala]m, and Karma[-mala] – the latter was not discussed by Nallasvami), which all impede the soul from getting right knowledge. However, Nallasvami's concern was to work out that Āṉava Mala, and not Maya, is the crucial and main impurity (Tam. mūla-malam) that encases the soul during its periodical existence in the world of Maya (Skt. sakala-avasthā), as well as during world-sleep (Skt. kevala-avasthā), until its final liberation. Āṉava Mala is "night and darkness"; it is the "cloud or cataract in one's eye".[83]

Āṉava Mala would vanish only when the "Light of Truth, ... entering body and soul, has melted all faults and driven away the false darkness", and when "the soul is fully enveloped in that Supreme Splendour".[84] This is "the soul's Śuddha or Nirvāṇa condition".[85] In this state, the soul is united with God, and Nallasvami quoted from the Tiruvācakam, a famous classical collection of Tamil Bhakti-songs, to illustrate the intense and emotional unity between the soul and Siva in the state of liberation.[86] However, even in this unity, the soul always remains categorically different from God:

> The soul is not a reflection nor a particle nor a spark of the Partless and Changeless Brahman, nor one with Him. God is other than the soul.[87]

Nallasvami made a very strong point against Advaita Vedanta when he further explained that "all religion and morality are sure to die, when we regard the soul the same as God"[88]. On this matter, he lined up with the Western Christian critique of Indian "Pantheism", when he approvingly quoted a long passage from a book of the well-known English Unitarian minister, Richard Acland Armstrong (1843–1906). This quote, for instance, contained the following statement of Armstrong: "Pantheism ... becomes deadly to vigorous religion and morality when it makes the

[83] Nallasvami Pillai 1911m: 305.
[84] Nallasvami Pillai 1911m: 305.
[85] Nallasvami Pillai 1911m: 305.
[86] Nallasvami quoted the 7th hymn of the "kōyiṟṟiruppatikam" in an English translation from *Siddhanta Deepika* 1 (1897/1898) 51, by an anonymous contributor ("P. A."), who is probably a Tamil (see also Nallasvami Pillai 1911g: 107; Nallasvami Pillai 1911l:251–252). Nallasvami did not use the translation of Pope, though he was familiar with it and quoted from it on other occasions (see Pope 1900: 222–223).
[87] Nallasvami Pillai 1911m: 306.
[88] Nallasvami Pillai 1911m: 306.

man's soul, the man's self, a portion of God"[89]. Nallasvami concluded that, in the end, it is Saiva Siddhanta with its "three planes of existence, or three centres, the plane of matter, the plane of souls and the plane of God",[90] which best takes up these conceptual challenges.

Nallasvami backed up his argument again with Vedanta Sutras, which also postulate "the difference between the Human Soul and the Supreme Soul"[91], and he discussed their treatment of the so called Mahavakya (Skt. mahāvākya) verses from the Upanishads (like, for instance, "tat tvam asi" / "thou art that"), the crucial scriptural foundation for Advaita Vedanta's teaching that brahman and atman (Skt. ātman) are identical. He argued that the Mahavakyas were not discussed in the first chapter of the Vedanta Sutras with regard to the theoretical foundation of categories, but in the third chapter in relation to the means of salvation. This is why they did not relate to a natural identity, but dealt with a union of God and soul based on the "consciousness of duality"[92] between the two. This argument culminated in the statement that the union of God / Siva and the soul is also called "advaita" in Saiva Siddhanta, and that the proper name for Saiva Siddhanta would be Saiva Advaita Siddhanta. Saiva Advaita Siddhanta was, of course, phrased in opposition to Advaita Vedanta, and "Saiva Advaita" is probably inspired by "Sivadvaita" (Skt. śiva-advaita), the designation for Srikantha's system.[93]

To explain this specific notion of advaita, Nallasvami referred to the peculiar concept of the soul in Saiva Siddhanta, which stands between matter (Skt. asat / non-being) and God (Skt. sat / absolute being) and belongs to neither of the two. However, the soul can be called "sat-asat", as both matter and God strive to conform the soul to their own image, and because it is a characteristic of the soul that it is unable to live for itself but must always attach itself to something or other. Only in the state of liberation does the soul become "sat" in union with God[94]:

> This nature of the soul consists in its becoming one with whatever it is united to, losing its own individuality, and its not being able to exist independently, except in union with one or the other. ... The soul identifies itself absolutely with the body or God ...[95]

Again, Nallasvami sought to reconcile this specific Saiva Siddhanta idea of the soul with Christian teachings. He cited Henry Drummond (1851–

[89] Nallasvami Pillai 1911m: 306 note. The quote is from Armstrong 1896: 60.
[90] Nallasvami Pillai 1911m: 307.
[91] Nallasvami Pillai 1911m: 306.
[92] Nallasvami Pillai 1911m: 307.
[93] Nallasvami Pillai 1911m: 305–306.
[94] See also Nallasvami Pillai 1911e: 67, and Schomerus 1912: 198–208.
[95] Nallasvami Pillai 1911m: 308.

1897), the Scottish evangelical scientist and theologian, who tried to settle the growing science-religion divide in the 19th century.[96] In a famous address on Christian sanctification, Drummond interpreted a Pauline verse from the New Testament (2 Cor. 3:18) in the general sense that the person is a mirror of the divine who, when reflecting the character of Christ, will become like Christ.[97] In this idea of the person as a mirror, Nallasvami saw a congenial expression of the Saiva Siddhanta notion of the soul. Nallasvami referred to this parallel in Drummond's writings also on other occasions,[98] calling it a "formula of sanctification" that he also identified in mirror metaphors in the Svetasvatara Upanishad and in Saiva Siddhanta writings.[99]

This peculiar notion of the soul is the key to the understanding of advaita in Saiva Siddhanta, which Nallasvami wanted to see as clearly distinct from Advaita Vedanta. He also made it clear that Saiva Siddhanta had nothing to do with the Visishtadvaita (Skt. viśiṣṭādvaita) Vedanta of Ramanuja (11-12th century), which was considered by contemporary Western Orientalists as the main theistic critique of Advaita Vedanta in the Indian tradition. Visishtadvaita Vedanta was and still is a living tradition in the Tamil context, where it is called Srivaishnava (Skt. śrīvaiṣṇava), and Nallasvami had apparently close contacts to some of its followers.[100] He also did not want Saiva Siddhanta to be explained in the categories of Madhva's Dvaita Vedanta (12-13th century).[101] However, Vishistadvaita and Dvaita Vedanta are clearly seen to have much more in common with Saiva Siddhanta than Advaita Vedanta. At one instance, Nallasvami explicitly emphasized that "there is much greater doctrinal harmony between Śaivaism and Vaishṇavism of Śrī Rāmānuja's school than between these and Vēdāntism of Śaṅkara's School".[102] He also

---

[96] See Bergunder 2005.

[97] See Nallasvami Pillai 1911m: 308, see Drummond 1891: 17–29.

[98] See, for instance, Nallasvami Pillai 1911h: 143–144; Nallasvami Pillai 1911j: 215–216; Nallasvami Pillai 1911l: 257–258.

[99] See Nallasvami Pillai 1911m: 309. He quoted Svetasvatara Upanishad II.14–15 and I.10 in Max Müller's translation (see Müller 1884: 242–243, 236), which is nevertheless altered in a way that shows some familiarity with the original Sanskrit text (for instance, instead of "all natures" he wrote "all tattvas") and also interpreted in Saiva Siddhanta terminology (for instance, instead of "freed from all fetters" he wrote "freed from all pāśa"). For Saiva Siddhanta, he cited Sivagnana Botham VIII, 3 in his own translation (Nallasvami Pillai 1984: 84).

[100] See Nallasvami Pillai 1911o: 359.

[101] Nallasvami Pillai 1911o: 358–359.

[102] Nallasvami Pillai 1911o: 358.

acknowledged the apparent similarities between Dvaita and Saiva Siddhanta when he reported his discussion with a Madhva follower.[103]

However, for Nallasvami, Saiva Siddhanta represented a fundamentally different way of thinking than the great Vedanta traditions, be it Advaita, Visishtadvaita, or Dvaita.[104] At the same time, he expressly called himself an "Advaiti" as "all Śaiva Siddhāntis call themselves strict Advaitis".[105] This was, of course, directed against the claim of Neo-Hindus and Western Orientalists that Advaita Vedanta and its concept of advaita comprise the central philosophy of Hinduism. Nallasvami's Saiva Siddhanta was a direct counterclaim against Neo-Hinduism.

Nallasvami argued, with reference to the second Sutra of Sivagnana Botham, that the true meaning of advaita is "anyō nāsti" or "ananya", i. e. "inseparable" but not unity or monism.[106] Advaita marks a "relation" which could be defined best by the phrase "neither one nor two"[107]:

---

[103] Nallasvami Pillai 1911o: 358–359. He referred to his exchange with P. Srinivasa Rao, Judge at the Civil Court in Madras.

[104] See also Nallasvami Pillai 1984: 15–33; Nallasvami Pillai 1911l: 244–272.

[105] Nallasvami Pillai 1911l: 244.

[106] See Nallasvami Pillai 1911m: 310. The Tamil transliteration for Sanskrit 'anyō nāsti' is 'anniyanātti'. As far as I can see, the Sanskrit word 'ananya' (usually 'ananniyam' in Tamil transliteration) is not used in Sivagnana Botham, but could, for instance, be found prominently in Sivagnana Siddhiyar XI.11 (see Nallasvami Pillai 1897–1902: 5:110; Schomerus 1981: 373–374).

[107] Nallasvami Pillai 1911m: 310. The first time Nallasvami quoted this phrase was in his comments on Sivagnana Botham II: "In Sivagnana Siddhi, Adwaitham is defined as o<u>n</u>r̲ākāmal, iraṇṭākāmal, o<u>n</u>r̲umiraṇṭumi<u>n</u>r̲ākāmal (neither one, nor two, nor neither)." (Nallasvami Pillai 1984: 18). Strangely, Nallasvami referred to the wrong source, as these lines are not from Sivagnana Siddhiyar. As Nallasvami gave also the original Tamil text, I could trace the quote to another Tamil work of Arunanti (Tam. aruṇanti), the author of Sivagnana Siddhiyar, called Irupa Irupatu (Tam. irupā irupatu) in chapter 20. Moreover, in his other writings, up until 1911, he never gave the correct source when quoting these lines (see, for instance, Nallasvami Pillai 1911d: 62; Nallasvami Pillai 1911h: 128), which hints that he learned this phrase through one of his Tamil pundits, without obtaining a clear reference. Whereas Nallasvami showed intimate knowledge of Sivagnana Siddhiyar, I could not trace any other quote from Irupa Irupatu in his writings up to 1911 (see also Nallasvami Pillai 1911m: 294, where Arunanti is only given credit for Sivagnana Siddhiyar, though in his short introduction to Sivagnana Siddhiyar from 1897 he acknowledged Arunanti as author of Irupa Irupatu, see Nallasvami Pillai 1897–1902: 1:2). This reinforces the impression that Nallasvami's exposition of Saiva Siddhanta in our text is mainly dependent on Sivagnana Botham and, especially, on Sivagnana Siddhiyar. However, the picture is complicated. In 1912/1913, Nallasvami published an English translation of Irupa Irupatu where he also gave due credit to the "famous Phrase" (Nallasvami Pillai 1912/1913: 450), but it seems that this intensive study of Irupa Irupatu was a latecomer. For Irupa Irupatu, see also Schomerus 1916.

Advaita, literally meaning not two, simply denies the separability or duality of God and soul and matter, but does not postulate Oneness ...[108]

Nallasvami backed this view on advaita with different authorities. To show its correspondence with the teachings of the Vedanta Sutras, he referred again to Srikantha's commentary,[109] and to Manilal Dvivedi (1858–1898) who had also stated that, in the Vedanta Sutras, advaita does not mean "one" (Skt. eka, abhinna) but "inseparable" (Skt. ananya).[110] Dvivedi was one of the leading contemporary proponents of Advaita Vedanta which he tried to reconcile with western materialism and Theosophical ideas to propose it as a scientific religion.[111] The reference to Dvivedi shows, once again, how Nallasvami tried to make his point through engaging the Neo-Hindu side.

Nallasvami then took on contemporary Western philosophy, quoting Alexander Bain (1818–1903), a Scottish Utilitarian and leading proponent of a scientific approach to psychology.[112] He alluded to Bain's discussion on the difficulties of thinking about the paradoxical and contradictory relationship between mind and body, resulting in Bain's statement "that there is not even an analogy to illustrate this unique union of mind and body"[113]. Nallasvami combined this argument of Bain with a look at the

---

[108] Nallasvami Pillai 1911m: 310.

[109] See Nallasvami Pillai 1911m: 310 note. Nallasvami referred without further explanation to Srikantha's commentary of the Vedanta Sutras II.i.22 (Sastry 1897–1906: 2:217–218), where Srikantha tries to go beyond conventional expressions of duality / non-duality. However, it should be noted that, in the passage which immediately follows (II.i.23), Srikantha explains, among other things, how the soul and the universe are emanations from Brahman; this marks one of the main differences between Srikantha's Sivadvaita and Saiva Siddhanta.

[110] Nallasvami Pillai 1911m: 310 note. Obviously, Nallasvami referred to passages like Dvivedi 1889: 35, 40–41); literally, it is indeed a convincing reference. It also shows that, in the circles around Neo-Vedanta and Theosophy, complex conceptions of advaita were discussed, a fact which is often overlooked when one takes Vivekananda's rather simple exposition of advaita as representative (for Vivekananda's conception of advaita, see, for example, Hatcher 1999: 47–70). However, in the end, Dvivedi's conception of advaita was shaped by the fundamental principles of Advaita Vedanta, which was irreconcilable to Nallasvami's Saiva Siddhanta views on God, soul and matter. This could best be seen in Dvivedi's refutation of Visishtadvaita and Dvaita Vedanta (see Dvivedi 1889: 68, 102–104).

[111] See also Thaker 1983.

[112] See Young 1990: 101–133.

[113] Nallasvami Pillai 1911m: 310 note. In other articles, Nallasvami had discussed Bain's idea in more detail, which shows that his reception of Bain is more than mere namedropping. See, for instance, Nallasvami Pillai 1911d: 53–59, 61–62; Nallasvami Pillai 1911e: 64–65, where Nallasvami also gave the quotation in full: "There is an alliance with matter, with the object or extended world; but the thing allied, the mind proper, has itself no extension and cannot be joined in local union. Now, we have a difficulty in providing *any form of language, any familiar analogy*, suited to this unique conjunction; in

Sanskrit tradition, where the close linkage between mind and body had occasionally been used to illustrate the relationship between God, soul, and matter. He quoted from the Brhadaranyaka (Skt. bṛhadāraṇyaka) Upanishad, where God is called the "soul" (Skt. ātman) that dwells in a "body" (Skt. śarīra), i. e. the "Universe of nature and man".[114] This led to another quote from the Aitareya Upanishad, which he understood in the sense that, within the Sanskrit tradition, the metaphor of body and soul could be further translated into the metaphor of consonants and vowels: "Its consonants form its body; its vowel, the soul."[115] However, Nallasvami argued that it was only in the Tamil tradition that the great conceptual potential of these metaphors were realised and deeper reflected upon. The Tamil grammar uses for vowels the word for soul (uyir), and for consonants the word for body (uṭal, mey). According to Nallasvami, this peculiarity was taken up by the Tamil proponents of Saiva Siddhanta and it helped them to develop a clear and comprehensive idea of advaita:

> The consonants cannot be brought into being unless the vowel supports it; and in union, the two are inseparable; and One is the word used in the oldest Tamil Grammar to denote the union of the two ... the vowel is not the consonant nor the consonant the vowel. God is one with the soul and the Universe, and yet without God, where is the Universe?[116]

It is at this point that Nallasvami explicitly brought in his Tamil context and the Tamil language as the basis of a superior philosophy. This is a key argument for him, which also figured centrally in some of his other

---

comparison with all other unions, it is a *paradox*, or *contradiction*." (Nallasvami Pillai 1911d: 53, directly quoted with slight alterations, especially regarding punctuation and use of italics, from Bain 1879: 136).

[114] Nallasvami Pillai 1911m: 310–311. He quoted Brhadaranyaka Upanishad III.7.3 and 22 in the translation of Max Müller (see Müller 1884: 133, 136), again with alterations that show familiarity with the Sanskrit original. It is noteworthy that Nallasvami, who frequently quoted these verses, on one occasion, explicitly discussed his differences from the translation of Max Müller (see Nallasvami Pillai 1911f: 95).

[115] Nallasvami Pillai 1911m: 311 (Aitareya Upanishad II.2.4.1, using Max Müller's translation, see Müller 1879: 22. However, one should note that the context does not seem to support Nallasvami's interpretation.).

[116] Nallasvami Pillai 1911m: 311. It is not entirely clear to me what Nallasvami means with the "oldest Tamil grammar". This should be *Tolkāppiyam*, but I could not trace an apt verse there, though the commentaries of *Tolkāppiyam* interpret the designation of vowel and consonant as soul and body often philosophically (see Kiruttinamurtti 1990: 75–77). The only Tamil grammarian that Nallasvami explicitly referred to seems to be Nannul, (Tam. naṉṉūl) with verse 204 ("'uṭalmēl uyirvantoṉṟuvatiyalpu.' 'It is a natural union when the vowel unites with the consonant as one.'" Nallasvami Pillai 1911n: 327, see also Nallasvami Pillai 1911l: 249 with a slightly different Tamil Sandhi and English translation). As Nallasvami's English translation has a clear reference to the word "one", probably this verse is meant by Nallasvami. For the meaning of Nannul 204 see Ilavarasu 1997: 117.

writings, where he included in detail various reflections on the letter 'A' in Tamil literature and especially in Saiva Siddhanta writings.[117] He made his point there in direct contrast to the Sanskrit tradition. The Bhagavadgita, for instance, he argued, might also have a verse such as: "Of letters, the letter A, I am"[118], but "we look in vain even in Śankara's commentary for the meaning we have tried to give it [in the framework of Tamil Saiva Siddhanta]"[119]. Based on these arguments elaborated elsewhere, he quoted again the second Sutra of Sivagnana Botham in our text in order to make his case in this direction: "You can indeed say God is One, without a Second, as when you say without the vowel 'A' no other letters exist."[120] This, taken together, led him to the strong conclusion that the specific Tamil aspect of Saiva Siddhanta should be of universal importance in answering the pressing religious questions of the time:

> This is a view of Advaitam or Monism, which is not ordinarily met with, which must appeal to the hearts and intelligence of the people of every nation and every religion and which I commend to your earnest consideration.[121]

With this principal appeal, Nallasvami ended his outline of the core teachings of Saiva Siddhanta, and added a very short excursus on the role of "practical religion" in Saiva Siddhanta. He introduced Saiva Siddhanta's four stages (Skt. mārga) on the way to liberation, but interpreted them inclusively as well as progressively. In its inclusive aspect they became different paths to suit the different spiritual needs of different people:

> When you want to approach God, you can approach Him as your Lord and Master [Skt. dāsa-mārga / servant's way], you can approach Him as your Father [Skt. putra-mārga / child's way], or as your Friend [Skt. saha-mārga / friend's way] or as your Beloved [Skt. san-mārga / true way]. The last is no mārga at all but where the One-ness is reached fully and finally. There is return to birth, while one is in the first three paths. And these paths are so adjusted in an ascending

---

[117] Besides Sivagnana Botham II, he also explicitly mentioned the first verse of the Tirukkural (see Nallasvami Pillai 1911d: 59), and first verse of Tiruvarutpayan (Nallasvami Pillai 1911d: 62).

[118] Nallasvami Pillai 1911d: 53. It refers to Bhagavadgita X,33; the peculiar wording and a comparison with the other contemporary translations makes it clear that he used the English translation by Annie Besant (see Besant 1984: 187). For the role of the Bhagavadgita in 19th-century India, see Bergunder 2006.

[119] Nallasvami Pillai 1911d: 59.

[120] Nallasvami Pillai 1911m: 312. He did not render his own published translation (cf. Nallasvami Pillai 1984: 12), but gave more of a paraphrase, which interpreted the verse in a way that neatly fits into the required meaning. It seems that these verses were very important for Nallasvami, as he gave further different interpretative translations in other articles (see, for instance, Nallasvami Pillai 1911k: 226; Nallasvami Pillai 1911l: 249).

[121] Nallasvami Pillai 1911m: 312.

scale to suit the intellectual, moral and spiritual development of the aspirant. The lowest and the highest have equally a place in this scheme and are given room for their development and progress. No one path is put in opposition to the other.[122]

He proposed this fourfold classification of Saiva Siddhanta against the common Vedantic understanding of four paths, which was, also with an inclusive interpretation, forcefully propagated by contemporary Neo-Hindu circles, i. e. Karmamarga, Bhaktimarga, Yogamarga and Jnanamarga.[123] However, according to Nallasvami, these latter four paths, which marginalized Tamil Saivism as Bhaktimarga, had "no logical scheme at all but involve cross division"[124]. The aspects expressed (Karma, Bhakti and Jnana) "are altogether essential" and together part of every stage in the Saiva Siddhanta classification. Once again, Saiva Siddhanta is established as superior to Vedanta. It has a better classification of religious practice and can easily include the concerns of the four paths of Vedanta.

After his detailed discussions, Nallasvami closed his argument with the statement that Saivism, through its interpretation in Saiva Siddhanta, could truly claim to be a "universal religion" in its own right, but with a strong foundation in the Sanskrit tradition that fundamentally challenges the inclusive and representative claim of Advaita Vedanta on Hinduism:

Saiva Siddhanta, as representing the old Hinduism and with its chief scripture, the Śvetāśvatara Upanishat and the Gīta, claims to be an eclectic philosophy and an universal Religion; and the various points I have brought out above will show how it brings itself into agreement with every shade of opinion, Religion, and Philosophy.[125]

To further prove the case, he cited "a few opinions of European Students"[126] about Saiva Siddhanta, and documents their praise for it in longer quotations. It is noteworthy that all the three authors he explicitly refers to are Christian missionaries with a scholarly interest in Saiva Siddhanta, namely G. U. Pope, F. Goodwill and W. F. Goudie.

Curiously, he did not end here but added a small passage on the "ethical basis" of Saiva Siddhanta, but admitted this topic "is not usually discussed in text-books on Religion [in Saiva Siddhanta]".[127] Nevertheless, he claimed that Saivism is "based on the Highest morality"[128], and

---

122 Nallasvami Pillai 1911m: 312.

123 For the notion of these four paths in Neo-Vedanta see, for instance, Vivekananda 1959: 1:108, 5:414, and, in slightly different terminology, Aiyar 1946: 105–106.

124 Nallasvami Pillai 1911m: 312.

125 Nallasvami Pillai 1911m: 313.

126 Nallasvami Pillai 1911m: 313.

127 Nallasvami Pillai 1911m: 314.

128 Nallasvami Pillai 1911m: 314.

its most important ethical foundation is the *Tirukkuṟaḷ*, though he also mentioned the "ahimsa doctrine" as the "chief pillar" on Saiva Siddhanta without explaining this further.[129]

Nallasvami and the discourse on universal religion in colonial India

This investigation into Nallasvami's thought shows that it is hardly adequate to call him and his ideas "indecisive" or "moderate". He claimed that Saiva Siddhanta was the true heir of the Sanskrit tradition and a universal religion of its own, like Christianity and Islam. Making "universal religion" the core concept, Nallasvami related to one of the major themes of the colonial discourse in India. This must be seen in the context of the cultural debates and transformation processes in 19th-century Europe and North America, which led to, as it is sometimes called, the "invention of World Religions".[130] However, it seems more appropriate to understand this "invention of World Religions" as a global discourse, because "creating, redefining, and standardizing religion has long been a political strategy linked to the making of national identities and the exercise of colonial power"[131]. As religion was part of the colonial discourse, the colonized had no choice but to relate to it. At the same time, the appropriation and application of the concept, in colonial non-Western contexts, was in itself also a transformation process that affected the discourse on religion as a whole, i. e. also in Europe and North America. In this way, the colonized were also part of the "invention" process, and religion should not simply be seen as a Western construction as is often done in scholarly discussion.[132]

In this line of argument, one can locate Nallasvami's application of the concept of "universal religion" to Saiva Siddhanta. Right from its beginning, *Siddhanta Deepika* gave ample space to the discussion on "religion" from a general theoretical perspective and, in numerous articles and editorial comments, the journal reflected contemporary scholarly debates. Two examples from the first volume (1897–1898) might illustrate this. The first volume saw the start of a longer series of articles by the Italian Jesuit Giorgio Bartoli, on "Evidences of Natural Religion", which gave a broad overview of contemporary theories on the history of religion, though with

---

129 Nallasvami Pillai 1911m: 315.
130 See Masuzawa 2005.
131 Peterson and Walhof 2002: 1.
132 See, for instance, McCutcheon 1997; Dubuisson 2003.

a Christian theological interpretation.[133] *Siddhanta Deepika* also reprinted the summary of a lecture by Robert Needham Cust (1821–1909), a former high ranking colonial official and then private Orientalist scholar with a passion for Christian mission, on "modern religious conceptions".[134] This painted the picture of a plurality of religions (Islam, Judaism, Hinduism, Zoroastrism, Buddhism, Confucianism) and discussed their recent transformation processes, and the rise of numerous reform movements, as a reaction to the challenge by Christianity and Christian mission. In general, one can say that the articles in *Siddhanta Deepika* are well informed, not only about the scholarly debates on religion, but also about the ways in which Christianity, Theosophy, and Neo-Hinduism were conceptualizing themselves as universal religions.

Nallasvami used the concept of "universal religion" against the background of his intimate knowledge of the contemporary Western debates on religion, and in awareness of its crucial role in the colonial discourse. He carefully discussed the different aspects of universal religion to find a proper space for the universal claim of Saiva Siddhanta within this discourse. Liberal Christian theologians and historians of religion in the West often focused on the divide between universal and missionary religions, on the one hand, and local or ethnic religions on the other hand. Universal religions, in this sense, were Christianity, Islam and Buddhism; however, in a second evaluation, Christianity was often considered to be the only religion that was truly universal in all aspects.[135] This position was explicitly refuted by Nallasvami in a longer statement in *Siddhanta Deepika* against the Haskell Lectures from 1898–1899 given by the well-known liberal Scottish theologian Andrew Martin Fairbairn (1838–1919), who was an advocate of this position.[136] Nallasvami insisted on another definition of universal religion:

> We demur to the definition of Universal Religion given by the Haskell Lecturer [Fairbairn]; and here is what we conceive to be the Universal religion: ... "That religion is the true which does not conflict with this religion and that, and yet reconciles all and stands supreme in the conscience of man." Whose supreme Ideal is such that, once seen, every Religionist can exclaim, "what is there here of

---

[133] See Bartoli 1897–1899. Bartoli was, at the time, a Jesuit missionary teaching at a college in Mangalore. Later, in 1909, after repeated accusations of being a modernist, he became a Protestant Waldensian minister.

[134] See *Siddhanta Deepika* 1 (1897/1898) 144. The text reprinted a summary of a congress paper from the Calcutta Review, but the content seems to be identical with a book published by Cust years earlier (see Cust 1891).

[135] See Masuzawa 2005.

[136] See, for instance, Fairbairn 1902: 230–236.

sect and creed, All is His Supreme Glory and Bliss", and perceiving which, even the hardest heart can melt in love and joy eternal.[137]

Nallasvami saw the core of universal religion not in its transnational reach and missionary activity, but in its inclusive potential to contain all the others, which he underlined with a well-known quotation from a Saiva Siddhanta classic. In that modern context, it meant for Nallasvami that other religions found their teachings included in Saiva Siddhanta. The inclusive interpretation of the four paths, mentioned earlier, served as a hermeneutical tool for claiming this universality of Saiva Siddhanta. Islam and Judaism could be understood as the servant's way (dāsa-mārga), Christianity as the child's way (putra-mārga) etc.[138] In this context also belongs the reprint of an article from the Rajput Herald in *Siddhanta Deepika*, which observes how religious and cultural life in England resembles, in many ways, that of a Saivite country.[139] This idea of Saivism as the inclusive fulfilment of all other religions emphasises another aspect of universal religion that was also present in the colonial discourse on religion. It was not so much highlighted by Christian theology or Western scholars of religion but became strong within currents that were rather critical of established Church Christianity or of Christianity in general. Forceful proponents of this aspect of universal religion were, for instance, American Transcendentalism and Theosophy and, on the Indian side, the Brahmo Samaj and, as we will see, Neo-Hinduism.[140]

However, the different features of universal religion were not understood as mutually exclusive within the global discourse of religion, but mark only a different emphasis. Accordingly, the aspects of having a universal reach and missionary engagement were also taken up by Saiva Siddhanta. Nallasvami's Saiva Siddhanta oriented its activities in several ways on the work of the Christian missions in India, especially the Bible societies.[141] Curiously, occasionally, it even claimed having a universal reach, as in an editorial of *Siddhanta Deepika* from 1911: "Now the Śaiva Religion is found in almost all parts of the world and the extent is very

---

[137] Nallasvami Pillai 1898/1899c: 214. Nallasvami gives no hint as to where both quotations are taken from, but for the first quotation the Tamil text is also given, so that it can be identified as part of Sivagnana Siddhiyar 8,13. In his full translation of Sivagnana Siddhiyar, the passage is rendered differently (see Nallasvami Pillai 1897–1902: 4:240). The quotation is also repeated in Nallasvami Pillai 1911m: 313. For an interpretation of the passage, see also Schomerus 1981: 309. The second quotation is not from the same passage, but I could not work out where it might be taken from.

[138] See Nallasvami Pillai 1911j: 220–221.

[139] Seesodia 1911/1912. See also Glasenapp 1922: 437. For Seesodia see also *Siddhanta Deepika* 13 (1912/1913) 50.

[140] See, for example, Jackson 1981; Figl 1993; Campbell 1980; Hatcher 1999.

[141] See Nehring 2003: 336–337.

wide as many other religion. We have adherents to this Faith everywhere."[142]

Related to the discourse on universal or world religions was also the question of what would be the religion of the future, and many made the claim that it would be their own. Occasionally, we find this claim even in Saiva Siddhanta, though it does not appear explicitly in a text written by Nallasvami himself. In the already mentioned editorial of *Siddhanta Deepika* from 1911, we also read: "We hope that in the near future our sacred Śaivism will become the universal religion ..."[143] This position of Saiva Siddhanta, as the religion of the future, was also voiced by Ponnambalam Ramanathan (Tam. poṉṉampaḷam rāmanātaṉ, 1851–1930), who acted two times as president for the central annual Saiva Siddhanta conference.[144]

After the World Parliament of Religions in Chicago 1893, the global religious discourse received an institutional expression in the form of interreligious conferences, which were irregularly held in many places in the aftermath of Chicago.[145] In 1909, a 'Convention of Religions in India' was accordingly organized in Calcutta through the initiative of the Vivekananda Society.[146] The invitation was reprinted in *Siddhanta Deepika*, and Nallasvami attended the convention as a representative of Saivism.[147] The article 'The Saiva Religion and Saiva Advaita Siddhanta Philosophy', which we discussed in the first part, was actually presented there by Nallasvami, and it was also reprinted in the congress volume, though in a slightly abridged version.[148] This context backs our interpretation that the claim of Saiva Siddhanta as a universal religion is the central theme of the text. It also shows, on the one hand, how this is embedded in the global discourse on religion and, on the other hand, that this claim has to be understood as a struggle for representation among different religious currents within the Indian context.

The programme of the convention, and its documentation in the conference volume, show the strong claim of Vivekananda followers to be the true representatives of Hinduism. The invitation was extended to five

---

[142] *Siddhanta Deepika* 11 (1910/1911) 523. The author is probably V. V. Ramana Sastrin.

[143] *Siddhanta Deepika* 11 (1910/1911) 523.

[144] See Ramanathan 1906: 124–126, see also Glasenapp 1922: 422. For biographical information on Ramanathan, see *Siddhanta Deepika* 13 (1912/1913) 286–290.

[145] See Klaes 2000.

[146] See Sen 1910. To my knowledge, there has been no scholarly research on this conference.

[147] *Siddhanta Deepika* 9 (1908/1909) 135–136.

[148] See Sen 1910: II.110–136.

religions, which were identified as "I. Hinduism ... II. Christianity. III. Islamism. IV. Zorastrianism. V. Judaism."[149] Hinduism was specified as having nine subdivisions: "(a) Buddhism (b)Jainism (c) Shaktaism (d) Vaishnavism (e) Saivaism (f) Sikhism (g) Brahmoism (h) Arya Samaj (i) Theosophy"[150]. The papers presented on Hinduism were expected to pick out these or other subdivisions as their themes. Only one paper in the conference volume dealt with "Hinduism" in general and this is from Swami Saradananda of Bellur Math, which had been founded by Vivekananda.[151] This was flanked by an "Introduction" of the Vivekananda Society, which was to give "A Short Account of the Evolution of Religious Ideas Beyond India".[152] Both texts made it very clear that the Advaita Vedanta, in the Neo-Hindu interpretation of Vivekananda, is the core of Hinduism as an inclusive universal religion. The introduction argued that the main feature of the "Aryan idea" is to assume the "Oneness" of all reality, as against the "ne-Aryan [non-Aryan] idea" which assumes "duality".[153] The Aryans were presented as the civilising factor of India, who acculturated also the other peoples of the subcontinent like, for instance, the "Dravidian tribes" of South India.[154] This Aryan idea "that there is but One"[155] found its contemporary expression in Vivekananda's teachings. The introduction concluded:

> In this Oneness is included all faiths, all dogmas. Each of them has its own place in the world. We must recognize this. Through this Oneness is the ideal of a Universal Religion realized. ... Let us hope for the day when this idea of Universal religion will shine upon mankind.[156]

Accordingly, Saradananda stated in his paper on Hinduism, man "begins his religious life with Dvaita" and "when he is comparatively advanced he experiences the Visishtadvaita ... and finally ends with the Advaita".[157]

In this framework, there was only derivative space for the articulation of a theistic, a Saiva Siddhanta, or a South Indian ("Dravidian") perspective. Hence, it is clear that Nallasvami's argument is directly made against this hegemonic representative claim of Neo-Hinduism. He accepted that advaita ("Oneness") is the supreme idea but twists the point,

---

[149] Sen 1910: I.5; see also *Siddhanta Deepika* 9 (1908/1909) 135.

[150] Sen 1910: I.5 (italics deleted); see also *Siddhanta Deepika* 9 (1908/1909) 135.

[151] See Saradananda 1910. In the conference proceedings, this paper was announced under the title "Sanatan Dharm" (see Sen 1910: I.10, 40.

[152] Vivekananda Society 1910.

[153] Vivekananda Society 1910: iii.

[154] See Vivekananda Society 1910: xxi.

[155] Vivekananda Society 1910: li.

[156] Vivekananda Society 1910: lix.

[157] Saradananda 1910: 207.

claiming that only Saiva Siddhanta has fully grasped its meaning and can truly incorporate all the other traditions and religions.

It is important to note that Nallasvami was very much aware of the Neo-Hindu representative claim on Hinduism, long before he went to Calcutta. When Vivekananda made his triumphant return from the West, he stopped for nine days in Madras in February 1897 and gave some speeches. Apparently, Nallasvami sent a delegation from Tiruppatur, where he was District Munsiff at the time, to meet Vivekananda in order to engage him into a critical philosophical conversation. However, the delegation was brushed off by Vivekananda after it dared to ask, as their first question, how the unmanifested can become the manifested.[158] Moreover, Nallasvami regularly read the journals of Vivekananda followers, especially the Madras-based English journals, *Brahmavadin* and *Prabuddha Bharata*.[159] There were even polemic exchanges between *Prabuddha Bharata* and *Siddhanta Deepika*. *Prabuddha Bharata* was edited (and mostly written) by B. R. Rajam Aiyar (1872–1898), the famous Tamil novelist, Vedantist, and Vivekananda supporter.[160] Rajam Aiyar had taken appreciative notice of *Siddhanta Deepika* in the October issue of 1897. But he also declared that the assumption of three principles in Saiva Siddhanta instead of one, as in Advaita Vedanta, would be useless "metaphysical wrangling", which evoked a strong reaction in *Siddhanta Deepika*.[161] In the February issue of 1898, Rajam Aiyar advertised several Tamil pamphlets as useful for "refuting the dualistic Saiva Siddhanta", which again brought a strong editorial reply in *Siddhanta Deepika* rejecting the notion that Saiva Siddhanta is "dualistic".[162] This shows that, in Madras, the Saiva Siddhanta revival had clashed with Vivekananda's renaissance of Advaita Vedanta almost from the beginning. The polemical engagement between the Tamil followers of Saiva Siddhanta and Neo-Hinduism, in the late 19th and early 20th century is

[158] Reminiscences of Swami Vivekananda by K. S. Sundarama Iyer, see appendix II: 369–374. The followers of Nallasvami have a strong oral tradition that a personal meeting between Nallasvami and Vivekananda took place (see Balasubramaniam 1965: ix, 122–125). To clarify that matter the two respective historical sources are given in the appendix of this book, see pp. 371–373.

[159] See, for instance, for references to Brahmavadin Nallasvami Pillai 1911b: 21–22, 27–28; Nallasvami Pillai 1911c: 42–43, 45, 48; Nallasvami Pillai 1911i: 173–174, 177, 179, and for *Prabuddha Bharata* Nallasvami Pillai 1911c: 43. As many journals exchanged copies, the Saiva Siddhanta office received regularly a variety of journals on religion and culture as complimentary copies, among them were most of the English speaking journals from sympathizers of Vivekananda, see, for instance, *Siddhanta Deepika* 6 (1902–1903) 24.

[160] For Rajam Aiyar see Aiyar 1946: 14–20; Blackburn 1998: 157–175.

[161] See *Siddhanta Deepika* 1 (1897/1898) 119–120.

[162] See *Siddhanta Deepika* 1 (1897/1898) 240.

unfortunately not yet well researched.[163] It is important to note that this early exchange was mainly about the issue of who would represent Hinduism; only later, in the mid-1910s, did the Dravidian issue become the major dividing theme in the religious confrontation of the two sides. Nallasvami himself also occasionally quoted Vivekananda in his writings, but he apparently avoided combining his harsh criticism of Advaita Vedanta with a specific dismissal of Vivekananda's positions.[164] *Siddhanta Deepika* even printed a short solemn obituary on the occasion of Vivekananda's death.[165] Seeing these strong interactions between the two sides, it seems quite certain that Nallasvami was at least familiar with some of the speeches that Vivekananda gave on his tour back to India in 1897. They had been published in *Brahmavadin* and *Prabuddha Bharata*,[166] but were also separately printed in pamphlet editions in Madras, and even a Tamil translation was available and duly announced in *Siddhanta Deepika*.[167] In the speeches of January and February 1897, Vivekananda repeatedly made bold claims regarding a universal religion:

> You have also heard, quite within recent times, claims put forward in favour of Christianity by a great friend of mine, Dr. Barrows, that Christianity is the only universal religion. Let me consider this question awhile and lay down before you my reasons why I think that it is the Vedanta, and the Vedanta alone that can become the universal religion of man, and that none else is fitted for that role.[168] ... Ours, as I have said, is the universal religion. It is inclusive enough, it is broad enough to include all ideals.[169]

---

[163] *Siddhanta Deepika*, for instance, reported significant polemical confrontations at two annual Vedanta conferences at Madras in 1913 and 1914, which even led to the situation where, in one instance, the followers of Advaita Vedanta "pelt stones at the Siddhantis from a distance" (see *Siddhanta Deepika* 13 [1912/1913] 481–483; 14 [1913/1914] 235–237).

[164] See, for instance, Nallasvami Pillai 1911b: 28; Nallasvami Pillai 1911c: 42; Nallasvami Pillai 1911h: 124, 128; Nallasvami Pillai 1911l: 268; Nallasvami Pillai 1911m: 294.

[165] See *Siddhanta Deepika* 6 (1902/1903) 30, and *Siddhanta Deepika* 13 (1912/1913) 285–287, where a tribute to Vivekananda's 50th birthday is reprinted.

[166] See Basu and Ghosh 1969: 505 (*Brahmavadin*/27.2.1897: 'Kumbakonam Address'), 603 (*Prabuddha Bharata*/March 1897: 'The Vedanta and its Application to Indian life' – Madras; 'The Sages of India' – Madras).

[167] See Muller 1897; Muller 1904; *Siddhanta Deepika* 1 (1897/1898) 288.

[168] Muller 1897: 96 (italics deleted); Muller 1904: 90. This is the Kumbakonam Address that is reprinted in the Complete Works, though with some alterations in the English style (Vivekananda 1959: III.182). John Henry Barrows was one of the organisers of the World Parliament of Religions in Chicago 1893 (see Ziolkowski 1993).

[169] Muller 1897: 168; Muller 1904: 160–161. This is the third Madras lecture with the title "The Sages of India", reprinted in the Complete Works (Vivekananda 1959: III.251–252. There is at least one more explicit statement on universal religion in the Madras lectures, see Vivekananda 1959: III. 279.

These quotations show clearly the use of the same strategy to conceptualize Advaita Vedanta as a universal religion that we found with Nallasvami for Saiva Siddhanta. Whereas the conceptual framework of a universal religion is very similar between Nallasvami's Saiva Siddhanta and Vivekananda's Advaita Vedanta, there are some interesting differences which should be noted. Vivekananda stated that "modern materialistic science can be acceptable, harmoniously with their religion, only to the Vedantins" and this was combined with "the wonderful rationalism of the Vedanta".[170] The scientific claim is made against orthodox Christianity as a seemingly unscientific, non-empirical, revelatory religion.[171] In connection with this, Vivekananda also elevated experience (Skt. anubhava) to a status of authority higher than scripture. This related to the concept of an inward experiential religion not dependent on scriptural revelation and outward practices.[172] Following this line of argument, Vivekananda was also critical of traditional rituals. He considered religious rituals the "kindergarten of religion", which are only secondary expressions and, as "concretized philosophy", limited in their importance to a pedagogical function.[173]

Nallasvami could not agree with this line of argument fully. He also referred to the contemporary knowledge of Western science, and he claimed for Saiva Siddhanta that "the latest discoveries in science could not shake its foundation"[174]. However, he never spoke of Saiva Siddhanta being itself scientific. The background for this might have something to do with the specific discursive constellation. Within the discourse of religion, identity or reconciliation between science and religion was usually claimed by non-theistic movements, like Spiritualism, Theosophy, Neo-Hinduism, or Neo-Theravada-Buddhism, which understood their own teachings as pantheistic, monistic, or non-dualistic.[175] They backed up their arguments with a Western critique of religion, especially of Christianity, from evolutionary materialism (Herbert Spencer, Ernst Haeckel etc.). They understood themselves as a religious version of contemporary philosophical monism, though without the materialistic implications of its counterpart in popular Western philosophy.[176]

Since Nallasvami defended a theistic tradition, he could not go along with this. Moreover, as he did not start his activities for Saiva Siddhanta

---

170 Vivekananda 1959: III. 184–185.

171 For the discursive context of the science and religion debate, and the critique of Christianity, see Bergunder 2005.

172 See Proudfoot 1985; Rambachan 1994; Nehring 2005.

173 See Vivekananda 1959: I.72, V.216, VIII.365.

174 Nallasvami Pillai 1911k: 242.

175 See Bergunder 2005.

176 See, for instance, Dvivedi 1889. See also Prakash 1999: 75–82.

before the late 1890s, it seems he was already aware of the new situation in the West, where the science and religion antithesis was widely overcome by Neo-Kantianism. Nallasvami did not view science as materialistic and anti-religious; when he mentions scientific positions, he calls them "agnostic" or refers simply to Neo-Kantian philosophy.[177] As we have seen, he used the Western Christian critique of pantheism to criticize Neo-Hinduism. This made it nearly impossible to relate Saiva Siddhanta, at the same time, to the idea of a scientific monistic religion. Moreover, because the Neo-Hindu understanding of Advaita Vedanta as the central philosophy of Hinduism was firmly embedded in the Orientalist understanding of the Sanskrit tradition, Nallasvami had to argue with scriptural evidence to show the opposite; this made it also very difficult for him to take an empiricist position like Vivekananda. He did not even relate Saiva Siddhanta to any kind of religious experientialism, and he rarely addressed the emotional side of Tamil Saiva Bhakti.

Another difference to Vivekananda relates to the position towards rituals. Saiva Siddhanta is well known for its complex ritualism, but, as already pointed out, Nallasvami largely left out this dimension. However, in contrast to Vivekananda, he could not outrightly devalue rituals. He seemed to be aware, though, that in constructing Saivism as a universal religion, he needed to have some critical position on rituals too:

> We cannot know God really by all our religious rites and performances, repetition of prayers and formulas by saguna or nirguna worship, with or without idols, and even by the highest yoga, except when His grace and Love fills us all and we lose ourselves in this Love. ... All our religious practices, ceremonies, forms and Shibboleths fall off from us, as the basket from the sleeper's hand, and they are of no consequence when we reach His seat.[178]

Whereas Vivekananda could easily relate to the long tradition of advaitic vedantic ritual criticism, the more ritualistic Saiva Siddhanta had many more problems coping with the criticism of ritual inherent in the contemporary global religious discourse. The different concepts of ritual criticism, in Neo-Hinduism and Saiva Siddhanta revival, are also an indication of the constraints on the power of the colonial discourse when it met strong conflicting traditions.

Though Nallasvami and his followers argued their case in an elegant, sophisticated and comprehensive manner, the universalist claim of Saiva Siddhanta to be the true heir of Hinduism was not accepted outside their ranks and did not gain permanent ground in the following decades. At least two setbacks are obvious. The colonial discourse on religion in India

---

[177] See Nallasvami Pillai 1911b: 25; Nallasvami Pillai 1911m: 308.

[178] Nallasvami Pillai 1911j: 216; Nallasvami Pillai 1911o: 358. See also Nallasvami Pillai 1898/1899a: 157.

was deeply shaped by the framework of Western Orientalism. This marks the first handicap for Saiva Siddhanta. Several studies have shown how Neo-Hinduism was able to achieve its strong plausibility by playing along the lines of Orientalist thinking, though often inverting its judgements.[179] Nallasvami was well aware of the current state of Western indological research. In the second volume of *Siddhanta Deepika*, we find a concise overview about the history of European Sanskrit scholarship,[180] and many new books by famous indologists like Max Müller or Paul Deussen were often immediately reviewed.[181] Nallasvami saw clearly how Neo-Hinduism profited from this relation to Orientalist thinking, and that Saiva Siddhanta simply did not fit into the picture of the 'mystic East'. It is interesting to read how sharply Nallasvami complained about it:

> The European who has learnt to read the books of one [Indian] school of philosophy only (all the books translated till now in English are books and commentaries of the Vedānta School), knows nothing of any other school of philosophy existing in India and what authorities they had, and has gradually come to deny the existence of even such; and young Indians educated in English deriving all their pabulum from such source have also been ignorant of any other phases of Indian Philosophy.[182]

The exclusionist effects of the Orientalist discourse are not an invention of postcolonial scholars; they were already realized by many marginalized and colonized people, a point which deserves more attention in future research.[183] In this situation, Nallasvami and his followers closely watched for any possible changes in the discursive constellation. As we have seen, Nallasvami's argument depended, among others, on a theistic interpretation of the Vedanta Sutras as against the Advaita Vedanta and, as already briefly mentioned, he especially emphasised Max Müller's late change of mind with regard to this. Only a few months after the publication of Max Müller's book on Ramakrishna, Nallasvami wrote an editorial under the title *Prof. Max Muller's conversion*. In his book on Ramakrishna, Müller had written that he was now "bound to acknowledge after

---

[179] See, for instance, King 1999; Dirks 2001; Bergunder 2004.

[180] See Ramanan 1898/1899.

[181] See, for instance, *Siddhanta Deepika* 2 (1898/1899) 238 (M. Müller, *Ramakrishna*, 1898); *Siddhanta Deepika* 13 (1912/1913) 142–146 (P. Deussen, *The System of Vedanta* [Engl. transl.], 1912).

[182] Nallasvami Pillai 1911i: 172–173, see also Nallasvami Pillai 1898/1899a: 157. Cf. also Vaitheespara 1999: 168–169, where another quotation is given which makes it clear that Vedanta, in that context, meant Advaita Vedanta.

[183] For another sharp critique of the exclusionist nature of the Orientalist discourse in India, see some remarks of C. Iyothee Thassar (Tam. k. ayōttitācar, 1845–1914) in the Tamil journal, *Tamiḻaṉ* (see Aloysius 1999: I.153, II.86). For an English translation of the respective passages, see Bergunder 2004: 72 fn. 21. See also Aloysius 1998; Geetha and Rajadurai 1998: 98–99.

Professor Thibaut's luminous exposition that Viśiṣṭādvaita interpretation is more in keeping with the Sutras of Badarayana."[184] Nallasvami considered himself vindicated, but also spoke of his impotence in changing the hegemonic discourse in India:

And it took him [Max Müller] nine years [since the publication of the first volume of Thibaut's commentary] to come round to face the real truth and acknowledge it. ... we have been claiming attention for Dr. Thibaut's view since 1895, and not even a single Indian writer condescended to notice it. Such is the firm-hold bigotry of this so-called liberal age.[185]

In another instance, *Siddhanta Deepika* drew attention to an anonymous review of Paul Deussen's *Allgemeine Geschichte der Philosophie*, in one of the leading English review journals. The German indologist, Paul Deussen, was known to Saiva Siddhanta revivalists as "the keenest expounder of Sankara in the West"[186]. The review criticized his opinion that Sankara "returned to the pure doctrine of the Upanishads", and his estimation of Advaita Vedanta as "still the creed of the majority of those Hindus who feel the need for a philosophical basis of their conception of the world". The reviewer complained:

The Professor speaks here more as a partisan than as a critic, ignoring the justifiable claims of some millions of e. g. Saivas and Ramanujiyas. We regret too that he has not studied at first hand the very interesting and valuable system of the Saiva Siddhantam which is the dominant creed of Southern India.[187]

However, this review probably did not come from an established European indologist, but from H. W. Schomerus, who belonged to the small group of Christian missionaries that had a scholarly interest in classical Tamil literature and Saiva Siddhanta.[188] These missionary scholars, especially G. U. Pope and Schomerus, tried to confront Western indology with the Tamil and Saiva classics, as can be seen in this review. Nallasvami and his followers sought them as allies. As already seen, Nallasvami presented their research and their positive judgement of Saiva Siddhanta

---

[184] *Siddhanta Deepika* 2 (1898/1899) 238. The quotation is from Müller 1899b: 71. The reference about George Thibaut is with regard to his translation of the Sankara commentary of the Vedanta Sutras in the *Sacred Books of the East* (see Thibaut 1890/1896, especially page c of the introduction in the first volume).

[185] *Siddhanta Deepika* 2 (1898/1899) 238.

[186] Ramanan 1909/1910: 48.

[187] Ramanan 1909/1910: 49 (italics deleted). The quotation is a reprint from the book review in *Luzac's Oriental List and Book Review* (London) 20 (January to December 1909) 1910: 2–3. Though the review is anonymous, the whole ductus of the arguments makes it is highly likely that it was written by H. W. Schomerus, cf. similar statements in Schomerus 1912: 5, 19–20, 176–177.

[188] For Schomerus in general, see Nehring 2003. Schomerus' German book on Saiva Siddhanta (Schomerus 1912) was reviewed in *Siddhanta Deepika* 14 (1913/1914) 92–93.

to confront mainstream Orientalist notions with conflicting and alternative Western scholarship. He invited Schomerus as a special guest to the fourth Saiva Siddhanta conference in 1909, and Schomerus' conference report was reprinted in *Siddhanta Deepika*.[189] Nallasvami even bought 100 copies of Pope's translation of the Tamil Saiva Bhakti classic, *Tiruvacakam* (Tam. tiruvācakam), to distribute it to interested people free of cost.[190]

However, Western indology at the time was well entrenched in Sanskrit studies, and the research on South India was simply ignored by prominent contemporary indologists. The few Tamil scholars were not able to make a difference, which Nallasvami was very much aware of when he wrote in an editorial:

> A European missionary gentleman wrote to us from England to say that he repeatedly pressed on Professor Max Müller and Monier Williams and others the claims of Tamil literature and Philosophy but that they had turned a deaf ear to his prayers.[191]

In the same way, the leading English speaking Indian elite, dominated by Brahmans, oriented themselves towards Sanskrit traditions and advaitic Neo-Hinduism, and largely ignored other currents. In 1911, a second 'Convention of Religions' was organized by the followers of Vivekananda in Allahabad. Nallasvami again participated and presented an impressive paper, which interpreted Saiva Siddhanta as a universal religion in relation to other religions.[192] However, no trace of any impact on the wider Indian context could be found. The failure to make a lasting effect is also illustrated by the fact that at the 'International Parliament of Religions', organized by the Ramakrishna Mission at Calcutta in 1937, no representative of Saiva Siddhanta presented a paper.[193]

The other great obstacle to the universalist claims of Saiva Siddhanta was its strong Vellalar base. All the important activists of the Saiva Siddhanta revival were from a Vellalar or related background. Though Nallasvami had close Tamil Brahman co-workers, like V. V. Ramana Sastrin, and also a wide range of Brahman sympathizers, it was to

---

[189] See Nehring 2003: 335–341.

[190] See Balasubramaniam 1965: 88.

[191] *Siddhanta Deepika* 7 (1906/1907) 27.

[192] See Nallasvami Pillai 1911o: 347. *Siddhanta Deepika* did not provide further information of the Allahabad convention. It seems also that no conference volume was published.

[193] See Ramakrishna Mission 1938. However, T. H. M. Sadasivayya spoke on "Vīraśaivism" and had a brief look at Saiva Siddhanta teachings, when tracing its historical roots. He referred to its special notion of advaita and made the argument in an identical way to that of Nallasvami. He probably, therefore, knew Nallasvami's writings (see Sadasivayya 1938: 434).

Theosophy and Neo-Hinduism that most English educated Brahmans were allied in the South Indian Tamil context. It does not appear as if many Brahmans joined the Saiva Siddhanta revival.

We also have hardly any evidence that the idea of Saiva Siddhanta as a universal religion was combined with an active policy of opening up its base to people from groups considered by Vellalars to be of lower societal status. The only incident that informs of a specific practical crossing of caste barriers is the positive report about a 'Pañchama Religious Association', with the name 'Śivanēsa Tirukūṭṭattār', which Nallasvami encountered during a 1911 lecture visit in Bangalore. Young men from that organisation sang hymns of the Tamil Saiva classic Tevaram (Tam. tēvāram) to the audience, and Nallasvami made it a point to visit their place.[194] However, it is not reported that this organisation became in any way part of the network of Tamil Saiva Siddhanta organisations coordinated by Nallasvami. On the other hand, caste discrimination and its impact on social inequality were openly discussed in the Saiva Siddhanta organizations, especially at the fourth central conference in Trichy 1909.[195] However, the main attitude was that of gradual and top down social reform as, for instance, suggested by Nallasvami in relation to the Nadar (Tam. nāṭār) discrimination: "If we are wise in our generation, we should give small concessions to these people gradually such as their entry into some of the inner enclosure and so on till all the restrictions are done away with."[196] Into this picture fits the plan by the central Saiva Siddhanta association to open a 'Nandanar school for the education of the Pañchama'[197] in 1910.

Dravidian historiography, Tamil identity, and the legacy of Nallasvami

It is somewhat illustrative that *Siddhanta Deepika* was discontinued in 1914, whereas the Justice Party and perhaps the Pure Tamil movement started in 1916. At this point, it is not possible to analyse the complex historical genesis of this development. Here, we will solely focus on the conceptual break from Nallasvami's idea of an inclusive, universalist Saiva Siddhanta to Maraimalai's decisively Dravidian understanding of Tamil Saivism and its history. However, this break was not a complete one, as the question of Tamil identity and Dravidian historiography were

---

194 *Siddhanta Deepika* 11 (1910/1911) 513–514.

195 See *Siddhanta Deepika* 10 (1909/1910) 258–259.

196 *Siddhanta Deepika* 3 (1899/1900) 47.

197 *Siddhanta Deepika* 11 (1910/1911) 431.

already discussed by Nallasvami himself and in his journal *Siddhanta Deepika*. It should be noted that Nallasvami defended, by all means, Tamil as a modern language, and forcefully fought for its place at the university.[198] Moreover, he displayed a very critical position against the Brahmanical caste system with its discriminatory effects, and adopted an explicit Dravidian understanding in his criticism of it:

> Brahmins tried hard to impose their fourfold distinction [in South India]; and portions of the South Indian community who display greater punctiliousness in the matter of caste are all people who have become more and more under the sway of Brahminism; and even now if there are instances of Pariahs entering temples and non-Brahmins officiating as priests ... they are vestiges of the older influences of non-Brahmins before they were subverted by the dominance of Brahmins ...[199]

In a remarkable editorial, he referred to the situation of the Nadars, which he personally knew from his own travel experience.[200] He wrote that "the restrictions imposed on the Shanars [i. e. Nadars] were not religious" but "political", and he called it "shameful" that this treatment should happen "in the name of our Religion and our God".[201] He saw the Nadars as a people that in the past had experienced not a religious subjection but a political one, which later was wrongly interpreted as religious. It is in this sense that he was also critical of the Nadars' claim to be Kshatriyas (Skt. kṣatriya), because it reinforced the Brahmanical varna (Skt. varṇa) framework, which he wanted to be discarded. He objected to the Kshatriya claim as "nobody would seriously talk of their being Kshattrias when they were pure Dravidians"[202]. One might speculate that this is also one reason why he nowhere discusses the caste status of the Vellalars, or comments on the then contemporary claim of Indian Vellalars to be Vaisyas (Skt. vaiśya).[203] Regarding caste, it seems clear that Nallasvami argued in line with the dichotomy of Dravidian / Tamil versus Aryan / Brahman. Here is also a basic difference to Vivekananda's position, who was undecided on the issue of caste but, in the end, tended to defend the Brahmanical varna system, while rejecting its discriminatory aspects.[204]

---

198 See Balasubramaniam 1965: 67–78.

199 Nallasvami Pillai 1898/1899b: 188.

200 See *Siddhanta Deepika* 2 (1898/1899) 119–120.

201 *Siddhanta Deepika* 3 (1899/1900) 47.

202 *Siddhanta Deepika* 3 (1899/1900) 48.

203 For the Vaishya-claim of Vellalar, see Hellmann-Rajanayagam 1989: 241; Vaitheespara 1999: 325–326, 481. However, in one of his articles, he provided a longer quote from P. Sundaram Pillai where the Vellalars are called "the flower of the Dravidian Race" (Nallasvami Pillai 1898/1899c: 112).

204 See, for instance, Bayly 1998: 101–104; Bayly 1999: 163–166. However, though Bayly admits that Vivekananda's writings also contain anti-caste statements (Bayly 1999:

This rejection of the Brahmanical varna system principally demanded the postulation of a specific Dravidian and pre-Aryan past without a varna system.[205] Nallasvami indeed proposed, explicitly, a Tamil race that migrated to India by sea "from Assyria and Asiatic Minor, the oldest seat of ancient civilization"; and he even claimed that he was "the first to broach the notion that the Tamilians had no sort of connection with the north or northern settlers and they never derived their letters or arts or civilization from the Aryans".[206] However, he himself did not elaborate on this matter further, though he consciously gave room to its discussion in *Siddhanta Deepika*.[207] Without explicitly distancing himself from it, he reproduced, in one of his own articles, quotations from P. Sundaram Pillai (1855–1897), who was perhaps the first of the English educated Tamil scholars from a Vellalar background who radically proposed a Dravidian Saiva non-Aryan past of the Tamils.[208] Sundaram was of the conviction that "most of what is ignorantly called Aryan Philosophy, Aryan civilization is literally Dravidian or Tamilian at bottom"[209]. Similar views were also unambiguously propagated by Ponnambalam Pillai. In the presidential address of the 7th central conference at Kanchipuram in 1912, he stated that the Dravidians already had a "high state of civilization all peculiarly our own – when the Āryans entered India",[210] and this Dravidian civilization did not know any caste discrimination.[211] Saiva Siddhanta was called by him the "Dravidian religion" that "had been perfected so as to become a cosmopolitan religion as it is now, so that it may embrace within its fold all the other religions in the world, by the time the Āryans entered India with the earlier and unsystematic portions of the Vedas"[212].

However, it is hard to reconcile this aspect of Dravidian historiography with Nallasvami's derivation of Saiva Siddhanta from the Sanskrit tradition and his broad outreach to the English educated elite of South Indian

166 note 47), she emphasizes, perhaps too much, the apologetic side. Vivekananda's critique of caste can already be found in some passages of his Indian addresses in Ceylon and South India in January/February 1897 (see Vivekananda 1959: III.132–133, 198–199, 267, 291–298).

205 For the general question of Aryan and Dravidian historiography within the colonial discourse in India see Ramaswamy 2001; Bergunder 2004.

206 Nallasvami Pillai 1898/1899c: 110.

207 These voices received special attention in the fifth volume of Siddhanta Deepika from 1901/1902. See, especially, Savariroyan 1901/1902. There was, for instance, also a longer extract from Sundaram Pillai's *History of the Religious Sects in Southern India* in *Siddhanta Deepika* 5 (1901/1902) 73–74. See also *Siddhanta Deepika* 5 (1901/1902) 157–161, 168–173.

208 For P. Sundaram Pillai see Vaitheespara 1999: 139–158.

209 Quote in Nallasvami Pillai 1898/1899c: 112.

210 Ponnambalam Pillai 1912/1913: 346 (italics deleted).

211 See Ponnambalam Pillai 1912/1913: 352.

212 Ponnambalam Pillai 1912/1913: 349–350.

Brahmans. Nallasvami seemed to be very aware of this problem and wrote in a 1906 editorial:

Following up our first article on the ancient Tamilian civilization, Pandit D. Savariroyan and his friends have opened up a dark page of South India's past and great credit is due to them for carrying on their work, undeterred by the unreasoning opposition and prejudices of a large number. And we have heard it – that we have lost the sympathy of a few of our well-wishers and friends by permitting the publication of such articles. But we will appeal to their sense of justice and fairness for once.[213]

The idea of a distinct Tamil history was apparently so important to Nallasvami that he even risked the established friendship of his Brahman supporters. However, in his philosophical expositions of Saiva Siddhanta as a universal religion, the idea of a Dravidian pre-Aryan past was nowhere explicitly reflected on. It is hard to believe that a systematic thinker like Nallasvami had no idea of how to relate the idea of a special and separate Tamil past to the history of Saiva Siddhanta. Only in one article, on the Svetasvatara Upanishat, did he write about the time between Buddha and Badarayana, the author of the Vedanta Sutras:

It was during this time ... that the blending of the Aryan and Tamilian in art and civilization and Philosophy took place (and we could not here consider how much was common to both and how much each gained from the other).[214]

From this quotation, one might guess that he considered the Vedanta Sutras the product of the contact between Aryan and Tamil philosophy, but he did not elaborate on it further. The following text of thc paragraph suggests, in a certain way, that Samkhya (Skt. sāṃkhya) and Yoga might be of Tamil origin, or at least had a strong Tamil counterpart. However, as we have already seen, Nallasvami made it clear that Saiva Siddhanta is neither Samkhya nor Yoga, but a "third school" different from them both.[215]

It is precisely here that Maraimalai went one step further. Basing his argument very much on the Samkhya tradition, he explicitly related Saiva Siddhanta to a specific Dravidian past. The difference of this approach to Nallasvami is well illustrated when looking at a paper which Maraimalai presented before the Theosophical Society in Calcutta in 1913.[216] The

[213] *Siddhanta Deepika* 7 (1906/1907) 29–30. The 7th volume was published after a three-year delay. Considering the unusual, explicit language about lost well-wishers, one might speculate that the journal got into financial trouble after extensively publishing the Dravidian perspectives in the 5th volume, because Brahman friends might have stopped giving support or paying their subscription.

[214] Nallasvami Pillai 1911h: 121.

[215] See Nallasvami Pillai 1911b: 32–33.

[216] See Vaitheespara 1999: 443–446.

context is similar to the paper of Nallasvami that we analysed in the first part, because Maraimalai is also speaking about Saiva Siddhanta to a North-Indian audience that views Advaita Vedanta as the central philosophy of Hinduism. Unlike Nallasvami, Maraimalai centred his whole argumentation around Samkhya as being the historical root of Saiva Siddhanta. For him, Samkhya is "the earliest and deepest fountain of philosophy"[217] and it had a deep impact on Buddhism and Yoga, but also on the Sanskrit tradition, like the Upanishads, the Bhagavadgita, and the Vedanta Sutras. However, it is Saiva Siddhanta that truly preserved the Samkhya tradition:

> Now as regards the relation of Sānkhya to Saiva Siddhānta I venture to say that in all and every important respect they are identical ... As you also see from this identity of these two systems, that the doctrine of Saiva Siddhānta entitle it to a claim of as great of antiquity as the system of Sānkhya has.[218]

One should not overlook that this line of argument is in many ways similar to Nallasvami's approach. Central parts of the Sanskrit tradition, such as the Upanishads, the Bhagavadgita, and the Vedanta Sutras, are claimed for Saiva Siddhanta by Maraimalai, though, in his case, it is because of their Samkhya imprint only. As in Nallasvami's case, this meant for Maraimalai that the Advaita Vedanta could no longer claim that its interpretation of these foundational classical texts was authentic or appropriate. Similarities can also be found in several specific philosophical positions on Saiva Siddhanta. Maraimalai explicated the specific understanding of advaita in Saiva Siddhanta in the same way as Nallasvami would have done it.[219] This is not self-evident, as Sundaram had characterized Saiva Siddhanta as "dualist", in his effort to separate a Dravidian or Tamil tradition of Saiva Siddhanta from an Aryan tradition of Advaita Vedanta.[220] Maraimalai clearly followed Nallasvami's more complicated argument.

However, highlighting Samkhya created a special problem, as Maraimalai himself acknowledged. Samkhya is an "agnostic" philosophy with no knowledge of a "Supreme Being".[221] One might speculate that this aspect deterred Nallasvami from searching in more detail for a Dravidian Samkhya tradition, as he was always making theism the most crucial and central aspect of Saiva Siddhanta and its historical predecessors. Marai-

---

[217] Maraimalai Adigal 1913–1914: 174.

[218] Maraimalai Adigal 1913–1914: 213–214.

[219] See Maraimalai Adigal 1913–1914: 185–188. A comparison between Nallasvami and Maraimalai, regarding their views on the philosophical tenets of Saiva Siddhanta, is an academic void.

[220] See *Siddhanta Deepika* 5 (1901/1902) 74, and Balasubramaniam 1965: 55–60.

[221] Maraimalai Adigal 1913–1914: 212, 214.

malai downplayed this aspect and explained that "Saiva Siddhānta, like the so called theistic Sānkhya or yoga of Patañjali, goes a step upward and maintains the existence of an all intelligent power from certain actual experiences of our inward life"[222]. This line of argument transformed God into a power that can be observed empirically and, hence, could be included into the system. The emphasis here is more on the rational justification of God, which goes along with Maraimalai's strong emphasis on the rational foundation of Samkhya. He accused the Sanskrit tradition of having diluted Samkhya rationalism by mixing it with a scriptural foundation, because "in the Vedanta Sutras the doctrines of Sankhya [were] assimilated and expounded, not based upon reason alone [as in the original Samkhya] ... but based upon the various passages of the upanishads"[223]. According to Maraimalai, Saiva Siddhanta had kept the rationalism of Samkhya, which led him to claim that Saiva Siddhanta and science were principally identical:

> To all those who seek after an exact knowledge of these six eternal verities [of Saiva Siddhanta], it must be very gratifying to note that the recent developments of western philosophy and physical science go every inch to prove the truth and value of all the fundamental doctrines that are peculiar only to Saiva Siddhanta but not to any other religion or philosophy, ancient or modern.[224]

This is a claim that Nallasvami avoided. It brings to mind the understanding of Advaita Vedanta as science in the writings of Vivekananda, which Maraimalai had intensively studied and compared with Saiva Siddhanta.[225] However, the main, directly traceable influence of this scientific claim came from Maraimalai's study of Western esotericism and especially Theosophy which, as already mentioned, also claimed an identification with science.[226] Against the background of this esoteric scientism, he understood Saiva Siddhanta as an occult science.[227]

In his later writings, Maraimalai's ideas on the Dravidian past became more articulate and combined with strong anti-Brahman sentiments.[228] It is often pointed out how strongly this Dravidian position of Maraimalai's Tamil Saivism became the ideological base for the early Justice Party and pre-Periyar Dravidian movement. However, a point often neglected is that this was also connected with a shift and transformation in the self-under-

---

[222] Maraimalai Adigal 1913–1914: 214.

[223] Maraimalai Adigal 1913–1914: 181.

[224] Maraimalai Adigal 1966: 14–15.

[225] See Vaitheespara 1999: 365.

[226] For Maraimalai's study of Western Esotericism see, for instance, Vaitheespara 1999: 334, 364–365.

[227] See Vaitheespara 1999: 367.

[228] See, for instance, his comprehensive treatise of Saiva Siddhanta from 1940 (see Maraimalai Adigal 1966).

standing of the Tamil Saiva Siddhanta revival. At least a comparison between Nallasvami and Maraimalai suggests this. It is a well established fact that the elder and influential Nallasvami took over some of the important revival initiatives of the younger Maraimalai. Nallasvami monopolized control over the central Saiva Siddhanta umbrella organization and the annual conferences it organized, which had been initiated by Maraimalai.[229] There is also evidence that Maraimalai had a strong personal animosity towards Nallasvami, whom he even once called a "drunkard" in his diary.[230] However, this personal rivalry and power struggle must not overshadow the conceptual differences at play, which exemplarily mark the plurality and changes within the Tamil Saiva Siddhanta revival in the late 19th and early 20th century.

Universalist interpretations of Saivism before Nallasvami in the late 19th century

The conflation of Saiva Siddhanta with a Dravidian identity started in the late 19th and early 20th century, interpreting and appropriating the contemporary Orientalist dichotomy of Aryans and Dravidians. P. Sundaram Pillai is perhaps the earliest exponent of this perspective and Maraimalai the most established.[231] However, as our analysis has shown, Nallasvami's understanding of Saiva Siddhanta as a universal religion was also dependent on Orientalist notions and the contemporary colonial discourse on religion in the second half of the 19th century. This raises the question whether Nallasvami's interpretation of Saiva Siddhanta as a universal religion marked a new development or whether it was part of a foregoing discursive context. Nallasvami himself seems to suggest that he was inspired by his teacher, Somasundara Nayakar (1846–1901), when he wrote in the obituary: "He used to frequently point out the universal character of the Siddhanta, how this was the whole, of which all other schools were but parts ..."[232] Although the work of Somasundara is not yet well researched,[233] it is doubtful if he already had a clear concept of Saiva Siddhanta as a universal religion. The same seems to be true for the 19th-

---

229 See Vaitheespara 1999: 383–396.

230 See Vaitheespara 1999: 395.

231 See Vaitheespara 1999: 32–33. See also Dirks 2001; Nehring 2003; Bergunder 2004; Trautmann 2006.

232 *Siddhanta Deepika* 4 (1900/1901) 205.

233 There is no academic biography, but for a good summary of his life and teachings see Vaitheespara 1999: 118–139.

century Saiva Siddhanta revival in Jaffna (Tam. yāḻppāṇam) around Arumuga Navalar (Tam. āṟumuka nāvalar, 1822–1897).[234]

There is one case that deserves special attention. It is related to the interpretation of the message of Ramalinga Adigal (Tam. irāmaliṅka aṭikaḷ, 1823–1874) after his death. Ramalinga was a major Saiva saint in the 19th century, but his characterization differs widely.[235] When T. Velayuda Mudaliar (Tam. toḻuvūr vēlāyuta mutaliyār), Ramalinga's foremost and long-standing disciple, published the first edition of Ramalinga's religious poetry in 1867, called the *Tiruvarutpa* (Tam. tiruvaruṭpā), he added a biographical poem in which he characterized Ramalinga as a Tamil Saiva Bhakti saint.[236] In the 1892 edition of the *Tiruvarutpa* Ramaswamy Mudaliar explained Ramalinga's life as that of a traditional Tamil cittar (Skt. siddha).[237] Yet, the Tamil nationalist interpreters of Saiva Siddhanta claimed Ramalinga, as well as Arumuga, as the founder of the whole Saiva Siddhanta revival, and he was held in high esteem by Maraimalai.[238]

Velayuda pleaded, some years after Ramalinga's death, in the 1880s, for a universalist understanding of Ramalinga's message. In 1882, Velayuda presented his new interpretation; he published a longer statement in the official journal of the Theosophical Society to introduce Ramalinga's universalist message:

> Among many other things he [Ramalinga] preached ... that the distinction between races and castes would eventually cease, and the principle of Universal Brotherhood be eventually accepted, and a Universal Brotherhood be established. ... In the year 1867, he [Ramalinga] founded a Society, under the name 'Samarasa Veda Sanmarga Sangham', which means a society based on the principle of Universal Brotherhood, and for the propagation of the true Vedic doctrine. I need hardly remark that these principles are identically those of the Theosophical Society.[239]

This remarkable statement sees Ramalinga's teachings in line with a universal religious outlook when it interprets its core as the "principle of

---

[234] See the article of Peter Schalk 'Sustaining the Pre-Colonial Past' in this volume: 106–130. See also Bate 2005, who looks into the concept of religion that Arumuga adopted.

[235] See Raman 2002.

[236] See Raman 2002: 193.

[237] Raman 2002: 193–194.

[238] For quotes in *Siddhanta Deepika* where Arumuga and Ramalinga are called the two founders of the Saiva Siddhanta revival see, for instance, 10 (1909/1910) 254, and 11 (1910/1911) 262. For Maraimalai's appreciation of Ramalinga, see Vaitheespara 1999: 321–331, 416–418, 440–441.

[239] *The Theosophist* 3 (1881/1882) 243. The whole text is on pp. 243–244 under the heading "Coming Events Foretold", and is reprinted in Adigal 1975: 611–616. It is also partially quoted in Raman 2002.

Universal brotherhood", and when he identifies it with the teachings of Theosophy, which are exemplary for the concept of a universal religion.[240] When this statement was published, Velayuda, who was working as Tamil pandit at Presidency College, and thus had some social standing, had already officially joined the Theosophical Society. He was not the only follower of Ramalinga who reached out for contacts with the Theosophical Society. Henry Olcott (1832–1907), the co-founder of the Theosophical Society, met "certain disciples and near relations" of Ramalinga in Bangalore in 1886, who apparently all supported this universalist and Theosophical interpretation of his message.[241] We also know that Casava Pillai, Inspector of Police in Nellore and prominent member of the Theosophical Society in the early years, had been deeply influenced by Ramalinga and was a friend of Velayuda.[242] Unfortunately, we do not have more information about these Theosophical Ramalinga followers. There are some indications that, in the 1880s, the Theosophical Society had many leading Tamil members of Vellalar or Chettiyar (Tam. ceṭṭiyār) background. This changed later on[243] and, during the 1890s, the Brahman domination, for which the Theosophical Society is now famous in the Tamil context, became slowly established and many of the early Vellalar and Chettiyar members were forgotten.

The universalist claim of Velayuda caused a harsh and strict refutation from the Brahmanical side. It was written by N. Chidambaram Iyer, who was a sympathizer of the Theosophical Society, a regular contributor to *The Theosophist*, and who especially appreciated Theosophical help in reviving Hinduism.[244] One of Chidambaram's major arguments was that the notion of a universal religion necessarily needs the idea of an impersonal God, which Ramalinga did not teach but which Velayuda wrongly

---

[240] Up until today, there is no scholarly study on Ramalinga, but Srilata Raman has recently worked on him (see Raman 2002) and plans to publish a monograph. The following interpretation keeps to Velayuda's interpretation and does not go back to Ramalinga's message itself. However, for an interpretation of the ambiguous terms 'samarasa' (Tam. camaracam) and 'san-mārga' in Ramalinga's works, see Dayanandan Francis 1990: 33–36. For the teachings of Theosophy on universal religion see, for instance, Campbell 1980; Figl 1993.

[241] See *The Theosophist* 7 (1885/1886) 747. See also Olcott 1895: 386–391 for a visit of Olcott to Bangalore, where he probably met the disciples and relatives of Ramalinga.

[242] See R. Casava Pillai: How a Hindu of Madras Interviewed a Mahatma at Sikkim. In: *The Indian Mirror* (Calcutta) Vol. 25 (1885) March 3, p. 2, and March 7, p. 2 (quoted from http://www.blavatskyarchives.com/pillai.htm, 08/2008).

[243] Browsing through the journal *The Theosophist* shows that, in the 1880s, numerous 'Pillais' and 'Mudaliars' were mentioned, which abruptly stopped in the 1890s.

[244] As this source is still unknown but very important for the understanding of Ramalinga's legacy, it will be reprinted in Appendix I: 359–368. Chidambaram Iyer became a member of the Theosophical Society in 1883 and died in 1892 (see *The Theosophist* 13 [1891/1892] xlviii).

implied that he did. Velayuda had characterized Ramalinga's understanding of God as: "that what men call 'God' is, in fact, the principle of Universal Love – which produces and sustains perfect Harmony and Equilibrium throughout all nature"[245]. Chidambaram understood this as an impersonal concept of God and confronted it with a contrary statement from one Venkatesa Iyer, whom he called the "most important Chela of Ramalingam Pillai, in fact one of the very few that even now strictly adhere to the instruction of the Guru"[246]. Chidambaram thus contested the privileged disciple status of Velayuda with the supposedly higher authenticity of Venkatesa Iyer, who had written in a letter to Chidambaram:

> He never said there was no personal God. He said there was but one God; that that God possessed all the attributes ever assigned to him by man in word or thought, and many other attributes; that the world was governed by persons chosen by Him for the purpose, and that he was one of the chosen few.[247]

Chidambaram used the testimony of Venkatesa to prove that Velayuda was wrong in implying an impersonal understanding of God in Ramalinga's message:

> The reply [of Venkatesa], however, shows that Ramalingam was a firm believer in a personal God and that he wanted to assume the position of a Saviour of mankind. ... Far from the views of Ramalingam Pillai being 'identically those of the Theosophical Society', you will observe that there is not one important point about which both parties would mutually shake hands; or one common ground except perhaps as to the obnoxious distinctions of caste in which Ramalingam Pillai was naturally much interested for this plain reason, viz., that he occupied, though by accident of birth, the lowest round of the ladder, or, in other words, he was a Sudra.[248]

This strong statement by Chidambaram could be interpreted as claiming, in no uncertain terms, Brahman superiority over religious questions. Venkatesa, the Brahman disciple of Ramalinga, was much more trustworthy than the Vellalar Velayuda, the "Sudra" (Skt. śūdra, Tam. cūttirar) disciple. The claim for universality was reduced to a "Sudra" protest against caste discrimination. Ramalinga is painted as a popular Bhakti saint who believed simply in a personal God, but went a little bit over the top with the claim that he is the saviour of mankind. However, the idea of universal religion could not be derived from theistic Saivism and the latter was also incompatible with Theosophy. It is interesting to note that in an editorial comment, probably written by Henry Olcott or H. P.

---

[245] *The Theosophist* 3 (1881/1882) 243; Adigal 1975: 612.
[246] *The Theosophist* 4 (1882/1883) 62. See Appendix I: 365.
[247] *The Theosophist* 4 (1882/1883) 61. See Appendix I: 361.
[248] *The Theosophist* 4 (1882/1883) 63. See Appendix I: 365.

Blavatsky (1831–1891), the other co-founder of the Theosophical Society, Velayuda was defended by stating that Ramalinga's message was, in principle, in harmony with Advaita Vedanta:

Since the above article was put in type Mr. Chidambaram has kindly sent us for inspection an original copy of a Tamil handbill (Notice) issued by Ramalingam about 10 years ago, together with his (Mr. C's) English rendering of the same. We find upon a careful examination of the Tamil what seems unquestionable evidence that the famous Sadhu believed in the God of the Adwaitees, i. e., a non-personal Universal Essence ...[249]

It is most remarkable that Velayuda, in his rejoinder, did not take sides between a personal or impersonal understanding, but tried to bring both together. The English summary of a Tamil letter written by him to the editors of *The Theosophist* contains the following passage:

It is nowhere pointed out in the Pandit's [i. e. Velayuda's] sketch that Ramalingam Pillai ever said that there is not a Personal God. Here may be [Velayuda] adduced in favour of the statement "That what men call 'God' is, in fact, the principle of Universal Love," a stanza from 'Thirumanthiram' ... "The ignorant say that Love and Brahmam are different. None know how love becomes Brahmam. After knowing that love is Brahmam one becomes absorbed in love and Brahmam." This is also shown in Ramalingam Pillai's works, viz., 'Arulperumjothi Akaval'&c. Nothing more is said in the sketch [i. e., Velayuda's first statement in The Theosophist] about a personal God.[250]

This debate between Chidambaram and Velayuda already showed up the difficulties of how to articulate a universal claim and maintain a theistic concept of God. As has been seen, this was a major theme in Nallasvami's writings, who even quoted the same famous verse from Tirumantiram, when he tried to explain that God is both nirguna and saguna in Saiva Siddhanta.[251] In this manner, then, the circle around Velayuda prepared the way for Nallasvami's later discussion about Saiva Siddhanta as a universal religion. Whether Nallasvami was personally aware of Velayuda's activities is not known, but it is likely, not least because Nallasvami had some contacts to Theosophical circles, though Nallasvami does not refer to Velayuda and Ramalinga in his writings. In any case, Velayuda's example shows, at least to some extent, that the concept

---

[249] *The Theosophist* 4 (1882/1883) 61 note. See Appendix I: 361.

[250] *The Theosophist* 4 (1882/1883) 63. Appendix I: 366. The English text, as related in a footnote, is "freely translated [from Tamil] into English by G. Subbiah Chetty Garu, F. T. S. who speaks in the third person." Soobiah Chetty (1858–1946) was one of the early non-Brahman members of the Theosophical Society (see Sarada 1991). The quote is from Tirumantiram 270, and one should note that the original has Siva (Tam. civam) instead of "Brahmam".

[251] See Nallasvami Pillai 1911m: 300; Nallasvami Pillai 1911p: 354.

of Saivism as a universal religion had already been part of the religious discourse in South India before Nallasvami.

Chidambaram's "Sudra" reference also hints at the later divide between non-Brahman Tamil Saivism and Brahman Neo-Hinduism and Theosophy. Velayuda himself also anticipated this later development. Though he argued against all castes in confrontation with Chidambaram and proclaimed Ramalinga's message as a universal one, he was, at the same time, a leading figure in a petition by Madras Vellalars to the census commissioner, which demanded that the Vellalars be granted a Vaisya instead of Sudra status.[252]

Theoretical implications

Orientalism and colonial discourse

Several groundbreaking studies have shown how the Western colonial representation reshaped Indian society in the 19th and first half of the 20th century.[253] The case of Nallasvami shows, in an exemplary fashion, how the Saiva Siddhanta revival was embedded in the colonial discourse. Western concepts of religion and the Orientalist representation of Hinduism and Indian traditions shaped the debates on Saiva Siddhanta, and any articulation that wanted to be heard had to relate to them. However, there is a danger in this approach, as it might too easily rely on a dichotomy between the colonizer and the colonized as something that shapes the discourse; whereas this dichotomy, in a strict theoretical sense, can only be understood as nothing more than being itself a discursive effect that needs critical treatment. As Stoler and Cooper have pointed out:

> Scholars need to attend more directly to the tendency of colonial regimes to draw a stark dichotomy of colonizer and colonized without themselves falling into such a Manichean conception. ... How to demarcate the boundaries of the 'colonizers' and analyse how those boundaries were produced is proving as elusive task as probing the multiple layers of oppositional discourse and politics. ... It does us no service to reify a colonial moment of binary oppositions ...[254]

It is in relation to this that Homi Bhaba has pointed to the hybridity of the colonial encounter.[255] With regard to South India, Eugene Irschick has even tried to go one step further by viewing the colonial discourse as a

252 See Velayudam Mudaliar 1880.
253 See, for instance, Inden 1990; King 1999; Dirks 2001.
254 Stoler and Cooper 1997: 3, 8, 9.
255 See Bhabha 1994.

multifaceted phenomenon to which all participants contribute.[256] Irschick was heavily criticized for calling this process "dialogue",[257] and one could indeed get the impression that he downplays the basic insight that any identity or subject positioning is an effect of power. However, in the same way, the dichotomous identity of colonizer and colonized is a product of the relationship of power. The critique of Irschick's dialogue concept, then, is itself in danger of constituting a step backward, towards reification of this dichotomy as constitutive of the colonial discourse and providing it with an external, extra-discursive framework, or, in other words, with what Derrida criticises as a "transcendental signifier". As Laclau and Mouffe have shown, on the one hand, identity positionings lead to dichotomies, as they demand an empty signifier to close the endless play of signification and, in that process, a negative "other" necessarily emerges. However, on the other hand, they have also pointed out that these dichotomies are always fragile and open to the subversion of the signifying processes by its participants; and it is this latter aspect that requires major attention in order to trace the discursive dynamics of power struggles.[258]

The South Indian situation, especially, demands a careful and cautious investigation. Ravindiran Vaitheespara has argued that, here, the list of the colonized is broadened into Brahmans and non-Brahmans, and the Orientalists into Sanskrit Orientalists and Missionary Tamil Orientalists.[259] Since this does not fit into the common scholarly view, which relies only on a simple dichotomy between colonizer and colonized, be it conventional history or Postcolonial theory, the "Dravidian movement ... is still largely presented as an aberrant if not peculiar phenomenon"[260]. However, this broadening is also dependent on Western Orientalist representations and needs to be looked at critically. Perundevi Srinivasan has warned that scholars on Tamil Saivism in colonial South India often assume dichotomies, like Non-Brahman Tamil / Dravidian Saivism versus Brahman Aryan / pan-Indian Advaita Vedanta as essential, "with the assumption that the chasm lying between the constructed categories is natural and forever"[261].

However, at the same time, it is important to acknowledge the "reality" of these constructed categories, as they have constituted the hegemonic discourse in the South Indian Tamil context since the 1920s. Nallasvami's universal claim for Saiva Siddhanta did not win general recognition. It

[256] See Irschick 1994. See also the article of Andreas Nehring 'Performing the Revival' in this volume: 12–29.

[257] Dirks 2001: 303–314.

[258] See Laclau and Mouffe 1991.

[259] See Vaitheespara 1999: 1–24; Vaitheespara 2006.

[260] Vaitheespara 1999: 3.

[261] Srinivasan 2006: 239.

was defeated by the rival claim of Neo-Hinduism to be the universal and representative religion of India. Neo-Hinduism fitted Western Orientalist representations and won a pan-Indian following among Indian English educated elites, who came from Brahmanical traditions or who looked at them as religious benchmarks. This also explains well why Nallasvami's concept of Saiva Siddhanta, as a universal religion and fulfilment of the Hindu tradition, did not attract much attention in the academic study of Hinduism – it simply did not fit into the established dichotomies, broadened or not. The result was a marginalization of Saiva Siddhanta. Mariasusai Dhavamony, in 1971, characterized this very well:

> One reason for this neglect [of Saiva Siddhanta and other theistic traditions] is that in India with the rise and spread of Neo-Vedāntism, which champions the cause of the advaita in order to suit the purpose of being as a sort of universal religion syncretising in itself all other great religions, bhakti was accorded a lower status ... Till recently the opinion prevalent among Westerners about Hindu religion was ... that its central idea is non-dualism. Hence, the theistic current in Hindu sacred writings which supplied the intellectual framework for the bhakti cults was thought to be of little consequence in the history of Indian religions.[262]

On the other hand, the Vellalars and other non-Brahman Tamil elites chose to follow an anti-Brahman agenda, which favoured a Tamil nationalist instead of a universal reading of Saiva Siddhanta; hence, Nallasvami's universalist approach fell also into oblivion here. However, it is not the scholarly task to reproduce the history of the victors but to recover the complexity of identity positions of the past. Any discourse is an articulation by *all* its participants and, in order to recognize its complexity, we need to reconstruct as many voices in it as possible. Neglecting the universalist position of Nallasvami does not do justice to the complex power struggles in colonial South India, or to the different strategies of Vellalar elites to come to terms with increasing Brahmanical domination in colonial society. The Tamil nationalist interpretation of Saivism was not the only option. One should also be aware that any scholarly critique of Tamil Saiva nationalism automatically undermines historically legitimated Vellalar-representative claims, and might itself be nourished by opposing interest groups, be it Tamil Brahmans, Tamil Dalits or Western researchers. There is hardly any escape from power struggles when it comes to identity representations,[263] but what is needed is an explicit reflection on these dynamics.

---

[262] Dhavamony 1971: 3.

[263] As this matter is highly sensitive and emotionally loaded, I purposefully resist giving references. However, the whole issue of representation in current scholarship on the Tamil context would need more explicit attention.

Invention of tradition?

The concept of universal religion is a product of the 19th century which took shape within Western debates on religion and became globalized in the wake of Western imperialism. This constellation is often understood as the imposition of something foreign onto an indigenous tradition, but behind this argument lies a notion of authenticity that cannot be upheld within an approach based on discourse theory. The colonial discourse is the constitutive framework for all participants and it is made up of their articulations; it is not a neutral meeting place for negotiation between previously separate and essentially different traditions. However, an important question remains: to what extent is Saiva Siddhanta's appropriation of the concept of universal religion shaped by its specific context? What Christopher Bayly has stated with regard to nationalism could also be applied to the concept of universal religion – as far as the 'theory' is concerned, continuity with concepts of the Saiva Siddhanta tradition would not be a necessary condition for the emergence of the nineteenth-century concept of universal religion in the Tamil Saiva context. It does not need to have been born out of some earlier and similar concepts of religious universalism. This does not mean that such traditions could not have existed, or that it is unimportant when they existed. Traditions have unintended, unexpected and sometimes profound consequences.[264] The important point here is that the role of tradition has to be specifically and strictly established historically. It is clear that Nallasvami, like Vivekananda, used traditional inclusive models to back up a universal claim. These inclusive models expressed the superiority of Saiva Siddhanta or Advaita Vedanta in relation to other Indian schools and they were then applied to the relationship to other religions. We have seen how Nallasvami took one of his definitions of true religion as that "which does not conflict with this religion and that, and yet reconciles all and stands supreme in the conscience of man" from a traditional Saiva Siddhanta source, but also how he transformed its meaning for a modern purpose.[265] In the same way, he took over the Saiva Siddhanta understanding of the four paths, but interpreted it in a new way. The question to what extent these traditions referred to have influenced Nallasvami's concepts, is a matter of assessment and not a matter of principal, as long as it is accepted that these traditional concepts have been reinterpreted by the Saiva Siddhanta revival. Nallasvami was also deeply influenced in his

---

[264] Bayly 2004: 219. The following paragraph contains mainly verbatim quotes from Christopher Bayly's discussion on nationalism applied to the concept of universal religion. For better readability the direct quotes are not highlighted.

[265] See on page 52.

interpretation of Saiva Siddhanta by the Saiva pandits of his generation. He had a certain preference for Sivagnana Siddhiyar as an authoritative source, and he wrote in the introduction to his translation of the text:

> Our Pandits fall shy generally of Sivagnanabotham, but this work [Sivagnana Siddhiyar] is more popular with them; and its words and phrases thoroughly permeate their speeches and writings, and one feels so far quite at home in Siddhiar, when one takes it up, after an acquaintance with writings and speeches of our Pundits [sic].[266]

In order to assess Nallasvami's dependence on the pandits, one would have to analyse his references to Saiva Siddhanta texts for their possible relation to established pandit interpretations of the time. Before that can happen, more scholarly research is necessary regarding the Saiva Siddhanta pandit traditions in 19th-century South India. A good start would be, for instance, an analysis of the 19th-century commentary on Sivagnana Siddhiyar by Subrahmanya Desikar, from the Thiruvadathurai Mutt.[267]

However, one has also to keep in mind that a strict historical approach has to be open to surprises with regard to specific traditions. It is a salient feature of Nallasvami's argument that he distances himself from Advaita Vedanta and claims the right understanding of advaita for Saiva Siddhanta. This claim assumes a clear demarcation between Advaita Vedanta and Saiva Siddhanta, but it is probably the Saiva Siddhanta revival itself which produced these clear cut boundaries, since there is plenty of evidence that the boundaries were somewhat blurred in the time previous. This phenomenon needs further investigation in future research. Karl Graul, director of the German Lutheran 'Leipzig Mission' and one of the early Western Tamil scholars, reported in 1855 about a Saiva Society that existed in Madras for some years and which held monthly meetings with lectures on Saiva classics. In relation to this "a Saiva Saint" (Germ. ein Saiva-Weiser) complained about the growing dominance of Smarta Brahmans who taught Advaita Vedanta among Tamil Saivites:

> They [the Tamil Saivites] think, the Advaita teachings and Saivism belong together, and the Smarta-Brahmans are nothing else than Saiva-Brahmans. That is why the Vellalar and other castes put aside their Saiva-Visishtadvaita books and study the Advaita texts, under the delusion that the latter contain the truth. They [the Smarta Brahmans] get quite a few proselytes here in the South among the Saivas – they draw them slowly away from the mandatory customs of their Saiva

[266] Nallasvami Pillai 1897–1902: 3:5.
[267] See Devasenapatti 1960: 14–15.

books, get them used to their own customs, and deprive their previous gurus of their entire income.[268]

This conflation of Advaita Vedanta and Saiva Siddhanta goes back at least to the 18th century, when the famous Tamil poet, Tayumanavar (Tam. tāyumāṉavar), whose poetry stands in between several different streams of Saiva and non-Saiva traditions, suggested a synthesis between Saiva Siddhanta and Advaita Vedanta, and coined the phrase "Vedanta-Siddhanta-Sama-Rasa" (Tam. vētānta cittānta camaracam / harmony between Vedanta and Siddhanta).[269] Tayumanavar was arguably one of the most popular Tamil Saiva poets of the 19th and early 20th century.[270] Nallasvami quoted regularly from his poems and called him "our saint"[271]. However, the Vivekananda follower, Rajam Aiyar, also highly appreciated Tayumanavar and understood him from the perspective of Advaita Vedanta.[272] These different receptions of Tayumanavar at the beginning of the 20th century somewhat echoed the earlier conflation of both traditions. It was also echoed in Nallasvami's incorporation of Srikantha's Sivadvaita Vedanta into his interpretation of Saiva Siddhanta, which he learnt from Venkatagiri Sastrigal, a Brahman scholar from Trivandrum, whom he called both "a Siddhanthi" and "follower of Sri Kanta Charya"[273]. Moreover, the only known commentary of Srikantha's system was written in Sanskrit by Appayya Dikshita (1552/53–1624), who apparently combined the basic convictions of Advaita Vedanta with the theistic concept of Saiva bhakti:

> As an advaitin release meant for him realisation of identity with Brahman; but this is not to be, so long as there continues in the world even a single unredeemed soul. Till the final release of all, individual release is but the attainment of being of Īśvara.[274]

In the late 19th century, it appears that this kind of hybridity was felt as problematic. In 1901, *Siddhanta Deepika* reported that the "exposition by the same man [Appayya Dikshita] of two apparently opposed systems [Advaita Vedanta and Saivism] has given rise to a great amount of debate and it is one of the vexed questions ever cropping up in the vernacular

---

268 Graul 1854–1856: IV.155. Perhaps the society is Saiva Siddhanta Sangam, with Ramasami Kavirayar as president, founded 1829 in Madras (Blackburn 2003: 109). See also Nehring 2003: 262.

269 See Isaac Tambyah 1925: xxii–xxx; Purnalingam Pillai 1929: 306–307; Lehmann 1935: 7–12; Shulman 1991.

270 See Lehmann 1935: 12–14.

271 See, for instance, Nallasvami Pillai 1911a: 3; Nallasvami Pillai 1911b: 34.

272 See Aiyar 1946: 14; Blackburn 1998: 160.

273 See Nallasvami Pillai 1984: ix, see also Vaitheespara 1999: 163.

274 Suryanarayana Sastri 1974: 4.

religious papers"[275]. This again shows how new boundaries became established that were, perhaps, formerly blurred. Even the reception of Vivekananda and his message among Tamil Saivites in Ceylon hints at this constellation. Vivekananda received a warm reception from Tamil Saivites at the Saiva Paripalana Sabai of Jaffna in 1897.[276] Tamil Vellalars had apparently also no difficulty in founding a 'Vivekananda Society' in Colombo in 1902, which laid much stress on Saiva traditions and Saiva Siddhanta. It is reported from the year 1907 that there were weekly classes on Sivagnana Botham under one R. C. Kailasa Pillai Mudaliar; and a member wrote to *Siddhanta Deepika* that he would be writing a paper on Tayumanavar, who "will be portrayed as the latest exponent of Siddhanta, preaching the quintessence of Vedanta"[277]. It seems this reconciliation with the Advaita Vedanta of Vivekananda's Neo-Hinduism lasted for quite some time, at least in the Ceylonese context. However, when S. Sabaratna Mudaliyar presented a paper on "The Advaita Philosophy" before the Vivekananda Society in 1911, he claimed that "pure Vedānta is Siddhānta"[278] in the sense that only the Saiva Siddhanta and not the "Māyāvādins" have an acceptable idea of advaita, and that "Māyāvāda" is nothing short of "Pantheism"[279] and its "theory of illusion" is unacceptable. His argument followed that of Nallasvami in nearly all details, but he was explicitly polemical against Vivekananda, which Nallasvami always avoided:

> No doubt, Svāmi Vivekananda was a great Sannyasin, and I may say, a great scholar too. So I may say of Sri Sankarāchārya also, whom I may even call a much greater man than Svāmi Vivekananda. But truth is truth and facts are stubborn, and I should not feel nervous to speak out what I think to be the truth.[280]

At least at this point, the chasm between Saiva Siddhanta and Neo-Hinduism was firmly established in the Ceylonese context too.

This should again make it clear that locating Nallasvami's concept of universal religion within the colonial discourse must also take into account his rootedness in the Indian traditions and their possible influence. However, the relevance of these traditions has to be shown in a strictly historical way and must not be apriorily assumed. Hence, this exposition of Nallasvami's thought has put great emphasis on the sources

[275] Siddhanta Deepika 4 (1900/1901) 196.

[276] See Sitrampalam 1994: 16.

[277] Siddhanta Deepika 8 (1907/1908) 225.

[278] Siddhanta Deepika 12 (1911/1912) 308.

[279] See Sabaratna Mudaliyar 1911/1912: esp. 309. 389–395. See also Sabaratna Mudaliyar 1913: 26, 28, 58–59.

[280] Sabaratna Mudaliyar 1911/1912: 395.

used by Nallasvami – to show how a comprehensive historical approach can be translated into concrete research.

Bibliography

Adigal, Uran (Tam. caṉmārkka tēcikaṉ eṉṉum ūraṉ aṭikaḷ). 1975. *Irāmaliṅka aṭikaḷ varalāṟu.* (1971) 2nd ed. Camayapuram: Camaraca caṉmārkka ārāycci nilaiyam.

Aiyar, B. R. Rajam. 1946. *Rambles in Vedanta.* (1905) Calcutta: S. P. League.

Aloysius, Gnanasigamony. 1998. *Religion as Emancipatory Identity. A Buddhist Movement among the Tamils under Colonialism.* New Delhi: New Age International.

——. (Tam. ñāṉ. alāyciyas), ed. 1999. *Ayōttitācar cintaṉaikaḷ.* 3 vols. Palayamkottai: Folklore Resources and Research Centre St. Xavier's College.

Armstrong, Richard Acland. 1896. *God and the Soul. An Essay towards Fundamental Religion.* London: Philip Green.

Bain, Alexander. 1879. *Mind and Body. The Theories of Their Relation.* (1872) (The International Scientific Series; 4). New York: D. Appleton.

Balasubramaniam, K. M. 1965. *The Life of J. M. Nallaswami Pillai.* Tiruchirapalli: J. M. Somasundaram Pillai.

Bartoli, G. 1897–1899. 'Evidences of Natural Religion', *The Light of Truth or the Siddhanta Deepika* 1–2: 1:131–134, 1:156–160, 1:185–188, 1:209–212, 1:237–239, 1:256–259, 2:18–19, 2:40, 2:65–66, 2:89–91, 2:134–139, 2:229–231.

Basu, Sankari Prasad and Ghosh, Sunil Bihari, eds. 1969. *Vivekananda in Indian Newspapers 1893–1902. Extracts from Twenty-Two Newspapers and Periodicals.* Calcutta: Bookland Private Limited.

Bate, Bernard. 2005. 'Arumuga Navalar, Saivite sermons and the delimitation of religion, c. 1850', *Indian Economic and Social History Review* 42: 469–484.

Bayly, Christopher A. 2004. *The Birth of the Modern World, 1780–1914. Global connections and comparisons.* Oxford: Blackwell.

Bayly, Susan. 1998. 'Hindu Modernisers and the "Public" Arena. Indigenous Critiques of Caste in Colonial India', in: William Radice, ed. *Swami Vivekananda and the Modernisation of Hinduism.* Delhi: Oxford University Press, 93–137.

——. 1999. *Caste, Society and Politics in India from the Eighteenth Century to the Modern Age.* (The New Cambridge History of India; IV,3) Cambridge: Cambridge University Press.

Bergunder, Michael. 2004. 'Contested Past. Anti-Brahmanical and Hindu nationalist reconstructions of the Indian prehistory', *Historiographia Linguistica* 31: 59–104.

——. 2005. 'Das Streben nach Einheit von Wissenschaft und Religion. Zum Verständnis von Leben in der modernen Esoterik', in: Eilert Herms, ed. *Leben. Verständnis, Wissenschaft, Technik.* Gütersloh: Gütersloher Verlagshaus, 559–578.

——. 2006. 'Die Bhagavadgita im 19. Jahrhundert. Hinduismus, Esoterik und Kolonialismus', in: Michael Bergunder, ed. *Westliche Formen des Hinduismus in Deutschland. Eine Übersicht.* (Neue Hallesche Berichte; 6) Halle: Verlag der Franckeschen Stiftungen, 187–216.

Besant, Annie. 1984. *Hints on the Study of the Bhagavad Gita.* (1906) 7th ed. Madras: Theosophical Publishing House.

Bhabha, Homi K. 1994. *The Location of Culture.* London: Routledge.

Blackburn, Stuart. 2003. *Print, Folklore, and Nationalism in Colonial South India.* Delhi: Permanent Black.

——. ed. 1998. *The Fatal Rumour. A Nineteenth-Century Indian Novel by B. R. Rajam Aiyar.* New Delhi: Oxford University Press.

Campbell, Bruce F. 1980. *Ancient Wisdom Revived. A History of the Theosophical Movement.* Berkeley: University of California Press.

Chaudhury, Ruma. 2004. *Srikantha's Philosophy of Monotheistic Vedanta.* Delhi: Global Vision Publishing House.

Cust, Robert Needham. 1891. *Clouds of the Horizon. An Essay on the Various Forms of Errors, which stand in the Way of the Acceptance of Real Christian Faith by the Educated Natives of Asia, Africa, America, and Oceania.* (1890) 2nd ed. London: Elliot Stock.

Dayanandan Francis, T. 1990. *The Mission and Message of Ramalinga Swamy.* Delhi: Motilal Barnasidass.

Devasenapatti, V. A. 1960. *Saiva Siddhanta as expounded in the Sivanjnana-Siddhiyar and its six commentaries.* Madras: University of Madras.

Dhavamony, Mariasusai. 1971. *Love of God According to Saiva Siddhanta. A Study in the Mysticism and Theology of Saivism.* Oxford: Clarendon.

Dirks, Nicholas B. 2001. *Castes of Mind. Colonialism and the Making of Modern India.* Princeton: Princeton University Press.

Drummond, Henry. 1891. *The Changed Life. An Address.* New York: James Pott.

Dubois, J. A. 1906. *Hindu Manners, Customs and Ceremonies.* 3rd ed. Oxford: Clarendon Press.

Dubuisson, Daniel. 2003. *The Western Construction of Religion. Myths, Knowledge, and Ideology.* (L'Occident et la religion <eng.>) Baltimore: Johns Hopkins University Press.

Dvivedi, Manilal Nabhubhai. 1889. *Monism or Advaitism? An Introduction to the Advaita-philosophy read by the light of Modern Science.* Bombay: Subodha-Prakasa Press.

Ekambaranathan, A. 2000. 'Kaleidoscopic Reflections of Saiva Icons – Somaskanda Murti', in: P. Krishnan, ed. *Facets of Saiva Siddhanta. Chennai: Department of Saiva Siddhanta.* University of Madras, 143–150.

Fairbairn, Andrew Martin. 1902. *The Philosophy of the Christian Religion.* London: Macmillan.

Figl, Johann. 1993. *Die Mitte der Religionen. Idee und Praxis universalreligiöser Bewegungen.* Darmstadt: Wissenschaftliche Buchgesellschaft.

Garbe, Richard. 1897. *The Philosophy of Ancient India.* Chicago: Open Court.

Geetha, V. and Rajadurai, S. V. 1998. *Towards a Non-Brahmin Millennium. From Iyothee Thass to Periyar.* Calcutta: Samya.

Ghose, Rajeshwari. 1996. *The Lord of Arur, the Tyagaraja Cult in Tamilnadu. A Study in Conflict and Accomodation.* Delhi: Motilal Barnasidass.

Glasenapp, Helmuth von. 1922. *Der Hinduismus. Religion und Gesellschaft im heutigen Indien.* München: Kurt Wolff Verlag.

Gonda, Jan. 1978. *Die Religionen Indiens. I. Veda und älterer Hinduismus.* (1960) (Die Religionen der Menschheit; 11) 2nd ed. Stuttgart: Kohlhammer.

Graul, Karl. 1854–1856. *Reise nach Ostindien über Palästina und Egypten von Juli 1849 bis April 1853.* 5 vols. Leipzig: Dörffling und Franke.

Griffith, Ralph T. H. 1973. *The Hymns of the Rigveda.* (1889) Delhi: Motilal Banasidass.

Hatcher, Brian A. 1999. *Eclecticism and Modern Hindu Discourse.* New York: Oxford University Press.

Hellmann-Rajanayagam, Dagmar. 1989. 'Arumuka Navalar. Religious Reformer or National Leader of Eelam', *Indian Economic and Social History Review* 26: 235–257.

Ilavarasu, Som (cōm. iḷavaracu). 1997. *Naṉṉūl eḻuttatikāram.* Ceṉṉai: Maṇivācakar patippakam.

Inden, Ronald. 1990. *Imagining India.* Oxford: Basil Blackwell.

Irschick, Eugene F. 1969. *Politics and Social Conflict in South India. The Non-Brahman Movement and Tamil Separatism, 1916–1929.* Berkeley: University of California Press.

——. 1994. *Dialogue and History. Constructing South India, 1795–1895.* Berkeley: University of California Press.

Isaac Tambyah, T. 1925. *Psalms of a Saiva Saint, being Selections from the Writings of Tayumanaswamy.* Madras: Diocesan Press.

Jackson, Carl T. 1981. *The Oriental Religions and American Thought. Nineteenth-Century Explorations.* Westport: Greenwood Press.

Kailasapathy, K. 1979. 'The Tamil Purist Movement. A Re-Evaluation', *Social Scientist* 7,10: 23–51.

Keith, Arthur Berriedale, ed. 1914. *The Veda of the Black Yajus School entitled Taittiriya-Samhita.* (Harvard Oriental Series; 18–19) Cambridge, Massachusetts: Harvard University Press.

King, Richard. 1999. *Orientalism and Religion. Postcolonial Theory, India and 'The Mystic East'.* London: Routledge.

Kiruttinamurtti, K. (Tam. kō. kiruṭṭiṇamūrtti). 1990. *Tolkāppiya āyviṉ varalāṟu.* Ceṉṉai: Ceṉṉai palkalaikkaḻakam.

Klaes, Norbert. 2000. 'Globalisierung und interreligiöse Zusammenarbeit', in: Klaus Krämer, Ansgar Paus, eds. *Die Weite des Mysteriums. Christliche Identität im Dialog. Für Horst Bürkle.* Freiburg: Herder, 377–403.

Laclau, Ernesto and Mouffe, Chantal. 1991. *Hegemonie und radikale Demokratie. Zur Dekonstruktion des Marxismus.* (Hegemony and Socialist Strategy <ger.>) (1985) Wien: Passagen Verlag.

Lehmann, Arno. 1935. *Die Hymnen des Tayumanavar. Texte zur Gottesmystik des Hinduismus.* (Allgemeine Missionsstudien; 19) Gütersloh: C. Bertelsmann.

M., K. M. 1879. *In the Woods. A Book for the Young.* London: Thomas Nelson.

Macdonell, Arthur Anthony. 1900. *A History of Sanskrit Literature.* New York: D. Appleton.

Maraimalai Adigal. 1913–1914. 'The Relation of Samkhya and Saiva Siddhanta', *The Light of Truth or the Siddhanta Deepika* 14: 174–188, 208–215.

——. 1966. *The Saiva Siddhanta as a Philosophy of Practical Knowledge.* (1923) 2nd ed. Madras: The South India Saiva Siddhanta Works Publishing Society, Tinnevelly.

Masuzawa, Tomoko. 2005. *The Invention of World Religions, Or, How European Universalism Was Preserved in the Language of Pluralism.* Chicago: University of Chicago Press.

McCutcheon, Russell T. 1997. *Manufacturing Religion. The Discourse on Sui Generis Religion and the Politics of Nostalgia.* New York: Oxford University Press.

Mehlig, Johannes. 1987. *Weisheit des alten Indien. Bd. 1: Vorbuddhistische und nichtbuddhistische Texte.* Leipzig; Weimar: Gustav Kiepenheuer.

Monier-Williams, Monier. 1875. *Indian wisdom, or, Examples of the religious, philosophical and ethical doctrines of the Hindûs, with a brief history of the chief departments of Sanskrit literature.* London: Allen.

——. 1883. *Religious Thought and Life in India. Part I. Vedism, Brâhmanism, and Hindûism.* London: John Murray.

Müller, Friedrich Max. 1879. *The Upanishads. Part I.* (Sacred Books of the East; 1) Oxford: Clarendon.

——. 1884. *The Upanishads. Part II. The Katha-Upanishad, The Mundaka-Upanishad, The Taittiriyaka-Upanishad, The Brihadaranyaka-Upanishad, The Svetasvatara-Upanishad, The Prasna-Upanishad, The Maitrayana-Brahmana-Upanishad.* (Sacred Books of the East; 15) Oxford: Clarendon.

——. 1899a. *The Six Systems of Indian Philosophy.* New York: Longmans, Green and Co.

——. 1899b. *Ramakrishna. His Life and Sayings.* (1898) New York: Charles Scribner's Sons.

Muir, John. 1873. *Comparison of the Vedic with the Later Representations of the Principal Indian Deities.* (1863) (Original Sanskrit Texts on the Origin and History of the People of India, Their Religion and Institutions; 4) 2nd ed. London: Trübner.

Muller, F. Henrietta, ed. 1897. *From Colombo to Almora, Being a Record of Swami Vivekananda's Return to India after His Mission to the West, Including Reports of His Lectures.* Madras: Vijayanti Press.

——. ed. 1904. *From Colombo to Almora, Being a Record of Swami Vivekananda's Return to India after His Mission to the West. Includes Reports of His Lectures and Replies to Addresses.* (1897) 2nd ed. Madras: Brahmavadin Press.

Murtti, A. K. (Tam. a. ki. mūrtti). 1998. *Caivacittānta akarāti.* Ceṉṉai: Tirunelvēli, teṉṉintiya caivacittānta nūṟpatippuk kaḻakam.

Nallasvami Pillai, J. M. 1896. *Light of Grace, or Thiruvarutpayan, of Umapathi Siva Charya.* (Translated with Notes and Introduction) Trichinopoly: Saiva Siddhanta Sabha.

——. 1897 1902. 'Sivagnana Siddhiyar of Arul Nandi Siva Chariya', *The Light of Truth or the Siddhanta Deepika* 1–5: 1:2–5, 1:27–28, 1:52–55, 1:77–80, 1:102–106, 1:125–126, 1:150–152, 1:177–180, 1:198–201, 1:246–249, 1:270–272, 2:7–9, 2:33–35, 2:55–56, 2:104–106, 2:151–152, 2:176, 3:5–6, 3:29–31, 3:53–55, 3:89–93, 3:113–114, 3:137–138, 3:161–164, 3:203–204, 3:236–238, 4:6, 4:30–32, 4:53–56, 4:77–80, 4:153–154, 4:237–240, 4:279–280, 5:1–5, 5:39–41, 5:57–62, 5:109–110, 5:162–164.

——. 1898/1899a. 'The Theological Situation in India', *The Light of Truth or the Siddhanta Deepika* 2: 156–158.

——. 1898/1899b. 'Mr. Justice Renade on "South India"', *The Light of Truth or the Siddhanta Deepika* 2: 187–190.

——. 1898/1899c. 'Prof. Fairbairn on the Philosophy of Religion', *The Light of Truth or the Siddhanta Deepika* 2: 214–215.

——. 1911a. 'Flower and Fragrance', in: J. M. Nallasvami Pillai, ed. *Studies in Saiva Siddhanta.* Madras: Meykandan Press, 1–4.

——. 1911b. 'An Another Side', in: J. M. Nallasvami Pillai, ed. *Studies in Saiva Siddhanta.* Madras: Meykandan Press, 21–34.

——. 1911c. 'The Nature of the Divine Personality' (1898) in: J. M. Nallasvami Pillai, ed. *Studies in Saiva Siddhanta.* Madras: Meykandan Press, 42–52.

——. 1911d. 'Vowels and Consonants' (1898) in: J. M. Nallasvami Pillai, ed. *Studies in Saiva Siddhanta.* Madras: Meykandan Press, 53–62.

——. 1911e. 'God and the World' (1898) in: J. M. Nallasvami Pillai, ed. *Studies in Saiva Siddhanta.* Madras: Meykandan Press, 63–70.

——. 1911f. 'Ashtamuhurtam', in: J. M. Nallasvami Pillai, ed. *Studies in Saiva Siddhanta.* Madras: Meykandan Press, 93–108.

——. 1911g. 'An Upanishat Text', in: J. M. Nallasvami Pillai, ed. *Studies in Saiva Siddhanta.* Madras: Meykandan Press, 104–108.

——. 1911h. 'The Svetasvatara Upanishat' (1901) in: J. M. Nallasvami Pillai, ed. *Studies in Saiva Siddhanta.* Madras: Meykandan Press, 109–145.

——. 1911i. 'The Union of Indian Philosophies' (1897) in: J. M. Nallasvami Pillai, ed. *Studies in Saiva Siddhanta.* Madras: Meykandan Press, 169–184.

——. 1911j. 'The Four Paths' (1906) in: J. M. Nallasvami Pillai, ed. *Studies in Saiva Siddhanta.* Madras: Meykandan Press, 202–222.

——. 1911k. 'The Personality of God' (1907) in: J. M. Nallasvami Pillai, ed. *Studies in Saiva Siddhanta.* Madras: Meykandan Press, 223–243.

——. 1911l. 'Advaita According to the Saiva Siddhanta' (1908) in: J. M. Nallasvami Pillai, ed. *Studies in Saiva Siddhanta.* Madras: Meykandan Press, 244–272.

——. 1911m. 'The Saiva Religion and Saiva Advaita Siddhanta Philosophy' (1909) in: J. M. Nallasvami Pillai, ed. *Studies in Saiva Siddhanta.* Madras: Meykandan Press, 273–315.

——. 1911n. 'The Nature of the Jiva', in: J. M. Nallasvami Pillai, ed. *Studies in Saiva Siddhanta.* Madras: Meykandan Press, 316–337.

——. 1911o. 'Saivism in Its Relation to Other Systems', in: J. M. Nallasvami Pillai, ed. *Studies in Saiva Siddhanta.* Madras: Meykandan Press, 347–360.

——. ed. 1911p. *Studies in Saiva Siddhanta.* Madras: Meykandan Press.

——. 1912/1913. 'Irupa-Irupathu of St. Arul Nandi Śivāchāriar', *The Light of Truth or the Siddhanta Deepika* 13: 199–202, 370–373, 397–399, 439–450.

——. 1984. *Sivagnana Botham of Meikanda Deva.* (1895) 2nd ed. Madras: South India Saiva Siddhanta Works Publishing Society, Tinnevelli.

Nehring, Andreas. 2003. *Orientalismus und Mission. Die Repräsentation der tamilischen Gesellschaft und Religion durch Leipziger Missionare 1840–1940.* (Studien zur Außereuropäischen Christentumsgeschichte (Asien, Afrika, Lateinamerika; 7) Wiesbaden: Harrassowitz.

——. 2005. 'Die Erfindung der religiösen Erfahrung', in: Christian Strecker, ed. *Kontexte der Schrift.* (Band II: Kultur, Politik, Religion, Sprache-Text) Stuttgart: Kohlhammer, 301–322.

Olcott, Henry Steel. 1895. *Old Diary Leaves.* 6 vols. Adyar: Theosophical Publishing House.

Peterson, Derek R. and Walhof, Darren R., ed. 2002. *The Invention of Religion. Rethinking Belief in Politics and History.* New Brunswick: Rutgers University Press.

Peterson, Indira Viswanathan. 1989. *Poems to Siva. The Hymns of the Tamil Saints.* Princeton, New Jersey: Princeton University Press.

Ponnambalam Pillai, T. 1912/1913. 'The President's Address of the Saiva Siddhanta Maha Samajam – Seventh Conference', *The Light of Truth or the Siddhanta Deepika* 13: 343–355.

Pope, G. U. 1900. *The Tiruvacagam or 'Sacred Utterances' of the Tamil Poet, Saint and Sage Manikka-Vacagar.* Oxford: Clarendon Press.

Prakash, Gyan. 1999. *Another Reason. Science and the Imagination of Modern India.* Princeton: Princeton University Press.

Proudfoot, Wayne. 1985. *Religious Experience.* Berkeley: University of California Press.

Purnalingam Pillai, M. S. 1929. *Tamil Literature.* (1904) 2nd ed. Munnirpallam, Tinneveli Dt.: The Bibliotheca.

Ramakrishna Mission, ed. 1938. *The Religions of the World.* 2 vols. Calcutta: Ramakrishna Mission.

Raman, Srilata. 2002. 'Departure and Prophecy. The Disappearance of Iramalinka Atikal in the Early Narratives of His Life', *Indologica Taurinensia* 28: 179–203.

Ramanan, V. V. 1898/1899. 'Modern Oriental Scholarship', *The Light of Truth or the Siddhanta Deepika* 2: 159–164.

——. 1909/1910. 'How Nilakantha's Bhashya is getting appreciated in the West', *The Light of Truth or the Siddhanta Deepika* 10: 48–50.

Ramanathan, Ponnambalam. 1906. *The Culture of the Soul Among Western Nations.* New York: Putnam.

Ramaswamy, Sumathi. 1997. *Passions of the Tongue. Language Devotion in Tamil India, 1891–1970.* Berkeley: University of California Press.

——. 2001. 'Ramains of the Race. Archeology, Nationalism, and the yearning for Civilisation in the Indus Valley', *Indian Economic and Social History Review* 38,2: 105–145.

Rambachan, Anantanand. 1994. *The Limits of Scripture. Vivekananda's Reinterpretation of the Vedas.* Honululu: University of Hawaii Press.

Ryerson, Charles A. 1988. *Regionalism and Religion. The Tamil Renaissance and Popular Hinduism.* (Series on Religion; 27) Madras: The Christian Literature Society.

Sabaratna Mudaliyar, S. 1911/1912. 'The Advaita Philosophy', *The Light of Truth or the Siddhanta Deepika* 12: 305–312, 389–396, 421–424.

——. 1913. *Essentials of Hinduism in the Light of Saiva Siddhanta.* Madras: Meykandan Press.

Sadasivayya, T. H. M. 1938. 'Virasaivism (The Religion of the Lingayets)', in: Ramakrishna Mission, ed. *The Religions of the World.* Calcutta: Ramakrishna Mission, I.432–440.

Sarada, S., ed. 1991. *Madame Blavatsky and Soobiah.* Madras: Adyar Lodge, The Theosophical Society.

Saradananda, Swami. 1910. 'Hinduism', in: S. N. Sen, ed. *The Proceedings of the Convention of Religions in India. 1909.* 2 vols. Calcutta: The Vivekananda Society, II.194–208.

Sastry, Alladi Mahadeva. 1897–1906. 'The Vedanta-Sutras with Srikantha Bhashya', *The Light of Truth or the Siddhanta Deepika* 1–7: 1:193–198, 1:217–222, 1:241–246, 1:265–270, 2:1–6, 2:25–30, 2:49–54, 2:97–103, 2:121–127, 2:145–150, 2:169–174, 2:193–198, 2:217–221, 2:240–246, 2:265–270, 3:1–4, 3:25–29, 3:49–52, 3:85–88, 3:109–112, 3:133–136, 3:157–160, 3:195–200, 3:231–235, 4:1–5, 4:25–29, 4:49–52, 4;73–76, 4:121–124, 4:145–148, 4:169–172, 4:189–192, 5:6–8, 5:33–39, 7:3–17, 7:41–50.

Savariroyan, D. 1901/1902. 'Some Disputed Points Cleared'. *The Light of Truth or the Siddhanta Deepika* 5: 78–81.

Schomerus, Hilko Wiardo. 1912. *Der Caiva-Siddhanta, eine Mystik Indiens.* Leipzig: J. C. Hinrichs'sche Buchhandlung.

——. 1916. 'Irupa Virupatu oder die Zwanzig in zwei Versmaßen von Arulnantisivacarya, aus dem Tamil übersetzt und mit Erläuterungen versehen', *Zeitschrift für Missionskunde und Religionswissenschaft* 31.

——. 1981. *Arunantis Sivajnanasiddhiyar. Die Erlangung des Wissens um Siva oder die Erlösung. Unter Beifügung einer Einleitung und Meykantadevas Sivajnanabodha aus dem Tamil übersetzt.* (Beiträge zur Südasienforschung; 49) 2 vols. Wiesbaden: Franz Steiner.

Seesodia, Thakur Jessarajsighjee. 1911/1912. 'Is England a Saivite Country?' *The Light of Truth or the Siddhanta Deepika* 12: 401–404.

Sen, S. N., ed. 1910. *The Proceedings of the Convention of Religions in India, 1909.* 2 vols. Calcutta: The Vivekananda Society.

Shulman, David. 1991. 'The Yogi's Human Self. Tayumanavar in the Tamil Mystical Tradition', *Religion* 21, London: 51–72.

Sitrampalam, S. K. 1994. 'Hindu Revivalism in Northern Sri Lanka During the Nineteenth Century. A Historical Perspective', *Journal of the Institute of Asian Studies* 11,2: 1–20.

Smith, David. 1996. *The Dance of Siva. Religion, Art and Poetry in South India.* Cambridge: Cambridge University Press.

Srinivasan, Perundevi. 2006. 'Can We Cross the Chasm? Agency and Orientalist Discourse in the Colonial Tamil Context', in: Chandreyee Niyogi, ed. *Reorienting Orientalism.* New Delhi: Sage Publication, 228–244.

Stoler, Ann Laura and Cooper, Frederick. 1997. 'Between Metropole and Colony. Rethinking a Research Agenda', in: Ann Laura Stoler and Frederick Cooper, ed. *Tensions of Empire. Colonial Cultures in a Bourgoise World.* Berkeley: University of California Press, 1–56.

Subba Row, T. 1994. *Philosophy of the Bhagavad-Gita. Four Lectures delivered at the Eleventh Annual Convention of the Theosophical Society, held at Adyar, on December 27, 28, 29 and 30, 1886.* (1912) 2nd ed. Madras: Theosophical Publishing House.

Suryanarayana Sastri, S. S. 1930. *The Sivadvaita of Srikantha.* Madras: University of Madras.

——. 1974. *The Sivadvaita-Nirnaya (An Inquiry into the System of Srikantha) of Appayya Diksita.* Edited with an Introduction, Translation and Notes. (1929) 2nd ed. Madras: University of Madras.

Thaker, Dhirubhai. 1983. *Manilal Dvivedi.* New Delhi: Sahitya Academy.

Thibaut, George. 1890/1896. *The Vedanta-Sutras with the Commentary by Sankara.* (Sacred Books of the East; 34, 38) 2 vols. Oxford: Clarendon.

——. 1904. *The Vedanta-Sutras with the Commentary of Ramanuja.* (Sacred Books of the East; 48) Oxford: Clarendon.

Trautmann, Thomas R. 2006. *Languages and Nations. The Dravidian Proof in Colonial Madras.* Berkeley: University of California Press.

Vaitheespara, Ravindiran. 1999. *Caste, Hybridity and the Construction of Cultural Identity in Colonial India. Maraimal Adigalar and the Intellectual Genealogy of Dravidian Nationalism, 1800–1950.* (Ph. D. thesis, University of Toronto) Toronto.

——. 2006. 'Christianity, Missionary Orientalism and the Origins of Tamil Modernity', in: Andreas Gross, Vincent Kumaradoss et al., eds. *Halle and the Beginning of Protestant Christianity in India.* Halle: Verlag der Franckeschen Stiftungen, II.973–1017.

Velayudam Mudaliar, T. (Tam. toḻuvūr vēlāyutamutaliyār). 1880. *Vēḷāṉ marpiyal.* Madras: Scottish Press.

Vivekananda Society. 1910. 'A Short Account of the Evolution of Religious Ideas Beyond India', in: S. N. Sen, ed. *The Proceedings of the Convention of Religions in India. 1909.* 2 vols. Calcutta: The Vivekananda Society, II.i–lx.

Vivekananda, Swami. 1959. *The Complete Works of Swami Vivekananda.* Mayavati Memorial Edition (Reprint). 9 vols. Calcutta: Advaita Ashrama.

Westcott, Arthur. 1903. *Life and Letters of Brooke Foss Westcott.* 2 vols. London: Macmillam and Co.

Young, Robert M. 1990. *Mind, Brain and Adaptation in the Nineteenth Century. Cerebral Localization and Its Biological Context from Gall to Ferrier.* (1970) 2nd ed. Oxford: Oxford University Press.

Younger, Paul. 1995. *The Home of Dancing Sivan. The Traditions of the Hindu Temple of Citamparam.* New York: Oxford University Press.

Ziolkowski, Eric J., ed. 1993. *A Museum of Faiths. History and Legacies of the 1893 World's Parliament of Religions.* Atlanta, Georgia: Scholars Press.

Zvelebil, Kamil V. 1975. *Tamil Literature.* (Handbuch der Orientalistik, II. Abteilung; 2,1). Leiden: E. J. Brill.

Ravi Vaitheespara

Forging a Tamil caste: Maraimalai Adigal (1876–1950) and the discourse of caste and ritual in colonial Tamilnadu

Vedachalam Pillai (Tam. vētācalam piḷḷai), better known by his pure-Tamil name, Maraimalai Adigal (Tam. maṟaimalai aṭikaḷ, 1876–1950), was without doubt one of the most important ideologues of the Tamil / Saivite revivalist movement – a movement that went on to play a key role in shaping the Tamil / Dravidian movement that followed. Maraimalai's importance was not simply due to the fact that he was one of the earliest and most prolific crusaders of a novel brand of 'Dravidian' Tamil-Saivism, but also because his work and writings had an enormous influence in inspiring a whole generation of writers, activists and organizations for whom he was a central figure. Beginning to emerge, as we are, from under the powerful shadow cast by the Dravidian movement on the scholarship of the Dravidian movement it is imperative that we move beyond viewing the Tamil-Saivite movement as a distinct if not inconsequential phase, which was later completely eclipsed by the entry of E. V. Ramasami and the Self Respect Movement, as contemporary scholars have often portrayed it.[1] Rather, it laid important ground work for what followed. It is from such a perspective that I have argued elsewhere that Maraimalai's reinscribing of Tamil-Saivism – following Talal Asad's understanding of religion and modernity[2] – was central to his re-imagining and re-inscribing of Tamil Saivism as the Tamil nation, and his discourse on caste was an essential aspect of this broader secularizing process.

Asad's focus on tracing historical changes in religious practices, where he suggests different disciplinary practices and technologies for the 'production of truth' in different historical periods, is quite useful for understanding Maraimalai's recrafting of Saivism. Particularly useful is his broad conceptualization of changes in 'faith' practices, from the medieval to the modern, where he suggests that the culture of medieval European Christianity, which he believes was centered on various social and disciplinary practices centered on disciplining the body (practices of pain and penance) gives way by the time of the Reformation to an understanding of 'religion' as above all a set of doctrines or belief system

[1] See for example, Pandian 1994; Venkatachalapathy 1994.

[2] See, especially, Asad 1993.

whose truth value subsequently gets opened up for debate in the emerging public sphere through the new 'rationalities' thrown up by Enlightenment and post-Enlightenment thought. Asad then locates the contemporary understanding of religion as a transcendent and unchanging 'essence' – something that is transhistorical and universal – to the impact of post-reformation history and its global spread through European expansion and colonialism. I argue that Maraimalai's understanding and deployment of Saivism and Saiva Siddhanta (Tam. caiva cittāntam, Skt. śaiva siddhānta) as a form of Tamil nationalism certainly signals a new understanding of Saivite practices, one that matches Asad's conceptualization of post-reformation understanding of religion.[3]

Although best known simply as the father of the Pure Tamil Movement, it is important to note that this label often serves to mask the complex genealogy of Tamil / Saivites, such as Maraimalai, for whom Tamil consciousness and Tamil identity were inseparable from their commitment to a renewed brand of Tamil-Saivism. Maraimalai's practice and reinscription of Tamil-Saivism, then, was certainly different from that of his predecessors, such as Ramalinga Adigal (Tam. irāmaliṅka aṭikaḷ, 1823–1874).[4] Most obviously, Maraimalai's re-visioning was very much inspired and influenced by certain strands of European and missionary Orientalist discourses that informed its anti-Brahmanism or Dravidianism. Put more simply, Maraimalai's revisioning was influenced by certain strands of what David Scott characterizes as the new European disciplinary and representational practices, typical of what he considers to be second empire colonialism.[5]

Not surprisingly, even such seemingly secular concerns as the question of caste hierarchy were central to Maraimalai's revisisioning and reinscribing of Tamil Saivism, language and culture; it, therefore, makes its appearance in almost all of his writings. Before one considers how Maraimalai reimagined and re-negotiated the question of caste and caste hierarchy, it is imperative that we at least briefly rehearse the political and socio-cultural developments of his time, against which one needs to locate the impetus for much of his work and writings. As is now well known, by the late 19th century, the complex balance and accommodation between the Brahman and dominant non-Brahman elites in the Tamil region was clearly under strain. The underlying social conflict began to manifest itself not merely at the level of competition for 'loaves

---

3 See Vaitheespara 2009.

4 Although Ramalinga's revival beginning in mid-nineteenth century could itself be said to be influenced by new currents brought about by the colonial impact, it still operated very much within a vernacular public space less influenced by European Orientalist currents.

5 See Scott 1994: 146.

and fishes', but also, more importantly, at the level of 'culture'. The emerging pan-Indian nationalism was clearly founded upon a number of cultural movements that, for the most part, reimagined an 'Aryo-centric', neo-Brahmanical vision of India, which provided the 'ideology' for this hegemonic project. In the Tamil region, such a vision and ideology was closely associated with the Tamil Brahmans and, especially, the Smartha Brahmans who were considered the strongest adherents of the pan-Indian Sanskrit-Brahmanical tradition.

Though neo-Brahmanical revivalist movements were clearly ascendant at the time, there were other revivalist movements, which included Tamil-Vaishnavite revival movements as well as the much neglected Neo-Buddhist movement founded by C. Iyothee Thassar (Tam. k. ayōttitācar, 1845–1914).[6] Sharing some common ground with Maraimalai's movement was the Tamil-Saivite revival movement, which had begun earlier in neighboring Jaffna (Tam. yāḻppāṇam), and advocated a form of Tamil Saivite revival less hostile to the Sanskrit tradition. This more conservative stream of Saivite revival can be viewed as continuing a tradition of accommodation reached between the non-Brahman Saivites and the Brahman tradition by the sixteenth century.[7] Such accommodation enabled the dominant non-Brahman Tamil caste, the Vellalars (Tam. veḷḷāḷar), to claim Sat Sudra (Tam. caṟcūttirar, "clean Sudra") status to distinguish and elevate themselves from the rest of the caste Tamils, who were all relegated to the Sudra (Skt. śūdra, Tam. cūttirar) category. This move enabled the Tamil Vellalars to lead and be heads of important Saiva Siddhanta monastries (Tam. maṭam) in the region, which, by the early modern period, had gained reputations as important guardians and centers for the dissemination of Saiva Sidhanta and Tamil.[8]

Mostly referred to in the extant scholarship as the conservative Saivites, what distinguished them from Maraimalai and his followers was that they claimed, at least in theory, to embrace both the Vedic Sanskrit tradition and the tradition of the Saiva Agamas (Skt. āgama, Tam. ākamam) as equally important, just as they regarded Sanskrit and Tamil as equally divine languages; although it is difficult to deny, even here, that the Sanskrit tradition clearly held greater sway. Reflecting such accommodation, as well as the increasing sway of the Sanskrit tradition, was the highly Sanksritized form of Tamil that was quite prevalent by the early part of the 19th century called Manipravalam (Tam. maṇippiravāḷam, Skt. maṇipravāla). Clearly, by the late 19th century, such accommodation with the Sanskritic tradition was beginning to be seen, at least by a segment of

[6] See, for example, the pioneering and excellent work: Aloysius 1998.
[7] Prentiss 1996: 231–257.
[8] Prentiss 1996: 231–257.

the non-Brahman intelligentsia, not so much as an accommodation but a gradual subversion and displacement of the original Tamil tradition. It is against such a socio-cultural background that we need to locate Maraimalai's work and writings.

To challenge and combat this rising hegemony of the Sanskrit-Brahmanical tradition, caste was an important vehicle for Maraimalai, just as it had been for his European missionary and indigenous predecessors.[9] Caste, then, became the principal interpretive tool or explanatory device through which Aryan-Brahman hegemony and its alleged subversion of the Tamil tradition could be explained. It fell upon Atigal, who was fast becoming one of the most important and respected men of Tamil letters at the time, to further elaborate and fine tune what some of his predecessors, such as Reverend Robert Caldwell and Sundaram Pillai, had helped set in motion.[10]

Caste, then, informs or is an important subtext in most of Maraimalai's writings. The vast majority of his writings are devoted, not surprisingly, to reversing the claim of the Indo-Aryan or the Aryan-Brahman as the progenitor of the great Indian civilization and, instead, to claiming that honour for the Tamils or the Dravidians. Maraimalai relied particularly on his keen knowledge of ancient Tamil literary works to effect this reversal, using essentially a form of literary history to argue his case. His early commentaries on the ancient Tamil literary works, such as *Mullaipāṭṭu* and *Paṭṭiṉappālai,* both of which he published in book form, were used to present his arguments.[11] It was, however, the brilliant lecture, later published in book form, that he delivered at the fourth Madurai Tamil Sangam, in the year 1905, entitled *Paṇṭaikkāla-t-tamiḻarum āriyarum* (*Ancient Tamils and Aryans*) that really attracted a great deal of public attention, and brought him the reputation as a valiant champion of the non-Brahman Tamils against the 'Aryan-Brahmins'.[12] All the ingredients of his revised perspectives on Tamil and Indian civilization and history are already evident in this early essay. Although the arguments he offers are quite complex what is especially striking, even in this early essay, is the easy slippage between caste and nation in the work. Thus, the words Arya Jati (Tam. cāti, Skt jāti) are used often as a blanket term for all Indo-Aryans and the term Tamil Jati to mean all Tamils.[13]

---

[9] The story of the Missionary-Orientalist genealogy of the Dravidian movement has been fairly well rehearsed in recent scholarship. See, for example, my earlier article on the subject, Vaitheespara 1999.

[10] Vaitheespara 1999.

[11] See, for example, Maraimalai Adigal 1998.

[12] Maraimalai Adigal 1965.

[13] Maraimalai Adigal 1965: 1–2.

If the vast majority of Maraimalai's writings on caste are either preoccupied with reversing the Indo-Aryan claim to superiority or simply condemning the evils of caste, Maraimalai also wrote a number of works where he offers a more systematic exposition of his views on the origins and evolution of caste. They are to be found in *Cātivēṟṟumaiyum pōli caivarum (Caste Discrimination and False Saivites)*[14] and *Tamiḻar nākarikam allatu vēḷāḷar nākarikam* (*Tamil Civilization or Vellalar Civilization*)[15] and, to a lesser extent, in his last major work *Tamiḻar matam (Tamil Creed)*[16]. Maraimalai also returned to focus entirely on the subject of caste in his novel, *Kōkilāmpāḷ kaṭitaṅkaḷ*[17], which depicts the precarious love affair between a former Brahman child-widow and a young Vellalar male against the background of determined opposition by members of the Brahman woman's family. Perhaps drawing from his own background as a child of an inter-caste marriage, Maraimalai manages to bring out, quite vividly, the every-day practices of caste discrimination set against the horrors and pathos of a caste-riven Tamil society, particularly as it gets played out in terms of family dynamics and gender relations, although, again, the predominant focus here is on the Brahman-Vellalar divide.

Taken together, it can be argued that Maraimalai's writings on caste sought to accomplish at least four major objectives. Firstly, reflecting his central preoccupation with displacing the Aryan-Brahman from the pinnacle of Tamil if not Indian society, Maraimalai sought to take back India from the Indo-Aryans and claim it as, essentially, a non-Brahman Tamil civilization. The central message is that it is to the non-Brahmin Tamils that we owe the high culture of India and not so much to the Indo-Aryan or Brahman. Secondly, Maraimalai sought to subvert the established order of the Varna (Skt. varṇa) hierarchy by dismissing as irrelevant or inappropriate the demeaning Sudra Varna category, to which all non-Brahman caste Tamils were assigned. Confirming this subversion of the established order even further, Maraimalai claimed for the Tamils the status as the originators of caste and offered up the system of caste as a peculiarly Tamil contribution to Indian society. Thirdly, Maraimalai refashioned and re-ordered the institution of caste in Tamil society on a new ethico-religious basis. Though positing the Tamil-Saivite Vellalar as the ideal counterpoint to the Aryan Brahman, he sought to subvert the Vellalar's ascriptive qualities and undermine the 'caste as essence' argument, so as to make the category Tamil-Vellalar much more broadly

---

[14] Maraimalai Adigal 1957a.
[15] Maraimalai Adigal 1975.
[16] Maraimalai Adigal 1941.
[17] Maraimalai Adigal 1957b.

inclusive. Fourthly, despite privileging the Tamil Vellalars in opposition to the Brahman, even as he sought to empty the 'Vellalar' of its ascriptive qualities, it is evident from his voluminous and passionate writings against the evils of caste that Maraimalai was primarily concerned with forging a unified 'Tamil-caste'. Despite privileging the agrarian-Vellalar as the natural ideal for his reimagined Tamil nation, it is important to note that he sought to open up membership into the Vellalar-fold to anyone who adhered to what he considered its ideals and ethics. The tremendous efforts that Maraimalai as well as his fellow activists expended on calling for reforms in temple administration, the administration of monastries (Tam. maṭam) as well as in fashioning new 'pure-Tamil' or non-Brahman rituals that could be used by all Tamils without the use of 'Aryan-Brahman' priests for every day ritual practices such as marriage, death and puberty, also attest that Maraimalai's efforts were primarily aimed at forging a unified Tamil-caste that could resist and contest the alleged inroads and challenges posed by the Aryan-Brahmans.[18]

Reclaiming India: History of India as history of the Tamils

Subverting the practice of reading the origins of Indian history from the Vedic corpus and the arrival of Indo-Aryans, Maraimalai begins his history much earlier, based on what he regards as the much older Tamil works, the *Tolkāppiyam* and *Tirukkuṟaḷ*.[19] They show the Tamils to have been a highly advanced civilization, spread as far north as the Himalayas and as far west as Afghanistan before the advent and arrival of small bands of 'uncivilized Indo-Aryans'. Given their small numbers, Maraimalai claims that they were easily subsumed within the larger Tamil / Dravidian population. In Maraimalai's phrasing, 'they were a small stream that joined the vast Dravidian ocean'.[20] People who pass off as Indians today, then, are the descendants of the admixture between the large population of Dravidians and the small bands of Aryans whom Maraimalai calls the Dravido-Aryans.[21] Relying a great deal on the

[18] It is, for example, evident from a cursory glance at the Tamil/Saivite journal, *Centamiḻ Celvi,* founded and run by many of Maraimalai's supporters and fellow activists, that reforming and fashioning a unified non-Brahman Tamil Saivite community was a central goal for them. There were even calls made in the journal for a *toṇṭar paṭai,* an army of devoted soldiers or workers for the cause.

[19] Maraimalai makes this argument even in his early work, Maraimalai Adigal 1965: 3.

[20] Maraimalai Adigal 1941: 4.

[21] Maraimalai Adigal 1941: 10. As for the case of existence of pure Aryans in India, Maraimalai was of the opinion that it is only in places such as Kashmir and segments of Rajputana that you find traces of pure Aryan stock.

selective use of contemporary European Orientalist, ethnological, philological and archeological works, Maraimalai offers what is essentially a racial and ethnological argument. Writing often in a rather polemical style and pointing to evidence from the early Vedic corpus, Maraimalai describes the incoming Aryans as uncivilized and prone to "living off the meat of wild buffaloes and goats" and sacrificing these dead animals to the numerous minor gods they worshipped. In an ironic reversal of extant accounts, Maraimalai describes these Aryan gods as resembling those that one can still find among the tribal peoples in India today, and as resembling the minor gods worshipped in Tamil regions by the lowest castes.[22] Unlike the Aryans who had come from colder, more intemperate climates, which for Maraimalai explains their rude state of civilization, the Tamils like all peoples who inhabit the rich fertile lands close to the equator had evolved into a highly developed, wealthy and complex society based on settled agriculture. Agrarianism, consistent with the then current British colonial rhetoric equating civilization with Agrarianism, was for Maraimalai the hallmark of all great civilizations around the world.[23] For Adigal, developments consistent with a wealthy agrarian civilization led to the evolution of kingship and an army to protect the people and their wealth, and also gave rise to great philosophers to impart wise government and wisdom to the people.[24] It was because Tamils were naturally hospitable that they had welcomed the Aryans, and even tolerated their barbaric customs, and only slowly tried to educate them in their own more peaceful and reflective philosophies. Hence, the difference between the crude ramblings found in the early Vedic corpus and the later more reflective philosophies found in such works as the Upanishads, Sankhya, Yoga and even the Vedanta Sutras, which are essentially all creations of the Tamil philosophers. In this vein, Maraimalai asserted that if the early Vedas are Aryan, Vedanta, as it is reflected in the philosophy of the Upanishads, is a Tamil creation.[25] These were, after all, written by the Tamil sages in order to educate the uncivilized and barbaric Aryans. Even Buddhism and Jainism, for Maraimalai, were invented by Tamil kings to curb the countless animal sacrifices and flesh eating practices of the incoming Aryans. The old name for India, Bharatavarsha (Tam. pāratavaruṭam, Skt. bhāratavarṣa), was for Maraimalai derived from the name of the descendant of the great Tamil kings of ancient India, Bharatan, who had led a coalition of the

[22] Maraimalai Adigal 1957a: 49.

[23] Maraimalai cites from Tilak's *Arctic Home of the Vedas* and HT Buckle's *History of Civilization* to make this argument. See Maraimalai Adigal 1957a: 6.

[24] Maraimalai Adigal 1957a: 50.

[25] He made such an assertion as early as 1905 in his lecture, *Paṇṭaikkāla-t-tamiḻarum āriyarum*. See, Maraimalai Adigal 1965: 45–47.

armies of ten Tamil kings to meet the incoming Aryans.[26] Thus, Maraimalai deftly reversed the conventional account of ancient Indian history, where the high culture of India is attributed to the Indo-Aryans, and claimed it instead for the Tamils. Also important to note here is that Maraimalai, in doing so, not only sought to reverse the conventional history of India but also to collapse the story of the ancient Tamils as Indian history into what is essentially Tamil history.

Jettisoning the Sudra label and reclaiming caste as a Tamil creation

A persistent preoccupation in Maraimalai's writings is, of course, his attempt to jettison the Sudra label to which all non-Brahman caste Tamils were relegated. Like Sundaram Pillai before him, Maraimalai felt particularly aggrieved by this demeaning label. In order to subvert this categorization of the caste-Tamils as Sudras, Maraimalai chose three lines of attack. The first was to provide, in rather florid and insulting language, the offensive meanings given to the word Sudra in the standard prescriptive Sanskrit legal texts, such as 'slave' and 'son of a whore', and rhetorically invite his Vellalar readers to choose which they found to be the most appropriate for them. His second line of attack was to discredit the recourse that the Vellalars had taken in adopting the term Sat Sudra (clean Sudra) to distinguish and elevate themselves from the rest of the Sudra and non-Sudra Tamils.[27] Arguing that such a category as Sat Sudra is hardly known outside the Tamil region, especially in northern Sanskrit legal texts, Maraimalai argued that Manu would certainly have not cared to differentiate between the Sudras and Sat Sudras.[28] He argued that the

[26] Bharatan's ancestors were the great kings of India, according to Maraimalai. Since the Tamils were wise in government and had very able kings who were called Arasar by the Tamils, the Aryans misread this word as Asurar, but from the meaning given to this word in the Rig Veda as head or authority, it is plain to Maraimalai that the Aryans accepted these Tamil kings as their heads or leaders. The kings and their families were referred to as Arasiniyar, which was modified according to the contemporary usage as Rajanyar. Here, it is evident that Maraimalai is providing kshatriya equivalence to the ancient Tamil kings. See, Maraimalai Adigal 1957a: 16–17.

[27] His most vitriolic writings were aimed at what he thought was this great insult. He was particularly outraged by the complacency of a contemporary Saiva Vellalar elite who, in his mind, despite being the great heirs of the architects and guardians of the highest civilization, had become so mired in ignorance to not even question this very insulting label. Taking recourse to the category of Sat Sudra to elevate themselves from the rest of the Tamil Sudras, by arguing that since they are vegetarian Saiva Vellalars they deserve to be put above the rest of the Tamil Sudras, hardly softened the insult.

[28] Maraimalai Adigal 1957a: 35.

fact that the term had been used in some Saiva Agamas is hardly any consolation since these were largely meant to be temple manuals, and only written a few hundred years earlier by temple priests in the South anxious over the patronage offered to the temples by wealthy Vellalars.[29] Finally, yoking his criticism of the Vellalars with his broader project for Tamil unity, he argued that it was only because these Vellalars were foolish enough to be misled by the Aryan Brahmans that they betrayed their own Tamil kith and kin, who had in the first place, through their hard work, made these Vellalars wealthy. It is in the same vein, Maraimalai argued, that instead of being grateful to these less fortunate Tamils the Vellalars, heeding the advice of Brahmans, had shown them nothing but contempt. He then again rhetorically posed the question, "Is it then small wonder that Lord Shiva had punished these Vellalars by getting the Brahmans to call them Sudras?"[30]

Having managed to subvert the established order of the Varna hierarchy, particularly as it pertained to the depiction of caste-Tamils as Sudras, Maraimalai was still left with the task of explaining how caste originated and entered the Hindu body polity. Consistent with his argument that the Vellalar and agrarianism was the source of all civilization in India, including the development of the complex division of labour, it was only a small step for Maraimalai to suggest that the institution of caste too originated and was developed by the Tamil Vellalars.[31] Maraimalai thus boldly asserted that it was the Tamil Vellalar king Manu who originated and introduced caste among the Dravido-Aryans, as a way to bring order and civilization to them.[32] Thus, caste had originated as an effort by the

---

[29] Maraimalai Adigal 1957a: 35.

[30] The real reason for this state of ignorance by the once proud Vellalars was quite obvious. It was because they had fallen victim to the lies of those posing as Aryan Brahmans and had lavished their wealth and power according to their advice. However, what was even worse was that, in so doing, these Vellalars had abandoned the precious Tamil groups who had made them wealthy and powerful in the first place by their hard work, and begun to look on them with disdain and contempt. See Maraimalai Adigal 1957a: 37.

[31] Not content to demonstrate that the Indo-Aryans, given their state of civilization, hardly required the necessary division of labour that had necessitated the system of caste, Maraimalai argued that there is no evidence of caste among the ancient Indo-Aryans. The only division that existed initially in the ancient period, according to Maraimalai, was over skin color between the incoming Aryans and the Tamils and hence the term Varna, which over time came to denote caste. Maraimalai Adigal 1957a: 41.

[32] Maraimalai cites from Matsyapurana and other works to argue that Manu was indeed a Tamil Vellalar king who had sat in meditation in the hills of Southern India. However, he argued that caste is certainly not mentioned in the early Vedas and even if there is mention of caste in later works, such as the Upanishad and Mahabaratha, it mostly takes the form of referring to various professions or conduct of individuals rather than to any ascriptive hierarchies. How then did caste originate? If there is no evidence of caste in the initial

Tamils to bring order to the mixed populations of Dravido-Aryans and had not really been intended for the Tamils. Why, then, do we find caste among the Tamils? It is here in his innovative reading of the origin and evolution of caste among the Tamils that one can see Maraimalai attempting to ethnicise caste, to subordinate his reading of caste to his project for the Tamil nation. At this point, it is interesting to digress briefly to consider Dilip Menon's recent observation about the distinctiveness of caste dynamics in Southern India in his excellent essay on caste and communalism. Menon makes two observations about why the south was distinctive. First, the missionary intervention had the effect of democratizing and opening up a space for lower caste and untouchable voices to be heard in the public sphere, unlike in northern India, so that caste was central to discourses of various religio-cultural movements. Second, "there was a tendency to ethnicise caste and work towards an internal unity and solidarity accompanied by a rejection of caste Hindu practices", unlike in the north where there are "attempts at upward mobility followed by adoption of higher ritual practices."[33] What I find most compelling is Menon's perhaps more innovative suggestion that caste struggle is so closely imbricated with movements for religious or communal solidarity. His observation that there was a tendency to ethnicise caste makes perfect sense in the case of Maraimalai. It is clear that Maraimalai's discussion of caste was very much in the form of an immanent critique and in the service of his broader project of ethicizing caste in the Tamil region and subordinate to it. I would also suggest, without being overly reductionist, that the various Hindu sectarian struggles in nineteenth-century South India may be viewed as closely imbricated with caste competition and struggles. They were efforts to refashion and reorder social hierarchies in culturally meaningful ways. It is from such an angle that Maraimalai's writings on caste are best understood.

Forging a Tamil caste: Reordering Tamil castes

If Manu had introduced caste among the Dravido-Aryans in order to civilize them, left unexplained was how caste originated among the

period of the arrival of Indo-Aryans and only much later is there evidence of caste in its elaborate form found, it was then simple logic to claim it was the advanced civilization of the Tamils that was responsible for its origins and elaboration. The institution of caste was then originated by the Tamil Vellalar king Manu, who had written the work Manusmriti in his efforts to bring order and civilization to the mixed population of Dravido-Aryans. Maraimalai Adigal 1957a: 42.

[33] Menon 2006: 16.

Tamils in the first place and how one was to explain the contemporary caste order among the Tamils. Maraimalai was faced with a formidable task. He would have to come up with a counter narrative that would adequately explain the reality of contemporary caste order among the Tamils, while still maintaining the twin objective of subverting the dominant Brahmanical view of caste and, at the same time, providing a counter narrative that could potentially unite all Tamils under a new hegemonic bloc. The way Maraimalai negotiated this, though bordering on the fantastic in places, was, nevertheless, quite creative and brilliant. In his counter narrative of caste in the Tamil country, Maraimalai sought to posit the Saiva-Vellalar as the ideal counterpoint to the Aryan-Brahman. Yet, as a radical Saivite and a passionate critic of the caste order, he was compelled to empty the Saiva Vellalar caste category of its hierarchic and exclusionary aspects and, instead, posit it as a much more fluid moral and ethical ideal. In this reframed caste grouping, membership in the Saiva Vellalar caste category was in theory open to all and depended more on meeting the ideals of vegetarianism, cleanliness (now redefined as moral and ethical virtues in addition to physical cleanliness), as well as education and spiritual practice.

In Maraimalai's narrative, everything begins with the Tamil Vellalar's discovery of agriculture as a way of life, portrayed here very much as an act of transcendence from their earlier primitive mode of hunting and living off the flesh of animals. It is the wealth and comfort that accrue from such a lifestyle that not only led to the proliferation of specialized professions, which ultimately led to caste differentiation, but also to the cultivation of moral and ethical virtues, which ultimately became the decisive factor in caste differentiation. Thus, through agrarianism, Vellalars were the earliest discoverers of the virtue of non-killing and vegetarianism, which became the first principle of caste differentiation. Later, other virtues associated with this agrarian lifestyle followed, such as cleanliness, now recast as both mental and physical cleanliness, propensity towards cultivation of knowledge and education, and the worship of God, and also, interestingly, the good moral conduct of the women of a caste.[34]

---

[34] Maraimalai's narrative of the origin of caste in Tamil society begins with the Tamil Vellalars and the rich agricultural Maruntham zones they inhabited. Adopting, again, an evolutionist paradigm for understanding social change among the Tamils, Maraimalai conceded that the very ancient Tamils lived mostly in forest and hill tracts and survived by hunting wild beasts with bows and arrows. It is in this period that Tamils began worshipping Lord Murugan and Valliammai as the gods of the hills. A more learned and wiser segment of this original population soon descended to the fertile river valleys, to plant crops and generally build a society around an agrarian culture. This segment, having discovered the benefits of settled agrarian culture and the wealth that came from it, also

As to caste differentiation in Tamil society, it is interesting that of the five caste groupings Maraimalai divides Tamil society into, the first three all emerge from the very same Vellalar stock that discovered agriculture. These evolved as a result of the professional differentiation such a wealthy and complex agrarian society required. Since the wealth generated by agriculture necessitated its protection, the institution of kingship and a warrior caste emerged to protect society and its wealth. Other institutions also emerged, such as temples, monastries all of which required various professionals such as *antaṇar* (sages / ministers), priests (such as *āticaivar), caivakkurukkaḷ nampiyār*, *paṭṭar,* and all of whom came from various segments of the same Vellalar stock.[35] Thus, priests and officiants of temples who now claimed Aryan Brahman status were, in reality, what Maraimalai depicts as Vellalar-Brahmans. Most of the Brahmans in Tamilnadu today are understood as the descendants of these Vellalar Brahmans. A segment of these original Vellalars also went into trade and came to be called Chettiyars (Tam. ceṭṭiyār), but again, for Maraimalai, they were in reality of the same Vellalar stock. Maraimalai provided as evidence the fact that they still "give and take women among themselves" and interdine.[36]

However, as Maraimalai goes down the Tamil caste order his arguments get much more convoluted and lack clarity. For example, the next tier in terms of caste hierarchy in Maraimalai's narrative of caste in Tamil society, after his first three categories of *antaṇar* (ministers / priests), *aracar* (royalty and their families), and *vaṇikar* (traders), are a much more heterogeneous grouping who have been generally described as *kīḻōr* (Inferiors) or *iḻintōr* (mean or disgraced people) as a result of their difficult life and poverty. Interestingly, Maraimalai includes, among this category, people of the original Vellalar stock who had first discovered agriculture, but who cultivate their own fields in contrast to the higher Vellalars who had it cultivated for them.[37] This category also includes, aside from those who did the various jobs demanded by the Vellalars, the eighteen non-Vellalar groups specializing in various crafts and trades.[38]

---

began to abjure killing and meat eating. Thus, the first division among the Tamils was between those who practiced non-killing and vegetarianism and those who practiced killing and meat eating. This ethics of non-killing was discovered by the top layers of the Tamil society (Vaitheespara 2009: 31). The wealth that accrued from this settled agrarian way of life also led to the further development of society and the proliferation of various specialized professions. To guard and protect the society kingship, an army arose. Temples and matams were built requiring priests and heads of mutts and ministers with titles such as *antaṇar*, *āticaivar*, *caivakkurukkaḷ*, *nampiyār*, *paṭṭar*.

[35] Maraimalai Adigal 1957a: 49–50.

[36] Maraimalai Adigal 1957a: 52.

[37] Maraimalai Adigal 1957a: 52.

[38] Maraimalai Adigal 1957a: 52–53.

Important to note here is that Maraimalai, despite this attempt at a detailed explanation of the ranking of Tamil castes, also attempts at the same time to underline that hierarchies or gradation only evolved due to professional differentiation and as a result of lifestyle rather than due to physical essences or birth. Attempting, thus, to frame his system of ranking on the basis of profession and ethics rather than birth, he suggests, for example, that it was simply due to the fact that the Vellalar *antaṇar* (priests) could afford to follow all the four virtues that he had underlined, such as vegetarianism, that they came to be regarded as the highest; and the Parayar and Pallar (Tam. paḷḷar) caste sadly came to regarded as the lowest since they could not follow these four virtues and, in addition, were in the habit of eating buffalo meat and beef aside from indulging in toddy (Tam. kaḷḷu). He went on to assert that, in future, such labels should only be based on people's profession and practice rather than simply due to their birth or ancestry.

This detailed attempt at an ethnological mapping of caste groupings in Tamil society was the exception rather than the rule. The major thrust of Maraimalai's work and writing on caste was to passionately argue against the practice of caste discrimination among the Tamils. Maraimalai, in fact, went to extraordinary lengths to argue against the practice of caste discrimination in many of his work and writings. He was particularly brilliant and persuasive in his efforts to provide his readers with detailed examples, culled from ancient and medieval Indian and Tamil literature, which not only pointed to evidence for caste mixing from the earliest of times, but also that some great writers and religious figures were a result of such unions. Much in the style of Ramalinga, who had founded his religious order on the principle of samarasa (Tam. camaracam) or equality, Maraimalai named the religious order that he founded the Samarasa Sanmarga Nilayam (Tam. camaraca caṉmārkka nilaiyam), insisting that discrimination on the basis of caste will not be tolerated in his order. Thus, even his detailed efforts at accounting for caste in Tamil society need to be read against his efforts, in the same work, to forge caste unity among the non-Brahman Tamils. In the same work, Maraimalai makes a strong appeal to the Saiva-Vellalar to embrace, into their fold, people from all castes (including intermarrying and inter-dining), as long as they indicate their willingness to adopt his Saivite ideals, such as vegetarianism and cleanliness.[39] Even those who do not fully conform to these practices are to be embraced and slowly encouraged to do so.

Warning of grave dangers if caste practices go unchecked in Tamil and Indian society, he offers the case of the contemporary Moplah uprising in neighboring Kerala as a warning. If the Nambudri and Nayar landlords

[39] Maraimalai Adigal 1957a: 87.

had treated their own lower caste Hindu workers well, he asks, "Would they not have assisted when the Muslim peasants attacked and skinned many of them (Hindus) alive?" He answers his own question by stating, "If not for the British intervention Kerala would now be a Muslim country" and adding, if not for the British, India "would be a graveyard for the Hindus".[40] If people continue to discriminate on the basis of caste and not help the lower orders, he warned, they would all eventually convert to Christianity, Islam or Buddhism and the "Hindu-race will disappear from India."[41] In a similar vein, he argues against the practice of denying entry into temples for the lowest castes in the Tamil region, stating that it is little wonder that so many of them have embraced Christianity and Islam in places such as Tirunelveli.[42] In a sub-chapter entitled *Teṉṉāṭṭu-t tirukōyilkaḷil tāḻnta vakuppār cilar viṭappaṭāmaiyāl nikaḻum tītu* (The evil of denying certain segments of the depressed castes in temples in South India), he wrote, "Is there a greater evil than the evil of considering a major segment of God's created beings as 'lower castes' and denying them entry into precisely the abode where God resides?"[43] His passionate advocacy of love marriage, as opposed to arranged marriage, was yet another indication of his more radical views on caste. Linking caste practices with the control of women and sexuality in a section entitled, *Cātivēṟṟumaiyāl tamiḻmātar paṭum koṭum tuṉpaṅkaḷum avaṟṟai oḻikkum vakaiyum* (The suffering of Tamil women due to caste practices and the ways to remove it), he carefully linked the oppression of Tamil women and their lack of freedom to the custom of arranged marriage on the basis of caste rather than on the basis of love. Going even further, he asserted that it is little wonder that children born to such oppressed and unfree women are born with little intelligence and strength and are of little use to society.[44]

What remains a paradox, then, is why he sought, despite his great animus against the practice of caste and his warnings of the grave dangers it posed to Tamil and Indian society, to privilege the Vellalars, even if it was merely at a symbolic level. If he was particularly incensed by the caste arrogance and practices of a segment of the conservative Tamil Vellalars[45] – some of whom had clearly inspired him to write his major

---

[40] Maraimalai Adigal 1957a: 114.
[41] Maraimalai Adigal 1957a: 114.
[42] Maraimalai Adigal 1957a: 115.
[43] Maraimalai Adigal 1957a: 122.
[44] Maraimalai Adigal 1957a: 128.
[45] Maraimalai was particularly creative in his critique of the conservative segments of Saiva Vellalars. He utilized a range of techniques, including humor. Imitating the conversations of one such group, "We are thirty household people; We only eat and mix among these thirty households; We won't go beyond and even wet our hands in another

work critiquing caste in the first place – why did Maraimalai privilege the Vellalars in his revamped narrative of caste in Tamil society or, for that matter, why did he equate Tamil civilization with Vellalar civilization as he did in his work *Tamiḻar nākarikam allatu vēḷāḷar nākarikam*? Maraimalai's foreword to a later work offers a clue to his reasoning. He mentions, as inspiration for writing the work on Vellalar Civilization (Tam. *vēḷāḷar nākarikam*), the tremendous reception his lectures on Tamil civilization had received not only in Jaffna, but also segments of the Tamil Diaspora communities in the Malayan Strait settlements[46]. Given the reputation of Jaffna as a Vellalar stronghold with Vellalar numbers constituting almost half its population by the late nineteenth century, it is hardly surprising that Maraimalai's privileging of the Tamil Vellalar as a counterpoint to the Aryan Brahman earned him an enthusiastic reception there. Maraimalai lists, as the second major inspiration for writing the work, the controversy that had erupted over a Chettiyar (Tam. ceṭṭiyār) journal claiming that since Chettiyars have been referred to as Vaisyas (Skt. vaiśya) they should not intermarry with the Sudra Vellalars, and the fact that numerous people had approached Maraimalai to settle this dispute once and for all.[47] These reflections by Maraimalai certainly confirm that, by the 1920's, he had begun to be considered, if not the 'organic intellectual', as an important authority for a significant segment of the non-Brahman Tamil / Saivite community; consisting of many liberal Saiva Vellalalar, as well as a host of allied upwardly mobile non-Brahman castes determined to contest Aryan Brahman hegemony rather than the internal bickering among the leading non-Brahman Tamil castes. This obvious and real constituency, on which Maraimalai depended for most of his patronage, may have certainly acted as a constraint against Maraimalai's more radical and iconoclastic goals. His strategy of privileging the Vellalars, while at the same time broadening the category of Vellalar, may have been due to such circumstances and factors. It would then appear that Maraimalai's privileging of the Tamil Vellalars, despite his great animus against caste, was motivated not so much by a single factor but a host of factors and considerations. Given the long history of agrarian dominance exercised by the Vellalars in the Tamil region, in which the ideology of Tamil-Saivism played a central role and which is well reflected in the Tamil literary sources including the

household", he questioned "how such practices benefit them or others." Asserting that such Saivites, in fact, behave much more disgracefully than others, he wrote, "How many such Saivites are indulging themselves in brothels! How many such people secretly indulge in English whisky, fried mutton and eggs! And how many are spending their time gambling..." Maraimalai Adigal 1957a: 108–109.

[46] See Maraimalai Adigal 1957c: 14.

[47] Maraimalai Adigal 1957c: 14.

Tolkāppiyam and Saivite Bhakti literature, it would have been difficult for Maraimalai to have ignored the Vellalar altogether. Even his recourse to using agrarianism, as the hallmark of Tamil civilization and virtue, against the nomadic, meat eating Aryan-Brahman, was no doubt a result of his rather uncritical dependence on these early Tamil literary sources. Finally, as mentioned earlier, Maraimalai's more radical and iconoclastic goals may have been tempered and constrained by the pragmatic reality of his support base, consisting largely of upper caste non-Brahman elites. Despite this tepid and constrained reformism, what is perhaps more important to note is that Maraimalai's work and writings were able to introduce a novel language and grammar of reform within the fortress of Tamil / Saivite orthodoxy, which was unthinkable only a century earlier and which no doubt help lay the groundwork for the much more radical reforms that accompanied and followed Dravidianism's rise as a major political ideology. It is then small wonder that one of the poems published at Maraimalai's death which attempts to grasp the mulitiple facets of his contribution reads: "Saiva Siddhantists have lost their true leader ..."[48]

Bibliography

Aloysius, Gnanasigamony. 1998. *Religion as Emancipatory Identity: A Buddhist Movement among the Tamils under Colonialism.* New Delhi: New Age International Publishers.

Asad, Talal. 1993. *Genealogies of Religion.* Baltimore and London: Johns Hopkins University Press.

Maraimalai Adigal (maṟaimalai aṭikaḷ). 1941. *Tamiḻar matam.* Madras: SISSW.

——. 1957a. *Cātivēṟṟumaiyum pōli caivarum.* (1911) Madras: The South India Saiva Siddhanta Works Publishing Society.

——. 1957b. *Kōkilāmpāḷ kaṭitaṅkaḷ.* (1921) Madras: The South India Saiva Siddhanta Works Publishing Society.

——. 1957c. *Māṇikkavācaka varalāṟum kālamum.* Madras: The South India Saiva Siddhanta Works Publishing Society.

——. 1965. *Paṇṭaikkāla-t-tamiḻarum āriyarum.* (1906) Madras: The South India Saiva Siddhanta Works Publishing Society.

——. 1975. *Vēḷāḷar nākarikam.* (1923) Madras: The South India Saiva Siddhanta Works Publishing Society.

——. 1998. *Mullaipāṭṭu ārāycci urai.* (1903) Ceṉṉai: Maṇivācakar patippakam.

Menon, Dilip M. 2006. *The Blindness of Insight: Essays on Caste in Modern India.* New Delhi and Chennai: Navayana.

Pandian, M. S. S. 1994. *Notes on the Transformation of Dravidian Ideology – Tamil Nadu C. 1900–1940.* Madras: Madras Institute of Development Studies.

[48] *Centamiḻ Celvi* on the death of Maraimalai by one Mr. Aa, Muthukumarasamy Pillia of Thenkasi. See *Centamiḻ Celvi*, October 1950: 95. (Translated into English by author).

Prentiss, Karen Pechilis. 1996. 'Tamil Lineage for Saiva Siddhanta Philosophy', *History of Religions* 35,3, February: 231–257.

Scott, David. 1994. *Formations of Ritual: Colonial and Anthropological Discourses on the Sinhala Yaktovil.* Minneapolis: University of Minnesota Press.

Vaitheespara, Ravindiran. 1999. 'Discourses of Empowerment: Missionary Orientalism in the Development of Dravidian Nationalism' in: Timothy Brook and Andre Schmid, eds. *Nation Work: Asian Elites and National Identities*. Michigan: University of Michigan Press.

——. 2009. 'Maraimalai Atigal and the Genealogy of the Tamilian Creed'. *Economic and Political Weekly*. Mumbai. 44,14 (04.05.): 45–51.

Venkatachalapathy, A. R. 1994. *Tirāviṭa iyakkamum vēḷāḷarum.* Madras: South Asia Books.

Peter Schalk

Sustaining the pre-colonial past: Saiva defiance against Christian rule in the 19th century in Jaffna

Introduction

The present formation in Jaffna (Tam. yāḻppāṇam, īḻam[1]), of the caste system, the religious ritual performance among Saivas (Tam. caivar, Skt. śaiva) and Christians, and the educational system are, in part, results of the Portuguese, Dutch and British colonial administrations (1504–1948). In this article, with special regard to Saivism (Tam. caivam), I shall focus on the 19th century, which falls within the period of the British colonial administration (1815–1948). The major figures of Saivism in Jaffna from the 19th century will be presented. They were guided by Arumuga Navalar (Tam. āṟumuka nāvalar, 1822–1897). Based on his works, I shall show how the followers of Saiva Siddhanta (Tam. caiva cittāntam, Skt. śaiva siddhānta) among the Vellalars (Tam. veḷḷāḷar), led by Arumuga, tried to defend and sustain a continuous tradition of Saivism based on the Agamas (Skt. āgama, Tam. ākamam) against the attacks of Christians and against the rise of alternative elites among Tamil speakers. One particular way of achieving this was by employing ritual formalism and traditionalism as indicators of orthodoxy and orthopraxis. I shall conclude by analysing Arumuga's network of thought, which connects concepts of Saiva Siddhanta with those of class, caste and ethnicity, though not with race. Arumuga, in contrast to the later Sinhala-Buddhist reformer in the South, Anagarika Dharmapala (Sinh. anagārika dharmapāla, 1864–1933), did not use racial and racialist categories.

Yāḻppāṇam is Tamil. In Singhalese, the city is today called Yapanaya and in English Jaffna. When speaking about Jaffna (yāḻppāṇam / yapanaya) today, we may refer either to a district, to a town in the wider non-technical sense, or to a Government Agent Sub-Division (SD) within Jaffna town. There is another neighbouring SD called Nallūr which shall also occupy us. It should always be made clear, when speaking of Jaffna, which area is intended.

---

[1] *Īḻam* is the Tamil toponym for the whole island along with *ilaṇkai*; *īḻam* should be distinguished from *tamiḻīḻam*. For these terms and other toponyms for the island see Schalk 2004b.

The oldest references – in the form of a 1435 inscription from Tirumaṇikuli of the name of the town Jaffna, which is also mentioned in the literary work *Tiruppukal̲* by Aruṇakirinātar from the 15th century – are South Indian. The town's name has been the subject of foundation myths based on speculative associative etymology. The age of the name is of course not the same as the age of the town, which is older. Up to the arrival of the Portuguese in 1621, Jaffna was an independent Kingdom[2] with a military presence in Van̲n̲i, fighting with the Kings of Nuvara (Kandy) for control of economic products, not least of elephants which were shipped from the Jaffna coast to South India and South East Asia. The Portuguese and Dutch included Jaffna in their administration, which comprised mainly of the coastal areas. The alleged range of political influence of the former Kingdom of Jaffna, together with the language geography of Tamil, is today the basis for the projection of the borders of the new state of 'Tamil̲īl̲am' by the Liberation Tigers of Tamil Eelam (LTTE).

In 1658, the Dutch took over the administration of the Portuguese, including Jaffna and the great fort built and finished by the Portuguese in 1636. The Dutch promoted the material interests of the Vellalar caste und used them in a divide-and-rule-policy. From the Dutch period stems the 19th century Vellalar opinion that the Jaffna district is the homeland of the Vellalars.

The British conquered the whole island in 1815 and in 1833 it was re-organised into an integrated system of administration areas. This was the precursor of the formation of the unitary state of the post-colonial government in the Constitution of 1972. The one-nation Sinhala-Buddhist state of Lanka (Sinh. laṃkā) is a post-colonial construction that has exercised a strong influence on succeeding governments.[3]

In 1827, 123 188 people were registered by the British in the Jaffna District, of which only 844 lived in Jaffna town. Statistics were not yet perfected at this period, but they do provide a rough guide to size. The largest caste in the district were the Vellalars, with 45 651 members, while the Brahmans (Tam. pirāmaṇar, Skt. brāhmaṇa) had 1 935. Of the total population, 15 359 were classified as "slaves" ("Covias", "Nalluas", "Pallas", slaves of the Burghers). Regarding religion: Protestants numbered 839, Roman Catholics 9 201, "Mahometans" 2 166, and "Heathen"

[2] For the Kingdom of Jaffna see Pathmanathan 1978: Part 1 (circa A. D: 1250–1450); Pathmanathan 1974; Pathmanathan 1979; Gunasinghe 1978. For the controversy among historians about this Kingdom, see Hellmann-Rajanayagam 2007: 191–259.

[3] For the formation of Sri Lanka as a colonial nation state, see Fernando 2008.

[= Saivas] were 110 982.[4] This slave based society was part of the living conditions when Arumuga was born in 1822 into a Vellalar clan.

The castes of Jaffna

Still today, we can identify about 20 interacting castes in the Jaffna district, all with precursors in the colonial period. We have to focus on this caste reality in order to understand, for example, the past and present official statistics about land distribution and landownership. Also, aspects of religious organisation were and still are, in part, determined by caste organisations. True, there is a strong resistance against caste formation, not only from the government, but also from human rights activists, Saiva and Bauddha enthusiasts, the present Dalits, and not least the LTTE. It has organised a program against *cāti* 'caste' including *cītaṉam* 'dowry'.[5] In the beginning of the 19th century, however, the caste system, including slavery, was unquestioned and spilled over even into the Christian mission.

Given the intensive tradition of dedication to education, the Jaffna district has had high literacy. The Christian mission had a decisive influence on the expansion of educational institutions from the 19th century on, but it was only in 1974 that the University of Jaffna was founded. The delay was due to political controversies.

The 18th and 19th-century official lists of castes enumerated about 50 interacting castes.[6] The reduction today to about 20 can be explained by the formation of mega-castes, by different ways of counting castes, and by the effect of the appearance of anti-caste ideologies.[7] Today, the Vellalar caste should be viewed as a mega-caste, which has included people of other castes that have disappeared as autonomous institutions.

Castes presented themselves to the public in the 19th century by showing their caste marks.[8] The most important caste, because of its numerical dominance of almost 50 % of the population, formerly and now, is the caste of the Vellalars, 'cultivators', which constitute the landowners', not

---

[4] *Return of the Population of the Island of Ceylon*. Compiled from the Separate Returns made by the Collectors of Districts to the Commissioner of Rebenue, in Pursuance of an Order of Government Bearing Date 27th January 1824 (Colombo: Government, 1824).

[5] For the social programme of the LTTE see Schalk 2007b: 31, 39, 46–48, 58, 102, 113.

[6] For a published list established by the Dutch in 1790 see Raghupaty 1987: 208–210. For the 19th Century see *Return of the Population:* 69–70. For the functioning and interaction of castes in the 20th century see Holmes 1980: 221–232, and David 1977: 203.

[7] For the formation of mega-castes see Holmes 1980: 236–237, and for the different ways of counting castes see Holmes 1980: 206.

[8] D'Alwis 1874. David 1977: 183–184.

the land labourers' caste. The term *veḷḷāṇmai* means 'cultivation'. The caste mark of the Vellalars is given as the standing brass lamp[9] or as the two-leaved lotus.[10] Jaffna was and still is an agricultural society, where control of land is the key to social control. Today, not all Vellalars are landowners. Some of them are proletarised and others have professions, which have nothing to do with landownership. In exile, the function of being a landowner has often become obsolete, but still, caste identity is kept alive, especially at times of marriage.

In 1824, the Jaffna district had the highest number of slaves in the island in proportion to its population, 12.46 % (Trincomalee 6.91 %, 0.28 %, Galle 0.18 %, Mannar 0.33 %, Cilau 0.15 %).[11] It is not clear whether these numbers refer to 'house people' or to 'slave people' or both (see below).

We have to consider that the South Indian castes are generally classified as *śūdra* in a pan-Indian perception, transmitted and upheld especially by sanskritisised Brahmans in South India. This is a powerful and unshakable pan-Indian classification going back to the *Dharmaśāstras*. There is little possibility for the Dravidian 'Sudras' (Skt. śūdra, Tam. cūttirar) to eliminate this or to undermine it by social climbing. This acceptance of being a Sudra has been internalised.[12] This internalising may not indicate an ambition for social climbing to the observer, but it does. It is a clear demarcation against the untouchables. This internalisation points at what the Dravidians are not. The Vellalars try to delimit themselves against those belonging to the fifth caste, which is the outcastes, the modern Dalits. They are, for example, *vaṇṇār*, washermen, *ampaṭṭar*, barbers, *naḷavar*, toddy tappers, *paḷḷar*, low caste worker, and *paṟaiyar*, drummers. These and some other castes were in the *tēcavaḻamai*, the customary law, classified either as *kuṭimakkaḷ*, 'house people', servants to the Vellalars, or as *aṭimakkaḷ,* 'slave people' like the *kōviyar*, family slaves, *cantar*, slaves in public service, *nallavar*, toddy tappers, and *paḷḷar*, family labourers to the Vellalars.[13]

The 'house-people' sold their labour to chosen or inherited Vellalar families for money or kind, sometimes lifelong. We would call this system bonded labour. The 'house-slaves' were forced to sell their body and life to the landowner. They were part of his property. Today Īḻam is ruled by Roman-Dutch law and the *kuṭi-* and *aṭimakkal* rhetoric is obsolete, but there is still bonded labour in Jaffna in a legal grey zone. It

9 Raghavan 1954: 139.

10 David 1977: 183.

11 See *Return of the Population.*

12 See Pfaffenberger who correctly applies the *śūdra* label in the title of his book: Pfaffenberger 1982.

13 On *kuṭimakkaḷ* see Raghavan 1954: 140–150.

should be mentioned that the social formation of Singhalese-Buddhist speakers is also related today to a caste system of their own. This plays a role in the formation of Buddhist monastic orders and in the identification of individuals in marriage pools, which includes the transfer of property by a system of dowry.

The Vellalar expansion in the religious sphere is limited by the Brahmans who of course are not classified as Sudras, but the Vellalars, with Arumuga in the forefront, who sustained the Agamas, have insisted upon a special consecration as Kurukkal (Tam. kurukkaḷ) that enables even Vellalars to serve in Agamic temples (Tam. kōyil). These Kurukkals compete with the Brahmans for positions in Agamic and non-Agamic Saiva temples (*kōyils*).[14]

A caste consisted and still consists of several *pakuti*s, 'sections', 'portions', 'allotments', 'divisions'. These are local organizations. Each consists of grandparents, parents, uncles and aunts, and their children, as a minimum. We would call it an extended family based on kinship, contrasting to assembled extended families based on friendship or common interest. Tamil speakers use the term *kuṭumpam*, 'household'. Its unity is usually demonstrated at the occasion of a marriage, and in the homeland even at death. It functions as a marriage pool. It is the *kuṭumpam* that sanctions the choice of partner, which again is decisive for the future of the couple and for their relations to the other members in the same *kuṭumpam*.

An important observation made by Karthigesu Sivathamby (Tam. kārttikēcu civattampi) is that *kuṭumpam* and *pakuti* overlap.[15] As castes are endogamous, the *kuṭumpam* is a guarantee for partners to be part of the same *pakuti*. As can be expected, arranged cross-cousin marriages are idealised. Dysfunctional love marriages are discouraged. This household system is not abolished in exile. It lingers on in a different way. Geographical distances are overcome by letters, faxes and emails that connect uprooted and dispersed 'households' all over the globe and even reach Jaffna in 'the motherland'. The *kuṭumpam* also lingers on as attractive fiction in romantic and nostalgic films and narrations.

One metaphorical Tamil word for 'wife' is *kuṭumpam*. The wife not only symbolizes the *kuṭumpam*, she is it. *Kuṭumpam* used for 'wife' is employed in spoken language and is even preferred to the pedantic *maṉaivi*, 'wife'. The use reflects the strength of endogamy and the aversion against exogamic relations. It is interesting to see that, where a *kuṭumpam* based on kinship is missing, another secondary *kuṭumpam*

---

[14] For Tiruñāṉacampantar see Schalk 2004a: 126–127, 177–178.

[15] Pfaffenberger speaks in this connection of micro-castes each of which jockeys for higher rank. See Pfaffenberger 1990: 186.

based on a common interest is formed. Temple communities today in exile sometimes form themselves in such a way.[16] The fact that a fictional *kuṭumpam* is invented if there is none shows the strength of this social formation that was and is the basis of caste in Jaffna. The strength of the *kuṭumpam* is also visible at funerals. It is the *kuṭumpam* that mourns. The LTTE has coined the expression *māvīrar kuṭumpam* for the clan of the killed fighter when mourning and grieving its 'Great Heroes' who died in battle for the establishment of 'Tamiḻīḻam'. The fading away of the *kuṭumpam,* due to social reform based on an individualised economy, will be the final blow to the caste system based on clans with a common economic interest.

In Jaffna, some of the temples were and still are run by a *pakuti* and on this social basis an annual religious *tiruviḻā*, 'holy festival', is organized in the villages lasting 1–15 days. Big festivals were and are organized by several *pakutis* of the same caste group. In a Vellalar village, for example, subordinated minority castes like *kōviyar*, the servants of the Vellalars, or the *karaiyār*, the fishermen, hold their own *viḻā*. If there are several *pakutis*, they elect a coordinator or elderman, who, as a symbol of his position, performs the ritual *tarppaipōṭutal*, 'wearing of the [sacrificial] grass'. It is formed to a ring that he wears on his right ring finger. This grass is usually used in purification rituals; in Sanskrit it is known as *dharbā*. The leader of the *pakuti* practising *taṟppaipōṭutal* may demonstrate the purity of the *pakuti*. The same ritual was and is practised in another context in the temple. The annual *viḻā* is a social event, where a *pakuti*'s status is demonstrated. Village problems are discussed, or the possibilities of marriage are examined.

In Jaffna the annual *viḻā* was and is still based on caste distinctions, but to avoid caste conflicts, different castes have their own *viḻā*. There was a movement in the 1960s and 1970s called "the temple entry movement" that was mobilised by untouchables in Jaffna;[17] its aim was to allow all lower castes to enter higher castes' temples. The Māviṭṭapuram temple was the symbolic bastion of attack. The movement was allegedly unsuccessful,[18] though I would argue that it was partially successful. The organising of the movement was a way of solving internal problems of a social split within the community of Tamil speakers, with the unexpected and undesired help of the external enemy, the Government of Sri Lanka. It had interfered already in 1957, under the banner of human and civil rights, with the *Prevention of Social Disabilities' Act* to prevent caste dehumanisation, and rejected in 1968, on this basis and with reference to

[16] See Schalk 2007a.

[17] Paffenberger 1970.

[18] This is the evaluation in Sivathamby 1990.

the problem in Jaffna organised by the temple entry movement, the application of the Federal Party for autonomy. Bryan Pfaffenberger's comment on this is relevant: still in the 1960s, at least part of the Vellalar community regarded the peninsula to be in essence a Vellalar preserve and relished partition as a means to stop the Colombo Government's intervention in pursuit of 'social reform' in Jaffna. This is true also in 2008, but we have to consider this part of the Vellalar community as a marginalised elite.

I referred above to the *tēcavaḻamai* as meaning 'custom of the country'. It contains customary law for the Jaffna district.[19] The Dutch administrators interviewed local chiefs and slaves and put in writing this law in Dutch in 1707, but it was retranslated into Tamil by twelve leading *mutaliyār*, 'headmen'. The Dutch introduced changes and so did the British later, who also made a new translation into English from the Dutch code. Section 4 in the formulation from 1707 says that all questions that relate to those privileges that subsist in the said province between the higher castes, particularly among the "Vellales" on the one hand, and the lower castes, particularly the "Covias", "Nalluas" and "Palluas", on the other, shall be decided to the said customs and the ancient uses of the province. During the time of Arumuga the *tēcavaḻamai* was still in use, with the exception in the part on the above section concerning slavery which was abolished by the British in 1844.[20]. This was a turning point for the Vellalars, where they lost control over parts of the caste-system and were unable to prevent social climbing and stop the formation of the Vellalars as a mega-caste.

The Dutch had exploited caste divisions, from which the Vellalars had profited, in the agricultural sector, especially in the cultivation of tobacco for export. During the British administration, international competition meant less profits on the tobacco market. Many Vellalars adapted to these circumstances and combined agriculture with new sources of income: English education that generated mathematicians, engineers, medical officers, lawyers, civil servants and politicians. The 'Colombo Tamil' was created, who had his residence in Colombo but still had a side income from his properties in Jaffna. It is this Tamil living in Colombo, recruited from the English educated elite in Jaffna, that has formed the image of the Tamil speaker who in disappointment of losing his privileges takes up arms against the Government of Sri Lanka. Even critical scholars took over this stereotyped and generalised image about Tamil speakers, suppressing thereby the fact that most of them belonged to a landless proletariat, suppressed by the Vellalars, by the British colonials

---

[19] For the history of this customary law see Tambiah 1958.

[20] Jayapalan n. d.

and by the Government Agents of the Governments of Sri Lanka who in Jaffna applied the laws of the central government. 1844 was a moment of choice among Tamil speakers to be for or against colonial culture in the cultural sector, including also the influence of Christianity in the educational field.

The Vellalars tried to indicate that they are *sat-*, 'true', which implies that the other castes belonging to the Sudra group are not *sat-*.

They are *a-sat*. This distinction was used by Arumuga, who, following an older tradition, did not relate it to specified castes, but to moral behaviour. Yet, as behaviour was related to caste, his classification was indirectly caste related. Sudras drinking liquor and eating meat were *a-sat*. The distinction was then applied to non-Vellalars, especially to proletarians who were connected with hard labour like the *nalavar* and *paḷḷar* and those engaged in killing. Such a caste is for example the *karaiyār*, fishermen, with a strong position in and around Valveṭṭituṟai. In spite of reforms still, in 1967, only 17 % of all temples in Jaffna were open to all castes.[21]

In the 20th century, low-castes were still not allowed to live near a temple, to draw water from the wells of high-caste families, to enter public places like a barber shop, laundries, cafés or use a taxi, to keep women in seclusion and protect them by enacting domestic rituals, to wear shoes, to sit on bus seats, to register their names properly so that social benefits would be obtained, to attend school, to cover the upper part of the body, to wear gold earrings, if male, to cut their hair, to use umbrellas, to own bicycles or cars, to cremate the dead, and to convert to Christianity or Buddhism.[22] Other references to harassments against low castes by the Vellalars have been collected by Dagmar Hellmann-Rajanayagam.[23]

Saiva Vellalar xenophobia

In turning to the 19th century we are faced with a complete dominance of Christian educational institutions; we have to search for Saiva and secular educational institutions. In 1816, American Missionaries were welcomed by the British Governor and only ten years later they had established a considerable mission in Jaffna consisting of hospitals and schools. This included the famous Batticotta (Tam. vaṭṭukōṭṭai) Seminary for collegiate education, with a dominance of students from the Vellalar caste, and an

---

21 Pfaffenberger 1994: 143.

22 For caste discrimination see Holmes 1980: 232–234.

23 Dagmar Hellmann-Rajanayagam 1993: 253.

emphasis on female education in the Girls School in Utuvil.[24] Arumuga, whose life work was influenced by Vellalar caste interests, reacted by establishing Saiva schools with a dominance of Vellalar students and his younger follower, Ponnambalam Ramanathan (Tam. poṉṉampaḷam rāmanātaṉ, 185–1930), started in the spirit of Arumuga the Ramanathan College which was the first school for Saiva girls situated not far from Utuvil, where the competing Christian school was situated. The Catholics, who had arrived already in 1621 in Jaffna, had 23 Catholic schools with 424 students in 1828.[25] Well-known schools are St. Patrick's College, established in 1850, and Holy Family Convent, a girl's school founded in 1862.[26] Dennis Hudson has pointed out that Arumuga wanted to prevent a development in Jaffna that had occurred in Tirunelveli, South India, where the Protestant mission had succeeded in converting a group of Vellalars and had formed a Christian caste of its own.[27] This intention is however not made explicit by Arumuga himself, though it can be reasonably ascribed to his way of thinking. Indeed, the Vellalar religious unity based on Saivism split already during the life time of Arumuga into a Christian and a Saiva section. The real threat emanated from those Christians who, after conversion, rejected or neglected the caste system.

In the second half of the 19th century a protest movement arose in Jaffna among a Saiva elite against the dominance of especially Christian education and Christian polemic against Saivism. The protest was not prospective, millennaristic or revolutionary; it was retrospective by turning towards sustaining an idealised pre-colonial past, and by erecting this past as a wall of defence and protection against the alleged threatening and foreign elements of spiritual culture that were presented by the Christian part of the colonial administration. An already existing Vellalar xenophobia was intensified.

The knowledge about this ideal past was not based on historical-critical studies of pre-colonial society, but on a Puranic tradition of narration, especially from the Tamil *periyapurāṇam* and the *kantapurāṇam* that identified as ideal rulers saints or at least saintly kings. Sainthood was the ultimate ideal. This past was part of aesthetics and religion; it was virtual, not differentiated and therefore not real, but exactly this constituted its seductive strength among some intellectuals in the 19th century in Jaffna. I would not call them nostalgics; they did not believe in a *paradise lost*.

---

[24] Sivathamby 1992; Pathmanathan 1986; Pathmanthan 1995.

[25] Sivathamby 1979.

[26] For the development of Catholicism in Yalppanam see Jayaceelan 1995; Sabaratnam 1995.

[27] Hudson1995b: 108–109.

They believed in a *paradise sustainable*. They saw themselves as actors, not as victims, but they had to pay a price for their defiant retrospection.

This reacting protest was proportional to the way dominance had been established by the colonial administration, not by violent extinction of Saivism as did the Portuguese, or by systematic suppression and segregation of Saivas in the colonial administration as did the Dutch who however exempted the Saiva Vellalar elite from this discrimination. The British established an inclusive domination of Western Christian culture over the local Saiva culture by making competent elites, among them Saiva elites and other competing possible elites, participate in, make use of and benefit from the material exploitation of the colonial administrative system. The defiant protest by de-monopolised Saiva Vellalars took therefore no violent anti-British forms, but had a clear and determined two pronged strategy in verbal communication: first to demonstrate the old age and highest value of Saivism to both Christians and apostates from Saivism to Christianity by presenting and cultivating Saivism in a specific sectarian interpretation of Saiva Siddhanta from the pre-colonial period, and second, to try to prevent the rise of new elites by sustaining the present elite's caste hierarchy, not least by a self-representation through ritual formalism and traditionalism. The top of this hierarchy were the Tamil educated pandits of the Vellalar caste, whose marker and self-image was Saiva Siddhanta as doctrine-and-ritual. They tried to prevent the undermining of Saiva Siddhanta (= of Vellalar ideology) in Jaffna by emerging competing castes, by the split of the Vellalars, and by the formation of the Vellalars as a mega-caste (but their efforts ended in their marginalisation in present Jaffna society of the 20th and 21st centuries). Arumuga gave this movement a special twist to which I now turn.

Most Tamil speakers in the whole of Īḻam belong nominally to his school of Saivism known as 'Caivacittāntam' in Tamil, 'Śaiva Siddhānta' in Sanskrit.[28] The present Western observer may evaluate it as both esoteric and eccentric, but it was not harmless seen from a social and political point of view. The tension between Agamic / non-Agamic was 'connected' with the pairings of both high caste / low caste and Tamil / non-Tamil in a series of persuasive identities (example: "a genuine Tamil is a Vellalar and his religion is Agamic Saivism"), or in persuasive homologies (example: the status relation of a genuine Tamil is that of a Vellalar to a low caste and of an Agamic to a non-Agamic form of Saivism, Vaishnavism [Tam. vaiṇavam, Skt. vaiṣṇava], or Christianity). The protesting movement was a "historic bloc" in the Gramscian sense (see below) that tried to cement the hegemony of Saiva orthodoxy in combi-

---

[28] Jaffna University has produced its own scholars in Saiva Siddhanta. See, for example, Nāṉakumaraṉ 1995.

nation with caste and ethnic consciousness both in a doctrinal and ritual discourse.

In Arumuga's work is a promotion of the interests of the Vellalars. This is not explicit in his texts, but explicit is his promotion of classical *varṇāśramadharma* in, for example, his work *civālaya-taricaṇa-viti* (see below), where *dharma* is understood as Saiva *dharma*. In his prescription, each caste has its proper way of worshipping, which implies caste segregation in the temple and among temples.

Arumuga Pillai

Arumuga Pillai (Tam. āṟumuka-p-piḷḷai) is known also as *nāvalar*, 'the orator', with the extended connotation of 'the learned', or simply as Arumuga Navalar Avargal (Tam. āṟumuka nāvalar avarkaḷ).[29] A common honorary high-sounding title in Tamilised Sanskrit is *śrīlaśrī āṟumuka nāvalar*. There is, of course, a Navalar road in present Jaffna and a special sanctuary for him close to the Nallūr temple to venerate his memory.[30] An annual Navalar 'solemnity' (Tam. nāvalar viḻā) is organized among his supporters even in exile. In 1971 the Government of Ceylon issued a stamp to commemorate him, and in 2003, in a period of cease fire, his 181st birthday was celebrated in Jaffna by his followers. When public commemorative monuments are erected over a person it is usually to save him from oblivion among the masses.

There are several images of Arumuga. The first image of him is as a saint following in the footsteps of the Nayanmars (Tam. nāyaṉmār*)*. Some of his dedicated admirers depict him verbally and visually as one of the followers of the Nayanmars, the Saiva leaders of *patti* (*bhakti*) whose biographies are summarized in the *periyapurāṇam*, one of Arumuga's favorite texts. He is depicted as a Saiva saint with *kṣavaram* 'tonsure', *tiripuṇṭaram* 'three marks' and *rudrākṣa* 'Rudra's eyes', which refers to a chain of beads. In a side sanctuary of the Nallur temple in Jaffna town he is depicted in a statue as if he was one of the Nayanmars among Nayanmars. On stamps and pictures distributed today he is almost one of the Nayanmars which is not completely absurd: his connecting of Tamil with Saivism goes back to Campantar.[31] Arumuga tried to associate himself

---

[29] His life and work has been described many times. Ambalavanar 2006: 6–14; Hellmann-Rajanayagam 2007: 141–167; Hudson 1995b; Hudson 1992b: 51; Hudson 1992a; Hudson 1995; Kailasapathi 1979; Pathmanathan 1986; Pathmanathan 2003; Perinpanayagam 1988; Sivathamby 1995; Sivathamby 1979.

[30] A picture of this sanctuary with the statue of the Nāvalar is in Schalk 2004a: 243, picture 41.

[31] See Schalk and Vēluppiḷḷai 2002: 430–445.

closely with the pre-colonial period in South India in the manner of a pious theologian; he seems to have 'gone native' by identifying himself with an idealized past, but traditionalism does not in all its forms exclude transformation of its content or of its form. There is no such thing as a *frozen* tradition, except for in ideological historiography with vested interests. Devadarshan Ambalavanar has rightly pointed out that in this image is included a consciousness of change: the historical Nayanmars hold palm leave books in their hands, but Arumuga is depicted with an open printed book. According to Devadarshan Ambalavanar there was an element of colonial modernity combined in his traditionalism to go public, in his case to go public with Saivism as as counter measure to the dominance of Christianity.[32] The image of him as a Nayanmar is and should be modified, but not disowned. It was part not only of Arumuga's self-understanding, but can also be used as an interpretative model by the historian for understanding him. I have come to the conclusion that Arumuga was not only traditionalistic, having a dedicated commitment and attraction to the past, but that he also was traditional, being a representative of a continuous past going back in certain aspects to the Nayanmars.

A second image presents him as being heavily influenced by colonial modernity. It ascribes to him the consciousness of a Vellalar climbing the social ladder within the colonial system, dependent on keeping an open mind for education, especially in English. Along with opening schools in Tamil medium, it is pointed out that he personally engaged in the formation of a school in Jaffna using English medium (but they do not say that his attempt was a failure). Arumuga realized, reportably, that for the Vellalars to survive, they had to adapt themselves to a certain degree to new circumstances introduced by the British. He taught himself and his followers to distinguish between the beneficial colonial administration and the destructive Christian mission. The element of co-operation with the central and centralizing worldly authorities consisting of Singhalese-Buddhist speakers is allegedly characteristic of him and his followers, especially with his promotion of the politician Ponnambalam Ramanathan. Ponnambalam Ramanathan's strategy was to highlight the blessings of British Rule,[33] but at the same time to pinpoint the intolerance of the Christian mission.[34] This was allegedly also Arumuga's main strategy. What Ramanathan stood for is ascribed to Arumuga.

The historian Sivasubramaniam Pathmanathan (Tam. civacuppiramaṇiyam patmanātaṉ) has pointed out that Arumuga did not exhibit anti-

[32] Ambalavanar 2006: 24, 152, 221, 405, 411.
[33] Ramanathan 1929: 30, 41, 76.
[34] Ramanathan 1929: 85–88.

British sentiments. Arumuga even believed the British Government had a capacity to govern the colonial subjects in accordance with the principles of natural justice.[35] Moreover, to substantiate this image of a modernising reformer, Arumuga is depicted as the creator of modern Tamil prose, the user of the printing press, the taking over of preaching, the promoter of girls' education, and of singing hymns like Christians, and the creator of a 'catechism'.[36] All this does not fit into the image of him being a follower of the Nayanmars.

This image is evidently not painted by historians with knowledge about pre-colonial Tamil culture, which could provide a differentiated background to these examples of Arumuga's dependence of colonial culture.[37] When discussing whether Arumuga was a reformer or sustainer, it is necessary to approach the subject as a historian with a solid knowledge of the pre-colonial period. There are some critical scholars, including myself, who interpret these elements as the result of a sustained pre-colonial past.[38]

The real problem is what 'inspired by Christianity' means. If it means learning from Christianity something new for Saivism, I must reject this statement, but if it means to be inspired to look for similar elements in the Saiva past, I agree. Arumuga looked for arms that could beat the enemy, the enemy's own arms. Christianity was an awakener that made Arumuga search for similar elements in the Saiva past pertaining to doctrine-with-ritual and to methods of propaganda. I say similar, not identical, because it is evident as shown by Bernard Bate that, for example, the pre-colonial *piracaṇkam* 'preaching' and Arumuga's colonial *piracaṇkam* were at variance.[39] It can be shown that his 'monotheism' is a sustainment of an Agamic modalistic image of a god from the pre-colonial period that is similar but not identical with a strict monotheism.[40] To sum up, in the past, Arumuga found elements *similar* to monotheism – the singing of hymns and preaching, etc. – but he paralleled them, he did not adopt them, to Christian forms knowing that they were effective in his campaigns. Parallels never meet. His pragmatism did not change his traditionalism.

Another image of Arumuga was painted to counteract the criticism of him for being a representative of a hegemonic caste and that his hidden

---

35 Pathmanathan 2003.

36 See, for example, Bate 2005.

37 See, for example, the many works by Ālvapiḷḷai Vēluppiḷḷai on *caivam*, *caiṉam* and *pauttam*. Example: Vēluppiḷḷai 1990.

38 Hellmann-Rajanayagam 2007: 147–162. See also the main thesis in Ambalavanar 2006.

39 Bate 2005. For the *piracaṅkam* see also Young and Jebanesan 1995: 177–180.

40 See Schalk 2004a: 90.

agenda was to promote this caste within the colonial administration. Instead, he is depicted without a hidden agenda as a purely *religious* reformer of Saivism which also includes elements of charity. This image was introduced by Ponnambalam Ramanathan in 1884 when he remembered Arumuga shortly after his demise in 1879 as "the champion reformer of Hindus in the Northern Province".[41] This characterization was again taken up as a title in V. Muttukumaraswamy's biography in 1965, *Sri La Sri Arumuga Navalar. The Champion Reformer of the Hindus*. The same author summarized this biography in a booklet in 1971 which has been distributed in both Tamil and English, thereby cementing the image of Arumuga as an idealistic 20th-century religious reformer fighting immorality.[42] The profile of this image is not only that Arumuga was open to British colonial modernity, but also that his intention was *religious* only, not socio-economic. His caste basis and caste interest are played down or hidden away. When he is said to fight social vices it is exemplified by meat eating and drinking alcohol, not about the economic exploitation of man by man in a system of bonded and slave labour.

In this image the element of fenced Saiva sectarianism is also not mentioned. Saivism has traditionally 16 sects and only one is promoted by Arumuga. Jaffna has a strong group of Virasaivas (Tam. vīracaiva, Skt. vīraśaiva) who have been marginalized.[43] Vaishnavas were despised by Arumuga. Jainas (Tam. caiṉa, Skt. jaina) were subject to disgust. Folk religion was condemned.[44] Therefore, not even his religious program is given in its totality.

His sectarian views on Saivism have been idealized by a group of pandits even today who involve the public in seemingly endless discussions about what is Agamic and non-Agamic. These discussions are coded forms for manifesting social stratification. The model case is the discussion of the Nallūr temple started by Arumuga's criticism of it for being non-Agamic.[45] Devadarshan Ambalavnar has made a meticulous examination of Arumuga's argumentation and has come to the conclusion that Arumuga's argumentation preserves – or as I say sustains – a pre-colonial tradition and that the temple committee that believes itself to be Agamic is dependent on non-Agamic reforms introduced in the colonial period.[46]

The activity of these *paṇḍitar* provokes the rise of critical voices against Arumuga and his legacy, above all from the Tamil left. They

---

41 Ramanathan 1929: 86.

42 Muttukumaraswamy 1971.

43 See Schalk 2004a: 83–88.

44 For folk religion, see Shanmugaratnam 1990; Susindirajah 1999.

45 For a presentation of this case, see Pathmanathan 2006: 336–374.

46 Ambalavanar 2006: 384.

criticise Arumuga's dedication to the upper caste [= upper class]. Other critical voices are the Virasaivas, and also some few Christians who fight still active intolerant sectarianism and casteism – with and without ultimate hidden religious and political motives.[47]

This image of Arumuga as a purely religious reformer is unhistorical. Caste was part of Arumuga's concept of religion when he accepted the concept of *varṇāśramadharma*. His Vellalar based negative evaluation of other castes is also evident. His caste agenda was not always hidden. To this we can add his covering metonymic language that makes his soteriology imply caste. He used the coded, specialized, seemingly apolitical, metonymic language of a Saiva theologian who speaks about social experiences of conflict in the hierarchical caste system in metaphors of a graded and hierarchical soteriology. The experience of social stratification is reproduced in terms of a graded and stratified soteriology. Soteriological terms are used to generate a semantic change from the social / political to the spiritual, thereby eliminating contingency about the former. One can refer to fire by speaking about smoke. This kind of metonymic language is typical for a traditional Gramscian intellectual who avoids confrontation and looks for consensus.

I suggest that we see Arumuga as a typical Gramscian traditional intellectual. Antonio Gramsci (1891–1937) examined especially the role of education in the formation of hegemonic groups and focussed upon the role of intellectuals. Some function as traditional and others as organic intellectuals. The traditional intellectual is allied with the dominant ideology and the ruling class. In Arumuga's case this is his Vellalar base in cooperation with the colonial administration, as illustrated by his promoting of Ponnambalam Ramanathan. In contrast, the organic intellectual belongs to an ascending class where he is formed and therefore is 'organic', genuine or authentic. Characteristic for a traditional intellectual is also his avoidance to identify himself with a specific group being allegedly above and beyond specific class interests. His language is coded. I have not yet found a passage where Arumuga identifies himself as *veḷḷāḷaṉ* (Vellalar). Arumuga, as a traditional intellectual who goes for consensus, saw himself as Saiva and the people as Saivas which seems to be specific, but which is not. There are 16 Saiva sects and Saivism was the ocean of Tamilness for him. Tamil Saivism ("Caivam") is a label not only for a religion, but also for a historic bloc (see below). In contrast, an organic intellectual honors his own caste-class identity.

The traditional intellectual attempts to establish and to maintain a distinction, difference and segregation between their *alta cultura* and 'the people's' *cultura populare,* which he does not acknowledge in its own

[47] See Hoole n. d.

right, but as serving the elites. The distinction is, in our case, expressed in the caste system and in a parallelized graded soteriology. An organic intellectual strives to overcome these differences by generalizing popular culture, when necessary, by a revolution. By introducing the concept of a Gramscian traditional intellectual it becomes clear that the attempt to depict him as a religious reformer only is an act of traditional intellectualism.

A fourth image has tried to affiliate him to specific political interests and make him an organic intellectual who, on the side of the people, initiated the present freedom struggle of the Tamil speakers. Attempts have been made to make him a Tamil patriot and connect him with the present Tamil Resistance Movement as precursor. In 1986, when the 107th Arumuga 'solemnity' (Tam. nāvalar viḻā) was observed, even in exile among Tamil speakers, the well-known lawyer Krishna Vaikunthavasan (Tam. kiruṣṇa vaikuṇṭavācaṉ) from London presented Arumuga as a patriot and freedom fighter to whom tribute should be paid by full support of the militant movement.[48] It should be noted that Vaikuntavācaṉ was not part of the Central Committee of the LTTE, or had any official function within the LTTE, but was a supporter who like many dedicated supporters allegedly can read the mind of Velupillai Prabhakaran (Tam. vēluppiḷḷai pirapākaraṉ, 1954–2009). The LTTE leadership is, however, alienated to Arumuga's program. Vaikunthavasan's exploitation of Arumuga's name for specific political ends is based on a misunderstanding of both the nature of thought of Arumuga and of the Tamil Resistance Movement. Arumuga's alleged seminal thoughts for the LTTE's cause can be easily declared void. His caste interest is counteracted today by the Tamil Resistance Movement. Also, his loyalty towards a central Government with a centralised political administration is contradicted. His was no political programme. He had no ethnic understanding in political terms or in territorial terms of a Tamil motherland / homeland, a federal or independent state. His adept follower, Ponnambalam Ramanathan, tried later in the 1920s to knead a homeland concept, but this step was never taken by Arumuga. The use of violent revolutionary means was alien to him. His contribution to an awakening of Tamil consciousness was seen from the ebony tower of Vellalar consciousness. His defiance was an expression of a class / caste specific Saiva Vellalar self-assertion. Evidently, he and his followers thought it possible to maintain some of the privileges from the Dutch period. This self-assertion again was not directed against Singhalese speakers or against the colonial system, but above all against Christians, Christian Vellalars and non-Vellalars, within his own society

[48] Vaikunthavasan 1986. There are more instances like this documented in Hellmann-Rajanayagam 2007: 142–143.

of Tamil speakers. Tamil speaking Christians were not only different believers, but also possible competitors within the caste system. Both were threatening the privileged position of the Vellalars from the period of the Dutch administration on. To sum up, I share the evaluation of Dagmar Hellmann-Rajanayagam that there is no straight line from Arumuga to recent aspirations for Sri Lankan Tamil independence,[49] if 'straight line' means a teleological development predetermined already in his alleged seminal thinking. What happened in the 20th century in the Tamil Resistance Movement was and is mainly determined by the British political administration of selected preferences of ethnicities according to their usefulness and by successive Sri Lankan Governments' insisting on a formation of a unitary state.

Formalism and traditionalism in Arumuga's works

Arumuga's mission to sustain, from the Dutch period on, the social-economic privileges of the Vellalars and their Saiva ideology of dominance was supported not least by his religious program in sustaining an Agamic past. I focus here especially on Arumuga's norms for Agamic ritual performance in Arumuga's texts. One is from 1873 and called *Caiva Question-Answer* (Tam. caiva-viṉā-viṭai). It is a small but 'loaded' book in two parts that is constructed in the form of questions and answers, like the Protestant catechism of Martin Luther. Therefore, a popular but also misleading 'translation' of *caivaviṉāviṭai* is 'Saiva Catechism', which is given even in the *Tamil Lexicon*. To give an example from the book: the first section is called *kaṭavul iyal*, ["the nature of the god"], and the first question and answer in this section is *ulakattukkuk karuttā yāvar?*["Who is the maker (creator) of the world?"] *civaperumāṉ* ["Siva, the Great"].[50]

Another important source for us is Arumuga's *civālaya-taricana-viti* ["The (Proper) Way to Worship at Siva's Abode (= temple)"].[51] Both books are excellent sources for a general study in ritual formalism and traditionalism, which hand in hand were means to achieve his aim. The formalisation of ritual counteracts attempts to change and to bind the involved to an acceptance of a social hierarchy. Traditionalism of ritual is

---

49 Hellmann-Rajanyagam 1989: 235.

50 Navalar 1993. For predecessors and successors of this book see Young and Jebanesan 1995: 180–181.

51 The "Catechism" is not yet translated, but *The (Proper) Way to Worship at Civaṉ's Abode (= temple)* is translated by Dennis Hudson in Hudson 1995a.

here part of a process to legitimate the positioning of the Saiva Vellalars on top of the caste hierarchy.

The framing as rituals by Arumuga of certain acts which seem secular to us, like urinating, reveals an interesting aspect of his thought. Arumuga believed in the power of rituals, in their ability to empower the ritual performer, provided the rituals are correctly executed. The reward is *puṇṇiyam* 'merit' which is a help in soteriological climbing. Arumuga saw it as his responsibility to inform the public about these rituals as assistants to salvation within a complex system of Saiva Siddhanta. He collected, from the tradition, prescriptions and proscriptions and published them in schoolbooks. These belong to a space other than the temple. They belong to a public space. It is the great merit of Devadarshan Ambalavanar to have demonstrated convincingly this specific adoption by Arumuga of colonial modernity, the shift from private to public space.[52] This adoption is not comparable to the saying *new wine, old bottles*, but is an example of the saying *old wine, new bottles*. True, the space is shifting and we can discuss further whether the content is affected from this shift, but Arumuga's stand is clear. He thought that the shift would not change tradition, but would lead to its spread. His acceptance of the printing press is therefore not a sign of becoming modern, but is an intensification of the spread of tradition, more specifically of a "historic bloc" in the Gramscian sense. In Gramsci's view, any class that wishes to dominate in modern conditions has to move beyond its own narrow 'economic-corporate' interests, to exert intellectual and moral leadership, and to make alliances and compromises with a variety of forces. Gramsci calls this union of social forces a "historic bloc". This bloc forms the basis of consent to a certain social order, which produces and re-produces the hegemony of the dominant class through a nexus of institutions, social relations and ideas. The historic bloc in the case of Arumuga was religion, Saivism, which he hoped to develop under the protection of the colonial administration and its modern school system on the basis of a system of social relations that we know as the caste system dominated by the Vellalars.

The two books prescribe in detail ritual behaviour in what is believed to be the tradition of the Agamas from the 12–14th centuries. In the given context of confrontation with Christianity we face a set of rituals expressive of retrospective defiant resistance against the efforts by the Christian mission and its supporters among Tamil speakers who allegedly were undermining 'pure' Saivism as the dominant ideology of the Vellalars. The two books were still used in schools up to the 1960s when the Government of Ceylon nationalised schools and introduced

---

[52] Ambalavanar 2006: 24, 221, 152, 405, 411.

schoolbooks controlled by a centralised administration in Colombo. Still today individuals of the generation that went to school up to the 1960s know by heart sections of these books. The rise of the Tamil resistance movement in the 1970s made these books an anachronism.

I shall now give some examples from the books, with reference to their formalism that reflects their particular style and genre. It should be noted that all the contained prescriptions are given without explanation. The first example refers to the right way of using *vipūti,* which is holy ash to be used as prescribed in the *caiva-viṉā-viṭai* first part, chapter 3. We do not learn any paradigmatic or aetiological myth that 'explains' religiously the use of *vipūti*. Arumuga does not appeal to a pious or rational understanding, but to the obeying of the authority of tradition. He gives orders. What follows is my summary of a part of this section.

Vipūti should be kept in a *campuṭam*, [a little silk bag or brass cuplike vessel] for smearing. One should smear it, facing the North or the East, taking care not to drop it on the ground. One should face upwards and uttering "Siva Siva", take the *vipūti* in the three central fingers of one's right hand, and smear it on one's forehead. One should smear it before going to sleep, after getting up from sleep, after washing one's teeth, while the sun rises or sets, after bathing, before and after meals. If one receives an *ācāriyār* 'teacher' or a *civaṉaṭiyar* 'devotee of Siva' one should worship them thrice or five times, bowing down and prostrating in front of them, and get up and receive the gift of *vipūti* with both hands. Then one should worship the masters as before. One should smear *vipūti* not facing them, but facing opposite to them. One should smear head, forehead, chest, navel, two knees, two shoulders, two elbows, two wrists, the left and right sides of the back between the shoulder blades, lower vertebral column, neck – 16 parts in all. Some leave out the back between the shoulder blades and mention the two ears. Some leave out elbows and wrists and have 12 places. The length of the *tiripuṇṭaram* on the forehead is from one extreme end of an eyebrow to the other. It is wrong to have longer or shorter marks. On the chest and the shoulders it should be six inches. There should be one inch space between each line. One line should not touch the other, etc. ...

It is understandable that Arumuga dedicates three pages to the art of applying *vipūti* and that he dedicates several pages to the art of carrying a *liṅkam*. It is however puzzling why he prescribes in detail the way how a male orthodox follower of Saiva Siddhanta should go to the toilet. A Saiva should rise two hours before the sun, and ease and purify himself at once. The place should be a hundred bows distance from a temple. The act must be done in silence, with the cord place on the right ear and the body covered from head to waist. If it be day-time, the person must face north, if night, the south. He must ask the gods of the place to retire by clapping his hands thrice. He must not look at the sun, moon, fire, cow, Brahmans, those waring the Saiva insignia, or women. He must keep his eyes fixed on the tip of his nose. He must not yawn, sneeze, or spit. The gods curse an uncovered head that will be split into a hundred fragments.[53]

The point here is that even in an extremely private situation there should be a consciousness of being a follower of Saiva Siddhanta. There is no private or reserved sphere that suspends the dedication to Siva. The other point is that these actions are framed as rituals which qualifies them – correctly performed – as instruments for gaining merit.

We can interpret the formalism and traditionalism of Arumuga as ways of defending orthodoxy, which refers here to the doctrinal teaching about the image of Siva and soteriology of Saiva Siddhanta in accordance with the Agamas. Orthopraxis refers to the correct ritual performance within Saiva Siddhanta in accordance with Agamas. Saiva Siddhanta has strong roots in this special collection of 28 texts from the pre-colonial period known as Agamas. They come under the category of Tantric texts. They prescribe what to believe according to Saiva Siddhanta, how to live and how to perform the rituals correctly. What is 'Agamic' is regarded as orthodox. Most of these texts in their Tamil version appeared in the 12th to 14th century AD in South India, and influenced the development of Saivism in Īḻam, too, not least through the work of Arumuga. Elsewhere, in 2004, I described Arumuga's work in relation to the South Indian tradition[54] and came to the conclusion that Arumuga, in contrast to Dharmapala, is traditional. Devadarshan Ambalavanar has also convincingly delivered an arsenal of arguments for that stand in 2006.[55] I see Arumuga as a Gramscian traditional intellectual whose tradition is not religion alone but a "bloc" of religion and specific caste interests.

Conclusion

The complexity of the hybrid Jaffna caste system demands an analysis. A caste in Jaffna is similar, not identical, to a class. A Tamil caste's dominance is founded not mainly on religious status like the varna (Skt. varṇa), but on economy, more specifically on landownership, and also on size. It deviates from class in its insistence on endogamy and in its fatalism that lets the status of birth determine an individual's destiny. The

[53] For a complete translation see Young and Jebanesan 1995: 181.
[54] Schalk 2004a: 88–95.
[55] Ambalavanar 2006: especially chapter VI.

economic foundation of landowning makes the Vellalars the dominant upper-class and the *aṭimakkaḷ* and the *kuṭimakkaḷ* suppressed landless classes. In order to uphold this class system on the moral and emotional level and to legitimate it, notions from the varna system have been introduced, like the concepts of purity and pollution as separators of social strata. This includes also notions in popular and official religion in the form of a ritual system of sacrifices that establishes the greatness of the Vellalar patron and the humble status of his servants and retainers.[56] Furthermore, there is the strong connection of caste to the extended family system under the name of *kuṭumpam,* whose solidarity is symbolised in religion in the form of a clan temple. Finally, there is the Vellalar specific doctrine that cast stratification, resulting in Vellalar hegemony in Jaffna, is an authentic expression of Tamilness including Saivism. The stratification of caste becomes a mirror of soteriological climbing. It also introduces a connection between social stratification and ethnic consciousness. The Jaffna caste system in the form of a purified Vellalar tradition, in the footsteps of Arumuga, is an attempt to unite religion, language, class, caste and ethnicity on to a caste hierarchy as a model for the lower castes. After Arumuga some leaders added the concept of race. Today this hybrid system is still upheld by a small group of Saivas who, however, in the context of the development initiated especially by the LTTE, appear as sectarian and atavistic.

In the case of the Buddhist Dharmapala we can safely say that he was not traditional, but that he was traditionalistic. He retrieved from the past of the Vamsic tradition clements which he connected with the modern development to facilitate its acceptance among Singhalese-Buddhist speakers, but he was not traditional in the sense that he was an exponent and representative of an unbroken Vamsic tradition. The Vamsic tradition had been reinvented by colonial historians first in the middle of the 19th century. In the 18th century the *mahāsaṃgha* had to travel to Siam to renew its lineage of the initiation of monks. Dharmapala was fundamentally a modernist, holding industrialising Japan as a model for the development of the island. He 'pasted' Vamsic references and allusions onto his program for modernity to legitimise its introduction in a conservative Buddhist society.

In contrast, Arumuga was not only traditionalistic, he was traditional also. He did not retrieve and paste, together with a group of Tamil intellectuals he sustained from the pre-colonial past a transmitted and still existing world view from the Puranic and Agamic tradition, which had been made available orally and in manuscripts for centuries, and in publi-

[56] For more on this, see Pfaffenberger 1982 and an abridged version in Pfaffenberger 1984: 17–18.

cations in print in the 19th century. In his case, modernity in the form of English colonial culture was forced upon him as a necessity for the survival of Vellalar hegemony in a colonial setting, but he used it selectively for his own purposes. He placed traditional Saiva education into the colonial school system. He remained like one of the Nayanmars living in the 19th century. He was not modern like "Colombotamils" settling in Colombo as Ponnambalam Ramanathan did, enjoying the benefits of colonial material culture, or like Dharmapala who had ideas about development through industrialisation, or like Dayananda Saraswati (1824–1883) who searched and found modern telecommunications and gravitational attraction mentioned in the Vedas. Arumuga realised that modern techniques like the printing press and a new public space like the school – even if they were not mentioned in the Tamil Vedas – could help him to sustain the past as a model for the present, not for the past's own sake, but because it contained what he as a traditional intellectual believed to be an empowering soteriology. He poured old wine into new bottles. This is how a tradition can be sustained when encountering changes. Some may call this a modernisation of tradition; I call it the sustenance of tradition.

Arumuga never went outside the Tamil language area. His knowledge about Europe was based on his studies of classical antiquity and of the early Christian tradition. He developed a pre-colonial native mentality. Coming too early for modernism actually saved him from becoming an anti-Sanskrit Tamil language purist and biological racist like some later Tamil leaders of the South Indian Dravidian movement and like the movement of the Singhalese-Buddhist Dharmapala. Language purism and racism became part of colonial modernity towards the end of the 19th century. Arumuga, however, has paid a price for his sustaining of tradition: his ideas today are a sectarian and exotic atavism in Jaffna marginalised by the LTTE, the Tamil left, the Dalit movement and democratic forces.

Bibliography

Ambalavanar, Devadarshan. 2006. *Arumuga Navalar and the Construction of a Caiva Public*. (Diss.) Cambridge: Harvard University.

Bate, Barnard. 2005. 'Arumuga Nāvalar, Saivite Sermons, and the Delimitation of Religion, c. 1850', *The Indian Economic and Social History Review* 42, 4: 469–484.

D'Alwis, James. 1874. 'Brand Marks on Cattle', *Journal of the Ceylon Branch of the Royal Asiatic Society*, Part 1: 60–63.

David, Kenneth. 1977. 'Hierarchy and Equivalence in Jaffna, North Sri Lanka: Normative Codes as Mediator', in: Kenneth David, ed. *The New Wind. Changing Identities in South Asia.* Paris: Mouton, 179–226.

Fernando, Jude Lal. 2008. *Dynamics of Essentialist Representation of Nationhood and the Politics of Interpretation: The Role of Religion in the Making and Unmaking of the Sri Lankan Nation-State.* (Diss.) Dublin: Irish School of Ecumenics.

Gunasinghe, P. A. T. 1978. 'S. Pathamathan. The Kingdom of Jaffna, Part 1 (c. A. D: 1250–1450). A Critical Review', *Sri Lanka Journal of Humanities* 5: 99–112.

Hellmann-Rajanyagam, Dagmar. 1989. 'Arumuka Navalar: Religious Reformer or National Leader of Eelam', *The Indian Economic and Social History Review* 26,2: 235–257.

——. 1993. 'The Jaffna Social System: Continuity and Change under Conditions of War', *Internationales Asienforum* 24,3–4: 251–281.

——. 2007. *Von Jaffna nach Kilinocchi. Wandel des politischen Bewusstseins der Tamilen in Sri Lanka.* (Beiträge zur Südaseinforschung. Südasien-Institut Universität Heidelberg; 199) Würzburg: Ergon Verlag.

Holmes, W. Robert. 1980. *Jaffna (Sri Lanka) 1980.* Jaffna: Jaffna College.

Hoole, Ratnajivan. n. d. *The Tamils: The Problem of Identity and Religion.* Unpublished manuscript.

Hudson, Dennis. 1992a. 'Winning Souls for Śiva: Arumuga Nāvalar's Transmission of Hindu Traditions in India and Abroad', in: R. B. Williams, ed. *A Sacred Thread. Modern Transmission of Hindu Traditions in India and Abroad.* Chambersburg: Anima Publications, 23–51.

——. 1992b. 'Arumuka Navalar and the Hindu Renaissance among the Tamils', in: Kenneth W. Jones, ed. *Religious Controversy in British India. Dialogues in South Asian Languages.* New York: State University of New York Press, 27–51.

——. 1995a. 'How to Worship at Śiva's Temple', in: D. S. Lopez, ed. *Religions of India in Practice.* Princeton: Princeton University Press, 304–320.

——. 1995b. 'Tamil Hindu-Response to Protestants: Nineteenth-Century Literati in Jaffna and Tinnevelly', in: Steven Kaplan, ed. *Indigenous Responses to Western Christianity.* New York: New York University Press, 95–123.

Jayaceelan, Joseph. 1990. 'Catholicism in the History of Yalppanam', *Lanka* 5: 103–115.

Jayapalan, V. I. S. 1983. 'Left Movements and the Caste Struggle in Jaffna', *Lanka Guardian* 5, 19: 8–10.

——. n. d. *Slavery and its Abolition in the Jaffna District.* Unpublished manuscript.

Kailasapathi, K. 1979. 'Arumuka Nāvalar: The Central Years (1834–1848)', *Navalar Number 1979.* Jaffna: St. Joseph's Catholic Press Jaffna: VI-XI.

Muttukumaraswamy, V. 1965. *Sri La Sri Arumuga Navalar. The Champion Reformer of the Hindus.* Colombo: Ranjana Printers.

—— (Tam. vi. muttukumaracuvāmi). 1971. *Śrīlaśrī ārumuka nāvalar. avarkaḷukku añcali intu camaya varalāṟṟil ipperuntakaikkuriya iṭam.* (Niṉaivu muttirai veḷiyīṭu, 29-10-1971)

Nāṉakumāraṉ, Na. 1995. 'Studies in Caiva Cittāntam', in: Peter Schalk, ed. *Studies in the Tamiḻ Cultural Heritage of Yālppāṇam, Īḻam (Lanka).* (Uppsala Studies in the History of Religions; 2) Uppsala: Uppsala University, 49–56.

Navalar, Arumuga (Tam. āṟumuka nāvalar). 1993. *Caiva viṉāviṭai. mutaṟ puttakam* (1873) Citamparam: Śrī āṟumukanāvalar caivappirakāca vittiyācālai aṟakkaṭṭaḷai, 1993.

Pathmanathan, Sivasubramaniam. 1974. *The Kingdom of Jaffna. Origins and Early Affiliations*. Peradeniya: Ceylon Institute of Tamiḻ Studies.

——. 1978. *The Kingdom of Jaffna*. Colombo: Arul M. Rajendran.

——. 1979. 'Kingdom of Jaffna – Propaganda? Or History?', *Sri Lanka Journal of Humanities* 5: 101–125.

——. 1986. 'Religion and Social Change in Northern Sri Lanka 1796–1875: Protestant Missionary and the Hindu Response', *Modern Sri Lanka Studies* 1,1: 15–42.

——. 1990a. 'Murukan the Divine Child: The Kantacuvamai Temple at Nallur', *Lanka:* 80–102.

——. 1990b. 'The Religious Tradition of the Kingdom of Yalppanam', *Lanka* 5: 43–79.

——. 1995. 'Protestant Christianity in Yalppanam', *Lanka* 5: 120–154.

——. 2003. *Arumuka Navalar and the Hindu Revival in Sri Lanka in the 19th Century.* Unpublished manuscript presented at Uppsala University.

——. 2006. *Hindu Temples of Sri Lanka*. Colombo: Thirukketheeswaram Temple Restoration Society.

Perinpanayagam, R. S. 1988. 'The Social Foundation of Educational and Economic Activity in Jaffna. Sri Lanka', in: M. Chitralega et al., eds. *Kailasapathi Commemoration Volume*. Jaffna: Jaffna University, 83–100.

Pfaffenberger, Bryan. 1970. 'The Political Construction of Defensive Nationalism: The 1968 Temple-Entry Crisis in Northern Sri Lanka', *The Journal of Asian Studies 49,1*: 78–96.

——. 1982. *Caste in Tamiḻ Culture: The Religious Foundation of Sudra Domination in Tamil Sri Lanka.* Syracuse: Maxwell School of Foreign and Comparative Studies.

——. 1984. 'Fourth World Colonialism, Indigenous Minorities and Tamil Separatism in Sri Lanka', *Bulletin of Concerned Asian Scholars*. 16,1: 15–22.

——. 1988. *Pilgrimage and the Technology of Life: Center and Other in the Logic of Jaffna Hindu Pilgrimage.* Unpublished manuscript 1988.

——. 1990. 'The Hindu Temple as a Machine, or, the Western Machin as a Temple', *Techniques et culture* 16: 183–202.

——. 1994. 'The Political Construction of Defensive Nationalism: The 1968 Temple Entry Crisis in Sri Lanka', in: Chelvadurai Manogaran and Bryan Pfaffenberger, eds. *The Sri Lankan Tamiḻs. Ethnicity and Identity.* Boulder: Westview Press, 143–168.

Raghavan, M. D. 1954. 'The Sociology of Jaffna – The Nalaver and the Koviar', *Tamil Culture* 3,2.

Raghupaty, Ponnampalam. 1987. *Early Settlements in Jaffna. An Archaeological Survey.* Madras: Raghupaty.

Ramanathan, Ponnambalam . 1929. *Select Speeches. Delivered in the Legislative Council of Ceylon. Vol. 1. 1879–1894.* Colombo: The Daily News.

Sabaratnam, A. 1990. 'The Hindu-Catholic Encounter in Yalppanam Today', *Lanka:* 103–116.

Schalk, Peter. 2004a. *God as a Remover of Obstacles. A Study of Caiva Soteriology among Īḻam Tamil Refugees in Stockholm, Sweden.* Uppsala: Acta Universitatis Upsaliensis.

——. 2004b. *īḻam<sīhaḷa. An Assessment of an Argument.* (Acta Universitatis Uppsaliensis, Historia Religionum; 25) Uppsala: Acta Universitatis Upsaliensis.

——. 2006. *cāvilum vālvōm. 'Auch im Angesichts des Todes werden wir leben'. Īḻamtamilesein im Krieg und in der Fremde.* Dortmund: Internationaler Verein Emigrierter Tamilischer Schriftsteller e. V.

——. 2007. 'Caivam – a Religion among Tamil Speaking Refugees from Sri Lanka', *Refugee Survey Quarterly* 26,2: 91–108.

——. 2007b. *Die Lehre der Befreiungstiger Tamilīḻams von der Selbstvernichtung durch göttliche Askese*. Uppsala: ACTA, 2007.

Schalk, Peter and Āḷvāpiḷḷai Vēluppiḷḷai, eds. 2002. *Buddhism among Tamils in Pre-Colonial Tamiḻakam and Īḻam. 1. Prologue: The Pre-Pallava and the Pallava period.* Uppsala: ACTA.

Shanmugalingam, N. 1990. 'From Ghora to Bhoga: Role Change and Rise of the Goddess Turkkai in Yalppanam', *Lanka* 5: 186–200.

Shanmugaratnam, N. 1990. 'From Ghora to Bhoga: Role Change and Rise of the Goddes Turkkai in Yalppanam', *Lanka* 5: 186–200.

Sivathamby, Karthigesu. 1979. 'Hindu Reaction to Christian Proselytization and Westernization in 19th Century Sri Lanka', *Social Science Review* 1: 41–75.

——. 1990. 'Divine Presence and / or Social Prominence – An Inquiry into the Social Role of the Places of Worship in Yālppāṇam Society', *Lanka* 5: 155–175.

——. 1992. *American Influence on Sri Lankan Tamil Social Life. A Note on the American Socio-Cultural Impact on Jaffna Tamil Society*. Unpublished Manuscript presented in Uppsala.

——. 1995. 'The Ideology of Śaiva –Tamil Integrality. Its Socio-Historical Significance in the Study of Yalppanam Society' (1990), in: Sivathamby, Karthigesu. *Sri Lankan Tamiḻ Society and Politics.* Madras: New Century Bookhouse, 61–72.

Sugirtharajah, Rasiah S. 2005. *The Bible and Empire: Postcolonial Exploration*. Cambridge, Mass: Harvard University Press.

Susindirajah, Swaminathan. 1999. 'Religiousness in a Saiva Village', in: K. Balasubramanian et al., eds. *Studies in Sri Lankan Tamil linguistics and Culture. Select papers of Professor Suseendirarajah.* Jaffna: University of Jaffna, 235–250.

Tambiah, H. W. 1958. 'The Law of Thesavalamai', *Tamil Culture* 7,4: 386–408.

Vaikunthavasan, Krishna. 1986. '107th Navalar Day Observed by Tamils', *New Life* 10, 38, 12 December: 19.

Veluppillai, Alvapillai. 1990. 'Religions in Yalppanam up to the Thirteenth Century', *Lanka* 5: 10–42.

Young, R. F. and Jebanesan, S. 1995. *The Bible Trembled. The Hindu-Christian Controversies of Nineteenth-Century Ceylon.* (Publications of the Nobili Research Library; 22) Vienna: Institute für Indologie.

Ulrike Schröder

No religion, but ritual? Robert Caldwell and *The Tinnevelly Shanars*

Introduction

When the Bishop of Madras, George Trevor Spencer (1799–1866), visited the south of his diocese in 1841, he also came to Mudalur, a Christian village in the South Indian district of Tirunelveli. On this occasion, he wrote in his diary:

> I want words to express my astonishment at all I see in this land of promise. The word of the Lord is covering it ... I unhesitatingly declare to all who are interested in the progress of the Gospel in India, that this is a land of promise. ... Here we have Christian villages – villages entirely Christian. It is a glorious sight ...[1]

In the decade before, the Society for the Propagation of the Gospel (SPG) had revived its mission in the south-eastern portion of Tirunelveli, as the Church Missionary Society (CMS) had done in other parts of the district.[2] The steadily growing numbers of converts to Christianity, especially from the Shanar / Nadar (Tam. cāṇār / nāṭār) caste, excited not only missionaries and bishops, but also mission propagandists in Britain. Like no other mission field throughout India, the claim of there being 'fields white to harvest' in Tirunelveli seemed true. Missionary magazines, as well as other Christian periodicals and even ordinary newspapers, were constantly filled with articles describing the success of Christianity in Tirunelveli and which depicted the 'customs' and 'religion' of the Shanars / Nadars. Therefore, in the public missionary discourse of the 19th century, the 'Tinnevelly Shanars' were probably the best known single caste in India besides the Brahmans.

The Anglican missionary Robert Caldwell (1814–1891) was the man who made the most important single contribution to this by writing an entire book entitled *The Tinnevelly Shanars.* His frequently quoted essay claimed to be much more than a mere ethnographic description. Its subtitle reads: *A Sketch of Their Religion and Their Moral Condition, and Characteristics as a Caste. With Special Reference to the Facilities and*

---

[1] Spencer 1842: 120.

[2] For the history of the CMS and SPG missions in Tirunelveli, see Pascoe 1901; Stock 1899; Appasamy 1923; Grafe 1990. The CMS had already started its work in Tirunelveli in 1816, through the efforts of James Hough, and in 1820 it sent its own missionaries to the district.

Hindrances to the Progress of Christianity Amongst Them.[3] Although primarily a theological work, Caldwell's book was quickly understood as one of the first ethnographic accounts of a South Indian caste and their religion. However, basically, it was only the product of Caldwell's first ten year's experience as a missionary in Tirunelveli. It is astonishing that Caldwell's book, *The Tinnevelly Shanars,* is to this day less known for its contents than for its impact on the emerging identity of Shanars / Nadars in the second half of the 19th century.[4] Aiming at the description of the Shanars as objects of Christian mission work, Caldwell ascribed to them a distinct religion that was separated from Brahmanical Hinduism and afforded points of contact to the Christian mission. His representation of the Shanars' religious and social identity, as well as his predominantly negative account of their 'moral condition', caused a wave of protest from Shanars / Nadars – a striking example of what happened to colonial and missionary representations of South Indian culture and religion once they left the hands of their inventors.

The context: The reorganisation of mission in Tirunelveli

When, in 1826/27, the SPG took over the mission field in Tirunelveli from the Society for Promoting Christian Knowledge (SPCK), there were almost no missionaries of British origin working in South India. For more than a century, the missionaries were Germans, provided by the Danish-Halle connection to the SPCK.[5] The introduction of British missionaries into mission work in South India brought a completely new kind of missionary to India. They no longer came from the tradition of German (Lutheran) Pietism, but were heavily influenced by the Evangelical Awakening and missionary movement in Great Britain, which developed from the 1790s onwards. Calvinism, the Evangelical revival, and British missionary debates constituted the background of men like Robert Caldwell, who came to Tirunelveli in 1841.[6]

---

[3] Cf. Caldwell 1849.

[4] For the impact of Caldwell's theories about South Indian culture and religion on discourses of identity in nineteenth-century colonial South India, especially among the Shanars/Nadars, and on the upcoming Dravidian movement, see Hardgrave 1969; Kent 2004; Vaitheespara 2000; and Vaitheespara 1998.

[5] For a recent overview of the history of the Protestant Tranquebar Mission in the 18th century see Gross, Kumaradoss, and Liebau 2006.

[6] For the social and theological background of British missionaries in India cf. Piggin 1984 and Potter 1974. For a general overview of the history of the British missionary movement see Porter 2004. The biographical sources on Caldwell's personal background are rather rare. The *Reminiscences of Bishop Caldwell*, published and edited by Caldwell's

The development of the missionary movement in Great Britain had led to the foundation of missionary societies that distinguished themselves along denominational lines. Fostered by the growth of independent church bodies in England and Scotland through the Evangelical Awakening, denominational identities were reshaped in Britain in the first half of the 19th century. For example, Robert Caldwell began his missionary career as a staunch Evangelical missionary of the London Missionary Society (LMS) and was heavily influenced by the moderate Calvinism of the new Scottish Congregationalism.[7] He took an active part in denominational debates about 'church principles' and 'church government' that also swept into the field of mission. Before coming to Tirunelveli in 1841, he decided to change his denominational alliance from the independent LMS to the Anglican SPG, which represented the opposite pole of denominational identity in Britain, namely the Anglican High Church establishment, which was largely non-Evangelical.[8]

Caldwell changed his denominational alliance not only because he disagreed with the LMS work in Madras. Like many Anglicans, he was attracted by the prospect of reviving a mission in Tirunelveli that could claim the tradition and success of their older 18th-century German predecessors, like Christian Frederick Schwartz.[9] Yet, the ways in which the new Anglican missionaries continued the work of the older mission resulted in a completely new concept of mission: they transferred the model of the Anglican parochial system into the mission field. This model relied completely on an ecclesiastical hierarchy and paternal supervision, infused by the Evangelical zeal for 'serious religion' in every-day practice.[10] The Indian congregations, which had come into existence before the reorganisation of the mission, had largely sustained themselves independently by Indian catechists and 'country priests', and

son-in-law, Joseph L. Wyatt (Wyatt 1894), do not provide much detailed information about Caldwell himself. For a recent biography of Caldwell see Kumaradoss 2007.

[7] As a student at the Glasgow Theological Academy, which was founded by two leading Scottish Congregational Evangelicals, Ralph Wardlaw (1779–1853) and Greville Ewing (1767–1841), Caldwell was most probably influenced by the "Scottish school of mission theory" (Stanley 2001: 19). His autobiographical remarks in *Reminiscences* show a tendency to downplay his Evangelical upbringing; see Wyatt 1894: 3 ff.

[8] Caldwell's position in these debates and his decision to join the SPG is reflected in his later remarks in *Reminiscences* (Wyatt 1894: 7 ff. and 62 ff.). Stanley (1996) provides an insightful analysis of Caldwell in the context of the denominational debates in Madras in the 1830s and 1840s. See also Copley 1997: 144 ff.

[9] Christian Frederick Schwartz (1726–1798) was considered the 'founder' of the 'Tinnevelly mission'. This view was enhanced by Caldwell in his works about the history of the Tinnevelly mission, see Caldwell 1880 and 1881.

[10] Cf. Caldwell 1857: 62, where he describes the method of "assembling the Christian inhabitants of every village every morning, and evening, for public prayer and catechization."

had been only occasionally visited by European missionaries. This led to the development of Christian congregations which were, more or less, firmly bound to the local religious context, but did, however, not fit to the ideals of the new missionaries. They established a system of mission stations that exposed the Indian Christians to a new order: organized as strongly hierarchical, it gave all authority to the missionaries as heads of their own missionary establishments. The apostolic and Episcopalian form of church government, as it was represented by the Church of England, was held to suit especially to India and to the 'genius of the Orient' in general.[11] The mission work modelled Tirunelveli as an ideal for the revivalist reorganisation of the Anglican Church in the first half of the 19th century. Therefore, the importance of Anglican mission in Tirunelveli exceeded the local or regional level of India and was of importance for the religious discourse in Britain as well. In 1858, Thomas Brotherton observed that "in no agricultural parish in England and Wales [are the people] so systematically, carefully and effectively instructed in the Christian doctrines [as are] the people in our Tinnevelly Missions."[12] Caldwell also ascribed the "success" of Christian mission in Tirunelveli to the parochial system:

> Much of the success realized in Tinnevelly has been owing to the personal influence of the Missionaries; and I am naturally led by what I have said respecting the introduction of the parochial system, to mention this here, for it is only by means of the parochial system that the personal influence of the Minister of Christ can systematically cooperate with the influence of the truth.[13]

The great increase in the missionary presence throughout the district from the 1820s onwards[14] posed a significant threat to the established order of Tirunelveli's society. It resulted in fierce struggles with the upper caste Hindu and Muslim communities. They were alarmed by the conversion of

---

[11] Cf. Stanley 1996: 411. Caldwell probably shared this idea when he wrote, in a letter home defending his change from the LMS to the SPG, "Should [I] be tied down to a system of Christianity which whether suited or not to England, is not, I believe, suited to India?" Letter, dated Madras June 20, 1841, cited in Wyatt 1894: 66.

[12] Pascoe 1901: 541 f., citing the *SPG Report* for the year 1858. Spencer wrote in his visitation journal of 1841: "I affirm it as my deliberate conviction, that the parochial system of the Church of England is in active operation in Tinnevelly. The plan pursued by the missionary clergy both here and in Travancore seems to me particularly well-adapted to accomplish their object. Their doctrine I have every reason to believe is simply, truly, and fully that of the Church of England, neither turning to the right hand nor to the left, but faithfully delivering that message which the Church has committed to them; while their discipline and the management of their congregations is wholesome, godly, and primitive." (Spencer 1842: 128 f.).

[13] Caldwell 1857a: 58.

[14] Between 1829 and 1850 the number of European missionaries (CMS and SPG) increased from 3 to 16 (6 SPG and 10 CMS Missionaries), cf. Pope 1850–51.

larger groups of Shanars / Nadars, including whole families and villages, into the folds of the missionaries, seeing the conversions as a threat to the social and ritual hierarchy of the South Indian society. In 1845, when Bishop Spencer was on his next visitation tour through South India, he received a petition from the villagers of "Streeveigoondum". They complained that the missionaries "make congregations of wicked Shanars and thievish Maravars, and the Pullers and Pariahs, who have always been our slaves and shoemakers, basketmakers, and other low-caste-persons, and teach them the Gospel, the Ten Commandments, and the other things."[15] In essence, the conversions were not, as the missionaries thought, an effect of their own agency, but part of the already ongoing emancipative movement of the Shanars / Nadars in order to escape from social and religious oppression by the dominant elites. Especially in the first half of the nineteenth century, the conversions in Tirunelveli were fuelled by local conflicts between landowners and peasants.[16] For many subaltern groups in South Indian society, the Christian mission provided an opportunity to flee from oppression and to benefit from the mission, which provided protection and education.

However, the massive missionary activities in Tirunelveli were indeed influential on local religious cults. For the missionaries, conversion included the strict proscription of demonolatric practices among the converts, as well as the systematic destruction of 'devil temples' (Tam. pēy kōvil) and other places of worship in those cases where whole village communities converted to Christianity. The destruction of temples – along with the confiscation or destruction of 'idols' and 'images' – or their conversion into places of Christian worship was frequently used by the missionaries as an indicator of their success. George Uglow Pope, who superintended the Sawyerpuram District of the SPG Mission, reported in 1845:

> I may also mention that since my appointment here 9 devil temples in this division of the district, have either been destroyed or converted into Christian prayer-houses, and that of the 22 villages in connexion with the mission, the whole of the most respectable and influential inhabitants are under instruction.[17]

Such demolitions evoked local resistance from Hindu organisations, like the Vibuthi Sangam and the Sadur Veda Siddhanta Sabha, which counteracted by destroying prayer houses and persecuting new Christians. As Robert Frykenberg noted, these tensions between Hindus and Christians

---

[15] Spencer 1848: 51.

[16] For an analysis of the social and economical condition of Tirunelveli in the nineteenth century see Ludden 2005.

[17] Pope 1845: 5.

in Tirunelveli led to a form of early Hindu-Christian communalism.[18] The incidents in Tirunelveli were taken to the courts at Madras, where the Hindu elite was already alarmed about the agency of Christian missionaries, and fuelled the heated debates in Madras newspapers about the question of mission and conversion. Tirunelveli was labelled the "emporium of missionaryism, flourishing under the auspice of the public servants of the Company" by Hindu critics.[19] The missionaries from Tirunelveli did not remain silent, but published a lengthy reply that disapproved of the allegation of interfering with 'devil-worship' by the deliberate destruction of "Peycoils".[20] It is interesting to note that Caldwell was among the signatories, though he mentions virtually nothing concrete about these incidents in his reports from Tirunelveli besides vague remarks about a "crisis in the history of the Missions in this province", caused by the "persecuting zeal" of "Hindooism".[21]
Another problem the missionaries had to face while operating in the 'mission field' was revivalist and sectarian movements, which sprang up in South India during the 19th century. The most prominent example was that of Ayyavali (Tam. ayyāvaḻi), which originated in South Travancore and was led by the Shanar / Nadar Muthukutty Swami (Tam. muttukuṭṭi cuvami, c. 1809-c. 1850), later known as Vaikunda Swami or Ayya Vaikundar (Tam. ayyā vaikuṇṭar).[22] In his first report from Tirunelveli, Caldwell reported that this movement also swept to the south of Tirunelveli and gained considerable influence in his mission district. He noticed that Muthukutty styled his message and mission method on the practice of the (mostly Evangelical) missionaries:

It is held that there is but one God, whose name is Narayana, 'The Predestinator,' 'the Master,' and whose mark or 'seal,' as it is styled, resembling that of the *Vaishnavas*, is worn on the forehead. Mootoocootty and his disciples, orgininally twelve, the inspired representatives of this deity, profess to foretell all events, to avert all calamities, and to cure all diseases by giving sick persons copious draughts of cold water. The followers of this system are required to renounce the

[18] For a historical reconstruction of these affairs, cf. Frykenberg 1976. The conflict between Hindus and Christians is also summarized in Suntharalingam 1974: 32 ff.

[19] "Hindoo Memorial: To the Honourable the Court of Director of the East India Company [Dated Madras, 7th October, 1846]." *Allen's Indian Mail and Register of Intelligence* 5/69, January 26, 1847: 41–44, p. 43. This statement was set up at a large public meeting on October 7, 1846 in Madras, to claim the violation of "civil and religious interests of the Hindoo community" by the missionary agency in the Madras Presidency, particularly in Madras and Tirunelveli. (For the background of the statement cf. Frykenberg 1976: 209 f.)

[20] Pettitt 1847: 44. Cf. also Appasamy 1923: 79 ff., and Stock 1899.1: 324.

[21] Caldwell 1847: 19.

[22] Muthukutty Swami had probably also come into contact with Christian ideas, as the LMS mission was active among the Shanars/Nadars in Travancore. Cf. Patrick 2003.

worship of devils to break their idols, to bring presents to the prophets of the sect for distribution to the poor, and to assemble every Sunday for what they style 'instruction' and 'prayer,' but which seem to me to be screaming and dancing. So greatly has this system prevailed among the heathens of the South, especially those of the Shanar caste, that it bids fair to supersede devil worship.[23]

It has to be kept in mind that the reorganisation of the mission in the 1830s and 1840s, and the conflicts in Tirunelveli that followed from this, constitute the historical background of Caldwell's book, *The Tinnevelly Shanars*. Another important element, though, was the prominence that the Tinnevelly mission had gained in public and, particularly, in missionary circles. The revitalization of the mission in Tirunelveli was presented to the interested public in Britain as the homemade success of SPG and CMS-Missions. The enormous amount of missionary reports that were published, in all major missionary magazines from the 1830s onwards, aimed primarily at raising funds for the Tirunelveli mission, but they also presented the Tinnevelly Shanars as a distinct group of people to a wider public in Britain. The encounter with Indian people, as the objects of colonial and missionary endeavours, did not only take place at the overseas frontier, but also in the home of the Empire – by disseminating images and descriptions of the 'Shanars' as 'Palmyra climbers' and 'devil worshipers'. Therefore, knowledge about the 'indigenous races' or the 'heathens' of the British Empire was not only accessible to the educated classes and colonial elite.[24] Missionary meetings were envisaged as a proper means to teach the ordinary citizen about the "homes, habits, and lot of remote nations", as a writer in the London Quarterly Review observed:

We cordially welcome the Missionary Meeting ... as an instrument of educating the people into a sense of fellowship with 'all sorts and conditions of men;' of acquainting them with the homes, habits, and lot of remote nations; of enlarging their minds, and infusing lofty sentiments ... The influence already exerted by this new element of social life has been great; for in some villages the Missionary Meeting is now the great annual festival; and many a small tradesman or rustic knows more of African or Polynesian life than London journalists.[25]

One could add here that this was certainly also true of India in general and of Tirunelveli in particular. The influence of missionary representations of Indian people and religion in the colonial discourse is quite well known. Nevertheless, I stress this point here for two reasons. First, as a part of the SPG-Series, *Missions to the Heathen*, Caldwell's book, *The*

[23] Caldwell 1844: 21 (italics in the original).

[24] Cf. Pennington 2005.

[25] "Reports of the Various Missionary Societies for the Year 1856." *London Quarterly Review* 7, October (1856): 209–261, 239.

Tinnevelly Shanars, was part of the SPG policy to disseminate knowledge and to arouse interest in Anglican missions throughout the British Empire.[26] Second, Caldwell's social and religious theories about the Shanars / Nadars draw directly and indirectly from the missionary discourse in general, and particularly from the Evangelical concept of religion that was dominant throughout the 19th century. We now turn to look at this second point, and, first of all, briefly consider the context of Caldwell's book, *The Tinnevelly Shanars,* within the SPG series and other journals.

The *Missions to the Heathen* series started in August 1844 with a collection of correspondence between George Uglow Pope (1820–1908), a missionary in Sawyerpuram, and the SPG officials in Madras (Madras Diocesan Council) and London. Pope reported about the group conversions of members of the Retti caste into his fold. During the next six years, no less than thirteen out of twenty three issues published were concerned with missionary reports and journals from Tirunelveli. The issues were so frequently reprinted that some earlier issues reached their ninth reprint after three years.[27] By far the most industrious contributors were the aforementioned Pope, of whom six reports from the Sawyerpuram Mission were published,[28] and Robert Caldwell, who contributed three reports from Idaiyangudi ("Edeyenkoody")[29] and his book about the Tinnevelly Shanars. The missionaries in Tirunelveli were also frequent suppliers of reports for other missionary periodicals published by the CMS and SPG, for example, the *Mission Field* and the *Colonial Church Chronicle and Missionary Journal.* The latter was especially designed to link the affairs of the Anglican Church at home with its missionary endeavours abroad. Here again, Caldwell and Pope were the main authors of lengthy reports about the Tinnevelly mission.[30]

---

[26] Cf. the review of SPG publications in: *Churchman's Monthly Review* (1846), 600–601. See also the preface of Earnest Hawkins, secretary of the SPG, in Caldwell 1844: iv.

Compared to other missionary societies, such as the CMS, the SPG started to publish its own periodicals and book series about its mission work relatively late. The first regular periodical was the *Quarterly Paper*, which was published from 1834 onwards. The *Mission Field*, which became the main periodical of the SPG in the second half of the 19th century, was started as late as 1856. According to Thompson, the *Missions to the Heathen* series together with its twin publication, *The Church in the Colonies* were intended to record alternately from the two fields of the Society's work, the ecclesiastical bodies in the colonies and the missions to the heathen. Cf. Thompson 1951: 109 and Pascoe 1901.2: 813d–816 for a complete list of SPG home publications.

[27] For example, the first issue of *Missions to the Heathen* (Pope 1844) reached its ninth reprint in 1847.

[28] *Missions to the Heathen* no. 1, 3, 7, 8, 12, 16.

[29] *Missions to the Heathen* no. 2, 10, 19.

[30] For example cf. Caldwell 1857, separately published as Caldwell 1857 and Pope 1849–50, Pope 1850–51.

The book, *"The Tinnevelly Shanars: A Sketch of Their Religion and Their Moral Condition, and Characteristics as a Caste ..."* was published in 1849 in Madras,[31] and republished in 1850 by the SPG as number twenty three of the series *Missions to the Heathen.*[32] Written for an English speaking public in Britain and India, it aimed primarily at promoting an interest in the Tirunelveli mission and collecting funds for it. In the following decades, it provoked the critique of members of the Shanar / Nadar community by its unflattering statements about their religion and their low 'moral disposition'. From the 1880s on, a war broke out – a war of petitions and counter petitions by different groups of Shanars / Nadars, Christians and non-Christians alike, that centred around the question of caste identity and the impact of Christian missionaries on the Shanar / Nadar community in Tirunelveli. Before turning to the repercussions of Caldwell's book, though, it is necessary to have a closer look at the book itself.

The Tinnevelly Shanars (1849)
as a ritual typology of 'demonolatry'

Theories of religion were never absent in the observation of local religious practices by missionaries like Robert Caldwell. Their remarks on 'superstitions' and 'idolatry' are, of course, no more than rough and stereotyped sketches of the local field. However, the importance of such accounts is not so much on their verifiability. Rather, they have to be understood from the perspective of category formation and comparative theories of religion which emerged at the colonial and missionary frontiers.[33] As Brian Pennington has observed:

> The construction of religion ... was more than an imaginative exercise involving category formation and descriptive discourses. It also involved the manufacture of actual religious ideas and practises for Christians and non-Christians alike. New religious ideas and practises appeared across the globe in places touched by British colonialism, and they conformed to the categories and descriptive habits of the emerging study of religion.[34]

---

[31] Caldwell 1849.

[32] Caldwell 1850. This edition of Caldwell's book contains numerous slight variations, additions and deletions, compared to the original edition of 1849. (Cf. also Hardgrave1969: 21). My references in this article are to the original edition from 1849.

[33] For this understanding of Caldwell's book, I am indebted to David Chidester's analysis of the history of comparative religion in Southern Africa as a "science of contact" that emerged out of colonial frontier situations. Chidester 1996.

[34] Pennington 2005: 24.

It is certainly true that Caldwell's book fits well in this frame, because it is a good example for this discursive liaison of description and missionary practice.

As noted before, Caldwell's earlier reports in the series *Missions to the Heathen* give an insight into his first observations on the local people and the religious context in Tirunelveli, prior to his book in 1849. A comparison of his different works about South Indian culture and religion indicates that his theories underwent a considerable development in the period between the 1840s and 1880s. For example, while he observed from the beginning the difference between the "orthodox system" of the Brahmans and the local religious practices of the lower castes in Tirunelveli,[35] which were depreciated as 'devil-worship' by the missionaries, in his later accounts he separated the Shanars / Nadars, and subsequently the Dravidians, on the basis of linguistic, racial, and particularly religious arguments from the dominant Brahmans / Aryans. Moreover, in his first report from the "Edeyenkoody Mission" (1844), he described devil worship only as a "primitive form of Hindoo superstition, on which the Brahmanical system afterwards grafted", but did not stress this point further in terms of a conceptual difference between two different systems of religion.[36]

Although Caldwell claimed to have gained his knowledge about the Shanars / Nadars from personal observation and local informants ("intelligent Hindus" and Shanars)[37], his book should not be read as a firsthand account of the local religious practices in Tirunelveli. As he admits in his description of the ritual of 'devil-dancing', he did not witness such ritual practices at close range.[38] Obviously, missionaries were not admitted to be present at such occasions, because their presence was considered to be inauspicious and an obstacle to the right performance of the ritual. Joseph Mullens, a missionary of the London Missionary Society (LMS), reported that missionaries had only seldom the opportunity of obtaining a sight of rituals like devil-dancing and sacrifices, as the people believed that "their devils cannot cope with Europeans."[39] According to Caldwell, Europeans

---

[35] Caldwell 1849: 7.

[36] Caldwell 1844: 6.

[37] Cf. Wyatt 1894: 84–85.

[38] Cf. Caldwell 1849: 20–21.

[39] Mullens 1854: 99, see also p. 112. Joseph Mullens (1820–1879) worked from 1843 till 1865 as a missionary in Calcutta, and from 1868 as Foreign Secretary of the LMS. He visited South India in the years 1853 and 1865–66 and published two books on South Indian missions: Mullens 1854 and 1863. His description of the mission among the Shanars/Nadars is mainly based on Caldwell, with whom he was personally acquainted. For biographical information on Mullens, see Sibree 1923: 57.

were attributed with immunity against the power of demons,[40] but probably the refusing of a European presence at such events was also an indication of the serious threat that the agency of Christian missionaries among the Shanars / Nadars posed to local religious cults.

If not derived from personal observation, Caldwell's ideas about the Shanars and their 'religion' were predetermined by the Evangelical (more specifically Calvinistic) concept of religion. As a missionary, his tacit axiom was the question of conversion, which, in the language of the Evangelicals, always meant the attainment of a personal conviction concerning God's salvation of humanity in Jesus Christ. Therefore, the parameters of his accession on the religion and culture of the Shanars / Nadars – and in general terms also to South Indian religion and culture – were primarily theological, even if they were combined with linguistic arguments and the intermixed language of "race", "class", and "nation".[41] The structure of the book indicates this more clearly: "True", or rather "genuine" religion could be detected and determined by the knowledge of a superior divine being (I.1.), the personal commitment to a future state of being ("spiritual condition" I.2.) and the effects on the "moral constitution" of a subject (II.). For Caldwell, the religion of the Shanars / Nadars had to be evaluated according to these terms. It is obvious that the close connection between mission theory and a theory of religion is already provided by the structure of the book, and that, more specifically, the theory of Shanar religion evolves out of his missionary ambitions. The main internal contradiction of his argument is, therefore, that while he is constantly stressing the (un)readiness of the Shanars / Nadars for Christianity due to their lack of any 'serious' or 'higher' religion at all, he is delineating a religious "system" of a lower degree that affords important points of contact to Christianity.[42]

According to Caldwell, the religious system of the Shanars / Nadars could be denoted as devil-worship or "demonolatry".[43] The latter term is used by Caldwell in an abstract sense. It indicates an attempt to systematize his cultural, historical and linguistical observations into a coherent theory of demonolatry. According to Caldwell, this religious system had

---

[40] Cf. Caldwell 1849: 16–17.

[41] Caldwell 1849: 4. This is not to deny the importance of Orientalist theories about Indian religions. Caldwell was, for sure, deeply influenced from the very beginning by his own studies of Orientalist theories of Indian religions and culture. But the relationship of Evangelical conceptions of religion and Orientalism needs to be more carefully considered than is currently done, at least when speaking of 'missionary orientalism'. For an analysis of Caldwell's Orientalist studies, see Vaitheespara 1998: 26 ff.

[42] Caldwell 1849: 18.

[43] Caldwell 1849: 12.

to be clearly separated from "Brahmanism", which was, for Caldwell, largely identical with Hinduism:

> Their connection with the Brahmanical systems of dogmas and observances, commonly described in the mass as Hinduism, is so small that they may be considered as votaries of a different religion. ... The mind of the Shanars has appeared to be a dreary void, a desert in which no trace of religious ideas is to be found. I have now to show how this desert has been peopled by a gloomy imagination with visions of goblins and demons. ... Demonolatry, or devil-worship is the only term by which the religion of the Shanars can be accurately described. ... Demonism in one shape or another may be said to rule the Shanars with undisputed authority. ... A large majority however of the devils are of purely Shanar or Tamil origin, and totally unconnected with Brahmanism.[44]

His attempt to describe demonolatry as a system totally different from Brahmanical Hinduism was motivated by considerable anti-Brahman reservations, which were shared by nearly all missionaries in India at that time. From the missionaries' point of view, Brahmanical Hinduism was liable for the caste system which was considered by the new British Protestant missionaries to be the greatest obstacle to Christian mission in India. Caldwell might have been also aware of the internal debates between Catholic and Protestant missionaries, like Abbé Dubios and James Hough, about the Catholic partiality for a mission among the higher castes.[45] But Caldwell's concern to construct a system of 'Shanar religion' independent from Brahmanism served primarily his missionary agenda, to utilize it as the soil on which the mission could plant its Christian tree. Therefore, his main argument was that demonolatry failed to be a higher form of religion at all, as it could not comply with the (Christian) criteria of religion. For example, the Shanars did not have any real knowledge about a God or any good divine being that was worshipped on a regular basis, as well as any apprehension of divine salvation, and the person's future state of being.[46] Whereas these failings could be considered as disadvantages at first sight, the absence of a higher religion was seen by Caldwell as an advantage for Christian mission:

> It must be obvious that the sincerity of the belief entertained by the Shanars in their demons, though productive of superstitious gloom and incompatible with a high caste of thought, is morally a more promising feature of mind than the conceited rationalism or universal scepticism of the Brahmanical higher castes, and capable of being turned to better account.[47]

---

[44] Caldwell 1849: 7, 11–13.
[45] Cf. Vaitheespara 2006: 43 ff.
[46] Cf. Caldwell 1849: 8 ff.
[47] Caldwell 1849: 43.

Caldwell's strategy, to construct demonolatry as a cohesive system, is worthy of consideration from a methodological point of view. His description of devil-worship is a reduction of the complex variety of South Indian religious practices and rituals to one uniform system. The first step he takes is the reduction of certain gods and divine beings to one "genus" of deity:

> I shall now mention some particulars illustrative of the opinions entertained respecting these demons and the peculiarities of their worship, as it exists at present. I shall not attempt to enter upon a minute description of the system, or exemplify it by specific illustrations; but shall confine myself to the more general object of furnishing the reader with a sketch of its salient points and more prominent characteristics, and helping him to form an estimate of its tendencies and effects. My description will therefore apply rather to the genus 'demon' than to any demon in particular – rather to the points in which all diabolical rites agree than to local or incidental varieties.[48]

Caldwell admitted that his account was somehow generalized, but it was exactly this method of generalization which enabled him to construct demonolatry as the prototype of non-Brahman, Tamil religion in South India. This religion, he believed, had been prevalent in South India prior to the immigration of Brahmans from the north.[49] Accordingly, his understanding of demonolatry is rather inclusive, as it includes the spiritual beings that were denoted as *pēy*, but also, to some extent, the Amman (Tam. ammaṉ) goddesses, which were typical of South Indian villages. Although Caldwell denotes the Amman goddesses as female "demons", the relationship between Amman-worship and demon-worship seems to be quite ambivalent.[50] On the one hand, he is aware of the strong relationship between village cults and the worship of *pēys*, including the fact that animal-sacrifices were part of both cults. On the other hand, he assumes that the worship of Amman goddesses did not belong to the original form of demonolatry, because the goddesses are seen as forms of Kali (Skt. kālī, Tam. kāḷi), thus providing for them a Brahman lineage. Hence, the worship of Amman goddesses becomes, for him, an example of the partial Brahmanisation of demonolatry over the course of time. Further, the two most important male deities in South India, Murugan (Tam. murukaṉ) and Aiyanar (Tam. aiyaṉār), are decidedly excluded by him from the concept of demonolatry, because of their clear connection with Brahmanical mythology. He only gives their Sanskrit names, "Subrahmanya" (Skt. subrahmaṇya, Tam. cuppiramaṇiyaṉ) and "Shástá" (Skt. śāstṛ, Tam. cāstā) without mentioning any particularities of their worship

[48] Caldwell 1849: 13.
[49] Cf. Caldwell 1849: 24.
[50] Cf., for example, Caldwell 1849: 13–14 and 23 ff.

in South India.[51] It is interesting that, in his article on "Demonolatry in Southern India" which appeared more than 30 years later (1886), he revised this classification in a significant way. Here, he included male deities, such as Aiyanar, as well as the female deities, such as the various forms of Amman, in the system of demonolatry, but clearly distinguished them as "semi-divine beings" from the devils / demons (*pēy*) as "semi-diabolical beings".[52] This is contrary to his arguments in *The Tinnevelly Shanars* (1849). In 1886, he gives a fuller account of at least one male deity, Aiyanar, and does not emphasise the opposition of Brahmanism and demonolatry to the same extent as he did before.[53] However, in *The Tinnevelly Shanars* the worship of spirits – and to some extent also that of Amman deities – provides the background for Caldwell's theory of demonolatry.

This reduction of different deities to one "genus demon" reinforced his claim that the Shanars / Nadars were a separate social entity with a distinct ritual identity. The second step, therefore, was the generalization of the variety of ritual practices connected with spirit worship and village deities. Caldwell took two rituals as the key practices of the system of demonolatry. The first is called "devil-dance" by him (Tam. cāmiyāṭṭam). The description of the devil-dance is chiefly used by him to show that the Shanars do not know any separate priesthood, but that this rite "may be performed by any one who chooses" and who, then, carries out the role of the priest.[54] He seems to acknowledge this indirectly as a positive aspect, since the presence of a strong religious authority – the Brahmans for example – was usually seen as a major obstacle to the success of Christian mission. In connection with the devil-dance he could, of course, not abstain from explaining the issue of demoniacal possession, which was one of the most striking features of the Indian religious context for the

[51] Cf. Caldwell 1849: 12.

[52] Caldwell 1886: 93 ff.

[53] Caldwell 1886: 93–94. Caldwell's article, which is partly a revision of his concept of demonolatry after a fierce conflict with the Shanar/Nadar community of Tirunelveli, cannot be discussed here at length, although there are significant differences compared to his argument in 1849. The most striking feature is his attempt to re-integrate the system of demonolatry into a broader concept of Hinduism, following Monier Monier-Williams' description of 'demon-worship' as an integral part of Hinduism (Monier-Williams 1883: 230–256). Citing Monier-Williams, Caldwell wrote: "In fact, a belief in every kind of demoniacal influence has always been, from the earliest times, an essential ingredient in Hindu religious thought." (Caldwell 1886: 92). In fact, this was a retraction from his earlier positions due to the protest of the Shanars/Nadars, who denied that their religion was not to be considered as part of Hinduism. The article was republished in the *Indian Evangelical Review* 14 (1887–88): 192–203. For the conflict between Caldwell and the Shanar/Nadar community see also the next paragraph.

[54] Caldwell 1849: 19–20.

missionaries.[55] Although he gives the typical rationalistic explanation, reducing the description to the performative acts of the ritual, the question of possession was nevertheless an ambivalent issue for the European missionaries. The possibility of 'real' demoniacal possession – understood as the presence of the devil in Christian terms – was never far from their mind. Hence, their descriptions very frequently display this ambivalence between the Christian devil (singular) and the local devils (plural). Edward Sargent's (CMS) short account of devil worship, which appeared also in 1849, can be seen as a good example:

> It is a curious question whether those who dance and are said to become possessed are really so in the strict sense of the word. The whole service is the service of the devil, and must, in a certain sense, be attributed to his influence and agency; but whether he so possesses their bodies and governs their minds as to make their volition and action not properly their own, but his, appears to me very questionable. From all that I have seen and heard, I should rather consider it as a voluntary excitement, which works itself up to a species of frenzy, and which gradually subsides as the party becomes exhausted.[56]

The second ritual, which Caldwell designates as the "offering of bloody sacrifices", becomes the key point in his construction of a coherent system of demonolatry and its ritual typology.[57] The description provided in this section differs substantially from that of devil-dancing; he does not give a very detailed account of the ritual performance, but goes on to introduce a theory about the genealogy of demonolatry as the original religion of the Tamil people. It is noteworthy that he does not use the term 'Dravidians' here, which was a few years later the key term in his

[55] See Kent 2004: 58 ff., for an insightful analysis of Caldwell's account.

[56] Sargent 1849: 61. It is worth mentioning here that, around 1850, a number of descriptions of devil worship in Tirunelveli appeared in periodicals and books. See, for example, Tucker 1848: vol. 2, chapter 4–5; Best 1849; and Pope 1850–51. Some of them, like Edward Sargent's description, are autonomous accounts, which describe similar features of the religious practices in Tirunelveli, but are virtually independent from Caldwell's book. Interestingly, Sargent does not seem to share Caldwell's idea of a coherent system of demonolatry, because he uses the term 'devil worship' without any systematic intention. His account is also rather differentiated compared to Caldwell's book, and is at least willing to differentiate between Amman and spirit cults.

Other descriptions of devil worship in Tirunelveli, which refer to Caldwell's book are, for example, Pettitt 1851: 476 ff.; and Mullens 1854: 96 ff. The latter reflects Caldwell's typology of Shanar ritual practice by stating that "the service presented to the demons is of two kinds, DEVIL-DANCING and DEVIL-SACRIFICE [sic]." (Mullens 1854: 98).

An Abridgement of Caldwell's book was reprinted by G. J. Metzger in the English edition of Bartholomäus Ziegenbalg's *Genealogy of the South Indian Gods* (Metzger and Germann 1869).

[57] Caldwell 1849: 21 ff.

Comparative Grammar of the Dravidian or South-Indian Family of Languages (1856).[58]

However, the idea of demonolatry as the "aboriginal" religion in South India, prior to the immigration of the Brahmans from the North, is already to be found in his earlier book (1849). According to Caldwell, the "origin of the Shanar Demonolatry lies in the unknown depths of antiquity. ... The worship of devils would seem to have been anterior to the Vedaic [*sic*] system itself."[59] He is arguing that demonolatry is not only more ancient than Vedic religion and subsequent Brahmanism, but not dependent on both in any way: "There are many direct reasons for assigning to demonolatry an origin independent of Brahmanism and anterior to its introduction into the Tamil country, or even into India."[60] The complex argument which follows tries to examine the religious antiquity of demonolatry by a combination of mythological evidences from Brahmanical Hinduism, contemporary theories of the history of religions, and linguistic and cultural observations. It is obvious that they serve Caldwell's intention to restore the historical antiquity and theological independency of demonolatry in India, which can readily be adapted for Christian mission:

> Here, in polished and metaphysical India we find a civilization but little raised above that of the Negroes, and a religion which can only be described as fetishism. And what exists in Tinnevelly is only a type of the social and religious condition of extensive tracts throughout India with which Europeans have not yet become familiar.[61]

The idea of adaptability of 'ancient', that is to say 'primitive', religions with Christian concepts is further enhanced by Caldwell's theory about the genealogy of animal sacrifices among the Shanars / Nadars. It is obvious that his definition of 'sacrifice' was dictated by the Evangelical notion of Jesus' death as sacrifice for the redemption from sin; the latter being primarily understood as offences which affected the moral consciousness of Christian believers:

> The sole object of the sacrifice is the removal of the devil's anger or of the calamities which his anger brings down. It should be distinctly understood that sacrifices are never offered on account of the sins of the worshippers, and that the

---

[58] Cf. Caldwell 1856. Appendix IV is entitled "Ancient Religion of the Dravidians". Parts of the text (pp. 521–522) were taken from his earlier book. Here, Caldwell used explicitly the term 'Dravidian demonolatry'. For his explanation of the term 'Dravidian', see pp. 26–28.

[59] Caldwell 1849: 24.

[60] Caldwell 1849: 25.

[61] Caldwell 1849: 29.

> devil's anger is not excited by any moral offence. The religion of the Shanars, such as it is, has no connection with morals.[62]

Indeed, nowhere else can Caldwell's Evangelical attitudes be seen more clearly than in his interpretation of sacrifice. What, one could ask, makes in the eyes of Evangelical missionaries, like Caldwell, such people better objects for the Christian mission than any devotee of 'higher' religions? Here, Caldwell's astonishing answer is that, even if there is no connection between belief and ethics in demonolatry, its theological adaptability exists primarily in the idea of substitution which lies behind the sacrificial rituals. Although he claims that the Shanars / Nadars do not explicitly know a theory of substitution, the ritual of bloody sacrifice is interpreted by Caldwell as a substitutional practice, which, implicitly, serves as a kind of 'praeparatio evangelica'. Aside from the historical and theological independence of demonolatry from 'higher Hinduism', its ritual practice is, according to Caldwell, the most important point of contact for Christian mission and the main reason for the success of Christian missions among the Shanars / Nadars:

> The Shanars have not intellect enough to frame for themselves a theory of substitution; but their practice and their mode of expression prove that they consider their sacrifices as substitutions and nothing else. ... It is sufficiently obvious that ... they are in a better position [than other Hindus] for understanding the grand Christian doctrine of redemption by sacrifice. ... The prevalence of bloody sacrifices for the removal of the anger of superior powers is one of the most striking [facts] in the religious condition of the Shanars, and is appealed to by the Christian Missionary with the best effect.[63]

Turning the idea of substitution into a historical fact, he even supposed that the animal sacrifices were themselves a substitution of the even more ancient "human sacrifices to the demons", which had prevailed in ancient times all over South India. Like many of his contemporaries, Caldwell believed the 'meriah' sacrifice of the Khonds, a tribe in the north-eastern parts of Madras Presidency, to be a vivid remnant of this history.[64]

A further point, which cannot be analysed here at length, is his account of the 'moral constitution' of the Shanars that follows in chapter two. As mentioned before, Caldwell attested that the Shanars / Nadars had a total

---

[62] Caldwell 1849: 21.

[63] Caldwell 1849: 22. In the introduction he writes: "There are certain facts and truths proper to Christianity, such as the doctrine of our redemption by sacrifice, which are peculiarly offensive to some of the Brahmanical sects, and are supposed to be offensive to the Hindu mind every where, but which convey no offence in Tinnevelly; where the shedding of blood in sacrifice and the substitution of life for life are ideas with which the people are familiar." (Caldwell 1849: 7).

[64] Cf. Caldwell 1849: 22. Consequently, he marked the Khonds as the "most primitive and least Brahmanized portion of the aboriginal Tamil race." (ibid.)

absence of any ethical consciousness ("morals").[65] However, the fact that this chapter makes up more than half of the whole book indicates that Caldwell's theory of demonolatry, evolved in chapter one, serves primarily as a prerequisite for the typical Evangelical agenda of Christian mission as moral and social improvement directed towards the lower classes of society. Caldwell, thus, writes in the beginning of chapter two:

> From the description now given of the religion of the Shanars, it will not be difficult to form an estimate of its moral results. The influence of religion in forming or modifying the character of nations is well known ... Nations are what their gods are. ... In considering the moral condition of the Shanars as affected by their demonolatry ... incidental light will be thrown on some correlative questions. Reasons will probably appear why Christianity has prevailed more amongst the Shanars than amongst higher castes; reasons why the Shanars as a class should be less bigotedly attached to their religion and more easily impressed by Christian teaching and influences than other Hindus; and reasons also why the style of character exhibited by the native Christians in Tinnevelly differs so considerably from that of the Christians of Tanjore and Madras.[66]

As Eliza Kent has observed, the missionary interest in social uplift did not stem from altruism alone, but was motivated by the theological presumption that the "low castes' depths of degradation made their material and spiritual uplift a persuasive index of the power of Christian faith. ... God's greatness was affirmed by his ability to lift up wretches from their lowly and benighted state."[67] Hence, missionary descriptions like Caldwell's book were always inclined to amplify the antagonism between the factual condition of its missionary objects and their own Evangelical ideals of 'moral religion'. The Shanars / Nadars were constructed as idealised representatives of a 'particular need' of the missionary agency for all lower caste groups in Tirunelveli, by means of adapting them to the common Evangelical narratives. Not only in the case of Caldwell, the peculiar dynamics of these narratives in Tirunelveli resulted from their strategy to represent Tirunelveli as a land without religion, which was at the same time the habitat of the devil(s) and, as Bishop Spencer said, the land of promise for the missionary endeavour. Caldwell's book is a good example of how missionary narratives about the Tirunelveli mission covered up this space between the devil and the devils, between the 'land without religion' and the 'field white to harvest'. Missionaries like Caldwell were well aware that the congruence between accounts of devil worship and Christian conceptions of the devil could be understood as

[65] Caldwell 1849: 11.
[66] Caldwell 1849: 32.
[67] Kent 2004: 52–53.

contrived.[68] Yet, he and other missionaries did not invest much effort into dissolving such identifications. Far from it, it had a massive impact on their missionary strategies. In an account of a (typical) dialogue between a missionary and a 'devil worshipper', written by George Uglow Pope, the missionary asks the devotee: "Have you never heard of holy and beneficient beings that protect the sons of men, and deliver them from the power of demons?"[69]

Caldwell's method of systematizing the religious practice of Shanars as demonolatry, and the temporal theories he then imposed on his findings, led to several consequences that I will now consider briefly in the end of this paragraph. First, he constructed the Shanars / Nadars as a coherent community with a distinct ritual identity, depending on their low caste status in South Indian society. As I have already indicated, Evangelical narratives had a preliminary tendency to locate the objects of their missionary concern at the lower ends of society, which, in turn, forced their emphasis on the necessity of social uplift. Caldwell's theory of demonolatry is, therefore, also a theory of lower class religion; based on the assumption that demonolatry was not only the most ancient religion of South India, but a typical example of the religious degradation of the lower classes. It is unsurprising that he shows no serious intention – if he had any – to differentiate between the Shanar / Nadars and other lower caste groups. He even admitted that he would go so far as to "include [sometimes] the whole of the lower classes of the local population under that predominating name",[70] and extended this claim by substituting demonolatry, occasionally, by the term 'Shanarism'.[71] His book adapted the Shanars / Nadars, therefore, not only to the Evangelical narratives, but also fixed their place on the social scale of South Indian society. His frequently cited words from the beginning of his book ascribe to the Shanars / Nadars a position at the lower end of social hierarchy:

> The caste of Shanars occupies a middle position between the Vellalers and their Pariar slaves. ... They may in general be described as belonging to the highest

---

[68] See, for example, Caldwell 1849: 12, where he writes: "When Missionaries allude to the devil worship prevalent in Tinnevelly, some persons seem to suppose that by the term 'devils' we mean the gods worshipped by the people; and that we style them 'devils' because their claims are supposed to those of the true God ... It is thought that we use the term in a controversial sense ... But ... in describing the *positive* [*sic*] portion of the religion of the Shanars as devil worship, the word used is not only the most appropriate one we know, but it exactly corresponds with the term used by the Shanars themselves. ... Consequently, demonolatry, or devil worship, is the only term by which the religion of the Shanars can be accurately described."

[69] Pope 1850–51: 60.

[70] Caldwell 1849: 4.

[71] Caldwell 1849: 34.

division of the lower classes, or the lowest of the middle classes: poor, but not paupers; rude and unlettered, but by many degrees removed from a savage state.[72]

This assignment became the bone of contention for Caldwell's Shanar opponents in the following decades.

Second, his method led him to the level of religious theory and comparative religion. Having separated demonolatry from its religious and cultural context in South India, he could even claim that the rituals and religious practices of the Shanars were to be compared to other forms of primitive religion, for example "fetishism" in Western Africa.[73] This introduced the Shanars / Nadars as a separate group, with distinct rituals and a distinct identity, into the field of global comparison. Although he asserts that there exists no common historical origin for both Shanar demonolatry and fetishism, "the two systems have a greater resemblance to one another than either of them has to any of the other religions of the heathen world."[74] It is telling to see how he constructs the similarity on the basis of a morphological comparison, referring to a fixed set of components, for example, the transformation of the spirits of the dead into demons, the same forms of worship ("frantic dances" and sacrifices), possession, exorcism, the absence of a regular priesthood, and of "every idea of revelations and incarnations."[75] Hence, demonolatry was for him not only a religion specific to South India, but also a translocal phenomenon that could be found, for example, also in Sri Lankan Buddhism.[76] Moreover, the Evangelical conviction that religion and morals were inextricably bound to each other enabled him also to treat demonolatry as a specific mentality, signifying a complete absence of any "morals" in parallel to "atheism" and "materialism".[77]

It is remarkable that he did not follow up his assumption of a structural identity between fetishism and demonolatry in his later works. A few years later, in his *Comparative Grammar of the Dravidian or South-Indian Family of Languages* (1856), he replaced it by a comparison with "shamanism" in Siberia, explaining that he had written his earlier book "before I was aware of the identity of the demonolatry of Siberia with that

[72] Caldwell 1849: 4.

[73] Caldwell 1849: 25.

[74] Caldwell 1849: 28.

[75] Caldwell 1849: 28.

[76] See Caldwell 1849: 27, where Caldwell asserts that the worship of devils could also affect higher religions, for example Buddhism: "The Buddhists of Burma and Ceylon have added to Buddhism the worship of indigenous demons, though nothing can be supposed more foreign to the genius of Buddhism than such a system." For an analysis of colonial representations of Singhalese religion and the ritual of "Yaktovil" in particular, see Scott 1994.

[77] Caldwell 1849: 36.

of Tinnevelly".[78] This enabled him to incorporate the theory of demonolatry into his broader theory about a common racial and linguistic origin of the Dravidians and Scythians in Upper Asia. It should be clear from these few remarks that his theory of demonolatry made up an essential part of his theory of the Dravidians, filling the gap of historical evidence for a uniform pre-Aryan and non-Brahman culture in Asia.

Casting and re-casting the Shanars: Reactions of the Tirunelveli Shanars / Nadars

In missionary circles, in India as well as in Britain, Caldwell's book was readily received as an exemplary testimonial of mission work in India. In a review, the *Madras Quarterly Missionary Journal* praised Caldwell for providing his readers with "something to read", in contrast to the overwhelming mass of missionary literature which bored its readers with patchy extracts from journals and diaries:

> In such a sketch the real work of the Missionary is made manifest; the many strange phases of human error which he has to oppose and dissipate are illustrated, we are enabled to enter into the arena of conflict and see unbelief set face to face with 'the truth as it is in Jesus,' and to anticipate its shameful retreat.[79]

The reviewer's call, for more accounts of missionary work in the style of Caldwell's book, indicates that missionary circles in India felt a demand for quasi-ethnographical accounts of their converts, which helped to overcome the conceptual lacks of standard Evangelical anthropology in the field of missions. Whereas in the following decades Caldwell's book gained recognition as a canonical work on South Indian religion and culture, absorbed as an integral part of colonial knowledge, the representation of Tirunelveli and the Tirunelveli Shanars by Caldwell and his epigones did not remain unanswered by Shanars / Nadars and other local groups, Christians and non-Christians alike. The battle about their customary ritual and social ranking in South Indian society during the nineteenth century is a good example, which displays the effects of colonial representations of Indian society and how the dynamics of representation and counter representation unmasked the dominance of cultural and religious paradigms in colonial discourse.

---

[78] Caldwell 1856: 521.

[79] 'Reviews and Notices of New Publications: 1. The Tinnevelly Shanars, a Sketch. By the Rev. R. Caldwell, Edeyengoody'. *Madras Quarterly Missionary Journal* 1,2 (1850): 123–128, p. 124.

As already mentioned, the general resistance to missionary activities was organised by the dominant caste groups in Tirunelveli. The more specific critique of Caldwell's book came from the side of the Shanars / Nadars, who disagreed particularly with the low social status Caldwell had ascribed to them, and with his claim that their religion was to be denounced as aboriginal demonolatry that had no connection with Brahmanical Hinduism. Parallel to Caldwell's preferred methods, theories about historical genealogy, linguistics, and ritual became the most important ingredients of their counter manoeuvre in the following decades. According to Hardgrave, the movement took its initial motivation from conflicts between Shanar / Nadar Christians and European missionaries in Tirunelveli.[80] Converts to Christianity challenged the paternalism of European missionaries and their narratives about Tirunelveli and the Shanars / Nadars in missionary publications. Arumai Nayakam Sattampillai (Tam. aṟumaināyakam caṭṭampiḷḷai, 1824–1919), a catechist of the SPG mission in Nazareth (Tirunelveli), took the lead in organising resistance to missionary dominance among Christian converts. He was dismissed from his post as catechist in the SPG mission after fierce debates with the local missionary in Nazareth, August Frederic Caemmerer. In reaction, he founded, in 1857, his own church, the 'The Hindu Church of the Lord Jesus', which he also called the 'Hindu Christian Church'. At that time it was probably the only independent Protestant Indian church in South India.[81]

In contrast to European theorists like Caldwell, Shanar activists claimed a different status – one *within* the Brahmanical varna (Skt. varṇa) system – as Kshatriyas (Skt. kṣatriya). This was based on the assumption that Shanars were descendants not of any aboriginal Dravidian race, but of the Pandya kings, once the powerful rulers of ancient South Indian kingdoms, who had lost their original social and ritual status over the centuries and were reduced to servitude.[82] According to Hardgrave, the writing of caste histories to prove this genealogy became one of the major activities of the emerging movement, resulting in the production of more than forty books, pamphlets and articles in the years following the schism in 1857.[83] This claim of a noble descent was further justified by an etymological re-interpretation of the word 'Shanar', which seemed to have a contemptuous meaning as a caste designation in the 19th century. The standard orientalist etymology interpreted Shanar as a derivation of

[80] As Hardgrave and Kent have both given detailed accounts of this movement, I confine myself here to a short summary of their findings. Hardgrave 1979; Kent 2004.

[81] For Sattampillai and his church, see Thangaraj 1971; Kumaradoss 1996; and Sugirtharajah 2005: 175–189.

[82] Cf. Surguner 1883: 17–18.

[83] See Hardgrave 1969: 78 ff. and Appendix III, for a full account.

the Tamil word for toddy, 'caru' (Tam. cāṛu), thus associating the Shanars with the production of alcohol from the Palmyra juice, which was considered a polluting business by the higher castes. In contrast, Shanar activists, like Samuel Sargunar, interpreted a variant of their caste name, 'canrar' (Tam. cāṉṟār), as a derivation of the Tamil word 'canror' (Tam. cāṉṟōr), frequently used in Sangam Literature. According to Sargunar, there it designated not only a 'noble' or 'learned' man, but their ancestors as a distinct group.[84] All these arguments were closely linked to a detailed criticism of Caldwell's book. Grasping precisely the major shortcomings of colonial knowledge production, Sarguner wrote:

> The whole of this discussion by the Bishop, so far as it relates to the Dravidians, is nothing but a mass of unadulterated falsehood, which appears to have originated with the Bishop's unsound and superficial knowledge of Tamil, combined with the imagination of his illogical mind, which too readily took it for granted that what it found to exist now had existed always, just as it believed [sic], as I have shown above, [and] that what was true of a few Shanars at or about Edeyengudi must be true of each of the Shanars all over the Tinnevelly District. ... It is none the less true ... that he has been a greater writer than thinker, and that his forte is to compare a dozen Grammars and Dictionaries of as many languages and boil down bundles of papers, be they Government records, Missionaries' letters, or copies of inscriptions, into forms of narratives.[85]

Yet, these claims were more than only a tug of war over words. The example of Sattampillai's Hindu Christian Church demonstrates that such counter representations did not remain in the sphere of mere words, but were also transferred to the field of ritual practice and religious identity. Based on the claim that Shanars / Nadars had originally a Kshatriya status and had to be called 'Nadars' as the correct name for their caste, Sattampillai and his followers challenged the image of Shanars / Nadars as a low caste community by a reconstruction of a ritual canon that served the religious needs of Shanar / Nadar Christians as Kshatriyas. They combined an adaption of Jewish rites from the Old Testament with the attempt to confer high caste moral and social norms upon the Shanar / Nadar community. As Eliza Kent has demonstrated, this implied substantial changes on gender relations within the Shanar / Nadar community, because the revaluation of matrimonial concepts was a central concern of

---

[84] Cf. Samuel Sarguner: *Dravida Kshatriyas* (1880), cited in Hardgrave 1979: 174. See also Surguner 1883: 6 ff. Hardgrave gives a detailed analysis of these "new mythologies" and the etymological evidence. According to him, these linguistic theories were even debated in public newspapers, for example, the *Madras Mail* in 1899.

[85] Surguner 1883: 5–6.

Sattampillai's agenda.[86] Sattampillai understood his Hindu Christianity as a true challenge to the Protestant missions in Tirunelveli. As Caldwell noted:

> They call themselves in their documents 'The Hindu Church of the Lord Jesus;' but amongst their neighbours they call themselves, and are generally called, the Nattar, or 'national party'. In their zeal for caste and Hindu nationality, they have rejected from their system everything which appeared to them to savour of a European origin. Hence they have abandoned infant-baptism and an ordained ministry. Instead of wine they use the unfermented juice of grapes in an ordinance which they regard as the Lord's Supper, and observe Saturday instead of Sunday as their Sabbath.[87]

The catechism Sattampillai wrote in 1890 was primarily a harsh critique of the Western concept of Christian religion, in which he accused the missionaries of mixing their national customs with Christianity. The appendices of his book were filled with carefully selected references to prove "Anglican national profligacy" and the "idolatry" of the old Saxons "quoted from the very words of the Europeans themselves".[88] Yet, Sattampillai's method not only mirrored the tune of missionary rhetoric adopted by Caldwell and others. Besides discrediting European Christianity, he used such statements to argue that Christianity was tampered with Western decadence, sexual immorality and materialism, which were contradictory to the "national customs" of the Hindus. Converts to Christianity were thus allowed to keep their respective traditions alive, based on the argument that in the time of ancient Christianity "the Gentile converts would be incorporated with the Jewish Holy Church, with the full liberty to practise such of their own respective national customs ... as would not violate but naturally be in accordance with the righteousness of the [Jewish] law ...".[89] Although Sattampillai's reconstruction of a Nadar Christianity with the help of Old Testament law and rituals was to a certain extent an idiosyncratic endeavour, it was much more oriented towards Brahmanical Hinduism than towards Jewish religion. He seems to have adapted only those rituals which were not objectionable from the point of view of Brahmanical Hinduism. For example, he demanded "sacrificial nourishments" to Jesus Christ during worship, but allowed only "*pure* offerings, that is, substances *not offensive* to any class of

[86] Kent 2004: 190–196 gives an excellent analysis of Sattampillai's concept of Indian Christian marriage and his role in the emerging discourse on Shanar/Nadar identity in the second half of the nineteenth century.

[87] Cited in Mullens 1863: 51–52.

[88] See the appendix of his book where he cites contemporary critics of Western culture at length to emphasise his argument. Sattampillai 1890: 30–47.

[89] Sattampillai 1890: 3–4. See also p. 7.

people."[90] Thus, the offering of "food, drink and perfumes [i. e. burning of incense]" during worship,[91] as well as the substitution of wine by grape juice during the Eucharist, indicate that the rituals in the Hindu Christian Church were clearly oriented towards Brahman standards.

The criticism of Caldwell and his book continued until the late 1880s and resulted in a war of petitions that was closely related to caste conflicts within the mission congregations. Furthermore, it was also related to the conflict between Caldwell and his fellow missionary Margöschis, in which Indian Christians of different castes were also involved. The petitions accused as well as supported Caldwell. They were written to different ecclesiastical and political authorities in Britain and India, which set the question of Shanar Christian and non-Christian identity again from the local to a global level of discourse. Besides the plea to withdraw the book entirely from circulation, the petitioners all shared the opinion that this was a debate on the issue of the 'respectability' of their caste, as well as a clear knowledge of the reception and reproduction of their image in Britain and in the missionary discourse in particular.

In the SPG archive there are no less than eight petitions filed, which were written in only two years between 1882 and 1884.[92] Each petition complaining about Caldwell was followed by one in favour of him. Both sides accused each other of deception and forgery in obtaining signatures.[93] By far the most interesting point concerning these petitions relates to how they mirror the effects caused by Caldwell's book and the debates among the parties involved; for example, about the role of missionaries. First, the authors were fully aware of the effects Caldwell's book had on the colonial discourse and their popularity as 'mission objects'. Gnanamutthu Nadar, Caldwell's most active and distinguished opponent in the course of the affair, observed that the circulation of Caldwell's book in Britain led the "enlightened world" to form a low opinion about Shanar Christians in Tirunelveli. The dissemination of this image through the work of various copyists made things much worse. He claimed that "every writer having read Bishop Caldwell's work writes as if he were quite sure of the non aryan and aboriginal origin of the Shanars, and their

[90] Sattampillai 1890: 12 (italics in the original).

[91] Sattampillai 1890: 12.

[92] All petitions are held in the archive of the United Society for the Propagation of the Gospel (USPG), Rhodes House Library, Oxford, Copies of Letters Received (CLR) vol. 52, henceforth cited as CLR 52. I am grateful to the USPG for permission to cite from their archives.

[93] This was claimed in a Petition of "Native Christians of Tinnevelly", July 25, 1883, CLR 52: 268 ff.

degraded condition. ... Every writer ventures to call the Shanars an aboriginal race which is far from being the fact."[94]

Moreover, one petition of the Shanar Christians argued that Caldwell's depiction of the Shanars / Nadars as a degraded caste provoked local Hindus as well as Christians to uphold their caste distinctions even more furiously: "Because they think, that this system is inquired into, and made much of, even by the European Missionaries."[95] They very clearly stated that this had led to an increased consciousness of Shanar identity among Hindus as well as Christians. The petitioners even went so far as to state that Caldwell and his book alone had – ironically – become the cause of the extraordinary caste consciousness amongst the Shanar / Nadar Christians and the greatest obstacle to the progress of Christianity in Tirunelveli. Finally, the wave of resistance Caldwell had to face from the Shanars / Nadars induced him to retract the book from further publication by the late 1880s, a fact providing powerful evidence that missionaries – and colonial representatives in general – were not always powerful enough to control the genies they let out of their bottles.

Conclusion

In this article I have sketched how, in the period between the 1840s and 1880s, the missionary agency and the reflection on it by local Shanars / Nadars in Tirunelveli, contributed to the emergence of a globalised colonial image of the Shanars / Nadars and, closely related, to discourses of identity among this particular South Indian caste group. Their claim for a higher social position in South Indian society strongly affected the formation of a transregional Shanar / Nadar identity in the decades to come after Caldwell.[96] To briefly sum up my argument, it is necessary to return to the question at the beginning of how the restructuring of the Christian mission in Tirunelveli necessitated missionary narratives about Tirunelveli and the Shanars / Nadars. These narratives were distinctly elaborated in Caldwell's book, *The Tinnevelly Shanars*. His book should be seen in the broader context of comparative theories of religion, as they emerged all over the world in fields of colonial conquest during the nineteenth century. As David Chidester has observed, in the case of comparative religion in colonial South Africa, the colonial reaction to the encoun-

[94] "Petition from certain Shanar Christians of Tinnevelly" (written by Y. Gnanamutthoo Nadar), May 19, 1883, CLR 52: 230.

[95] "Petition from certain Shanar Christians of Tinnevelly" (written by Y. Gnanamutthoo Nadar), May 19, 1883, CLR 52: 231.

[96] See Hardgrave 1969.

ter of alien peoples and their culture was a shift from a denial to a 'discovery' of their religions. Accordingly, the evolution of comparative theories about 'indigenous' religions was linked to the implementation of control on colonial frontier zones.[97] It should now be clear how this entanglement of the global and local levels of discourse helped Caldwell to galvanise the local missionary agency with a comparative religion approach and, in return, helped discourses of identity among Shanars / Nadars to take place at the intersection of regional as well as global levels of colonial discourse.

Bibliography

Appasamy, Paul. 1923. *Centenary History of the C. M. S. In Tinnevelly.* Palamcottah: Printing Press.

Best, James Kershaw. 1849. 'Devil-Worship in Tinnevelly.' *Parochial Missionary Magazine* 2: 190–191.

Caldwell, Robert. 1844. *Mission of Edeyenkoody, in the District of Tinnevelly, and Diocese of Madras.* [Part One] 8th ed. 1847. (Missions to the Heathen; 2) London: SPG.

——. 1847. *Mission of Edeyenkoody, in the District of Tinnevelly and Diocese of Madras. Part Third: Report of the Rev. R. Caldwell, 1846.* 1st ed. (Missions to the Heathen; 19) London: SPG.

——. 1849. *The Tinnevelly Shanars: A Sketch of Their Religion and Their Moral Condition, and Characteristics as a Caste. With Special Reference to the Facilities and Hindrances to the Progress of Christianity Amongst Them.* Madras: R. Twigg.

——. 1850. *The Tinnevelly Shanars: A Sketch of Their Religion, and Their Moral Condition and Characteristics, with Special Reference to the Facilities and Hindrances to the Progress of Christianity Amongst Them.* (Missions to the Heathen; 23) London: SPG.

——. 1856. *A Comparative Grammar of the Dravidian or South-Indian Family of Languages.* London: Harrison.

——. 1857a. *Lectures on the Tinnevelly Missions, Descriptive of the Field, the Work, and the Results: With an Introductory Lecture on the Progress of Christianity in India.* London: Bell and Daldy.

——. 1857. 'Progress of Christianity in India: The Tinnevelly Missions No. I-VII.' *Colonial Church Chronicle and Missionary Journal* 11: 88–103, 129–136, 177–186, 244–253, 286–296, 332–345, 365–378, 494–510.

——. 1880. *The First Centenary of the Tinnevelly Mission.* Palamcottah: Church Mission Press.

——. 1881. *Records of the Early History of the Tinnevelly Mission of the Society of Promoting Christian Knowledge and the Society for the Propagation of the Gospel in Foreign Parts.* Madras: Higginbotham.

——. 1886. 'On Demonolatry in Southern India', *Journal of the Anthropological Society of Bombay* 1,1: 91–105.

[97] See Chidester 1996: 1–29.

Chidester, David. 1996. *Savage Systems: Colonialism and Comparative Religion in Southern Africa*. Charlottesville: University Press of Virginia.

Copley, Antony. 1997. *Religions in Conflict: Ideology, Cultural Contact and Conversion in Late-Colonial India*. Delhi: Oxford University Press.

Frykenberg, Robert E. 1976. 'The Impact of Conversion and Social Reform Upon Society in South India During the Late Company Period: Questions Concerning Hindu-Christian Encounters with Special Reference to Tinnevelly', in: Cyril H. Philips, ed. *Indian Society and the Beginnings of Modernization: c. 1830–1850*. London: School of Oriental and African Studies, 187–243.

Grafe, Hugald. 1990. *The History of Christianity in Tamilnadu from 1800 to 1975*. Erlangen: Verlag der Evangelisch-Lutherischen Mission.

Gross, Andreas, Kumaradoss, Vincent Y., and Liebau, Heike, eds. 2006. *Halle and the Beginning of Protestant Christianity in India*. Halle: Verlag der Franckeschen Stiftungen.

Hardgrave, Robert L. 1969. *The Nadars of Tamilnad: The Political Culture of a Community in Change*. Berkeley: University of California Press.

——.1979 'The New Mythology of a Caste in Change', in: Robert L. Hardgrave, ed. *Essays on the Political Sociology of South India*. New Delhi: Usha Publications, 164–188.

Kent, Eliza F. 2004. *Converting Women: Gender and Protestant Christianity in Colonial South India*. New York: Oxford University Press.

Kumaradoss, Y. Vincent. 1996. 'Negotiating Colonial Christianity: The Hindu Christian Church of Late Nineteenth Century Tirunelveli.' *South Indian Studies* 1: 35–53.

——. 2007. *Robert Caldwell, a Scholar-Missionary in Colonial South India*. Delhi: ISPCK.

Ludden, David. 2005. *Early Capitalism and Local History in South India*. New Delhi: Oxford University Press.

Metzger, G. J., and Germann, Wilhelm, eds. 1869. *Genealogy of the South-Indian Gods: A Manual of the Mythology and Religion of the People of Southern India, Including a Description of Popular Hinduism, by Bartholomaeus Ziegenbalg. Freely Translated into English, and Enriched with Various New Additions and an Index by G. J. Metzger*. Madras: Higginbotham.

Monier-Williams, Monier. 1883 'Demon-Worship and Spirit-Worship', in: Monier Monier-Wiliams, ed. *Religious Thought and Life in India. Vol. 1: Vedism, Brahmanism, and Hinduism*. London: Murray, 230–256.

Mullens, Joseph. 1854. *Missions in South India Visited and Described*, London: W. H. Dalton.

——. 1863. *A Brief Review of Ten Year's Missionary Labour in India, between 1852–1861, Prepared from Local Reports and Original Letters*. London: Nisbet.

Pascoe, Charles Frederick. 1901. *Two Hundred Years of the S. P. G.: An Historical Account of the Society for the Propagation of the Gospel in Foreign Parts, 1701–1900*. 2 vols. London: Society for the Propagation of the Gospel.

Patrick, G. 2003. *Religion and Subaltern Agency: A Case-Study of Ayya Vali, a Subaltern Religious Phenomenon in South Tiruvitankur*. Dissertation Series, Vol. 2. Chennai: Department of Christian Studies, University of Madras.

Pennington, Brian K. 2005. *Was Hinduism Invented? Britons, Indians, and the Colonial Construction of Religion*. Oxford: Oxford University Press.

Pettitt, George. 1847. 'The Tinnevelly Missionaries to the Editor of the Madras Athenaeum [Republished from the Madras Athenaeum, November 23, 1846]', *Allen's Indian Mail and Register of Intelligence* 5,69, January 26: 44–45.

——. 1851. *The Tinnevelly Mission of the Church Missionary Society*. London: Seeleys.

Piggin, F. Stuart. 1984. *Making Evangelical Missionaries 1789–1858: The Social Background, Motives and Training of the British Protestant Missionaries to India*. (Evangelicals & Society from 1750; 2) Abingdon: Sutton Courtenay Press.

Pope, George U. 1844. *Mission of Sawyerpooram in the District of Tinnevelly and Diocese of Madras [Part One]*. 9th ed. 1847. (Missions to the Heathen; 1) London: SPG.

——. 1845. *Mission of Sawyerpooram. Part Third. Report of the Rev. G. U. Pope, January 1845*. 4th ed. 1847. (Missions to the Heathen; 7) London: Society for the Propagation of the Gospel.

——. 1849–50. 'Missions of the Church in Tinnevelly No. I-IV', *Colonial Church Chronicle and Missionary Journal* 3: 246–252, 281–287, 361–369, 441–450.

——. 1850–51 'Missions of the Church in Tinnevelly No. V-VIII', *Colonial Church Chronicle and Missionary Journal* 4: 55–65, 121–125, 201–206, 281–287.

Porter, Andrew. N. 2004. *Religion Versus Empire? British Protestant Missionaries and Overseas Expansion, 1700–1914*. Manchester: Manchester University Press.

Potter, Sarah Caroline. 1974. *The Social Origins and Recruitment of English Protestant Missionaries in the Nineteenth Century*. Ph. D., University of London.

Sargent, Edward. 1849. 'Some Account of the Devil-Worship Practised in the Province of Tinnevelly, South India, by the Rev. Edward Sargent, Church Missionary at Suviseshapuram' *Church Missionary Intelligencer* 1,2–4: 34–37, 60–62, 84–85.

Sattampillai, Arumai Nayakam. 1890. *A Brief Sketch of the Hindu Christian Dogmas: By A. N. Suttumpillai, Alias S. A. Nayaga Nadan*. Palamcottah: Shunmuga Vilasam Press.

Scott, David. 1994. *Formations of Ritual: Colonial and Anthropological Discourses on the Sinhala Yaktovil*. Minneapolis: University of Minnesota Press.

Sibree, James. 1923. *London Missionary Society: A Register of Missionaries, Deputations, Etc. From 1796 to 1923*. 4th ed. London: London Missionary Society.

Spencer, George John Trevor. 1842. *Journal of a Visitation to the Provinces of Travancore and Tinnevelly, in the Diocese of Madras, 1840–1841*. London: Rivington.

——. 1848. *Journal of a Visitation Tour in January and February 1845, through the Missionary Stations of the S. P. G. In the South-Eastern Portion of His Diocese*. (Missions to the Heathen; 9) London: Society for the Propagation of the Gospel.

Stanley, Brian. 1996. 'The Reshaping of Christian Tradition: Western Denominational Identity in Non-Western Context', in: R. N. Swanson, ed. *Unity and Diversity in the Church: Papers Read at the 1994 Summer Meeting, and the 1995 Winter Meeting of the Ecclesiastical History Society*. Cambridge: Blackwell, 399–426.

——. 2001. 'Christian Missions and the Enlightenment: A Reevaluation', in: Brian Stanley, ed. *Christian Missions and the Enlightenment*. Grand Rapids: Eerdmans, 1–21.

Stock, Eugene. 1899. *The History of the Church Missionary Society: Its Environment, Its Men and Its Work*. 4 vols. London: Church Missionary Society.

Sugirtharajah, Rasiah S. 2005. *Bible and Empire: Postcolonial Explorations*. Cambridge: Cambridge University Press.

Suntharalingam, R. 1974. *Politics and Nationalist Awakening in South India, 1852–1891*. Tucson: University of Arizona Press.

Surguner, Samuel. 1883. *Bishop Caldwell and the Tinnevelly Shanars*. Palamcottah: Pillai.

Thangaraj, M. Thomas. 1971. 'The History and Teachings of the Hindu Christian Community Commonly Called Nattu Sabai in Tirunelveli', *Indian Church History Review* 5: 43–67.

Thompson, Henry Paget. 1951. *Into All Lands: The History of the Society for the Propagation of the Gospel in Foreign Parts, 1701–1950*. London: SPCK.

Tucker, Sara. 1848. *South Indian Sketches: Containing a Short Account of Some of the Missionary Stations, Connected with the Church Missionary Society in Southern India, in Letters to a Young Friend. Part One: Madras and Mayaveram. Part Two: Tinnevelly, Travancore Etc.* 2 vols. 3rd ed. London: James Nisbet.

Vaitheespara, Ravindiran. 1998. Caste, Hybridity and the Construction of Cultural Identity in Colonial India: Maraimalai Adigal and the Intellectual Genealogy of Dravidian Nationalism, 1800–1950. Ph. D. Dissertation, University of Toronto.

——. 2000. 'Discourses of Empowerment: Missionary Orientalism in the Develoment of Dravidian Nationalism', in: Timothy Brook and Andre Schmid, eds. *Nation Work: Asian Elites and National Identity*. Ann Arbor: University of Michigan Press, 51–82.

——. 2006. 'Christianity, Missionary Orientalism and the Origins of Tamil Modernity', in: Andreas Gross, ed. *Halle and the Beginning of Protestant Christianity in India; Vol. 2: Christian Mission in the Indian Context*. Halle: Verlag der Franckeschen Stiftungen, 973–1017.

Wyatt, Joseph L., ed. 1894. *Reminiscences of Bishop Caldwell*. Madras: Addison & Co.

Mary E. Hancock

Landscapes of Christianity in colonial South India: The matter of Hindu ritual and Christian conversion, 1870–1920[1]

Introduction

The introduction of Protestant Christianities to South Asia relied heavily on the work of British and North American missionary women. Scholarship on their efforts has illuminated the role of missionization in British imperialism, explored the cultural hybridity of Christian subjects, both Indian and Eurowestern, and problematized the embodied, affective and gendered dimensions of these transformations.[2] This article builds on this scholarship by relating colonial Christianity's globalization and vernacularization to the materiality of both Christian and Hindu traditions, as it shaped the process of Christian conversion and the formation of gendered, racialized Christian subjects. I focus on the proselytic activities of American women of the Methodist Episcopal Church (North) in Tamil south India, between 1870 and 1920, dates which correspond to the florescence and decline of the women's mission movement in the United States. Methodists, by 1869 the largest Protestant denomination in the U. S., provide a useful case study, first because of their early and intense interest in India as a mission field and the associated scale of Methodist women's participation in mission and, second, because of Methodism's activist theology, with its focus on the pragmatic and material contexts of everyday life.

The period between 1870 and 1920, besides bracketing a phase of relative autonomy for Methodist women in mission, was also a critical time for the consolidation of anti-colonial nationalisms and contemporaneous social reform movements, many launched by and on behalf of South Asian women and with goals of modernization. In this volatile

[1] I thank Michael Bergunder, Joseph Muthuraj, Andreas Nehring, Vakulabharanam Rajagopalan, Ulrike Schroeder, Ravindiran Vaitheespara, and A. R. Venkatachalapathy for their helpful comments. I thank the archivists at the General Commission on Archives and History of the United Methodist Church at Drew University for their assistance, and I gratefully acknowledge the grant from the Interdisciplinary Humanities Center at the University of California, Santa Barbara, which supported the archival research for this article.

[2] Bergunder 2008; Bowie, Kirkwood and Ardener 1993; Burton 1994; Burton 1999; Flemming 1992; Forbes 1986; Haggis 1998; Haggis and Allen 2008; Hill 1985; Kent 2004; Ramusack 1992; Robert 1996; Singh 2000; van der Veer 1996; Viswanathan 1998.

environment, American Methodist missionaries occupied conjunctural positions – identifying racially and culturally with India's colonizers, even while allying themselves, at times, with Indian social reformers and nationalists.[3] Consistent with both the interventionism of the American ideology of 'manifest destiny' and the millennialism of Methodist religiosity, they promoted an implicitly racialized Christian modernity that was communicated not simply as a worldview, but was meant to be enacted behaviorally and spatially.[4] This modernity claimed the home as its stage and encompassed individualism, companionate marriage, rationalized home management, hygiene and temperance, and women were its privileged exponents.[5] Elements of Christian modernity were absorbed and reworked within nationalist autonomy movements (pan-Indian and regionalist, including Dravidian) and in those social reforms, such as the promotion of women's education and widow remarriage, temple entry, and child marriage prohibition, that were sometimes aligned with nationalist causes.[6] The late nineteenth-century fiction of Krupabai Satthianadhan, for example, illustrated how feminist aspirations for higher education and personal autonomy could be woven into notions of Christian subjectivity.[7]

This article examines the circulation of key tropes of domesticity and femininity, associated with discourse on the zenana, in Methodist writing during this critical period. Zenana was the term used by Eurowestern missionaries and colonizers to refer to the women's quarters of elite Hindu and Muslim homes throughout South Asia, but it also connoted other practices of gender seclusion, such as veiling. Consistent with Orientalism's feminization of Hindu and Muslim society, it served as a powerful, gendered metaphor for what missionaries regarded as South Asia's uncolonized interior spaces. A key feature of missionary practice from the early nineteenth century, zenana work referred to the mixture of evangelism and instruction in domestic arts and reading that Christian missionary women engaged in during visits with women in elite Hindu and Muslim homes. Although British churchwomen's role in the zenana

---

[3] Statement of Social Principles Adopted by the Methodist Federation for Social Service, 1908; Methodist Women in War Work, 1910–1930; Records of the Women's Division of the General Board of Global Ministries, 2604-3-7:07, General Commission on Archives and History of the United Methodist Church, Drew University, Madison, New Jersey. The generally progressive effects of Christian conversion – educational advancement, a richer civic life, self-sufficiency, spirituality – were noted by Hume 1894.

[4] Oldham 1914: 131–142; 150. See also Cramer 2004; Hill 1985.

[5] 'Dr. Pentecost on Women's Work in India', *Heathen Woman's Friend* 25,6 (1894), 101–103; Hume 1894.

[6] Chakrabarty 1996; Chatterjee 1989; Chatterjee 1993; Hancock 2001; Jayawardena 1995; Murshid 1983; Nair 1996; Uberoi 1996.

[7] Satthianadhan 1998a; Satthianadhan 1998b.

mission has received considerable scholarly attention, my investigation of American participation sheds light on their relatively understudied roles and contributes to pragmatic approaches to conversion, by attending to the ways that the transnational circulation of the rhetoric of the zenana – its spatial, material and embodied dimensions especially – framed contemporary understandings and practices of conversion. I am interested, particularly, in the letters, reports, and essays of Grace Stephens, the Anglo-Indian superintendent of the Methodist Episcopal Zenana Mission from 1886–1919. While few conversions were attributable to zenana work, the model persisted among American Methodists as a device for framing the embodied and material dimensions of Christian conversion and subject formation and Grace Stephens' activities in Madras were hailed specifically as demonstrations of the success that the zenana mission could yield. In this article, I use Grace Stephens' writing as a lens to examine the ways that the conversionary capacities of zenana work – located in its pragmatic and embodied dimensions – were represented in the Methodist imaginary.

Pragmatic approaches to conversion

The materiality of Hindu praxis, exhibited in its ritual transactions and its attention to images and figural representations, is often contrasted with the separation of matter and spirit thought to pervade Judeo-Christian and Islamic traditions. The materiality that characterizes Indian Christianities, in styles of worship, dress and representation is treated as an effect of the Hindu context – it is deemed to represent the vernacularization of the Renaissance and post-Reformation forms of Christianity introduced by Eurowestern missionaries. In this article I argue that, rather than being an effect of Hinduism, it represents the uneasy confluence of and dialogue between the competing materialities of *both* Hindu and Christian praxis.

The conversionary dynamic of Protestant traditions has often been theorized using linguistic models. Susan Harding, for example, describes conversion as an internal dialogue that culminates in the substitution of one language for another.[8] Within Protestantism, language is the privileged medium by which humans come to know and share in God's divinity and this perspective, drawing on the Platonic and Hebraic suspicion of imagery, has tended to shape scholarship in ways that have occluded attention to the spatial and material media by which Protestant Christianities are enacted.[9] Increasingly, however, historians of Christian-

[8] Harding 2001: 57.

[9] McDannell 1995: 8–13.

ity are attending to the pervasiveness and persistence of its material dimensions and, using the theoretical and methodological tools of visual culture, media studies, architecture and art history, and ethnography, are exploring religion's materiality comparatively.[10]

Colleen McDannell observes that the material culture associated with religion is infused with and acts as a carrier of values, ideas, and sentiments.[11] It comprises artifacts (humanly produced objects), landscapes, architecture and art, and the human body, both in its capacity to represent cosmological domains and moral principles and in its service as a vehicle of religious identity, practice and communication. She argues that making sense of popular religious expression requires attention to Christianity's materiality, for example, the valuation of medals and scapulas by Roman Catholics, the centrality of family bibles in the domestic culture of Victorian Protestants, Christians' emotional attachments to religious prints, relics and other memorabilia, and even the commercial circulation of artifacts such as prayer cards and lawn ornaments.[12] The recognition of Christianity's material dimension, moreover, offers an opportunity to reframe its entwinement with colonialism and global capitalism in ways that do not reduce religious expression and affect to reflexes of capitalism, but treat them as part of core dynamic of production, exchange, consumption systems that formed infrastructure of colonial expansion.

To an important extent, some of these insights have already made their way into South Asian scholarship. While not explicitly theorizing the material mediation of religion, attention to the corporeal and pragmatic aspects of Christian conversion can be found in colonial historiography and in ethnography. Feminist historiography, for example, has analyzed gendered bodies as media of a Christian imaginary and the colonial modernity that it portended.[13] Conversion, in this context, is understood as a dynamic ensemble of embodied practices, artifacts and social spaces in which Hindu and Christian elements intermingled. Some of this scholarship has aimed to illuminate gendered, sexualized and racialized dimensions of colonialism as these have unfolded in processes of Christian conversion and practice.[14] Other works, using ethnographic evidence, have dealt with vernacular Christianities, especially the 'Hinduization' of Christianity in South Asian contexts.[15]

---

[10] McDannell 1995; Morgan 2005; deVries 2001.
[11] McDannell 1995: 2.
[12] McDannell 1995: 18–57, 67–102.
[13] Burton 1994; Haggis 1998; Hill 1985.
[14] Haggis 1998; Hill 1985; Kent 2004.
[15] For example, Busby 2006; Mosse 2006.

Pragmatic approaches to conversion would be enriched, I contend, by expanding the scope to include the material mediations through which the two religious traditions interacted. By examining the work of American missionaries and southern Indian converts through the lens of material religion, I aim first to understand the spatio-material and embodied contexts of conversion and ritual praxis in which gendered and racialized Christian modernities were mediated. And in dealing with the role of American missionaries in shaping Indian Christianities, I hope to contribute to our understanding of the genealogy of Christian traditions in India.

My presentation begins with a brief overview of Protestant missionization of the nineteenth and early twentieth centuries, highlighting the roles played by Methodists and the imbricated discourses on Hindu domesticity and femininity – captured in the trope of the zenana – that propelled their work. I then move to a discussion of how the zenana, in spatial and material terms, figured in the process of Christian subject formation, looking at prescriptive discourses that American and Anglo-Indian Methodists produced. I follow with an analysis of the processes that the zenana mission entailed – both the materiality of zenana work in India and the transnational circulation of material artifacts and persons that sustained that work – using Grace Stephens' writings as principal sources. As this article represents an early stage in my research on this topic, I will end with provisional observations and questions, rather than fully formed conclusions. My sources include missionary periodicals (mainly *Heathen Woman's Friend*, later renamed *Missionary Woman's Friend*), missionaries' letters and reports, and the memoirs, essays, novels authored by missionaries and by Indian Christians.

"Woman's work for woman": American Methodist missions in Southern India

Several centuries of Christianization efforts in southern India had preceded the arrival of Protestant missionaries in the nineteenth century. The establishment and diversification of Christian sects, such as the Syrian, Thomist and Jacobite traditions, dated from the early centuries of the common era. By the early seventeenth century, Roman Catholicism was well established in conjunction with Portuguese exploration and settlement of the eastern and western coasts of the peninsula. It was only in the early eighteenth century that Protestant missionization began, with the 1706 establishment of the German Lutheran mission at Tranquebar, the location of the Dutch East India Company's fort and factory. Other denominational missions followed a century later (from 1813), when the British East India Company amended its charter to allow for proselytization and mission education in its territories. These efforts were led by English evangelicals, including members of the Church Missionary Society and Wesleyan Methodists, both of whom established bases of activity in Madras.[16]

Three years after the Company opened its settlements to missions, American Congregationalists, under the auspices of the American Board of Commissioners for Foreign Missions established missions in Ceylon and, in 1835, in Madurai. Other American denominations, including Methodists, established mission boards and women's auxiliaries around this time as well, spurred by evangelical revivals during the first half of the century. It was not until 1856, however, that William Butler, an American affiliated with the Methodist Episcopal Church (North), established an independent mission station in the northern Indian town of Bareilly. This was followed by increased activity, independently and in cooperation with British organizations and the American Board, in a number of northern and central Indian locales and in the southern cities of Madras and Bangalore. This included the Tamil Methodist Church, founded in Vepery following the revival of 1874, which had been led by William Taylor.

Over the latter half of the nineteenth century, the expansion of Protestant missions in India were supported by and, in turn, helped nurture the women's missionary movement in the U. S. The first organization, the interdenominational Women's Union Missionary Society, was founded in 1861 and other denominational boards followed, including, in 1869, the Women's Foreign Missionary Society of the Methodist Episcopal Church. During 1880s, several mission institutes were established in the U. S., offering training in Biblical studies, mission history, and practical fields such as home economics and nursing.[17] Denominational and interdenominational women's societies flourished and provided financial and material support for the work of women missionaries and, by 1890, women constituted about sixty percent of the total American mission force, with the Women's Foreign Missionary Society, itself, supporting about fifty missionaries in India by the end of the nineteenth century.[18] Many of the societies maintained publication divisions, which were responsible for the preparation of tracts and

[16] Methodist Churches were established in Royapettah (1819), Black Town (1822), St. Thomas Mount (1829).

[17] The most important Methodist institute was the Chicago Training School for City, Home and Foreign Missions.

[18] Robert 1996: 130.

reports, as well as a raft of periodicals, which mixed travelogue-type accounts with reports on mission life, educational features and administrative notes. By the 1920s, the women's mission movement had contracted, due to the rise of conservative, self-styled fundamentalisms within American Protestantism. With that, support for foreign missions diminished sharply. With a drop in recruits and the absorption of women's boards by the general denominational governing boards, the women's missionary movement soon came to a halt.

With this general historical outline in mind, we can take a closer look at *how* American women participated in mission. Paralleling their roles in other Protestant sects, Methodist women initially entered the mission field as wives of ministers and evangelists. Many had prepared for missionary life through seminary education, though their ability to fully immerse themselves in the work of mission stations was limited by their domestic duties. Women entered the field as full-fledged missionaries (evangelists, teachers, medical missionaries) only in the 1860s, supported by newly formed women's boards and in response to concerns about the plight of women in 'Oriental' religions (Hinduism, Islam, Buddhism, as well as Shinto and Confucian sects), whose degradation was felt to be emblematized in customs such as foot-binding, child-marriage, and gender seclusion practices.

India held a special attraction for evangelical women. Its "religious standards" reportedly ensured that the "deepest degradation of womanhood" persisted.[19] The wife of India's first Methodist Episcopal missionary, Clementina Butler, felt that missionary women were necessary for Indian women's progress and was one of the founders of the Woman's Foreign Mission Society.[20] She nonetheless credited her husband with having spurred this movement, noting in her memoir that he had "received a 'glorious vision' that he should take in girls orphaned during the uprising and that Methodist women should organize to educate the orphans and do mission work among Indian women secluded in zenanas."[21]

From the early nineteenth century, the zenana had been a key trope in missionary discourse. Women missionaries sought first, to puncture Orientalist stereotypes that depicted the zenana as a space of debauched luxury and expose it, instead, as a light-deprived prison that bore no resemblance to a true home.[22] This remained a persistent theme, with one

[19] Montgomery1910: 56.

[20] Robert 1996: 126.

[21] Butler 1929.

[22] 'Professional Visit to a Zenana of a High-Caste Brahman', *Heathen Woman's Friend* 1,10 (1870): 2–5; Page 1887: 121–124; Page 1888: 183–185; Butler 1903: 135–136. This strategy was common among other Protestant denominations; a Congregationalist

writer exclaiming in 1907 that even in wealthy households, "the rooms are *bare,* the cement floors are uncovered. There are no pictures, no books, no family gatherings! A house you see, not a home."[23] Secondly, they meant to proselytize within the zenana. The seclusion of Hindu and Muslim women, coupled with their importance in maintaining and transmitting religious traditions within the domestic sphere, made it imperative that special efforts be made to convert women in order to effectively Christianize the subcontinent. Methodists and other activist Protestants developed a rubric, "woman's work for woman", for this model.

During the 1880s, the zenana mission was further systematized among American Methodists through the introduction of deaconess training, following a model popularized earlier in Germany. Deaconesses were women committed to lives of service, mainly in the cities of their home countries and abroad. Influenced by the home economics movement in the U. S. and in keeping with Methodism's activist theology, they combined evangelism with the delivery of medical, educational and social services. Deaconesses received training in both Bible studies and in relevant social, medical and applied sciences (e. g., nursing, home economics) and, like Catholic nuns, they remained unmarried and wore a distinctive uniform.[24] By 1900, there were forty deaconesses working in India, twenty-one of whom were from the U. S.[25] The remainder comprised Indian and Anglo-Indian Bible women, teachers and evangelists. Several of India's more prominent Methodist missionaries were deaconesses, including Isabella Thoburn, the American founder of Thoburn College, Lucknow, and Grace Stephens, the Anglo-Indian who headed the Methodist Episcopal Zenana Mission from 1886–1919, whose work I explore further below.

The years between 1870 and 1920, therefore, were marked by an acceleration in women's missionization and by active institution-building. American Methodist women, with the support of the Women's Foreign Missionary Society, established mission stations across India (Lucknow, Calcutta, Cawnpore, Bombay, Moradabad, Bareilly, Naini Tal, Pithoragarh, Madras and Bangalore), most of which were affiliated with or adjacent to existing mission stations. In those locations, they maintained

missionary stated that the disheveled sitting room in one wealthy home "would have shamed a very negligent housekeeper at home." Sisson: 1872.

[23] Denning 1907.

[24] See also, 'The Value of Women's Work and Influence', *Heathen Woman's Friend* 13,3 (1881): 61–62; Page 1887; 'Reform in Hindu Homes', *Heathen Woman's Friend* 23,4 (1891): 81–82; Fisher and Maskell 1898; 'Bishop Thoburn on Deaconess Work in Southern Asia', *The Deaconess Advocate* 15 (1899): 9.

[25] Thoburn 1899.

orphanages, schools and clinics, trained native evangelists, catechists and Bible women, and carried out house-to-house evangelization under the rubric of zenana work.

The remainder of this article deals with the activities that zenana work comprised as well as the means by which the zenana, as trope, was deployed and circulated in accounts of conversion. I begin with the role that the mission station landscape played in this work.

Mission stations and domestic modernity

Mission stations were headquarters for the day-to-day work of missionaries, as well as object lessons in Christian domesticity.[26] Missionary periodicals regularly featured articles about day-to-day activities at the stations and about their construction and expansion. In Tamil south India, Methodist women maintained their principal mission station, the Methodist Episcopal Zenana Mission, in Madras city. Like other stations, the Madras mission was a space of Eurowestern civic and material culture within a cityscape that was a checkerboard of colonial and indigenous settlement spaces. Erected in Vepery, one of the city's original residential suburbs and long a home to European and Anglo-Indian families, the complex abutted other Christian institutions including Doveton College, the London Mission, the Wesleyan Mission House, and the Tamil Methodist Church.

Over the 1880s and 1890s, under Grace Stephens' supervision, the Madras Zenana Mission station was expanded from a residence-cum-office to a complex that accommodated educational activities and an orphanage. By 1899, with support from the Baltimore and Northwestern Branches of Women's Foreign Missionary Society, a spacious compound of six buildings had arisen.[27] It included two reception areas for those members of the public seeking assistance; one, Bethesda, served poor and low-caste visitors and the other, Nicodemus, was reserved for higher status persons. Soon after its completion, Nicodemus also served as a residence for high-caste Christian converts. The Baltimore Memorial housed mission offices and work spaces, while the fourth structure, a Deaconess Home, served as a missionary residence. The last two build-

---

[26] Montgomery 1910: 160. See also, Bruce 1874. The "object lessons" afforded by native Christian homes were of equal importance: 'Social Settlement Element', *Heathen Woman's Friend* 26,4 (1895): 110.

[27] 'Dedication of Mission Buildings at Madras' in Eugene Smith, ed. *The Gospel in All Lands*. New York: Missionary Society of the Methodist Episcopal Church (1900): 178–179.

ings provided space for the orphanage (the Harriet Bond Skidmore Memorial) and nursery. Outside the complex were the modest brick cottages of The Colony, built as homes for Indian Christians employed by or affiliated with the mission.

With its bungalow-styled structures and spacious gardens, and its proximity to other Christian institutions, the complex demarcated a built environment of vernacular Christian modernity that resembled other, contemporaneous mission stations in Asia, Africa and the Pacific. Bungalows, European adaptations of Bengal's rural architectural forms, had long been emblems of colonial hybridity throughout the British empire.[28] The local Christians in whose hands much of the stations' daily operations lay were also hybrid in matters of clothing, language, domestic practices and frequently racial affiliation. Indeed, consistent with other racialized institutions of colonialism, American missionaries opined that, despite their "suspicious, sensitive, vain, untruthful and extravagant" character, mixed race persons, Anglo Indian and Eurasian, were more effective agents of Christianization because of their cultural and linguistic affiliation with the indigenous populace.[29] The supervising bishop of the Methodist Episcopal Church in South and Southeast Asia, William Oldham, lamenting the one hundred million souls "untouched" by Christianity, advised missionaries:

> Eurasians are the connecting link between foreign missionaries and the heathen world. The quality of your assistants greatly influences the effectiveness of your missionaries. The Eurasians have a far-reaching influence.[30]

The mission's Anglo-Indian superintendent, Grace Stephens, typified the ambiguity of this racialized category. With her Western clothing and reliance on English, she signaled her identification with the white American and British Methodists who helped maintain the mission, thereby reinforcing its Eurowestern character. She, as well, distanced herself from Indian Christians, whom she usually described in letters and reports as

---

[28] King 1995.

[29] 'English Work,' 'India, 1908–1913' Records of the Women's Division of the General Board of Global Ministries, 2604-3-5: 04, 05, General Commission on Archives and History of the United Methodist Church, Drew University, Madison, New Jersey.

[30] Oldham Typescript, Records of the Women's Division of the General Board of Global Ministries, 2604-3-5: 04, General Commission on Archives and History of the United Methodist Church, Drew University, Madison, New Jersey. 'India, 1908–1913', Records of the Women's Division of the General Board of Global Ministries, 2604-3-5: 05, General Commission on Archives and History of the United Methodist Church, Drew University, Madison, New Jersey. Similarly, the Women's Home Missionary Society of India was founded in 1905 "to rouse the Eurasian and Anglo-Indian community in India to a sense of duty and privilege to give the Gospel message to the heathen." 'The Home Missionary Movement of India', *Missionary Woman's Friend* 37, 11 (1905): 396–397.

"natives". Like other missionaries, she described "native" homes and religiosity with metaphors of darkness and "natives", themselves – if not given to trickery (as was the case of Brahman priests) – as "child-like". She remarked often on adult women's love of toys, such as dolls, for example.[31] Stephens, nevertheless, strategically *dis*-identified with her American and British sponsors in other instances. She routinely designated herself "India's Own" in her official communications and wrote that she "had been called by God to be a missionary in my own land."[32] She also used familial terms to categorize her relations with the other Indian Christians associated with the mission, referring to herself as the "mother" of the large mission "family." Photographs encapsulate this ambiguity, typically showing her in Eurowestern dress, seated, and surrounded by standing Indian Christians – men, women and children. Her hybridity was thus a matter of strategic acts of identification and dis-identification with different racialized categories, rather than a matter of syncretism or stable recombination.

A starker demonstration of the racial dynamics of the colonial missionary enterprise can be seen in the ways that missionaries monitored and commented upon the bodies of converts. Eliza Kent has written extensively about the cultural logics of dress and other kinds of self-fashioning among the low caste Bible women in the Madurai area who were charged with much of the day to day work of evangelization.[33] The high-caste female body was also a signifier, especially for western audiences. Pandita Ramabai is a well-known exemplar of this phenomenon. A less familiar (and more unsettling) case was that of a Brahman convert, Sooboonagam Ammal, who toured the U. S. with Grace Stephens in 1900 and 1901. I discuss Grace Stephens' account of the conversion, presented in her book, *Sooboonagam Ammal*, in greater detail below. Here, it is sufficient to note that although Sooboo, as she was known, was taken to the U. S. to testify to the "splendid work" of the missionaries, she remained in these reports virtually voiceless – quite unlike Pandita Ramabai, who produced a substantial corpus of letters, articles, and essays. Sooboo's conversion was re-presented in the U. S. not with her own words, but by her repeated performance of the hymn that she reportedly sang when she had been publicly baptized in Madras (1895), "Jesus, I my cross have taken." She signified less the outcome of an engagement with Christianity than the *possibility* of conversion, her

[31] For example, Stephens 1903: 305–307.

[32] Missionary Roll Call, Records of the Women's Division of the General Board of Global Ministries, Mission Bio Reel, entry 2179: Grace Stephens. General Commission on Archives and History of the United Methodist Church, Drew University, Madison, New Jersey.

[33] Kent 2004: 150–163.

unadorned body conveying Christian personhood through the absence of the jewels and substances of Hindu womanhood.

Distinctions of race, gender and status were entangled, similarly, in the mission's character as a social space. The Madras station, like others, was intended as an exemplary Christian home (albeit headed by a woman) whose cleanliness and rationalized time-discipline would educate neophyte Indian Christians about the flaws in own homes and lifeways and the promise of Christian modernity. The object lessons of the mission station were also meant to encourage a particular form of respectability in behavior, dress and marriage customs, which had come to be associated with a Christianized bourgeoisie.[34] This is apparent in the Mission's separate reception sites for elite and poor visitors and in its architectural plan – a Eurowestern core surrounded by a perimeter of mediating space made up of habitation sites of Indian Christian villagers. Thus, despite the critique of caste hierarchy that missionaries often proclaimed, the space of the mission often materialized and preserved the inequalities of status and class. It was, in short, an island of Christian modernity – a refuge, laboratory and classroom where new forms of Christian domesticity could be displayed and enacted, where missionaries themselves could be protected from the sources of moral and physiological contagion that they perceived around them, and where edifying contrasts between the zenana and the Christian home could be drawn.[35]

Transformation from within

If the mission station was an emblem of a Christian future, the 'Oriental' home was crucible in which corrupted tradition had to be encountered and subdued. Indeed, as I have implied, the object of the missionary's attention not just the woman but woman within space of the home. Missionaries in India recognized temples as equally 'corrupt' but, with the memory of the 1857 Rebellion still fresh, realized that they were not penetrable without significant resistance and possibly violent consequences. Admittedly, temple precincts were preferred as sites for public evangelization because of the density of commercial and social life that they anchored and missionaries attentively documented temple rituals in letters and reports.[36] It was in homes, however, where the incremental,

---

[34] Kent 2004: 9–12, 127–129.

[35] For example, 'Kolar', *Heathen Woman's Friend* 27,2 (1895): 32–33.

[36] For example, Butler, 'Idols and Shrines in India', *Heathen Woman's Friend*, 1, 3 (1869): 19–20; 'The Holy Rivers of India', *Heathen Woman's Friend* 1,10 (1870): 87–88; 'Worship of Siva', *Heathen Woman's Friend* 2,4 (1870): 44–45; 'Brahmins at Prayer',

sustained work of Christianization was undertaken, and domesticity that furnished the tropes of proselytic rhetoric.

American Methodist women, like most mid-nineteenth-century Americans, understood homes to be generative spaces of (always-already racialized) nationhood and maintained that women exerted influence on society through Christian homes, as mothers and "queens of the house."[37] The domestic world of the white middle classes illustrated a sphere of feminine influence and nurture capable of yielding the masculine citizens and soldiers of the nation. In these intimate spaces of modern Christian aspiration, the fruits of technological progress were yoked to a racialized worldview, framed by millennialist teleology. For, though cloaked in sentimentality, homes were laboratories in which promises of modernity could be implemented – in scientific home management, social settlement work and even architectural experiments.[38]

Seen through this lens, the key to Christianizing 'heathendom' lay in transforming the domestic sphere – creating spaces of Christian modernity whose positive contagion, exerted in hygiene, mothercraft, companionate marriage, education and Christian piety, had the power to cure heathen society of its moral and physiological ills. Indeed, while missionaries targeted the zenana in effort to penetrate and rework caste and Hinduism, colonial authorities, social reformers, and nationalists also sought to map and reorganize domestic space and its gendered subjects and relations.[39] While such practices were formalized in home science education in the 1910s, they buttressed mission practice and discourse from its outset. And the trope of the zenana continued to be deployed as metonym for 'Oriental' corruption in missionary discourses over the nineteenth and early twentieth centuries, encouraging donations and spurring young American women to commit to missionary life.

Zenana work

Given their understanding of the zenana as an icon of heathendom, it is no surprise that missionaries identified zenana work as a critical feature of South Asia's mission field. For their part, Methodist missionaries in India wrote confidently about the influence that Hindu and Muslim

---

Heathen Woman's Friend 4,7 (1872): 389–390; 'Jagganath Temple', *Heathen Woman's Friend* 17,12 (1886): 293–295; 'Goddess Kali', *Heathen Woman's Friend* 20,1 (1888): 1–3.

[37] Beecher 1869.

[38] Hayden 1981.

[39] Hancock 2001.

women exerted in the home, even while asserting that they were 'trapped,' and 'oppressed' by doctrines that were both internalized by women and congealed in the oppressive space of the home, itself.[40] The zenana, in this sense, was not a neutral container, but served as the spatial referent for the 'heathen woman' and the corrupt traditions, mores and material artifacts, including spaces of domestic worship, that formed the constitutive matrix of womanhood. The zenana work prescribed for missionaries comprised home visits and zenana parties – social gatherings for local women held in makeshift zenanas in missionary compounds.

Madras city was home to one of the late-nineteenth century's foremost proponents of the zenana mission, Grace Stephens, who was lauded in Methodist publications as a model for Methodist activism. In 1891, an anonymous author in *Heathen Woman's Friend* described the efforts of Stephens and her sister, Mrs. E. Jones:

> Their period of service is not comparatively long, but they have contrived to compress within it results that others would have needed many long years to achieve. Christian sympathy and patience is the only witchcraft they employ to gain access to the hearts of the women of Hindu households, who everywhere receive them with open arms. ... caste, that adamantine chain which binds a Hindu hand and foot, and which it is though only a giant can break, is being shivered to pieces by the quiet teachings of Miss Stephens ...[41]

The author rhapsodized about the outcomes of Stephens' zenana work: the greater consideration shown by husbands toward wives, improved child-rearing, and the abandonment of superstition. Their efforts yielded only a handful of actual conversions, however. Rather than emphasizing outcomes in terms of conversion, therefore, Stephens and other zenana workers reported on the numbers of homes visited. She began in the mid-1880s with fourteen homes; in 1891, she mentioned having two hundred zenana pupils; and, by 1895, it was estimated that five hundred zenana women were regularly visited by her and her workers.[42]

Zenana work – geared to upper castes – never yielded large numbers of conversions, with mission historian Helen Montgomery judging it, in 1910, to have had "disappointing results"[43] Much more success in numbers of conversions had been achieved through schooling and other kinds of social settlement work among working classes and those designated as untouchable.[44] Despite this, as well as some missionaries' deep misgivings about its costs in time, money and labor, the zenana mission

---

[40] Hume 1894; Montgomery 1910: 45–81.
[41] 'Reform in Hindu Homes', *Heathen Woman's Friend* 23,4 (1891): 82.
[42] Stephens 1886: 116–118; Stephens 1891: 50–52; Rudisill 1905: v.
[43] Montgomery1910: 110.
[44] Kent 2004: 16–19.

persisted, often in the hands of local Bible-women. To consider why this was the case, I shift to a discussion of the rhetoric of the zenana, and its illustration of the constituent processes and material signs of conversion.

Opening the zenana

Missionaries understood zenana work as both behavioral and material transformation and usually described it using spatial metaphors: the zenana, 'dark,' 'window-less,' 'prison-like' was to be 'opened' through missionary labors, its inmates brought into sensory contact with a 'light-filled' exterior world. The incremental changes wrought by zenana work, initiated by comparisons of domestic activities and personalized interaction, constituted a standard conversion narrative and provided the warrant for continued investment by mission boards and auxiliaries.

Zenana work in Madras began in 1863 with the efforts of Anna Satthianadhan, an Indian Christian who had married into that well-known Indian Christian family. Satthianadhan's daughter-in-law, the writer Krupabai, provided a fictional characterization of the transformative effects of zenana work in *Saguna*, describing how one Hindu woman's (Radha) initial resistance to the visits of missionary women gradually gave way before the persuasive power of Christianity:

> Radha, busy at her work, would scarcely notice them at first, but afterwards she took pride in showing them what she knew in the way of cooking, and would make them taste her different preparations, and was gratified at their praise. Soon she was induced to visit them in return, and was in a bewilderment of joy of seeing so many queer looking nice things in the bungalow. The pretty fancy work caught her attention at once, though she never would have anything to do with reading. "Those are magic letters", she would say, shaking her head, "and Christianity is tied in the books". ... Her mind was often troubled and she had secret misgivings regarding her belief in shastras and idols. ... She also noticed the transforming effect of Christianity on her husband. His gentleness, kindness, and patience unconsciously set her thinking ... Gradually she succumbed to the strong influences of Christianity.[45]

As Satthianadhan's account suggests, comparisons, implicit and explicit, between 'heathen' and 'Christian' homes lay at the heart of zenana work. Missionaries themselves engaged in such comparisons in their letters and reports. More important, they also encouraged elite women to make such comparisons by exposing them to elements of Christian modernity. Krupabai Satthianadhan gave voice to such comparisons in her writing. In *Saguna*, she provided ample testimony about the object lessons of the

[45] Satthianadhan 1998b: 61.

missionary home and its materialization of desirable personhood and way of life; she testified, also, to the disclosure of divine agency in natural landscapes.[46]

As Satthianadhan's novelistic account implied, it was quotidian efforts that set the stage for Christian subject-formation. During zenana visits, ostensibly to teach women reading and needlework, missionaries described their own 'Christian homes,' they sang hymns, witnessed and sometimes read from bibles or tracts. They often attempted to leave bibles and tracts in these homes because numbers distributed were indices of missionary success.[47] It was not simply the quantity of bibles in circulation that mattered, however; missionaries also recognized the *agency* of bibles in process of conversion. The possession of a bible, in the first place, signified Christian personhood (e. g., as suggested by the moniker, 'Bible-woman') and converts' deep emotional attachments to their bibles were frequently reported in missionaries' letters.[48] Secondly, bibles and other tracts were invested with capacities to trigger action. The Women's Foreign Missionary Society Annual Report of 1908–1909, for example, describes a Brahman being diverted from his intention to renounce by the accidental acquisition of a page of a Christian song book: "he purchased a powder to dye his white garments yellow. The tradesman wrapped the powder in a piece of paper, formerly a page of a Christian songbook; the Brahman read the song. Not understanding it, he sought a missionary for explanation and by the truth of the song was led to 'peace, perfect peace'."[49]

The issue of the agency of non-human actors in the process of Christian conversion can be explored further by returning to Grace Stephens' paradigmatic account of high-caste conversion, *Sooboonagam Ammal*, which I introduced above. This text merits attention on account of its capture of the materiality of conversion, figuring it as a series of

---

46 Satthianadhan 1998b: 62, 70 f., 139.

47 Badley 1889; Stephens 1890: 222–224.

48 For example, Thomas 1870; 'Another Zenana Convert', *Heathen Woman's Friend* 2,11 (1871): 121–122.

49 'Fortieth Annual Report of the Women's Foreign Mission Society of the Methodist Episcopal Church, 1908–09', Baltimore: Women's Foreign Missionary Society of the Methodist Episcopal Church (1909): 8. 'Annual Reports, 1891–1940' Records of the Women's Division of the General Board of Global Ministries, 2598-2-5: 03, General Commission on Archives and History of the United Methodist Church, Drew University, Madison, New Jersey. Congregationalist missionaries similarly reported "remarkable instances of conversions by means of a Bible or part of one, accidentally obtained. One poor man begged for the whole Bible saying that the scrap he held in his hand, which contained little more than the verse, 'the blood of Jesus Christ His Son cleanseth us from all sin' had done him more good than all the books he had ever read." 'Plan of Study', *Light and Life for Women* 10,3 (1880): 113.

substantive exchanges (among human and non-human actors) in the course of which both the Hindu body and domestic space were replaced by Christian counterparts.

The narrative began by contrasting Hindu and Christian bodies and homes. The moral etiquette of the Brahman household, anchored by the seclusion of women and sustained by spatial and behavioral boundaries was captured in Stephens' allusions to the "severe lessons" learned during her visits. She reported on the visual barriers that prevented her from seeing kitchens, the behavioral norms of commensality that restricted her sharing of meals, her confinement to homes' outer, mediating spaces during visits, and the various prohibitions on physical contact with her hosts.[50]

The book's opening also conveyed the hybridity of Stephens own racialized identity. She sought identification with her American readers by signaling her discomfort with Hindu domesticity. She presented other facts, however – details of Hindu ritual praxis, as noted above – that distanced her from that readership. She underscored the strength of Sooboo's dedication to Hindu lifeways, for example, by describing her desire to be "sealed" or branded (a form of body modification among some Brahman communities), and by references to the various, "magical" powders with which she marked her body, to her endowment of a village temple and to the numerous "idols" and "pictures" that she worshipped.[51] In these passages, Stephens displayed an easy familiarity with phenomena introduced to shock American readers, in keeping with her self-proclaimed status as "India's Own".

Having established the materiality of Hindu religiosity, Stephens anticipated Sooboo's conversion, rendering it as an embodied and spatialized process:

> As we think of all this young life and all these things, and see her now in our home, we wonder if she can be the Sooboonagam Ammal of the past. No more fasting days and nights for salvation! No more bathing in seas and rivers to be saved from sinful pollution! No more the visiting of temples, nor the drinking of holy water! No more the giving of large sums of money for prayers to the priests and temples! No more the sacred powder and marks of worship on face and arms! No more the lighting of lamps, the penance, and all the rites prescribed by heathen priests! No more the proud, lofty look, the look of disdain and contempt for a Christian! No more the "touch-me-not" Brahman! But now our Sooboonagam sings most touchingly ... "Come to Jesus", ... "Nothing but the Blood of Jesus" ... "Jesus, I my cross have taken" ...[52]

[50] Stephens 1896: 2–5.
[51] Stephens 1896: 14 f., 20.
[52] Stephens 1896: 20 f.

With the contrast between Christian and Hindu lifeways illustrated, Stephens continued with a step-by-step account of Sooboo's conversion. She framed it as a transfer between two morally charged domestic spaces – Sooboo's Hindu home and the Christian domesticity of the mission compound. The seeds of Christianization, we learn, had been planted with a bible that had been left in Sooboo's home in course of zenana work.[53] We are told that she lost her desire for "idol worship", her rejection finally sealed by an omen, a scorpion's presence among deity figures.[54] Following several visits to the mission compound in 1894 and 1895, Sooboo experienced a catharsis – leaving behind her possessions (clothing, jewelry, idols, pictures), she fled to the compound where Stephens' extended Christian "family" was celebrating Christmas. She announced that she had come as "God's Christmas gift" and presented Stephens with a power-laden token of her commitment:

> She now took from her person the only thing she did bring, and gave it to me. It was the little metal box containing the sacred powder given by the priests as a sign that she had been sealed by them, and which ... she had to wear always about her person. In giving me this box, with the powder, she said she gave up her all – caste, heathenism, idolatry, everything.[55]

Sooboo then took up residence at the mission compound. Her family meanwhile mourned her departure and, when she confirmed her intention to leave, Stephens reported that they performed a funeral for her, using an effigy fashioned from clay. Once she became a resident in the mission compound, Sooboo was publicly baptized and took up work as an evangelist and teacher. In her new home, she dutifully served her Christian "family", carrying out household tasks and, more important, providing in her person an emblem for the success of zenana work in India and abroad.[56]

The "Blessed Magnet", as Stephens called Sooboo in recognition of her supposed influence on other women, resided for several years in the Nicodemus House on the mission compound. Sooboo, though consumed by her devotion to Jesus, retained (we are told) the "child-like" but nonetheless "superior" demeanor that missionaries attributed to zenana women. She also continued to live and work in partial seclusion – occupying the designated zenana house on the mission compound and traveling to homes in a carriage, accompanied by a "protector." Some ten years after the events described in the book, there were reports that

---

[53] Stephens 1896: 22 f.
[54] Stephens 1896: 25, 28.
[55] Stephens 1896: 43, 46–47.
[56] Stephens 1896: 103.

Sooboo left the compound to return to her family, though the references in Methodist periodicals and publications are almost non-existent.

Sooboo, who remained largely voiceless in the account, represented what Stephens claimed were hundreds, if not thousands, of "secret Christians", women, she said, who retained the outward trappings of Hindu identity but who had surrendered to Christianity in their hearts. For example, in an 1887 report, Stephens described viewing a family's *pūjā* room during one of her zenana visits and reported, with satisfaction, that the women had given flowers to the workers after having offered those flowers to the deity.[57] Stephens interpreted a standard act of redistribution of *prasāda* as a sign of the women's disregard for the ritual. This anecdote may be indicative of a misinterpretation on Stephens' part, but based on her familiarity with Hindu ritual, it is more likely a rhetorical strategy. If, in effect, any Hindu woman could be a secret Christian, then any act of Hindu practice could justify zenana work, even without the quantifiable evidence of a public conversion.

Stephens also used the narrative to elaborate on one of the important aspects of material Christianity and its constituent processes – the resignification of Hindu artifacts as Christian. These exchanges occurred from the first appearance of the bible in Sooboo's home to the cathartic moment when she relinquished her box of "powder" to Stephens. This theme was reiterated in the supplemental portions of later editions of the book, in which Sooboo's success as a zenana worker was hailed.[58] Like Stephens, she managed to acquire a "trophy", a photograph of a priest, probably a Sankaracarya. This image had been gifted to her by one of the legions of secret Christians that zenanas were claimed to harbor. Ironically, the photograph depicted one of Sooboo's own relations – her mother's brother – thus indexing the distance she had come from Hindu to Christian.

In other writings, Stephens detailed the materiality of Christian conversion in more general terms. She described secret Christians' reluctance to allow catechisms and bible portions to be placed near their domestic altars.[59] In another article, she described the death and burial of a zenana convert who had chosen to remain in her home, rather than join the mission station "family". After intervening to make sure that "nothing of marks of the Devil were put on her", she observed that Christian workers laid the woman's body on the home's verandah.[60] Stephens maintained that the corpse's presence was morally beneficial: "It was

---

57 Stephens 1887: 286–287.
58 Stevens 1905: 118.
59 Stephens 1890a: 222–224.
60 Stephens 1890b: 248.

good for them to come and see that Christian body" for it opened the hearts of that "heathen family."[61] And, recognizing that conversion necessitated the exchange of Hindu artifacts for Christian, she described the baptism of a Hindu priest in this way: "... as he stood for baptism I washed the hideous 'Swami marks' from his brow; and on removing his priestly yellow garment, Mrs Rudisill gave him a 'white robe;' I now have many of his sacred, priestly belongings."[62] Another article, "A Remarkable Conversion", described the exchange of "magic books" for bible that marked a renunciant's conversion to Christianity.[63]

As already noted, it was difficult to assess the efficacy of zenana work, as conversions were few and secret Christians were difficult, if not impossible, to tabulate accurately. Perhaps to justify its continuation, a more readily quantifiable operation was introduced to supplement one-on-one home visits. This was the zenana party. Here, again, Stephens acquired a reputation as the foremost proponent of this type of missionary endeavor.[64]

Zenana parties were introduced in 1891 to bring local Hindu and Muslim women to mission stations.[65] A temporary 'zenana' was fashioned, using curtains and existing architectural features, and women were entertained there with contests and games, gift distribution and snacks.[66] While hymns were often sung and prayers offered, the event was not a religious service in any explicit sense; the intent was, rather, to expose elite women to the Christian modernity that suffused the domestic world of the mission compound.

Just as zenana visits introduced Christian artifacts into Hindu homes, the parties also involved transfers of material artifacts. Stephens' parties were held as adjuncts to the mission's Christmas celebrations, and served as occasions to convey Christian religious principles and tie them to material objects and to a gift mode of exchange. These events, moreover, constituted a nexus for exchanges that were transnational in scope. chapters of the Women's Foreign Missionary Society in the U. S. assembled Christmas boxes that were sent to the mission stations. Dolls and harmonicas were among most coveted items; supplies for sewing and needlework projects, such as scissors, thimbles, needles, crochet hooks, and ribbons, were also included.[67] During the parties these artifacts, along

[61] Stephens 1890a: 249.
[62] Stephens 1896: 105.
[63] Stephens 1895a: 96.
[64] Montgomery 1910: 113.
[65] The first reference that I found was Ninde 1891: 159–161.
[66] Ninde 1891: 159–161; Stephens 1891.
[67] 'What to Send to India', *Heathen Woman's Friend* 19,12 (1888): 328; Hughes 1889; Stephens 1891; Stephens 1893: 3–5; Stephens 1895b: 5–6; Stephens 1903: 305–307.

with bibles, were awarded as gifts for recitation and singing. And, although artifacts of Christian domesticity were distributed, the party also offered opportunities for the display of the Hindu artifacts in Stephens' collection.[68]

The numbers of attendees, usually in the hundreds, were remarked upon in mission reports.[69] These numbers, like those of bibles and tracts distributed and homes visited, provided indices of the efficacy of the Christian mission. And, while numbers of secret Christians were unverifiable, the accounts of the parties helped sustain the trope of the secret Christian with their claims that such parties nurtured the faith of the many secret Christians who were among the guests and that the parties helped plant the seeds of Christian conversion in others.[70] Despite their exclusivity, the parties were also asserted to be "caste levellers." Stephens maintained that the women who visited the compound on these occasions mingled freely and without regard for the behavioral restrictions that ordinarily obtained. This she presented as evidence of the inroads that Christian modernity was making.[71]

If artifacts of U. S. domesticity were imported for zenana parties, there were also material artifacts of Hinduism that circulated outside the mission field. The Hindu artifacts that converts relinquished as signs of transformation were, in some cases, presented by missionaries to their sponsors and supervisors as religiously-charged souvenirs. In 1894, a Mrs. E. P. Stevens described the Christian conversion of a Tamil renunciant named Appaswami, attributing that transformation to books that Grace Stephens had given him. Convicted of his sin, he "surrendered to Miss Stephens ten books on magic, one magic slate, three books written on sacred leaves and bound by sacred thread, and was then baptized." She quoted Stephens's letter: "I wish you could have seen Appaswami as he brought the books to me and seen him as I put the Holy Bible in his hand as an exchange."[72] Despite the books' considerable monetary value, Stephens initially elected to keep them, "as a sacred trust", but later reconsidered and implored Mrs. Stevens to accept them as signs of Christianity's advancement in India.

---

68 Stephens 1893.

69 'Twenty-third Annual Report of the Women's Foreign Mission Society of the Methodist Episcopal Church', Baltimore: Women's Foreign Missionary Society of the Methodist Episcopal Church, 1892, in 'Annual Reports, 1891–1940', Records of the Women's Division of the General Board of Global Ministries, 2598-2-5: 03, General Commission on Archives and History of the United Methodist Church, Drew University, Madison, New Jersey.

70 Stephens 1895b: 5–6.

71 Stephens 1895b: 5–6.

72 Stevens 1895a: 96.

Grace Stephens also enclosed lithographs and cloths, metonyms of the Hindu domestic interior, in some letters to her supervisors. A letter to Dr. North, dated December 1, 1916, included a lithograph of the Jagannatha, Balarama and Subhadra, produced by Ravi Varma Press, as an enclosure: "I am enclosing in this a worshipped paper. Think of the people worshipping a thing like that and what it means now for them to have a place of their own erected for God."[73] In another letter to North, dated August 17, 1917, she wrote, "I am sending you a handkerchief used by the Hindoos here, with the gods and goddesses on it. Just think of a handkerchief like this being used in America!"[74]

Personalized interactions such as these were complemented by activities that incorporated a wider public. The zenana was kept alive in Americans' imaginations through embodied practices in the United States. An article in *Heathen Woman's Friend* described zenana parties being held to "stimulate more zeal in our work."[75] American women, dressed in saris, hosted these affairs at which returned missionaries spoke about zenana life. These activities were meant, like many of the study assignments carried out by auxiliaries, to have a pedagogical thrust, which they did by enabling an active and material imagination of the mission field. There were, as well, other portable icons of the zenana that enjoyed transnational circulation. More than twenty years before Stephens sent Hindu souvenirs to her American supervisors, another missionary, Rev. Thomas Craven, prepared photographic prints of Hindu and Christian women, which emphasized their contrasting dress and demeanor. One, a "Hindoo woman of the middle class" is "robed in full costume, displaying the abundance of ostentatious ornaments on her forehead, fingers, and toes as well as in her nose." The other picture was presented as a contrast to Hindu decadence: it was, he wrote, "a sweet, modest, intelligent face of a Christian ... convert ... from the upper ranks of Hindoo society." He urged Americans, be they merely collectors of curios or those interested in advancing the cause of foreign missions, to decorate their homes with these pictures:

[73] Letter from Miss Grace Stephens to Dr. North, December 1, 1916. 'Mission Correspondence, 1912–1949', Records of the Women's Division of the General Board of Global Ministries, 1113-1-1, General Commission on Archives and History of the United Methodist Church, Drew University, Madison, New Jersey. On the reverse of the lithograph, Stephens had written, "The three greatest gods in India. Brahma in the centre, Vishnu and Siva on the sides. This paper has been worshipped by the people."

[74] Letter from Miss Grace Stephens to Dr. North, dated August 17, 1917 'Mission Correspondence, 1912–1949', Records of the Women's Division of the General Board of Global Ministries, 1113-1-1, General Commission on Archives and History of the United Methodist Church, Drew University, Madison, New Jersey.

[75] Reed 1895: 64–65.

> We would like to know of a set of these photographs being in every American home. They cannot fail to contribute ... to an abiding interest in the people of India. Wherever they [the pictures] go, they will furnish a reply to such as say there are no good results from foreign missions.[76]

Zenana work (parties and visits) and its circulating icons thus were key features that sustained the potency of India in the missionary imaginary. The zenana was represented as the matrix in which Hindu materiality and womanhood were inextricably bound together and, as such formed dynamic core of the interlocked systems of caste and Hindu religiosity. Despite gaining few converts or even being able to measure their efficacy, accounts of the interior world of the zenana and missionaries' incremental penetration of it remained staple features of letters and reports. These narratives were complemented, as well, by the circulation of material and visual artifacts within and outside mission field, all of which helped sustain Americans' emotional, moral and financial investments in Indian missions.

Conclusion

It is apparent, from this brief overview, why the zenana claimed the imaginations and affective commitments of American Protestants. The zenana's status as a metonym for what missionaries described as 'heathendom' is affirmed in the frequency and content of articles in missionary periodicals and in the letters, reports and essays of both American missionaries and Indian Christians. These sources reveal missionaries' understanding of upper-caste Hindu women's bodies as media through which Hinduism and caste were continuously regenerated and sustained. At the same time, both their resistance and submission to Christianity were also framed in embodied terms. These broadly shared perspectives were focused and intensified by Methodism's pragmatic and activist orientation. Methodist women missionaries' evangelism was accompanied by efforts to reorganize and reform Hindu domestic spaces through the incremental changes associated with zenana work and by modeling Christian domestic order in their own residences and institutions.

I have suggested in this article that American Methodists' zenana mission in India, both its conduct and its representation in missionary discourse, persisted despite its cost and low conversion counts because of its power as a rhetorical trope. Grace Stephens' writings were particularly

[76] 'India Photographs', *Heathen Woman's Friend* 14,8 (1883): 182.

influential. Her accounts repeatedly invoked the image of the zenana as a space in which the material signs of Hinduism and Christianity were locked in battle and in which secret Christians awaited salvation. Indeed, within this frame, any Hindu whose home had been entered by missionaries could be interpolated as a secret Christian. It could be argued that this simply served to justify the continuation of the mission station in Madras and to enhance Stephens' own reputation. There is more to this, however. Her attention to the material signs of conversion encoded principles of material Christianity that I argue were deeply entwined in the Methodist imaginary. The artifacts of Christian modernity – bibles, tracts, hymnbooks, needlework tools – were understood as agents in their own right, with the power to penetrate the resistant sheath of Hindu custom. The artifacts of Hindu religiosity (rendered as 'tradition' in relation to Christian modernity) could, in turn, be resignified as "trophies", collectibles that embodied the transformative effects of conversion and represented the 'others' against which American Methodists framed their own Christian subjectivities. If social settlement work among poor and low-caste communities yielded greater numbers of converts, zenana work yielded the most potent icons of conversion – "magic powders", books, pictures, and "idols" – and, more important, gave missionaries access to Hindu women who were thought to be the fulcrum on which caste and Hinduism rested.

Insights about the pragmatics of conversion can be gained through these accounts. Existing models of Christian conversion have emphasized its linguistic dimension and treat Christian subjectivity as an interior, psychological state. In this article, building on recent scholarship on material Christianity, I have focused instead on material media of Christian subject formation, suggesting that conversion be considered as a process comprising material exchanges and embodied performances that rely on, reproduce and rework gender, racial and class codes. Conversion may be a matter of translation, but it is also a matter of *matter*, of materiality – of artifacts, landscapes, and buildings, as well as the bodies of its human emblems and agents. Bibles, songbooks, domestic space and accoutrements (from embroidery tools to pianos) comprised the material and performative matrix of colonial Christianity and mediated the encounters between Christian and Hindu persons and institutions. This perspective offers a useful supplement to scholarship on the linguistic dimensions of conversion. It also problematizes the cultural and racialized hybridity sometimes attributed to converts by framing their self-presentation as temporally unfolding (and reversible) strategies of identification and dis-identification, reliant on material and performative media. As such, conversion may be theorized, following generally on

Judith Butler's work, as an embodied performance that is situational, transactional and negotiated and that contributes to the formation and sedimentation of relational subjectivities, be they associated with gender, race, class and / or nation.[77]

The picture of the colonial missionary project that I have outlined in this article invites further questions both about the materially mediated interactions between different religious traditions in colonial contexts and, more specifically, about the ramifications of the American missionary presence in India. How do the material transactions and exchanges documented in Indian Christianity compare with those of other missionary encounters, in Africa, East and Southeast Asia, and the Pacific? What insights about colonial expansion and power might be yielded by attention to material religiosity? How did American Protestant denominations influence the formation of Indian Christianities? Did American Protestant missionary practice intersect with emerging discourses on racial identity and difference in the U. S.? In India? These are questions that I can gesture toward at this point, but they may be worth further examination as we consider the manifold ways in which colonialism in South Asia brought about the reworking of the material organization of everyday life.

Bibliography

Badley, M. 1889. 'Female Education in India', *Heathen Woman's Friend* 21,1: 8–10.

Beecher, Catherine. 1869. *The American Woman's Home.* New York: J. B. Ford.

Bergunder, Michael. 2008. *The South Indian Pentecostal Movement in the Twentieth Century*. Grand Rapids: Eerdmans.

Bowie, Fiona, Kirkwood, Deborah and Ardener, Shirley, eds. 1993. *Women and Missions: Past and Present.* Oxford: Berg.

Bruce, H. J. 1874. 'The Mission House at Rahuri', *Light and Life for Woman* 4,3: 89–92.

Burton, Antoinette. 1994. *Burdens of History: British Feminists, Indian Women, and Imperial Culture, 1865–1915.* Chapel Hill: University of North Carolina Press.

——, ed. 1999. *Gender, Sexuality and Colonial Modernities*. London: Routledge.

Busby, Cecilia. 2006. 'Renewable Icons: Concepts of Religious Power in a Fishing Village in South India', in: Fenella Cannell, ed. *The Anthropology of Christianity.* Durham: Duke University Press.

Butler, Clementina. 1903. 'Inside the Zenana Curtain', *Missionary Woman's Friend* 35,4.

Butler, Clementina. 1929. *Two Empires and the Kingdom.* New York: The Methodist Book Concern.

Butler, Judith. 1993. *Bodies that Matter: On the Discursive Limits of 'Sex'.* New York: Routledge.

[77] Butler 1993; Butler 1997.

——. 1997. *Excitable Speech: The Politics of the Performative.* New York: Routledge.

Chakrabarty, Dipesh. 1996. 'The Difference-Deferral of a Colonial Modernity: Public Debates on Domesticity in British Bengal', in: David Arnold, David Hardiman, eds. *Subaltern Studies VIII: Essays in Honour of Ranajit Guha.* Delhi: Oxford University Press.

Chatterjee, Partha. 1989. 'The Nationalist Resolution of the Women's Question', in: Kumkum Sangari, Sudesh Vaid, eds. *Recasting Women: Essays in Indian Colonial History.* New Delhi: Kali for Women.

——. 1993. *The Nation and Its Fragments: Colonial and Postcolonial Histories.* Princeton: Princeton University Press.

Cramer, Janet. 2004. 'White Women and Religion: Colonial Discourse in the U. S. Women's Missionary Press, 1869–1904', *Howard Journal of Communication* 14, 4: 209–224.

Denning, Margaret. 1907. 'Scenes in the Zenana', *Missionary Woman's Friend* 39,11: 390.

deVries, Hent. 2001. 'In Media Res', in: Hent de Vries and Samuel Weber, eds. *Religion and Media.* Stanford: Stanford University Press.

Fisher, Fannie and Maskell, M. 1898. 'Kolar India', *The Deaconess Advocate* 14: 11 f.

Flemming, Leslie. 1992. 'New Humanity: American Missionaries; Ideals for Women in North India, 1870–1930' in Margaret Strobel and Chaudhuri Nupur, eds. *Western Women and Imperialism: Complicity and Resistance.* Bloomington: Indiana University Press.

Forbes, Geraldine. 1986 'In Search of the "Pure Heathen": Missionary Women in Nineteenth Century India', *Economic and Political Weekly* 21, 17: WS2–WS8.

Haggis, Jane. 1998. 'Good Wives and Mothers or Dedicated Workers? Contradictions of Domesticity in the "Mission of Sisterhood", Travancore, South India,' in: Kalpana Ram, Margaret Jolly, eds. *Maternities and Modernities: Colonial and Postcolonial experiences in Asia and the Pacific.* Cambridge: Cambridge University Press.

Haggis, Jane and Allen, Margaret. 2008. 'Imperial Emotions: Affective Communities of Mission in British Protestant Women's Missionary Publications c1880–1920', *Journal of Social History* 41, 3: 691–716.

Hancock, Mary. 2001. 'Home Science and the Nationalization of Domesticity', *Modern Asian Studies* 35: 871–903.

Harding, Susan. 2001. *The Book of Jerry Falwell.* Princeton: Princeton, 57.

Hayden, Dolores. 1981. *The Grand Domestic Revolution: A History of Feminist Designs for American Homes, Neighborhoods and Cities.* Cambridge, MA: MIT Press.

Hill, Patricia. 1985. *The World their Household: The American Woman's Foreign Mission Movement and Cultural Transformation, 1870–1920.* Ann Arbor: University of Michigan Press.

Hughes, M. 1889. 'Christmas at the School in Madras', *Heathen Woman's Friend* 20,11: 290 f.

Hume, Robert. 1894. 'What Gain for Women in India in Twenty-five Years?' *Heathen Woman's Friend* 25: 292–293.

Jayawardena, Kumari. 1995. *The White Woman's Other Burden: Western Women and South Asia during British Rule.* New York: Routledge.

Kent, Eliza. 2004. *Converting Women: Gender and Protestant Christianity in Colonial South India.* New York: Oxford University Press.

King, Anthony. 1995. *The Bungalow: The Production of a Global Culture.* Revised edition. New York: Oxford University Press.

McDannell, Colleen. 1995. *Material Christianity: Religion and Popular Culture in America*. New Haven: Yale University Press, 8–13.

Montgomery, Helen. 1910. *Western Women in Eastern Lands*. New York: The Macmillan Company.

Morgan, David. 2005. *The Sacred Gaze: Religious Visual Culture in Theory and Practice* Berkeley: University of California Press.

Mosse, David. 2006. 'Possession and Confession: Affliction and Sacred Power in Colonial and Contemporary Catholic South India', in: Fenella Cannell, ed. *The Anthropology of Christianity*. Durham: Duke University Press.

Murshid, Ghulam. 1983. *The Reluctant Dubutante: Response of Bengali Women to Modernization, 1849–1905*. Rajshahi: Sahitya Samsad.

Nair, Janaki. 1996. *Women and Law in Colonial India: A Social History*. Delhi: Kali for Women.

Ninde, Mary.1891. 'A Zenana Party', *Heathen Woman's Friend:* 22,7.

Oldham, W. F. 1914. *India, Malaysia and the Philippines: A Practical Study in Missions*. New York: Eaton and Mains.

Page, Anne. 1887. 'Zenana Work', *Heathen Woman's Friend:* 19,5.

——. 1888. 'Zenana Work', *Heathen Woman's Friend:* 19,7.

Ramusack, Barbara. 1992 'Cultural Missionaries, Maternal Imperialists, Feminist Allies: British Women Activists in India, 1865–1945', in Strobel and Chaudhuri, eds. *Western Women and Imperialism: Complicity and Resistance*. Bloomington: Indiana Univ. Press.

Reed, Horace. 1895. 'Zenana Party in Illinois', *Heathen Woman's Friend* 27,3.

Robert, Dana.1996. *American Women in Mission: A Social History of Their Thought and Practice*. Macon, GA: Mercer University Press.

Rudisill, A. W. 1905. 'Introduction', in: Grace Stephens, *Sooboonagam Ammal*. Baltimore: Peters Publishing: v.

Satthianadhan, Krupabai. 1998a. *Kamala: The Story of a Hindu Child-Wife*. Delhi: Oxford.

——. 1998b. *Saguna: A Story of Native Christian Life*. Delhi: Oxford.

Singh, Maina. 2000. *Gender, Religion and the 'Heathen Lands': American Missionary Women in South Asia, 1860s–1940s*. New York: Garland.

Sisson. 1872. 'India-First Experiences', *Light and Life for Heathen Woman* 2,8: 340–342

Stephens, Grace. 1886. 'Zenana Work in Madras', *Heathen Woman's Friend* 18,5.

——. 1887. 'Madras', *Heathen Woman's Friend* 18,11.

——. 1890a. 'Zenana Work and Its Results', *Heathen Woman's Friend* 21,9: 222–224.

——. 1890b. 'The Christian Burial of a Madras Zenana Worker', *Heathen Woman's Friend* 21,10.

——. 1891. 'A Madras Zenana Party', *Heathen Woman's Friend* 23,3.

——. 1893. 'Another Zenana Party', *Heathen Woman's Friend,* 25 3.

——. 1895a. 'A Remarkable Conversion', *Heathen Woman's Friend* 26,4.

——. 1895b. 'Christmas Festivities in Madras', *Heathen Woman's Friend* 26,1.

——. 1896. *Sooboonagam Ammal*. Madras: Methodist Episcopal Publishing House.

——. 1903. 'A Step Forward', *Missionary Woman's Friend* 35,9.

Stevens, E. B. 1905. 'Supplement I', in: Grace Stephens, *Sooboonagam Ammal*. Baltimore: The Peters Publishing and Printing Company.

Thoburn, Isabella.1899. 'Deaconesses in India', *The Deaconess Advocate* 15: 11.

Thomas, M. A. 1870. 'A Day in the Zenana', *Heathen Woman's Friend* 2,2: 13 f.

Uberoi, Patricia, ed. 1996. *Social Reform, Sexuality and the State*. Contributions to Indian Sociology Occasional Studies, No. 7. New Delhi: Sage.

van der Veer, Peter. ed. 1996. *Conversion to Modernities: The Globalization of Christianity*. New York: Routledge.

Viswanathan, Gauri. 1998. *Outside the Fold: Conversion, Modernity and Belief*. Princeton: Princeton University Press.

Torsten Tschacher

Witnessing fun: Tamil-speaking Muslims and the imagination of ritual in colonial Southeast Asia

Introduction

Of all the far-reaching transformations of Tamil society in the nineteenth and early twentieth centuries, the migration of thousands of Tamil-speakers to Southeast Asia may be said to be the least noted. From the perspective of South Indian history, migration to Southeast Asia was mainly an economic event, the most important social effect of which was the departure of large numbers of individuals to another land.[1] The main theme of South Indian migration has been 'settlement' and the formation of 'diasporic' communities, for whom India increasingly became a dim memory rather than social reality.[2] Yet, the histories of South Indians on both sides of the Bay of Bengal are not so easily disentangled, at least not as far as the colonial period is concerned. In the course of the nineteenth century, individuals shifting from India to Southeast Asia and back again were generally moving within the same, mainly British and French imperial space, uninhibited by the national boundaries which increasingly limited movement from the mid-twentieth century onwards. Steamships increased the numbers of passengers that could take the journey to Southeast Asia, as well as the speed of that journey. And the rise of Tamil-language newspapers in Southeast Asia in the 1870s brought Southeast Asian news to the door-steps of readers in South India.

Far from constituting separate domains, Tamil societies in South India and Southeast Asia remained linked through the circulation of goods, ideas, print media, and not least individuals, creating distinct but connected historical trajectories that cannot easily be separated. Investigations of the socio-cultural transformations experienced and effected by Tamil-speakers in colonial Southeast Asia, thus, need not only to be placed in the wider context of changes affecting Tamil-speaking populations in the nineteenth and early twentieth centuries, but also has to be seen as being a fundamental part of the history of these changes, without which our understanding of processes of change and

[1] A noteworthy exception to this trend is Rudner 1994.

[2] Cf., for example, Arasaratnam 1979, Sandhu 1969, Sandhu and Mani 1993, as well as the relevant country overviews in Lal 2006.

transformation in South Indian history remains partial at best. The challenge in studying South Indian societies in colonial Southeast Asia lies in tracing the peculiar patterns of convergence and divergence between developments seen in these societies and the wider historical processes of South India, as well as Southeast Asia.

This chapter is a first attempt at studying one such process of transformation among one particular community of South Indians in colonial Southeast Asia, namely the changing ways of representing and imagining ritual among Tamil-speaking Muslims settled throughout Southeast Asia, but particularly in the British colonies of the Straits Settlements and Burma. Beginning in the late-nineteenth century, Tamil-speaking Muslims in Southeast Asia began to utilize print-media to put forward and contest diverse visions of identity and belonging. Religion played an important role in the discourse generated by these media, and shifting images of Muslim ritual were part of the way in which Tamil-speaking Muslims created public spaces for themselves in the Southeast Asian environment. Investigating these images is therefore a useful entry into studying wider socio-cultural transformations, underway among Tamil-speaking communities in colonial Southeast Asia.

Being at home abroad: Tamil-speaking Muslims in colonial Southeast Asia

The engagement of Tamil-speaking Muslims with Southeast Asia was already several centuries old by the early nineteenth century.[3] In the Straits Settlements, these formed substantial populations in the early nineteenth centuries. In 1826, 'Chulias', as Tamil-speaking Muslims in Southeast Asia were often called, made up 10 % of the population of Melaka, while a census conducted in Singapore in 1849 showed that, even thirty years after the founding of the British settlement, almost 80 % of the Indians residing in Singapore were Muslims, again forming almost 10 % of the total population.[4] Tamil-speaking Muslims were engaged in a number of occupations, especially as traders, clerks, and manual laborers.

During the nineteenth century, networks of Tamil-speaking Muslims spread throughout most of Southeast Asia. Towns and cities on or close to the west coast of the Malay Peninsula had the largest concentrations but, in the course of the nineteenth century, important inland towns, such as Kuala Lumpur or Ipoh, increasingly attracted settlement. This process

[3] For a recent discussion and bibliography, cf. Tschacher 2009.

[4] Figures for Melaka quoted in Nordin 2007: 173; figures for Singapore taken from Jackson 1850: table II.

was even more pronounced in Burma, were the British conquest facilitated the movement of Tamil-speaking Muslims from the coast up the Irrawaddy as far as Mandalay, so that by the early twentieth century they were "scattered throughout Burma, in villages and towns".[5] They also remained active in the wider world of archipelagic Southeast Asia, which came increasingly under Dutch dominance in the nineteenth century. The expansion of Tamil Muslim networks is perhaps most striking on the Southeast Asian mainland, where, in addition to Burma, Tamil-speaking Muslims came to settle in most of the political, cultural and economic centers, such as the kingdom of Siam or French Indochina. The establishment of French hegemony over what was then called 'Indochina' attracted Muslims from French colonies in South India to Vietnam and Cambodia. In 1927, the Bengali intellectual, Suniti Kumar Chattopadhyay, noted Tamil-speaking Muslims settled in Hanoi, Hue, Saigon and Phnom Penh on board of a ship bound for Haiphong.[6]

Yet, what makes the colonial period so interesting for a historian of Tamil-speaking communities is that, for the first time, a Tamil-language publishing industry produced books, pamphlets and newspapers in Tamil from Southeast Asia, which were mainly aimed at an audience settled in the region. Muslims did not only participate in this industry, but were amongst its pioneers. Any study of socio-cultural transformations among Southeast Asian Tamil-speaking Muslims, therefore, has to take account of this body of source material.

The story of Tamil publishing in Southeast Asia seems to have begun in Singapore in 1872, with the publication of a collection of poetry entitled *Muṉājāttuttiraṭṭu* by Mukammatu Aptulkātiṟuppulavar of Nagore.[7] Within the next three decades, Tamil publishing increased in scope throughout the Straits Settlements and, from the 1890s onwards, also in Burma. Muslims participated in this process to a great extent as authors, publishers, printers, and consumers of printed books and newspapers. In Singapore, the first Tamil printing presses not owned by Europeans were run by Muslims.[8] Around 1873, Ci. Ku. Makutūmcāyapu established Denodaya Press, which published Tamil, Malay, and English publications well into the twentieth century.[9] Another press that occasionally published Tamil publications was owned by the Jawi Peranakan Company,

[5] Yegar 1972: 29–44, quote on p. 41.

[6] For Siam, cf. Mani 1993; for Indochina, cf. More 2000, Ner 1941: 152–153, Pairaudeau 2006; Chattopadhyay's account can be found in Bose 2006: 247–248.

[7] Mukammatu Aptulkātiṟuppulavar 1872.

[8] For a general account, see Jāpar Muhyittīṉ 1990.

[9] The last printed book connected with his name was a Malay publication of 1908; Proudfoot 1993: 615; regarding the foundation of the press, cf. *Ciṅkainēcaṉ* (25 June 1888), "Nam pattirikai", 206.

whose owner, Muḥammad Sa'īd, had started *Jawi peranakan* in 1876, the first successful Malay-language newspaper, and also served as a trustee of the main Tamil mosque in Singapore.[10] These two printing presses also published the first Tamil newspapers in Singapore, of which only one, *Ciṅkainēcaṉ* (1887–1890), published by Denodaya Press, has survived complete. The situation was similar in Penang, where the first Tamil newspaper, *Vittiyā vicāriṇi*, was published in 1883 by one of the most important Tamil Muslim poets of the nineteenth century, Kulām Kātiṟu Nāvalar (1833–1908).[11] While probably only a very limited number of copies were printed, the geographical circulation of these newspapers is all the more impressive. *Ciṅkainēcaṉ* had subscribers in towns of the Malay Peninsula, Sumatra, Java, Siam, the Mekong delta, and India. About thirty years later, another Muslim-run Tamil newspaper from Singapore had agents in various towns of the Malay Peninsula, Sumatra, India, and even Makassar on Sulawesi.[12]

It was in these newspapers, and other printed publications, that Muslims put forward their ideas and visions of Muslim ritual as well as its relation to the specific context of colonial Southeast Asia that it was enacted in. These texts are not the only but they are certainly the richest source for the performance of Muslim ritual, or rather, the way it was imagined among Tamil-speaking Muslims in Southeast Asia. There are of course other sources which complement our knowledge of these ritual practices. British sources, both newspapers as well as court records, do occasionally address Muslim ritual practice. These accounts were mostly created when, in some way or another, Muslim conceptions of ritual propriety conflicted with the social order envisioned by the colonial state and European settlers, and thus have to be used with care. Yet there are other, visible reminders of past and usually also present ritual activity of Tamil-speaking Muslims in the towns of Southeast Asia. These are the mosques and shrines constructed by Tamils, defining and claiming space for the conduct of ritual, and thus of central importance to the imagination of ritual space. It is to these visions of ritual space that we first turn our attention to.

---

[10] Ahmad 1965: 43 (the name is misspelled 'Syed' in this source), Birch 1879: 51–52, *Ciṅkainēcaṉ* (25 June 1888), "Ma-ḷa-ḷa-śrī, Muṉṣi Mukammatu Cayītu", 206.

[11] Birch 1879, *Ciṅkainēcaṉ* (9 June 1890), "Kuṟṟamillātavaṉyāvaṉ?", 186, Samy 2000: 94–97, 101, 117, 137–138; *Ciṅkainēcaṉ* and a single issue of *Ñāṉacūriyaṉ* are available in the Lee Kong Chian Reference Library, Singapore.

[12] *Ciṅkai ñāṉōtayam* (12 June 1907), "Ējaṇṭukaḷ", [unpaginated], *Ciṅkainēcaṉ* (25 June 1888), "Nam pattirikai", 206; lists of subscribers of *Ciṅkainēcaṉ* were published on August 8, 15 and 22, September 5 and 19, October 10 and 17, November 21 and December 12, 1887.

Transcending localities: The imagination of ritual space

Many Muslim rituals can be performed anywhere, provided the place fulfills basic requirements of ritual purity. Yet, nevertheless, some ritual space is demarcated by more permanent structures, and of these the mosque is undoubtedly the most central to Muslim ritual life. The importance mosques had for Tamil-speaking Muslim communities in Southeast Asia becomes evident from the large number of mosques founded by them. One of the most long standing of their settlements in Southeast Asia, Kampong Pali in Melaka, was tellingly named after its mosque (Tam. paḷḷi), rather than after the ethnic group that inhabited the *kampong*, as in the case of other quarters of Melaka.[13] At least seven mosques were established by Tamil-speakers in Singapore, and others at least included South Indians among their founders. Similarly, in Penang, it has been claimed that 22 out of an estimated 67 mosques on the island were established by Indians or Jawi Peranakan.[14] The founding of mosques was an even more urgent concern in mainland Southeast Asia, where the majority population was Buddhist. In December 1887, Tamil-speaking Muslims in Singapore were requested to donate for the construction of a mosque in the Siamese town of Cantappōṉ (perhaps Chanthaburi), and mosques were similarly founded in Burma and Vietnam.[15]

The importance attached to mosques is also mirrored in some of the Tamil-language sources of the period. A poem about a journey to Singapore and Johor, undertaken in 1909, notes various mosques in Singapore, Johor, Melaka and Kuala Lumpur, which the poet visited.[16] In a letter published in *Ciṅkainēcaṉ* in 1888, one Singaporean resident voiced his vision of an ideal mosque

> As a place of rest for those who spend long days praying to God, praised is He and exalted, for those who conduct dhikr [ritual recollection of God; T. T.], for those who engage in other acts of worship, for the scholars and savants, and for

---

[13] Nordin 2007: 141.

[14] For Singapore, cf. Ahmad 1965: 43–61; for Penang, cf. Fujimoto 1988: 79; 'Jawi Peranakan' denotes a person of mixed Indian-Malay parentage, or simply an Indian well integrated into Malay networks.

[15] *Ciṅkainēcaṉ* (12 December 1887), "Aṟivippu", 97, More 2000: 121–122, Taylor 2007: 118, 214, Yegar 1972: 43–44.

[16] Ṣeyku Muhammatu Pāvalar 1910: 9 (stanzas 47, 51), 10 (stanza 55), 16 (stanzas 93–94), 19 (stanza 109), 23 (stanza 131), 24 (139–142).

mendicant fakirs, as well as a site where the Imam [leads] the congregation every day without fail.[17]

This image of the mosque as the central node of Muslim ritual was threatened, however, for the letter was published as part of a campaign to get Singapore's Tamil-speaking Muslims to finance the necessary renovation of the main Tamil mosque in South Bridge Road before parts of it collapsed.[18] Debates about the proper administration of mosques were common among Tamil-speaking Muslims in Southeast Asia. Already by the 1880s, tensions about the administration of the South Bridge Road mosque were simmering, and rumors were being spread about the performance of Muḥammad Sa'īd, the owner of the Jawi Peranakan Company, as trustee.[19] At the same time, similar debates and litigation regarding the administration of the Masjid Kapitan Kling caused several enquiry commissions to be set up in Penang; the same process repeated itself in the 1930s with regard to the Chulia Mosque in Rangoon.[20] In the Straits Settlements, these disputes led to most endowments made by Tamil-speaking Muslims to be taken over by endowment boards controlled by the colonial state. This process was objected to by some Muslims, but others, such as the editor of *Ciṅkainēcaṉ*, considered state-intervention to be indispensable.[21]

Another aspect of the imagination of the mosque as a ritual space seems surprising at first glance, namely, the strong connection of mosques with ethnicity. Mosques are of course open to any Muslim and the situation in colonial Southeast Asia was not different. Yet, nevertheless, specific mosques were clearly identified with certain ethnic groups, who formed the majority of the congregation of a mosque and whose language dominated preaching and other religious activities. Mosques, such as the Chulia Mosque in Rangoon or the Masjid Kapitan Kling in Penang, were already identified with Tamil-speakers through their name. In Singapore, the mosque in South Bridge Road, often simply called the 'Big Mosque' (Tam. periyapaḷḷivāyil) in Tamil, was known to the British as the 'Kling Musjid'.[22] This identification of the mosque with South Indians (Malay.

[17] *Ciṅkainēcaṉ* (29 August 1888), "Periyapaḷḷivāyil", 40; *paratēciyākiya pakkīrkaḷ* may also be rendered as "sojourning paupers" rather than "mendicant fakirs". All translations are my own unless noted otherwise.

[18] *Ciṅkainēcaṉ* (8 August 1887), "Kaṭitam", 28, (15 August 1887), "Cavuttu piriṭciṟōṭ kuttupāp paḷḷivāyilaippaṟṟiya potu viṣayam", 29, (22 August 1887), "Cavuttu piriṭciṟōṭ kuttupāp paḷḷivāyilaippaṟṟiya potu viṣayam", 33; the mosque is nowadays known as Masjid Jamae (Chulia).

[19] *Ciṅkainēcaṉ* (25 June 1888), "Ma-ḷa-ḷa-śrī, Muṉṣi Mukammatu Cayītu", 206.

[20] Fujimoto 1988: 86–90, Khoo 2002: 303–308, Yegar 1972: 43–44.

[21] Cf. *Ciṅkainēcaṉ* (25 February 1889), "Paḷḷivāyilkaḷum tēvālayaṅkaḷum", 134.

[22] *The Singapore Free Press* (21 December 1865), "On the 15th instant ...".

keling) was clearly shared by the local Tamil-speakers: in one article, this mosque as well as the Māriyammaṉ Temple next door were said to "belong to the Klings who came from India".[23]

The identification of mosques with ethnic groups was not only envisioned in texts, but actually expressed by architecture. Most of the early mosques and shrines founded by Tamil-speakers in Southeast Asia share a common architectural style, combining Southeast Asian style buildings with square minarets and the use of decorative niches on the façade. While some of these features go back to Malay or Deccan Muslim architecture, the assemblage undoubtedly invokes the architecture of South India's most holy Muslim site, the Nagore Dargah. Examples are the South Bridge Road Mosque (Masjid Jamac [Chulia]) in Singapore, the Keramat Dato Koya in Penang, the Koyu Masjid in Mandalay, as well as at least one mosque in Saigon.[24] Interestingly, this style seems later to have given way to a more eclectic style, including European and Indo-Saracenic elements. Khoo interprets the reconstruction of the Masjid Kapitan Kling in Penang in a neo-Mughal style in the 1910s as an "architectural expression of empire", the result of the take-over of the mosque by the Endowment Board and the imposition of British tastes on mosque architecture throughout British Malaya.[25] Yet, the changing tastes of Muslim elites seem to have played a similarly important role. The Masjid Abdul Gafoor in Singapore, with its highly eclectic Europeanized architecture, was completed before the endowment was taken over by the Endowments Board in 1927.[26] To Muslim elites in colonial Southeast Asia, new architectural styles may have signified many things, among them modernity, loyalty to the British Empire, past Islamic grandeur, and the transcendence of ethnic boundaries among Muslims.

Mosques were not the only structures marking ritual space. Shrines for Muslim saints were and still are a common sight in many Southeast Asian towns. As in the case of mosques, some of these shrines were constructed by South Indians, reproducing a peculiar South Indian architectural style. Perhaps the most striking case of marking off a particularly South Indian ritual space through a saint shrine is that of the branch shrines of the Nagore Dargah, South India's most popular Muslim saint shrine, which presently exist in Penang and Singapore dating back to the early-nineteenth century.[27] In the colonial period, these shrines were the focus of intense devotional practices, culminating in yearly festivities which

---

[23] *Ciṅkainēcaṉ* (25 February 1889), "Paḷḷivāyilkaḷum tēvālayaṅkaḷum", 134.

[24] Cf. Alfieri 1997: 10–15, Ghulam-Sarwar 1989: 34–35, Lee 2002: 82–83, Pairaudeau 2006: 202.

[25] Khoo 2002: 309.

[26] Lee 2002: 90–93.

[27] Ghulam-Sarwar 1989: 34, Lee 2002: 80–81.

attracted thousands of devotees. In Penang, valuables vowed to the saint were thrown into the sea and believed to be washed up in Nagore a few months later. Acehnese devotees of the saint preferred the more mundane method of handing their gifts, pledged to the saint, to Indian traders for conveyance to Nagore.[28] In 1888, Singaporean devotees (including the Jewish Katz Brothers!) raised $ 1,500 to purchase a crystal chandelier to be sent to the Nagore Dargah in India.[29] That Shāh al-Ḥamīd of Nagore was venerated as a protector of seamen and navigators only helped the spread of his cult.

Far from remaining limited to their respective localities, saints thus played an important role in imagining Muslim space for mobile communities of Muslim traders and seamen in the Bay of Bengal.[30] Consequently, saints and the rituals connected with them also played an important role in the imagination of ritual, if in other ways than in the case of mosques. The main mode of imagining a saint and the connected ritual procedures was through poetry. The late-nineteenth and early-twentieth centuries saw an unprecedented rise in the production of literature on Muslim saints in Tamil.[31] The increase in the production of saint-related literature complicates the perception that the introduction of print led to a strengthening of exactly those tendencies in Islam inimical to the veneration of saints.[32] Print did certainly contribute to such tendencies. But the Tamil evidence shows that far from shying away from print, devotees utilized it vigorously to glorify their saint.

This predominance of devotional poetry, including poetry about saints, is clearly visible in Southeast Asia. The first book published from Singapore, Mukammatu Aptulkātiṟuppulavar's *Muṉājāttuttiraṭṭu*, was a collection of devotional poems about God, the Prophet, as well as a number of mainly South Indian saints. Similar collections of poetry were published throughout Southeast Asia in the late-nineteenth century. In Singapore, Ki. A. Vu. Cevattamaraikkāyar published *Malākkāp piravēcattiraṭṭu*, a poem about the pilgrimage (*jiyārattu*) of a Singaporean gem-trader to the tomb of a saint buried on the island Pulau Besar near Melaka, in 1886. Ten years later, another collection of poetry by Mukammatu Aptulkātiṟuppulavar was published, including some poems

[28] Snouck-Hurgronje 1906, I: 217–219; the observation on Penang is found in the footnote on p.218 made by the translator.

[29] *Ciṅkainēcaṉ* (16 January 1888), "Nākūr tarukāvukkāka paḷiṅkuc ceṭiviḷakku", 118.

[30] Cf. Tschacher 2006.

[31] Cf. More 2004: 202–295, Uvais and Ajmal Kāṉ 1991.

[32] Cf. Robinson 1996, Robinson 1997.

from his earlier collection.[33] The situation in Penang was similar. In 1890, Mukammatu Cultāṉ Maraikkāyar's *Patānanta mālai* was published, a collection of poetry very similar to the two collections by Mukammatu Aptulkātiṟuppulavar from Singapore, with a focus on the saints of the town of Porto Novo in India. Some years later, Kōcā Maraikkāyar published the *Piṉāṅku, uṟcava tiruvalaṅkārac cintu*, a poem on the annual procession held in Penang in honor of the Nagore saint.[34] As late as the Japanese occupation during World War II, a Tamil translation of five Arabic panegyrics in praise of various saints was published in Singapore.[35]

A central concern of all these collections is the space over which the saint has authority, and this space – usually a specific town or some part of such a town – plays an important role in the arrangement of the collection. The ritual recitation of such poems allowed diasporic groups of traders to connect with their hometown and its saints periodically, thereby connecting spaces through ritual performances. The compilation of songs about different saints from different places in a single collection served to imagine these places as part of a common Islamic geography of sacred sites and connected rituals. The most striking example is the collection *Kīrttaṉattiraṭṭu* of 1896. Beginning with songs addressed to God, the Prophet, and 'Abd al-Qādir al-Jīlānī, the collection proceeds to songs in praise of saints of various towns in the Kaveri-Delta, beginning with Nagore. This poetic journey through South India's geography of saints ends with the exaltation of three Singaporean saints. The most important of these saints, Sikandar Shāh, was addressed in a poem written in a Tamilized Malay printed in Tamil script.[36] In the earlier collection, *Muṉājāttuttiraṭṭu*, Sikandar Shāh had similarly been represented as Singapore's central saint, but in a much more South Indian idiom:

---

[33] Cevattamaraikkāyar 1886; Mukammatu Aptulkātiṟuppulavar 1896. I have to thank the Roja Muthiah Research Library, Chennai, for allowing me access to and supplying me with copies of Cevattamaraikkāyar 1886.

[34] Mukammatu Cultāṉ Maraikkāyar 1890; Kōcā Maraikkāyar 1895; the latter text has 1895 as year of publication on the English title-page, but 1 Sha'bān 1313 AH (17 January 1896) on the Tamil one.

[35] Ceyyitu Muhammatu 1942 (?). I could not find the year of publication mentioned, but the name 'Syonan-to' for Singapore shows that it was published during the Japanese occupation. The date of publication is taken from Chan 2008: 249 (entry 1815).

[36] Mukammatu Aptulkātiṟuppulavar 1896: 48.

O Sikandar Ṣāḥib,
Enveloped by fame,
Who graciously came [to us] so that the City of Singapore,
Engulfed by the Ganges,
May see [him],[37]

Give support and always protect [us],
Whenever [we] are subject to the deceitful nets of those ladies,
Covered with garlands
Which surround [their] breasts.[38]

Another poem, published in 1910, about a journey to Singapore and Johor, does not only mention the saints and their shrines, but also rituals like the recitation of the *fātiḥa*, the first chapter of the Koran, performed at the shrines of Ḥabīb Nūḥ and Sikandar Shāh in Singapore and at tombs of members of the royal family in Johor.[39]

In addition to the more permanent marking of ritual space through permanent structures, and by writing poetry about this space, there was also a temporary marking off of ritual space in the course of rituals through processions. In both Penang and Rangoon, processions were taken around the streets during the annual festival of the Nagore saint, much as is still done in Nagore.[40] The *Muṉājāttuttiraṭṭu* of 1872 contained a 'picture-poem' or *cittirakavi* on the saint of Nagore in the shape of a processional chariot (Tam. iratapantam).[41] A report on a disturbance which occurred during the Nagore festival in Singapore in 1857 does not mention processions, but a temporary fencing off of space in front of the Singaporean branch-shrine of the Nagore Dargah.[42]

Yet, the most spectacular inscriptions of ritual space on the cityscape of the Straits Settlements were the annual *muḥarram*-processions. Despite the fact that virtually all Tamil-speaking Muslims are Sunnites, *muḥarram*-processions were highly popular, not only in the Straits Settlements, but also in India, commonly drawing the ire of nineteenth-

[37] *ciṅkainakar kāṭci peṟa vantaruḷum ... cikkantar cākipē* would more commonly translate as 'Sikandar Ṣāḥib ...who graciously came to obtain the sight of the City of Singapore', but in the light of the common trope of 'obtaining the sight of' (*terici-*) a saint or his tomb (cf. Ṣeyku Muhammatu Pāvalar 1910: 7 (stanza 40)), the above translation seems more probable.

[38] Mukammatu Aptulkātiṟuppulavar 1872: 19 (stanza 19).

[39] Ṣeyku Muhammatu Pāvalar 1910: 7–8 (stanzas 40–41), 10 (stanza 58), 19 (stanza 110).

[40] For Penang, cf. Ghulam-Sarwar 1989: 33, Kōcā Maraikkāyar 1895; for Rangoon, cf. the evidence provided by the *Iraṅkōṉ nākūr kantūrip pāṭṭu* discussed below.

[41] Mukammatu Aptulkātiṟuppulavar 1872: 90 and illustration on p. 92 [unpaginated].

[42] *The Singapore Free Press* (26 February 1857), "Coroner's Inquest", statements of Arthur Pennefather and Charles Cashin.

century Sunnite scholars.[43] In the Straits Settlements, the most peculiar aspect of these processions was their control by two 'secret societies', the 'White Flags' and the 'Red Flags', which existed both in Penang and in Singapore.

The rivalry between these two groups led to frequent quarrels and riots during the processions. In the 1860s, both cities experienced major riots which led the authorities to take a much tougher stance against processions. The Penang riot of 1867, which lasted for ten days, was much more severe than the disturbances in Singapore in 1864. Yet what makes the Singapore case so interesting is the fact that the ritual background of the disturbance becomes much clearer if compared to the Penang case.[44] At the root of the disturbance lay three acts of ritual provocation of the 'White Flags' by the 'Red Flags'. Firstly, in 1864, the 'Red Flags' seem for the first time to have taken precedence in the processions, an honor usually granted to the 'White Flags'. Secondly, the 'Red Flags' in 1864 marched down Cross Street in daytime, apparently the center of 'White Flag' territory. Thirdly, they destroyed the "symbol of the Mohamedan religion", possibly the *tābūt* of the 'White Flags', the processional image of Imām Ḥusayn's tomb.[45] The leader of the 'Red Flags', Saiboo Attai, was quoted as stating before the procession that "I want my procession to go down Cross Street".[46] Obviously, the disturbance arose over a conflict about ritual 'honors', a common phenomenon also in nineteenth-century South India. British observers noted the importance of processions in ritual ranking, though unsurprisingly, they interpreted this only as a vain desire of the members of 'secret societies' "to surpass their rivals in the grandeur of their public displays". In this, they felt supported by the poorer Indians, who were "deprived of one-third of their earnings to pay for the mummeries".[47]

While *muharram*-processions receded in many places in Southeast Asia in the course of the second half of the nineteenth century, they were continued in South India, and Tamil-speaking Muslims settled in Southeast Asia maintained an interest in them. In 1888, a letter was published in *Ciṅkainēcaṉ,* from Porto Novo in India, describing a disturbance during the annual *muḥarram*-procession in that town. The author of the

[43] Cf. e. g. Sayyid Muḥammad 1963: 505–506, Uwise 1990: 212–213; for a detailed description of *muḥarram*-rituals by a nineteenth-century Urdu-speaking South Indian Sunnite cf. Shurreef 1991: chapter XV.

[44] Cf. Mahani Musa 1999: 162–166.

[45] Cf. *The Singapore Free Press* (19 April 1866), "Criminal Session" (quote by Ninamsah), cf. also *The Singapore Free Press* (23 November 1865), "The following is ...".

[46] *The Singapore Free Press* (19 April 1866), "Criminal Session" (quote by Ninamsah).

[47] *The Singapore Free Press* (19 October 1865), "We publish with pleasure ..."; cf. also *The Singapore Free Press* (19 April 1866), "The following Copy ...".

letter claimed that such disturbances occurred year after year at processions, as 'factions' (Tam. kakṣi or kaṭci) based in different streets came to compete with each other. The letter-writer from Porto Novo also noted, with a mixture of disdain and irony, that when some youths began to attack the police during the disturbance, the 'big men' (Tam. periyamaṉitar) stopped their own fight in the alleys and turned to watch the 'fun' (Tam. vēṭikkai), as if "a street-fight is pleasing [lit. cooling] to the eye".[48] It is this depiction of rituals as spectacular events that perhaps most characterizes the imagination of rituals in the colonial period.

Spectacular amusements: Rituals as events

Prior to the nineteenth century, the imagination of rituals in texts was predominantly normative and prescriptive. Texts focused more on what was to be done in a ritual (and what not) than on the description of the performance. Some texts dealt extensively with questions of religious import, including rituals. Poems continued to be produced into the nineteenth century, such as Kātiṟu Mukiyyittīṉ Aṇṇāviyār's *Pikhu mālai* of 1863.[49] Yet, from the late nineteenth century onwards, prose became the main medium in which religious obligations and ritual norms were discussed. Such works could cover the prime acts of Muslim worship comprehensively, as in the manner of the *Pikhu mālai*, or they could focus on a specific issue, such as prayer or marriage laws. There were even tracts addressed peculiarly to women and children.[50] Some such works were also published in the Straits Settlements, such as a tract dealing with the conduct of a Sufi novice (Arab. murīd) in question-and-answer form.[51]

Yet the nineteenth century was to bring major changes to the way ritual was imagined in texts. The normative texts did of course not vanish, but they were soon complemented by a new vision of ritual, one that seems at least partly to be connected to a new type of texts, namely newspapers.

---

[48] *Ciṅkainēcaṉ* (26 November 1888), "Kaṭitam", 84.

[49] Kātiṟu Mukiyyittīṉ 1990; this poem was published with a commentary by Kulām Kātiṟu Nāvalar in 1901.

[50] Cf. Shu'ayb 1993: chapter 6, Tschacher 2001: 23–33; a translation of one of the most important religious manuals of the period is Sayyid Muḥammad 1963.

[51] Ṣākumukammatu 1878; in the copy utilized by me, which is kept in the Lee Kong Chian Reference Library, Singapore, the year of publication seems to have been stamped onto the copy at a later date. Nevertheless, the year 1878 is consistent with the fact that the book must have been printed before the death of Muḥammad Sa'īd in 1888 when the press was still called 'Sa'īdī Press'; after his death, it was usually called 'Jawi Peranakan Press', cf. Proudfoot 1993: 605, 633.

To put it in modern parlance, rituals in the nineteenth century became 'events'. Rituals were now not simply practices that needed to be normatively regulated, but that could actually be described and reported about. This was true of a whole plethora of ritual practices and performances. The most elaborate coverage was reserved to the two main Muslim holidays, *'īd al-fiṭr*, at the end of the fasting month, and *'īd al-aḍḥā*, in commemoration of Abraham's willingness to sacrifice his son, which takes place during the *hajj*. The Singaporean newspaper *Ciṅkainēcaṉ*, for example, regularly published articles and whole supplements on these days. Articles on *'īd al-aḍḥā,* for example, consist of a mélange of praises of the holiday and the *hajj*, stories and depictions concerning the rewards for those who practice these rituals, and admonitions regarding the rules to be observed.[52] What was new about these publications was not their content (indeed, the editor commonly 'recycled' material published in earlier years), but the temporal connection between the performance and the publication, linking the text to the actual 'event' in a different manner than was the case in religious handbooks.

This becomes even clearer when looking at less 'normative' rituals, such as the holidays of certain saints or the celebration of the birthday of the Prophet. In these cases, despite the fact that news about these rituals was much shorter than in the case of the main holidays, we are presented with much more circumstantial evidence, such as the organizers of the ritual, time, place, participants, etc.[53] A good example is provided by the following short notice published in the bi-monthly *Ciṅkai ñāṉōtayam,* regarding the annual holiday of 'Abd al-Qādir al-Jīlānī celebrated in 1907: "The *mawlid*-assembly of Jakata Caṟkuru Kuttupu Ṟappāṉi Mukiyittīṉ Aptul Kātiṟu Jīlāṉi Āṇṭavar was performed and completed in an auspicious manner for eleven days by people possessing every good quality at the piece-good shop of Mr. Yā. Cultāṉaptulkātiṟumaraikkāyar".[54] The same issue contained a long letter by someone who attended the proceedings, furnishing many more details about the proceedings of this holiday, including the names of those who financed the assembly each day, the food served and gifts distributed, the number

[52] *Ciṅkainēcaṉ* (29 August 1887), "Hajjup perunāḷ", 37, (13 August 1888), "Ītul aluhā veṉṉum hajjup perunāḷ", 26, *Ciṅkainēcaṉ anupantam* (5 August 1889), "Ītul aluhā veṉṉum hajjup perunāḷ". For a similar type of publication concerning *'īd al-fiṭr,* cf. *Ciṅkainēcaṉ* (27 May 1889), "Nōṉpup perunāḷ", 185.

[53] This did not prevent the editor of *Ciṅkainēcaṉ* from 'recycling' passages even in these short articles; cf. *Ciṅkainēcaṉ* (12 December 1887), "Mavulitu", 97–98, *Ciṅkainēcaṉ* (19 November 1888), "Mavulitu", 78.

[54] *Ciṅkai ñāṉōtayam* (12 June 1907), "Mavlītu", 116.

of guests, and the names of some noteworthy participants.[55] Similarly, sermons given by visitors from India would be noted in newspapers. Conversely, when the controversial publisher P. Daud Shah (Pā. Tāvutṣā) visited Malaya in 1925, his journal, *Tārul islām,* informed readers in India where and about what topic he had delivered sermons.[56]

The greater focus on rituals as 'events' initiated by the newspapers also seems to have had a close correspondence in poetry. Increasingly, poems began to be composed not only about specific saints, but about the rituals and festivals conducted in honor of specific saints at specific places. In Hindu poetry, the genres of *kīrttaṉam* (a devotional song) and *vaḻinaṭaiccintu* (songs of travelers, including pilgrims), in which indeed many of these Muslim poems were composed, provide some parallels to this trend as early as the seventeenth century.[57] Yet, the poems composed in the late-nineteenth and early-twentieth century seem to have become much more specific than their predecessors. The first such poem written in Southeast Asia, entitled *Kūttāṉallūr, aptulmukammatucākipolipēril kantūriccintu*, still deals with the annual festival of a saint buried in India.[58] But with the publication of Kōcā Maraikkāyar's *Piṉāṅku, uṟcava tiruvalaṅkārac cintu* in January 1896, we get for the first time a poem about a festival enacted in Southeast Asia, namely the annual festival of the Nagore saint as celebrated in Penang. A similar, though much shorter poem, *Iraṅkōṉ nākūr kantūrip pāṭṭu*, was written about the Nagore-festival in Rangoon by Pō. Nā. Cīṉi Muhammatu Pāvalar.[59]

What characterizes these poems is their attention to the specifics of place and time. Thus, Kōcā Maraikkāyar follows the procession through Penang, describing route, sights, and people along the way. In one stanza a whole catalogue of native fruits is given, which abounds in Malay words for fruits in general as well as specific fruits.[60] Similarly, the author of the *Iraṅkōṉ nākūr kantūrip pāṭṭu* describes not only the actual ritual proceedings, the procession and its route through Rangoon as well as the mosque, but also the festive crowd and the "shops where gaudy girls sell peanuts, puffed rice, and round rice flakes".[61]

---

[55] *Ciṅkai ñāṉōtayam* (12 June 1907), "Maulītukkaḷari", 137–138.

[56] *Ciṅkainēcaṉ* (13 May 1889), "Kōṭṭār, Hāji Ceyku Mukiyittīṉ Ālim ibuṉu Ceyku Mukammatu Leppai Ālim Cākipu", 178 [printed as p.179], *Tārul islām* (March 1925), "Ellāṅkā"vil jumĀp piracaṅkam", 135, (April 1925), 183–185, (May 1925), 232, (June 1925), 275, (July 1925), 326–327 [all under heading "Malāy nāṭṭil namatu āciriyar"].

[57] Cf. Zvelebil 1974: 221–224.

[58] Mukammatu Aptulkātiṟuppulavar 1872: 73–88; the poem was republished in Mukammatu Aptulkātiṟuppulavar 1896: 49–58. I quote from the latter edition.

[59] Kōcā Maraikkāyar 1895; Cīṉi Muhammatu Pāvalar's poem is printed in Cītakkāti Tamiḻppaṇik Kaḻakam 1980: 60–62; the exact date of this poem is unclear.

[60] Kōcā Maraikkāyar 1895: 21 (stanza 29).

[61] Cītakkāti Tamiḻppaṇik Kaḻakam 1980: 61 (stanza 3).

These images of ritual proceedings and their surroundings should not be taken to be 'realistic'. While there is a clear tendency towards giving these poems a 'local' flavor, the poems are still highly formalized and full of conventional tropes, which include the novelties and 'exotic' items on display during festivals. One of these 'novel' items that apparently all poets wished to insert into their description of these festivals were globe-lamps, designated with the loan-word *kuḷōppar*, usually as part of a general section on the lamps that illuminate the shrine where the festival takes place.[62] While the imagination of ritual was extended to include depictions of the novel and the exotic, these were immediately conventionalized into new tropes that poets could follow in crafting what were after all highly 'traditional' poems.

What is striking about these poems describing an individual festival is, furthermore, their glorification of the spectacular and carnivalesque. For British observers, 'native' festivals and processions were simply "orgies", "absurdities" and "great nuisances", which blocked up public roads, threatened the safety of the city through the innumerable torches carried, and kept the police from going its rounds.[63] In contrast, Tamil poetry on Muslim festivals celebrated all those aspects which the British abhorred. Take the following example from the *Iraṅkōṉ nākūr kantūrip pāṭṭu*:

See:
They pray to Allah, the Only One, speaking 'Amen';
The scholars gather and recite *mawlid*;
Say, isn't the food excellent?
'The Indian[64] gentleman is a good man', say the Burmese
and place their offerings straight away;
There the poets sing their lively poems,
In honor of Qādir Ṣāḥib Walī.
[See] the wrestlers' wrestling bouts,
And [observe] the fun of simple young men arguing,
And [watch] the fencers' show, with sticks a few feet long,
And also [note] the poem sung by Cīṉi Muhammatu.[65]

The central term, repeated several times in this stanza, is *vēṭikkai*, 'fun, amusement, show'. The displays of wrestlers and fencers are seamlessly

[62] Cītakkāti Tamiḻppaṇik Kaḻakam 1980: 60 (stanza 1), Kōcā Maraikkāyar 1895: 3 (stanza 2), Mukammatu Aptulkātiṟuppulavar 1896: 49, Ṣeyku Muhammatu Pāvalar 1910: 4 (stanza 21).

[63] *The Singapore Free Press* (12 October 1865), "The leading men ..." (absurdities), "The orgies ..." (orgies), (19 October 1865), "We publish ..." (nuisances); cf. also *The Singapore Free Press* (26 May 1842), "We learn that ...", (19 April 1849) "Below we give ...".

[64] *kallā*, from Burmese *kala*, 'Indian'.

[65] Cītakkāti Tamiḻppaṇik Kaḻakam 1980: 61–62 (stanza 4).

integrated with the more narrowly ritual and religious acts of worshipping God, placing offerings to the saint, and reciting panegyric poetry. Already in the refrain (Tam. pallavi) of this poem, we are told about the festival that "the amusements (Tam. vēṭikkai) there are manifold".[66] The other poems as well put much stress on visualizing the festival for their audience, and the *Piṉāṅku, uṟcava tiruvalaṅkārac cintu* describes it as the grace of the saint "to take on a joyful mind and to see the coming of the holiday which occurs in Penang".[67]

These descriptions of the spectacular nature of these festivities were not only imagined by poets, but were also part of the perception of participants, as the statement of a young coolie, Meerah Hoossain, during the inquest held upon the 1857 disturbance at the festival of the Nagore saint in Singapore, shows. He stated that he had left his house at Kampong Glam that evening "for the purpose of witnessing the fun at Telook [sic] Ayer".[68] The festival attracted a large number of people, who, beside participating in the ritual, also took pleasure in the other diversions from their daily drudgery offered by the festival. One witness, probably Urdu-speaking, stated that he had been "sitting down close to the Mosque at the time listening to the Music".[69] Other coolies took the opportunity and tried to turn the festive mood into some additional money for themselves, such as a young man stowing cargo on ships who sold coffee during the festival.[70] Even Englishmen "went out to see the Kling play", describing the music, dances, and even a small roundabout which were all part of the celebrations.[71] Even those who were critical of such pageants could not but notice that they obviously provided 'fun', or *vēṭikkai*, to those who participated in them.[72]

It seems reasonable to conclude that, in the course of the nineteenth century, it became more and more common among Tamil-speaking Muslims to give voice to a vision of rituals that went beyond the normative and prescriptive to grant space to the experiential aspect of rituals. The rise of newspapers and literary genres that allowed such an individuation of rituals against their normative background certainly

---

66 Cītakkāti Tamiḻppaṇik Kaḻakam 1980: 60 (*pallavi*).

67 Kōcā Maraikkāyar 1895: 5 (stanza 5).

68 *The Singapore Free Press* (26 February 1857), "Coroner's Inquest", statement of Meerah Hoossain.

69 *The Singapore Free Press* (26 February 1857), "Coroner's Inquest", statement of Fatey Allee Shah.

70 *The Singapore Free Press* (26 February 1857), "Coroner's Inquest", statement of China Tomby.

71 *The Singapore Free Press* (26 February 1857), "Coroner's Inquest", statement of Charles Cashin.

72 Cf. *The Singapore Free Press* (19 October 1865), "We publish ...", *Ciṅkainēcaṉ* (26 November 1888), "Kaṭitam", 84.

speeded this process along. For Tamil-speaking Muslims in Southeast Asia, this also made it possible to use the new medium of print to carve out a peculiar niche for describing their own vision of rituals and festivals by describing the distinctive and exotic surroundings and items, but most of all, the peculiar people and individuals which joined in the celebrations.

Ritual participation: Images of individuals and communities

What about the people who organized or simply just participated in ritual activities? One of the salient features of the textual record is the concern it places on speaking about individuals and communities who engaged in ritual. Even more noteworthy is that much of this attention is directed toward ritual procedures that most Muslims at that time would have considered supererogatory: participation in the daily prayers, fasting, or the sacrifice on *'īd al-aḍḥā* are not noted, but the funding of feasts and *mawlid*-assemblies, the participation in processions, and the gifts and donations made to a shrine or mosque are recorded. Lists of donors were a common sight in newspapers of the period, no matter if the object of the donation was a mosque in Siam, a crystal-chandelier for the Nagore Dargah, a feast on the birthday of the Prophet, or an assembly for the recitation of panegyric poetry in honor of 'Abd al-Qādir al-Jīlānī.[73] While the prescribed ritual practices were the duty of any Muslim, and thus not worthy of any further notice if performed properly, these supererogatory rituals provided the opportunity to do additional good deeds and simultaneously project one's identity as a generous Muslim to the wider community. As testaments of the period prove, this wish persisted beyond death: several testaments included provisions for funding annual feasts and *mawlid*-recitation.[74]

But the newspapers were not the only way to project individual participation in communal rituals. Poetry could similarly imagine the participation of individuals in a ritual. The most striking example is the *Piṉāṅku, uṟcava tiruvalaṅkārac cintu*, which does not only depict the sights along the route of the procession, but is populated by dozens of Tamil-speaking Muslims, often identified by occupation and hometown, who went along the procession, such as "valued, prosperous

[73] *Ciṅkainēcaṉ* (12 December 1887), "Aṟivippu", 97, (16 January 1888), "Nākūr tarukāvukkāka paḷiṅkuc ceṭiviḷakku", 118, (18 November 1889), "Ṟacūluṭaiya mavlitukkaḷaṟi", 78, *Ciṅkai ñāṉōtayam* (12 June 1907), "Maulītukkaḷari", 137–138.

[74] Cf. e. g. Kyshe 1885, I: 269, *The Straits Settlements Law Reports* (1936): "In *re* Abdul Guny Abdullasa, deceased", 108.

Yūcupukkaṉi, handsome Kātiru Cākipucapuṟali together with worthy Meytīṉ, and honorable Mukammatukkaṉi, conducting the procession".[75] Similarly, the main poem of *Malākkāp piravēcattiraṭṭu* is not simply in honor of a saint, but depicting the pilgrimage of one particular named individual, the gem-trader Tā. Mīṟācākipu, to the tomb of Ceykicumāyīl Oliyullā in Melaka.[76]

In naming individual participation in ritual activities, newspapers and poems came, in some respects, to play a role not unlike that of the inscriptions of earlier years. Indeed, a newspaper can be seen as a very apt medium to record the 'fluid' and impermanent exchanges typical of supererogatory Muslim ritual in colonial Southeast Asia.[77] There is no reason to doubt that individuals considered the mention of their names as people financing a ritual as important for both their religious as well as social status. 'Self-advertising' does not seem in any way to have been considered distasteful. Rather, potential donors were actively lured by the prospect to have their names made public.[78] But this does of course not mean that this was the only reason for publishing individuals' names. In the case of the *Piṉāṅku, uṟcava tiruvalaṅkārac cintu*, one may perhaps argue that, through the medium of the poem, those individuals mentioned in it came to participate perpetually in this imagined procession.[79]

Individuals could also be censored through the same media if their behavior was considered to be improper. Thus, in 1889, *Ciṅkainēcaṉ,* in a long article, warned its readers about one Aptulkapūr, who claimed to be raising funds for the construction of a mosque in Singapore's Little India, but who in the eyes of the newspaper was only searching for new means to enrich himself. History decided in favor of Aptulkapūr, for the mosque which was finally constructed on the specified site in the early twentieth century is nowadays called Masjid Abdul Gafoor and was declared a national monument in 1979.[80]

It was not only individuals, though, who sponsored rituals and were consequently mentioned in texts about ritual. For the first time, late-nineteenth-century sources allow us to gain a better understanding of the corporate aspect of ritual performances among Tamil-speaking Muslims. The corporate groups who engaged in funding rituals were apparently usually based on occupation or hometown, or in some cases both. The

---

[75] Kōcā Maraikkāyar 1895: 4 (stanza 3).

[76] Cevvattamaraikkāyar 1886: 22-34.

[77] Cf. Narayana Rao, Shulman and Subrahmanyam 1992: 67–72.

[78] Cf. *Ciṅkainēcaṉ* (12 December 1887), "Aṟivippu", 97.

[79] For the question of 'self-advertisement' in medieval Tamil inscriptions, cf. Orr 2006: XVI.

[80] Lee 2002: 90–93, *Ciṅkainēcaṉ* (17 June 1889), "Cuṇṇāmpuk kampattup paḷḷivāyilum ciṟāṅkūṉṟōṭ maiyattukkollaiyum", 193.

most salient group in our sources of the period is the boatmen. In 1857, the imam of the Nagore Dargah shrine in Singapore mentioned "each separate class of people having a night set apart during the festival for their particular observance", and that, during one of the nights, the ritual proceedings were organized by the boatmen.[81] Thirty years later, *Ciṅkainēcaṉ* commented that since about the late 1860s the boatmen[82] had set the income of six ferryboats aside to finance annually the performance of *mawlid*-poetry and a feast on the birthday of the Prophet, as well as the festivals of 'Abd al-Qādir al-Jīlānī and Shāh al-Ḥamīd of Nagore.[83] Other occupational groups appear as well in the evidence. Thus, in 1889, the festival of 'Abd al-Qādir al-Jīlānī was organized jointly by warehouse coolies and police peons, while on the other end of the social spectrum, the chief merchants of Tirumalairayanpattinam (then called Grande-Aldée), near Karaikkal, organized a similar event on the same occasion in 1907.[84]

One final striking feature of the imagination of ritual among Tamil-speaking Muslims in colonial Southeast Asia is the strong sense of ethnic diversity and at times something I would call the 'ethnicization' of ritual, i. e. the ascription of ritual practices not to 'religions' but to ethnic groups. These tendencies resulted both from the much more cosmopolitan character of the metropolises of colonial Southeast Asia as compared to the small towns of the South Indian countryside that Tamil-speaking Muslims hailed from, and also from the practice of the colonial state to structure its relationship to Asian communities in terms of 'race', rather than 'caste' as was the case in India.[85]

In the poetry of the colonial period, the most important expression of this ethnic consciousness is the depiction of the participation of diverse ethnic groups in various ritual performances. We have already seen this in the stanza from the *Iraṅkōṉ nākūr kantūrip pāṭṭu* quoted above, where Burmese devotees of Shāh al-Ḥamīd of Nagore are depicted as placing offerings for the saint. In another stanza of the same poem, we hear of Chinese and Bengalis wandering about the festival site.[86] The *Piṉāṅku,*

---

[81] *The Singapore Free Press* (26 February 1857), "Coroner's Inquest", statement of Emaum Saib Lebbay.

[82] *tammāṅkukkārap piḷḷaikaḷ*; *tammāṅku* < Malay *tambang*, ferryboat.

[83] *Ciṅkainēcaṉ* (12 December 1887), "Mavulitu", 97; cf. also *Ciṅkainēcaṉ* (19 November 1888), "Mavulitu", 78, (18 November 1889), "Ṟacūluṭaiya mavlitukkaḷaṟi", 78.

[84] *Ciṅkainēcaṉ* (2 December 1889), "Kantūri", 86, *Ciṅkai ñāṉōtayam* (12 June 1907), "Maulītukkaḷari", 137–138.

[85] Cf. PuruShotam 1998; it should be noted, though, that Tamil-speakers in Southeast Asia at that time often denoted both the concept of 'race' as well as that of 'caste' with the term *cāti* or *jāti*; cf. e. g. *Tārul islām* (August 1925), "Em Malāy nāṭṭu aṉupavam", 342, *malāy jātiyār*, 'Malays'.

[86] Cītakkāti Tamiḻppaṇik Kaḻakam 1980: 62 (stanza 5).

urcava tiruvalaṅkārac cintu is even more concerned with ethnic variety. Already in Cevattamaraikkāyar's preface (Tam. cirappuppāyiram) to the poem, Penang is described as an "attractive city excelling in the beauty of Malay women".[87] In the poem itself, two stanzas of a total of 44 lines list the ethnic groups that participate in the festival. The first of these stanzas presents a more 'realistic' picture of the ethnic groups present in Penang, including e. g. Malays, Klings (here obviously meaning Tamil-speaking Muslims), Chinese, Hindus, Chettiyars (Tam. ceṭṭiyār),[88] Bengalis, Japanese, Andhras,[89] Paraiyars (Tam. paraiyar), Malabarians, and Portuguese,[90] incidentally illustrating the inclusion of 'ethnic', 'religious', and 'caste' groups under the term *cāti*. In the second stanza, the poet presents ethnic groups according to a more traditional concept, that of the *patiṉeṇpūmi* or 'eighteen countries' (here called the *patiṉeṇjāti* or 'eighteen communities').[91] Part of this cosmopolitan *imaginaire* was also the use of local words. The Burmese, venerating Shāh al-Ḥamīd, call him by the Burmese word for 'Indian', *kala*, while the reader of the *Piṉāṅku, urcava tiruvalaṅkārac cintu* is informed beforehand that the poem contains words from many languages such as Arabic, Persian, Hindi, Malay, English, and Chinese.[92]

The link between ethnicity and ritual was also made in other contexts. As already mentioned, certain mosques in the cosmopolitan centers of colonial Southeast Asia came to be associated with specific ethnic groups. Similarly, the link was made between certain ritual practices and the ethnic groups conducting them. One example would be the practice of Mandi Safar, the taking of a purifying bath on the last Wednesday of the month of Ṣafar. In 1889, *Ciṅkainēcaṉ* published a note stating that "all the Malays and Javanese staying in Kampong Glam celebrated Mandi Safar in Geylang on last Wednesday with very curious distractions [*vēṭikkaikaḷuṭaṉ*]".[93] In 1925, Daud Shah was less positive about what he heard regarding Mandi Safar: "It goes without saying that there is no Muslim seeing the disgraceful things going on at this [Mandi Safar] who does not shed blood from [his] eyes".[94] However different their perspectives, both sources agree in identifying the practice particularly with Malays, which is especially interesting since Mandi Safar has come

---

87 Kōcā Maraikkāyar 1895: preface, 2.

88 If *nakarattiṉar* stands for *nakarattār*.

89 *kōraṅki* probably stands for 'Coringhi', a term used for Telugu-speakers in Burma; cf. Yegar 1972: 118.

90 *tōrppokkīcu* should be *pōrttokkīcu*.

91 Kōcā Maraikkāyar 1895: 4–6 (stanza 5–6).

92 Kōcā Maraikkāyar 1895: preface, 8.

93 *Ciṅkainēcaṉ* (28 October 1889), "Caparmaṇṭi", 66.

94 *Tārul islām* (August 1925), "Em Malāy nāṭṭu aṉupavam", 346.

to be interpreted as an example of the influence of Indian practices on Malay culture.[95]

Yet there was another actor in the discourse linking ethnicity and ritual – the colonial state. As mentioned, the British colonial government put a much greater stress on the concept of 'race' than on 'religion'. This led to cases where colonial discourse privileged the interpretation of a ritual as 'ethnic' rather than 'religious'. This is especially salient in the case of the practice known as *kantūri* in Tamil and *kenduri* in Malay. In both languages, the term predominantly signifies a ritual feast, though the occasion for such feasts may differ. In Malay, almost any feast with a vaguely 'religious' connection may be designated as *kenduri*, such as feasts at life-cycle events or in memory of the dead. In Tamil, the term signifies especially feasts on the holiday of saints, and as a consequence, it is often employed as signifying the holiday as such.[96]

The practice came to the notice of the British through the medium of wills. The seminal court case for the future engagement of the colonial state with *kantūris*, *Fatimah & Ors. v. D. Logan & Ors.*, happened in 1871. The case dealt with the will of Mahomed Noordin, a wealthy and influential South-India-born merchant in Penang.[97] While none of the people involved in the case had brought up the issue, the judge questioned whether a trust set up to provide for various annual 'kandoories' on the anniversary of the testator's decease was charitable according to the law, since only then could a perpetual trust be set up. Though the judge conceded, "I have no means of knowing the meaning of the word kandoorie except from the context", he decided that the trust was void, for he was unable to see "how it can be of any public utility to give feasts".[98] This decision triggered several other cases, since the descendants of testators now saw a chance to have the property that constituted a trust for *kantūris* to be transferred to them by having the trust declared void.[99] In one of these cases, a definition of 'kunduri' was given as "[a] 'Kunduri' *is a Malay word* signifying a feast".[100] This case apparently established a connection between the term *kantūri* and Malays, which led to a quite unexpected result in another case, decided in 1936, with refer-

---

[95] Cf. Nagata 1993: 521, Singaravelu 1984.

[96] For the Malay usage, cf. McAllister 1990: 27–30, Snouck-Hurgronje 1906, I: 214; most accounts of Tamil Muslims simply explain the term with reference to a saint's festival (cf. Bayly 1989: 143, More 2004: 123), but the original meaning as feast is evinced by the *Kantūri paṭalam* of the *Atapu mālai*, a nineteenth-century poem discussed below; cf. Sām Naynā Labbay n. d.: 76–78 and also Shurreef 1991: 164–165.

[97] Kyshe 1885, I: 255–272; for more on Mahomed Noordin, cf. Fujimoto 1988: 59–62.

[98] Kyshe 1885, I: 269.

[99] Cf. Kyshe 1885, I: 580–581, Kyshe 1890: 212–213.

[100] Kyshe 1890: 212; emphasis mine.

ence to a will from Penang dating to 1908. In his will, the testator Abdul Guny Abdullasa had provided for the annual performance of three ceremonies on the birthday of the Prophet and the holidays of 'Abd al-Qādir al-Jīlānī and Shāh al-Ḥamīd, which included the recitation of prayers by 'Lebays'[101] and the distribution of food – exactly the type of rituals that *Ciṅkainēcaṉ* would have called a *kantūri*.[102] Yet, while the party challenging this trust in court claimed that the ceremonies indeed constituted *kantūris* and that the trust was thus void, the judge thought otherwise: "There is, I think, a clear distinction between the ceremony enjoined and 'kandoories'". The judge gave a couple of reasons for his opinion, such as stating that the ceremonies were not meant to perpetuate the name of the deceased and that the distribution of food was just incidental to them. "Moreover", he added, "the deceased ... *was not a Malay*".[103] The close association in British eyes of *kantūris* with Malays ultimately led to Tamil *kantūris* being recognized as charitable, but not under the name *kantūri*.

'This-worldly' intercessions Rituals and the muted discourse of reform

Justifying his decision to consider Mahomed Noordin's trust for *kantūris* to be void in 1871, the judge lamented that, though the will had stated that these celebrations were "according to the Mahomedan religion or custom", "[n]o evidence was given ... whether they are enjoined by the Mahomedan religion".[104] Had the judge attempted to enquire more deeply into the matter, the answer may not have been straightforward. It has been claimed that the nineteenth and twentieth centuries witnessed "a shift in the focus of Muslim piety from the next world to this one".[105] An element of this shift was the increased tendency to criticize practices which were not perceived to be enjoined by canonical Muslim sources and those which aimed at improving a person's status in the afterlife, such as the creation of endowments for *kantūris*. What about such 'reformist' discourse among Tamil-speaking Muslims in colonial Southeast Asia? The simple answer is that there is currently not much evidence of such discourse, at least as far as the period before World War I is concerned. It

[101] The term 'Labbai' (*leppai*) originally denotes a type of minor religious functionary, and not a Muslim sub-community, as usually claimed; cf. Tschacher 2009: 52–53.

[102] *Ciṅkainēcaṉ* (2 December 1889), "Kantūri", 86.

[103] *The Straits Settlements Law Reports* (1936): "In *re* Abdul Guny Abdullasa, deceased", 111; emphasis mine.

[104] Kyshe 1885, I: 269.

[105] Robinson 1997: 1.

would be wrong to assume that a 'reformist' discourse was unknown among Tamil-speaking Muslims in Southeast Asia. Quite in contrast, *Ciṅkainēcaṉ* regularly published articles on important reformers, such as Jamāl al-Dīn al-Afghānī.[106] But the stress in these was on political and general educational revival, not on the reform of ritual. Indeed, *Ciṅkainēcaṉ* clearly supported practices such as feasting in honor of saints or intercessory beliefs.[107]

Tamil-speaking Muslims did not remain untouched after the reformist discourse gained in strength among the Malays after 1900. Indeed, one of the most strident Indonesian reformers, Ahmad Hassan (d. 1957), was a Singapore-born Tamil Muslim.[108]

It may thus be that further research will uncover more evidence for 'reformist' discourse among Tamil-speaking Muslims in Southeast Asia. Much may also have been lost, as such discourse often articulated itself through pamphlets and handbills that have not survived.[109] Yet, even in the reformist sources that did survive, little is said about debates concerning ritual. Daud Shah, else a severe critic of practices such as the celebration of *kantūris*, remained silent about such issues in his travelogue of his journey to Malaya in 1925, reserving all criticism of ritual for Malay practices such as Mandi Safar, dramatic performances, and the Ronggeng dance.[110] In the exchange of handbills and the 'Muslim Libel Case', caused by Daud Shah's visit to Singapore, questions of doctrine and religious authority were debated, but hardly any ritual controversies, apart from a statement during the Libel Case by the defendant about the first plaintiff that the latter would ask "what would happen if you do not pray" when reminded that the Koran asked Muslims to pray.[111] An important Tamil Muslim community-leader, in post-independence Singapore, remembered in his memoirs that as a young man in the 1930s he had campaigned against diverse practices such as certain marriage customs, the practice of separate mosques for members of different parties (Tam. kaṭci) from the same town, or becoming the disciple of wandering holy men, and that Muslim and non-Muslim reformers had been delivering speeches, but had apparently met with only limited success before World War II.[112]

One example of the muted character of 'reformist' discourse in the imagination of ritual among Southeast Asian Tamil-speaking Muslims, in

---

[106] Cf. *Ciṅkainēcaṉ* (17 October 1887), "Ceyku Jamāluttīṉ", 68.
[107] Cf. e. g. *Ciṅkainēcaṉ* (29 August 1887), "Hajjup perunāḷ", 37.
[108] Federspiel 2006: 31–33.
[109] Cf. More 2004: 282–288.
[110] *Tārul islām* (August 1925), "Em Malāy nāṭṭu aṉupavam", 345–346.
[111] Mallal 1928: 113.
[112] Meytīṉ 1989: 15–21.

the colonial period, is the whole complex of *mawlid* or *mawlūd*, referring both to the celebration of the Prophet's birthday and the recitation of poetry in honor of the Prophet and saints on various holidays. In late-nineteenth-century South India, these practices had been challenged by groups such as the North Indian reform movement Ṭarīqa-i Muḥammadiyya, which had first reached Madras in the 1830s.[113] Consequently, 'traditionalist' scholars attacked the followers of the Muḥammadiyya, usually dubbed 'Wahhābīs' by their 'traditionalist' opponents, for opposing devotional practices.[114] An interesting case is the poem *Atapu mālai*. This poem is usually ascribed to the scholar Sām Shihāb al-Dīn b. Sulaymān, generally claimed to have passed away in 1709. The criticism of diverse practices contained in this poem has led some authors to contend that Sām Shihāb al-Dīn b. Sulaymān was a forerunner of nineteenth-century reform movements.[115] But these claims fail to take proper account of the poem, for the *Atapu mālai* is neither simply a 'reformist' poem, nor likely to date to before the nineteenth century, since it contains a scathing criticism of 'Wahhābīs' in fifteen stanzas (Tam. vahhāpip paṭalam).[116] It is more likely, therefore, that the poem was written not too long before it was first printed in 1875,[117] and that Sām's name was used to add authority to the work. In stanza 12 of the *Vahhāpip paṭalam*, the poet denounces opposition to the recitation of *mawlid* in no uncertain terms, while at the same time affirming his faith in intercession:

All persons,
  Who assembled in groups and excellently recited the Prophet's mawlūd,
  Causing joy[118] for the beautiful Prophet,
Will obtain intercession [shafā'a] in future.
While all the excellent great people recite [mawlūd],
  Longing intensely with desire,
The Wahhābīs forsake and repudiate [them] as fools,[119]
And went astray.[120]

---

[113] Cf. Bayly 1989: 228, Pearson 2008: 61.

[114] Cf. e. g. Sayyid Muḥammad 1963: 297.

[115] Cf. e. g. More 2004: 122–124; More seems to draw all his knowledge about the poem from a single secondary article. For the dates of Sām, cf. Shu'ayb 1993: 140.

[116] Sām Naynā Labbay n. d.: 131–135.

[117] Cf. More 2004: 230, Uvais and Ajmal Kāṉ 1991: 5.

[118] The word *napiyuvappuṇṭāki* literally only means 'joy having arisen for the Prophet', but in the context is better translated as causative; the whole phrase could also be translated "causing desire for the Prophet".

[119] I assume that *māṭṭumaṉitar*, lit. 'cow-people', is a term of abuse here rather than meaning 'cowherds', on the line of the term *māṭṭuttaṉam*, 'boorishness'. It would be possible to take the phrase as *māṭṭum maṉitar*, 'people who attach themselves to' or who

As we have seen, late-nineteenth century Tamil authors and newspapers in Southeast Asia were generally supportive of such practices, and gave them coverage. There is little evidence that any opposition to the practice existed, apart from a single note published by *Ciṅkainēcaṉ* in 1889. Reporting about the feasting and *mawlid* recitation for 'Abd al-Qādir al-Jīlānī on his annual holiday, the newspaper also noted that some Muslims had refused to donate money for the proceedings:

> [Some] Tulukkars behaved recklessly by saying that they would not give the money to conduct this arrangement. Has the saint's matter come to pass without being performed because they did not donate? Has it not been conducted even more excellently than in other years?[121]

The editor gave no space to state the reason for the Tulukkars' actions, and we are therefore left to wonder whether it was a case of 'reformist' resistance, or simply of some people trying to keep their savings for other purposes. In any case, such incidents do not seem to have been too common. Matters may have been different in the 1930s, when the author of a book about the Prophet published in Singapore found it necessary to insert a chapter on the requirement (Tam. vēṇṭiyatu) to celebrate the Prophet's birthday. Significantly, the author does not mention the recitation of poetry, but rather advises Muslims to recount the life and deeds of the Prophet.[122] While this may be taken as an example of a shift in the image of the Prophet from the 'Perfect Man' of the Sufis to a 'perfect person',[123] more mundane concerns may have been behind the suggestion, for the author advises his readers to make his book known to others and to distribute it so that Muslims may know about the Prophet's life. The popularity of *mawlid* recitations does not seem to have been threatened.

Conclusion

What were the changes and transformations which took place in the imagination of ritual by Tamil-speaking Muslims who sojourned and settled in colonial Southeast Asia? The evidence presented in this article allows us to gauge some of these transformations, but also some of the

---

'comprehend', which would not change the import of the stanza, but also not fit too well with the reportive clitic *–ām* that follows the phrase.

120 Sām Naynā Labbay n. d.: 134 (stanza 12).

121 *Ciṅkainēcaṉ* (2 December 1889), "Kantūri", 86; the term *tulukkar*, 'Turks', is sometimes used derogatorily.

122 Hāji Cikkantar 1933: 58–59.

123 Robinson 1997: 10.

continuities with the past. Furthermore, while some transformations seem to have been common to the ritual *imaginaire* in both South India and Southeast Asia, others appear to have been peculiar to the latter region.

Perhaps the central transformation that occurred in the imagination of ritual was a series of processes one might subsume under the heading 'individuation'. Rituals increasingly came to be imagined as being part of a particular spatial, temporal, and social context. The specific processes we have identified in this article concern the construction of specific ritual actions as 'events' which could be reported in newspapers and poems, the concern with locality in newspapers as well as the literature about specific saints and shrines, the stress on the spectacular and festive nature of ritual occasions, and the note that was taken of the individuals and groups that conducted, sponsored, or participated in ritual activities.

This process of 'individuation' was accompanied by a similar process of conventionalization of the imagination of ritual. While rituals were situated in a specific spatial, temporal, and social context, the way they were thus situated became standardized. Certain architectural styles were replicated all over Southeast Asia to mark off ritual spaces used by Tamil-speaking Muslims, poems followed similar conventions in describing festivals and rituals, and lists of donors and their donations took the same format whether they were published as parts of newspapers or books. Indeed, it was through these conventions that ritual practices could be individualized, by placing them in relation to similar practices through the use of a repertoire of shared, conventionalized images.

Some of these processes were shared between South India and Southeast Asia, such as the increase in the production of songs on particular shrines and festivals. One development that seems to have been peculiar to Southeast Asia, though, was the heightened awareness of ethnic difference. The ascription of an 'ethnic' identity to mosques and shrines and its inscription in architectural styles, the linking of ritual practice and ethnicity, and the importance of ethnic diversity in the depiction of ritual, characterize the Southeast Asian imagination of ritual in contrast to that of South India, even though there are connections between the depiction of ethnic variety in Southeast Asian sources and that of caste variety in South Indian ones.

There were of course also continuities with the past imagination of ritual. Beside the 'individuation' of ritual noted above, ritual continued to be imagined through idealized and normative texts. But perhaps the most peculiar 'continuity', if we may call it thus, is the persistent stress on what Francis Robinson would call 'other-worldly' modes of Muslim piety, on devotional practices, saints, and the belief in intercession. What makes this 'continuity' so peculiar is that this mode of Muslim piety seems to have experienced an upsurge through exactly the medium that is usually associated with its demise, namely, print culture. The evidence of the Tamil ritual *imaginaire* of the colonial period complicates the narrative of Muslim reform in the nineteenth and twentieth centuries.

In conclusion, it should be stressed again that what has been presented here is not a study of the transformation of ritual itself. We have little knowledge how rituals were actually conducted, which rituals were conducted, what kind of tensions arose from them, and which transformations took place. What we have left is only the record of how certain elite sections of society imagined ritual, and what changes took place in the period and localities under consideration. This record, though, allows us to gain a better insight into the changing mentalities of these elites, and in the way that South Indian and Southeast Asian histories linked up, converged, and diverged again.

Bibliography

Ahmad bin Mohamed Ibrahim. 1965. *The Legal Status of the Muslims in Singapore.* Singapore: Malayan Law Journal.

Alfieri, Bianca Maria. 1997. 'Il complesso religioso di Nagore nel Tamil Nadu'. In: Bianca Maria Alfieri et al., eds. *In memoria di Francesco Gabrieli (1904–1996)* (Rivista degli studi orientali; 71, Supplemento n. 2) Roma, 3–31.

Arasaratnam, Sinnappah. 1979. *Indians in Malaysia and Singapore.* 2nd ed. Kuala Lumpur: Oxford University Press.

Bayly, Susan. 1989. *Saints, Goddesses and Kings: Muslims and Christians in South Indian Society 1700–1900.* Cambridge: Cambridge University Press.

Birch, E. W. 1879. 'The Vernacular Press in the Straits', *Journal of the Straits Branch of the Royal Asiatic Society* 4: 51–55.

Bose, Sugata. 2006. *A Hundred Horizons: The Indian Ocean in the Age of Global Empire.* Cambridge, Mass.: Harvard University Press.

Cevattamaraikkāyar Nāvalar, Ki. A. Vu. 1886. *Malākkāp piravēcattiraṭṭu.* Ciṅkappūr: Tīṉōtayavēntiracālai.

Ceyyitu Muhammatu Cāhipu, Maulavi. 1942 (?). *Javāhiṟul kamsa(h) eṉṉum pañca irattiṉa mālaikaḷ.* Syonan-to [= Singapore]: Cavut intiyaṉ piras.

Chan, Fook Weng, compiler. 2008. Catalogue of Rare Materials in Lee Kong Chian Reference Library. Edited by Ang Seow Leng, Noryati Abdul Samad and Ong Eng Chuan. Singapore: National Library Board.

Cītakkāti Tamiḻppaṇik Kaḻakam. ed. 1980. *Nel: Iḷaiyāṅkuṭi ilakkiyaṅkaḷ – tokuti-1.* Iḷaiyāṅkuṭi: Cītakkāti tamiḻppaṇik kaḻakam, ṭākṭar cākir ucēṉ kallūri.

Federspiel, Howard M. 2006. *Indonesian Muslim Intellectuals of the 20th Century.* Singapore: Institute of Southeast Asian Studies.

Fujimoto, Helen. 1988. *The South Indian Muslim Community and the Evolution of the Jawi Peranakan in Penang.* Tokyo: ILCAA, Tokyo Gaikokugo Daigaku.

Ghulam-Sarwar Yousof. 1989. 'Lasting Charisma', *Pulau Pinang* 1.2: 30–35.

Hāji Cikkantar, Ci. 1933. *Muhammat napi (sal) avarkaḷ carvalōka ca̱rkurunātar (1352-m varuṭa jaṉaṉatiṉappiracuram)*. Ciṅkappūr: Intiyā nāval ṭippō.

Jackson, Louis S. 1850. 'Census of Singapore and Its Dependencies, Taken under Orders of Government in the Months of November and December 1849', *The Journal of the Indian Archipelago and Eastern Asia* 4, February: Tables I & II (following p. 106).

Jāpar Muhyittīṉ, Mu. 1990. 'Ciṅkappūr tamiḻ muslimkaḷiṉ ilakkiyappaṇi', *Aintām ulaka islāmiyat tamiḻ ilakkiya mānāṭu – Kīḻakkarai: Ciṟappu malar,* 117–122.

Kātiṟu Mukiyyittīṉ Aṇṇāviyār. 1990. *Fikhu mālai: ṣāfiī vaḻimuṟaiyiṉariṉ caṭṭattokuppu.* Edited by Kē. Es. Caiyitu Mukammatu Aṇṇāviyār. Ceṉṉai: Ciṅkaip patippakam.

Khoo, Salma Nasution. 2002. 'Colonial Intervention and Transformation of Muslim Waqf Settlements in Urban Penang: The Role of the Endowments Board', *Journal of Muslim Minority Affairs* 22,2: 299–315.

Kōcā Maraikkāyar. 1895. *Piṉāṅku, uṟcava tiruvalaṅkārac cintu.* Piṉāṅku: "Kim Cēyk Hiyāṉ" eṉṉum acciyantira cālai.

Kyshe, James William Norton, ed. 1885. *Cases Heard and Determined in Her Majesty's Supreme Court of the Straits Settlements 1808–1884.* 3 vols. Singapore: Singapore and Straits Printing Office.

— 1890. *Civil, Ecclesiastical, Habeas Corpus, Admiralty and Bankruptcy Cases: Criminal Rulings and Magistrates' Appeals.* (1885-1890) (Cases Heard and Determined in Her Majesty's Supreme Court of the Straits Settlements 1808–1890; 4) Singapore: Singapore and Straits Printing Office.

Lal, Brij V., ed. 2006. *The Encyclopedia of the Indian Diaspora.* Singapore: Editions Didier Millet.

Lee, Geok Boi. 2002. *The Religious Monuments of Singapore: Faiths of Our Forefathers.* Singapore: Landmark Books.

Mahani Musa. 1999. 'Malays and the Red and White Flag Societies in Penang, 1830s-1920s', *Journal of the Malaysian Branch of the Royal Asiatic Society* 72,2: 151–182.

Mallal, Bashir A., ed. 1928. *Trial of Muslim Libel Case.* Singapore: C. A. Ribeiro & Co.

Mani, A. 1993. 'Indians in Thailand', in: Kernial Singh Sandhu and A. Mani, eds. *Indian Communities in Southeast Asia.* Singapore: Institute of Southeast Asian Studies: 910–949.

McAllister, Carol. 1990. 'Women and Feasting: Ritual Exchange, Capitalism, and Islamic Revival in Negeri Sembilan', *Research in Economic Anthropology* 12: 23–51.

Meytīṉ, A. Nā. 1989. *Neñcil patinta niṉaivuc cuvaṭukaḷ.* Kumpakōṇam: Tōḻamaip patippakam.

More, J. B. Prashant. 2000. 'Pathan and Tamil Muslim Migrants in French Indochina', *Pondicherry University Journal of Social Sciences and Humanities* 1,1+2: 113–128.

— 2004. *Muslim Identity, Print Culture and the Dravidian Factor in Tamil Nadu.* Hyderabad: Orient Longmant.

Mukammatu Aptulkātiṟuppulavar. 1872. *Muṉājāttuttiraṭṭu.* Singapore: J. Paton, Government Printer.

——. 1896. *Kīrttaṉattiraṭṭu.* Ciṅkappūr: Jāvippirāṇākkaṉ acciyantiracālai.

Mukammatu Cultāṉ Maraikkāyar. 1890. Patānanta mālai. Piṉāṅku: Piṉāṅku anṭu sṭereyṭs piras.

Nagata, Judith. 1993. 'Religion and Ethnicity among the Indian Muslims of Malaysia', in Kernial Singh Sandhu, A. Mani, eds. *Indian Communities in Southeast Asia.* Singapore: Institute of Southeast Asian Studies, 513–540.

Narayana Rao, Velcheru, Shulman, David and Subrahmanyam, Sanjay. 1992. *Symbols of Substance: Court and State in Nāyaka Period Tamilnadu*. Delhi: Oxford University Press.

Ner, Marcel. 1941. 'Les Musulmans de l'Indochine française', *Bulletin de l'École Française d'Extrême Orient* 41: 151–202.

Nordin Hussin. 2007. *Trade and Society in the Straits of Melaka: Dutch Melaka and English Penang, 1780–1830*. Copenhagen: NIAS Press and Singapore: NUS Press.

Orr, Leslie. 2006. 'Preface', in G. Vijayavenugopal, ed. *Putuccēri mānilak kalveṭṭukkaḷ: Pondicherry Inscriptions: Part I: Introduction and Texts with Notes*. Pondicherry: Institute français de Pondichéry and École française d'Extrême-Orient: I-XXVII.

Pairaudeau, Natasha. 2006. 'Indo-China: Vietnam, Laos and Cambodia', in Lal, Brij V., ed. *The Encyclopedia of the Indian Diaspora*. Singapore: Editions Didier Millet: 200–203.

Pearson, Harlan O. 2008. *Islamic Reform and Revival in Nineteenth-century India: The Tarīqah-i Muhammadīyah*. Delhi: Yoda Press.

Proudfoot, Ian. 1993. *Early Malay Printed Books: A Provisional Account of Materials Published in the Singapore-Malaysia Area up to 1920, Noting Holdings in Major Public Collections*. Kuala Lumpur: Academy of Malay Studies and The Library, University of Malaya.

PuruShotam, Nirmala Shrirekam. 1998. 'Disciplining Difference. Race in Singapore', in Joel S. Kahn, ed. *Southeast Asian Identities. Culture and the Politics of Representation in Indonesia, Malaysia, Singapore, and Thailand*. Singapore: Institute of Southeast Asian Studies: 51–94.

Robinson, Francis. 1996. 'Islam and the Impact of Print in South Asia', in Nigel Crook, ed. *The Transmission of Knowledge in South Asia: Essays on Education, Religion, History, and Politics*. Delhi: Oxford University Press: 62–97.

— 1997. 'Religious Change and the Self in Muslim South Asia since 1800', *South Asia* 20,1: 1–15.

Rudner, David West. 1994. *Caste and Capitalism in Colonial India: The Nattukottai Chettiars*. Berkeley: University of California Press.

Ṣākumukammatu Aptulkātiṟu Jeyiṉuttīṉ. 1878. *Muṟītuviḷakkameṉṉum irattiṉaccurukkam*. Ciṅkappūr: Sayīti yēntiracālai.

Sām Naynā Labbay. n. d. *Adab mālai* [edition in Arabic script]. Madrās: Maṭba' shāh al-ḥamīdiyya.

Samy, A. Ma. 2000. *History of Tamil Journals (19th Century)*. Translated by A. Marichamy. Chennai: Navamani Pathippakam

Sandhu, Kernial Singh. 1969. *Indians in Malaya: Some Aspects of their Immigration and Settlement (1786–1957)*. Cambridge: Cambridge University Press.

Sandhu, Kernial Singh and Mani, A., eds. 1993. *Indian Communities in Southeast Asia*. Singapore: Institute of Southeast Asian Studies.

Sayyid Muḥammad b. Aḥmad Lebbai 'Ālim al-Qāhiri al-Kīrkari. 1963. *Fat-hud-dayyān fi fiqhi khairil adyān (A Compendium on Muslim Theology and Jurisprudence)*. Translated by Saifuddin J. Aniff-Doray. Colombo: The Fat-ḥud-dayyān Publication Committee.

Ṣeyku Muhammatu Pāvalar, V. A. 1910. *Ciṅkai juhūr pirayāṇak kummi*. Nākapaṭṭaṇam: "Hamītiyyā" accukkūṭam.

Shu'ayb, Tayka. 1993. *Arabic, Arwi and Persian in Sarandib and Tamil Nadu: A Study of the Contributions of Sri Lanka and Tamil Nadu to Arabic, Arwi, Persian and Urdu Languages, Literature and Education*. Madras: Imāmul 'Arūs Trust.

Shurreef, Jaffur. 1991. *Qanoon-e-Islam, or the Customs of the Mussulmans of India; Comprising a Full and Exact Account of Their Various Rites and Ceremonies, from the Moment of Birth till the Hour of Death.* Translated by G. A. Herklots. Delhi: Asian Educational Services.

Singaravelu, S. 1984. 'The Malay-Tamil Cultural Contacts with Special Reference to the Festival of Mandi Safar', *Tamil Civilization* 2,2: 71–80.

Snouck-Hurgronje, Christiaan. 1906. *The Achehnese.* 2 vols. Translated by A. W. S. O'Sullivan. Leyden: E. J. Brill.

Taylor, Philip. 2007. *Cham Muslims of the Mekong Delta: Place and Mobility in the Cosmopolitan Periphery.* Singapore: NUS Press and Copenhagen: NIAS Press.

Tschacher, Torsten. 2001. *Islam in Tamilnadu: Varia.* Halle: Institut für Indologie und Südasienwissenschaften der Martin-Luther-Universität Halle-Wittenberg.

——. 2006. 'From Local Practice to Transnational Network – Saints, Shrines and Sufis among Tamil Muslims in Singapore', *Asian Journal of Social Science* 34,2: 225–242.

——. 2009. 'Circulating Islam: Understanding Convergence and Divergence in the Islamic Traditions of Ma'bar and Nusantara', in R. Michael Feener and Terenjit S. Sevea, eds. *Islamic Connections: Muslim Societies in South and Southeast Asia.* Singapore: Institute of Southeast Asian Studies: 48–67.

Uvais, Ma. Mukammatu and Pī. Mu. Ajmal Kāṉ. 1991. *Islāmiyat tamiḻ ilakkiya nūl vivarakkōvai.* Maturai: Maturai kāmarācar palkalaik kaḻakam.

Uwise, M. Mohamed. 1990. *Muslim Contribution to Tamil Literature.* Madras: Fifth International Islamic Tamil Literary Conference.

Yegar, Moshe. 1972. *The Muslims of Burma: A Study of a Minority Group.* Wiesbaden: Otto Harrassowitz.

Zvelebil, Kamil V. 1974. *Tamil Literature.* Wiesbaden: Otto Harrassowitz.

C. J. Fuller and Haripriya Narasimhan

The agraharam: The transformation of social space and Brahman status in Tamilnadu during the colonial and postcolonial periods[1]

In Madras in 1917, the non-Brahman Justice Party's newspaper compared the Brahman-dominated Indian National Congress to an 'agraharam' (Skt. agrahāra, Tam. akkirakāram), an exclusively Brahman residential quarter.[2] Moreover, according to Pandian, 'agraharam' was the commonly used metonym for Brahmin power in colonial Tamil Nadu',[3] but how much can be read into this is unclear; maybe critics just wanted a good simile for Brahman monopolistic cliques. Certainly, the rich and powerful Brahmans dominating politics and the nationalist movement at the time were not living in agraharams, but in new houses in Madras, such as the splendid mansions built in prime locations like Luz Church Road in Mylapore.[4] Admittedly, Mylapore was and is a distinctively Brahman part of the city; nevertheless, Luz Church Road was never an agraharam and we doubt if anyone thought it was.

On the other hand, the journalist who complained about Congress probably thought that many of his non-Brahman readers would have personally experienced abasement in an agraharam and would easily grasp his point. According to Geetha and Rajadurai, who discuss disputes over access to Brahman streets in Madras and an agraharam in a village outside the city,[5] non-Brahmans in the early 1900s "were angered and irritated beyond measure by such open avowals of superiority".[6] Indeed, it seems likely that non-Brahmans' day-to-day experience in agraharams may have been a real cause of widespread visceral anti-Brahman feeling, even though other authors – despite some comments about Brahman

---

[1] Research was carried out among Eighteen-Village Vattima Brahmans in Tippirajapuram in September 2005–March 2006, in the US in September 2006, and in Chennai and other Indian cities in January–April 2007, August 2007, and January–March 2008; Haripriya Narasimhan did most of the research, although Chris Fuller accompanied her for part of the time. This article was written by Fuller, although we have discussed it together extensively and it represents our joint views. We thank the Economic and Social Research Council, which has supported all the research.

[2] Pandian 2007: 93–94.

[3] Pandian 2007: 101.

[4] Pandian 2007: 68–69.

[5] Geetha and Rajadurai 1998: 57–59.

[6] Geetha and Rajadurai 1998: 61.

'arrogance' –[7] do not mention it in histories of the non-Brahman movement, which mainly focus on inequalities in education, employment and political representation. By 1917, though, the agraharam as a bastion of traditional Brahman status and power was beginning to be undermined by modern change and by the end of the twentieth century, agraharams inhabited predominantly by Brahmans, let alone exclusively by them, were rare. But they have not entirely disappeared and even today the agraharam is a significant institution in some parts of contemporary Tamilnadu.

The agraharam

The multiple meanings of 'agraharam' and allied terms partly express the complicated history of Brahmans in the Tamil countryside since medieval times.[8] At least by the nineteenth century, though, the primary meaning of 'agraharam' was an exclusively Brahman residential street or quarter. Moreover, it is probably (though not certainly) the case that in all Tamil 'wet-zone' villages in the river valleys where Brahmans were dominant – 'Brahman villages', for short – Brahmans, both landlords and others, invariably lived in agraharams. An agraharam was spatially demarcated from the *ūr*, the main village settlement area occupied by non-Brahmans; the untouchable Adi Dravidars (Tam. ātitirāviṭar) – today's Dalits or Scheduled Castes – lived in separate 'colonies', *cēri*, at the exterior of the village. Agraharams were also found in older urban areas; in Chennai, for instance, mostly rather decrepit agraharams still exist in localities such as Mylapore, Triplicane and Georgetown.

By the early twentieth century, the rural agraharam was an institution starting to decline, as more and more Brahmans were migrating from villages to towns and cities. The scale of Brahman emigration varied among regions; in the Kaveri delta, where Brahman landlords were most numerous and prosperous, emigration was generally slower and later than in the Palar, Vaigai and Tambraparni river valleys, but within any one region there was probably considerable variation from place to place. For nine Brahman villages, there is a significant amount of published evidence; in addition, we have recently collected material on Tippirajapuram and other Kaveri delta villages inhabited by the Eighteen-Village Vattimas (Tam. vāttimar), a Smarta or Aiyar subcaste. The information about Brahman emigration in these studies is summarised elsewhere.[9]

[7] Geetha and Rajadurai 1998: 61–62; Baker 1976: 28; Barnett 1976: 22.
[8] Stein 1980: 145.
[9] Fuller and Narasimhan 2008a: 173–176.

The first detailed ethnography of an agraharam, by Gough, is based on fieldwork carried out in Kumbapettai, near Thanjavur, in 1951–1952 and 1976. Not far from Kumbapettai is Sripuram, which Béteille studied in 1961–1962. These two authors' publications tell us most about what life was like in a still exclusively Brahman agraharam in the mid-twentieth century. Thyagasamuthiram, near Kumbakonam, whose agraharam was in decline, was studied in less detail in 1957–1958 by Sivertsen. There is no detailed ethnography from the pre-Independence period.

In Kumbapettai between 1952 and 1976, Brahman household numbers fell from 36 to 33. The net Brahman decline was therefore small, but there was considerable movement in and out. In 1952, the agraharam was exclusively Brahman but, by 1976, it also contained eight non-Brahman families;[10] in 2005, when we visited Kumbapettai briefly, the agraharam housed only six Brahman families, who were outnumbered by non-Brahmans. In Sripuram, whose Brahman landlords were mostly richer than Kumbapettai's, the agraharam contained 92 Brahman households and had no non-Brahman residents in 1961–1962,[11] although many Brahmans were leaving the village. Emigration has continued, but the agraharam has not declined as much as might have been predicted, so that in 2005, Brahmans still occupied more than half its houses. Thyagasamuthiram's agraharam was still exclusively Brahman in 1957–1958, but it contained only 13 households; 30–40 households had left since around 1900, and the "greater part of the [agraharam] is now in ruins".[12] By 2007, only two poor Brahman households remained in Thyagasamuthiram and much of the agraharam was still more or less ruined, as were its Vishnu and Siva temples.

Gough[13] wrote a compact description of the Kumbapettai agraharam and its restrictions in the early 1950s that we summarise here. Non-Brahman and Adi Dravidar labourers came to the back door of a Brahman house to collect their wages, and Adi Dravidars did not enter the agraharam street – nor of course its temples – at all. Brahmans conversely did not enter the untouchables' *cēri*, not only to avoid pollution but also because Adi Dravidars believed that if they did, the whole of their street would suffer serious misfortune. Brahmans could enter non-Brahman houses and some men did so to have sex with non-Brahman women, but they could not eat in them and had to bathe before re-entering their own homes. Non-Brahmans had earlier been excluded from Brahman houses, but by the 1950s they worked in them as servants, but did not enter the

[10] Gough 1989: 240–245.
[11] Béteille 1965: 26.
[12] Sivertsen 1963: 28, 33, 66.
[13] Gough 1955: 49–50.

kitchen. Non-Brahmans had also been forbidden to wear footwear in the agraharam or while standing before a Brahman, but at the time of Gough's fieldwork two assertive non-Brahman schoolboys deliberately walked through the agraharam in shoes. Here we may also mention that in Thyagasamuthiram in the late 1950s, similar restrictions applied: untouchable Paraiyars (Tam. paṟaiyar) were debarred from the agraharam street, whereas non-Brahmans could walk along it, but only in bare feet and without carrying umbrellas.[14]

By the 1970s, the rules about pollution and caste interaction in Kumbapettai "had become much more attenuated".[15] Thus, for instance, almost all older Brahmans still avoided the *cēri*, but younger men were much less bothered about it. In 1952, house sales to non-Brahmans "would have been strenuously resisted",[16] but in 1976, some non-Brahmans lived in the agraharam and they could all freely move through it; moreover, in the context of a political dispute, the Kallars (Tam. kaḷḷar) actually displayed their contempt for the Brahmans by driving their own cattle through the agraharam.[17] By this time, too, children of all castes attended the village school in the agraharam, even though the presence of Adi Dravidar children, who were formerly banned from it, still offended both the Brahmans and non-Brahmans.[18] Thus inter-caste relations were far from harmonious, but, crucially, Brahmans had lost a lot of their former power, so that they could no longer control the other castes' access to their once exclusive agraharam and merely complained. In 2005, as far as we could tell on a brief visit, relations between Brahmans and non-Brahmans in the agraharam were fairly relaxed, but there was antipathy towards allegedly aggressive, disrespectful Dalits; in Kumbapettai, like most if not all villages, Dalits still live in their own colonies and never move into agraharams.

In Sripuram, too, by the early 1960s, the Brahmans had lost many of their former prerogatives. Nonetheless, as Béteille was often told, he was the only non-Brahman who had ever had access to their houses and had eaten in them,[19] and the Brahmans strongly objected to the very idea of non-Brahmans living in the agraharam, usually on the grounds that they eat meat and fish.[20] Non-Brahmans never went to worship in the Vishnu temple located within the agraharam.[21] The village school at one end of

[14] Sivertsen 1963: 35.
[15] Gough 1989: 357.
[16] Gough 1981: 159.
[17] Gough 1989: 325.
[18] Gough 1989: 248.
[19] Béteille 1965: 9.
[20] Béteille 1965: 29.
[21] Béteille 1965: 39.

the agraharam was, however, attended by non-Brahman and Adi Dravidar pupils.[22] Brahmans hardly ever entered the Adi Dravidars' *cēri*, and the idea that they could cause misfortune also prevailed in Sripuram.[23] Yet the old order had been sharply challenged. Thus on 26 January 1950, when India became a republic, a local non-Brahman politician took a group of non-Brahmans and Adi Dravidars on a march through the agraharam to the Vishnu temple entrance. It was unprecedented, and the Adi Dravidars' participation "was not only ritually polluting, but it also brought social humiliation on the Brahmins. A decade before the event an Adi Dravida could be tied to a tree and beaten by any Brahmin for a similar offence". On this occasion, though, the Brahmans realised that times had changed and did nothing.[24]

In 2005, when we visited Sripuram, we met an elderly Brahman widow who was unusually conservative. She had come to live in Sripuram after her marriage in 1946 and had never once been to the non-Brahman central area of the village. Although non-Brahmans first bought or rented houses in the agraharam around 1980, she still disapproved of them, saying that they have dirty habits and that the agraharam's character had disappeared. Her views echoed that of another old lady in Yanaimangalam, near Tirunelveli, where the agraharam now contains only a minority of mainly poor Brahmans, who flatly declared that "this village is now ruined".[25] Our informant in Sripuram also reported that the Brahmans have now decided not to sell or rent any more houses to non-Brahmans; we have been told about identical agreements in other agraharams, such as nearby Kalyanapuram, locally renowned as an agraharam that has not declined, where we were told that about 90 houses were still owned by Brahmans (though some are unoccupied) and only about six belong to non-Brahmans. Whether such agreements will hold is uncertain, however, because – as sceptical Brahmans said – many urban residents no longer care about agraharams and sell or rent their empty houses to the highest bidders. Nonetheless, the very existence of the agreements shows how some Brahmans today are belatedly trying to reassert control over agraharams where they retain a significant presence.

Our evidence about the agraharams of the Eighteen-Village Vattima subcaste is consistent with that from elsewhere, for example, in the restrictions on low-caste access and their relaxation during recent decades. As their name indicates, this endogamous subcaste is presumptively defined by the 18 villages in which its members have mainly lived

---

[22] Béteille 1965: 43.
[23] Béteille 1965: 35.
[24] Béteille 1965: 152.
[25] Mines 2005: 2.

as the dominant group; in fact, almost everyone agrees about 16 villages, but the list is completed by picking from several more.[26] In addition to Tippirajapuram, which has been studied in detail, we collected basic data on visits to 16 villages and have some information on a few more. Five or six villages – or more precisely their agraharams – are regarded as the most important owing to the size of their Vattima population and the landed wealth of their leading families. Konerirajapuram was the largest Vattima settlement and it has a famous, ancient Siva temple; Mudikondan has been the richest, at least during most of the twentieth century; the other important agraharams are Anandatandavapuram, Sengalipuram, Tippirajapuram and, less certainly, Vishnupuram. Each of these agraharams used to contain between about 55 and 120 Vattima households; today, the numbers have roughly halved in all of them, although the numbers of non-Vattima Brahmans and non-Brahmans vary considerably. In Tippirajapuram, Brahmans collectively form a large majority of the population, mainly because so many non-Vattima Brahmans live there, whereas Brahmans (mostly Vattimas) are only about half the population in the other important agraharams. In the Vattimas' less important agraharams, their numbers were always lower – between 20 and 50 households – although Tediyur was an exception, with around 120 households. In all these agraharams, Vattima numbers have now fallen to 15 or less, sometimes only two or three, and other Brahman households are similarly few in number. Moreover, most Vattima villagers are old; some elderly men have always been agriculturalists and some have retired from urban employment, but almost all middle-aged and younger people are living and working in towns and cities, either in India or overseas. In most agraharams, a lot of old Brahman houses are empty or even ruined. In most agraharams, too, there are not many non-Brahman families, but a very unusual case is Tediyur, where nearly 100 Vattima houses have been sold to Muslims, regarded by the majority of Tamil Brahmans as unacceptable residents of an agraharam (in contrast with Christians, who are generally tolerated). In Tediyur, though, as the Brahmans and Muslims we met were keen to emphasise, each group attends the other's ceremonies, and relationships between them do indeed appear cordial.

Tippirajapuram

Tippirajapuram is about seven kilometres from the town of Kumbakonam. As already implied, Tippirajapuram is an unusual agraharam because its inhabitants are still mostly Brahmans. The agraharam is a

[26] Fuller and Narasimhan 2008b: 736.

square formed of North, South, East and West Streets; a short extension of South Street, Sannidhi Street, leads to the Vishnu temple in the south-west corner. Behind North Street runs the River Tirumalairajanar, a distributary of the Kaveri. The agraharam contains 129 houses occupied by 95 households – the rest being empty – of which 82 (86 per cent) are Brahman, 11 (12 per cent) are non-Brahman and two are of unknown caste. Of the 82 Brahman households, 34 are Eighteen-Village Vattimas and the remainder belong to other Brahman subcastes, mostly Aiyar. Among the Brahmans, the Vattimas are the dominant group, especially the six 'big families' (*periya kuṭumpam)*, each with its ancestral house; one was the first Vattima family to settle in the village, but the others have also been there for a long time. Each of the six families used to have large landholdings, although a couple of them lost a lot a generation or two ago owing to extravagant spending. Even today, though, all these old landed families retain much of their ancestral status and respect for them has not faded away. The six families' ancestral houses are on South Street, whose 31 households include 20 Vattimas, 10 other Brahmans (some actually on Sannidhi Street near the temple) and one non-Brahman. South Street (together with the adjacent ends of East and West Streets) is the pre-eminent section of the agraharam and a key feature of Tippirajapuram is the opposition between it and North Street, where the four Vattima households are outnumbered by 27 other Brahman and five non-Brahman households. Comparable internal status divisions are fairly common in large agraharams.

In Tippirajapuram, South Street's pre-eminence is reinforced by the location of the Vishnu temple. Tippirajapuram's Siva temple is in the opposite corner of the agraharam; its side entrance is at the eastern end of North Street, but its front entrance is on the main road running parallel to East Street. In Tippirajapuram, unlike most agraharams, the two temples' positions actually correspond to an ideal Hindu norm, whereby Siva is in the north-east and Vishnu in the south-west. More typically, though, they also exemplify a distinction found in many agraharams, for Vishnu's temple can only be approached by walking right through the agraharam, whereas Siva's is easily accessible from outside it and has therefore always been open to non-Brahman devotees, including those who live in Tippirajapuram's non-Brahman area on the other side of the main road from the agraharam. This distinction in turn constitutes Vishnu as purer and more Brahmanically orthodox than Siva, who is more closely linked in Tamil popular Hinduism to non-Sanskritic, village deities,[27] even though both gods are served by Brahman priests responsible for their Sanskrit liturgy and vegetarian worship. In Tippirajapuram today, the

---

[27] Fuller 1992: 43, 48.

caste composition of worshippers at the two temples is still different, because very few non-Brahmans (and no Dalits) go to Vishnu's temple, whereas many non-Brahmans (and possibly some Dalits) go to Siva's. Incidentally, in a fairly typical asymmetry, for the Brahmans the agraharam alone is synonymous with Tippirajapuram, whereas the other side of the main road is just the nameless non-Brahman streets, but for the non-Brahmans Tippirajapuram comprises the settlements on both sides of the road.

One reason why so few non-Brahmans go to Vishnu's temple is because they have to walk along South Street to reach it. Local people correctly assume that many Brahmans living on this street would prefer non-Brahmans to avoid it, even though they cannot openly object, and most non-Brahmans do not want to be discomfited by disapproving Brahmans watching them from the front of their houses. As far as most Vattimas are concerned, South Street is their street and because they are the dominant group in the agraharam, it is right and proper that this street should be kept as traditionally Brahmanical as possible. The non-Vattima Brahmans on North Street harbour considerable resentment against the South Street Vattimas and have mixed feelings about whether North Street is a better or worse place to live. Some people prefer it because it has a more mixed population and they can be more relaxed about purity and pollution rules, whereas others dislike it for those same reasons. One Brahman woman living on North Street even described it as 'adulterated' by non-Brahmans.

The difference between the two streets is symbolised by their surfaces, for South Street is made of sand and North Street is a metalled road. Partly because it is a through route, North Street was surfaced with tar several years ago, but then the local panchayat decided to surface the other streets as well. The late chairman of the City Union Bank (which was founded and is still mainly controlled by Vattimas), who was then the most powerful man in the village, lived in South Street and successfully objected to the plan to surface it. In 2007, the panchayat actually started to tar West Street from its northern end, but when the road workers neared the southern end, where several Vattima houses stand, including the home of one of Tippirajapuram's richest landlords, the Vattimas got the work stopped. Thus the tarred surface covers only part of West Street and none of South Street (or East Street) has been altered. Sand is preferred partly because it is just traditional, but also because it deters outsiders' vehicles and supposedly encourages people to walk respectfully through the agraharam.

Because it is a through road, all sorts of people use North Street, but the incidents that have caused outrage among both Brahmans and non-Brahmans are when Dalit funeral processions have moved along it accompanied by the sound of drums. Many years ago, such a procession would have gone along the riverside path behind the houses on North Street, but it is now blocked with rubbish. It is, however, the drumming, which apparently started in the 1990s, rather than the procession itself, that is regarded as most outrageous. A non-Vattima Brahman living in North Street was discussing the matter with a non-Brahman who is influential in Tippirajapuram; the latter said that surely no Dalit would play a drum in an agraharam, but the Brahman retorted that he had heard someone in the procession shout out for the drums to be played, which he assumed – probably correctly – to be deliberately provocative. When asked by another Brahman why he had said nothing, he replied: "Those days are over. Times have changed. I have no power to say anything." The crucial feature of these incidents is that both Brahmans and non-Brahmans are equally hostile to Dalits, who are accused of behaving aggressively, and that they also believe that they can do nothing about it. On the other hand, though this is speculation, given that North Street is a metalled thoroughfare with a fairly mixed population, the Dalits themselves may not regard it as a proper agraharam street.

On some land close to the Siva temple at the end of North Street, which a non-Vattima Brahman had sold to a non-Brahman, a developer planned to build a 'marriage hall' (*kalyāṇa maṇṭapam*). Vattimas, led by the rich landlord mentioned above, successfully took legal and other action to block this plan, so that in 2007 a shopping complex was under construction instead. The main objection was that crowds of non-Brahmans, with their 'dirty' habits, would come to the hall and cook meat there for wedding feasts (although in fact they normally serve vegetarian food on these occasions). The state of South Street, however, concerns the Vattimas much more and – following an initiative by the late bank chairman – they have ostensibly agreed (as in Sripuram and Kalyanapuram) not to sell any of its houses to non-Brahmans. The chairman's son, now a leading figure in Tippirajapuram, said that even though Vattimas in the agraharam are selling land, they are not selling their houses, preferring to keep them closed, although at least one elderly Vattima expressed scepticism about whether an agreement to refuse to sell to non-Brahmans could last. On the other hand, a non-Brahman on West Street did say that his attempt to buy a Brahman's house on Sannidhi Street had been thwarted by the owner's mother, who flatly declared that they would not sell to non-Brahmans, even if they were vegetarians. Sometimes, to mollify Brahmans, non-Brahmans who buy agraharam houses claim that they will not cook meat in them so that they remain pure; in Tediyur, even some Muslims are said to observe this restriction.

Although many houses in Tippirajapuram are unoccupied, none have fallen down and the agraharam is unusual in having no ruined buildings. Many houses largely retain their original design, although some have had internal modifications. A traditional Tamil house is typically long and narrow; it has a relatively small frontage on the street, but behind the front door it extends a long way. At the front is a veranda (*tiṇṇai*); the door at the back of the veranda opens on to a courtyard (*mittam / muttam / muṟṟam*) partly open to the sky, surrounded on three sides by a hall (*kūṭam*). At the back of the hall in a corner is a cupboard – the domestic shrine or 'puja shelf' – containing small images or pictures of the deities. Behind the hall is the kitchen and behind that is the 'second portion' (*reṇṭām / iraṇṭām kaṭṭu*), a storeroom for food known as the 'daughter-in-law's room'. At the rear of the house is a yard with a well, bathrooms, and an area used for cooking large festive meals. Behind the rear section are a cowshed and a garden, extending to the far end of the site, where there is a back door. In a large house, there may also be extra rooms off the hall, a separate shrine room, a separate granary, and so on; the biggest houses have an upper storey as well.[28]

In the past, the space of a Brahman house was clearly graded according to its relative purity, as well as markedly gendered. The veranda, outside the front door, was the least pure area, where visitors, including non-Brahmans, were received. In Vattima houses in Tippirajapuram until fairly recently, men mainly stayed on the veranda and in the hall, and only went into the kitchen to eat. Women remained in the kitchen, the storeroom (especially daughters-in-law) and the back half of the house. The kitchen was also the pure centre of the house, which was closed to anyone of lower status, including members of the family suffering pollution, especially menstruating women who were secluded in the back yard. As women did not go to the front of the house, they had to use the back door, like low-caste servants visiting their Brahman masters.

Today, the rules about access to Vattima houses, and about male and female space within them, are much less strictly observed than they were. For example, women as well as men now frequent the hall and courtyard, and sit on the verandas chatting and watching people go by, but, as older women recall, this never happened a generation or so ago. Menstruating women are no longer confined to the rear of the house and can sit in the courtyard, although they do not cross the threshold into the street. Most women regard their increased freedom of movement as a definite improvement on the past. Many Vattimas today also have non-Brahman

[28] Narasimhan n. d.; cf. Reiniche 1981.

servants who enter the kitchen, which they formerly did not, and non-Brahman visitors are no longer restricted to the veranda. As a foreigner, Fuller was initially surprised to be invited to look round many Vattima houses, sometimes including the kitchen; in a few houses, he has even eaten in the kitchen. In contrast, he was rarely invited into the homes of Brahman temple priests in Madurai in the 1970s or 1980s, although this altered in the 1990s, at more or less the same time as among the Vattimas.[29] Another notable change is that people now rarely use the back doors and the lanes running behind the houses, except for menstruating women and girls, who may go to work or school by leaving at the back. Mostly, though, the lanes have become overgrown and filthy, unlike the streets that are kept clean.

Notwithstanding the significant changes that have occurred, today's visitor to Tippirajapuram, especially South Street, enters an agraharam that is more visibly 'traditional' than most because it is still predominantly occupied by Brahmans who want to keep it that way. Quite a lot of non-Vattima Brahmans in Tippirajapuram used to live in agraharams now taken over by non-Brahmans. They moved to Tippirajapuram because they want to live in a place where Brahmans are the majority; Brahmans, they say, are peaceful, intelligent, well-educated, clean in their habits and devout, and they care for their temples. Some non-Brahmans in Tippirajapuram also prefer to live there for the same reasons; thus a Chettiyar (Tam. ceṭṭiyār) widow living on East Street said she liked the 'peace' and 'spirituality' of the agraharam, and another Chettiyar couple on North Street praised Tippirajapuram as "calm" and "good for the children's future", although they added that the Brahmans "still hate us", even if they pretend otherwise. The Chettiyar widow's daughter and her husband are the only non-Brahmans on South Street, where they manage the primary school in a house there. They have adopted a Brahmanical outlook themselves, so that the wife, unlike other non-Brahman women in Tippirajapuram, observes menstrual pollution strictly, insisting that it would be wrong not to do so, because a menstruating woman should not walk on the agraharam streets.

Not everyone in Tippirajapuram accepts all this at face value, however. The village is full of gossip and many critics of the Vattimas, both Brahmans and non-Brahmans, castigate them as hypocrites keeping up appearances, claiming that a lot of men on South Street drink alcohol inside their houses. Stories about Vattima men (and even occasionally women) having affairs with non-Brahmans also circulate. It is impossible to tell how much of this gossip is well-founded. Perhaps more significantly, some people in Tippirajapuram blame the Brahmans, especially

[29] Fuller 2003: 67 f.

Vattimas, for breaking their own purity rules – for example, by letting non-Brahman servants into their kitchens – and thereby allowing the agraharam to decay. Some of these conservative critics are actually non-Brahmans, who say that Brahmans should know the importance of adhering to their own rules in order to preserve the agraharam's way of life.

As Vattimas all acknowledge, however, the greatest threat to Tippirajapuram's survival is not broken purity rules, but emigration by Brahmans who are selling land and giving up agriculture, and instead pursuing educational and employment opportunities in urban areas. Among the 85 Vattimas resident in Tippirajapuram in 2005–2006, there were only three children under 16, whereas 51 men and women were aged 60 or over. Among the 155 other Brahmans, however, there were 29 children and 34 people over 60, so that the demographic position is more balanced. In their other villages, the Vattimas' situation is generally worse and prognoses for the future correspondingly more pessimistic; as one woman in Anandatandavapuram put it, her agraharam has no daughters-in-law, so that it will be extinct in the next generation. The economically active children and grandchildren of elderly villagers are almost all living and working in Chennai, other towns in Tamilnadu, other cities across India or overseas, especially America. In this respect, Tippirajapuram is distinctive only because, in the rest of the Vattima villages, emigration occurred earlier and on a greater scale, though Tippirajapuram has also seen more immigration from non-Vattima Brahmans, mainly because it is conveniently close to Kumbakonam. Yet Vattimas as a whole do retain stronger village roots than many, if not most, Tamil Brahmans. The Eighteen-Village Vattima subcaste is small and still overwhelmingly endogamous,[30] which contributes to its survival as a distinct group, but many Vattimas assume that because their subcaste is defined by its villages, its viability would be seriously threatened if all their villages – especially the most important ones, including Tippirajapuram – ceased to be Vattima settlements entirely. But not all Vattimas agree or care; many living in urban areas, especially outside Tamilnadu, are not particularly concerned about subcaste endogamy and have no interest in village life. Younger urban women especially tend to dislike villages, which they see as too conservative and restrictive. Among the Eighteen-Village Vattimas, there is therefore a lot of debate about the value of their agraharams and rural life, but those still living in villages are particularly preoccupied by the issue.

[30] Fuller and Narasimhan 2008b.

Temple renovation rituals in Tippirajapuram

One important consideration is that even urbanised Vattimas living far away normally retain familial links with their ancestral village's Vishnu and Siva temples. As is common throughout Tamilnadu, the costs of temple rituals are met by dividing them into a series of shares, typically defined by days of the month or within a festival (for example, daily worship on the first day of every month, or all rituals on the second day of a particular festival). Sponsorship of a ritual share (known as a *maṇṭa-pappaṭi*) is a right belonging to a particular individual or family and is inheritable. In Tippirajapuram's temples, there are no shares without sponsors (and hence none available for newcomers) and all Vattimas guard their shares jealously, as they also do in other villages, including those where hardly any Vattimas now live. Hence numerous Vattima emigrants send money to relatives or temple priests to pay for rituals in their ancestral villages, so that links to temples survive even when land and houses have been sold. The practice in other agraharams varies; for example, in Thyagasamuthiram in 2007, one of the resident Brahmans was still receiving money for rituals in the decrepit Siva temple, whereas in Kumbapettai by the 1970s, some festivals in the Vishnu and Siva temples were no longer celebrated because emigrant Brahman sponsors sent no money for them.[31]

The significance of temples is prominently displayed in renovation rituals (*kumbhābhiṣeka / kumpāpiṣēkam*). Especially since the early 1990s, these grand and expensive rituals have been celebrated in numerous temples, large and small, throughout Tamilnadu.[32] Ideally, renovation rituals should be held every twelve years, though the interval is often longer. In Tippirajapuram, they were held for both temples on one weekend in February 2008: Vishnu's on Friday and Siva's on Sunday. (Previous renovation rituals had been held for Vishnu's temple in 1978 and 1995, and for Siva's in 1891, 1919, 1940, 1952, 1973 and 1996.) There are minor differences between renovation rituals in Vaishnava and Shaiva temples, and in small temples the rituals are shorter and simpler than in major ones like the Minakshi temple in Madurai.[33] The fundamental structure, however, is always the same: the divine power (*śakti*) within the temple's images is transferred into water-pots; a series of oblations (*homa*) into sacrificial fires is made in order to generate power that is conducted into the water; at the end of the ritual – the *kumbhābhiṣeka* itself – the pots are emptied over the temple's towers

---

[31] Gough 1989: 355.

[32] Fuller 2003: 120–125.

[33] Fuller 2003: 7–18; Fuller 2004.

and pinnacles, and the images inside it, so that the enhanced power in the water flows back into those images.

For this article, the participants in the renovation rituals, rather than the rituals themselves, are most germane. First of all, money is important, because this must be raised to pay for the repair and redecoration work, as well as the rituals, in advance. An elderly, well-respected Brahman who is not a Vattima is president of the Vishnu temple committee in Tippirajapuram and he was one of the first people to donate a large amount of money; a few other non-Vattima Brahmans and a handful of non-Brahmans in Tippirajapuram gave smaller sums. All Tippirajapuram Vattima family members, wherever they now live, were asked for large donations and they gave freely, especially the younger people living in America, so that the amount raised was around 25 lakhs (Rs 2.5 million), considerably more than the total cost of around 18 lakhs. Publicly, Vattimas said that they were glad to receive donations from anyone, but at least some non-Vattimas claimed that actually they were not, because they wanted complete control over the renovation rituals. The Vishnu temple, it should be mentioned, is a private temple owned by Vattimas. The Siva temple is a public temple controlled by the Tamilnadu government's Hindu Religious and Charitable Endowments Department, but as far as the Vattimas are concerned, they are still in charge; in practice, the HR&CE Department did nothing for the renovation except give formal permission for it.

The committee in charge of the money and renovation contracts was chaired by a Vattima, but the most prominent figures at the rituals themselves were three other Tippirajapuram Vattimas: the rich landlord who has already been referred to, an engineer and company director who has recently retired and alternates his residence between a house on South Street and another near Tirucchirappalli, and the younger son of the late bank chairman who is himself a bank executive residing in Kumbakonam, although he visits Tippirajapuram regularly where his mother still lives on South Street. At each key ritual, these three men – or sometimes the late chairman's elder son, whose seniority afforded him precedence over his younger brother – took the primary roles as patrons of the fire-sacrifices or leaders of the processions carrying the water-pots; after the water had been poured to complete each renovation ritual, they went in procession with some of the water to their houses. In other words, according to a template that is standard in Tamil temple rituals, these Vattima men assumed the 'royal' role of ritual patron, the classical *yajamāna*, and also received the 'honours' (*mariyātai*) that are a patron's due.

The three men's prominence relegated other Vattimas to a secondary place, which not all of them were happy about, but for the Vattimas as a whole, the conduct of both renovation rituals manifested their complete, well-organised control of events, as well as their pre-eminence in the agraharam. All this was reinforced by the presence of at least 130 Vattimas, mostly relatives of Tippirajapuram residents, who travelled from Chennai and elsewhere to attend the rituals, as well as by the free meals that were provided every day to demonstrate Vattima generosity. At the celebrations of Radha and Krishna's marriage, the Radhakalyanam, at which men danced in the Vishnu temple on the Saturday morning, and of Parvati and Siva's marriage, for which women brought her wedding presents on the Sunday evening, Vattimas also took the leading roles. Of course, Vattima pre-eminence displeased many other people in Tippirajapuram, especially North Street's non-Vattima Brahmans, very few of whom ate the free meals amid complaints that they were never properly invited and were not really welcome anyway. Significantly, too, the non-Brahmans who attended the rituals, in greater numbers in Siva's temple than Vishnu's, always sat or stood behind the Brahmans, and in this context their lower-caste status was unmistakably displayed. It was particularly plain at the ritual performed by Brahman women only, mostly Vattimas, to protect Parvati and Siva from the evil eye by throwing rice over their images, which they did before giving their wedding presents; many non-Brahman women watched this ritual, but none could take part, even though a few gave presents. All in all, by the end of three days of renovation and marriage rituals, Vattima control over the two temples and Vattima dominance over the agraharam, as well as the 'big man' status of the three leading figures, had been publicly displayed and reasserted. As we have seen, this did not please all Eighteen-Village Vattimas, let alone all other Brahmans in Tippirajapuram, although all of them, even if vicariously, were parties to a collective assertion of Brahman prerogative in an agraharam that has not declined like so many others have.

Conclusion

Until the early twentieth century, when the 'great exodus' of Tamil Brahmans that "transformed a rural class into an urban class"[34] was under way, the majority of Brahmans – especially high-status, wealthy landlords – lived in rural agraharams. In Brahman villages in Tamilnadu, social space was hierarchically segmented into three parts – Brahman

[34] Dupuis 1960: 51.

agraharam, non-Brahman *ūr* and Adi Dravidar *cēri* – with a sharpness hardly found anywhere else in India, except in parts of coastal Andhra Pradesh. Moreover, Brahmans were in many respects above and apart from the society constituted by the non-Brahman bulk of the population, so that in key respects Brahman superiority was formed not by unequal relationships with inferiors, but precisely by their independence from inferiors.[35] In a different way, of course, untouchables were below and apart from the rest of society. As Béteille's monograph[36] most plainly showed, caste – or more precisely these three caste groupings and the relationships or non-relationships between them – were mapped on to and constituted by the space of the village with a firmness and clarity that could have escaped nobody living there.

Rural Dalits still live in their own colonies, but agraharams, as exclusively Brahman spaces, have disappeared, so that one fundamental dimension of a rural social structure that had probably lasted a millennium practically collapsed during the twentieth century. Heated arguments between the caste groups about the 'making of public space' had been going on in Tamilnadu since the early twentieth century, especially in urban contexts.[37] In villages, though, change was most marked after Independence. Then a semi-private Brahman space became an increasingly public multi-caste space, as non-Brahmans started to walk along agraharam streets freely, with or without footwear; Dalits followed suit and began to go to the front doors of Brahman houses, although for many years older Dalits in particular remained reluctant to walk through agraharams. Non-Brahmans also gained access to Vishnu temples inside agraharams, although many still do not worship there, and Dalits hardly ever do. (In some agraharams, Brahmans reportedly closed the Vishnu temples, rather than open them to non-Brahmans.) Sooner or later, non-Brahmans (but not Dalits) started to live in agraharams; all agraharams now have some non-Brahman residents and in many they outnumber the Brahmans. Brahmans have also progressively relaxed restrictions on non-Brahman access to their homes, so that private domestic space has become relatively more open, following the conversion of the agraharam's streets into public space.

The primary cause of this social transformation in villages has been urban migration, as more and more Brahmans have been 'pulled' to the towns and cities by new opportunities in education and salaried employment, and 'pushed' by indebtedness and land sales, exacerbated after Independence by land reforms, as well as by their self-proclaimed

[35] Cf. Fuller 1992: 18.
[36] Béteille 1965.
[37] Geetha and Rajadurai 1998: 51–62.

inability to turn themselves into modern, efficient farmers. After Independence, too, Brahman political power in rural areas was undermined by the rise of the non-Brahman movement. Nonetheless, the post-Independence pressure on Brahmans came after many of them had already left the villages, so that their own falling numbers were a critical factor in their loss of power. Also salient, of course, is the general process of 'secularisation', whereby Brahmans and others have become less and less preoccupied with ritualistic caste and purity rules, not only in towns and cities but also, though rather later, in villages as well. Overall, though, in the history of Brahman villages since the beginning of the twentieth century, the most striking feature is not lower-caste resistance to inequality and exploitation, but the way in which Brahmans themselves overwhelmingly brought about the decline of their agraharams. In so doing, they dissolved the spatial segregation that was so vitally constitutive of their hierarchical superiority within rural society.[38]

Tamil Brahmans as a whole are now a predominantly urban and indeed urbanised community, and many of them retain little if any connection with their ancestral villages, so that the Eighteen-Village Vattimas are unusual in doing so. Furthermore, outside the Kaveri delta region, only a few villages with a sizeable number of Brahmans probably exist today, although the available evidence is too scanty to be sure. Even within this region, Tippirajapuram is an unusual agraharam because its Brahman population is still so large, although this may remain the case owing to Tippirajapuram's proximity to Kumbakonam, which attracts Brahmans working in the town who find it a convenient place to buy or rent accommodation. Among the Eighteen-Village Vattimas' agraharams, Tippirajapuram is exceptional, too, because it is still clearly dominated by the subcaste, but even the most optimistic Vattimas, like the young bank executive, do not expect their dominance to survive for longer than one more generation. The more numerous pessimists think it may end sooner, as hardly anybody will come back to replace the old people now living there, although a few urban Vattimas might conceivably retain their houses as country homes, a possibility now being discussed by some urban, middle-class Brahmans.

In a few other Vattima agraharams without large Vattima populations (e. g., Kundalur, Maratturai, Molaiyur, Puliyur), temple renovations have been undertaken recently, sponsored by city-dwellers originally from those places. Throughout Tamilnadu, it is now common for temples in agraharams (e. g., Kalyanapuram), as well as in non-Brahman villages, to be renovated at the expense of migrants from the villages or by the latters' descendants, who may never have spent any time at all in their

---

[38] Fuller and Narasimhan 2008a: 176.

own 'native places'.[39] In Tippirajapuram, though, the renovation rituals in February 2008 were in part an assertive demonstration of continuing Vattima and Brahman status and power in the agraharam today. This assertiveness has to be understood in relation to the Brahmans' position within Tamilnadu, which has generally been enhanced since around 1990, partly because for a variety of reasons anti-Brahmanism has been declining as a political force, but also because economic liberalisation and globalisation have benefited the urban middle class amongst whom Brahmans, including Vattimas, are very well represented. It is in this broader context that Tippirajapuram's Vattimas, easily able to raise money for the renovations, could try to show that they are there to stay, committed to the two temples and unwilling to sell any more houses to non-Brahmans, at least in 'traditional' South Street. If the pessimists among them are correct, these manifestations of Vattima assertiveness in Tippirajapuram, which are paralleled in some other agraharams like Sripuram, should probably be seen as a last gasp of the old regime, but they nevertheless show that – despite the Tamil Brahmans' transformation into a migratory, urbanised population, as well as all the other changes associated with modernity – the agraharam as the grounded, physical expression of age-old Brahman claims to caste superiority is not yet extinct.

Bibliography

Baker, Christopher J. 1976. *The Politics of South India, 1920–1937*. Cambridge: Cambridge University Press.

Barnett, Marguerite R. 1976. *The Politics of Cultural Nationalism in South India*. Princeton: Princeton University Press.

Béteille, André. 1965. *Caste, Class, and Power: Changing Patterns of Stratification in a Tanjore Village*. Berkeley: University of California Press.

Dupuis, Jacques. 1960. *Madras et le Nord du Coromandel: Etude des Conditions de la Vie Indienne dans un Cadre Géographique*. Paris: Librairie d'Amérique et d'Orient, Adrien-Maisonneuve.

Fuller, C. J. 1992. *The Camphor Flame: Popular Hinduism and Society in India*. Princeton: Princeton University Press.

——. 2003. *The Renewal of the Priesthood: Modernity and Traditionalism in a South Indian Temple*. Princeton: Princeton University Press.

——. 2004. 'The Renovation Ritual in a South Indian Temple: the 1995 Kumbhābhiṣeka in the Mīnākṣi Temple, Madurai', *Bulletin of the School of Oriental and African Studies* 67: 40–63.

---

[39] Gough 1989: 249 f.; Mines 2005: 128–129.

Fuller, C. J. and Haripriya Narasimhan. 2008a. 'From Landlords to Software Engineers: Migration and Urbanization among Tamil Brahmans', *Comparative Studies in Society and History* 50: 170–196.

——. 2008b. 'Companionate Marriage in India: the Changing Marriage System in a Middle-Class Brahman Subcaste', *Journal of the Royal Anthropological Institute* (N. S.) 14: 736–754.

Geetha, V. and S. V. Rajadurai. 1998. *Towards a Non-Brahmin Millennium: from Iyothee Thass to Periyar*. Calcutta: Samya.

Gough, Kathleen. 1955. 'The Social Structure of a Tanjore Village', in: McKim Marriott, ed. *Village India*. Chicago: University of Chicago Press, 36–52.

——. 1981. *Rural Society in Southeast India*. Cambridge: Cambridge University Press.

——. 1989. *Rural Change in Southeast India, 1950s to 1980s*. Delhi: Oxford University Press.

Mines, Diane P. 2005. *Fierce Gods: Inequality, Ritual, and the Politics of Dignity in a South Indian Village*. Bloomington: Indiana University Press.

Narasimhan, Haripriya. n. d. *'In-Between, like Trisanku': Menstrual Pollution among Tamil Brahmans*. Unpublished manuscript.

Pandian, M. S. S. 2007. *Brahmin and Non-Brahmin: Genealogies of the Tamil Political Present*. Delhi: Permanent Black.

Reiniche, Marie-Louise. 1981. 'La maison au Tirunelveli (Inde du sud)'. *Bulletin de l'École Française d'Extrême Orient* 70: 21–57.

Sivertsen, Dagfinn. 1963. *When Caste Barriers Fall: a Study of Social and Economic Change in a South Indian Village*. Oslo: Universitets Forlaget.

Stein, Burton. 1980. *Peasant State and Society in Medieval South India*. Delhi: Oxford University Press.

Gnanasigamony Aloysius

Vicissitudes of subaltern self-identification: A reading of *Tamiḻaṉ*

Oru paica tamiḻaṉ / Tamiḻaṉ[1]

The setting is the northern part of *tamiḻakam* (the Tamil country), the period is the second half of colonialism, and the caste / community we are concerned with has been known commonly as the Paraiyars (Tam. paṟaiyar), an important subalternised and excluded one among many such. The social formation of the northern districts, particularly those of the Arcot, had been marked by a relatively low level of Brahman impact. These areas, by and large dry, had been peopled by marginal farmers of mostly toiling castes, but leading mostly subsistence lives. In this way they had preserved their relative autonomy, both in economy and culture, until the emergence of Madras under the British, which brought in the Brahman politics to the whole of the Tamil speaking world. This was in sharp contrast, for example, to the kind of Brahman feudalism that was entrenched and prevalent in the Cauvery and Tamirabarani valley areas further south.[2] The second half of the colonial period was characterised simultaneously by Brahman consolidation everywhere, multifaceted awakening among the colonially subalternised castes, and the governmental intent to move away from its stranglehold by Brahmanism.[3] Also, the installation of modern institutions based on the rule of law gave a promise of new opportunities for the emergence of the relegated social groups. Those who came to be known as the Paraiyars, not without ambiguity, constituted an important segment of the population, not only in terms of their numbers but also in the power they wielded in pre-modern culture-knowledge spheres – in Tamil literature, medicine, and in the sacred through traditions of several forms of asceticism.[4] Though these spheres of influence had largely disappeared under the corrosive dynamics of time, the institutional modernity promised by colonialism

[1] *Tamiḻaṉ* (incorporating *Oru paica tamiḻaṉ* and *Tamiḻaṉ*, registered with the Madras Government for the period between 1907–1914 under the editorship of Iyothee Thassar at Chennai, and *Tamiḻaṉ*, registered with the Mysore Government for the period between 1926–1933 under the editorship of Gabriel Appaduraiyar at Kolar Gold Fields, both the journals with different serialization).

[2] Baker 1984; Ludden 1985; Washbrook 1993; Perumal 2000.

[3] Aloysius 1997.

[4] Thurston 1907.

provided a sure context for members of this caste to resuscitate themselves individually as well as collectively. In other words, the totality of circumstances was such that prolific articulations and activities, expressive of subaltern subject-formation, could certainly be foreseen. Particularly remarkable was the way the Paraiyar communities of the northern districts, in late colonialism, took to the print-word, as a means of socio-political as well as religio-cultural awakening and mobilization, belying the timeless 'depressedness' attributed to them.[5]

Oru paica tamiḻaṉ was launched on 19 June 1907 by C. Iyothee Thassar (Tam. k. ayōttitācar, 1845–1914) as a weekly news magazine from Royapettah, Chennai, and printed at the Buddhist Press of one Adimoolam. Soon enough, the journal acquired a press of its own – Gautam Press – through the generosity of the recently empowered men of the community from the Kolar Gold Fields. Though the journal was a collective effort of several men and women – "philosophers, natural scientists, mathematicians and literateurs" – "in order to teach justice, right path and truthfulness to people who could not discriminate between the excellent, mediocre and the bad", it was Iyothee Thassar who was the dominant inspiration and guiding hand behind it. Under his charismatic leadership, the journal was also seen as a mobilisational tool of the new Buddhist movement among the subalternised classes. The journal was called simply *Tamiḻaṉ* in its second year and continued to come out week after week without fail for the rest of the editor's life, carrying a wealth of information on current events, interpretations of Tamil history, religion and culture, and continuous polemics against the dominant religio-cultural as well as socio-political discourses of the time. It was also the rallying point for all the Buddhist revivals and retrievals that were going on through the initiative of the men and women of these communities. The imprint of the multifaceted and versatile genius of its editor, a Tamil savant, Siddha medical Practitioner, confirmed rationalist and Buddhist reconstructionist, with an unrelenting rage against all societal injustices and a passion for egalitarian reconstruction of the society with equal and dignified status in it for the subalternised classes, is unmistakable in every one of the issues and every page of the issues of *Tamiḻaṉ*.

With the untimely death of Iyothee Thassar on May 5, 1914, the first and the foundational phase of the journal was over. When it reappeared on June 17 of the same year, it was Pattabiram, the eldest son of Iyothee Thassar, who became the editor. *Tamiḻaṉ* survived under the new editorship till 1917 when it ceased publication. The exact circumstances under which it was stopped and the controversy, if any, between him and others remain obscure. In 1921, through the efforts once again of the men of

[5] Perumal 2000.

Kolar Gold Fields, where the mobilization of the community was strongest, the journal reappeared. Though it was published by V. P. S. Moniyar from Pudupet, Chennai, it was edited by Gabriel Appaduraiyar, a Tamil pandit from the Kolar Gold Fields. Such a cumbersome arrangement could not continue for long and within a year the publication stopped once again. However, the mobilisational energy of the Paraiyar communities of the Northern districts had not yet been exhausted. Along with the increase in the rate of power-devolution from colonialism, and the rise of those known as 'non-Brahmans,' revitalization took place and the fragmented movement regrouped. The printing press was shifted to Kolar Gold Fields under the banner of Siddharta Publishing House, with B. M. Rajarathinam as the publisher. G. Appaduraiyar once again became the editor. In July 1926, *Tamiḻaṉ* reappeared from the Kolar Gold Fields and ran for a total of nine years up to 1935. In its seventh year, 1932, the journal was stopped temporarily through a Government Order issued due to the complaint of some Muslims whose sentiments had been hurt by remarks in an article. When it resumed in November, the same year, we see the journal without a formal editor and being managed by its publisher with active help from Iyyakannu Pulavar and M. V. Ponnaiah. During the ninth year, *Tamiḻaṉ* was reduced to half its size and appeared fortnightly till it was finally closed down.[6]

Paṟaiyaṉ versus Tamiḻaṉ

If the last quarter of the nineteenth century could be narrowed down as the period in which the subaltern classes of Northern *tamiḻakam* showed definite signs of awakening and incipient mobilization, then we could already witness among them a dichotomous way of self-perception or identification. Already, in the seventies and the eighties, Iyothee Thassar was active in the Nilgris, organizing the people and petitioning the government for re-identification of this community in the census as Original Tamils. The year 1891, however, was crucial. Rettaimalai Srinivasan (Tam. iraṭṭaimalai cīṉivācaṉār, 1860–1945) announced the formation of Paraiyar Mahajana Sabai in the presidential town of Chennai. In that same year, Iyothee Thassar came forward from the Nilgiris, the summer capital of the presidency, with Dravida Mahajana Sabai and addressed a mass petition to the Congress Committee to be forwarded to the government. The very first item of the ten demands put up by the petition was that those who use the term 'Paraiyar' – a contemptuous term that hurt the sentiments of the people – should be

[6] The historical details concerning the journal are taken from Aloysius 1998.

made guilty of the crime of defamation.[7] In the following year, he attended the annual conference of the Madras Mahajana Sabai, as the representative of his organization, and experienced the trauma of a 'swift and unanimous' rejection of his demand for temple entry for the so-called Paraiyars. In 1893, Srinivasan launched a journal called *Paṟaiyaṉ,* with the clearly articulated objective that unless the members of the community came forward, recognizing themselves as well as declaring openly that they are indeed Paraiyars, they would never get liberated but remain in serfdom and poverty. By this time Iyothee Thassar had put in a stint with *Tirāviṭa pāṇṭiyaṉ,* a journal run by John Ratnam (1846–1942), another ideologue of the same community. Subsequently, Iyothee Thassar also submitted a monster petition to the government, demanding that they be recognized as a distinct entity of 'Dravidians' and that representatives be appointed for and from among them in public and administrative bodies. He was also to complain later that, while these collective efforts took place, another disruptive activity had been let loose by some members of the community mobilized under the specifically contemptuous label, namely Paraiyar, appended to them by the enemies.[8] Presumably it was this activity, a mass rally displaying banners with the term Paraiyar written on them, which took place in the year 1895, which is narrated by Srinivasan in a celebratory manner.

It was after these prolonged and contrasting acts of social positioning that the incident involving the two stalwarts took place, which has become part of the lore among the mobilized sections of the subaltern classes. Srinivasan speaks of the incident in his short autobiography without, however, mentioning the name of Iyothee Thassar. The precise roles of these two persons in the incident, however, is yet to be extricated from the un-researched pages of history. Possible rivalry between the two for leadership and the influence of their different personal endowments alone could not explain their confrontational social posturing. It was in and through all this, and perhaps much more, that the inherent contradiction of the subaltern situation itself surfaced as different self-identifications. Srinivasan's insistent and repeated naming of the subalterns as the Paraiyars was apparently too much for the social sensitivity of Iyothee Thassar. A formal complaint of injury, under the offence of defamation, seems to have been made at the local court either by himself or on his behalf. The presiding officer took cognizance of the offence and decreed a fine of Rs.100 on the editor of *Paṟaiyaṉ*. Srinivasan mentions, suggesting his own popularity, that crowds had come to attend court on that day wearing head bands with the word Paraiyar written on them and

[7] *Tamiḻaṉ* 1909, 3: 14–15.
[8] *Tamiḻaṉ* 1908, 2: 50.

that someone in the crowd paid the fine. Shortly after, through the initiative of Iyothee Thassar and Colonel Olcott, a school was established for Dravidian children in Adyar. In the same year, 1898, Iyothee Thassar traveled to Ceylon, took Buddhist *dīkṣā* there, returned and set up the Sakhya Buddhist Society. R. Srinivasan, despite himself being Buddhist, was provoked by this public Buddhist posturing and the beginnings of an organization; he censured Iyothee Thassar publicly and challenged the character of his activities.[9] The journal *Paṟaiyaṉ* was subsequently closed down in 1900, when Srinivasan moved out of the country. However, the Paraiyar Mahajana Sabai seems to have continued for sometime even in the absence of its leader.[10]

It was against this background that Iyothee Thassar launched his *Oru paica tamiḻaṉ* in 1907. However, as will become clear, the name *Tamiḻaṉ* was not fortuitously chosen. *Tamiḻaṉ* carried on a relentless hermeneutical battle against the word Paraiyar as a term of collective identification for the subaltern communities, parallel with a tortuous and multi-pronged search for a 'common' or 'neutral' alternative appellation, expressive of certain clear ideological positions.[11] In this search the term *tamiḻaṉ* (a Tamilian) / Dravidian certainly loomed large. Srinivasan's formulation of the subaltern public identity as *paṟaiyaṉ* (a Paraiyar) was sensitive to their stark existential reality, 'the given' of the contemporary social politics. Emancipation, in his scheme of things, was premised on the public acknowledgement of the social reality; there would be no shying away from it, but perhaps this also implied an element of acceptance of the situtation. Such a project could be said to be informed by a hard and even shrewd sense of political pragmatism, undisturbed by larger or even long term considerations. Iyothee Thassar's agenda and his search for an alternative, on the other hand, was characterized by an anxiety to challenge and transcend the given situation as an indispensable condition for subaltern emancipation. The transcendence that the editor of *Tamiḻaṉ* aimed at, as his subsequent and prolific explanations amply show, was for the entire social polity, either as India / Bharata Nadu (Tam. pārata nāṭu) or more often as the Tamil speaking world, to encompass but also move beyond the specifically subaltern. It was this, his politico-cultural idealism, which erupted from within his astounding knowledge of history and culture, which characterized all his writings. Whether or not he has been successful in meeting the pragmatic challenge posed early by Srinivasan will be explored below.

---

[9] Aloysius 1998: 50.

[10] Details concerning R. Srinivasan are taken from his undated *Autobiography*. For those on Iyothee Thassar, see Ponnovium 1962.

[11] *Tamiḻaṉ* 1907, 1: 12.

Paraiyar, Panchama and depressed classes

The congruence of power and culture in the context of Indian nationalist consolidation became heavily biased towards the non-transformed but regrouped and revitalized Brahmans. Other cultural streams, in defensive reaction, became also relatively closed and rigid, but they were clearly excluded and subalternised, or their inclusion as a subordinate was sought within the emergent power-scheme. This configuration was indeed in keeping and in continuity with the 'genius' of the pre-modern Brahman dominance itself: each cultural fragment was to have a space, certainly, but a graded subordinate one at that, patterning after the *varṇa vyavasthā* of Vedic antiquity and sanctity. With such a 'modernised' tradition, the caste / community(s) in discussion – the Paraiyar – found itself at the outer most circle of exclusion and the bottom most rung of subordination.

The near monopolistic ascendancy to power of the Brahmans in Madras meant that the rest of the population became, in a general sense, alien to and excluded from the new power-scheme. It was in this context that the term Paraiyar surfaced in northern *tamiḻakam*, with enormously loaded but negative meaning and import. All that was considered obnoxious, contemptible and to be shunned by 'decent' humans came be called and likened to the Paraiyars.[12] The term was also deployed in the normal social discourse as an adjective – *paṟaiya* – which could be added on to anything contemptuous and despicable.[13] The meaning of the term, when used within the dominant discourse as an adjective, became somewhat diffuse and, one suspects, acquired two layers: primarily, it referred to the more or less specific and numerically strong caste(s) of Paraiyars; secondarily, it was also intended to encompass the entire non-Brahman (Tamil-Dravidian) population, albeit in an attenuated way.[14] The term Paraiyar in this sense, during the period under discussion, became a concept with a double focus: the specific Paraiyar community at its core to be sure, but also referring to a socio-political principle of mass exclusion. Here, one could note that the basic social division that emerged in *tamiḻakam* of that period was between Brahmans and Sudras (Skt. śūdra, Tam. cūttirar). The latter term, Sudra, covered in an undifferentiated way the entire non-brahman population. The 'popularity' of the term Paraiyar within the Brahmanical discourse indicated that it was conceived as an alternative, or at least a parallel term, to that of Sudra, and that it not only was intended to exclude a specific caste(s) but was also to operate as a principle for excluding the masses as a whole. It is to be remembered

[12] *Tamiḻaṉ* 1907, 1: 21; 1909, 2: 32.
[13] *Tamiḻaṉ* 1909, 2: 49.
[14] *Tamiḻaṉ* 1909, 2: 49.

that, if the early decades of the twentieth century already showed signs of individual communities becoming conscious of themselves being excluded, and if there were alredy attempts to compete for a better status, there certainly was an overwhelming commonality of exclusion from power and, to a certain extent, an experience of fraternity, loosely and somewhat ambiguously referred to as non-Brahmans.[15]

In other words, the exclusionary effort of the Brahman forces of the early twentieth century had, as its target, not only the specific community(s) of the Paraiyars but also the 'Tamils / Dravidians' in general, who were heirs to hoary non / anti-Brahman / Aryan cultural traditions and who also, as a fairly distinct group, emerged as a rival to the monopoly exercise of power in modernity. The achievement of this exclusion was sought by the Brahman forces in terms of a single Paraiyar / Sudra discourse. To the Brahman, the term meant *parāyar* or the alien other, irrespective of real or alleged internal differentiations.[16] While subsequent politics meant such an ambitious effort was unsuccessful and the nebulous commonality of all non-Brahmans, that is the Dravidians, itself vanished, it was at this point of time, however, that the Tamils / Dravidians in general, certainly including the specific Paraiyar communities, were maligned and excluded as the Paraiyars. It is only with this background explanation, of the dominantly given Paraiyar identity, that one can comprehend the breadth and depth of, as well as the passion behind, Iyothee Thassar's de-constructional as well as re-constructional efforts regarding identification.

The given identity of the Paraiyars by the dominant forces was also buttressed by a couple of other allied identities in response to the pressures of the times. One was that of the Panchamas (Tam. pañcamar). This ascribed a specific discriminating identity to a cluster of castes, indicating already the unreal character of the indiscriminate Brahman aspiration of mass exclusion. If the term Paraiyar seemed to attenuatedly encompass an amorphous mass of Dravidians, the term of Panchama was in contrast a reference to a fairly clearly demarcated group within that mass. A forerunner of the later term 'untouchables', the term and identity of the Panchamas brought together certain unevenly developed groups, including the Paraiyars. Such clubbing of disparate and differentially developed castes under a single category was also intended to fix groups in their

---

[15] *Tamiḻaṉ* 1909, 3: 14.

[16] *Tamiḻaṉ* 1908, 2: 14. A Brahman friend with much hesitation and after a good bit of coaxing explained 'their' meaning of the term 'Paraiyar', which was *para* (other than) and *aiyar* (Brahman), meaning the rest of the population.

'appropriate' places within the new society, which with the dawn of modernity ran into the real danger of becoming socially homogenized.[17]

These then were the major terms used for identities that the subaltern groups of northern *tamiḻakam* found themselves saddled with as they became self-aware during the late colonial period. As identifications that were not self-determined, these terms expressed the harsh material and non-material reality of plain non-congruence with power or at best attenuated congruence, falling far short of the subaltern aspirations. The editor of *Tamiḻaṉ*, in the regrettably short seven years of publication of the journal, set himself to the task of unpacking these identifications and, through that very task also, of repacking a different set, presumably self-determined. The methodology he chose for the task was 'historicization'. This meant the historical contextualization of what was projected by the dominant as meta-historical or culturally essentialistic. It was a process of de-reification through which the cultural was systematically exposed to show that it had been basically constituted by the political through the activities of specific human agencies operating in history. This historical interpretation was aided by a multi-level and critical hermeneutics, as well as textual exegesis, for which Iyothee Thassar was eminently equipped. The task, which began only with a few terms of subaltern identity, expanded into a process of deconstruction of the whole range of new socio-political identifications that had emerged in the public domain of the period. It ended up proposing a fresh and alternative look at the history and culture of the subcontinent in general and that of *tamiḻakam* in particular. In the course of this comprehensive intellectual exercise he never hesitated to draw upon what today has come to be known as orientalism. His concern was not so much to avoid or absorb mechanically whatever was coming from this source but to critically deploy it in order to establish his own argument and concern, which certainly was not those of the Orientalists.[18] While his extensive explanations and convincing rebuttals would go a long way to recasting several basic questions concerning the history and culture of the larger society, on the existential issue of strategic re-identification of the specific social groups his efforts brought to surface many hidden tensions inherent in the very conditions of subalternity.

---

[17] *Tamiḻaṉ* 1909, 2: 38.

[18] The substantial thesis of Iyothee Thassar as laid out in the next section, it is to be noted, is a direct counter to the Orientalist notion of the subcontinent as an organic-spiritual unity based on Sanskritic-Brahmanical views.

Paṟaiyaṉ versus Pārppāṉ

The primary insight of Iyothee Thassar, which found overwhelming resonance among the subalterns, was that their current experience of negative congruence between power and culture was not only morally reprehensible in the light of emerging modernity but also, when viewed against the advancing historical sciences, a plain distortion. As a confirmed rationalist, he looked for the human agency that brought about such a situation and found it in that group of people who at that time identified themselves as the Brahmans (Tam. pārppār*)*. It was the Brahmans, along with those who accepted and abided by their guidance, that were responsible for the subaltern identification and condition of the Paraiyars, Panchamas and depressed classes, constituting a negative congruence with power. It is the Brahmanical self-identification, as affirmative congruence with power, that identified the Paraiyar as having a negative congruence with the same power.

Iyothee Thassar consistently pointed out and relentlessly challenged the real life Brahman resistance to subaltern emergence in the new spheres of land allotment, education, employment and political representation.[19] This Brahman resistance was carried out systematically in the name of presumably timeless and, hence, inviolable *ācāram* (caste-specific way of life). His accusatory formulation is sharp: "Wherever the *pārppāṉ* (Brahman) is to profit, there is no *ācāram*, but when the *paṟaiyaṉ* makes a slightest move, the same *ācāram* becomes an insurmountable obstacle."[20] This is how the Brahman transcended his specific-naked identity to acquire a universal one, transcending the national, while the *paṟaiyaṉ*'s identity became more and more shameful, albeit at times they were the object of pity and benevolence.

Secondly, Iyothee Thassar pointed out that not only every concrete attempt of the subaltern to move out of their power-deprived cultural status towards minimum power was resisted, but they were, as along with the larger society, constantly reminded of their powerless; that is, contemptible Paraiyar identification was used as a strategy of reinforcing the status quo. This Paraiyar identification cropped up every where: street signs of *paṟaiccēri*, *paṟaiyar teru* were errected in public places as though to forewarn people of some danger ahead;[21] boards of no entry for Paraiyars were announced in public eating places, temples, and other specific areas; the foreigners were told by their Brahman teachers of

---

[19] *Tamiḻaṉ* 1909, 2: 33; 1909, 2: 34; 1910, 3: 40; 1910, 4: 29; 1911, 4: 39; etc.
[20] *Tamiḻaṉ* 1908, 1: 38; 1908, 1: 50.
[21] *Tamiḻaṉ* 1909, 2: 32.

language of the degraded status of the Paraiyars,[22] and the Brahman newspapers were liberal in the use of the term Paraiyar as an adjective to refer to objects to be avoided, to the contemptible and dangerous. One finds a relentless war being waged in the columns of *Tamilan* against the local Brahmans and their nationalist-mouthpiece *Cutēca mittiran*. Our editor was ever alert to the latter's patterned reporting of events, its casteist slant and slur, as well as anti-subaltern prejudice; and he promptly took these to task, with elaborate explanations, in his own journal.[23]

Thirdly, Iyothee Thassar sensed that there was a particular virulence when it came to the question of those whom the Brahman had termed as the Paraiyar. Opposition to the emergence of the Paraiyar by the Brahmans had been unanimous as well as insistent. The Paraiyar was his special target; the Paraiyar seemed to be also the very personification of depravity. The Brahman pretensions of pollution / untouchability, as applied to a whole set of 'untouchable castes' including the Paraiyars, was insufficient to explain their manifest feelings towards this particular group. There seemed to be something more than met the eye here. The social behaviour of the Brahmans at the time failed to give a clue to our editor. He therefore set himself to thinking and also looking into the history and traditions in order to get a clue to the phenomenon of the Brahman's animosity towards the Paraiyars.

Several years of study, research and consultations, according to his own account, lead him to the conclusion that the antagonism between the Brahman and the *paraiyan* is a result of ancient enmity between the two, on account of their antagonistic socio-religious ideals and ideologies. The main thesis of our editor, in barest outline, runs thus: quite early in the formative period of the subcontinent there arose the Sramanic (Tam. camaṇ, Skt. śramaṇa) tradition, whose pinnacle of achievement was the Buddha, which sought to and succeeded to a great extent in setting up an ideal in the social life of the people, as distinct from and against, the human-natural tendency of following one's instincts. This ideal – a cluster of social-relational values – embodied in the Buddhist prescriptions, came to characterize and set apart the 'human' from everything else and elevated it to the status of the potentially divine. This was the single major, chronologically first, and consciously mobilized force of humanization – developing a humane society – in the subcontinent and elsewhere. Around this basic force also developed 'culture', in a multi-dimensional sense, leading to the flourishing of arts and crafts. But soon there arose an 'alien' counter-force, identified subsequently as the Aryan-Brahman, which for the sake of sectarian power and privilege initiated a

---

[22] *Tamilan* 1908, 2: 14; 1908, 2: 29, 1909, 2: 39.

[23] *Tamilan* 1908, 1: 30; 1: 38; 1: 46; 1: 50; 2: 1; 2: 19.

long drawn-out war of ideals and ideology with far reaching consequences. This Brahman ideology was ascription-based and instinctual-naturalist, in contrast to that of the Sramanic which was achievement-based and rational-humanist. If valorization and celebration of birth (breed) and its circumstances, with implied immutability of group-social status and dignity, characterized the Brahmanical, the Sramanic, in contrast, could be recognized by its emphasis on what one achieves in life (for the benefit of humanity at large), implying the possibility and desirability of change and elevation of individual-worth accordingly. This contestation, while primarily being of values, ideals and views of life, was also for the hegemony of specific social forces: the indigenous versus the alien. Both these terms, however, are to be interpreted in a double sense as referring to the geographical / ethnic as well as to moral evaluation. Also, the dichotomy refers less to essentialised and ascriptive blocks and more to ideological choice and commitment to principles by individuals in social practice. In this macro scheme, one could recognize an intertwining of two strands: first, the superimposition of the alien 'Aryan-Brahman' on the indigenous 'Dravidians'; second, the subsumption of the moral-humanistic (Buddhist) basis under the naturalistic-instinctual (Brahman). In the socio-political context of Iyothee Thassar, with the relative success of the Brahmanical – the resurfacing of the varna (Skt. varṇa) ideology – under the colonial auspices, however, it was the latter strand that came to the fore for contestation, as expressed in *Tamiḻaṉ*, while the former merely gave an additional legitimacy. This double imposition in the subcontinental history, culture, and tradition has effectively distorted beyond recognition all identifications relating to the social as part and parcel of the larger attempt to achieve sectarian hegemony. The result has been that what appears on the surface is not the real; hence, the need for historical-critical deconstruction as well as reconstruction to arrive at the truth and moral critique.[24] It is within this long and also long-forgotten course of such macro-ideological contestation in history that Iyothee Thassar locates all of the relevant and changing socio-religious phenomena of the subcontinent, including the crucial issue of social identifications.

[24] *Tamiḻaṉ* 1913, 6: 39. For Iyothee Thassar's elaborate treatment of the distortive transformation of the sub-continental history and culture, see his *Indirar Desa Charittiram* first serialized in *Tamiḻaṉ* and subsequently edited in Aloysius 1999. An academic parallel to this construction could easily be worked out of the writings of Pande 1978; Joshi 2007; Oppert 1972 and several others.

Who is a Paraiyar? Who is a Brahman?

Who, then, is a Paraiyar? Iyothee Thassar offers several but mutually coherent interpretations. Paraiyars are indeed *parāyar*, meaning alien, but they are alien to what and whom? They are alien to the despicable and deceptive Brahman way and view of life.[25] If this is so, Paraiyar then is a positive identification. To be alien to the Brahman / casteist way of life implies no mean status. But again, if Paraiyar means alien in the Brahman lexicon is he indeed so? Rightly speaking, it is the Brahman, through the then practice of varna-casteism, who is alien to both the genuinely historical as well as politically legitimate. Research had shown that these Brahmans came from outside at a time when the universal moral was already entrenched and prevailing among the people. Within the system of meaning in vogue among the Tamils, *pa̱rai* meant drum; so Paraiyar ought to refer to those who beat the drums. Just as there are scores of identifications in Tamil to indicate the numerous occupations within society, the term Paraiyar should also mean those who are engaged in beating the drums. If so, how could Tamil savants, Siddha practitioners, advisers to royalties of old, current teachers, engineers, magistrates, Rai Bahadurs, and Srestadars, be degradingly and contemptuously identified as Paraiyars?[26] A Chakkiliyar (Tam. cakkiliyar), for example, can be called so as long as he is engaged in stitching leather, but when the same person having given up the job has become a teacher or an engineer, how could he still be called Chakkiliyar?[27] The term Paraiyar also means "those who announce", taking its meaning from the *koṭuntami̱l* (Malayalam) usage of *pa̱rai* meaning to say. Iyothee Thassar located his interpretation in the thick of the ideological-ethnic struggle in history. When those who came from without were on their business of distorting the already established religio-moral, by duping the illiterate petty kings and ignorant people and thus attempting to establish their hegemony of sectarian privileges, they constantly had to confront and run away from the moral leaders of the people who relentlessly intervened and exposed the interloper's trickery, greed and falsity. The latter were also chased away by villagers who threw cow dung at them. This practice gave rise to fear among the aggressors and, while fleeing, they began shouting that Paraiyars (those who expose the truth about them) were approaching.[28] And this is how those who stood steadfast in their universalist moral ideal from among the original Dravidians, who unceasingly confronted the

---

[25] *Tami̱la̱n* 1908, 2: 14.
[26] *Tami̱la̱n* 1908, 1: 38; 1909, 2: 30.
[27] *Tami̱la̱n* 1909, 3: 18.
[28] *Tami̱la̱n* 1908, 1: 30; 2: 15; 1909, 2: 30.

pretenders, came to be known and eventually downgraded as the Paraiyars.

The Paraiyars, along with several others, were also identified as untouchable. Who is an untouchable? Quoting from the teachings of ancient literature, the editor explained that one should not come in physical contact with leprosy and cholera patients and those who suffer from poisonous poxes; one should not go near also traitors, backstabbers and murderers, the bad social elements. Apart from and against this, if one taught that one should not touch more than six crores of decent and dignified people, the reason could not be anything other than hatred, jealousy and even fear. Even if one who identified themself as a Brahman suffered from any of these contagious sicknesses, or is a habitual offender of the above description, by his behaviour he too would become unfit for human interaction.[29] Iyothee Thassar also pointed out that, in ancient times, it was those who identified themselves as Brahmans who were treated as untouchables and unapproachables or *mlecchas* by the generality of upright men and women.[30] Because of his nefarious activities and his immoral way and view of life, the Brahman was considered inauspicious and polluting, and whenever he entered any settlement of the Sramanas and Sakhyas he was chased away by throwing cow dung at him.[31]

Besides, it was argued, the Brahman practice of untouchability is plainly selfish and opportunistic, and there is nothing spiritual and not even ritual about it. This is so because the Brahman practices untouchability only whenever it is to his advantage and not otherwise.[32] He has no sense of pollution when physical work is to be extracted, food-materials are to be prepared, or on entering the local liquor joints, or even when he is excited sexually.[33] Untouchability, on the other hand, comes into strict and consistent practice when the Paraiyar wants to worship in the temple, enter the public school for learning, or to get paid employment. Our editor also observed that if the Paraiyar is rejected and resisted with ferocious consistency as a polluting object, the same consistency is not seen when the Brahmans deal with social groups which are numerically small, ever-obedient, non-challenging and also cannot be said to be more hygienic.[34] From all of this, Iyothee Thassar drew his own conclusions: the Brahman practice of untouchability has nothing to do either with spirituality or hygiene. On the other hand, its selective and opportunistic

[29] *Tamil̲an̲* 1910, 4: 15.
[30] *Tamil̲an̲* 1909, 2: 30.
[31] *Tamil̲an̲* 1910, 4: 15.
[32] *Tamil̲an̲* 1908, 1: 38.
[33] *Tamil̲an̲* 1907, 1: 28.
[34] *Tamil̲an̲* 1908, 2: 1; 1910, 4: 10.

application indicated both hatred and fear. If the Paraiyar was to be let inside the temple, for example, he would instantly recognize the divinity within as his own and come to realize how the Brahmans had robbed him also of his god and religion; if the Paraiyar was let into the newly bourgeoning public sphere, he would easily become a threat to the Brahman dominance – because they (the Paraiyars) were of good status once and, given the opportunity, they would with ease spring back to rival supremacy.[35]

Clubbing together a few castes on the basis of their alleged 'backwardness' and giving them a distinct identification in the early part of the twentieth century was indeed a preliminary step for their later preferential treatment. It was a step that the newly empowered Brahmans were prepared to take as a concession to the pressures of contemporary politics. It was, in their calculations, a lesser evil, consisting of merely sharing a minimum of material resources – reservation – than conceding even an iota in ideological or cultural hegemony. Again, such a concession could easily mute, if not entirely divert, the sharp focus and counterthrust that the Brahmans were subjected to during that period. Thus emerged the identification of Panchama to refer to a cluster of castes, including that of the Paraiyars. *Tamiḻaṉ* challenged the term on its meaning: are these the remnants of the five Pandavas (*pañcapāṇṭavar)* of old, or victims of famine (*pañcam*), or constituted of the five elements (*pañcupūtiyam*) or indeed thrashed and scattered as cotton (*pañcu*) or those who lived along the banks of the five rivers (*pañcanati*)?[36] There was no response. As suggested earlier, the main opposition of *Tamiḻaṉ* was to the clubbing itself – bringing together differentially developed groups within a common identification. Iyothee Thassar was quick to point out that such clubbing and single identification were directed against the 'most developed' (hence a real threat) amongst them, that is, the Paraiyars.

The 'Panchama' soon gave way to the 'depressed classes' of the emerging dispensation. These classes would now be the legitimate object of pity, condescension (a form of contempt?), and welfare engagement for the dominant. The Brahmanical approach was learning to adjust to the unavoidable oncoming of democratic politics. It would now speak and act on behalf of the subaltern as befitted the liberal ruler. The internal rivalry among groups within the dominant classes, as to how to go about this noble task of 'representation' and 'upliftment', was to constitute the substance of 'democratic politics'. With this, the place of the subaltern within the new scheme and the acceptable concession for the demand of power

[35] *Tamiḻaṉ* 1908, 2: 23.

[36] *Tamiḻaṉ* 1909, 2:38.

congruence was being finalized and determined. First of all, they were identified by the dominant as the depressed, in contrast to itself as the developed. The most important characteristic of being depressed in the context was not poverty;depressed connoted absence of ideological / cultural resources to the extent even of plain lack of human dignity. The demand, then, was that those who are identified so, accept such a determination. If they did, space, albeit marginal, would be allotted to them. It was ironical, in the emerging context of the times, that even such a demeaning prescription was an empowerment for several groups on the ground. But it was certainly not so for the Paraiyars, who were regrouping and beginning to articulate through *Tamiḻaṉ*. Identification as the depressed classes for them meant structural consolidation of their already degraded societal status within the new Brahman power scheme. Accordingly, Iyothee Thassar rejected unambiguously and with passion this new identification. In a series of articles, he challenged the very notion of the depressed and uplift as the solution applied to the Paraiyars, and pointed out the hidden trajectory of such identification. He perceptively noted that running in close parallel to the new discourse of the depressed was the identification of 'low caste' in contrast to that of the identifier as the 'high caste'. Often enough, the two were interchangeably used, leading to the new identification of the depressed castes, to the chagrin of *Tamiḻaṉ*.

What was worse, however, was the Brahman claim and clamour for uplift of these depressed classes. How could one believe that the caste-affirming groups are going to uplift the caste-rejecting groups? It is like the tiger shedding tears becausc the goat is getting wet in the rain. It was these very people whose behaviour had caused the degradation and despoiling of the simple folk; and it was incredible that they now claimed to be working for their uplift. They preached that it is their karma that has made them born as 'depressed'. If so, through which and whose karma were they to be uplifted? When some from the so-called depressed themselves attempted to move towards a better life, they were obstructed in all possible ways by these very same people. In depression and uplift both, it appeared, the dominant Brahman would be the centre and subject. All talk of uplift was merely opportunistic and a method of self empowerment and employment. It is primarily intended to prevent the self-initiative of the so-called depressed, it was claimed, and maintain them in their present degraded status. Finally, as a true Buddhist, Iyothee Thassar challenged, can any one really uplift another? If one can uplift another, by the same token he could also bring down the other, in which case the uplift itself cannot be real or genuine.[37]

[37] *Tamiḻaṉ* 1909, 2:31; 1910, 3: 48; 4: 13; 1911, 4: 48; 1912, 5: 46.

The identification of the other is invariably implicated with or indeed a corollary of self-identification. Identifications such as Paraiyar and lower caste are indeed counter-opposites of self-identifications such as Brahman and upper caste. Satisfactory debunking of the former cannot be achieved without deconstructing the latter within a single and coherent framework. Thus Iyothee Thassar turned this around and demanded to know, who is this so-called 'Iyer' (Tam. aiyar) class that wants to uplift the depressed class?[38] One who protects all life as one's own; one who has attained all knowledge; one who excels in discernment; one who is generous and moral; one who has transcended caste-discrimination and jealousy and promotes human unity; one who does not go after another man's wife, or grab another's property or consumes intoxicating liquor even if available freely, he is the 'Iyer' class. Needless to say, Iyothee Thassar is here enumerating those Buddhist moral qualities which he does not find in those who had emerged as the Brahman. 'Iyer' class really means the noble, which is also the higher because of its behaviour; the term 'Iyer' refers to this only, it personifies or at least ceaselessly strives towards those above-mentioned qualities. An 'Iyer' is not born but becomes one through self-discipline, good conduct, and universal compassion, renouncing particularly the despicable distinctions of caste. A Brahman is then seen as one who exudes the fragrance of holiness – compassion, inclusion, selflessness – achieved through long years of practice. And this has been possible for one or two in a million. A Brahman is an identification of an individual's *sādhanā* and not an ascriptive attribute of a family or caste. Just as the ruler is called Kshatriya (Skt. kṣatriya, Tam. kṣattiriyar), farmers and merchants, Vaisyas (Skt. vaiśya, Tam. vaiciyar), and those using their limbs as tools work to create things, Sudras, a Brahman is one who is suffused with universal compassion and engaged in inclusive emancipation. Identifications are about what one does and not how one is born. Only such a Brahman is a true (*yatārttam*) Brahman and others are merely Brahmans in disguise (*vēṣam*). Those among the Tamils who were identifying themselves as Brahmans and uppercaste, according to *Tamiḻaṉ*, were neither, in terms of spiritual engagement, genuine, nor, in the historical sense, authentic. They are not even the original Brahman intruder, but locals who had taken to caste-ideals in view of the privileges it brought were merely imitations in a double sense. In other words, they were only *pārppār*. The term *pārppār*, with a tinge of contempt, is Iyothee Thassar's consistent and favorite term to refer to those self-called Brahmans, and it is his contribution to the lexicon of modern Tamil social history.[39]

[38] *Tamiḻaṉ* 1911, 4: 47.

[39] *Tamiḻaṉ* 1908, 2: 7; 2: 13; 1909, 2: 30; 2: 31.

Another newly emergent, but natural looking identification, against which the editor of *Tamiḻaṉ* sharpened his insights was that of the 'Hindus / Hinduism' along with allied terms such as 'Sanatan dharm' and 'Arya Dharm'. Iyothee Thassar relentlessly pursued these categories to explain and expose that they were merely meaningless terms, which could not be put on a par with similar identifications such as Christian, Muslim or Buddhist, and had no historical basis and no contemporary use.[40] Hindus / Hinduism is merely an alternate term to that of the Brahman / Brahmanism and as such it does not refer to any group or individual beyond those who accept and abide by the authority of the Brahmans and practice caste.[41] The term was also opposed point by point for those who had chosen to identify themselves as Buddhists.[42] These identifications, used as a support to the basic social-relational identifications of Brahman and Paraiyar, were only of recent origin, he argued, thanks mainly to the British overlordship.[43]

Underlying all these different identifications is the foundational term 'caste', which rose to tremendous socio-political salience during the late colonial period. Its Tamil equivalent is *cāti*. Within the Brahman lexicon the term meant an ascriptively constituted social group and, as an attribute to an individual, it referred to the group into which one is born. It was considered as a datum of nature or divinely ordained. The only reasonable attitude then towards this was to accept and abide by its conditionalities as given. But Iyothee Thassar exegetically worked out another, presumably genuine, meaning: the Tamil word *cāti* is originally a verb and only derivatively becomes a noun. In its verb-form *cāti* means to achieve, articulate and to act. A man is known by what he achieves / articulates and the way he acts. If one achieves righteous behaviour, he is of good / high *cāti*, unrighteous behaviour then bad / low caste. In the same way if one articulates Tamil, he is of Tamil *cāti*, if Telugu, Telugu *cāti* and so on. Also, if and when one is engaged in the act of tilling the soil, then he is a Vellalar (Tam. veḷḷāḷar), stitiching leather, a Chakkiliyar, beating a drum a Paraiyar and so on. He would be known as this or that *cāti* (caste) only when and as long as he was engaged in that particular type of activity or articulation.[44] Therefore, there is nothing natural, given or divine about it, on the other hand it is very much within one's own

---

[40] *Tamiḻaṉ* 1910, 4:1; 1912, 6: 17.

[41] *Tamiḻaṉ* 1911, 4: 37.

[42] *Tamiḻaṉ* 1910, 4: 28; 1911, 5: 18.

[43] *Tamiḻaṉ* 1908, 1: 45; 1: 47. The colonial construction of 'Hinduism', echoing the early insights of Iyothee Thassar, is a raging theme among scholars today. See for examples, Thapar 2004 and King 2008.

[44] *Tamiḻaṉ* 1908, 1: 36; 1911, 4: 39; 1913, 6: 38.

choice or social constraints. It is a matter of history and historical mutation.

Āti Tamiḻar, casteless Dravidians and Purva Buddhists

Earlier explanations of the terms, *paṟaiyaṉ* and *tamiḻaṉ*, already hinted at the subaltern oscillation in constructing its identity in modern times. The oscillation was indeed multi-directional, as will be explained. From within the very Brahmanical identification of the subaltern as the Paraiyar, Iyothee Thassar tried to extricate the ambivalences inherent in the situation and, out of these, sought to propose ways of constructing genuine identifications. Accordingly, Iyothee Thassar, early on, conceived of the identification *tamiḻaṉ* for the subalterns. It was a critical conception in the sense that certain criteria were made conditional for the appropriation of such an identification: a *tamiḻaṉ* is one who neither believes in nor practices *cāti ācāram* (caste-way of life). This condition is derived from two sources: history and politics. Historically, the Tamils originally neither believed in nor practiced *cāti*. *Cāti* meant, as suggested above, what one articulates or does. But *cāti* related to birth-circumstances was introduced by the so-called Aryan-Brahmans. So the critical conception of *tamiḻaṉ* was a historical retrieval. Secondly, modern times were meant to be based on equality, as the British taught. The British were only reminding the people of its own original ethos of Buddhist-egalitarian encompassment. To consider some as high and some others as low offends righteousness. It is against human nature, which demands a common-equal identification of all. However, the harsh reality was that many of those who, in a descriptive sense, were identified as the Tamils have took the parppan and became believers in and practitioners of caste. In order to distinguish the one from the other, the prefix *āti* was added. The casteless Tamil is the *āti tamiḻaṉ* in the double sense of the word, first as well as genuine / original. *Cāti* (casteist) *tamiḻaṉ* is only a *pāti* (half) *tamiḻaṉ* and, hence is merely the *mīti* (residual) *tamiḻaṉ*.

With the classification of the south Indian languages as a distinct group and their identification as Dravidian by the nineteenth-century linguists and philologists, particularly Robert Caldwell, the name Dravidian for the people of the peninsula became prevalent among the burgeoning intelligentsia of the land. This was also set in contrast to what was becoming hegemonic in the Northern parts of the country – the Aryan – thanks to the collaborative efforts of the Brahmans and the Orientalists there. While the notion of the Aryan became a racial theory and debates raged as to the origin, nature, and political implications of the alleged race and its spread, both within and without the country, *Tamiḻaṉ*, particularly its editor, was quick to seize the internal and real implications of the rising concept for the mass of the working people. The internal-real face of the Aryan in the context of the early twentieth century was indeed caste; and its racial dimension as well as its origin and other related questions were all merely of peripheral significance. Iyothee Thassar effectively challenged the term itself and pointed out that as it was pronounced *āriyaṉ* it had no meaning in Tamil, and the real term was *ariyaṉ* meaning rare and noble as applicable to all who demonstrate nobility of deed and character. He also explained that the real import of its contemporary construction was to legitimize, through camouflage, the sectarian and exclusive congruence of power and culture that was taking shape then, and also to consolidate the ideology of ascriptive discrimination within the emerging society. In this context, the Dravidian took on the opposite socio-political meaning of upholding the principle of evaluation of human worth according to deeds. He appropriated the term to serve his purpose on hand, of identifying the new community at the level of modern politics. The Dravidian in *Tamiḻaṉ* is accordingly a non-caste or even anti-caste political principle of egalitarian and inclusive unification – an ideal power-culture-congruence.

Keeping with the hoary tradition of this land, of presenting the social as the religio-cultural, Iyothee Thassar also sought to extricate the religious dimension of subaltern self-identification. In fact, his main thesis, as elaborated above, is a weaving together of the social as well as the religious dimensions as the eminently or sacralised social, which in other words is the human-moral dimension. The concrete context, however, was the colonially abetted rise, spread and consolidation of the Brahmanical principle of ascriptive discrimination as the time immemorial religion of Hinduism.[45] If ascriptive discrimination of the social, camouflaged as religious Hinduism, indicated the Brahmanical congruence between power and culture, it met its counter in Iyothee Thassar's egalitarian encompassment as the essence of Buddhism, signaling the legitimate and modern form of power-culture-congruence. Simultaneous to his self-identification, Iyothee Thassar was also attempting, in the teeth of overwhelming and combined opposition, to redefine the identity of the sub-continental history, culture, and tradition as a whole. He mustered numerous pieces of historical and linguistic evidence available to him to build up a logically coherent case of continuity / identity with the Purva / Sakhya Buddhists. The pictures of the Buddha and Buddhism that emerge out of the columns of *Tamiḻaṉ* are not foreign to the Tamil speaking world. The moral religion and its

[45] Thapar 2004.

founder are suffused with the very essence of all that is best in Tamil / Dravidian literature, culture and tradition. In Iyothee Thassar's idea of the ancient subcontinent, prior to the coming of the caste-pretenders, it was the Tamil / Dravidian that was prevalent everywhere. The present day Paraiyars are indeed the ideological (and also biological?) descendants of Sakhyamuni. Because of their social-ethical tenacity and resolute resistance, they now stand outside caste as outcaste. They are in a true sense the 'remnant'; but, in the course of reconstruction of the identity / ideology, this religion, in the pages of *Tamiḻaṉ,* is retrieved and projected as open-ended and inclusive just as it was in the beginning, inviting all who believe in and commit themselves to the ideology of casteless-ness – universal compassion and encompassment.

From the ideologised notion of the *paṟaiyaṉ* to Purva Buddhist through *tamiḻaṉ* / Dravidian, there is sameness or continuity in identity. The different inclusive identifications that Iyothee Thassar proposed are but different aspects – literary-cultural, historical-social and ethical-religious – of one and the same identification. As contemporary and contesting identifications, they are all similarly informed by the basic principles of choice and openness. The conceptual elaboration of the subaltern self-identification thus, in the columns of *Tamiḻaṉ*, is hermeneutically rich, interpretatively complex and ideologically refreshing. Such a presentation was possible, as suggested above, on two counts: first, the intellectual equipment of the editor – Iyothee Thassar – was indeed extraordinary. In fact, it is his thought that comes across forcefully in the pages of the journal as long as he was alive. Second, the overall political mobilization at all levels was only in its beginning, and confrontation between groups and forces was just taking shape; this provided enough space and time for the contestants to work out their own ideas and strategies. However, it needs to be said that despite the fact that Iyothee Thassar had conceptually elaborated a convincing and liberative identificational trajectory in one stroke both for the subalterns and the subcontinent, his own concrete agenda of self-identification as emancipation, though substantial, could only be realised on a limited scale, through his own Chadhi Pedhamattra Dravida Mahajana Sababai and Sakhya Buddhist Society.[46] What happened to the different dimensions of the conceptual edifice, in the time of fast moving devolution of power and competitive politics, can be seen in the second phase of *Tamiḻaṉ*.

[46] *Tamiḻaṉ* 1908, 2: 19; 1909, 2: 50; 3: 14; 3: 15; 3: 16; 3: 17; 3: 20; 3: 21; 3: 24; 3: 25; 1911, 4: 34.

Transitions and transformations

When *Tamilan* resurfaced, in Kolar Gold Fields in the year 1926, the socio-political scenario of *tamilakam* was vastly different on many counts, and this fact had its influence on the multi-dimensional process of subaltern self-identification and its expression through the revived journal. Most important among the changes, as far as the issue on hand is concerned, was the colonial devolution of power – the move of power away from the alien and towards the pluralistically and contestatiously defined native culture. Through a series of well-designed steps in 1909, 1919, and 1930, the British were fast relinquishing its hold over the land, society and culture. This created a widespread scrambling for power among all groups but near-panic reaction among the subalterns who, with more than sufficient reason, feared the worst in the event of an abrupt British withdrawal. The period of relative ease, intellectual search, conceptual elaboration, and fine tuning of articulation had gone, and it was now time for collective and clinching action. It was a now or never situation, particularly for those at the bottom of the society.

Secondly, there was the firm and clear emergence of the internal face of the rising nationalism, as articulated primarily by Gandhi but also several other leaders.[47] The arrival of this person on the scene, at least as far as the struggling subalterns were concerned, openly signaled what they had always suspected and feared, that the raising of the banner of nationalism by the colonially regrouped and revitalized Brahmans was to impose an internal 'discipline' a la the traditional varna mode.[48] Hence, from now on, the subaltern struggle for identification was going to be not merely against the traditional Brahmans, but against the 'nationalists' with all the practical disadvantages and moral defensiveness involved in such an endeavor. Yet, the situation had also given birth to a counter in the personality of Bhim Rao Ambedkar, who could respond, retaliate, and counter-articulate on behalf of the subalterns, at the level of pan-Indianism. While the subalterns of Northern *tamilakam* had their own particularities of highly contextualized social-historical development, the recent rise, spread and consolidation of Brahmanism in the political sphere under the auspicious of colonialism had created a certain measure of homogeneity in subalternisation across the land and this, even with minimal conscious collaboration among the scattered groups, had given birth to a commonality of political purpose and a mobilisational agenda among them.

---

[47] Gandhi 1962.

[48] Guha 1991.

Thirdly, one confronts a spectrum of inter-related changes taking place within *tamiḻakam* of this period: the rise of non-Brahmanism in general, the coming to power at the regional level of the Justice Party in particular, subsequent to the reforms of 1919, the emergence of the Self-Respect Movement under the leadership of E. V. Ramasami along with his powerful weapon, *Kuṭi aracu*, and finally a multi-faceted process of Tamil revivalism attempting to unify the linguistic territory. Such a spectrum of change, objectively, ought to have gone in favour of the subaltern struggle for self-identification, and in fact it did to a certain extent in several spheres. However, in the contexts of the overarching emergence of Brahman-nationalist hegemony at the larger and determinative level, and the marginal nature of economic differentiation and diversification on the ground, and not least, the sectarianism of the groups involved, several ambiguities came to characterize the relationship of the subaltern struggles to these parallel forces.[49]

Fourthly, the times were also characterized by a proliferation of journalistic endeavors by similarly and not-so-similarly placed communities and castes across Tamil society. The new *Tamiḻaṉ* had to take note of this development and to negotiate with them as an added dimension of the process. This certainly was a welcome development in the Tamil public sphere. There had emerged journals claiming to represent the entire Tamil / Dravidian society, *Kuṭi aracu* and *Tirāviṭaṉ*, and also those specifically addressing individual caste-concerns, *Nāṭārkula mittiraṉ, Vicuva nēcaṉ, Muslīm nēcaṉ* and several others. Scores of individuals, both men and women, emerged as authors and writers, contesting, supporting, correcting and suggesting through multiple and creative-imaginative ways the current structuration of power congruences or social identities. All these were necessarily reflected in *Tamiḻaṉ*.

Fifthly, within the subaltern communities themselves, there had emerged the first generation of leadership which could articulate and assert the subaltern concerns, both within society but also in the State, as members of legislative and executive bodies – R. Srinivasan, Swami Sahajananda, M. C. Rajah, Veeraiyan, L. C. Guruswamy, Madurai Pillay, V. G. Vasudev Pillai, Appaduraiyar, Annapoorniammal, V. I. Munusamy Pillai, Periyasamy Pulavar, N. Sivaraj and Meenambal Sivaraj, to name only the most prominent ones. While this emergence had boosted the

---

[49] It is often forgotten that subalternity in India is not articulated as a single point or moment in a bipolar situation but is layered in hierarchies. If the bottom-most social layer could claim to be the most oppressed and a 'classical' case of subalternity, the other layers below the topmost could also claim, though with attenuated truth, oppression including the characteristic lack of self-determination. Here, the Adi Dravidars, Dravidars, all of them claimed the position of subalternity vis-à-vis their domination, severely complicating the situation.

morale of the identificational struggles of the people at large to quite an extent, it had also injected the inevitable murky dimensions of competitive and calculative politics, further fragmenting the already non-unified struggles.

Sixthly, at the level of the journal itself, the difference in the character of editorship also came to matter. While G. Appaduraiyar was also a Tamil pandit and had been initiated into this particular mode of social politics by his predecessor, he did not have his intellectual stature or moral authority. Among the colleagues of Iyothee Thassar he had been but a junior. All those who had participated in the earlier *Tamiḻaṉ* do not seem to have rallied around the revived venture for some obscure reasons. The journal owes it success no less to the efforts and sacrifices of its indefatigable and committed printer-manager-publisher, B. M. Rajarathinam of Kolar Gold Fields. The confluence of these and similar other factors explain how the new *Tamiḻaṉ* came to be what it was and also how it came to express the concerns of subaltern self-identification the way it did. If the earlier *Tamiḻaṉ*'s identification was pre-dominantly in conceptual mode and secondarily in mobilisational / concrete and marginally imaginative mode, the later's orientation was first mobilisational, then imaginative and, thirdly, conceptual.

Identifications: From the conceptual to the concrete I

Sometime during the year 1914, probably after the death of Iyothee Thassar, the Madras legislative passed a resolution to the effect that the terms Paraiyar and Panchama, as they signify degradation and contempt, were not to be used in reference to specific communities and, instead, the term Adi Dravidar (Tam. ātitirāviṭar) should be used.[50] Subsequently, a government order was issued to record the names of different communities for official purposes, as desired by the groups concerned.[51] And, finally, a resolution moved by M. C. Rajah in the year 1922 settled the issue, at least at the level of the law and administration, in favour of the term Adi Dravidar.[52] This certainly was a victory for the struggling subaltern groups of Northern *tamiḻakam*. *Tamiḻaṉ*'s initiative certainly did play a leading role in this change of identification, just as earlier its efforts had made the government recognize a Buddhist community in census operations and allot a separate place in the burial ground in

---

[50] *Tamiḻaṉ* 1928, 3: 12.
[51] *Tamiḻaṉ* 1929, 4:7.
[52] Pillai 1922.

Chennai.[53] The new identification was, in a true sense, self-identification – a name that the subaltern groups had given to themselves.[54]

If, on the whole and for several practical purposes, the term Adi Dravidar was used by almost all groups, there was still continued discussions and debates about it. A small core group persisted in the line of thinking of Iyothee Thassar and insisted that *tamiḻaṉ* is the proper and appropriate identification: the new editor Appaduraiyar, his daughter, Annapoorniammal, who had emerged as an ideologue on her own right, and M. Ponnu, who was a powerful satirist, spearheaded this line. Appaduraiyar wrote a lengthy essay on the question, "Why *tamiḻaṉ* is the appropriate name for the subalterns", and it was also published as a separate pamphlet and circulated.[55] This group opposed vigorously those who thought otherwise, particularly those who sought to identify the subalterns as Hindus or Adi Hindus.[56] This latter identification was championed by no less a person than Swami Sahajananda from within the community, and whose credentials of honesty, dedication and sacrifice for the cause were certainly beyond dispute.[57] An Adi Dravidar Mahanadu even passed a resolution for change of name to Adi Hindu.[58] Valluvars, a sub-group which had traditionally looked after the intellectual and liturgical needs of several and even non-subaltern communities, claimed exemption from the term Adi Dravidar being applied to them.[59] Another respectable leader, V. G. Vasu Deva Pillai, continued to insist that there should be no difference of identification among the Dravidians and suggested that the prefix Adi was not necessary.[60] He had even announced the inauguration of a Dravida Mahajana Sabai. There erupted also a prolonged controversy, particularly in the southern part of *tamiḻakam* and in Ceylon, among those of the community traditionally known as Sambavars (Tam. cāmpār / cāmpavar). They insisted that the identification of Adi Dravidar for all subalterns groups, even of Paraiyars alone, was insufficient and that they ought to identify, organize and mobilize themselves specifically as Sambavars. The lengthy debates that went on for some time, between those who insisted on particularist identity and those who advocated a more inclusive one, not only remind one

---

[53] *Tamiḻaṉ* 1908, 2: 31.
[54] Anbu Ponnovium 1992 in an essay on N. Sivaraj suggests, referring to *Iraṅkōṉ piravēcattiraṭṭu*, that the term Adi Dravidar was in use for the subaltern communities as early as the middle of the nineteenth century.
[55] *Tamiḻaṉ* 1927, 2: 6; 1928, 2: 31.
[56] *Tamiḻaṉ* 1928, 2: 31.
[57] *Tamiḻaṉ* 1928, 2: 30.
[58] *Tamiḻaṉ* 1928, 2: 30; 2: 32.
[59] *Tamiḻaṉ* 1927, 2: 6.
[60] *Tamiḻaṉ* 1928, 2: 31.

of the earlier controversy between Iyothee Thassar and R. Srinivasan narrated above, but also anticipate some of the points being raised today in the problem of sub-caste classification and reservation. For the Sambavars pointed out that, in the name of unity and inclusiveness as Adi Dravidars, the Sambavars were systematically being ignored when it came to the question of appointing members to the governmental bodies.[61] Groups also raised the issue that, no matter what identification, the actual situation was not going to change and therefore concrete steps are more necessary to remove degradation than endless discussions as to the mere naming.[62]

The subalterns could identify themselves differently and they could even compel the government to recognize the new identification, but it is another thing to be able to stop the continued other-identification by the powerful within society. Yet, in the changed situation they could now take legal action against those who continued to use the term Paraiyar for the subaltern individuals and groups. Defamation cases sprang up in different places, particularly where the groups were better mobilized, against the derogatory use of the term Paraiyar, and in most cases the verdict was in favour of the subalterns and the culprits were fined.[63] The subalterns are the staple object of exploitation by the elite; they are not to be left alone particularly when they show signs of spontaneous emergence; they need to be controlled, contained and transformed to continue to serve the dominant. This had been the original idea behind the identification of the other as the Paraiyar, Panchama, Candala, etc. This hegemonic process of determination through definition was not to end that easily! Having emotionally blackmailed and successfully defeated the claims of the subaltern groups across the land as formulated and forwarded by Ambedkar, the new Gandhian-nationalist era identified the so-called untouchables as 'harijans'. The term at once sought to express the condescension and pity of the dominant castes and indicated the place and promise it had planned for these groups. It was also a warning for the subalterns not to leave the overall religious mode of politicking that Gandhi successfully, with some cooperation from the Muslims, was setting up. The awakened subalterns of *tamiḻakam*, however, were quick to sense the trap of the new identification. The last two years of the journal indicate the mood of the people who had closely participated in the historical confrontation between Gandhi and Ambedkar, most of them standing behind and supporting the latter. Gandhi was told in no uncertain terms to withdraw the new identification. The people painfully realized

---

[61] *Tamiḻaṉ* 1929, 3: 50; 3: 51; 4: 10; 4: 12; 4: 18; 4: 23.

[62] *Tamiḻaṉ* 1927, 2: 11; 2: 15.

[63] *Tamiḻaṉ* 1927, 2: 7; 2: 12; 1928, 2: 37; 2: 48; 3: 11; 3: 14.

how quick the Brahman journals were in taking to the Gandhian identification of the subalterns, and expressed the necessity to nip it in the bud before it stuck to them. The term was invariably found disgusting and degrading: it was a Vaishnava name, it was the name of the lowest castes in India according to Alberuni, it would perpetuate untouchability rather than end it and any way Gandhi had no business using it. When he visited *tamiḻakam*, he was pressed everywhere through petitions for its immediate withdrawal. To which, all he could respond, naively, was that an untouchable man himself had suggested it.[64]

Identifications: From the conceptual to the concrete II

The first major issue came up when it was noticed that the educational institutions under the Pachchaiappan Trust, Chennai, were consistently refusing admission to Adi Dravidar children, on the principled basis of their not being Hindu and that the Trust was set up only for the Hindus. The legitimate grievance of the thus excluded community was highlighted by leaders, readers, and others in various forums. The majority of the trustees, however, insisted and asked the High Court, in which a case was pending, to declare whether the Adi Dravidars were Hindus or not. When the court eventually declared that they were Hindus, the obstacle was removed and the children were admitted. The point, however, was that the spokespersons of the community, in the course of their struggle to move closer to the domains of power and privilege, were forced to argue against their own erstwhile stand and aggressively stated claims that they were not Hindus. The editor also had to write an editorial affirming that the Adi Dravidars were indeed part and parcel of the Hindu community. In the context of their previous, long and tortuous elaboration of their non-Hindu and specifically Buddhist identity, the resolution of the problem could be considered either a defeat or victory. It was indeed thought of as victory, but one could notice also a certain defensiveness in the presentation of their case.[65] Incidentally, it is to be noted that the local problem of the Pachchaippan Trust was not unconnected with the emergent nationalist pattern of permitting the Adi Dravidar's access to their rights as conditional on their allegiance and acceptance of 'Hinduism'. The public acknowledgement of the fact and the court decision necessarily cut into the conceptual freedom and self-respect of the Adi Dravidars, while simultaneously indicated the route of 'emancipation' acceptable to the dominant. In addition, the increased readership

[64] *Tamiḻaṉ* 1932, 7: 4; 7: 9; 1933, 7: 25; 8: 4; 1934, 8: 27.
[65] *Tamiḻaṉ* 1927, 2: 3; 2: 4; 2: 6; 2: 7; 1928, 2:21.

and participation of the Christians and also of Adi Dravidars of the southern districts, as well as of Ceylon, who were not party to the near-consenual emergence of the Buddhist community in the period of Iyothee Thassar, had relegated the importance of the Buddhist identity to a separate and somewhat marginalized engagement in the new *Tamiḻaṉ*.

Sometime in August 1928, an incident occurred that boosted the identificational processes of the various social groups. Kuppusamy, an active Buddhist and social organizer of the village of Angambakkam, earlier having encountered a number of obstacles from the local dominant community to his mobilisational efforts, was suddenly attacked by a mob. Defensive action and repeated warning failed to disperse the crowd. The military man, then, with his service rifle, shot dead three members and injured several in the crowd and he promptly informed the police station of the incident. He was arrested and proceeded against for the crime of murder. For *Tamiḻaṉ* this was a family problem and the journal itself took a mobilisational mode: sent its own team of investigators to find out the truth, attended court, closely monitored the proceedings and systematically reported them and collected financial contributions for expenses. When the lower court decreed a life sentence, the journal assisted in the appeal to the High Court, which declared him not-guilty and set Kuppusamy free. The community celebrated the release in a series of receptions organized for the champion of the downtrodden. For a whole year or so the issue of Angambakkam Kuppusamy resounded wherever *Tamiḻaṉ* was circulated and injected a new vitality to the community in the process of its self-identification.[66]

Another very important local issue, which had taken much of the space in *Tamiḻaṉ,* was the conflict between the Adi Dravidars and Kallars (Tam. kaḷḷar) / Nattars (Tam. nāṭṭār) of the Ramanathapuram district, particularly, the Devakottai area. These latter, a la Brahmans, considering themselves as better born, had been accustomed to extract slave-like obedience and services from the Paraiyars and Pallars (Tam. paḷḷar) for quite some time. The situation was made worse by the fact that the Kallars insisted that the slavery of the so-called low born be also obvious and manifest in food, dress, habitation and cultural practices. They could not understand that these groups were not any longer Paraiyars and Pallars of old, but had transformed themselves into Adi Dravidars and Devendrakula Vellalars (Tam. tēvēntirakkula vēḷāḷar). That is, they had re-identified / self-identified themselves and hence begun to eat, dress and live like anybody else. This was not acceptable to the those who thought that the traditional pattern of dominance would and should continue for ever: the Adi Dravidars were prevented access to public places, children

[66] See *Tamiḻaṉ* issues 7 to 46 of the 3rd year, 1927–1928.

were sent back from schools, their newly constructed schools were demolished, women's jackets were torn off, men beaten up for wearing full-length dress and refusing to do free menial services. In May 1930, the Kallars held a mass meeting of their own and drafted an elaborate code of conduct for the subaltern groups. Susequent systematic terror was let loose against those who defied it. Self-identification is nothing if not first and foremost self-respect and ultimately self-determination. The Adi Dravidars and also the Devendrars of the area responded to the situation: they were learning the democratic-legal methods of struggle and the effective use of the modern means of mobilizing support. The entire Tamil-subaltern world rose in sympathy: letters, articles, petitions, comments and condemnations poured in. The regional government was moved, through the issue being raised in the Legislative Assembly, to appoint an enquiry commission. Respectable men of other castes came to intervene and hold reconciliation meetings. In all this, *Tamiḻaṉ* moved along with the process through relentless reporting and mobilizing support. The journal had established direct contact with the local leaders, A. S. John, T. Ponnaiah and V. Arumugam. The services and sacrifices of these selfless persons were reported and lauded. A repeated comment that came up in the columns concerning the issue was the backing and support that the dominant caste was receiving from the Brahmanical police and other executive officers of the area. The process of reconciliation that was held, sometime in early 1931, at least for a time moved the area out of focus. But the relation between the Kallars and the subaltern castes in the entire Ramanathapuram district continued to remain tense. A tiny speck of hope too had flickered in the midst of the gloom. The Self-Respect Movement had also percolated in the area, so much so there were a few Kallars who took the side of the subalterns and suffered for it.

The names of Meiappan and Vedappa were noted specifically for their sacrifices. During the whole period of the struggle, about a year, the pages of *Tamiḻaṉ* became the testing ground for the performance of the emergent leaders both of the subaltern and others. They were all found wanting in performance in comparison to their own grandiose promises, at least on this issue.[67]

Identifications: From the conceptual to the concrete III

A complexity of issues – Simon Commission, Round Table Conferences and Pune Pact – presented itself as the context par excellence of the movement of power from the alien to the native culture, and an occasion

[67] *Tamiḻaṉ* 1930, 5: 25; 1931, 5: 30; 5: 40; 6: 3; 6: 6; 6: 7; 6: 11; 6: 13; 6: 21.

for a decisive struggle on all fronts towards the desired identification. The major parties concerned – the Brahmans-turned-nationalists, the politicized Muslims and the minorities, the mass of scattered and semi-organized but unevenly positioned subalterns and also the imperialists – considered the occasion as the determining moment of reconfiguration of power for the future in the subcontinent and were prepared to stake their claims. It was in the middle of the nineteen twenties, when the time for the start of this mega process of devolution was approaching and already the parties were getting ready for the ensuing controversies, that *Tamiḻaṉ* was re-launched (1926). For various reasons it ceased circulation in 1934. It was during this period of eight or so years that the social polity of India was in great turmoil around this complexity of issues and, finally, a more than rough sketch of things to come was made. *Tamiḻaṉ* participated in the process wholeheartedly as a stake-holder, and did the utmost possible to ensure that some power at least percolated downwards to the culture it represented. If a single issue that could summarily interpret the contribution of the journal is to be identified, it is this issue of devolution of power through the Commission, Conference and Pact. We have voluminous material on the single most important event of modern India seen through the eyes of the subaltern communities and that too in their own articulations. The subalterns did speak!

When the nationalists announced their non-cooperation with the Royal Commission, the subaltern groups of *tamiḻakam* were quick to recognize a lacunae, which they could with maximum advantage fill. Hectic activities began all across the province to mobilize the people to welcome the Commission, present memorandums and petitions, and generally to cooperate with it in all possible ways. Not that there was no dissenting voice. The few groups that had been working on the margins of the nationalist movement became either silent or did express their opinion in a subdued manner. Particularly the groups from Ceylon, which had been articulate participants in the columns of *Tamiḻaṉ* on slightly tangential lines, in clear indication of a different trajectory of development there, did put forth the view that unity with the nationalists was the proper route for emancipation. However, they were effectively and voluminously countered. Most of the participants, however, rallied around the editor Appaduraiyar, who turned the journal into an active weapon of mobilization. It is to the credit of the journal that at no point of time did it attempt to stifle a dissenting voice. While cooperation with the Commission was in the air with all the non-Brahman groups of the province, it acquired an additional edge and urgency in the case of the Adi Dravidars of *tamiḻakam* for two reasons: one, their own long history of organization, struggle, and to an extent success in bringing about a minimal identification of power with culture in terms of what came to be called later 'reservation;' and two, the emergence of a powerful voice in the person of Ambedkar, in and through whom the local groups found identification with a larger struggling mass everywhere. The journal also kept track and reported more systematically now developments on the issue in other places. Through all these counter activities at least one thing was achieved: the existence of groups earlier called untouchables or depressed classes could not anymore be wished away as mere creations of the colonial policy of divide and rule, and, in the concrete context of congruence of power with blatantly sectarian-Brahman culture, it would be minimum diplomacy to recognize their distinct conditions as appropriate for, at least, nominal power-sharing. The question that came to the fore now was the mode of such sharing of power.

Were the subaltern political representatives to be elected through the separate subaltern electorate or through a joint-common electorate from constituencies reserved for them? On this question the subaltern leaders, both local as well as pan-Indian, apparently were neither of one or firm mind. There seemed to have been some indecisiveness on their part based on real-life dilemmas. Some reflection would easily show that this dilemma was only another version of the same dilemma that has been plaguing the subaltern political consciousness from its very inception. If a separatist posturing would, in the course of time, tend to fix and tie them down in that very location, albeit self-chosen, and prove to be to their own disadvantage, in joining together on the other hand, they would, as experience time and again had shown, be overwhelmed by the still antagonistic dominant forces with the sure loss of the very purpose of struggle. What then was the appropriate level and mode of separateness as well as joint-ness for the subaltern social groups? And how could such a level and mode be given a legal-institutional shape? The ideologues were seen shifting position from forum to forum. They were indeed thinking aloud and testing for reactions from the masses. Differences in the personalities, perceptions and political equations of the leaders, at all levels, could not also be ruled out. However, when Ambedkar cast his lot finally for a separate electorate, most of the organized groups of subalterns, including many which were either indecisive or had been silently going along with the nationalists in *tami̲lakam*, fell in line solidly behind him. His position of a separate electorate for the subalterns easily achieved hegemony among the people concerned. All those who opposed it, irrespective of their creditable antecedents, were condemned as traitors to the cause. The big casualty was M. C. Rajah, the veteran of subaltern politics not only of Tamilnadu but elsewhere also. The participants of *Tami̲la̲n̲* showed no hesitation or compunction in throwing him overboard. The journals, both local and from Ceylon, which took positions against that of Ambedkar were criticized ruthlessly. Of course, scores of pages and extreme bitterness were reserved for taking to task and tearing to pieces Gandhi for his anti-subaltern, pseudo-spiritual and varna upholding stand. The few murmurs against such an irreverential and satirical treatment meted out to the great personality were easily muted. For the entire period of the Round Table Conferences, and the Pune Pact articles, critical and creative voices, condemning the stubbornness and debunking the sectarianism of Gandhi continued to pour in. On the positive side, full support to Ambedkar and R. Srinivasan was mobilized: meetings were organized everywhere and telegrams dispatched expressing faith in their leadership, affirming their position in the negotiations, and explicitly denying the representative capacity of Gandhi.[68] The bitterness with which the caste Hindus, through Gandhi, fought against the subaltern proposal did convince the masses that they indeed were on the right rack in their struggle for congruence with power. But success there was not going to be. Finally, when Ambedkar had to give in, under the heavy pressure of emotional blackmail, and accept the joint electorate in reserved constituencies, *Tamiḻaṉ,* unlike several other struggling groups elsewhere, by and large recognized the harsh reality of the situation and sympathized with the great subaltern leader.[69]

Self-respect as the foundational dimension of all identificational activities of *Tamiḻaṉ* is the appropriate note on which this selective and interpretative reading of the journal could conclude. *Tamiḻaṉ* was relaunched a year after *Kuṭi aracu* of the 'Self-Respect Movement' started publication. *Tamiḻaṉ* also ran parallel to *Tirāviṭaṉ* (since 1917), the mouthpiece of the ruling Justice Party. These journals not only ran parallel to one another, they constituted a spectrum of a single socio-political thrust, challenging and seeking to change the emerging configuration of power. This of course did not mean that they did not have differences, sometimes serious, among themselves in perception, priority and formulation. Nor did these differences fail to register themselves in the columns of *Tamiḻaṉ*.

The massive Self-Respect Movement led by E. V. Ramasami, from the middle of the nineteen twenties, is certainly, with all its limitations and ambiguities, crucial in understanding the transformation of the structure and culture of Tamil society in modern times. However, that the move-

[68] Irschick 1986, citing bureaucratic sources, says that R. Srinivasan and N. Sivaraj supported the cause of a joint-electorate.

[69] On this issue of the Simon Commission etc., and that of the subsequent self-respect, it has not been possible to specifically document this, as the relevant materials are spread throughout the journal.

ment itself was but an edifice constructed on the foundations laid much earlier by castes and communities far below the social scale than those which eventually came to constitute it, is hardly recognized or recorded. If the specific formulation of self-respect, which came to dominate the Tamil scenario, was peculiarly the movement's own, the substance and issues of what constituted self-respect could be found scattered in the forms of actual struggles several decades before across the Tamil speaking world. Ever since the intellectual and mobilisational efforts of Iyothee Thassar and his companions and E. V. Ramasami's association with them came to be known, it could legitimately be said that even the specific formulation of the movement owes much to the activities of the so-called Paraiyars of Northern *tami̱lakam*, right from the turn of the century.

The core elements of self-respect as formulated by Iyothee Thassar, in the columns of Chennai *Tami̱la̱n*, springing as they did from the very bottom of the social scale and reaching out to embrace the entire society in all its dimensions, were in several aspects more comprehensive than what Ramasami in later times could articulate in the context of a more fragmented society and in the midst of highly competitive politics. As a much more widespread and popular movement, the latter brought together under its umbrella several unevenly positioned castes and communities, not all of whom were inspired with the same degree of commitment and enthusiasm for the cause; there were within the movement individuals and groups with different and often ambiguous goals and aspirations. Despite these limitations, when Kolar *Tami̱la̱n* was relaunched in 1926, it found colleagues already in the field manifestly with similar vision and mission – in *Kuṭi aracu* and to a lesser extent in *Tirāviṭa̱n*. The three, at least at the level of ideology, could and indeed did articulate in unison on crucial issues. One can sense the feelings of comfort and security of the writers in *Tami̱la̱n* when reciting the litany of these three names, in one breath as it were, in discussing the issues immediate to the subaltern life – that they were not alone but together in the struggle for the cause of self-respect. Examples of actual collaborations are spread out in the columns of the journal: reports, articles and speeches were lifted from the other journals to be published here; *Kuṭi aracu*'s publications were given free publicity; the self-respect journals and publications could be subscribed to and bought from *Tami̱la̱n*'s office; the leader of the movement, Ramsami, was generally accepted as the staunch and unwavering supporter of the subaltern causes. As the days progressed the pages of *Tami̱la̱n* came to be filled with general and contextual writings, both critical and creative on self-respect and its correlate *camatarmam*.

However, beneath all this camaraderie and collaboration, one could read in between the columns, as it were, a thin but continuous line of underlying resentment against the larger movement which inevitably was having an ambiguous impact on *Tamiḻaṉ*. That *Tamiḻaṉ*'s generosity towards the other journals was not being sufficiently reciprocated; that the Self-Respect Movement was not always forthcoming in censuring the non-Brahman atrocities on the Adi Dravidars; that on issues crucial to the subalterns, often enough they had to go it alone; that *Tamiḻaṉ* was but an inferior partner in the struggle and all co-operations seemed to originate from one side only; that *Tamiḻaṉ*'s patronage came exclusively from the Adi Dravidars etc. – comments and observations to these effects did crop up in the journal as time progressed and the Self-Respect Movement began to achieve a local hegemony of sorts, with the corresponding waning of the current phase of the distinct subaltern movement.

The fact of the matter was that the specific experience of subalternity by the Adi Dravidars was more radical and comprehensive, and this reflected in their rather demanding and differential understanding and aspiration of self-respect as expressed through the columns of *Tamiḻaṉ*. Their immediate and existential problem was untouchability, which was acquiring ever newer dimensions and was being practiced by the rest of the entire society, albeit originated, formulated and sustained primarily by the Brahman elements. However, within the generalized mobilization for self-respect against the Brahman imposition, the extra edge of the subaltern experience and its corresponding self-respect aspirations tended to get blurred. This is how, despite Ramasami's strident and radical critique of Brahmanism, the movement as a whole has been identified as non-Brahman from the perspective of the Dravidars who were against the Brahmans in a limited political sense, instead of anti-Brahman from the point of view of the worst sufferers, the Adi Dravidars, or even of its chief ideologue, Ramasami. Further, the movement itself was recognizing that the Brahmanical pattern of power-congruence, that is caste, was not weakening. In response, the demand was for a proportionate sharing of power and resources within the existing framework. With this latter strategy coming to the fore, the primary goal of the movement – the abolition of caste – tended to get relegated. On this issue of the proportionate share of power within the existing framework, mobilization had advanced even more in the case of the Adi Dravidars at the hegemonic pan-Indian level. Splintering and splitting the varna-affected masses into ineffective and mutually antagonistic fragments was greatly to the advantage of the dominant Brahman forces; and graded power-congruence was a discourse that the same forces could countenance, negotiate with and even encourage. However, there was an undercurrent of understanding among the subalterns that it was the abolition of varna / caste that would prove of maximum, wholistic and secure benefit for its worst victims and its relegation, in turn, would affect them most. If the non-Brahman castes could not wait for the abolition of the varna principle of social relations to appropriate the homogenized power, much less could the Adi Dravidars located at the receiving end from all quarters. This was certainly a dilemma for all caste-affected groups, but understandably much more for the Adi Dravidars. The concept of self-respect did bring all the victims of Brahmanism together. Yet there were, in addition to the unevenness within, active and effectively hegemonic forces of pan-Indian Brahmanism, which the Self-Respect Movement, both of the Adi Dravidars as well as the Dravidars, had to confront and cope with.

Conclusion

In the wake of the systematic devolution of power by the imperial British on the one hand, and against the backdrop of the Sanskrit-Brahmanical's inexorable and near-monopolistic congruence with the same power on the other, the subaltern social groups of Northern Tamizhgam made a sustained bid, in the early decades of the twentieth century, to re-identify themselves both conceptually and concretely, in order to bring about a minimal congruence between power and the culture they represented. This article has attempted to selectively narrate the story and interpretatively highlight the dilemmas involved in such a process of identification, as found expression in the columns and pages of *Tamiḻaṉ*. The dilemmas, it has been seen, arose both from the general situation of subalternity, as well as its particular historical manifestation in the sub-continent of late colonialism.

If iteration or utterance are expected to bring about a change of discourse, in the case of the subalterns it does so only attentuatedly and indirectly. Iyothee Thassar's comprehensive, largely coherent and compelling re-iteration did, to an extent, destabilize the dominant discourse of the time within the Tamil-speaking world, and laid the moral-intellectual foundation for the mobilization of not only the so-called Paraiyar communities but also the larger Tamil / Dravidian population as well. To the subaltern communities it also delivered a new self-identification – Adi Dravidar, in the place of that of the despised Paraiyar. However, it was in the course of concrete action, particularly during the second phase of the journal, that the limitations, as well as the ambiguities and tensions, within the existential situation of the subalterns came to the surface.

The most significant aspect of the dilemma sprang from the complex realization that, while on the one hand, substantial, systematic and secure emancipation for those at the very bottom of the social scale can come about only with the larger change in the very terms of dominance, it is much too idealistic on the other hand, not to appropriate the small-little, evanescent, distorting and even eventually counter-productive emancipatory fragments made available at the moment within the existing pattern of dominance. From this basic dilemma flows several others, at the levels both of ideological formulation as well as strategic mobilization: should the subalterns primarily concern themselves with the change of the system or only with their own separatist-emancipation? What is the appropriate mobilisational strategy – inclusive or exclusive? If exclusive, how does one escape from slipping into the same old ghetto-like and branded identification? If inclusive, who is it to be inclusive of to begin with, and how does one avoid getting submerged in concerns not immediate to oneself? What is the ultimate goal of subaltern endeavours – perpetuation and promotion of a separatist identity or to merge within a larger identity? If the latter, what exactly is this larger identity? Dilemmas such as these do come to be debated within the movement; and such debates cannot be said to be free of group or personal, sectarian / selfish interests. What is not to be missed, however, is the alert, active and hegemonic presence of the dominant forces, engaged in the ceaseless process of thwarting or co-opting the subaltern agenda. The result of all these, and much more, is the contesting plurality of conceptualization as well as mobilization among the subalterns themselves, leading to a general frustration of their own efforts. Subaltern reiteration and mobilization, with these and similar limitations, do bring about emancipation for themselves and also change in the larger society. However, such change was often not what was envisaged, or not holistic or secure, in the sense of being structurally consolidated.

Opening up the debate on inclusive *tami̲la̲n* or exclusive *pa̲raiya̲n* identity, the journal registered in its columns and pages all the vicissitudes involved in such a process of subaltern self-identification. There was a continual search for an appropriate but also effective inclusive identity all through the life of the journal – *tami̲la̲n*, *tirāviṭa̲n*, Buddhist and even Hindu. It is pertinent, in that context, to remember that the possible identification as 'Indian' was no where on the horizon, not even of the dominant forces. Quotidian life and politics, as well as the concrete emanicipatory project, necessitated the distinctions – Paraiyars or Adi Dravidars to even Adi Hindus. The fact that debates on both sets of identities were inconclusive, indicates the existential dilemma of the groups involved. In operationalisation, both these sets seemed to engender problems that are not easily dealt with. Another aspect of the same historical problem pertains to the sphere of ground level politics. If the human agency behind the degraded and despised Paraiyar identity was unerringly and convincingly identified as the Brahmanical, its day-to-day reproduction, however, was effected largely by the Brahmanically determined non-Brahmanical. The re-identification process of the subaltern had to ceaselessly understand the ambivalent dynamics of, posture itself vis-à-vis, and negotiate with, this 'non-Brahmanical'. When the non-Brahmanical agency gradually achieved some sort of local hegemony under the very identification of Dravidian, the conceptual edifice of Brahmanically caused degradation began to lose salience. However, it was realized simultaneously that the non-Brahmanical agency also found it comfortable to exercise its local dominance, more often than not through the very same terms as the Brahmanical. Iyothee Thassar's early offer of cooperation with the emerging non-Brahmanical agency, conditioned on its comprehensive anti-Brahmanism, in the light and experience of subsequent (despite several positive) developments, was found to be losing relevance. It was again, in this context, that even the self-chosen identification of Adi Dravidar also began to appear as alien and as the 'other-given'. Numerous changes, both cultural and structural, finally came to mark the social polity of the sub-continent from the 1930s onwards and the most important among them, at least as far as the subalterns were concerned, was the political emergence of Ambedkar. An understanding of what followed, of the new directions and renewed attempts at self-identification, needs to be seen within the former context that has been discussed here.

Bibliography

Aloysius, Gnanasigamony. 1997. *Nationalism without a Nation in India.* Delhi: Oxford University Press.

——. 1998. *Religion as Emancipatory Identity.* Delhi: New Age International.

——. (Tam. ñāṉ. alāyciyas), ed. 1999. *Ayōttitācar cintaṉaikaḷ.* 3 vols. Palayamkottai: Folklore Resources and Research Centre St. Xavier's College.

——. 2004. *Dalit-Subaltern Emergence in Religio-Cultural Subjectivity: Iyothee Thassar and Tamil Buddhism.* New Delhi: Critical Quest.

Arooran, N. K. 1980. *Tamil Renaissance and Dravidian Nationalism.* Madurai: Koodal Publishers.

Baker, C. J. 1984. *An Indian Rural Economy 1880–1955. The Tamil Nadu Countryside.* Delhi: Oxford University Press.

Fraser, Nancy. 2008. *Social Justice in the Age of Identity Politics*. New Delhi: Critical Quest.

Frykenberg, Robert Eric. 1993. 'Constructions of Hinduism at the nexus of History and Religion', *Journal of Interdisciplinary History*, 13, 3: 523–550.

Gandhi, M. K. 1962. *Varnashrama Dharma*, Ahamedabad: Navjivan Publishing House.

Geetha, V. 1993. 'Rewriting history in the Brahmin's Shadow: Caste and the Modern Historical Imagination', *Journal of Arts and Ideas*, 25–26: 127–137.

Gettha, V. and Rajadurai, S. V. 1993. 'Dalit and Non-Brahmin Consciousness in Colonial Tamil Nadu', *Economic and Political Weekly*, 28: 2091–2098.

Gramsci, Antonio. 1971. *Selections from Prison Notebooks*. Quintin Hoare and G. N. Smith, eds. New York: International Publishers.

Guha, Ranajit. 1991. *A Disciplinary Aspect of Indian Nationalism*. Santa Cruz: Merill Publications.

Irschick, Eugene F. 1969. *Politics and Social Conflict in South India: the Non-Brahmin Movement and Tamil Separatism, 1916–1929*. Berkeley: University of California Press.

——.1986. *Tamil Revivalism in the 1930s*. Madras: Cre-a.

——. 1994. *Dialogue and History Constructing South India, 1795–1895*. Delhi: Oxford University Press.

Joshi, L. M. 2007. *Brahminism, Buddhism and Hinduism*. New Delhi: Critical Quest.

King, Richard. 2008. *Orientalism and the Myth of Modern Hinduism*. New Delhi: Critical Quest.

Ludden, David. 1985. *A Peasant History of South India*. Delhi: Oxford University Press.

Oppert, Gustav. 1972. *On the Original Inhabitants of Bharatvarsa or India*. 1893. Delhi: Oriental Publishers.

Pande, G. C. 1978. *The Samana Tradition*. Ahmedabad: L. D. Institute of Indology.

Perumal, S. 2000. *People's Movements and Tamil Publications – 1850–1950*. Vellore: Megalai Publications.

Pillai, Perumal (Tam. perumāḷ piḷḷail). 1922. *Ātitirāviṭar varalāṟu*. Chennai: Victoria Press.

Ponnovium, Anbu. 1962. 'Pandithar Ka. Iyothee Thassar', *Ambedkar* issue dated 15-08-62.

——. 1992. 'N. Sivaraj', *Aravurai*, 1, 6: 7–10.

Srinivas, M. N. 1966. *Social Change in Modern India*, Hyderabad: Orient Longman.

Srinivasan, R. (Tam. iraṭṭaimalai cīṉivācaṉār). No date. *Jīviya carittira curukkam*.

Thapar, Romila. 2004. *Imagined Religious Community*. New Delhi: Critical Quest.

Thurston, Edgar. 1907. *Castes and Tribes of Southern India*. Madras: Government Press.

Washbrook, D. A. 1993. 'Land and Labour in the late 18th Century Colonial South India: The Golden Age of the Paraiahs?', in: Peter Robb, ed. *Dalit Movements and Meaning of Labour in India*. Delhi: Oxford University Press.

A. R. Venkatachalapathy

'More Kshatriya than thou!' Debating caste and ritual ranking in colonial Tamilnadu[1]

> It is gratifying to note that the ethnological struggle on the part of the several castes of Southern India for social supremacy in the scale of God's creation is, in my opinion, not altogether without "a soul of goodness" in that it contributes, to no small extent, to enrich the knowledge of the students of the anthropology of the Baratha Kanda, although it is viewed as a sign of an unhealthy state of society by those, of whom I am one, who would like to see the equilibrium of social happiness never disturbed.[2]

In this article I seek to recover and analyse an ideological conflict between two castes in colonial Tamilnadu. In the early decades of the twentieth century a series of acrimonious debates, leading up to even court cases, occurred between two castes each of which not only claimed Kshatriya (Skt. kṣatriya, Tam. kṣattiriyar) status for itself but also contested the other's claim to it. Caste conflict, often marked by violence, is by no means novel in Indian society. That the two populous castes of Nadars (Tam. nāṭār) and Vanniyars (Tam. vaṉṉiyar) aspired to Kshatriya status is well known in the literature. However what marks out the little-known debates that I unearth and discuss here is the fact that these two castes do not inhabit the same region. In the process of Sanskritising and claiming a higher status in the caste hierarchy, M. N. Srinivas observes that "occasionally a caste claims a position which its neighbours are not willing to concede".[3] The assumption or suggestion here seems to be that the caste(s) that contest the claim are physical neighbours. Nadars predominantly live in the four erstwhile southern districts of Kanyakumari, Tirunelveli, Madurai and Ramanathapuram, while the Vanniyars are the most populous caste in the northern districts of Chingleput, North Arcot, South Arcot and Salem districts. The only region where these two castes live in any proximity is the working class neighbourhood of North Chennai, viz., Royapuram, Vannarapettai and Thondaiyarpettai.

---

[1] K. A. Manikumar commented on an earlier draft. Bernard Bate subjected the article to detailed criticism. The late Tha. Kovendhan, Mamani and A. Thiruneelakandan provided help with source material. All translations from Tamil sources are mine.

[2] T. Balasundara Mudaliar, 'Opinions' in Arumuga Nayakar 1907: 11.

[3] Srinivas 1966: 6.

Nadars faced the brunt of organised violence, especially at the hands of upper caste Nairs (Tam. / Mal. nāyar) and Vellalars (Tam. veḷḷāḷar) in the early part of the nineteenth century (in the Kanyakumari region) and at the hands of the Maravars (Tam. maṟavar) (in the south Pandya country) in the late nineteenth century (the place names of Kalugumalai, Kamudi, Sivakasi have become metaphors for caste violence not only in Nadar memory but in Tamil collective consciousness as well)[4]. In these cases there is little evidence of ideological argument and only brute physical force prevailed. But the debates I discuss here were carried out exclusively in the emerging public sphere through the medium and modality of print, and were mediated by colonial forms of knowledge.

Before I embark on the exercise of tracing and narrating these debates, a brief summary of the changing status of Nadars and Vanniyars in the context of the colonial transformation is in order. During the nineteenth century, as is now very well known, the transformation of Tamil society was marked by the improved means of communication and transport, wider marketing networks, the incursion of the state in the farthest reaches of society and economy, newer economic opportunities, western education, and the rise of a new elite class within each community.

In his classic work on the history of Nadars, Robert Hardgrave Jr lucidly narrates their dramatic and exemplary rise from a position barely above the so-called untouchables to a position of vast economic, social and political power in less than a century.[5] From pursuing the stigmatised occupation of toddy-tapping, Nadars, through a complex process of engagement with Christianity and colonialism, became a major trading caste in the late nineteenth century. By the 1860s, buttressed by the newly acquired wealth, Nadars adopted new social and ritual practices – they turned to vegetarian diet, adopted teetotalism, wore the sacred thread, applied sacred ash, changed their sartorial and coiffure styles, including golden jewellery for women – and began to claim Kshatriya status. They constructed an origin myth for their caste and claimed that they were the descendants of the Pandya kings. Hardgrave counts at least 40 books extolling the high status and greatness of the Nadars in the seventy five years after 1857.[6] Soon they attempted to enter Sanskritic temples, which was thwarted not only by the violence of Maravars but by the colonial

[4] In 1895, the Nadars of Kalugumalai village were prohibited by the zamin of Ettaiyapuram from conducting street processions and, in the ensuing riots, many Nadars were killed and their homes looted. In 1897, Nadars attempted to enter the Siva temple in Kamudi in Ramanathapuram district. A suit was filed, which the Nadars lost. In 1899, there was major conflict between Nadars and Maravars in Sivakasi, which resulted in the sack of the Nadar settlement and many murders.

[5] Hardgrave 1969. Also see Templeman 1996.

[6] Hardgrave 1969: 78.

legal-judicial system as well – a situation that did not formally change until late in the colonial period. Caste associations based on communal solidarity and enterprise rarely seen among other castes underpinned the rise of Nadars. The kinship organisation of *uṟaviṉmuṟai*, the subscription system of *makimai*, etc., were used to construct temples, schools and public wells. An attempt was made in 1895 to found the Kshatriya Mahajana Sangam, a provincial level organisation, but floundered, and it was not until 1910 that the Nadar Mahajana Sangam was formed.[7] The community's association with the Non-Brahman movement, both in the justice and self-respect phases, greatly enhanced the political position of the Nadars, culminating in the spectacular rise of K. Kamaraj as 'king-maker' both in the provincial and, later, in the national Congress.

Vanniyars, despite their growing political power in northern Tamilnadu since the reservation agitation in the 1980s and the rise of Pattali Makkal Katchi with its shrewd negotiation of electoral politics in a situation of fragmented polity, are yet to have their Hardgrave, or even a Dennis Templeman. Based largely on secondary sources – especially Thurston, census reports and contemporary newspaper reports and interviews – the Rudolphs sketched the rise of Vanniyars in their classic work *The Modernity of Tradition*.[8] A community made basically of agricultural labourers and tenant farmers, the Vanniyars, despite the proximity to the presidency capital of Madras, have by no means matched the spectacular rise of the Nadars. This is not to gainsay the significant mobility that the community had enjoyed in colonial Tamilnadu. Even by the first census in 1871, Vanniyars had claimed Kshatriya status as descendants of the fire races[9] with the publication of *Cāticaṅkiracāram*. By 1891 the *Vaṉṉiyakula viḷakkam (A Treatise on the Vanniya Caste)* was published. Their caste association, the Chennai Vannikula Kshatriya Mahasangam, was established as early as 1888.

Both Nadars and Vanniyars entered the emerging public sphere through the medium of print and caste associations. The earliest Nadar journals were *Cāṉṟōrkula tīpam* (1889) and *Cāṉṟōrkula vivēkapōtini* (1909). By 1897 the first Vanniyar journal, *Akkiṉikula kṣattiriya mittiraṉ,* had been launched by A. Subramania Nayagar, who figures prominently in the debates of the 1910s and 1920s. These were followed by *Akkiṉikulatittaṉ* (1908), *Vaṉṉiyakula kṣattiriya tīpam* (1912), *Vaṉṉikula mittiraṉ* (1913), *Kṣattiriyaṉ* (1923), *Kṣattiriya cikāmaṇi* (1923) and *Vīrapārati* (1927).[10]

---

[7] Hardgrave 1969: 130–131.

[8] Rudolph and Rudolph 1967.

[9] Kshatriyas were said to have three lineages (Skt. kula): the solar (Skt. sūrya), the lunar (Skt. candra) and the fire (Skt. agni, Tam. akkiṉi).

[10] Kavirinadan 2005: 11–12.

Even though the print runs of these journals were small, they made a deep impact on the identity of these communities.[11]

The proximate reason for the mobilisation of these castes in the late nineteenth century was the census. The Vanniyars demanded the dropping of the name 'Palli' (Tam. paḷḷi) and wanted to be returned as 'Vannikula Khsatriyas' (Tam. vaṉṉikula kṣattiriyar). The Nadars similarly did not want to be called 'Shanar' (Tam. cāṇār). The demand for a revised nomenclature was premised upon a certain view of Hindu social structure which was being codified by colonialism. This drew upon the Orientalist knowledge that was being recovered, produced and defined using new disciplines such as history, ethnography, epigraphy, etymology, philology and lexicography. Traditional notions of caste hierarchy coalesced with the Orientalist vision of a normatively ordered Indian society. This was so especially in relation to caste as varna (Skt. varṇa) – a theoretical construct –, as distinct from caste as jati (Tam. cāti, Skt. jāti) – a functioning social unit and determined by endogamy.

While caste as jati was certainly a lived reality of indigenous society, caste as varna – a more theoretical construct – had limited currency in Tamil society. While the four-fold varna (Tam. nālvaruṇam) as a phrase had usage, the slots of Kshatriya and Vaisya (Skt. vaiśya) varnas were empty in the Tamil caste structure. This explains, for instance, the phenomenally erudite Sivagnana Munivar, writing in the eighteenth century, being forced to claim a superior and 'clean' status for his Vellalar caste by calling it Sat Sudra (Tam. caṟcūttirar) to distinguish it from other lowly Sudras (Skt. śūdra, Tam. cūttirar). By the late nineteenth century, at the height of the Orientalist moment, we find many castes, as part of their upward mobility, claiming higher status by wanting to be assigned a new varna – either Kshatriya or Sudra.[12] The Vellalars claimed Vaisya status for themselves and produced the very influential *Varuṇa cintāmaṇi.*[13] Similarly, Nadars and Vanniyars claimed the non-existent Kshatriya varna status. History bears out that these claims for a higher varna status never succeeded. But even the cul-de-sacs of history can often deepen our understanding and it is in this hope that this article explores the now-forgotten debates between the Nadars and Vanniyars.

---

[11] David Washbrook argues that "... twenty-three years after the foundation [1888] of their Vannikula Kshatriya Sangham, the wealthy Pallis had convinced remarkably few of their depressed brethren to join their campaign (in the 1911 census, 89 per cent of the caste continued to return itself as Palli)". Washbrook 1975: 171 and endnote. This is completely beside the point.

[12] The much maligned Viswakarma caste, quite exceptionally, claimed Brahman status!

[13] Kanakasabhai Pillai 1925. The book carried forewords from as many as two dozen people of various castes. C. Subramania Bharati, the iconic Tamil poet, wrote prefaces to only two books in his lifetime and *Varuṇa cintāmaṇi* was the first.

I

From the available evidence the first salvo in the war of the Kshatriyas appears to have been fired in 1907.[14] Ka. Arumuga Nayagar's elaborate Vanniya interpretation of the history of varnas and the place of Vanniyar in it (the volume runs into about 400 pages), *Varuṇa taruppaṇam* (The Mirror of Caste),[15] devotes the last section of the book to refuting the claims of other castes to higher, especially Kshatriya status. After putatively establishing the Vanniyar claim to Kshatriya-hood, *Varuṇa taruppaṇam* devotes about 10 pages exclusively to demolishing Nadar claims for Kshatriya status. *Varuṇa taruppaṇam* first provides a detailed account, through a verbatim reproduction of Justice Benson's judgment, of the Kamudi temple entry movement and its ultimate failure. Consistently using the derisive word 'Shanar' to refer to the Nadars, *Varuṇa taruppaṇam* emphatically states that "there is no evidence to show that the Shanars are of the Kshatriya lineage or that they come in the line of Pandya and Chola kings".[16] Refutation of caste status cannot of course be without recourse to etymology and philological exegesis! *Varuṇa taruppaṇam* argued that 'Nadan' (Tam. nāṭāṉ) meant "the un-approached or unapproachable" and that 'Gramani' (Tam. kirāmaṇi)[17] derived from 'grama-anniyan' (Tam. kirāma-aṉṉiyaṉ) or "outcaste to the village"[18] – clearly assigning the Nadar status to outside the caste fold.

But this refutation is not without sociological merit, though couched in patronising terms, when *Varuṇa taruppaṇam* goes on to observe that:

> Even though toddy-tapping is the customary caste occupation [of the Nadars], with education, enterprise and wealth they have captured trade. ... As their status had risen due to their wealth they have tried to elevate themselves in the religious temple rituals as well. But in their efforts to equate their status with those of other castes they should not usurp the freedom of the castes above them. They should strive to rise among themselves [?]. If their efforts are in this direction without

---

14 In an appendix to his work on the Nadars, Hardgrave provides a chronology of Nadar caste histories in which he lists an 1892 work entitled 'Pallihal Vayappu' (= *Paḷḷikaḷ vāyāppu*) (A Refutation of the Palli Caste?) by one K. Shanmuga Gramani. I have not been able to trace this work. Since Hardgrave also does not cite or quote it, one can barely guess its content.

15 The Rudolphs misdate this volume to 1901 and also wrongly attribute it to T. Ayyakannu Nayagar. They also indicate that the place of publication is not known, while it was in fact published from Madras. Rudolph and Rudolph: 50n.

16 Arumuga Nayagar 1907: 378.

17 Gramani is a toddy-tapping caste in northern Tamilnadu. In the colonial period, through the familiar process of aggregation, Gramanis came to coalesce with Nadars, many of whom were migrating to the colonial city of Madras. The aggregation was more political than social and rarely included marriage.

18 Arumuga Nayagar 1907: 379.

harming others not only will the fair-minded sympathise with them but they can also win the protection of law courts.[19]

Finally, *Varuṇa taruppaṇam* rested its case with the words:

> Some later day 'wise' men, akin to imprisoning the wind in a pot, published books that the Shanars were Kshatriyas. But all these books contradict one another. Following our earlier arguments it is clear that they are neither Kshatriyas nor Vellalars. As stated in the tivākaram and piṅkalam [two authoritative medieval verse dictionaries] they rank below the Sudras.[20]

The arguments and insinuations of *Varuṇa taruppaṇam* were carried over in a few years by *Śrī vaṉṉi vamca pirakācikai.*[21] This short catechism was written by Salem Ardhanareesa Varma (1874–1964), a man of many parts and a stalwart in the politics of the Vanniyars.[22] In his long career spanning over seven decades, Ardhanareesa Varma wrote copiously (he composed the only known verse elegy on Subramania Bharati's death), published journals, took part in nationalist agitation and organised Vanniyars. Basing himself on *Cāticaṅkiracāram* and *Varuṇa taruppaṇam,* Ardhanareesa Varma explicated the ideas of Vanniyar superiority in questions and answers apparently for the benefit of 'boys'. After providing an etymology of 'Vanniyar' (Tam. vaṉṉi / Skt. *vahni* = fire, and Skt. ja = born of), the catechism elaborates the proliferation of castes by *anuloma, pratiloma* and *saṃkara* marriages. Finally it settles down to refuting the Kshatriya claims of some lower castes such as Paravar, Maravar and Vadugar (Tam. vaṭukar), including Shanar. With reference to the Nadars it rephrases the etymological arguments of *Varuṇa taruppaṇam* and ridiculed the Nadars for calling themselves *cāṉṟōrkula kṣattiriyar*, "a caste (*kulam*) that does not occur in any textual authority".[23]

Interestingly there is no evidence to suggest that the gauntlet was picked up by the Nadars until many years later. It was the Kammalars who went to court in the Salem Sub-divisional Magistrate's court immediately after the first edition was published in 1912. The case however was dismissed as the magistrate observed that "it is difficult to

[19] Arumuga Nayagar 1907: 378.

[20] Arumuga Nayagar 1907: 318.

[21] *Śrī vaṉṉi vamca pirakācikai* appears to have been first published in 1912 and reprinted the very next year. I have followed the 2007 reprint edited by V. Balakrishnan.

[22] Shanmugasundaram 1995 is the only available biography on him. Though sloppily written it contains a wealth of information.

[23] *Śrī vaṉṉi vamca pirakācikai:* 32–33.

obtain sensible replies from the plaintiff. ... I do not believe that there are defamatory words in the book".[24]

Vanniyar intellectuals seem to have continued with their tirade against Nadars and their Kshatriya status. It appears that the *Vaṉṉikula mittiraṉ*, edited and published by A. Subramania Nayagar from the Perambur Barracks region of North Madras, was at the forefront of this attack. A. Subramania Nayagar, who began his career as a printing apprentice, had risen to be a journalist and activist in Vanniyar politics. He seems to have wielded considerable influence on the Vanniyar working class of the region with its large number of textile mills. He also seems to have evinced antiquarian interests and had started collecting material for his histories and genealogies of Vanniyars, including the *Vaṉṉiya purāṇam,* from a very early age.[25] He was also instrumental in commissioning, printing, and publishing many works which provided intellectual ammunition for the Vanniyars' Kshatriya guns.

September 1919 saw the publication of two journals devoted to Nadar uplift and organisation. *Kṣattiriya mittiraṉ*, published from Thondiarpettai in North Madras, was edited by T. Vijaya Duraisamy Gramani.[26] The journal was certainly published until 1925 (volume six) but I have been unable to find when it ceased publication. T. Vijaya Duraisami Gramani was prominent in the debates concerning the caste and he authored a number of works on Nadar history and culture: *Āriya kṣattiriyakula viḷakkam* (1910), *Namatu kula toḻil yātu?* (1922), *Kṣattiriyar* (1923), *Namatu kula toḻil* (1926), *Nāṭār eṉṉum col ārāycci: Araca kulattai kuṟittu eḻutiya or pirapantam* (1927). Some of these works were originally serialised in the *Kṣattiriya mittiraṉ*. The other journal, *Nāṭārkula mittiraṉ*, began its career as a monthly and later became a bimonthly and then a weekly. After the first few years, when it showed Indian nationalist leanings, it became an important mouthpiece for E. V. Ramasami's Self-Respect Movement within the community. It was edited by S. A. Muthu Nadar and ceased publication only in 1931. Both these journals played a leading part in the acrimonious debate with the Vanniyar journals, *Vaṉṉikula mittiraṉ* and *Kṣattiriyaṉ*.

---

[24] *Śrī vaṉṉi vamca pirakācikai:* appendix. It is interesting to note that Kammalars with their Brahman pretensions were often in the forefront of disputing caste claims, starting from the famous Chittoor Adalat Court case (1818) to the use of 'Achari' as a caste suffix (during the first Rajaji ministry). The above case, however, seems to strengthen M. N. Srinivas' assertion: 'Normally Sanskritisation enables a caste to obtain a higher position in the hierarchy. But in the case of the Smiths [kammalar] it seems to have resulted only in their drawing upon themselves the wrath of all the other castes.' Srinivas 2002: 202.

[25] See his preface, dated 12 June 1955, to *Tirukkaivaḷam* (Subramania Nayagar 1955).

[26] I have been able to consult volumes I, II and VI. I remember with gratitude my mentor, Tha. Kovendhan, who brought this journal to my notice.

Vaṉṉikula mittiraṉ was started in 1913 and appears to have continued until 1930. As indicated earlier, it was edited and published by A. Subramania Nayagar. *Kṣattiriyaṉ*, edited by Ardhanareesa Varma, was published from Salem as a monthly. After two abortive attempts to run this journal, he revived it in Chennai when he moved to the city in January 1925. While one issue of *Vaṉṉikula mittiraṉ* has survived (a bumper issue containing the June, July, August and September numbers of 1924) nobody seems to have traced even a single issue of *Kṣattiriyaṉ*. Our information of the articles in the Vanniyar journals comes, apart from the single bumper issue mentioned above, from the refutations published in the two Nadar journals. Thankfully, Vijaya Duraisamy Gramani had the habit, something he prided himself upon and challenged his adversaries to emulate, of reproducing verbatim the opponents' views before proceeding to demolish them.

The very third number (November 1919) of *Kṣattiriya mittiraṉ* carried "A Warning to *Vaṉṉikula mittiraṉ*".[27] Adverting to the insinuations that Nadars and Gramanis were not Kshatriyas and that there were no textual authority to prove this status, Vijaya Duraisamy Gramani stated that "abusing other castes is the habit of the unlettered" and asked it to desist from such abuse immediately.

It was only towards the end of 1919, years after the publication of *Śrī vaṉṉi vamca pirakācikai*, that the Nadars seem to have taken notice of it. In the very next issue of *Kṣattiriya mittiraṉ* a detailed refutation of the book appeared by one Ne. Mu. Sha. Shanmugasundara Nayanar of Vannarapettai, Chennai. Ridiculing the claim that only Vanniyars (the derogatory word Palli is used) belong to the Agnikula Kshatriyas and that all royal dynasties including the Chera, Chola, Pandyas, the Kerala kings, and the Vijayanagara kings are their kin, the author also criticised the invidious nature of the book when the nationalist movement was going on towards uniting all the people. Stating that he was writing an elaborate refutation of the book with the title *Vaṉṉikku varuṇaṉ* (Rain on the fire), he claimed that many of the notaries who had provided opinions and prefatorial comments had been misled and that they were now willing to set the record straight by writing for the new volume.[28] (Writing in 1924, in the context of litigation against Nadar journals, A. Subramania Nayagar claimed that he had ignored this particular piece as being too ridiculous to require a refutation.[29])

---

27 *Kṣattiriya mittiraṉ*, 1,3, November 1919: 93.

28 *Kṣattiriya mittiraṉ*, 1,4, December 1919. 123–124.

29 *Vaṉṉikula mittiraṉ*, 'Tiruñāṉacampanta ceṭṭiyār maṉṉippu kaṭitam', June–September 1924.

After these two pieces of writing in *Kṣattiriya mittiraṉ* there appears to be a lull for a few years in the debate, or at least the issues of the journals have not survived. In the first number of volume VI (September 1924) there appears a refutation of the writings in *Kṣattiriyaṉ*. By this time the bulk of the journal is taken up by the Nadar-Vanniyar debate. As stated earlier, Vijaya Duraisamy Gramani published Ardhanareesa Varma's accusations verbatim and then proceeded to contradict them. It appears to be a continuation of published work in earlier numbers, which unfortunately have not survived. In the absence of these files, it is not clear when the tirades had actually been revived. It can probably be dated to early 1924.

An important point in the revived debate turned around the semantics of the words 'Sandror' (Tam. *cāṉṟōr*) and 'Nadar'. While the Vanniyars contended that it meant 'noble' people in general, the Nadars claimed that it referred exclusively to their forbears. Another twist to the semantics was the etymology: while Vanniyars claimed that the term came from *cāṟu* meaning 'toddy' the Nadars contended that it came from *cāl* or 'abundance' and later extended to mean 'noble character'. While Nadars treated *nāṭu* as a noun (meaning 'country' and by extension its rulers), Vanniyars treated it as a verb ('to seek' and its antonym to 'avoid')!

Kṣattiriyaṉ had also thrown a wager of Rs 500 to any one who could prove that the term Sandror referred to the Nadars. *Kṣattiriya mittiraṉ* countered it by saying that now that it had demonstrated this meaning he should, "if he was a true-born upper-caste Palli", not only republish his refutation but send the wager amount immediately.

If the Nadars' association with the palm tree and tapping toddy came in for consistent criticism and derision the Nadars in turn always used the term Palli, deeply detested by the Vanniyars, to refer to them. In a quick counter move *Kṣattiriya mittiraṉ* also went into the origins of the word 'Palli' and claimed that it came from the word *paḷḷam* (pit) and played on this sense of the word to denigrate Ardhanareesa Varma.[30]

The response from Ardhanareesa Varma seems to have been swift. In the 23 July 1924 issue of *Kṣattiriyaṉ* he raised the wager to a thousand rupees. The *Vaṉṉikula mittiraṉ* had also by then joined the issue. One S. Krishnaswamy Iyer raised many questions in an open letter to *Kṣattiriya mittiraṉ*. He asserted that the evidence cited by the Nadars thus far were 'shameful' and that their arguments relied on:

> Mere word play not befitting intelligent people ... All you have done so far is to keep repeating the three words, cāṉṟōr, nāṭār and kirāmaṇi. ... Even the words

[30] *Kṣattiriya mittiraṉ*, 6,1, September 1924.

kōṉār, cēṉaikkāraṉ, aruntati-kulam and cāmpāṉ [all lower caste names] appear majestic. ... Therefore mere wordplay won't do.

He raised seven questions. These questions revolved around the antiquity of the titles that the Nadars claimed, the traditional occupation of toddy-tapping, the absence of ruler-ship in terms of zamins, palayams, etc., the prohibition of entry into temples and the lack of literary works on Nadars.[31]

The sole surviving issue of *Vaṉṉikula mittiraṉ* also carries a refutation by M. S. Subramania Iyer, a journalist and author of several works of vicarious nationalism (the expression of nationalist sentiment and rhetoric by writing about the past wherein the enemy figure is Muslim rather than overtly criticising British colonialism), including a book extolling the bravery of Rajput kings. Written in response to an attack on his book, *Rājaputtira vijayam,* by one Murugadasan in the pages of *Nāṭārkula mittiraṉ*, he argued that there the division of Surya Kulam, Candra Kulam and Agni Kulam among kings did not exist; he asserted that Vanniyars were indeed of the Agni Kulam. He added that, based on the "vulgar essays" by Vijaya Duraisamy Gramani "some Nadar friends are raising pointless arguments".[32]

Vijaya Duraisamy Gramani now attempted to reply to the questions of both Ardhanareesa Varma and M. S. Subramania Iyer point by point and posed the counter question of the antiquity of the Vanniyar titles such as Nayagar, Varma, Boopathy, etc.[33]

While a modicum of intellectual and social decorum was maintained in the pages of *Vaṉṉikula mittiraṉ* and *Kṣattiriya mittiraṉ*, no punches seems to have been pulled in *Nāṭārkula mittiraṉ*. One S. S. Sankaralinga Nadar, writing in the pages of *Nāṭārkula mittiraṉ* offensively termed the writings of Ardhanareesa Varma as *ampaṭṭaṉ kuppai* (waste bin of the barber)! He also quoted offensive proverbs and popular sayings about Vanniyars. In a number of places Ardhanareesa Varma's frequent change of names – Varma, Nayagar, Rajarishi, etc. – came in for much ridicule. Vanniyar accusations and innuendoes about the fiasco of Kamudi temple entry and the sack of Sivakasi seem to have particularly rankled in the minds of the Nadars.[34]

Nāṭārkula mittiraṉ carried a series of articles by Murugadasan and Sankaralinga Nadar. It asserted that, contrary to their claims to royalty, Vanniyars descended from Kuravar (Tam. kuṟavar) and Vettuvar (Tam.

---

[31] *Vaṉṉikula mittiraṉ*, June–September 1924.

[32] *Vaṉṉikula mittiraṉ*, June–September 1924.

[33] *Kṣattiriya mittiraṉ*, 6,1, September 1924.

[34] *Nāṭārkula mittiraṉ*, 15 September 1924. See articles by Sankaralinga Nadar and Nathan.

vēṭṭuvar) tribal communities, ate snails and crabs, remarried widows and had loose morals. The culture of the poor Vanniyars in the Royapuram and Vannarapettai region of North Madras – their poor hovels, their squalor, irregular baths, immodest attire, wearing of ornaments made of brass, the women addressing the men folk in the singular, etc. – was ridiculed: "they conduct a whole marriage in fifteen rupees"![35]

The tenor and the trajectory of the debate, if you could call it that, inevitably led to the courts and litigation. Both Nadar journals were sued by the Vanniyars. In April 1924, A. Subramania Nayagar and A. Balasundara Nayagar (the son of the author of *Varuṇa taruppaṇam*) sued T. Vijaya Duraisamy Gramani and Thirugnanasambanda Chettiar for defamation at the Chief Presidency Magistrate's Court, Egmore, Chennai. The prefatorial poem by Vijaya Duraiswamy Gramani, written for Thirugnanasambanda Chettiar's *Vaṉṉikku varuṇaṉ* and republished in the February 1924 number of *Kṣattiriya mittiraṉ,* was the subject of dispute. In the hearing on 7 May 1924, Thirugnanasambanda Chettiar apologised but Vijaya Duraisamy Gramani did not appear and the case was adjourned. In the next hearing on 30 May 1924, Vijaya Duraisamy Gramani appeared in court with the issue of *Kṣattiriya mittiraṉ* carrying Thiruganasambanda Chettiar's apology. This is the version of the events provided by *Vaṉṉikula mittiraṉ* which claimed victory.[36]

Kṣattiriya mittiraṉ gives a very different story. Vijaya Duraisamy Gramani claimed that he did not at first notice A. Subramania Nayagar's pamphlet wherein he had drawn attention to the alleged defamatory remarks. Only after the legal notice was served had he consulted a lawyer. The following reply was sent: "My client is not in a position to understand a reference to the February part of *Kṣattiriya mittiraṉ*, which passage you refer to as defamatory to the Vanniya community ..." To further replies, Vijaya Duraisamy Gramani's lawyer maintained the line of incomprehensibility. I have been unable to find out the outcome of this particular litigation.[37] But suffice it to say that, given the nature of the case, whatever the outcome, each party could claim victory.

A few months later, in January 1925, another case was filed at the Second Presidency Magistrate's Court in George Town, Madras. The article "Varma vamcattār", wherein many derogatory comments were made about the poor Vanniyars living in the North Chennai region, was the bone of contention. The author of the article, Sankaralinga Nadar, and

---

[35] *Nāṭārkula mittiraṉ*, 22 September 1924. See articles by Sankaralinga Nadar and Murugadasan. See also the continuation in the subsequent issue dated 29 September 1924.

[36] *Vaṉṉikula mittiraṉ*, 'Tiruñāṉacampanta ceṭṭiyār maṉṉippu kaṭitam', June–September 1924.

[37] 'Policu kōrttum Tiruñāṉacampanta ceṭṭiyārum', *Kṣattiriya mittiraṉ*, 6,2, October 1924.

S. A. Muthu Nadar, the editor of *Nāṭārkula mittiraṉ* which carried it, were sued.[38] Meetings were organised, especially by Vanniyars, to campaign for the case.[39] The case dragged on for many months with frequent adjournments. The hearings were further delayed by the death of S. A. Muthu Nadar's wife. Campaigns were launched in the pages of *Nāṭārkula mittiraṉ* to garner financial support for the legal expenses.[40] Two defence committees were formed in Madurai and Chennai by Nadars.[41] The case seems to have stirred up widespread interest in the community. Reports in the newspapers reproduced in *Nāṭārkula mittiraṉ* indicate that large crowds gathered in the court.[42] But it was clear that the *Nāṭārkula mittiraṉ* was on the defensive.[43] The verdict in the case was finally delivered in early July 1925. The magistrate found the defendants guilty of defamation and imposed a fine of Rs 201. However S. A. Muthu Nadar stated in the court that he would prefer an appeal.

I have not been able to trace any further information on this. The virtual print war between the Vanniyars and Nadars also seems to have come to an end. Interestingly, however, no overt and tangible evidence for past animosity has survived. Even during the 1950s, when a political understanding was reached between Congress, then led by K. Kamaraj (Nadar) and the Vanniyar parties, Commonweal Party and Tamilnadu Toiler's Party, the signs were barely discernable. In the course of my oral histories with intellectuals of the Nadar community, and even some Vanniyar intellectuals, no one was aware of these disputes of the last century. Caste stereotypes of course prevail in the Royapuram region, but apparently these do not draw from this history.

The acceptance by the census authorities of the preferred nomenclature viz., Nadar and Vanniyar in the 1921 census, and the discontinuation of caste as a category in the 1931 census, perhaps put an end to the print war. Further, by the mid-1920s, the radical anti-caste Self-Respect Movement, led by E. V. Ramasami, had begun to take hold of the Nadars;[44] and Ramasami did not mince words when it came to rejecting the caste system as a whole and ridiculing claims to Kshatriya status. For instance, addressing a conference of the 'untouchable' caste of Pallars (Tam.

---

[38] *Nāṭārkula mittiraṉ*, 1 December 1924.

[39] *Nāṭārkula mittiraṉ*, 5 January 1925.

[40] *Nāṭārkula mittiraṉ*, 9 February 1925.

[41] *Nāṭārkula mittiraṉ*, 2 March 1925.

[42] However, S. A. Muthu Nadar states in his unpublished diary (entry dated 11.2.1925) that 100 Nadars and 20 Vanniyars turned up at the court (I am grateful to A. Thiruneelakandan for this reference).

[43] See the letter of Sankaralinga Nadar, one of the defendants, in *Nāṭārkula mittiraṉ*, 2 February 1925.

[44] For a rich study of Nadars in the Self-Respect Movement see Rajadurai 1992.

paḷḷar) or Devendrakula Vellalars (Tam. tēvēntirakkula vēḷāḷar) in September 1929, Ramasami was quite forthright in ridiculing the Sanskritising efforts of various castes.

You want to call yourselves Vellalars. Vanniyars want to call themselves Kshatriyas. Chettiyars want to call themselves Vaisyas. What for? All these amounts to only degrading yourselves ... Nadar masses too have taken to Aryan ways by wearing the sacred thread across their chests. When I exhorted them to tear away the sacred thread one friend asked me, "It has taken so long for our struggle to wear the sacred thread succeed and now you are asking us to take it away even before the thread has got dirty?" The desire to call oneself Kshatriya, or Vaisya, or Vellalar and wear the sacred thread only means that there is a caste above one's own and conceding that that caste is superior.[45]

All this no doubt contributed to the fizzling out of these debates.

II

Why dig up the past and resurrect pointless debates? Even contemporaneously this issue was raised. With their own axe to grind, both *Kṣattiriya mittiraṉ* and *Nāṭārkula mittiraṉ* published an open letter by a Vanniyar, S. Packirisami Padaiyachi, a driver from Rangoon, who claimed that he was sending it to the Nadar journals as the Vanniyar journals did not publish it.

Even though there are learned men in our community, they are wasting their time in unwanted affairs and pointless debates. ... When a number of our community men are wallowing in depraved activities, a few from Salem proclaim "I am a Kshatriya, I am Kshatriya" in a manner opposed to truth. We do not have the Kshatriya blood, valour or custom in us; therefore we are not really Kshatriyas. Brahmins have written about our tradition in such terms. It is despicable that we should glory in such meaningless-ness ... Therefore, the present unwanted debates should be spurned and we should work for the benefit of our people.[46]

If this was the view of a member of the community we have a similar position being articulated by an intellectual from outside the two communities. In the recently unearthed diaries of the highly respected Tamil scholar Na. Mu. Venkataswamy Nattar we find the following entry for 10 July 1925.

Three numbers of the monthly Kṣattiriya mittiraṉ arrived today. ... The Nadars are calling themselves Kshatriyas. Similarly the community of Pallis or Padaiyachis (Tam. paṭaiyācci) too claim to be Kshatriyas. I am neither happy nor

[45] Anaimuthu 1974: III.1607.

[46] *Kṣattiriya mittiraṉ*, 6,1, September 1924 and *Nāṭārkula mittiraṉ*, 3 November 1924.

unhappy by such Kshatriya claims. Let them happily make these claims. But, in my humble opinion, the evidence that they present to call themselves Kshatriyas fly in the face of wisdom and common sense. Further, both these communities call themselves Kshatriyas while denying that to others. The struggle that these have waged for this title is not a little. Whatever has been written by Padaiyachis condemning the Sandror and by Sandror on Padaiyachis evoke disgust. If only they make these claims to increase the prestige of their community and inspire them to uplift rather than to abuse others it would not be objectionable.[47]

On the face of it, of course, Venkataswamy Nattar's position sounds sensible. But when one recollects that he used a similar logic in his work on the history of his own caste, *Kaḷḷar carittiram*, this necessarily sounds hollow.

It is in the very nature of caste as a system that not physical but notional ranking, in a theoretical structure, is at the root of such conflicts.

III

By the mid-nineteenth century, the British colonial state had launched a massive exercise to collect and organise systematic knowledge about the colonised. The first decennial census of 1871, delayed by about a decade by the uprising of 1857–1858, made a major impact on the way Indians saw their status and rank in the caste order. As Bernard Cohn has pointed out, "Most of the basic treatises on the Indian caste system written during the period 1880 to 1950 was written by men who had important positions ... as census commissioners".[48] If the colonisers' view was shaped by the census, the census in its turn had an even bigger impact on the rising modern intelligentsia of various castes. The data of early census on caste, organised on the principle of rank within the caste order ('social precedence' in the words of Herbert Hope Risley), and even the very nomenclature of the caste itself, created quite a stir among the emerging Western educated elite of the various upwardly mobile castes. In the case of both Vanniyars and Nadars, both contested their designation as Pallis and Shanars respectively. At the time of the very first census itself, Vanniyars produced *Cāticaṅkiracāram* to stake their claim for a different nomenclature and a ranking of their preference. Nadars too followed a similar path. However, it was not until 1921 that the change was conceded. By the next census it had even dropped the ranking of castes.

[47] *Nāvalar nāṭṭār tamiḻ uraikaḷ*, Vol. 21, Chennai, 2007: 88.
[48] Cohn 1987: 242–243.

Caste associations proliferated at this time and these were in the forefront of petitioning the government to concede their demands in regard to the census. The texts and the arguments produced and adduced – though ostensibly based on tradition – were anything but that. The information, the categorisation and disciplines that they invoked were deeply inflected by Orientalism.

The first set of authorities that they invoked was Sanskrit texts: *Puruṣasūktas*, the *Dharmaśāstras* (with precedence given to Manu), and various other Puranas. In the case of Tamilnadu, along with these Sanskrit texts, a range of Tamil texts, newly entering the medium of print, were cited. The entire range of Sangam literary texts, and later verse dictionaries / thesaurus or *nikaṇṭus*, was cited. In fact, each caste picked up one or the other *pirapantam* or minor literary works as a text glorifying their caste. (*cilai-e̲lupatu* in the case of Vanniyar.) The Tamil and Sanskrit texts often gave very conflicting views, but they were reconciled by intellectual sleights.

We know that, since the late eighteenth century, Orientalists evinced a keen interest in various orthographies. The decipherment of the Ashokan Brahmi script by James Prinsep was undoubtedly a major intellectual achievement which effectively inaugurated the field of epigraphy in India. By the later nineteenth-century stone inscriptions were being systematically collected. In the debates we discussed above we find these caste intellectuals frequently taking recourse to various copper plate grants, stone inscriptions and palm leaf manuscripts. Such pre-modern written artefacts were privileged as historical documents that were assumed to provide unmediated access to the past. Here it is important to underline the new status given to history. Even though history was being taught in schools and colleges at that time, history as a discipline had not yet emerged; and certainly there was no professionalisation of the practice of history. History-writing was still the preserve of antiquarians, crackpots and vicarious nationalists (with a considerable degree of overlap!). To my mind, these caste genealogies used inscriptional material as sources much earlier than any professional historian – it certainly predates the use of epigraphs by P. Sundaram Pillai to mark "some milestones in the history of Tamil literature" and date "the age of Thirugnanasambanda". Oral history and proverbs were also extensively used.

Palm-leaf manuscripts were the jokers in the caste historians' pack. Apparently long-lost and mutilated manuscripts were pulled out of nowhere and published. The 1934 edition of the *Van̲n̲iya purāṇam* published by A. Subramania Nayagar is a good example of this. Some caste groups openly commissioned the writing of caste Puranas. The life of

Mahavidwan Meenakshisundaram Pillai, the prolific nineteenth-century poet, is replete with instances of such commissioning.

Another intellectual discipline that was frequently employed in the exercise of claiming higher caste ranking was etymology. Even though India's long history of linguistic analysis, with pinnacles of achievement such as Panini and *Tolkāppiyam*, was aware of word origins and (as Thomas Trautmann has demonstrated) words were classified as *tatsama, tadbhava* and *deśya*, etc. based on origins,[49] the specialisation of etymology concerned with word-roots was a new intellectual method, extensively used and abused in colonial India. Therefore, we need to include folk etymology ("sound etymology is not sound etymology" as the saying goes) within this rubric. In our case, both Nadars and Vanniyars, indulged in a free use of etymology to not only claim higher status for themselves but also to condemn the other to a lower status. Even when their etymology descended to mere wordplay and ingenuity – their analysis of transformation of words over time fly in the face of all established etymological, historical and historical geographical principles – the exalted status of the new discipline itself is not in question. Both sides acknowledged and indulged in it. T. Vijaya Duraisamy Gramani wrote a whole series of articles on *Nāṭār eṉṉum col ārāycci* (A treatise on the word 'Nadar') in his *Kṣattiriya mittiraṉ*, which was later published as a book. *Nāṭārkula mittiraṉ* also published a series of articles titled *Vaṉṉiyar eṉṉum col ārāycci*, wherein the same etymological method was used to decry Vanniyar claims to Kshatriya-hood.

Lexicons and dictionaries were also extensively cited and contested. Both sides criticised the famous Rottler and Winslow and later dictionaries for wrong word origins and derogatory definitions.

Not only history, but anthropology and ethnography as well were invoked in the disputes over caste ranking. Both sides looked up to colonial ethnographers and Orientalists. James H. Nelson, Gustav Oppert, Eugen Hultzsch, Herbert Hope Risley, not to speak of Edgar Thurston, were special favourites. However, it needs to be added that a great amount of selectivity and opportunism was involved. As *Varuṇa taruppaṇam* observed even when it was citing colonial authorities for its own purposes:

> When Tolkāppiyam and other texts written thousands of years ago state that the Vellalars are Sudras how can one cite the works of English scholars written 50–60 years ago as authorities?[50]

[49] Trautmann 2006: 157–161.

[50] Arumuga Nayagar 1907: 370.

The knowledge foundation of the caste histories and the disputes – sources, authorities, epistemes, methods, disciplines – were undoubtedly inflected and mediated in and by colonial discourse. This is by no means an earth shattering revelation but fully borne out by the debates and documented in this article.

IV

The debates documented and analysed in this article throw new light on struggles to re-negotiate caste status and ranking in colonial Tamil society. While the much-abused (in both senses of the word) concept of Sanskritisation has its use as a starting point to understand processes for negotiate caste ranking it has to be invoked with a keen awareness of the reality in a specific context. Opposition to claims for a higher ranking need not necessarily come from physically proximate communities but from adjacent castes in the hierarchy, even when they are separated by a wide distance. The re-negotiation of caste ranking, deeply embedded in a colonial discourse, drew from a wide range of sources, both indigenous and foreign. They were mediated by Orientalism and other colonial forms of knowledge.

Bibliography

Anaimuthu, V. (Tam. vē. āṉaimuttu), ed. 1974. *Periyār ī. ve. rā. cintaṉaikaḷ*. 3 vols. Tiruchirappalli: Thinker's Forum.

Arumuga Nayagar, K. (Tam. kā. āṟumuka nāyakar). 1907. *Varuṇa taruppaṇam*. Ceṉṉai: Star of India Press.

Cohn, Bernard. 1987. 'The Census, Social Structure and Objectification in South Asia', in: Bernard Cohn, *An Anthropologist Among the Historians and Other Essays*, Delhi: Oxford University Press, 224–254.

Hardgrave, Jr., Robert L. 1969 *The Nadars of Tamilnad: The Political Culture of a Community in Change*. Berkeley: University of California Press.

Kavirinadan (Tam. kāvirināṭaṉ), ed. 2005. *Akkiṉikula tittaṉ itaḻ tiraṭṭu*. Vol. 1. Ceṉṉai: Aṉṉal veḷiyīṭu.

Kanakasabhai Pillai, Kudalur (Tam. ku. kaṉakacapai piḷḷai) 1925. *Varuṇa cintāmaṇi*. (1901) Ceṉṉai: Taṉiyāmpāḷ vilācam acciyantiracālai.

Rajadurai, P. (Tam. pu. irācaturai) 1992. *Cuyamariātai iyakkattiṟku nāṭārkaḷ āṟriya toṇṭu*. Virutunakar: Iḷamāraṉ patippakam.

Rudolph, Lloyd and Rudolph, Susanne. 1967. *The Modernity of Tradition: Political Development in India*. Bombay: Orient Longman

Shanmugasundaram, K. (Tam. ka. caṇmukacuntaram) 1995. *Kaviccinkam rājariṣi arttanārīca varmā*. Ceṉṉai: Pe. kantacāmi nāyakar kalvi aṟakkaṭṭaḷai.

Srinivas, M. N. 1966. *Social Change in Modern India*. Berkeley: University of California Press.

——. 2002. *Collected Essays*. New Delhi: Oxford University Press.

Subramania Nayagar, A. (Tam. ā. cuppiramaṇiya nāyakar) 1955. *Tirukkaivaḷam*. Ceṉṉai: Ā. cuppiramaṇiya nāyakar.

Templeman, Dennis. 1996. *The Northern Nadars of Tamilnadu: An Indian Caste in the Process of Change*, Delhi: Oxford University Press.

Trautmann, Thomas. 2006. *Languages and Nations: the Dravidian Proof in Colonial Madras*. Berkeley: University of California Press.

Washbrook, David. 1975. 'Development of Caste Organisation in South India', in C. J. Baker, D. A. Washbrook, *South India: Political Institutions and Political Change, 1880–1940*. Delhi: Macmillan.

Heiko Frese

Soliloquizing Brahmans: Questions to a Telugu journal from the late 19th century

Proposal

The purpose of this article is to consider identities created or represented in historical sources. Is there something like a stable core of the self, a flavour, some kind of *rasa*, which is or was able to find its way from a once 'real' life into documents, to linger there until it is extracted or (re)discovered by historians? Is it possible for individuals or groups of people, united by common cultural attributes, to actively represent themselves through essentialist expressions and to 'know' about their identity? If the constitution of a social identity is an act of power,[1] how are these processes represented in history? What, moreover, is the 'way' of such a process of identification? Are there not identities read into texts, as well as read out of them? What does the discourse allow me, as a historian, to say about this, if I want my words to be accepted and understood as a part of its reality?

The concept of identity put forward here is inspired by the historical sources used; it is not an essentialist, but a strategic and a positional one. It does not, therefore, assume a stable core, unfolding from beginning to end through the ups and downs of history without change. If such a conception were transferred to a broader 'cultural' identity, the position taken in this article is not the 'collective or true self hiding inside the many other, more superficial or artificially imposed 'selves' which a people with a shared history and ancestry hold in common"[2] and which suggests a unchanging oneness underlying other, superficial differences. On the contrary, identities here are never unified, but often intersecting and antagonistic. They are subject to a radical historicization, and are constantly in the process of change and transformation. What one finds in the journal analyzed in this article are historical developments which disturb any fixed notion of the culture in focus. In fact, apart from a struggle about questions concerning social reform, the debates which dominated the intellectual world were about whether or not contemporary identities invoke an origin in the historical past with which they seem to correspond. I would argue that identities revolve around questions of using the

[1] Laclau 1990: 31.
[2] Hall 1994: 393.

resources of history, language and culture in the process of becoming rather than being.

Identities are constituted within, not outside discourse. Tradition, whether 'invented' or not, has to be read not as an endless reiteration but as a changing sameness; it cannot be a return to where one came from, but a process of accepting and agreeing with one's routes. Identities are narrations, but certainly the fictional nature of narrativization does not weaken its discursive effectiveness, even though the process of becoming a part of a story takes place, at least partly, in the imagination.

Identities are produced in specific historical contexts, within specific discursive formations and practices, by specific enunciative strategies. Rather than being the marker of a non-changing, 'naturally' constituted unity, they arise within the play of specific modalities of power, and are more the product of the marking of difference and exclusion. They are constructed through difference. This means that it is only through the relation to the other, the relation to what it is not (what it lacks), to its outside, that its 'positive' meaning (its identity) can be constructed. It is their ability to exclude that essentially makes identities work, their ability to push beyond their margins what they are not. 'Successful' identities affirm themselves only by repressing that which threatens them. This, again, necessarily means that the constitution of a social identity is an act of power.[3]

Identities are permanently 'in danger', never complete, representing a never ending constructing and deconstructing play of power. They are constructed in or through *différance* and constantly destabilized by what they leave out. They create subjects which can be spoken, and are points of contemporary attachment to the subject positions which discursive practices construct. As the results of successful articulations of the subject into the flow of discourse, they are the positions which the subject is bound to take up, although it always 'knows' that they are representations. Representation is constructed across a 'lack', across a division, from the place of the other, and thus can never be appropriate ('identical') to the subject processes which are invested in them. This, on the one hand, of course, cannot be thought of as one-sided, and on the other hand, to repeat again, has to be understood as a process. So it seems *identification* 'signifies' more adequately what all this is about: the relation of the subject to discursive formations as an articulation.[4]

---

[3] Laclau 1990: 31.

[4] And all articulations are properly relations of 'no necessary correspondence': See Laclau 1990: 35.

Evidence

The reform movements in Andhra, during the second half of the 19th century, are associated with the name of Kandukuri Viresalingam (Tel. kandukūri vīrēśaliṅgam, 1848–1919). It was he who initiated and led these movements, organizing them ideologically as well as in practice.

Kandukuri Viresalingam was born in Rajahmundry, in 1848, and died there in 1919. He was not only a social reformer, but is nowadays widely recognized as the father of modern Telugu literature. He was the author of poems, novels, plays, dramas, essays and satires, and translated Sanskrit and English literature into Telugu. Being among the first literary critics in Andhra, he published a history of Telugu literature (*Kavula caritra*, 1886), which was used in schools and colleges, and an even today well-known autobiography (*Sviya caritramu*, 1915). He was very active in the field of early Telugu journalism and published a number of journals, most of them being vehicles for his ideas on social reform.

Apart from the range of his activities, what distinguished Viresalingam from most other social reformers and scholars of his time was his commitment to action. In contrast to other scholars, who were primarily trying to sanction social reform by quoting appropriate passages from classical Sanskrit texts, he became famous within his own lifetime for his attempts to change certain practices in Telugu society.[5] He performed more than forty widow remarriages, started two homes for widows in need and opened two girls' schools. Even though he did not achieve much and many of his projects ended in relative failure, his actions were recognized as significant by contemporaries and later leaders and scholars.[6]

Viresalingam's most successful journal was *Vivēka vardhani* (The Growth of Wisdom), which began publication in 1874 in Rajahmundry. With around 200 subscribers it belonged to the most read Telugu journals of the 19th century.[7] Next to scholarly articles, it spread Viresalingam's ideas about social reform, with moralistic and polemical essays which were aimed primarily at his fellow Brahmans, to criticize their prejudices, backward oriented traditions and shortcomings. In the beginning, powerful British individuals were also his targets, but as his dependence on British officials increased in time he focussed on Indian public figures.[8] In general, Viresalingam was, on the one hand, trying to 'import' from

---

[5] *The Hindu*, September 5, 1913.

[6] In 1911, J. Gurunatham published the first biography of Viresalingam in the English language, thus laying the foundation stone of his ongoing fame in literature and science.

[7] Leonard 1991: 158.

[8] For an extensive discussion of Viresalingam's life, see Leonard 1991.

western culture what he thought were its best features which, on the other hand, added to his other concern for the improvement of the Indian 'nation', a term frequently used by him in his writings.[9]

Of significant importance and closely related to his activities concerning social reform were Viresalingam's literary works. He not only changed the landscape of Telugu literature by introducing new forms of literature, like novels, short stories and modern dramas, but played a major role in the revolution of the language itself. The Telugu used in premodern literature had mostly been a highly sanskritised language, the so-called *grānthika bhāṣa*, which was for the average Telugu speaker unintelligible. Even though Viresalingam was proficient in this – he published, for example, a Telugu version of the Mahabharata in 1879 – he decided that Telugu literature should be comprehendible and started to write in colloquial Telugu, *vyavahārika bhāṣa*. In the 1880s, Viresalingam completely turned away from classical Telugu and wrote only in the colloquial variant. This also paved the way for the 'meteoric rise' of Telugu from a medium of communication to a marker of identity.[10]

The main tool for distributing his ideas and promoting a different language of literature for Viresalingam were his journals, where many of his literary works were published before appearing in book form. Though they can hardly be compared to the form and influence newspapers and journals have nowadays, their discursive power should not be underestimated. As new sites of communication and representation, vernacular journals in 19th-century India sought to be influential. It is evident from their contents that the authors' or publishers' primary purpose was to spread ideas and information to people already gained for their cause or to fight differently-minded journals. A well-known example comes from Viresalingam's own context. A year after he had begun publishing his first reform journal, *Vivēka vardhani,* Kokkonda Venkataratnam (Tel. kokkoṇḍa veṅkaṭaratnam, 1842–1915), an orthodox Brahman who was a teacher at the Presidency College in Madras, started *Hāsya vardhani* (Growth of Laughter), also a monthly. As a leader of conservative circles, which strictly opposed social reform, he used this journal as an instrument to attack the ideas presented in *Vivēka vardhani.* In reaction to this, Viresalingam added, another year later, a supplement to his journal called *Hāsya sanjīvanī* (Bringing Laughter to Life), to attack Venkataratnam's ideas.

---

[9] Vīrēśaliṅgam 1951–52.7: 323–447.

[10] As described by Mitchell 2004. Nevertheless, even in the 20th century, many orthodox thinking people did not consider texts in the colloquial language to belong to the canon of Telugu literature. See Frese: in print a.

An important context for the evolution and contents of Telugu journals of the late 19th century was the social reform movements founded in Andhra, originally initiated in Bengal by activists like Rammohan Roy and Keshub Candra Sen. Sen had given a lecture in Madras in 1864, which had such an effect that it led, in the same year, to the founding of Veda Samaj, a monotheistic reformist society, which also brought out a journal, *Tattvabōdhini*. In their statutes, one finds already an explicit statement against the "superstitions and absurdities which at present characterise Hindu ceremonies",[11] which represents one of the fundamental positions that all social reform movements in Andhra had in common. Around 1869, the society was renamed and became the first Brahmo Samaj in South India.

The other main concern of the reformist thinkers was the status of women in Indian society. As mentioned above, Viresalingam attempted to improve the situation especially of young widows, and he also started a movement against the caste of courtesans (*veśya* or *bogam-vāḷḷu*) who, in his eyes, led a sinful life. These agitations became known as the *Widow Remarriage* and *Anti-Nautch* movements and were mainly supported by Indians with a western education, for their moral concepts were heavily influenced by Victorian values.

In the year 1878, Viresalingam founded, in Rajahmundry, the first Prarthana Samaj of Andhra. It was a local branch, in many ways connected with its prototype, the Brahmo Samaj in Madras. Yet, the parameters were slightly different. Not only was it led by the most active and influential social reformist of the whole region, but the town of Rajahmundry also provided particularly favourable conditions for the projects of the reformers. The city, situated in the delta of the Godavari River, was directly ruled by a British collector and had a government college with an Englishman as principal. This resulted in a wider acceptance of western education and less support for traditional scholarship. Additionally, a recent dam construction, by Sir Arthur Cotton (1803–1899), had enhanced the fertility of the area significantly and led to greater wealth, especially amongst the upper castes. Their children had the chance to receive an English education, which was a promising precondition for a successful career.

The colonial government, which observed the developments of public opinion and the changes in the social sphere closely, did not oppose social reforms and was far from making the lives of the reformers difficult. The ideas behind their activities matched the ideology of the Raj: they implied that the Indians accepted moral inferiority. Viresalingam was even awarded the title Rao Bahadur, which was the second lowest on the scale

[11] Bose 1994.1: 171–175.

of titles awarded by the British, but it was awarded only rarely at that time and usually only to distinguished chairmen of municipal councils or to lawyers who had performed some outstanding public service.

In 1891, Viresalingam helped to establish two Telugu journals. One was *Cintāmaṇi*, a literary journal, which was regionally successful in stimulating the composition of Telugu novels, the other, *Satya saṃvardhani* (Growth of Truth), was the mouthpiece of the Prarthana Samaj of Rajahmundry. The latter was a bilingual (English and Telugu) monthly, and saw its first issue released on 31 July. It was run by students of the Prarthana Samaj, but Viresalingam is said to have supervised the publishing and personally checked the Telugu articles.[12] The editors were S. Mṛtyunjaya Rāo and R. Veṅkaṭa Śivuḍu, who also wrote some of the English articles. Viresalingam had allowed them the use of the *Vivēka vardhani* Press, where his journal of the same name was printed.

Satya saṃvardhani was, according to its subheading, "mainly devoted to Religious, Social and Moral topics". Its opening article, titled "Ourselves", says:

> For some time past, the attention of the members of the Rajahmundry Prardhana Samaj has been occupied with the problem of finding a clue to the miserable condition of the lower orders of society. The absence of periodical journals in these parts calculated to convey useful information to the people, together with the want of effort on the part of the educated to bring up the less enlightened brethren of the community, has all the more urged us to undertake this work of publishing a Monthly Journal – the Satya Samvardhani. Our humble object in starting this periodical is to show our ignorant brethren the necessity of having a true Religion, and not only to point out to them the pernicious influence of some of our customs over the social and moral well-being and progress of the community, but to propose, as far as we honestly know, remedial measures to those evils. The Satya Samvardhani, then, discusses these important questions – Religious, Social, and Moral – chiefly in simple Telugu, and earnestly attempts to bring the minds of people to Truth and Virtue. It is almost needless to state that ours is a humble position, and, as such, we look to the public – especially the well-wishers of the country and the educated – for hearty support. Feeling sure that our appeal for encouragement will not be heard in vain, we commence the paper with the assurance that our Almighty Father will guide us inspite of every obstacle and hindrance.[13]

It is surprising that one of the first sentences speaks of an "absence of periodical journals", knowing that *Satya saṃvardhani* was printed at the same press as *Vivēka vardhani*, which had started as a monthly in 1874 but become a weekly in the meantime. Yet, this hints at the religious commitment of the publisher(s); they obviously wanted to make a

[12] Veṅkaṭa Śivuḍu 1931: 31.
[13] *Satya saṃvardhani*, Vol. I, No. 1, July 1891: 1–2.

difference. *Vivēka vardhani* was a political magazine, with an occasionally ferocious Viresalingam attacking vehemently anyone who behaved in a way not meeting his standards. In contrast, *Satya saṃvardhani* presented its ideas in a much smoother way. Only from time to time were there articles condemning social practices that should be subject to reform, such as child marriage to much older men. Most of the contents of *Satya saṃvardhani* consist of theistic prayers, which provide examples of how to behave and try to link Christian and Hindu topics.[14]

That the journal was bilingual did not mean that the Telugu portions were translations of the English articles or the other way round. Usually, there were not more than one or two articles in English, situated at the beginning of the journal, and the by far greater number of pages was dedicated to Telugu. The English articles almost always dealt with moral or religious topics, like the "Sweetness of Prayer"[15] or "Practical Religion"[16]. Some reports of annual meetings are in English and, interestingly, also the 'acknowledgements', that is, the list of subscribers. Their names are given in European script, naturally leading to variations of one and the same name in transcript. The Telugu parts also include several articles about religious and moral topics in every issue, but also biographical articles (like those of R. Tagore[17] or Ramabai Sarasvati[18]), dramas with moralistic messages, and the "news and notes" section, mostly with English headings and Telugu contents.

The articles never gave the name of their authors at the end. As mentioned above, the journal was managed by a group of students, who also wrote the articles; but who was responsible for which contribution remains unsaid. On the other hand, the office-bearers of the Prarthana Samaj were officially announced in the journal when they were elected, which took place once a year (for example, in July 1892, with Viresalingam as the president, Mṛtyunjaya Rāo as the Secretary, Srīrāmulu as the treasurer, etc.[19]). So the 'literary activity' stayed anonymous, whereas the names of functionaries were announced.

The subscribers of the journal mostly came from the region, although there were some who lived as far away from Rajahmundry as Rangoon in Burma. The subscription rate was 12 Annas per year, a single issue cost 2 Annas. 'Supporters' were asked 4 rupees for an annual subscription, 'patrons' 12 rupees. It is striking that about 90 percent of the subscribers

---

[14] For example by speaking about Jesus and Caitanya as examples for "love and forgiveness" in Vol. 1, No. 5, November 1891.

[15] *Satya saṃvardhani*, Vol. 2, No. 2, August 1892.

[16] *Satya saṃvardhani*, Vol. 2, No. 3, September 1892.

[17] *Satya saṃvardhani*, Vol. 1, No. 11, Mai 1892.

[18] *Satya saṃvardhani*, Vol. 1, No. 12, June 1892.

[19] *Satya saṃvardhani*, Vol. 2, No. 1, July 1892.

were Brahmans, one finds only very few names which hint at other castes. There are some Kapus and Reddis among them, and some British people, but only one Muslim appears during all the years the journal was published. Moreover, titles seem to have been of considerable importance. Those who had obtained a M. A. or B. A., of which there were many, took care to have it mentioned in the list of subscribers.[20] This again hints at the high standard of education of those who read this (and other) journal(s).

At the top of the list of subscribers, the names of some patrons keep reappearing. They supported *Satya saṃvardhani* over the years with donations, which obviously helped a lot in the overall project of editing and producing the journal. Among them were the Zamindar of Polavaram, the Rajas of Parlakimidi, Madugula and Vishakhapatnam. These rulers or landlords played an interesting role in the Andhra of the 19th century. They were often rulers who no longer were bestowed with royal powers and owed their position as a 'quasi-king' to a silent agreement with the colonial rulers. Though they were not allowed to wield much political power, they upheld the character of their courts as centres of culture and 'royal atmosphere'. As they understood the risks of acting in a political way, they shifted their activities to the vast arena of culture, and patronized poetry and music, as well as supported traditional scholars and poets. Such, mainly orthodox scholars and poets revived Sanskrit learning and elevated the rulers to a royal status with their writings, for example, by linking their genealogies with legendary rulers of the past.[21] In addition, the rulers often supported social reform by founding English schools or, as in this case, giving money to reform journals.

To my knowledge, *Satya saṃvardhani* was published over a period of ten years, from 1891–1901. Due to the early death of its editor, S. Mṛtyunjaya Rāo, in February 1895, the journal ceased publication at the beginning of 1895 and returned only two and a half years later. It then appeared irregularly for some time, with interruptions and incomplete volumes (there is no Volume 7 at all), until it became a regular monthly again in April 1899.

I now turn to discuss statements of identity which are related to the publishers and readers of *Satya saṃvardhani*, and especially to (their) caste. What was the imagined readership of the authors? What did the authors reveal about themselves? In what way was (their) caste

[20] Viresalingam seems to have set quite some value on his title Rao Bahadur. For example, he reprimanded a former student for omitting it in a personal letter. See Leonard 1991: 161.

[21] For a concrete example of the 'story' of a historiographical text and how it worked in the context of colonial rule, see Frese: 2003 and Frese: in print b.

represented, what belonged or did not belong to the identity of Brahmans (for it is mainly Brahmans that I am talking about here)? It is, of course, impossible to present something like a summary of the contents of a journal which appeared over a decade. Presented here are some examples from journal articles, which to my eyes reflect the identificatory statements continuously featured in the journal.

As mentioned, *Satya saṃvardhani* was never decidedly political. It is obvious that the authors did not regret certain developments which had come from Europe, such as the printing press or the railway; on the contrary, it was seen as a blessing.[22] European culture was respected: dance performances in the West were regarded as completely different from those of nautch girls, for they 'belonged to another culture' and were thus acceptable.[23] A sense of some pride shines through when an article, on funeral practices in England, mentions that people in Liverpool and London had begun to burn their dead and credits this to the Indian example.[24] Critical voices targeted at the colonial rulers do not exist in *Satya saṃvardhani,* although positive statements about the British are relatively rare.

There are no reports about 'events' in the sense of news coverage one finds in newspapers or journals nowadays. A few news items are sometimes mentioned at the end of an issue, yet only in the form of marginal notes. Apart from social events touching the very heart of the concerns of the authors (like marriages of elder men with young girls), even these short notes, never consisting of more than a few sentences, seem to hint at the matter of social reform. The victims of a castaway, close to the Andaman Islands, are rescued by prisoners who risk their lives (which displays an unexpected moral attitude);[25] missionaries and common people from England give money to help the poor in India who suffer from a drought, whereas rich Indians do not give anything.[26] *Satya saṃvardhani* presents itself as thoughtful and reflective, interpreting rather than presenting events.

This careful strategy is also visible when the authors give reasons as to why reforms should be undertaken, or better, why reforms were not against tradition. Throughout the journal there are steadily reoccurring references to classical (sometimes legal) texts, either mentioned to support their cause or, much more often, to emphasize that there are no objections in the Sastras (Skt. śāstra) against remarriage, the education of

[22] *Satya saṃvardhani*, Vol. 2, No. 5–6, November–December 1892.
[23] *Satya saṃvardhani*, Vol. 3, No. 3–4, September–October 1893.
[24] *Satya saṃvardhani*, Vol. 1, No. 10, April 1892.
[25] *Satya saṃvardhani*, Vol. 1, No 7, January 1892.
[26] *Satya saṃvardhani*, Vol. 1, No 7, January 1892.

women, and other such matters. One of the first issues of *Satya saṃvardhani* seems to be largely a reaction to criticism, presumably expressed by the elder fellow citizens of the young authors. There is an explicit statement that they are in no way criticizing the Sastras. On the contrary, social reform, especially in the case of widow remarriage, recovers only what had been lost in the dark ages of history. Widow remarriage is, it is argued, also for the purpose of the nation, because, if widows remarry, there is no need for them to become prostitutes. Finally, the authors offer to discuss matters.[27]

Nevertheless, although the tone in *Satya saṃvardhani* sometimes seems reluctant and defensive, it was still a reform journal. This meant that the behaviour of contemporary citizens was criticized and traditions were questioned; and not by the government or any renowned person, but by a group of young students. It was certainly known that Viresalingam stood behind the authors and was not only responsible, to a certain degree, for the contents of the journal, but also for the way the authors thought. Yet, was it acceptable or taken serious – a group of young men who wanted to tell their elders and betters how to behave?

In order to be more convincing, the arguments brought forward in connection with the examples quoted in the journals were based on reason and common sense. Again and again, it is pointed out that it could not be right for a 50-year-old man to marry a young girl, and the meaning of marriages between children – for example, an eight-year-old boy and an infant of only three months – is questioned.[28] Statistical arguments are produced: because of the great number of widows and because it is not unusual for men to have more than one wife, there are simply more possible husbands than wives within a subcaste (*śākha*). So, late marriage (or widow marriage) would help much to improve the situation and lessen the incongruity.[29] 'Technical' problems are discussed: if girls are too small for the palanquin in which they have to be carried, they might fall down or start crying; so some other girl would have to sit inside to hold the bride, but then the people watching could not know who is who.[30]

Furthermore, of course, classical texts are quoted – there was no child marriage in the Vedas,[31] and Manu, as well as other law texts, say that remarriage is not a problem.[32] If this is thought to be insufficiently relevant, the English also give a good example of how things should be,

---

[27] *Satya saṃvardhani*, Vol. 1, No. 3, September 1891.
[28] *Satya saṃvardhani*, Vol. 4, No. 6, June 1895.
[29] *Satya saṃvardhani*, Vol. 4, No. 2–3, August–September 1894.
[30] *Satya saṃvardhani*, Vol. 8, No. 7, January 1900.
[31] *Satya saṃvardhani*, Vol. 8, No. 7, January 1900.
[32] *Satya saṃvardhani*, Vol. 4, No. 2–3, August–September 1894.

as they marry only when they are grown up.[33] Finally, examples from other parts of India are cited: in Mysore a bill is passed that girls under 8 and boys under 14 are no longer allowed to marry, and the new law is sanctioned by scholars;[34] in Maharashtra the government also decides on a minimum age for marriage,[35] and so on.

The first two issues of volume four are almost completely dedicated to marriage and present long articles about what one should consider before marrying. Again, first of all, one should not marry too young, and the husband should be five-six years older than the wife. It should also be a conscious decision by the couple for each other, the degree of education should be similar and, as mentioned at several other instances, it is 'healthier' not to marry relatives (or as far away from close relatives as possible). Onc argument which repeatedly turns up in support of this is that the union of Hindu women with Mughal men resulted in strong progeny. Finally, the articles offer practical suggestions: as marriages among Brahmans tend to be very expensive, one could marry a widow for nothing; that a marriage between widow and widower should make sense, or between widow and orphan (as they also have a low status in society). In this way there would be less child marriages. After all, it is argued, if women are not allowed to remarry, men should not be in a better position.[36]

There is no topic of reform which is as dominant in the journal as that of marriage. Even the other main reform concern of the publishers, the abolishment of nautch performances and prostitution, does not occupy that much space. It is simply condemned from time to time in short notices when people hire nautch girls, but detailed articles are uncommon. In one letter to the editor, a reader says that officials from the government witnessed dance performances by nautch girls and could not see anything objectionable, so there is yet no law against it. This is criticized by the editors. They say that what the officials had experienced was an 'innocent' version, staged to mislead the British.[37]

Even though Viresalingam and his followers never started an official 'movement', the question about what Hindus, and especially Brahmans, should do in the society the reformers had in mind and what was inappropriate, is repeatedly discussed in *Satya saṃvardhani*. It was obviously a major concern of the publishers and is very often referred to, not always in specific articles, but mostly between the lines or in marginal remarks.

---

33 *Satya saṃvardhani*, Vol. 2, No. 5–6, November–December 1892.
34 *Satya saṃvardhani*, Vol. 3, No.1, July 1893.
35 *Satya saṃvardhani*, Vol. 3, No. 2, August 1893.
36 *Satya saṃvardhani*, Vol. 4, No. 1–3, July–September 1894.
37 *Satya saṃvardhani,* Vol. 3, No. 3–4, September–October 1893.

Next to the two explicitly defined pillars of the reformists, widow remarriage and anti-nautch, critique of customs, rituals and traditional behaviour appears almost everywhere. This offers, among other things, insights into indigenous perspectives on caste and society in general.

The diagnosed snobbishness of Brahmans, shown by treating other castes or even their own wives as creatures by far inferior, is the evident bone of contention for the authors to publish their comments and reform suggestions. In letters to the editor, even subscribers tell about their personal experiences with Brahmans. One reader expresses his lack of understanding about the fact that it was not allowed to mention the name of an untouchable while having a meal with Brahmans. Interestingly (or rather naturally), the author of this letter was a Brahman himself.[38]

Of course, ritual pollution was a major concern of the authors – it is not acceptable for a society which is proud of its knowledge about nature, history and humankind to cling to something like rituals of purification after having had contact with a person from a lower caste.[39] On the contrary, restrictions of all kinds should be abolished. In a speech, held in March 1893, in the Christian College in Madras, K. Subbarao pleaded for a universal commensality, the abolishment of the prohibition of sea voyages, and so on.[40] Moreover, every kind of work, it was argued, possesses dignity, and it is thus possible for everybody to pursue any profession. Caste specific professions are a construction of the society and should not exist.[41]

Such pleas for social reform are often embedded in literature presented in a literary form. For example, a fictive dialogue between a traditionalist and a reformer revolves around rituals and the question as to whether Sudras (Skt. śūdra, Tel. śūdra) should worship Brahmans or not. Although the conversation does not result in any distinct appeal, the intention of the authors, that these things should at least be discussed, is clearly visible.[42] Elsewhere, in a one-act play, *Hindumatsabha*, the 'contrast' between Brahmans and Hinduism is picked out as the central theme. One is not defined or determined by the other – so in a way the author claims that Brahmans are not Hindus.[43]

In a similar vein, one article says that Brahmans are lying all the time and are guilty for many a drawback in Indian society. In general, Indians suffer from a low self-esteem and an atmosphere of mistrust is predominant everywhere. Yet, the responsibility for all this is put by the

[38] *Satya saṃvardhani*, Vol. 1, No. 8, February 1892.
[39] *Satya saṃvardhani*, Vol. 2, No. 7, January 1893.
[40] *Satya saṃvardhani*, Vol. 2, No. 8, February 1893.
[41] *Satya saṃvardhani*, Vol. 4, No. 6, June 1895.
[42] *Satya saṃvardhani,* Vol. 5, No. 6, June 1895.
[43] *Satya saṃvardhani*, Vol. 2, No. 3, September 1892.

article onto the shoulders of the foreign peoples of the past who conquered India, or parts of it, because the defeated had to find tricks and techniques to survive, and lying was one of them.[44]

The Brahmans are not only liars, it was said, but some of them have no understanding of what they are doing. The pandits reciting verses from the Vedas do not know the meaning of those texts; they monotonously repeat what they had once learnt by heart. This means that whole rituals are 'without meaning', for other people involved also cannot understand the contextual background.[45] Thus Brahmans even propagate rituals or techniques which are not only unintelligible, but against all rationality. As an example, the authors present the description of a ritual which a husband has to put into practice if he wants to go on a journey and prevent his wife from having sexual intercourse with other men. As the moral conceptions of the Indian society in the late 19th century were far from liberal, the picture of a man rubbing certain kinds of powders into the sexual organs of his wife while she slept surely had an effect.[46]

Finally, idolatry, heavily connected to Brahman practices, was under fire. A range of remarks and articles condemns every kind of idol worship. The true God, it was argued, does not speak through wooden or stone images.[47] Idolatry is something for people in Africa, it was said, which was obviously regarded as a backward, primitive continent. What, asks the author, would be the difference if people in India do the same?[48] An interesting statement, for certainly not only Brahmans would have been touched by this. Were the authors aware of the implications of their critique?

More than once, one finds references to other parts of India in *Satya saṃvardhani*, especially when the authors intend to highlight the improvable state of things in Andhra. The most interesting example is a 'comparison' between Malayali and Telugu Hindus, firstly because it does not really seem to present a critical view, at least this is not obvious, and secondly, as expected, it mainly presents facts about Brahmans. For that reason, it also belongs to the statements about what Brahmans were and were not (should do and should not do). Though it comes across as not entirely neutral, it seems first of all to be presented for the sake of information. In a journal which fights superstition, the contents of this article appear at least unusual. So one should not, it is stated therein, have an argument with the wives of Brahmans, or give salt and buttermilk to

[44] Of course this means Muslims were responsible, an accusation which appears more than once. *Satya saṃvardhani*, Vol. 2, No. 11, May 1893.

[45] *Satya saṃvardhani*, Vol. 8, No. 7, January 1900.

[46] *Satya saṃvardhani*, Vol. 2, No. 3, September 1892.

[47] *Satya saṃvardhani*, Vol. 5, No. 4, November 1896.

[48] *Satya saṃvardhani*, Vol. 8, No. 6, December 1899.

the neighbours after dawn. One should wear white clothes, take a bath before the meals and avoid saying goodbye if one leaves friends on Sunday, Tuesday or Friday nights. Women should stay at home; one should keep an umbrella closed and carry it in the left hand with its top down, and so on.[49] All in all, this article, though presented as a serious contribution, seems to have an almost satirical character.

The authors of *Satya saṃvardhani* present themselves as determined, but not as perfect. So, they are open to criticism and do not hesitate to publish self-critical statements in their journal. In a letter to the editor, a reader asks why, after five years of *Satya saṃvardhani*, not much has changed in society.[50] Especially when, beginning with volume six, *Satya saṃvardhani* faced financial problems and then ceased publication for two and a half years, brief apologetic articles turned up in several volumes, complaining baldly about the obstacles the publishers had to struggle with.[51] Later, one author almost admits defeat, by saying that it is really difficult to enforce social reforms in one's own society.[52]

Other journals are also mentioned, regularly in an advertisement-like way at the end of issues and sometimes also with a comment. When the *Truthseeker*, a conservative Telugu monthly, was started in Rajahmundry in 1893 by a Muslim, the authors express their disappointment that the author, who criticizes the charity and social reform societies, but owed his own education to such an institution.[53] On the other hand, they neutrally acknowledged the foundation of a conservative society, without any negative comment.[54]

Reassurance

Satya saṃvardhani, in its form and content, is similar to quite a number of journals which emerged at that time. It can be called a reform journal that sought to convey messages of change to its readership. But did it achieve its aims?

The history of Andhra Pradesh tells us that if there was success, it was very limited. As said above, Viresalingam and his followers managed to inspire a few dozen widow remarriages, but that apart there were hardly

---

[49] *Satya saṃvardhani*, Vol. 8, No. 3, September 1899.

[50] *Satya saṃvardhani*, Vol. 6, No. 1, July 1897.

[51] As a consequence of the failure of subscribers to make payments, from May 1900 onwards, issues of the journal were only delivered by the V. P. service. *Satya saṃvardhani*, Vol. 8, No. 11, June 1900.

[52] *Satya saṃvardhani*, Vol. 9, No. 2, August 1900.

[53] *Satya saṃvardhani*, Vol. 2, No. 3, September 1892.

[54] *Satya saṃvardhani*, Vol. 3, No. 7–8, January–February 1894.

any palpable changes. The performances of nautch girls continued to take place, and Brahmans did not start to eat with Untouchables. Yet one effect was highly visible: it opened up a new space for a new quality of enunciative strategies, and initially *Satya saṃvardhani* and other journals acted as a catalyst for other journals. The last quarter of the 19th century witnessed an eruption of new journals. Of course, these were not only reform journals, but also journals dedicated to such subjects as literature, revivalist and caste issues, medicine, and many such others. However, this occupation of a new discursive space was, historically, the most striking development in connection with *Satya saṃvardhani*: The possibility of wielding power one day, to be part or the centre of a discourse.

At the beginning of this article I mentioned that the sources, the journals, had inspired and modified my understanding of identity. This will have become clearer by now if one reads all these statements and / or articulations as part of a picture the authors of *Satya saṃvardhani* composed. It is far from coherent, and even if one assumes a traditional or historical core or essence of identity (but where would that be gained from?), it is simply shattered here. Oppositions rule the scenery, a struggle for what and how one should be or not be.

It is worth reiterating that *Satya saṃvardhani* was a journal for Brahmans made by Brahmans. Although it claims to speak for the whole of society no other caste except Brahmans is mentioned. The only antipode, it seems, of which at least the name from time to time is visible – as people in history, as another religious group – were Muslims. Certainly there were other castes among the subscribers, especially those Reddis and Kapus, but the overwhelming majority belonged to one Varna only. This, therefore, excludes the idea that a group of underprivileged people used a new media to articulate 'unrealistic' demands; the authors, for sure, knew what they were doing.

Throughout *Satya saṃvardhani* they list markers of identity, thus *identifying* what a Brahman is and should be, and at the same time excluding what a Brahman is not and should not be. In fact, Brahmans could do and be anything: work in all professions or not, touch anybody or not, be polluted or not, be liars or not, know the Vedas or not, even be Hindus or not. Accepting that the authors of *Satya saṃvardhani* did not suggest completely absurd things all the time, the range of possible identifications for Brahmans was manifold and antagonistic. Their identity, if assumed, is deconstructed into contextual signifiers, which do not allow the creation of a safe picture. What the spectator learns here is that 'caste' (Brahman) was empty, for it could contain anything.

The struggle, which is visible through these sources, is to fill the emptiness with a given content – to suture the rift of the discursive centre and to create hegemony. The empty, incomplete character of the discourse is the driving factor, the emptiness makes discourses possible. Power comes into play, not only the power to construct a discursive formation, but also as a power-struggle between formations.[55]

Antagonisms work as the 'symbol of my non-being',[56] of what keeps the (political) project from obtaining a positive identity and thus establishing hegemony. So the antagonistic relationship, what keeps one from oneself, is the only type of identity one can obtain. "The outside is not merely posing a threat to the inside, but is actually required for the definition of the inside. The inside is marked by a constitutive lack that the outside helps to fill".[57]

For this reason, the Brahmans within this journal still needed and created an identificatory outside, but here it was defined 'among themselves'. It becomes evident that 'being Brahman' was something which needed negotiation, a question sufficiently urgent to dominate the contents of not only *Satya saṃvardhani,* but more than 30 other journals.[58] What were the answers to the 'impossible' project that aimed at the end of contingency, towards "the realization of a society fully reconciled with itself"[59]? This, alas, is the topic of another story, for here and now the concern is to end with an appropriate question.

Bibliography

Bose, P. N. 1994. *A History of Hindu Civilization under British Rule.* (1894) Delhi: Low Price Publications

Frese, H. 2003. 'Strategische Historiographie? Anmerkungen zu Orissa und der Mackenzie Collection', in: S. Conermann und J. Kusber, eds. *Studia Eurasiatica. Kieler Festschrift für Hermann Kulke zum 65. Geburtstag.* Schenefeld: EB-Verlag.

——. in print a. 'Identities of Scattered Archives: Histories of Telugu Literature in the 19th and 20th Centuries', in: H. Harder, ed. *Nationalist Ideology and the Historiography of Literature.*

——. in print b. 'The Attack of the Present on the Remainder of Time. Some Remarks on Historiography from 19th Century India', in: K. Veluthat and G. Dharampal-Frick, eds. *Interpreting Early India* (Proceedings of the Seminar Held at the South Asia Institute, Heidelberg, 2006).

——. in prep. *Fragments of Identity: Early Telugu Journals and their Rise to Power.*

Gurunatham, J. 1911. *Viresalingam, the Founder of Telugu Public Life.* Rajahmundry: Gunneswararao Bros.

---

[55] See Laclau 1996.

[56] Laclau and Mouffe 2001: 125.

[57] Torfing 2004: 11.

[58] These journals will be discussed in Frese: in prep.

[59] Laclau 1996: 69.

Hall, S. 1994. 'Cultural Identity and Diaspora', in: P. Williams, L. Chrisman, eds. *Colonial Discourse and Postcolonial Theory. A Reader.* New York: Harvester Wheatsheaf.

Laclau, E. 1990. *New Reflections on the Revolution of our Time.* London: Verso.

——. 1996. 'Why do Empty Signifiers Matter to Politics?', in: E. Laclau, *Emancipation(s).* London: Verso. 36–46.

Laclau, E. and C. Mouffe. 2001. *Hegemony and Social Strategy: Towards a Radical Democratic Politics.* (1985) London: Verso.

Leonard, J. G. 1991. *Kandukūri Vīrēśaliṅgam (1848–1919): A Biography of an Indian Social Reformer.* Hyderabad: Telugu University.

Mitchell, L. A. 2004. *From Medium to Marker: The Making of a Mother Tongue in Modern South India.* Unpublished Dissertation. Columbia University.

Torfing, J. 2004. 'Discourse Theory: Achievements, Arguments and Challenges', in: D. Howarth and J. Torfing, eds. *European Politics: Identity, Policy and Governance.* Basingstoke: Palgrave Macmillan, 1–32

Veṅkaṭa Śivuḍu, R. 1931. *Śri Vīrēśaliṅga Saṃsmṛti.* Guntur.

Vīrēśaliṅgam, K. 1951–52. *Kandukūri Vīrēśaliṅga Krita. Granthamalu.* Rajahmundry: Hitakāriṇīsamājamu.

Vakulabharanam Rajagopal

Anti-reform discourse in Andhra: Cultural nationalism that failed[1]

This article discusses the religious and cultural ideas of Kasibhatta Brahmayya Sastri (Tel. kāśībhaṭṭa brahmayya śāstri, 1863–1940), an orthodox Brahman scholar from coastal Andhra Pradesh who lived and functioned in the late nineteenth and the early twentieth centuries. The source that has been used is an anthology of essays that Sastri published in 1911 by the title of *Upanyāsa payōnidhi*.[2] Sastri began to write in the early 1880s, just about the time when an English college was started in Rajahmundry, an important coastal town. He had already learned the English language by that time, and embarked upon a serious study of Hinduism and Sastras (Skt. śāstra). He thereafter began to teach students what he learned and also started to write articles for journals. *Rāja yōgi*, a journal published from Kakinada, carried several of his articles. At the time of publication of the book, Sastri had been giving speeches about the Dharmas of *ārya mata* at several places, set up many sabhas, and was editing a monthly journal by the title of *Ārya mata bōdhini*.[3]

Kandukuri Viresalingam (Tel. kandukūri vīrēśaliṅgam, 1848–1919), the most prominent westernizing social reformer of Andhra, was the intellectual that Sastri disputed head-on; so much so, that it would be quite appropriate to describe Sastri as anti-Viresalingam. Viresalingam's ideas of westernizing social reform enjoyed their heyday during the late nineteenth century, with many English-educated students and young men joining his ranks.[4] Brahman and other upper caste students who came

---

[1] I am thankful to Rakesh Pandey, Heiko Frese, Raghurama Raju and Velcheru Narayana Rao for comments on a previous draft of this article.

[2] Calapatiravu 1911. The book (472 pp.) [in the following: *Upanyāsa payōnidhi*] contains 43 essays covering subjects from religion, Hinduism, Brahmoism, puranic themes, etc.

[3] This information about the author has been provided in the preface to the book by Nandiraju Calapatiravu. The editor unveils in the preface a more ambitious plan to publish all of Sastri's writings. He says that speeches and writings of Sastri on religious matters will come out in one or two more volumes, his essays on Telugu language and literature will appear in two or three volumes, and two additional volumes will comprise his other miscellaneous writings. As far as is known, this ambitious plan of publication appears to have fallen through.

[4] The editor of *Upanyāsa payōnidhi* remarks that the 'Dravidian' students of Madras did not respond as favourably to westernizing ideas. That the project of the so-called 'social reform' did not have as much success in the Tamil region as it did in the Telugu region is also a point made in Irschick 1969.

under Viresalingam's influence showed several signs of western influence, such as cutting their hair, eating without taking the ritual bath, being indifferent to perform *sandhya vandana*, and opposing image worship. Even during this phase, though, there were orthodox intellectuals who seriously opposed his ideas, well-known among them being the figure of Kokkonda Venkataratnam (Tel. kokkoṇḍa veṅkaṭaratnam, 1842–1915). Venkataratnam began to critique the new ideas and changes in his journal, *Āndhra bhāṣa sanjīvanī*, but the journal did not have the wide circulation of Viresalingam's journals, *Vivek-avardhani* and *Hāsya sanjīvanī*. Moreover, Venkataratnam wrote a prose that was quite difficult and inaccessible to the ordinary reader.[5]

The last quarter of the nineteenth century was also the time when the Europeans, on the one hand, and the Theosophists, on the other, began to publish extensively on the greatness and glory of Hinduism. As a result of these ideas, and also due to the impact of the spread of political nationalism, the situation of favourable climate to westernizing reform began to undergo a change in the early years of the twentieth century. The English-educated sections and their leaders began to fall out with Viresalingam, and increasingly adopted a programme of reform on nationalist lines. The change was quite dramatic in 1907, the year when Andhra felt the reverberations of Bengal's Swadeshi Movement. It was also during this year that the fiery Extremist leader from Bengal, Bipin Chandra Pal, toured and lectured in several towns in the Telugu districts and made a huge impact.

I have closely read Sastri's various essays in *Upanyāsa payōnidhi*, culled his views on various topics and issues, and made an ordering and classification of them in order to explore whether a coherent worldview of the author can be presented. Details about his early life experiences, formative influences and intellectual evolution would be valuable to make sense of his worldview, but such information is not available at present. I will first outline the various elements of his worldview below, so that an adequate ground will be available for later discussion, and then appraise the anti-reform discourse that Sastri took part in and led.

Responses to the critiques of Hinduism

Hinduism is not polytheistic: that Hinduism was a polytheistic religion was a critical observation made by several people, including critics from Islamic and Christian backgrounds. There were two possible responses to this critique: one, was to accept that Hinduism is indeed polytheistic and

[5] For a detailed account of Viresalingam's ideas and activities, see Ramakrishna 1983.

maintain that there was nothing wrong with that; the other, was to deny that Hinduism was polytheistic. Sastri, like several religious reformers of the colonial period, preferred the second response. The second response partially accepted the criticisms leveled against Hinduism by other religionists, such as the Christians, and an attempt was made to redefine Hinduism and provide a new interpretation of it in the light of the critiques.

In the opening essay of the book entitled 'Ganadhipati', Sastri argues that while it is sometimes thought that there are several gods and goddesses in Hinduism and Vighnesvara (Ganesa) is but one of them, he is only one of the several manifestations of the same *parabrahma* or *paramātma* (single supreme God).[6] The *parabrahma* is sometimes called Brahma, at another time Vishnu, and at yet another Ganesa. If you ask which one of these statements is correct, the answer has to be that all those statements are correct. They are all different names of the same God. If you ask, why call the same God by different names, Sastri maintains that there is much merit in that practice. The supreme God has multiple characteristics and each of these characteristics is captured by a specifically-named god, and even so, the entire gamut of the supreme God's characteristics is impossible to capture.[7]

In support of the above argument, Sastri cites the opinions of one Rev. Robertson, Monier-Williams, and the famous Brahmo reformer, Keshub Chandra Sen. The quote from Keshub Chandra Sen is provided here:

> Hindu idolatry is not to be altogether overlooked or rejected. As we explained some time ago, it presents millions of broken fragments of God. Collect them together, and you get the indivisible divinity. Their idolatry is nothing but the worship of a divine attribute materialized.[8]

Hinduism is not a closed religion: Sastri alludes to a prevalent opinion at the time among the English-educated in India that the Christians, because they are open and broad-minded, have widely disseminated their religious ideas among all sections of the people. The same set of people also maintained that the Hindus, being conservative, have closed the doors of their religion to the outside world. As a result, ordinary people in India have

---

[6] *Upanyāsa payōnidhi:* 11–12. Sastri goes on to say that the ancient Hindus went all the way to the 'nether' land of the Americas and exported some of their religion. Apparently, Mexicans worship a god looking similar to Ganesa, and this was observed by Alexander von (Baron) Humboldt.

[7] *Upanyāsa payōnidhi:* 3–5.

[8] *Upanyāsa payōnidhi:* 8. Keshub's difference from other Brahmo reformers – his positive evaluation of Sri Ramakrishna – has been noted in Chatterjee 1995.

remained in a state of ignorance. Sastri expresses his strong disapproval of this opinion.[9]

Hinduism is not the only religion with a large number of sects: Sastri says that it is common for the Christian missionaries, who came to India for proselytization, to argue that there are far too many sects in Hinduism. Closely following the missionaries, Brahmos agree with the Christian missionaries on this point. To refute the charge that this feature is true only of Hinduism, Sastri provides a list of 154 sects which were in existence in Christianity in England at that time. He remarks further that it is not uncommon among them for the members of one sect to kill those of another.[10]

Greatness of Hinduism

Hinduism is a living religion: if a question is posed as to which one is the living religion of India, Sastri says the answer has to be that it is Hinduism. Among religions prevalent in India at his time, he mentions Hinduism, Buddhism, Christianity, Islam and Brahmoism. Noteworthy religions, in his opinion, are Hinduism, Christianity and Brahmoism. Buddhism, once a significant religion, had now been fully absorbed and incorporated into Hinduism. Islam had stagnated and was found to be in a derelict state. The discerning eye would detect that even Christianity and Brahmoism were in a decaying state. Yet, there is a characteristic of obduracy about them, so that they appear as surviving to the people who are practicing them. Max Müller, whom Sastri quotes, had described the characteristics of a living religion in the following terms.

A religion which is not able thus to grow and live with us as we grow and live is dead already. Definite and unvarying uniformity so far from being a sign of honesty and life is always a sign of dishonesty and death. Every religion, if it is to be a bond of union between the wise and the foolish, the old and the young must be pliant, must be high and deep and broad, bearing all things, believing all things, hoping all things, enduring all things. The more it is so the greater its vitality, the greater the strength and warmth of its embrace.[11]

Hinduism is ancient, strong and resilient: according to Sastri, it is universally acknowledged that Hinduism is an ancient religion. Compared to it, Christianity and Islam are fairly recent. About the recency of Christianity, a quotation from Leslie Stephen is provided: "It (Christian-

---

[9] *Upanyāsa payōnidhi:* 29–30.
[10] *Upanyāsa payōnidhi:* 380.
[11] *Upanyāsa payōnidhi:* 19.

ity) has only existed during a relatively brief period of the whole history of the race, and then only among a small minority."[12]

However, ancientness is not the only virtue of Hinduism. A noteworthy religion should also stay strong and resilient. It should remain intact with its integrity preserved, withstanding the various attacks and sieges launched on it from the outside. This strength informs only Hinduism and no other religion in the world.

Despite ceaseless attacks on it from other religions, Hinduism has recoiled and prospered. Attacked from one direction by Islam, which wielded the sword, and from another direction by Christianity, which shot the cannon, and attacked internally by Brahmoism, Hinduism has survived by showing resilience, and had even began to make its influence felt in England and the United States.[13]

Hinduism is continuous and unbroken: the Hindu religion has continued through history without any interruption. Not many religions can claim such ancient and unbroken history, says Sastri. To strengthen this claim, he quotes from the Bengali nationalist, Romesh Chandra Dutt:

> For it may be truly said that in India alone we see the faiths and traditions of the long past still unbroken and still instinct (sic) with life and vitality. The ancient faiths of Egypt, Babylon are now things of the past and the religion of ancient Greece and Rome leaves only its poetry and art ... Among the Hindus only the link between the present and the ancient past remains unbroken.[14]

Hinduism is tolerant: only a religion that is true and robust can afford to be tolerant. Needless to say, only Hinduism fits such a bill, claims Sastri. This is what Rammohun Roy had to say on the issue: "It is well known to the whole world that no people on earth are more tolerant than the Hindus, who believe all men to be equally within the reach of Divine beneficence, which embraces the good of every religious sect and denomination."[15] In support of the position that Hinduism is tolerant, Sastri also provides the statements of Max Müller, Carsten Niebuhr and Monier-Williams.

Another quotation from Abbe Dubois is provided to demonstrate the point effectively:

> When I had to build or restore a church, it was very often from Brahmans that I obtained the site and the necessary building materials. ... But to return to the matter in hand, many people have attributed to narrow-mindedness and intolerance the excessive care which Brahmans take to exclude strangers from their temples and religious ceremonies. For my part, I think their only motive is

[12] *Upanyāsa payōnidhi:* 36.
[13] *Upanyāsa payōnidhi:* 38.
[14] *Upanyāsa payōnidhi:* 39.
[15] *Upanyāsa payōnidhi:* 40.

to secure themselves from the approach of men who from the way in which they live, and from the clothes which they wear, are in their eyes in a perpetual state of defilement.[16]

Suitability of Hinduism for India: Sastri argues that Islam and Christianity are helpful for people who are *ajña* (ignorant or ordinary), but not for people who are *prajña* (enlightened or capable). Even so, in their methods of devotion, there is no scope for image worship in their religions, so they are not even useful for the *ajña*. Hinduism is superior because it has methods of devotion suitable both for *ajña* and *prajña*.[17]

Critiques of Christianity

In the same essay, where Sastri argues that Hinduism is a living religion, he makes critiques of other religions including Christianity. In his estimation, Christianity is not a religion in a good shape. It has declined completely in its land of birth, Palestine. For some time, it prospered and proliferated in Europe and the United States, but even there it has entered a phase of steep decline. As awareness is advancing in the world, people, both the ignorant and the enlightened, are losing faith in Christianity. The reason for this is that the characteristics of a living religion, as described by Max Müller, are not present in Christianity. Since there is no image worship, it does not appeal to the ignorant. Since it does not have a philosophical depth, it cannot appeal to the enlightened. This explains its decline. To support his contention, Sastri quoted from a variety of sources, including from Max Müller, who said:

> It was because attempts were made from very early times to narrow and stiffen the outward signs and expressions of our faith to put narrow dogma in the place of trust and love. That the Christian Church has often lost those who might have been its best defenders and that the religion of Church has almost ceased to be what before all things, it was meant to be a religion of worldwide love and charity.[18]

Another citation is provided from the *Saturday Review*: "In the presence of the scientific religions – Brahmanism, Buddhism, Judaism and Muhammadanism – it has signally failed, and there is no prospect of an eventual victory."[19]

---

[16] *Upanyāsa payōnidhi:* 42.
[17] *Upanyāsa payōnidhi:* 20.
[18] *Upanyāsa payōnidhi:* 21.
[19] *Upanyāsa payōnidhi:* 21.

Critiques of Brahmoism

Puranic Hinduism vs. Vedantic Hinduism: *Īśvara vādi*, a Brahmo journal made a distinction between 'puranic' Hinduism and Upanishadic Hinduism, and further claimed that the former is followed by the general populace, whereas the latter is what the Brahmo Samajists followed.

Sastri disapproves of this distinction and argues that the two are not different and that there is an underlying unity between them. The Vedas have both the *karma kāṇḍa* and the *jñāna kāṇḍa*. The *Dharmaśāstras* teach the *karma kāṇḍa* and the Puranas teach the *jñāna kāṇḍa*. Therefore, if Puranas can be said to teach the meaning of the Vedas, it implies they can be purported to teach the sequel to the Vedas as well, namely the Upanishads. In support of his view, Sastri quotes from the *Vāsiṣṭhasmṛti*, *Pañcaratnavyākhyā*, *Pratāparudriyamu* and *Sahityaratnakaramu*. Additionally, he also cites from Rammohun Roy, Keshub Chandra Sen and Romesh Chandra Dutt.[20]

Vedantic Hinduism is available to all, contrary to the claim of some Brahmos: one of the critiques that some Brahmos leveled against Hinduism was that only the yogis, sages and the renouncers were eligible for receiving the *brahma jñāna*. Those Brahmos also claimed that, for the first time, such *brahma jñāna* was made available to the householders and ordinary people through the teachings of the Brahmo Samaj. Sastri refutes this view and argues that there are scores of examples in puranic lore of ordinary people and householders who achieved the *brahma jñāna,* without ever leaving the mainstream of society.[21]

Problems with the notions of 'virtue', 'evil' and 'rebirth' in the Brahmo discourse: Sastri takes elaborate issue with Viresalingam over the enunciation of some basic concepts of religion.[22] An important text in question is *Upanyāsa mañjari,* written by Viresalingam. In the text, Viresalingam acknowledges the necessity of religion. He also acknowledges that there are certain essential functions that religion serves in society, and one of these is to promote virtuous behaviour among members of society. Religion deters individuals from the commission of folly / evil (*pāpa*) by talking not only about the problems that arise from such behaviour in this world, but prescribing punishment for *pāpa* in the other world.

---

[20] *Upanyāsa payōnidhi:* 351–363.

[21] *Upanyāsa payōnidhi:* 436.

[22] Viresalingam's own articles on religion, which Sastri critiques in his book, are found in *Upanyāsa mañjari*, Rajahmundry, 1951. This is clearly a reprint of the book published before 1911, date of Sastri's book. I have however been unable to get hold of the precise date of publication of Viresalingam's book.

Viresalingam elaborates on this issue. He says that whenever a person commits a good act, he (or she) is seized by a feeling of happiness. Alternatively, whenever a person commits a bad act, he is overtaken by a feeling of unhappiness. However, he does not think such unhappiness is adequate punishment for those who commit bad or evil acts. One of the grounds for such a view is the observation that some bad people are quite successful, prosperous and consequently happy, whereas some good people lead poor, difficult and unhappy lives.

However, Viresalingam does not consistently hold to this position. At other places where he writes, he seems to think that the consequences of evil actions in this life and world are somehow serious enough for committers of such evil actions. He goes on to argue that only the virtuous person will receive the mercy or the kindness of God and achieve happiness in this life. Even if a person made much money by practicing illegitimate means, he will not have achieved happiness. Whenever he thinks about the means he adopted in making that money, his conscience would be plagued by guilt and negatively impact on his feeling of well-being. That is the reason why even if someone appears outwardly happy and successful, he is probably not 'really' happy.

Sastri detects an inconsistency between the above two positions of Viresalingam. Viresalingam is not clearly standing by the position of punishment in the other world for the evil actions of this world. Such a categorical position is present only in puranic Hinduism where there is a concept of hell (*naraka*), and where there are specific forms of punishment earmarked for specific crimes. Therefore, Sastri argues, if Viresalingam still insists on the necessity of religion and the essential functions it serves (such as deterring the commission of evil in this world), he would be much better off following puranic Hinduism.

Viresalingam also has other problems with certain Hindu theological beliefs, according to Sastri. For Viresalingam, if you accept the theory of karma, you cannot really answer the question of how people assumed the differential forms or births they did at the time of the origin of the world. Since God is neutral, impartial and not differentiating, he would not have allowed for such unevenness. The theory, therefore, becomes logically untenable. Additionally, Viresalingam argues, there is no mention of rebirth in the Vedas, and therefore it is not significant for the Hindu faith.

God, a merciful being or entity, could not be blamed for the existence of *pāpa* in this world, or for the faults of human beings, or for human suffering. In other words, Viresalingam seeks to rescue God from any responsibility for the existence of *pāpa* in the world. In doing so, he virtually dismisses the concept of *pāpa* and merely looks at it as the flip side of *puṇya*. It is humans themselves who are to blame for the existence of *pāpa*, and they become responsible in that way by defying God's diktat for virtuous behaviour.

A possible reason, according to Viresalingam, why God might want to punish the evildoers, is to maintain peace and order in the world and to promote virtue. This is akin to the laws of punishment that a king might enforce in a kingdom. But then, when a king punishes, he does so on the basis of laws that he has already enacted and made public. In this case, punishment has a deterrent effect on the offender and would carry an instructive value for other potential offenders. But in God's case, are people familiar with what his law is? Viresalingam is uncomfortable with this ambiguity, claims Sastri, and seeks to overcome it in a clumsy fashion by positing that 'conscience' may be taken as the manifestation of God's will or law. This resolution is however not entirely satisfactory, since conscience, only subjectively experienced, can be an inaccurate and unreliable indicator of God's law. Therefore, Viresalingam's dissatisfaction with the ambiguity implicit in the theory of God's punishment in the other world for man's follies committed in this world remains unsorted. When a punishment is unspecified, it becomes arbitrary, argues Viresalingam, and does not lead to the desired effects of punishment – regret, penitence and reformative attempt by the culprit, and does not have instructional value for others.

Sastri detects in Viresalingam an implicit critique of God's method of dealing with evil and evil-doers. He does not appear to be in favour of punishing the offenders in the other world, nor does he accept the theory of rebirth. Such views seriously compromise Viresalingam's claimed status as a Hindu and his posturing as a defender of religion, feels Sastri.[23]

Brahmoism is not Hinduism: Sastri cites the following grounds for arguing that Brahmoism is not Hindu. 1) All indigenous religions of India until now have accepted 'rebirth', and any religion which does not do that is not Hindu. 2) All Hindu faiths maintain that the 'soul' or atman (Skt. ātman) resides in flora and fauna, and even rocks and mountains, whereas Christianity maintains that only humans have a soul. Brahmoism, like Christianity, believes that only humans have souls, and therefore it is not Hindu. 3) Hindu religions maintain that karma is beginning-less. Christianity maintains that the world has a beginning. Similarly, Brahmoism also maintains that the world has a beginning, and karma, if it exists, must also have a beginning – therefore it is not Hindu; 4) Hindu religions prescribe image worship for the ordinary, though they admit that it is unnecessary for the yogis and *jñānis*, whereas Christianity proscribes image worship for anyone. Similarly, Brahmoism also decries image worship by anyone. 5) Hindu religions approve of the methods of *karma*,

---

[23] *Upanyāsa payōnidhi:* 52–59, 317–325.

bhakti and *jñāna* – Christianity approves of only the method of *bhakti*. Similarly, Brahmoism also approves only *bhakti*. 6) Hindu religions also accept the female principle as God, but Christianity strongly disapproves of this, as does Brahmoism. 7) Hindu religions understand manas (mind) as a tool and atman as the tool-bearer. Religions such as Christianity do not explicitly acknowledge atman. They mistake manas for atman. Similarly, Brahmoism also regards only the manas as atman.[24]

Brahmoism has no book: Sastri says that the fundamental principles of Brahmoism are not systematically expounded in any place. Also, there is no book that serves as the basis of the religion.

He adds that the Brahmos do not read the Indian religious books, nor are they interested in the history of Indian religions. They only read books on Christianity and its history, and using the yardsticks of the Christian religion they criticize Hinduism. They keenly follow Protestantism, a breakaway group from Christianity, and attempt to apply some of its principles to critique Hinduism.[25]

Social Customs of Brahmos: the distinction that the Brahmos have sought to draw are not simply in terms of religious beliefs but even of rituals and rites of passage. When the child of a Brahmo friend died, Viresalingam put the body in a coffin and buried it in the garden of its parent. It was not buried in the customary burial ground. This is an un-Hindu practice, according to Sastri.

Brahmoism is for a large part an imitation of Christianity, claims Sastri. Brahmos have set up rooms and halls for carrying out worship, in the manner of Christians. This is totally unlike the way Hindus worship their gods. Brahmos are cutting their hair like Christians, which is why Brahmoism has come to be called a 'hair cropping religion'.[26]

Decline of Brahmo Samaj: that the Brahmo Samaj is in a serious state of decline is attested by none other than an important leader of that organization, Pandit Sivanatha Sastri. The reason for this decline of popularity, according to Sivanatha Sastri, is the absence of image worship in Brahmoism without which it has failed to become popular among the people. Sivanatha Sastri adds:

> The Brahmo Samaj has neglected the masses and has mostly confined its attention to the educated classes, but the question is – is it making any notable progress amongst those educated few? This is the question to which I beg to draw your attention this evening.[27]

---

24 *Upanyāsa payōnidhi:* 351–355.
25 *Upanyāsa payōnidhi:* 351–355.
26 *Upanyāsa payōnidhi:* 351–355.
27 *Upanyāsa payōnidhi:* 27.

Sivanatha Sastri is lamenting that, unlike in the past, educated people are no longer attracted to it. On the other hand, they are turned away from it. He also laments that attendance at the Brahmo public meetings is progressively dwindling (Kasibhatta Brahmayya). Sastri injects that the reason for the decline of the Brahmo Samaj is that it has neither the sublime Vedanta nor the facility of image worship. On the other hand, Hinduism has both the *jñāna mārga* / Vedanta suitable for the enlightened (*prajña*) and image worship that is suitable for ordinary worshippers (*ajña*).

Reintegration into Hinduism: Brahmo Samaj is a sect that has split from Hinduism. After a certain period of independent existence, it is disappearing as an independent faith, claims Sastri, and is now in the process of getting absorbed back into Hinduism. As the individuals who converted initially to Brahmoism increased their knowledge of the world, they were not happy with their 'little' religion and began to come back to their religion of origin. Prominent among those who made that transition in recent times is Bipin Chandra Pal. This shows the vitality and greatness of Hinduism.[28]

Religious idiom as the basic Indian idiom: in an essay entitled 'Religion', Sastri begins with a discussion of the theoretical understanding of the concept and mentions the views of Kant, Fichte, Hegel, Comte and Paine. He then alludes to the popular view that the religious idiom is the basic idiom of Indian society, which he agrees with. According to the Indian understanding, he says, morality is part of religion; so are knowledge of the soul, devotion, release from worldly attachment, social duty, and worldly knowledge. In other countries, one or a few of these various dimensions are part of religion. In India, all these dimensions have become part of religion, which is why 'religion' stands out as the most important feature of Hindu society. However, superficial observers have caricatured Hindu society by saying that sitting, standing, sleeping are all part of religion in India.[29]

Importance of religion in modern life: Viresalingam insisted on the need for obtaining indubitable and verifiable knowledge in the field of religion, just as the method of science had been applied to gain reliable knowledge about the external and material world. Just as we use our experience and intellect to understand the world, we may use the same faculties to find out truth about religious matters as well. Since the Vedas are based on the least reliable form of evidence of oral transmission, Viresalingam says, we may corroborate them with our own experience and exercise our own intellect in arriving at their reliability. This is the

[28] *Upanyāsa payōnidhi:* 341–350, 420.

[29] *Upanyāsa payōnidhi:* 13–15.

criterion that he used to refute the Srutis, Smritis, Puranas, and other religious literature of Hinduism.

There is an ambiguity about the positioning of Brahmoism – is it a sect / division internal to Hinduism or does it claim an independent status outside the fold of Hinduism? Brahmos, in order to make their message more effective, initially claimed the status of insiders.[30] Legislation that the Brahmos pressed the colonial government to pass in 1872, Sastri says, effectively nailed this ambiguity and settled that they are indeed outside the fold of Hinduism. The opening statement of the legislation proclaims:

> Whereas it is expedient to provide a form of marriage for persons who do not profess the Christian, Jewish, Hindu, Mahammadan, Parse, Buddhist, Sikh or Jain religion, and to legalize certain marriage the validity of which is doubtful, it is hereby enacted.[31]

Sastri argues that this legislation for the first time in Indian history inaugurated the custom of a 'civil' marriage. He has two important critical remarks to make about the legislation. First, that marriage which had been a religious sacrament up until that point of time had been desacralized and made into a secular contract. And second, that the help of religious outsiders and alien rulers had been sought to bring about reform in Hindu social customs.

Need for social reform
Acknowledgement of Rammohun Roy's positive role

Sastri takes the occasion of the demise of Pratap Chandra Majumdar in 1905, an important leader of the Brahmo Samaj, to ruminate over the role of the Brahmo Samaj, and especially the contribution of its founder, Rammohun Roy.

Sastri acknowledges the need for reform in any society. Since human nature is fickle and vulnerable, every society will have its own set of objectionable practices, and critiques of such practices are healthy for a society. The practice of Hinduism came to be dominated by *karma*

---

[30] Sastri says that, in recent years (presumably the first decade of the twentieth century), some people in Rajahmundry got rid of their sacred threads. Even Viresalingam removed his. When there was a public meeting in the town on the question of religious reform, Nyapati Subba Rao, an erstwhile associate of Viresalingam and now a nationalist, spoke at the meeting and said that those who wanted to reform Hinduism should stay within its fold and make the attempt. He called Brahmoism un-Hindu and criticized certain individuals who claimed the status of Hindu social reformers for leaving the fold of Hinduism and joining Brahmoism. *Upanyāsa payōnidhi:* 60–61.

[31] *Upanyāsa payōnidhi:* 452.

anuṣṭhāna, and some of its more salient features became obscure to the people at large. During the early colonial period, when Christianity was in the process of rapidly spreading, some dogmatic people among both Christians and Muslims began to equate Hinduism with image worship. Some Indians, under the influence of the above-mentioned religions, also came to regard it in such terms. To refute this misperception, and to bring about changes in the practice of Hinduism, Rammohun Roy founded a new religion by relying on *jñāna mārga*. During Roy's time, it was observed that some healthy practices in Hinduism had fallen into ill repute and dysfunction. Hinduism was indeed plagued by external observances, multiple karmas, superstitious beliefs and other societal malpractices. People momentarily forgot the principles of *ārṣa mata* evolved from the Vedas. In order to bring about a change in this situation, Roy preached the new religion.

While some of the negative features were indeed present, Sastri argues that there is no need to jump to the conclusion that Hinduism was in a state of incorrigible decay, or that *ārṣa mata* had declined irreversibly, or that the principles of Hinduism fell into unsalvageable disrepute. The phase of decline of a religion is a cyclical process that happens to all religions in the world. All of them can do with a cleanup from time to time, and that is exactly what the early Brahmo Samaj attempted to do.

In the following cycle of regeneration, Hindus learned the principles of their religion afresh from Ramakrishna, Vivekananda and Annie Besant. They rejected wholesale the unwanted features that crept into Hinduism and resumed the practice of their religion in accordance with the dictates of the *ārṣa mata*. They also acknowledged that Rammohun Roy preached the purest principles of Hinduism and followed them. There is little new that Hinduism needs to learn from other religions. In fact, no other religion contains the sublime practices and lofty ideals present in Hinduism.[32]

Social and political reform

There are some social reformers today, says Sastri, who argue that political reform is not possible until social reform is completed. Rammohun Roy had never subscribed to this opinion. In fact, he was the one who laid the foundation for all the political reforms that the Indian National Congress is currently demanding. He undertook constructive reform activity without ever leaving either his religion or caste.[33]

---

[32] *Upanyāsa payōnidhi:* 341–350.
[33] *Upanyāsa payōnidhi:* 418.

Contradictions in Brahmo practice

When Viresalingam conducted the first Brahmo wedding in Andhra, it was expected that there would be a stark difference with a Hindu wedding. However, it turned out to resemble a Hindu wedding in most ways, claims Sastri. There are four important rituals in a Hindu matrimonial ceremony – *kanya dāna*, *maṅgaḷa sūtra dharaṇa*, *pani grahana*, and *sapta padi*. The so-called first Brahmo wedding, conducted by Viresalingam, ironically incorporated all of these important Hindu rituals.

Moreover, there was also the issue of dowry. Viresalingam and others had in the past waxed eloquently about the need to get rid of extravagant expenditure for weddings and also about putting a stop to the system of dowry. Contrary to such preaching, extravagant expenditure was lavished on the wedding and dowries (gifts) were handed out to both the bridegroom and the bride.[34]

Problem of Widows: if one were to go by what Viresalingam has written, one would think that the travails of widows in India are so grave that they would not be tolerable by humans (and only perhaps by demons). The actual situation of widows in India is not as bad as made out by him, argues Sastri. The evidence available from books written by civilized people, popular songs, poems, adages, etc. points to the respectful position enjoyed by the widowed daughters in their parental homes. In stating thus, Sastri does not mean to deny that widows have problems. There are problems with every state of being, and so also with this particular state of being. Problems are unavoidable. The biggest drawback for widows is that they have been deprived of husbandly love and companionship. This crucial drawback can indeed be highlighted and it can of course be argued that remarriage is important for widows. Other drawbacks are relatively minor in comparison to the main one. It is not right to argue that society persecutes the widows. They are only treating the widows in a suitable way. Hindus had other-worldly (*āmuṣmika*) objectives in mind in having the widows stay that way.[35]

Need for a balanced approach: Viresalingam's first novel, *Rājaśēkhara caritramu*, also among the earliest novels published in Telugu, has as its target audience Europeans. This novel does not appear to have been written with only the Indian (Telugu) readers in mind. Sastri feels it to be so because there are several descriptions in the text that are obvious to the native reader, and therefore do not merit a separate mention. It appears to

---

[34] *Upanyāsa payōnidhi:* 458–469.

[35] The prevalent discourses on women and widowhood in Andhra, as well as in other parts of India, are discussed at length in Rajagopal 2003: 377–402.

have been written for the purpose of telling non-Indians about the customs and practices of India.

When one is writing for a native audience, one-sided representations, whether positive or negative, are all right. But when one is writing for a foreign audience, says Sastri, one needs to practice balance, and represent both positive and negative features of the society. Is there nothing good at all about Indian society? Is there a society anywhere in the world which does not have even a trace of negativity?

Some preliminary reflections

The editor of *Upanyāsa payōnidhi* remarks in his preface that the articles in the volume are directed to make an appeal to educated Indians, which presumably means Indians literate in both Telugu and English. The 'method' of writing adopted by Sastri, notes the editor, relies on logic (*yukti*) as the primary basis, opinions of westerners as the secondary basis, and provision of examples from ancient Hindu literature such as the Vedas, Upanishads, Puranas as the third or tertiary basis for the arguments provided therein. This remark of the editor tallies with our observation and reading of the contents of the book.

This, however, raises further questions. Can we classify and understand Sastri as an Orientalist, that is, an Indian intellectual who came under the strong influence of the ideology of Orientalism (at least that variety of Orientalism with origins in European thought that draws sharp distinction between West and India and holds up India as comprising several positive or even superior features)? It would seem thus if one looks at the European writers such as Max Mueller, Robert Caldwell, Abbe Dubois, Monier-Williams, H T Colebrook, Warren Hastings, Baron Humboldt, etc. who have been invoked and quoted extensively in the articles.[36] He read British journals such as the *Saturday Review.* Sastri also engaged actively with the Brahmo discourse of the time by staying in touch with journals in English, such as the *Indian Messenger*, *Social Reformer* and journals in Telugu, such as *Īśvara vādi* and *Satya vādini.* The Brahmo discourse was influenced by another variant of Orientalism – an ideology that marked out the difference between the West and India, but one that upheld the superiority of Western culture and sought the reform or

[36] "Riding the growing political participation and exposure to new forms of communication, both of which had been effectively deployed for social reform in the earlier generation, cultural nationalists soon became a significant presence in Indian public life. They were the first orientalists that the Orient itself produced in defence of the Orient." (Nandy 2001: 18).

transformation of Indian culture in the image of the West. To the extent that Sastri sometimes grudgingly concedes the validity of the Brahmo critiques, as when he writes about the interventions of Rammohun Roy, it may be inferred that he came under the influence of the second variant of Orientalist thought as well.

Yet, the issue is more complicated. The generation of English-educated Indians of the late nineteenth century, who were influenced by the variants of Orientalist thought, relied heavily on European translations and interpretations of Sanskrit works on Hinduism. They did not have the language training or orientation for an independent access to classical works in Sanskrit and the Indian languages. Sastri should not be put into this category. He learned English well enough to use the Orientalist sources for his purposes, but it seems, from a perusal of his writings, that he was strongly trained in the Indian intellectual traditions and knew the classical literature of Sanskrit and Telugu rather well.

This being the case, we can make sense of Sastri as someone who was part of an influential Brahmanical discourse on Indian society, conducted both in Sanskrit and the regional languages that predated colonial rule. This discourse continued into the nineteenth century, though perhaps in a much more circumscribed fashion owing to the changes in the political context, through the scholarly and pedagogical work of a small number of Brahmans. Indigenous forms of social power and knowledge were progressively undermined as the nineteenth century progressed, though in the earlier phase of the beginning of the century it appeared as if such discourses received reinforcement from the colonial rule. Undermining of the privileges, ritual and social power of the Brahman elites, in addition of course to the ideological issues involved in the Christian attacks on Hinduism, drove the traditional and Brahman elites to fashion the language of cultural nationalism. Sastri's arguments about the ancientness, strength, resilience and superiority of Hinduism can be made sense of as the anti-colonial and nationalist perspective of a fading Brahman elite.

The ideology of nationalism, in the instance of India, can be elucidated in terms of multiple dimensions – namely economic, cultural and political. The founding of the Indian National Congress in 1885, in my estimation, cannot be understood as the arrival of political nationalism. Political nationalism, formulated in the language that calls for an overthrow of the British rule, is a development of the twentieth century. The Moderate leaders of the early Congress, critical though of the economic impact of colonial rule, were far too quiescent and loyal to colonial rule to go anywhere near political nationalism. On the other hand, they believed that British rule, albeit with some changes and corrections, would help India in the best possible way given the circumstances.[37] Their brand of nationalism may be characterized as economic nationalism.[38]

There was a rise in cultural nationalism as well in the late nineteenth century, though this happened largely outside the purview of the Indian National Congress. The critiques of a westernizing social reform project, defence of image worship and puranic Hinduism, cow protection movement, the debates that occurred over the Age of Consent Act of 1891, are all instances indicating this phenomenon. Rejection of the superiority of western / European culture and the extolment of Indian culture, and the defence of the Indian culture and customs from interference by external entities, such as the colonial state, are some salient features of cultural nationalism. Cultural nationalism has been said to occur prior to the occurrence of political nationalism in the Indian context.[39]

Cultural nationalism is also a political project. It is an engagement in the ideological tussle between the supporters of colonialism and its opponents. The authenticity or integrity of an intellectual position is necessarily, in this battle, subordinated to the political objective of defeating the rival ideological position. In this battle, Viresalingam was ranged on the opposite side of Sastri and in the company of the apologists of colonial rule. Viresalingam admitted to practicing eclectic and sometimes inconsistent methods to achieve his objective. When it suited him, he used the Sastras to defend his positions, and when it did not, he invoked the yardstick of reason. It seems that Sastri was similarly eclectic in his approach. He used European scholarship, which had a certain respectability at that time, for the sake of his political objective. Invoking it would make his appeal to the English-educated Indian readers more effective. If his invocation of European scholarship is indeed tactical, then the influence of Orientalist thought on him might be somewhat less significant that what one would at first think. Another noteworthy feature of Sastri's writings is that he intelligently deployed the critiques of Christianity by Christians themselves, and likewise critiques of Brahmoism by Brahmos themselves, to score his own polemical points.

At least some elements of Sastri's critique, such as the view that not everything has always been wrong within Indian society, or the view that there is no need to judge Hinduism by the standards of Christianity, would make an appeal to at least a section of postcolonial critics. How-

[37] An excellent account of the politics of the early Moderate leaders can be found in McLane 1977.

[38] The discourse of economic nationalism can be found in Naoroji 1878; Naoroji 1888; Naoroji 1901; Ranade 1898; Dutt 1904.

[39] For this argument, see Partha Chatterjee 1995. I would add that economic nationalism preceded cultural nationalism.

ever, his is a brand of cultural nationalism that clearly did not succeed. One might briefly speculate why this was so.

I have argued elsewhere, on the basis of my reading of evidence from the history of modern Andhra, that cultural and political nationalisms need not always go together.[40] There was a brief period, roughly between 1905 and 1915, when political nationalism paid lip service to cultural nationalism.[41] That moment passed soon enough, and several new groups and castes who joined the Indian national movement found that an agreement with the Western and the Christian critiques of Indian society significantly helped the cause of their social and political mobility.[42] Participation in the newly available modern political space was the key to achieving social mobility. That space became available sometimes through nationalist politics and at other times through the colonial state's electoral and legislative institutions. These new communities were clearly staking out a claim for a share in the power of the new Indian nation-state, due to emerge in the future. A case in point are the leaders of the non-Brahman movement in Andhra who combined repudiation of Hinduism with fairly vocal support for nationalist politics. There was also a relatively weaker trend of pro-colonial and non-Brahman Justice Party politics. It was, therefore, not just about claims on political power in a future national-political formation, but also a fight for political space under the existing colonial political regime.[43]

Sastri's model of cultural nationalism failed because it never really addressed the question of caste. There are very few references to the issue of caste in *Upanyāsa payōnidhi.* Caste was of course an important issue in the discourse on Indian society by that time. The Christian missionaries highlighted it, and reform groups such as the Arya Samaj addressed it. Sastri also was aware of the question, for he was far too familiar with the ideas and the activities of the Christian missionaries. Perhaps he was bothered by the discomfort of not possessing a satisfactory resolution to the question. Moreover, his notion of a 'public' consisted of 'educated Indians', which in turn meant members of the upper castes and especially Brahmans.[44] Issues of upper caste / Brahman domination had not yet crept

---

[40] Rajagopal 2005.

[41] A biography of Viresalingam, fairly critical of his pro-colonial politics, appears during this phase. See Gurunadham 1911.

[42] There is much commonality between the Christian and lower-caste critiques of Indian society even today.

[43] Along with the Justice Party, the nationalist Congress also took part in legislative politics under the colonial regime under the guise of the Swaraj Party. Later, it openly contested the elections in 1937.

[44] Sastri's limited imagination of the 'public' was in keeping with the times. When the leaders of the early and Moderate Congress spoke of an Indian 'public,' they excluded

into the discussions of the public sphere in Andhra / Telugu. They would do so, with increasing frequency and stridency, from the second decade of the nineteenth century. While there were some conversions to Christianity from the lower castes, they were most likely thought of as not significant enough to take into consideration. The appeal of the Brahmo Samaj was mainly to the members of the upper castes, and likewise, the appeal of their most trenchant critic, Sastri, also confined to that group. Curiously, therefore, both the Brahmo reformers and their orthodox critics shared a common ground in this respect, namely the target group of their appeal.

In the absence of a critical engagement with this important issue of Indian society, cultural nationalist ideology became confined to discussion in the proceedings of Sanatana Dharma Sabhas. These groups continued to function in the twentieth century even after the rise of political nationalism, and made some noises from time to time, such as at the time of the passing of the Sarda Act of 1929.[45] However, their brand of cultural nationalism, invariably identified with orthodox Brahman ideology, failed to inspire confidence in the upwardly mobile and politically aspiring lower-caste groups in Indian society. It was doomed to failure and insignificance.

Bibliography

Calapatiravu, Nandiraju, ed. 1911. *Upanyāsa payōnidhi.* Eluru: Manjuvani Press.

Chatterjee, Partha. 1995. *Nation and Its Fragments: Colonial and Postcolonial Histories*, New Delhi: Oxford University Press.

Dutt, Romesh Chunder. 1904. *Economic History of India.* New York: Franklin.

Gurunadham, J. 1911. *Viresalingam: The Founder of Telugu Public Life.* Rajahmundry.

Irschick, Eugene F. 1969. *Politics and Social Conflict in South India: The Non-Brahmin Movement and Tamil Separatism 1916–1929.* Berkeley: University of California Press.

McLane, John R. 1977. *Indian Nationalism and the Early Congress.* Princeton: University Press.

Nandy, Ashis. 2001. *Time Warps: The Insistent Politics of Silent and Evasive Pasts.* Delhi: Permanent Black.

Naoroji, Dadabhai. 1878. *Poverty of India.* London: Vincent Brooks, Day and Son.

——. 1888. *Poverty of India: Papers and Statistics.* London: W. Foulger

——. 1901. *Poverty and un-British Rule in India.* London: Swan Sonnenschein.

most of the rural population, all women, and a large section of the urban population. When they asked for representation on the governing or advisory bodies of state, they were stopping well short of asking for fully representative government. See Seth 1999.

[45] This legislation raised the minimum age at marriage for girls to fourteen. Orthodox Hindus protested that it interfered with indigenous Hindu customs.

Rajagopal, Vakulabharanam. 2003. 'The Rhetorical Strategy of an Autobiography: Reading Satyavati's Armacaritamu', *The Indian Economic and Social History Review* 40,4: 377–402.

——. 2005. 'Fashioning Modernity in Telugu: Viresalingam and His Interventionist Strategy', *Studies in History* 21,1: 45–77.

Ranade, M. G. 1898. *Essays on Indian Economics*. Bombay: Thacker.

Seth, Sanjay. 1999. 'Rewriting Histories of Nationalism: The Politics of "Moderate Nationalism" in India, 1870–1905.' *The American Historical Review* 104,1 (February): 95–116.

Ramakrishna, V. 1983. *Social Reform in Andhra*, New Delhi: Vikas Publising House.

Velcheru Narayana Rao

Multiple lives of a text: The *Sumati śatakamu* in colonial Andhra

The nineteenth century was undoubtedly a particularly eventful period in Indian history. This was the century when British rule in India consolidated itself and – after the turbulence of 1857–58 – eventually emerged confidently, not just as the inheritor of the fortunes of a trading company that had 'accidentally' found India falling into its lap, but as an agency that had accepted the responsibility to bring India from barbarity into a civilized state. Interactions between Britain and India – the former at the peak of its civilizational achievements and the latter in a perceived state of decline – produced monumental results that are open to varieties of interpretation. India received from British rule the mixed benefits of industrialization, English education, print culture, the ideas of the Enlightenment, Victorian sensibilities, Christian morality and a number of other features which add up to a phenomenon that may be called colonial modernity. And these ideas led in turn to a momentous paradigm shift in Indian thought and a world-view resulting in the formation of what we call modern India.

I want to focus on two features among the many that are said to have ushered in modernity: one is print and the other is public education. In this essay, I examine the impact of both of these new developments on Indian text-culture. The Gutenberg revolution and its influence on India is too large a subject for me to cover in a mere essay, so I want to be modest in studying the fortunes of one text, the *Sumati śatakamu*,[1] a Telugu work, through the nineteenth and twentieth centuries. By means of examining this one text and its use in public education, I will present the epistemological shifts that colonial modernity brought about in Indian text-culture. I have called this 'colonial modernity' to distinguish it from another modernity India had experienced before the colonial version, a subject about which I have written elsewhere.[2]

---

[1] Sreenivas Paruchuri and V. S. T. Sayee found and made accessible in record time a number of printed texts of *Sumati śatakamu* dating from the early decades of the 20th century, as well as many obscure secondary sources. Macca Haridasu gave me a copy of his notes about the manuscripts of *Sumati śatakamu*. I am deeply grateful to them for their assistance. Manuscripts of SS were inaccessible to me when I wrote this article. My conclusions should therefore be considered tentative and subject to revision after further research. Parts of this essay draw upon Narayana Rao and Subrahmanyam 2008: 25–65.

[2] See my afterword to Apparao 2007.

One of the responsibilities that the East India Company undertook was to open schools to teach the natives so they might grow up to be upright subjects. The responsibilities of public instruction gave new powers to the government – of deciding what to teach. By that time, those Indian intellectuals who were trained in English and were enjoying the benefits of their education by landing lucrative jobs in the service of the English East India Company were already convinced of the superiority of British culture. There was a general agreement in their minds that Indians lack morals. Vennelakanti Subbarao (1784–1839), translator for the *Sadr adālat* of the Madras Presidency, a Telugu Niyogi Brahman who rose to the highest post a native could aspire to in the East India Company administration at the time, felt that Indian children should be taught two things: namely, grammar and morals. When he was appointed to the Madras School Book Society, he submitted a report in 1820 on the state of teaching in schools. Addressing the need for teaching morals he recommended that "tales extracted from different books composed chiefly of morals written in modern languages" should be prescribed for study.[3]

From nīti to morals

Scholars in the service of the East India Company began to scramble for suitable books in Telugu to teach morals to schoolchildren. The closest word they found to 'morals' in Telugu and Sanskrit was *nīti*, which had some overlap with the English word in colloquial usage. Assuming that the semantic range of *nīti* and morals were similar, they looked for available texts that could be used to teach *nīti* to school children. The pandits who were associated with the East India Company were competent in Sanskrit and classical Telugu. Based on the general consensus among them that *Pañcatantra* stories were best suited for children, Ravipati Gurumurti Sastri retold them in Telugu in 1834 for classroom use. In 1853, Cinnaya Suri rewrote them in what he considered grammatically proper Telugu, under the title *Nīti-candrika*.[4] The *Pañcatantra* is a well-known book of fables in Sanskrit. Vishnuśarman, its author, had vowed to educate the three idiot sons of a king to make them experts in government

[3] Subbarao 1976: 65–75.

[4] The circumstances that led the *Pañcatantra* fables to be taught to school children are not clear. We, however, know that Cinnaya Suri, who worked as Telugu Headmaster in the Madras University, wrote these fables in a grammatically-acceptable high-flown Telugu. He gave his book a title in English, *Neeti Chandrika or Moral Stories*, which he "Respectfully Dedicated as A Mark of Respect" to A. J. Arbuthnot Esq. Secretary to the Madras University, and College of Fort Saint George. Virabhadra Rao 1986: 239–240.

in six months and wrote this book for that purpose, and not exactly to teach them morals.[5] Problems of cultural translation are already apparent in the choice. *Nīti* is a concept for which as Arthur W. Ryder, the translator of *Pañcatantra* into English perceptively notes, there is no equivalent in European languages:

> The word *nīti* means roughly "the wise conduct of life." Western civilization must endure a certain shame in realizing that no precise equivalent of the term is found in English, French, Latin, or Greek. Many words are necessary to explain what *nīti* is, though the idea, once grasped, is clear, important and satisfying.[6]

The concept of *nīti* in these stories relates to political policy and strategies suitable for worldly success. It is not in any way related to moral instruction as was understood by colonial administrators, or Christian intellectuals. But this did not deter scholars from teaching these stories for that purpose.

A Telugu book on nīti

In 1846, Puduri Sitarama Sastri (Tel. pudūri sitārāma śāstri) compiled his famous *Pědda bāla śikṣa*, (or the "big book to teach small children"). This book, reprinted again and again for decades, contains moral sayings composed by the author. *Nīti* now acquired a new meaning as a code of morals. Some of the moral sayings Sitarama Sastri included in his book appear as though they are paraphrased from a book called *Sumati śatakamu,* (hereafter *SS*).[7] A version of *SS* was first published in 1870 by Adi Sarasvati Mudranalayamu,[8] a family firm which later became the well-known publishing house, Vavilla Ramaswami Sastrulu and Sons.

[5] Olivelle 1997.

[6] Ryder 1962: 5.

[7] See Sitarama Sastri 1916: 46–47. In their preface, the publishers of this book say that they reprinted the 1847 edition free from the errors and alterations that crept into many of its reprints and published it exactly as it was in 1847 "with only minor changes."

[8] Nidadavolu Venkata Rao, in his preface to *Sumati śatakamu* (Venkata Rao 1966: 62), reports that the first edition of *PSS* was published by Adisarasvati on April 20, 1868. Such precise information with the date and month of publication is an unusual piece of knowledge about any book in Telugu, more so about a book published almost a hundred years ago, and Vennkata Rao does not say how acquired this information. The year of publication is repeated by Macca Haridasu in his *Tathyamu sumatī: parisodhana vyasālu*, (Haridasu 1984: 67) and Arudra in his *Samagra āndhra sāhityam* (Arudra 2002: Vol. 1., 224.) I have not found the 1868 edition in any library, nor have I been able to ascertain from any scholar that this edition actually exists. I take the 1870 edition of *PSS* to be its first edition, until the reported 1868 edition is located.

This edition (hereafter the *PSS*) became popular and was printed by a number of publishers again and again, mostly with no publication dates.

In the course of time, a number of verses from this book began to appear in text-books prescribed for grade school students. *Ānanda vācakamu,* a Telugu text book for the 3rd grade, compiled in 1930,[9] and approved for school use by the director of public instruction contains ten verses from the *PSS* under the heading *nīti padyamulu,* moral verses.[10] Some publishers issued the *PSS* with a sub-title: "Morals suitable to be taught for boys and girls", but there is an awareness on the part of at least some editors that *PSS* is not actually a book of morals, and many of its verses are unsuitable to be taught to young children. One of the volumes of the *PSS* printed in 1922[11] carried instructions to teachers on how to teach the verses and separated the verses that should be taught from those that should not be taught, but a glossary and notes were provided for all the verses anyway.[12]

A guide to success

To put the matter simply, the *Sumati śatakamu* is a guide to success in worldly life, in the same class as the Sanskrit *Pañcatantra, Hitopadeśa,* and *Nītisāra*, but without their high profile. It is a humble text by an unknown author, more applicable to real life in villages, written in simple verses that are easy to memorize.

Beginning from the thirteenth century, a number of books on *nīti* were written in Telugu. Verses from these books often served as authoritative sources to provide strategies for success in life for upper-caste men who aspired to be kings. While most *nīti* books concern the conduct of kings, ministers, armies, spies, etc., *SS* differs somewhat from such books in its content. Despite occasional references to kings, the focus of *SS* is the

---

[9] This book was actually compiled in 1920 by Kuchi Narasimham and Panuganti Lakshmi Narasimha Rao, even though the edition I have is dated 1930. I was not able to find any older elementary school readers, but it is possible that *SS* verses appeared in them as well.

[10] Schoolbooks do not give their sources, but the verses included in them are identical with verses in PSS.

[11] *Sumati śatakamu* 1922. A number of editions of *PSS* from 1913 on, are spelled *Sumatī śatakamu,* with a long /ī/, which is how the title *PSS* is pronounced in popular Telugu. Scholars who insisted on grammatically correct Telugu, who most probably edited the first edition of *PSS* spelled it with a short /i/.

[12] During the early decades of twentieth century a large number of books were written for school children teaching them *nīti*, morals. Between the years 1916–1930, a cursory search yielded 92 books on *nīti* such as *Nīti padyamulu*, moral verses, and *Nīti kathalu,* moral tales and so on. (I thank Sreenivas Paruchuri for this information.)

typical Andhra village with its local landlord, a few Brahmans, people of other upper castes, and courtesans. The *SS* is not the product of a king's court, nor was it intended for people in the court.

The *SS* is in sum a manual for success in life for upper-caste men. It is characterized by its proposal for uninhibited enjoyment of wealth and pleasure. In particular, the *SS* is concerned with sexual pleasure. A number of verses extol sexual enjoyment and belittle those who do not enjoy sex. Women are classified as wives or as courtesans. A courtesan never loves any man, no matter how handsome and skilled in the art of love he may be. Even wives do not care for a husband who does not earn money. As a general rule, the *SS* tells you that a woman should never be trusted, and a man should never confide in her. Without her husband's surveillance, a wife will certainly turn to prostitution. While a housewife is neither trusted nor loved, she is, paradoxically, respected as a goddess, as the magical source of all riches. The goddess of riches refuses to stay in a house where women cry. The man who causes grief to his wife risks losing the family's wealth. Although housewives are treated as goddesses, widows are treated as unworthy of respect. A household should be managed by a wife, not a widow, who is considered to be dangerous.

Socially, the *SS* presents a world of interdependence and tensions, of cooperation and mistrust. Considerable attention is given to the king, but it is likely the book is not dealing with any major rulers. Pompous words like *bhūpāluḍu*, "ruler of the earth", and *maṇḍalapati*, "lord of the country", are used to describe them. Men from literate castes served as their scribes and ministers. A number of verses in *SS* relate to them. For instance, a kingdom without a competent minister is like an elephant without its trunk. Scribes are advised not to serve a king who is himself literate. A scribe should never trust another scribe. He should be strong and never appear harmless. In the world of the *SS* each caste has its inherent defects, and a person's qualities are determined by birth. A *kṣatriya* is difficult to please, a *vĕlama* is undependable, a goldsmith is not trustworthy, a *komaṭi* is a liar. Even Brahmans are censured; a *vaidiki* lacks worldly wisdom, and a *karaṇam* is too full of stratagems to be trusted. Literary skills are extolled; to be able to write good poetry is valued highly but teaching the beauty of poetry to an idiot is like blowing a conch before a deaf person.

Low castes, in particular, are denounced. A low-caste person is variously referred to as *durjāti*, "bad caste person", *nīcuḍu,* "low person", *aviveki*, "unwise man", *pāmaruḍu,* "ignorant person", and *mūrkhuḍu*, "fool". By nature, they are dishonest. Friendship with them is foolish. If a low-caste person happens to be literate, he should be avoided like an elephant in rut. Low-caste people are specifically discouraged from saving money; their savings are always confiscated by kings, just as honey saved by bees is taken by people passing by. As a general principle, money exists for enjoyment or for charity. If a fool saves money without enjoying it himself or donating to deserving people, then it is confiscated by kings, stolen by thieves, or lost into the bowels of the earth.

Although the message of the *SS* is largely amoral, it does contain what appear to be moral sayings. For instance, desiring sex with another man's wife is wrong, stealing others' wealth is bad, anger is a person's worst enemy, and so on. In general, the *SS* conforms to the traditional scheme of Hindu life in which the four goals of *dharma, artha, kāma,* and *mokṣa* are evenly balanced. Everything thus has its place.

A man receives rewards or punishments according to his actions in previous lives. If he performed charitable deeds in his previous life, he is rich in this life, whether or not he works. If he was not generous in his previous life, he is poor in this life, no matter what he does to escape from poverty. In general, everything spoils: love ends in enmity, growth leads to destruction, low prices are replaced by high prices, and happiness is transformed into grief.

Probable readership of the SS

By the seventeenth century, a considerably large section of Brahmans known as *karaṇams* took to political occupations and jobs that required worldly skills instead of the usual Brahman profession of studying religious texts and conducting religious rituals. All of them were literate, some of them were scholars, and composed superior poetry in Telugu. They were good diplomats, and proud of their scribal skills with competence in multiple languages and scripts. They were not always associated with a king's court but an imagined royal court served as a model for their behavior. They composed a substantial body of poetry during this period. To attest to their writing skills, they made copies of their work and promoted them without much support from royal patrons. They were respectfully called *mantris,* ministers of kings, even when they actually did not serve a king. This seems to be the community that produced the *Sumati śatakamu.* True to their nature of not appearing important, but always managing affairs from behind the scenes, the *karaṇam* author[s] of *Sumati śatakamu* did not sign his name.

Despite their humble appearances, the self image of *karaṇams* is quite interesting. One of the verses about a *karaṇam* says:

He writes and reads and speaks intelligently.
He listens to what people say inside and out.
He interprets foreign languages to the king,
and controls the assembly if it goes out of line.
He says the right words and makes hearts unite,
and sees right away, honesty from trickery.
He can bring people together and separate them again
or favor enemies and offer them the throne.
He is humble, dignified, skilled and giving.
That's what a good mantri should be.

Karaṇams are portrayed as confident of their skill in manipulating matters to turn any situation favorable. They can make impossible things possible with their diplomatic skills:

If the king is against you, you need to be friends with the scribe.
When the god of death Yama was angry and declared a person
dead, "gatāyu", didn't Chitragupta, his scribe, change the 'ga' into a 'śa'
and make him live a hundred years, a 'śatāyu'?

The *SS* devotes a number of verses to *karaṇams*. However, the *karaṇams* the *SS* talks about seem to refer to the small group of persons employed in the hereditary position of a village revenue accountant – rather than the broad class mentioned above. *SS* also has several verses against the goldsmiths (*agasālĕ* caste). A legend that has acquired some acceptance, told by the noted intellectual Arudra,[13] is that in 1145 CE, a certain Rama Pradhani removed goldsmiths from *karaṇam* positions in some 6,000 villages and employed the Brahman *niyogis* in their place. Reading this legend and the negative representation of goldsmiths in the *SS,* Arudra suspects a certain opposition between *karaṇams* and goldsmiths, whereas Macca Haridasu suggests that the author of *SS* was most certainly a *karaṇam* revenue-accountant from the *niyogi* sub-caste of Brahmans.[14] An earlier scholar Vanguri Subbarao (1924) also thought that the author of *SS* was perhaps from the caste of *karaṇams*, (*mantri kulam*) though he does not categorically say that the author of the *SS* was a *karaṇam* revenue-accountant himself.[15]

Whatever the historical truth value of Arudra's reading of this legend, there is a prominent group of *niyogis* called *āruvela vāru*, the six thousand. We don't know the real origin of this name, but in Andhra most village revenue-accountants belonged to this group, which was known for their pride and self-confidence. The poet Kaṅkaṇṭi Pāparāju, (mid 18th century), who came from this group writes in praise of them:

---

13 Arudra 2002: vol. 1, 227–228.
14 Haridasu 1984: 52–54.
15 Subbarao 1924.

They steal the hearts of the members of the courts
of any king with their learning.
They give like the wishing tree, the ocean of milk, the legendary Karṇa and Bali.
They are known for doing good deeds with no ulterior motive.
They make the impossible possible to help the master they serve.
They break the pride of any enemy that stands up to them –
such are the qualities of the six thousand.[16]

However, a close reading of the verses of the *SS* does not seem to support the idea that the author is a *karaṇam* revenue-accountant. The book is critical of the *karaṇam* accountants just as it is critical of all other castes. Its negative representation of goldsmiths reflects the general mistrust of this community prevalent in Andhra and does not reflect any conflict between the Brahmans and goldsmiths. In fact, the *SS* does not seem to carry any personal views of the author, whoever he might be. The text only represents the general perceptions of upper-caste men, their prejudices included. All we can say is that this text is the product of a larger community of upper-caste scribes – whom we may call *karaṇams*. Later in the essay I will discuss the different versions of the *SS* that circulated among different groups of people.

Śataka genre

The *SS* is called a *śataka*, which is a genre containing a notional 100 verses (*śata*). Conventionally it has 108 verses, the first of which begin with the syllable *śrī*, a feature that makes the *śataka* auspicious. Verses in the *śataka* genre are unrelated to each other in terms of a narrative sequence but they are all composed in one kind of meter and carry a common word or phrase at the end of each verse. This is always a vocative, addressing a person or a deity, sometimes the author of the *śataka* himself, and is called *makuṭa*, or crown. The *makuṭa* is the only unifying feature that binds the disparate verses in a *śataka* into one single text. A *śataka* often gets its title by the *makuṭa*, thus the present text is called *Sumati śatakamu* because each of its verses ends in the vocative *sumatī*. *Śatakas* were usually composed by one poet but were almost never read from beginning to end as one unit. Modern scholars classify *śatakas* by their theme – such as *bhakti śatakas*, (which contain verses of devotion to one Hindu god or the other), *nīti śatakas* (which speak of *nīti*), *śṛṇgāra śatakas* (with erotic verses) and so on.[17] The independent nature of the verses in a *śataka*, and their readability make them easy to

[16] Pāparāju 1970: 5.
[17] For instance, see Gopalakrishna Rao 1976.

memorize and recite. Some verses may become more popular than others, and their oral communication from person to person introduces a number of structural and lexical changes in the process. I will have more to say about these changes later.[18] People who recite the verses of a *śataka* sometimes tell legends about the author and his life. Later in the essay we will learn a few legends about a supposed author of the *SS*. The available manuscripts of the *SS* are fragmentary. There is not one manuscript that contains all the verses – we don't even know how many there were to begin with.[19]

C. P. Brown and the SS

Charles Philip Brown (1798–1884), an employee of the English East India Company, who took a great interest in the study of Telugu language and literature, had an enormous influence on Telugu scholars. Born to evangelical parents in Calcutta, he spent a total of thirty-four years in two equal periods of seventeen years each in India, during which time he served the East India Company in several administrative capacities. He devoted most of his energies to learning Telugu, and trying to 'revive' Telugu literature. Brown's understanding of a literary text was grounded in the nineteenth-century European concept of a fixed, unified text. A text found in fragments or otherwise corrupted, had in his view to be carefully copied from several manuscripts, collated and corrected for inaccuracies and scribal errors. It could then be printed and made available to readers. Print was new to Andhra and Brown himself was largely instrumental in making Telugu texts available in print. Most texts in Telugu literature, which had some nine hundred years of continuous literary production, did not appear in manuscripts that were 'clean' enough for Brown to accept them as authentic. Furthermore, manuscripts were not easily available to Brown when he sought to collect them. Had he lived among Telugu people and tried to gain a proper understanding of the literary culture of this language, he would have had some sense of their textual practices.[20]

[18] In several cases, only a small number of verses survived from which scholars inferred the rest of the *śataka*. It is hard to say if the author wrote only a few, or if only a few survived from a complete text.

[19] Haridasu 1984 and Arudra 2002 inform us of ten manuscripts of *SS*, each of which has a different number of verses, in the Oriental Manuscript Library in Madras. Haridasu reports another four manuscripts from Saraswati Mahal Library at Tanjavur. An additional 50 verses are reported in *Āndhra sāhitya pariṣat patrika*, August-September, 1938.

[20] Brown wrote in his autobiography: "I never mixed with Hindu society, feasts or celebrations, and except those who worked with me I had few Hindu acquaintances. Indeed I was rarely visited by natives; and I was considered a deliberate enemy of the Hindu

However, Brown did not pause to think if the text-culture in Telugu was different from his own. The absence of the kind of texts he had expected assured him that Telugu literature was in a state of decline. His limited knowledge of Telugu coupled with his confidence in the superiority of Western culture made him comfortably assume the responsibility to save this literature.

Brown's interest in the *SS* developed neither because he was attracted to its *nīti* sayings nor because he thought it was an important text, but because it was written in a simple language that was easy for him to learn.[21] His interest in the text as a useful tool for a beginner like him to learn Telugu as a foreign language prompted him to have a pandit produce a version with a glossary so he could understand the text easily. As he read the text, he began to translate it into English, apparently as part of his exercise to learn Telugu. He collected the *SS* verses in 1832 from some ten manuscripts. Following the methods employed by European philologists in restoring Greek and Latin texts, he had different manuscripts collated by eliminating spurious, blemished or corrupted readings. Thus he created a version of 150 verses and printed it in 1842 with his English translation for 85 of them. No information is available as to how many copies were printed, but scholars have not been able to trace even one copy of this initial edition. The only evidence that Brown printed this edition comes from an advertisement for the book in 1842 reported by Macca Haridasu.[22] In 1973 the Andhra Pradesh Sahitya Akademi eventually published Brown's version again from his manuscript. I refer to this text hereafter as the *BSS*.

While we know about the manuscript sources of the *BSS*, we do not know anything about the manuscript sources of the *PSS*. If Adisaraswati based its 1870 edition on a manuscript, it is not reported anywhere. The two major changes in the Adisaraswati edition are that the verses are ordered alphabetically and the spelling confirms to what is by then accepted as the literary standard with features such as the silent nasal marks *(arthānusvāras)*. None of the manuscripts of the *SS* carries these features. Later reprints of the *PSS*, either clearly followed the 1870 edition, or more likely later editions of Adisaraswati, which appeared under the imprint of Vavilla Ramaswami Sastrulu and Sons. The 1870 edition of

idolatry." Brown and Reddy 1978: 58–59. Peter Schmitthenner describes in some detail the problems Brown faced in acquiring Telugu manuscripts, Schmitthenner 2001: 94–100.

[21] It is apparent that Brown assumed *nīti* meant morals, since he included *SS* among texts he thought were written "principally on morals." See Brown 1827: 9. But later he lost interest in *SS* and concentrated on Vemana's verses which were equally easy for him to read and appealed to him for their attack on Brahmans and practices of Hindu society. Schmitthenner 2001: 72–78.

[22] Haridasu 1984: 67.

the *PSS* contains 105 verses, but at some point of time after that the *PSS* acquired a few more verses, the most important of which is a prayer verse at the very beginning, *śrīrāmuni daya cetanu*, (by the kindness of god Rama), which includes the customary auspicious syllable *śrī* and a colophon verse, attributing the authorship to Bhimana (Tel. bhīmana). Some editions carry a word-by-word explanation following each verse *(ṭīka)* and a prose summary of the verse *(tātparya).*[23]

Alphabetizing is not common in Telugu; in fact only two more *śatakas,* both of which are printed much later than the *PSS,* are alphabetized.[24] As is well known, even dictionaries were not alphabetized until the 19th century. One suggestion is that this is based on *akṣarâṅkagadya,* ritual verses composed for Siva, where the verses are alphabetized. Another suggestion is that alphabetization is a Jaina influence and that a Jaina monk called Sumati is the author of *SS.* These suggestions are tantalizing at best, and have no real basis to follow through.[25] It is also interesting to note that no manuscript of the *SS,* nor the edition created by C. P. Brown are alphabetized, nor do they carry the standard spelling as the *PSS* does.

The name *SS* and the *makuṭa* refrain at the end of each verse was a strong enough indication that all these free-floating verses were generally perceived as belonging to one single text. However, it is the *PSS* that gave it a concrete unity, by making it a book, and truly a *śataka*, with the generic requirement of 108 verses, and with the auspicious syllable *srī* beginning the first poem and a colophon attributing the authorship of the text to Bhimana.[26] The text is further enhanced by the arrangement of the verse in alphabetical order. I located on the internet scanned fragments of a palm leaf manuscript from the Theosophical Society Library at Adyar.[27] This manuscript contains among its early verses, but not as its first verse, the prayer poem to Rama that begins with the words, *śrīrāmuni daya cetanu,*"by the kindness of god Rama", which, as we have noted, is printed as the first verse in the *PSS* sometime after 1870. Arudra and Haridasu report that they did not find this poem in any of the manuscripts they had seen. The Adyar manuscript looks interesting because it is the

[23] The prayer verse appears in *PSS* 1913, and the colophon verse appears in *PSS* 1962, though I know these verses must have been included much earlier.

[24] The two are: *Bhāskara śatakamu*, attributed to Mādayyagāri Vĕṅkanna in collaboration with his younger brother. Sarma 1987, and Venkatarayakavi 1982: 76–123.

[25] Venkata Rao 1966: 64, suggests the influence of the Saivite *Aṣarâṅkagadya;* Kolavennu Malayavasini (oral communication) suggests Jain influence; and *Sumati śatakamu* 1962 suggests a Jain monk, Sumati, as a probable author of the *PSS.*

[26] According to Arudra 2002, this colophon verse is in the palm leaf manuscript no. 1810 in the Oriental Manuscript Library at Madras.

[27] http://www.gutenberg-e.org/kam01/adyar_sumati/ This is palm-leaf manuscript no. 74882, placed on the internet probably by Michael Katten.

only one that contains the prayer verse, and because it seems to record verses that are closest in style to the *PSS*. However, the verses in the Adyar manuscript are not ordered alphabetically, nor does the spelling conform to the standard given to them by Adisarasvati. Unfortunately, the scanned fragments of the Adyar manuscript are not legible enough for me to make definitive comments.

Features of oral transmission

All the *PSS* verses show features of oral transmission compared to the *BSS* which contains a large number of verses in a literary style. One might say that all Telugu literature before the 20th century is oral in the sense that all verses were recited or sung, but I am making a distinction here between texts that were passed from person to person in a written form and those that were transmitted orally. The verses of the *PSS* were circulated orally, whereas most of the verses in the *BSS* were circulated through writing. In effect, there were two different kinds of transmission – oral and written. Inevitably the verses that entered the oral transmission process spread among a larger community than the ones that remained in writing. Both communities were literate, and both were upper caste. The community amongst whom the verses of the *BSS* were circulated was inhabited by scribes who had a penchant for preserving knowledge in writing. The other community among whom verses of the *PSS* were orally circulated was more accustomed to orality, and was much larger. These verses were good conversation-pieces and were often quoted to legitimize a viewpoint. Upper-caste men in village circles quoted verses in imitation of scholars who quoted from Sastras (Skt. śāstra). It was customary to learn the verses orally from a person who had memorized them, and an orally quoted verse had a much higher authority than one written down.

Such oral transmission brings about significant structural changes in the text, which I call oralization. Every single verse of the *PSS* carries features of oralization, which I will elaborate on below. If one person in the chain of oral transmission happened to be a scribe and wanted to have a written copy of an oralized verse, he wrote it as he had heard it, but the verse continued in oral circulation. In fact, one can find several oralized verses in the *BSS,* which as we know, is a collated version from many manuscripts. For convenience I use the *BSS* to illustrate literary features and the *PSS* to illustrate features of oralization.[28]

The metrics of kandamu

In order to discuss the features of oralization in the *PSS* verses, and contrast them with the literary features in the *BSS*, let me briefly present the metrics of *kandamu,* the meter in which all the *SS* verses were composed.[29] This is a meter comprised of four lines where a long syllable has a value of two *mātras* while a short syllable has a value of one. A *gaṇa* (cluster of syllables) used in *kandamu* could consist of two long syllables, or one long syllable and two short syllables, or four short syllables. The first and third lines are composed with three such *gaṇas* while the second and the fourth lines are composed of five. The second syllable of each of the four lines should use the same consonant or consonant cluster. This is called *prāsa*. In the second line and the fourth line, the first syllable of the first *gaṇa* and the first syllable of the fourth *gaṇa* should be euphonically similar. This is called *yati*. A list of syllables that are euphonically similar to each other is given in books on meter. The metrics of *kandamu* are presented below as an abstract diagram, where X represents the *yati* and the asterisk represents the *prāsa* and each length of straight line represents a *gaṇa*.

—— *—— ———— ————
X—*——— ———— ———— X———— ————
—— *—— ———— ————
X—*——— ———— ———— X———— ————

The following is a *kandamu* verse in roman transcription with each syllable separated with spaces. Here, the consonant cluster in the second syllable of each line, /ll/ is the *prāsa.* The first syllable of the first and the fourth *gaṇas* in lines two, /gŏ/ and /ko/, and five, /tĕ/ and /tĕ/, are the *yati.*

a *ll*u ni man ci ta nam bu nu
*gŏ ll*a ni sā hi tya vi dya – *ko* ma li ni ja mun
pŏ *ll*u na dañ ci na bi yya mu
*tĕ ll*a ni kā ku lu nu le vu – *tĕ* li yu ra su ma tī

[28] Brown collected every manuscript available to him without regard to the style of the verse and collated them all into *BSS.* Therefore *BSS* includes some verses which look like *PSS* verses.

[29] The metrics of *kandamu* are minimally presented here, leaving out details which are not relevant to this discussion.

Features of the PSS

An important feature of the *PSS* is the absence of enjambment; there are no run-on lines in its verses. In recitation each short line is one segment, while each long line, broken at the *yati*, makes two segments. Each segment begins with a new word. Rarely does a word extend over two segments. In recitation, it is customary to pause at the end of each segment before picking up the next segment. Since the syntactic structure of the poem corresponds to the pauses at the end of each segment, the meter in *PSS* reinforces the meaning, and the meaning reinforces the meter. Reading *PSS* verses breaking at every segment has given rise to a style of reading *kandamu* now considered by literary people as school-boyish. Another feature of the *PSS* is its simplistic observance of *yati,* using simple euphony as a guiding principle.

A significant feature of the style of the *PSS* is its extensive use of filler words. A filler word does not make a specific semantic contribution to the verse; it only helps to fulfill the meter. Filler words almost always occur where the metrical restrictions of *prāsa* and *yati* must be observed. For example, of the 108 verses in the *PSS*, 71 verses use a filler word; 52 use fillers in *yati* places, while 19 use filler words in *prāsa* places. Following is a list of words that occur in the *yati* place:

ilalo	“on the earth”
bhuvilo	"
mahilo	"
medini	"
vasudhanu	"
ĕrugumu	“know” (imperative)
tĕliyura	"
nayam’idi	“this is right”
mari	“and”
nikkamu	“it is true”
tathyamu	"
siddhamu	“that’s how it is”
sahajamu	“it is natural”
gadarā	“is it not?”

Filler words are viewed by scholars as *vyartha padas*, “useless words.” However, in the oral tradition, they have great value; they are predictable and make the verse easy to memorize. They reduce the semantic burden while preserving the euphonic beauty and the metrical structure of the poem.

A number of the *PSS* verses are built on a repetitive formulaic syntax, which helps memorization beyond the devices of *prāsa* and *yati.* For example, a string of negative imperatives followed by a declarative sentence is very common in the *PSS*. The following verse is an example (the *yati* is shown in italics and the *prāsa* is shown in capitals):

naVVakumī sabhalopala
*na*VVakumī talli daṇḍri – *nā* thula toḍan
naVVakumī parasatito
*na*VVakumī vipravarula – *na*yam'idi sumatī

Do not laugh in the assembly.
Do not laugh with your father, mother or master.
Do not laugh with another man's wife.
Do not laugh at a sacred Brahman.
Sumati, that's the right thing to do.

Also note, the final segment begins with a filler word, *nayam'idi*, thus saving the poet from having to choose a meaningful word that begins with a /na/.

Features of literary style

In contrast to the oralized style of the *PSS*, literary style is compact; it does not use filler words. Complex combinations of *yati* and *prāsa* as well as long and involved sentences are normal features of the literary style. Complexity rather than spontaneity, and manipulation rather than fluidity of phrases, are the predominant qualities of a literary style. A literary stylist works at a slower pace than an oral versifier and therefore has the time to choose his words with an aim to build a tightly composed verse. For an oral versifier, meter and syntax fuse into one structure that organizes both his language and the verse at the same time. For the literate poet, meter structures the verse but not always his language. Therefore, in a literary composition syntax tends to be relatively free from meter. To illustrate this point, I will present a verse, in the same meter, *kandam*, in which all the *SS* verse are composed, written by a literary poet of the first order, the 13th century Tikkana. This poem doesn't need to be translated; just a look at the complex structure of long Sanskrit compounds running into the next line, with *yati* and *prāsa* syllables embedded in them, shown here with strings of syllables with no spaces, visually demonstrates the point (the *yati* is shown in italics and the *prāsa* is shown in capitals):

triBHuvanaśukadṛḍhapañjara-
*vi*BHavamahitunaku tri*vi*shṭapanirmo-

kaBHujaṅgapatiki sakalajagad-
*a*BHinnarūpunaku bhāvan*â*tītunakun.[30]

None of the *SS* verses, the *PSS* or the *BSS* have this kind of high literary style. At no time did the *SS* include verses of great literary complexity. But we can see a literary style in many of the the *BSS* verses, though it is much simpler than Tikkana's verse shown above. Let me take the following verse from the *BSS as* an example (the *yati* is shown in italics and the *prāsa* is shown in capitals):

trāSUnu veśyayun' ŏka samam
au SAndehimpavalavad *'a*vanīsthalilo
vīSAm badhikamb'ĕccaṭan
o SArigāk andu mŏgguc *'u*ṇḍunu sumatī

Listen Sumati, a courtesan is like a balance. She tilts to the side which has a little more gold.

The syntax of this verse camouflages the metrical structure. A detailed breakdown of the metrical units and syntactical units of the verse would facilitate examination of this feature.

Metrical Units	Syntactical Units
1. trāsunu veśyayun'ŏka sama	1. trāsunu veśyayun'ŏka samam'au "A courtesan and a balance are one kind"
2. m'au sandehimpavalava	2. sandehimpavalavad' "There's no doubt about it"
3. d'avanīsthalilo	3. avanīsthalilo "on this earth" (filler word)
4. vīsamb'adhikamb'ĕccaṭa	4. vīsamb'adhikamb'ĕccaṭano "wherever there is a little more (gold)"
5. no sarigāk'andu mŏggu	5. sarigāk' "without being level"
6. c'uṇḍunu sumatī	6. andu mŏgguc'uṇḍunu "to that side (she) tilts"
	7. sumatī "wise man" (vocative)

On the metrical side of the chart, the four lines of the poem are divided into six segments to reflect the way it is recited. On the syntactical side,

[30] Tikkana, *Srīmadāndhra-mahā-bhāratamu,* 4.1.33.

one can see the first clause extends by one syllable beyond the first segment of the verse into the second segment where a new clause begins with the *prāsa* syllable /sa/. If a pause is made at the end of the clause to complete the meaning, the euphony of *prāsa* is affected. If, on the other hand, no pause is made so the euphony of *prāsa* is preserved, the clarity of the meaning is compromised. A similar situation occurs at the end of the fourth segment and at the beginning of the fifth segment. The last word, *ĕccaṭano*, extends into the fifth segment where a new clause begins with the *prāsa* syllable. Clearly, this verse cannot be read adopting the same style of recitation as a *PSS* verse.

The only oral feature of this verse is its use of the filler word *avanīsthalilo*, "on this earth", which, however, is a less easily understood Sanskrit phrase, compared to similar filler words in *PSS*. We don't find this verse in the *PSS*. It did not enter the oral transmission process, apparently because the metrical structure was not amenable to easy alterations to suit oralization.

Let me take a verse found in the *BSS* and show how it changes in the *PSS* to suit an oralized style. First, the verse from the *BSS:* (*yati* marked in italics)

dānamb'ivvani kuḍuvani
*vā*ni dhanamu rājacora*va*hnula jerun
gānala nīgalu gūrcina
*te*niya tĕravarula jeru *tī*runa sumatī

Listen Sumati, a person who does not enjoy or share his wealth, will lose it to the king, thieves, or fire, like honey which bees gather in the forest is taken by the passers-by.

This verse has a long Sanskrit compound, *rājacoravahnulu*, "kings, thieves, or fire", extending across the two segments of the second line and absorbing the identity of the *yati* syllable /*va*/, which would have been clearly demarcated in an oralized verse. Furthermore, the verse is a tightly constructed in one long, somewhat complex sentence, which never happens in *PSS*.

Let us see how this verse is transformed in oral transmission though the meaning remains the same. Here is its *PSS* counterpart: (*yati* marked in italics.)

tānu bhujimpani yarthamu
*mā*navapati jeru gŏnta *ma*ri bhūgata mau
gānala nigalu gūrcina
*te*niya yŏru jerunaṭlu *ti*ramuga sumatī

Listen Sumati, if you do not enjoy your wealth, some of it goes to the king, and the rest is lost into the earth, like the honey the bees gather in the forest is taken by others, sure and certain.

Two advantages result from this change. First, the long Sanskrit compound *rājacoravahnula* with the *yati* hidden in it, is eliminated. It is inconvenient for a reciter to remember a long compound which sweeps through two segments of a line particularly if it hides the *yati* syllable. He uses the *yati* as a memory landmark for the segment of the verse that begins with it. Therefore, the long compound is replaced by a line which is broken into two parts which are synchronous with the two segments they cover:

*mā*navapati jeru kŏnta *ma*ri bhūgata mau

The use of the filler word *mari* makes it easy to remember the *yati*. The second change is made in the fourth line. In the *BSS jeru tīruna* is one word that extends across two segments. In *PSS* the segments are clearly broken, facilitating oralized recitation.

teniya tĕravarula jeru tīruna sumatī (BSS)
teniya yŏru jerunaṭlu tiramuga sumatī (PSS)

In the *PSS* text, a filler word, *tiramuga* ("surely") begins the sixth segment. The *BSS* version of the line has a more complex arrangement in which the clause *tĕravarula jeru tīruna*, "like (honey) goes to passers-by", extends across two segments of the line across the *yati* place. Also, the lexical choice of *tĕravarulu*, "passers-by", is indicative of the interest of the literary stylist who wants three similar "t" sounds repeated in the same line for alliteration, which does not interest the oral reciter, who would prefer regularity and symmetry in a verse.

However, the stylistic gap between these two poems is too wide to permit a precise mapping of the process of transition of literary style into an oralized style. A better opportunity for observing this transition is provided by examination of the following two verses in the *BSS* and the *PSS*. Here are verses with the lines numbered for reference (*yati* syllables are in italics):

BSS:
1. mantri gala vāni rājyamu
2. *ta*ntrambula jĕḍaka śāśva*ta*mbai nilucun

3. mantri vihīnuni rājyamu
4. *ja*ntrapu kīl'ūḍinaṭlu *ja*rugunu sumatī

PSS:
1. mantri gala vāni rājyamu
2. *ta*ntramu cĕdak'uṇḍa nilucu *ta*racuga dharalo
3. mantri vihīnuni rājyamu
4. *ja*ntrapu kīl'ūḍinaṭlu *ja*rugadu sumatī

The variations in these two texts are limited to lines 2 and 4. The variations in line 2 are of two kinds. One is stylistic while the other is syntactic. The word *śāśvatamb'ai* ("permanently") in the *BSS* text extends across two segments of the line. The first segment of the line ends at *śāśva* and the next segment begins with *tambai*. A customary pause in oral recitation at the end of each segment would break the word unnaturally and awkwardly into two parts: *śāśva* and *tamb'ai*. If, on the other hand, the line is recited as one unit, the euphony between the initial *ta*- and the *ta*- in the *yati* place in the middle of *śāśvatamb'ai* loses its emphasis. Furthermore, it is inconvenient to memorize a line that does not have the usual break at the end of each segment.

A reciter resolves these problems by making appropriate changes in the text. A rephrasing of the text with the filler word *taracuga dharalo* ("frequently in the world") restores the break at the end of the first segment. The change makes the poem easy to memorize and recite.

As may be seen from the discussion above, the preferences of the literary style are very different from those of the oral style. A literary poet considers it more artful to compose a tight verse in which *yati* places are filled with meaningful words, not fillers. He avoids breaking at the end of each segment and aims at more complex line movements; his *yati* and *prāsa* places are usually hidden in long words. A literary stylist considers it artless to compose verses that break at every joint. Such composition is compared to the weaving of a fish basket, *cepala buṭṭa*, loose with a lot of holes in it. The use of filler words to satisfy *yati* and *prāsa* is especially undesirable because they show that the poet does not have a mastery over meter, and is rather led by it. The literary features discussed above were greatly admired by learned poets who scorned oral poetry.

The other variation in line 2, which is syntactic, is the result of a change in dialects. The *BSS* has *tantrambula jĕḍaka*, whereas *PSS* has *tantramu cĕḍak'uṇḍa*, both meaning "without losing administrative efficiency." Old Telugu uses both negatives freely while modern Telugu retains the non-progressive non-finite negative (the *–aka* form) for the specialized use of indicating a condition for an inevitable consequence; the progressive non-finite negative (the *–akuṇḍa* form) is used in all other situations. The following sentences are acceptable both in Old Telugu and modern Telugu since the clause ending with the *–aka* form marks a condition, an inevitable consequence which is revealed in the principle clause. Here are a few examples to illustrate this point:

Modern Telugu:
vānalu *leka* paṇṭalu poyāyi
"The crops failed for lack of rain."
tiṇḍi *leka* prajalu bādhapaḍutunnāru
"People are suffering for lack of food."
nidra *cālaka* kaḷḷu baruv'ĕkkāyi
"The eyes are heavy because of lack of sleep."

Old Telugu:
vānalu *leka* panṭalu poyinavi
"The crops failed for lack of rain."
tiṇḍi *leka* prajalu bādhpaḍucunnāru
"People are suffering for lack of food."
nidra *cālaka* kaḷḷu baruv'ĕkkinavi
"The eyes are heavy because of lack of sleep."

The following sentences, which use-*aka* forms, acceptable in Old Telugu, are not acceptable in modern Telugu because the event indicated by the finite verb is not an inevitable consequence of the event indicated by the non- finite.

Old Telugu:
atanu nāto *cĕppaka* vĕḍalipoyĕnu
"He left without informing me."
ī pustakamu *caduvaka* māṭlāḍakuḍu
"Do not talk without reading this book."
ī goḍa *paḍipoka* nilucunā?
"Does this wall stand without falling?"

Consequently, these sentences have to be rephrased with the *–akuṇḍā* form in modern Telugu:

Modern Telugu:
atanu nāto *cĕppakuṇḍā* veḷḷipoyāḍu
"He left without informing me."
i pustakam *cadavakuṇḍā* māṭlāḍakaṇḍi
"Do not talk without reading this book."
i goḍa *paḍipokuṇḍā* nilustundā?
"Does this wall stand without falling?"

Preference for the *–akunṇḍā* form in the *PSS* indicates the influence of modern syntax on the reciter. The *–aka* form is syntactically obsolete and is consequently rejected in favor of the modern *–akuṇḍā* form. The process is perhaps not deliberate but a natural propensity of the reciter to adopt a modern syntax. This brings into focus an important change that enters into an orally transmitted text: its syntax gets updated with time.

A comparison of verses in the *BSS* and the *PSS* suggests that most variations fall into the two categories discussed above: 1) stylistic variations introduced to render the verse easier to memorize and recite, and 2) dialectical variations to update the grammar of the verse.

Occasionally, a line or two in a verse composed in an especially intricate literary style becomes unintelligible to the oral reciter. In such instances, the line is altered to make it more intelligible, even if it results in a change in meaning. The following verse exemplifies this:

BSS:
kāraṇamu leka navvunu
preraṇamunu leni prema priyaratikeḷul
pūraṇamu leni būrĕlu
vīraṇamunu leni pĕṇḍli vṛtharā sumatī

Listen Sumati, a laugh without a reason, love play with a woman who is not aroused, dumplings without (sweet) stuffing, and a wedding without music – these are futile.

The second line of the verse is difficult for the oral reciter not only because of the Sanskrit compound *priyaratikeḷul* ("love play with / of the beloved") but also because of the number of *pra* sounds. The *PSS* alters the line:

peraṇamunu leni lema prthivīsthalilo

The oralized style brings in the filler words *prthivīsthalilo* ("in the earth") to replace the difficult compound *priyaratikeḷul* in the second segment of the line. This change also makes it easy to remember the segment, because it begins with the *yati* syllable. But now the line means "a woman who does not have a blouse." This change works perfectly for the oral reciter because it reflects a new style of wearing stitched clothes that came into vogue around the 17th century because of the cultural influence of Persianized Islam. Upper caste women began to wear blouses, which the lower castes did not adopt.[31] A woman without a blouse is therefore low caste and not desirable.

[31] New styles, from a foreign, likely Persian influence in the sixteenth century made sewn clothes popular among the upper castes in Andhra. Brahman men, however, did not wear stitched clothes when they performed religious rituals.

Popularity of the SS

In economics, Fisher's Equation in relation to the Quantity Theory of Money states that the velocity of the circulation of money should be factored in while measuring the quantity of money in use.[32] A million dollars kept in a safe for one year has a value of zero, while a dollar bill that changes hands a million times in one year does the work of a million dollars exchanged just once. A similar measure applies to the social impact of literature. A poem by a scholar-poet which is read by an elite group has less influence on popular ideas than a poem by a minor poet which is read, remembered and recited by a large community. In the world of ideas, the *PSS* was like a dollar bill that changed hands a million times while the verses of great poets were like a million dollars kept in a safe, or perhaps transacted just once in a while. The popularity of a book is usually established by the number of press runs and copies sold. This standard, of course, is not valid in the oral tradition. The *PSS*'s popularity indicates the general acceptability of its ideas to the community in which they circulated. Some verses of the *PSS* appear to be metrical restatements of well-known proverbs, and accepted prejudices, while other verses seem to carry the wisdom imparted by the poet. The epigrammatic nature of the text, the simplicity of the language, the prescriptive tone of the verses, and above all their immense quotability imbued the *PSS* with the power of a Sastra in the popular mind.

Critical editions of SS and authorship of SS

Another concept that became acceptable to Indian literary scholars during the colonial period is that every text must have a unique and historically identifiable author. It is true that in our own experience a text comes into existence because an author writes it. The sequence is as follows:

author > text > reader.

In pre-colonial India, with its oral tradition and written culture operating in tandem, the situation was somewhat different. Here the author does not necessarily write the text. Rather it may well be the other way around: the text writes the author. For instance, a text received by its listeners / readers as an epic / *itihāsa*, generates an author of superhuman powers like the sage Vālmīki for the Ramayana. If the same text is read as bhakti / devotional text, a text that gives religious merit to its readers, the

---

[32] Fisher's equation, used in the quantity theory of money is: MV = PT, where M represents the money supply, V represents the velocity of money, P represents the average price level and T represents the volume of transactions in the economy.

author is given a different 'biography'. This Vālmīki is a bandit who turns into a sage by repeating Rama's name. In effect, if a text changes its function, the author changes along with it.[33] A number of legends are told about authors of texts in the oral tradition. Such legends about an author mark an important shift in the meaning of the text, or indicate a new status to which the text is elevated. Legends about authors are in effect parts of the text. But the new concepts of an original author and an Ur-text led to such questions as who the author of *Sumati śatakamu* was and where and when he lived. The next task would be to establish the Ur-text by the original author, free from interpolations and spurious verses. Legends told about authors were of no use for the new scholars of literature, because they were unhistorical. C. P. Brown trained a number of scholars who worked under him in the methods of collating texts, and creating 'authentic editions'. Following Brown's ideas, the search for 'authentic editions' and reliable information about the real 'authors' became a major occupation for scholars of literature. It is striking that these scholars rejected concepts of author and text from their own culture. As late as 1988, Arudra, the influential poet and historian of Telugu literature writes in his magnum opus *Samagra āndhra sāhityam* (comprehensive history of Telugu literature):

> We need to produce a critical edition *(samśodhita-prati)* of the *Sumati śatakamu* to find out what interpolations the scribes indulged in, and this in turn would also resolve the question of authorship.

From the early decades of the twentieth century, scholars began to argue whether Baddĕna or Bhimana was the author of the *SS*. Those who argued in favor of Bhimana, based their belief on a poem found in some manuscript copies of the *SS*.[34] Furthermore, Kūcimañci Timmakavi (mid 18th century) identifies Bhimana as the author of the *SS,* in his *Sarvalakṣaṇsārasaṅgrahamu,* a book on meter. The following is the poem:

srī karamuga bhīmana munu
lokamunaku bŏgaḍagā vilokinci madin
brākaṭamuga sumatiki mati
cekūḍaga sumatinīti cĕppadŏḍaṅgen

Auspiciously Bhīmana, while the people admired him, thought well in his mind to teach good sense to Sumati and began to tell *Sumati-nīti.*

---

[33] This idea, presented all too briefly here, needs a longer essay, which I am writing.

[34] Haridasu 1984 identifies this verse in manuscript No. 1810 from the Oriental Manuscript Library, Madras (now Chennai). Unconfirmed reports say that all Telugu manuscripts from this library were moved to the Oriental Manuscript Library, Tirupati.

Note that here the text is not called *Sumati śatakamu* but *Sumati-nīti,* a name that brings to mind *Baddĕ-nīti,* a text scholars agree was written by Baddĕna. Interestingly, the same poem also appears at the end of several printed *PSS* texts.

However, Manavalli Ramakrishna Kavi, Vanguri Subbarao, N. Venkata Rao and other scholars argued that Baddĕna composed the *SS*. They base their arguments on the following verse from Baddĕna's *Nītiśāstra-muktāvaḷi*, a book of *nīti* verses:

śrīvibhuḍa garvitāri
kṣmāvaradaḷanopalabdhajayalaksmīsam
bhāvituḍa sumatiśatakamu
gāviñcina proḍa gāvyakamalāsanuḍan

I am the lord of the goddess of wealth, honored by the goddess of victory for destroying the proud enemy kings, and I am the expert composer of *Sumati śatakamu* and the creator of many other poems.

Bhimana vs. Baddĕna

However, not much is reliably known about Baddĕna. Scholars, such as Vedam Venkataraya Sastri and Manavalli Ramakrishna Kavi, suggest that he was a king of a principality in Andhra during the 11th–12th century. His book, *Nīti-śastra-muktāvaḷi*, is also known as *Baddĕ-nīti*. In this small book of 162 verses, he follows the tradition of such Sanskrit books as *Kāmandaka*, which prescribe the code of conduct for kings and courtiers. He was clearly a scholar competent in writing a well-turned verse, and a person with considerable understanding and perhaps experience in the political strategies of running a kingdom. His book seems to have been popular among the class of people who aspired to kingship or worked for kings. In any case, we know that Madiki Singana (14th century), the editor / compiler of the *Sakala-nīti-sammatamu*, included in his volume as many as 38 verses from *Baddĕ-nīti,* which indicates Baddĕna's popularity among the class of people who were politically minded.[35]

Not much is known about Bhimana either, if such a person ever existed. Legends told about him say that he lived in the village of Vemulavāḍa. His mother was a Brahman widow who conceived him after the death of her husband. She went to the Bhīmeśvara-śiva temple in Daksharama along with a group of women who had husbands. When they all asked the god for a son, she naively followed their example and asked for a son as well. The God Bhimesvara (Skt. bhīmeśvara) blessed her and gave her a

[35] See Narayana Rao and Subrahmanyam 2008: 26–65.

son. But because of his suspected illegitimacy, the young boy was badly treated by people in the temple town. One day he demanded that his mother tell him who his father was. She told him that the god Bhimesvara in the temple was his father. Angry that god Bhimesvara had never showed up to admit his paternity nor had ever taken care of him, the boy rushed into the temple with a big rock in his hands. He stood before the god and yelled, "Are you my father? If so, speak or I am going to hit you with this rock." The god Bhimesvara, who was himself a big rock *liṅga,* spoke: "Son, I am your father. From now on, no one shall ever call you a bastard. If anyone does, you may teach them a lesson. I give you the power to curse or bless. Whatever you utter will come true. You will be known as *śāpānugraha-samartha*, 'one who can curse and bless as well'."

From then on, everything Bhimana uttered came true because his power derived from god. Once, the young boy was expelled from a feast by Brahmans who objected to the presence of a bastard in their company. Bhimana angrily said:

annam'antā sunnam'avāli.
appāl'annī kappal'avāli.
ayyal'andarū kŏyyal'avāli.

The rice should become lime.
The sweet cakes should become frogs.
All the men should turn into wood.

Instantly his words came true, and all the rice turned into a heap of lime and frogs began to jump across the dinner plates, and the offending Brahmans turned to wood. Others in the room fell at the feet of the young boy asking for forgiveness. Bhimana then uttered a reversal of the curse and everything turned to normal. Other legends about Bhimana tell of how kings who ignored him lost their kingdoms and regained them only after repenting.[36] Śrināthuḍu (in the 15th century) includes Bhimana at the head of a chronologically-ordered list of several great Telugu poets who preceded him.[37] Piṅgaḷi Sūranna, of the late 16th century, refers to Bhimana as one who reportedly wrote a bi-textual narrative poem *Rāghava-pāṇḍavīyamu*, a single text that can be read as the *Ramāyaṇa* and the *Mahābhārata* as well, the like of which he (Sūranna) was commissioned to write.[38] Appakavi (in the 17th century) mentions Bhimana's name in the context of telling a legend about Bhimana's

---

[36] A good source for legends about Bhimana is Seshayya 1959–1971: vol. 1, 208–265.
[37] Śrināthuḍu 1969.
[38] Sūranna 1968: Pīṭhika, verse 11.

rivalry with Nannaya (11th century).[39] None of the above authors who invoke Bhimana's name give any verifiable information about him.[40] Their knowledge of Bhimana was probably based on legends and not necessarily on any hard facts. However, the fact that they mention his name clearly indicates that Bhimana's name was revered as early as the 15th century, that he was respected as a legendary poet, feared and honored as a poet of super-human powers.

Rival claims of authorship become meaningful when they are related to the mode of transmission and to the clientele of the *SS*. For *karaṇams* who wanted this text to be treated as authoritative guide to success, an author like Baddĕna would be preferable because he has the stature of a wise ruler. However, for the oralized *PSS*, which became popular among a larger readership and acquired the status of a Sastra, an author with superhuman powers like Bhimana would be preferable. All Sastras in Sanskrit were written by people who were known only from legends. One important point that needs to be noted here is that a real person called Bhimana need not actually exist for a legend to be generated about him. An historical evidence one way or the other does not make any difference for those who believe that he existed. Legends of his birth and his superhuman powers make him the right kind of a person to authorize a Sastra. Such an author allows for a consistency in legends about him and the possibility for him to live over many centuries.[41]

Nor was *SS* the only text attributed to Bhimana to elevate the status of the text. A book on meter of unknown date, *Kavijanâśrayamu*, perhaps written by a certain Malliya Recana, is popularly known as Bhimana's work. Appakavi, clearly says *Kavijanâśrayamu* is Bhimana's work. However, one of the manuscripts carries several prefatory verses where Bhimana says that he wrote the book for Recana and made it look like Recana himself wrote it. Recana is said to be a Jaina that belongs to a merchant (*vaiśya*) caste. Scholars went to town with the problem of authorship, when Jayanti Ramayya Pantulu edited *Kavijânāśrayamu* and published it with his preface defending Bhimana's authorship.[42,43] Other

---

39 Appakavi 1962: Pīṭhika, 44.

40 Arudra identifies nine different Bhimanas and complicates this matter even further.

41 The Telugu literary tradition speaks of at least one other invented person: Tenali Ramalingadu, who is said to be active in the court of Krishnadevaraya, the emperor of Vijayanagara, and about whom a number of stories are popularly told. For more about this poet, see Narayana Rao and Shulman 1998.

42 Nidadavolu Venkata Rao adds another wrinkle to the already tangled question of authorship of this text on metrics. Citing the fact that one of the many titles Baddĕna uses to refer to himself in his *Nīti-śastra-muktāvali* is Komaru Bhima. Venkata Rao argues that people may have called Baddĕna by his title Bhima(na) when they identified him as the author of *Kavijanâśrayamu*. This argument does not explain why this particular title, among many titles of Baddĕna, came to be chosen.

scholars that entered the debate and defended Recana's authorship include such famous names as Kandukuri Viresalingam and Arudra. The fact is that during pre-colonial times this work was consistently called *Bhīmana-chandamu*, the metrics of Bhimana. Arudra picked up on the caste status of Recana and strongly argued that attributing the text to Bhimana was a Brahman conspiracy against merchant castes and Jainas. Now the debate included caste and religion in addition to nineteenth-century ideas of text and author. It would be more logical to argue that *Kavijanâśrayamu* needed an elevated status as the first infallible prescriptive book, i. e. a Sastra on meter and the name of Bhimana provided such a status to the work.

I would imagine that the community of *Niyogis*, who initially made the *SS* their own, apparently found it very comforting to see that it had acquired such a high status, and they found no reason to interfere with Bhimana's authorship, while they themselves believed the text was authored by Badděna. It is interesting to note that the verse that attributes authorship of the *SS* to Badděna is in a high literary style, whereas the verse that claims Bhimana as the author has the features of the oral style, with filler words and segment breaks.

Conclusion

The *Sumati śatakamu* has traveled a long way from *nīti* to morals. Most people in Andhra today do not even remember that the *SS* was a guide to *nīti*, as a policy for success for upper-caste men. The epistemological shift that colonial thinking has brought about was more or less thorough in this regard. *Nīti* in Telugu usage now only means morals.

In this essay, I have tried to demonstrate the effects of the epistemological shifts that colonial education brought about in the concepts of texts and authors in India. Using the *Sumati śatakamu* as an example, I indicated that such Western ideas are unsuitable to understand the nature of Indian texts. I have also suggested that legends about authors and texts cannot be dismissed as unhistorical, and that they are valuable sources to understand the nature of indigenous text-culture. During the past several decades, especially under the influence of the postmodern ideas of Foucault and Derrida, a new thinking has effectively dismantled most of the nineteenth and early twentieth-century concepts of texts and authors. Scholars have used postmodern ideas effectively to revise our understanding of Indian texts as well. I have tried to argue in this essay that indigenous concepts of texts and author in India are, in themselves,

[43] Bhimakavi 1959.

already very sophisticated and can be efficiently employed for a better understanding of Indian text-culture.

Bibliography

Anantāmātyuḍu. 1962. *Bhojarājīyamu*. Madras: Vavilla Ramaswamy Sastrulu & Sons.

Appakavi, Kākunūri. 1962. *Appakavīyamu*. Gidugu Ramamurti, Utpala Venkata Narasimhacharyulu, and Ravuri Dorasami Sarma, eds. Madras: Vavilla Ramaswamy Sastrulu & Sons.

Apparao, Gurujada. 2007. *Girls for Sale: Kanyāśulakam, a Play from Colonial India*. (Translated from Telugu by Velcheru Narayana Rao.) Bloomington: Indiana University Press.

Aqil, Raziuddin and Chatterjee, Partha. 2008. *History in the Vernacular*. Ranikhet: Permanent Black.

Arudra. 2002. *Samagra Āndhra Sāhityam*. (1988) 4 vols. Hyderabad: Telugu Akadami.

Badděna. 1962. *Nītiṣāstramuktāvaḷi*. Ramakrishna Kavi, Manavalli, ed. Tanuku. Narendranatha Sahitya Mandali.

Bhīmakavi, Vemulavāḍa. 1959. *Kavijanâśrayamu*. (1917) Jayanti Ramayya, ed. Kakinada: Andhra Sahitya Parishattu.

Brown, C. P. (ed. and tr.). 1973. *Sumati Śatakam*. C. R. Sarma, ed. Hyderabad: Andhra Pradesh Sahitya Akademi.

Brown, C. P. 1827. *Āndhragīrvāṇacchandamu: The Prosody of the Telugu and Sanskrit Languages Explained*. Madras: The College Press.

Brown, C. P. and Reddy, G. N., ed. 1978. *Literary Autobiography of C. P. Brown*. Tirupati: Sri Venkateswara University.

Gopalakrishna Rao, K. 1976. *Āndhra Śataka Sāhitya Vikāsamu*. Hyderabad: Published by the author.

Haridasu, Macca. 1984. *Tathaymu Sumatī*: Pariśodhana Vyāsālu. 2002. Karimnagar: Indu Pracuranalu.

Narayana Rao, Velcheru and Shulman, David. 1998. *A Poem at the Right Moment: Remembered Verses from Premodern South India*. Berkeley: University of California Press.

Narayana Rao, Velcheru and Subrahmanyam, Sanjay. 2008. 'History and Politics in the Vernacular: Reflections on Medieval and Early Modern South India', in: Raziuddin Aquil and Partha Chatterjee, eds. *History in the Vernacular*. Ranikhet: Permanent Black.

Olivelle, Parick (tr). 1997. *Pañcatantra*. New York: Oxford University Press.

Pāparaju, Kankaṇṭi. 1970. *Uttara Ramāyaṇamu*. Madras: C. V. Krishna Book Depot.

Ryder, Arthur W., tr. 1962. *The Panchatantra*. (1956) Chicago: University of Chicago Press.

Schmitthenner, Peter. 2001. *Telugu Resurgence: C. P. Brown and Cultural Consolidation in Nineteenth-century South India*. Delhi: Manohar.

Seshayya, Caganti. 1959–1971. *Āndhra Kavitaraṅgiṇi*. 14 vols. Kapilesvarapuramu: Hindu Dharmasastragranthanilayamu.

Sitārāma Śāstri, Pudūri. 1916. *Pěddabālasiksha*. Madras: Vavilla Ramaswami Sastrulu & Sons.

Srīnāthuḍu. 1969. *Kaśīkhaṇḍamu*. Madras: Vavilla Ramaswami Sastrulu & Sons.

Subbarao, Vanguri. 1924. *Śataka Kavula Caritramu*. Narasapuram: Kamalkutir Press and Publishers

Subbarao, Vennelakanti. 1976. *The Life of Vennelacunty Soobarow (Native of Ongole) as Written by Himself.* (1873) Sikindrābādu: Śrī Bhārati Pracuraṇalu.

Sumati Śatakamu. Madras: Adi Sarasvati Mudranalayamu, 1870.

Sumatī Śatakamu. Ed. by Scholars. Kakinada: Karra Accayya, 1913.

Sumati Śatakamu. With a commentary by Gundu Raghava Diskshitulu. Bezawada: Marutiram and Company, 1922

Sumatī Śatakamu. Rajahmundri: Madeti Sanyasayya, 1923.

Sumati Śatakamu. Madras: Vavilla Ramaswami Sastrulu & Sons, 1962.

Sūranna, Piṅgaḷi. 1968. *Rāghavapāṇḍavīyamu*. Madras: Vavilla Ramaswamy Sastrulu & Sons.

Venkata Krishna Sarma, Chennubhatla, ed. 1987. *Bhāskara Śatakamu*. Kurnool: Balasaraswati Book Depot.

Venkata Rao, Nidadavolu. 1966. *Śatakasampuṭamu*, Part I. Hyderabad: Andhra Pradesh Sahitya Akadami.

Veṅkaṭarāyakavi, Polipĕddi. 1982. 'Veṇugopala Śatakamu', in: K. Gopalakrishna Rao, ed. *Adhikṣepa Śatakamulu*. Hyderabad: Andhra Pradesh Sahitya Akadami: 76–123.

Virabhadra Rao, Kottapalli. 1986. *Tĕlugu Sāhityamupai Inglīshu Prabhāvamu*. 2nd revised edition. Secunderabad: Published by author.

Viresalingam, Kandukuri. 2005. *Āndhra Kavula Caritramu*. Hyderabad: Visalandra Publishing House.

Appendix I

T. Velayuda Mudaliar vs. N. Chidambaram Iyer on the message of Ramalinga Adigal (From: *The Theosophist* 4 [1882/1883] 61–64)

THE UTTERANCES OF RAMALINGAM PILLAI

The communication from an esteemed brother, Mr. Velayudam Mudalliar, F. T. S., Tamil Pandit in the Madras Presidency College, which appeared in the THEOSOPHIST for July last, has been excepted to by Mr. N. Chidambaram Iyer, of Trivadi, Madras Presidency, who sends us his criticisms thereupon, together with a joint reply to certain questions of his addressed to a well-known *Chela,* or pupil, of the late Ramalingam Swami. The gentleman says, in a private note to us, that he has "the greatest respect for the Adept Brothers, for the Founders of the Theosophical Society, and for Ramalingam himself, who was no doubt a great man in his own way." He fully believes in the existence of the Brothers, and appreciates the work done by our Society "in so far as it tends to awaken in the minds of the Hindus a respect for the wisdom and learnings of their eminent ancestors." So far, well; but having thus wreathed his rapier with flowers he then makes a lunge with it at the Founders' ribs. "But, I do not at all approve," says he, "either their *indirect attempts* to spread Buddhism in the land of the Hindus, or the apathy with which the elite of the Hindu community view the evil that threatens to seriously injure the religion of their forefathers." This – if we may be pardoned the liberty of saying so – is rhetorical nonsense. The public discourses and private conversations of Colonel Olcott in India will be scrutinised in vain for the slightest evidence upon which the charge of Buddhistic propagandism could be based. That work is confined to Ceylon. His addresses to Hindus have so faithfully mirrored the religious and moral sentiments and aspirations of the people, that they have been voluntarily translated by Hindus into various Indian vernaculars, published by them at their own cost, and circulated all over the Peninsula. They have – as abundant published native testimony proves – stimulated a fervid love for India and her glorious Aryan past, and begun to revive the taste for Sanskrit literature. As for the tone of this magazine, it speaks for itself. Take the thirty-nine numbers thus far issued, and count the articles upon Buddhism in comparison with those upon Hinduism, and it will be found that while confessedly an esoteric

Buddhist, yet the Editor has taken great pains to avoid anything which might look like an Indian propagandism of that philosophy. For two years our Colombo Branch has been publishing a weekly paper – the *Sarasavi Sandaresa* – in advocacy of Buddhism, yet we have carefully abstained from quoting its articles lest we might depart from our rule, of strict impartiality. No, this charge must be ascribed to that orthodox prejudice which, under every phase of religion, begets intolerance and runs into persecution. It may amuse our critic to learn that some narrow-minded Buddhist bigots in Ceylon regard Colonel Olcott as scheming to break down orthodox Buddhism by gradually introducing Hindu ideas about the Soul, and he was publicly called to account because we use the mystic syllable OM on our Society documents and call ourselves *Theo*-sophists! So, too, an eminent Mussalman gentleman among our Fellows was soundly rated by his still more distinguished brother, because he had joined a body of persons banded together to Aryanise Islam!

Following is the correspondence sent us by Mr. Chidambaram; together with the rejoinder of Mr. Velayudham, to whom we submitted it for comment. It scarcely proves the former's case, but still, despite its length, we make place for it to give both sides the chance to be heard. – ED.

THE CORRESPONDENCE

TRIVADI, July 27, 1882.

"My dear friend,

A certain gentleman has recently published certain statements about your celebrated Guru Ramalingam Pillai which I am slow to believe as being wholly correct, and which I know is not the whole truth about the man. Of the numerous disciples of the man there is none who has made such fearful sacrifices in every way as you have done and none so faithful as you are to his cause. For you are I think the only one perhaps that even now declines to quit the very quarters that once witnessed the fame of this remarkable man. Having spent besides, the whole of your time, both day and night, by the side of the man, no one appears in my eyes better fitted than yourself to give a correct account of that man's views and aims.

I therefore wish to draw your attention to the following points, and I have too great confidence in your strict adherence to the cause of truth to doubt for a moment that you will write anything but what is wholly true."

It is not desirable that anything which is not wholly true, and which is not the whole truth, should be published touching the memory of a great man.

Yours sincerely,

N. CHIDAMBARAM IYER.

To Venkatesa Iyer, Vadalur, S. Arcot District.

GREAT LIGHT OF MERCY.

Questions asked by N. Chidambaram Iyer, and replies thereto by the Members of the Shadantha Samarasa Sudha Sanmarga Satya Dharma Sabha of Uttaragnanasittipuranam, otherwise known as Vadalur or Parvathccpuram, in the District of South Arcot in the Madras Presidency.

Q. 1. Did your Guru say that before long the esoteric meaning of the Vedas and Shastras would be revealed by Mahatmas in the North to foreigners?

A. Our Guru said that people in the North were more orthodox than those in the South, and therefore more corrigible, and that he had been sent down by God for the purpose of evangelizing men possessing a black (ignorant) mind with a white (clean) body. *Vide* note (a.)

Q. 2. Did he say that the fatal influences of the Kaliyug would be neutralized in about 10 years?

A. He said that the time was close at hand when God would appear on earth and play on it; that as men had ceased to love virtue, they, as well as animals, would suffer innumerable miseries which, however, would soon be removed by God, by whose power all men would be brought under the sway of his blessed reign. (b.)

Q. 3. Did he not believe in a personal God, especially in Siva, and does he not refer in his works to God as having appeared before him in a physical shape?

A. He never said there was no personal God.[1] He said there was but one God; that that God possessed all the attributes ever assigned to him by man in word or thought, and many other attributes; that the world was governed by persons chosen by Him for the purpose, and that he was one of the chosen few. (c.)

Q. 4. After he had gone into Samadhi and the doors of the room were closed by his orders, was the room opened and the place examined a year

[1] If he had believed in a personal God would he not have so declared? Since the above article was put in type Mr. Chindambaram has kindly sent us for inspection an original copy of a Tamil handbill (Notice) issued by Ramalingam about 10 years ago, together with his (Mr. C's) English rendering of the same. We find upon a careful examination of the Tamil what seems unquestionable evidence that the famous Sadhu believed in the God of the Adwaitees, i. e., a non-personal Universal Essence; and that the wonders he promised to his followers were only to be enjoyed by Siddhas, or Yogis. – ED. T.

later? You told me that the Collector of South Arcot and a member of the Madras Revenue Board at one time asked permission of yourself and others in charge of the room to open it, and that permission was refused. When was this? Was it before or after the expiration of a year from the 30th January, 1874, when your Guru entered on his Samadhi?

A. He said that if his followers should at any time find him apparently lifeless, they should not, thinking him to be dead, either burn or bury him. One day in the month of January, 1874, we found that the breathing had stopped, and for four days we continued to pay our customary respects to him. We then found it necessary to close the doors owing to some disturbance set on foot by some of his followers. Then followed some further disturbance by the police. Some three months after, on the receipt of the police occurrence report, Mr. J. H. Garstin, the then Collector of South Arcot, and Mr. George Banbury, the then Member of the Revenue Board, visited the spot and asked for permission to open the doors, which was, however, refused, and the gentlemen went away evidently satisfied with our conduct. On the 30th month we found the lock opened. A certain bold man entered the room and reported that he found the body of our Guru. *We were not prepared to credit his word.* He subsequently died after suffering many miseries. (d.)

Q. 5. Did he say that after going into Samadhi he would go to Europe or America in his physical or astral body and work there? Did he say that persons from Russia and America would come and preach in India the doctrine of Universal Brotherhood which he was forced to give up for want of support?

A. He said that Europeans would try to take possession of the Vadalur Dharmasala, but will not eventually do so; *that God meant to take him to countries where white men live, as Europe and America; that rumours would reach us that he was seen in those countries; that though this will certainly be true,* no attempt should be made to find him out, and that it was his wish that his followers should not quit the Dharmasala at Vadalur.

He also said that before the advent of God there would be witnessed certain miracles on earth and that all should not be surprised at or deceived by them. (e.)

Q. 6. Did not your Guru predict, as certain Astronomers have since done, that in the course of some 20 years, the greater part of mankind would be carried away by death, and that actuated by a desire to avert this calamity he was endeavouring hard to soothe the wrath of the Almighty? In fact was not this the main aim of his life and of the Sabha started by him?

A. The main object of our Guru was, that all men should enjoy the blessings he himself enjoyed. We find that his prayer to the Almighty was to the effect that he should be the means of imparting such blessings to the world at large. The aim of the Sabha is that every one should try his best to find out truth and act accordingly. (f.)

Q. 7. What was his object in advising his followers to bury the dead bodies of their relations?

A. It should not be supposed that to one that had the power to raise the dead burning would make the task more difficult than burying. It is a sin in us to destroy the body created by God. Learned men say that even where life is extinct the life principle never leaves the body, and that therefore to burn such body would be murder. Besides, as the natural wish is that the dead should return to life in their identical bodies, it is not proper to destroy such bodies. Besides, we know that certain great men, after they enter on their Samadhi, remain with their bodies for a long time. We have seen that the bodies of persons who were considered to be ordinary men, remained free from decay after burial; and as it is difficult to find out the real excellence and virtue of certain persons, it is always safe and advisable to bury the dead as a general rule. (g.)

Q. 8. Was not your Guru serious when he said in the Notice circulated by him that those that frequent his Sabha would witness the phenomena of the dead returning to life and of the old becoming young? You will remember having given me a Tamil copy of the Notice for translation into English.

A. To *witness* the phenomena mentioned in the Notice at the time of their actual occurrence, two things are necessary – 1st, Body (or long life); 2nd, Certain powers. To possess these it is necessary to pray to the Almighty. The Notice in question was issued for the purpose of awakening in men a *desire to acquire* the said requisites. (h.)

Q. 9. Was your Guru a believer in a future birth? Was it not the opinion of your Guru that when a man dies everything in him dies with him, and that Nirvana or Moksha consists in the preservation of this physical body from dissolution?

A. There *is* a future birth. To one that has learned to preserve his body from dissolution there is no future birth. The truth of this will become apparent when the matter is fully analyzed and examined. (i.)

Q. 10. With what object was that huge building erected at a cost of over half a lakh of rupees? With what object was that huge blank book got up which is still preserved under lock and key? (j.)

A. As the building is of service in the elucidation of those principles that throw light on the Nature of God, the obstacles in the way of seeing Him and the means of overcoming these, it resembles a map or plan.

Again, our Guru told us that one day we should find the blank book fully written up, that the writing should be viewed as the Samarasa Veda of the Sabha, and that the Summum Bonum of life and the means of attaining it would be mentioned in it.

The above, we have to remark, will not be clear and satisfactory to those that do not deeply go into the subject.

VENKATESA IYER.

A. SABAPATHI, GURUKKAL.

S. NAYANA REDDIAR.

20th Avani, Chithrabanu.

Notes by N. Chidambaram

(a) Question No. 1 is plain enough. From the reply it does not appear that Ramalingam Pillai ever said that "the esoteric meaning of the Vedas and other sacred books of the East would be revealed by the Mahatmas in the North to foreigners," as stated by Pandit Velayudum Mudalliar. – (Vide pages 243 and 244 of the last July issue of the THEOSOPHIST.)

(b) This sounds not unlike the expected advent of Christ by the Christians. I doubt whether the Founders of the Theosophical Society or the Adept Brothers themselves at all share in some such expectation. It is not improbable that the Pandit himself, judging from the signs of the time, was led to the opinion which he ascribes to his Guru. [Here follow some irrelevant remarks by the writer which, being based upon flagrant misinformation as to our Society and, moreover, couched in objectionable language, are omitted. – ED. T.

(c) This and reply to question No. 2 do not seem to indicate that in Ramalingam Pillai's opinion, "what men call God is in fact the principle of Universal love which produces and sustains perfect harmony and equilibrium throughout all Nature," as stated by the Tamil Pandit.

(d) From this it is evident that it is not true that the "door was locked by his orders," as stated by the Pandit, nor "the only opening walled up." It is also clear that the place was not "opened and examined a year later," but fully 30 months later, nor is it true that "there was nothing to be seen but a vacant room," for there was the body of Ramalingam Pillai as reported by the only eye-witness that had the courage to enter the room and examine it, though this is discredited by those that chose to remain without.

(e) Question No. 5 is plain enough. It does not appear from the reply to it that Ramalingam Pillai ever "exclaimed that the time is not far off when persons from Russia and America will come to India and preach the doctrine of Universal Brotherhood." Nay, more; the last sentence of the reply, if it means anything at all, would seem to show that the Sabha is not prepared to "appreciate the grand truths" preached by foreigners, nor are they inclined to attach any importance, agreeably to the instructions of their Guru, to the "many wonders worked by the Brothers who live in the North."

(f) Questions No. 6 to No. 10 were suggested to me by various discussions which I had with Venkatesa Iyer, the most important Chela of Ramalingam Pillai, in fact one of the very few that even now strictly adhere to the instruction of the Guru, and who, unlike the Tamil Pandit, gave up years ago his lucrative profession as a practitioner at a mofussil bar and now resides at Vadalur. Question No. 6 is plain enough; still a direct reply to it has not been vouchsafed. The reply, however, shows that Ramalingam was a firm believer in a personal God and that he wanted to assume the position of a Saviour of mankind.

(g) Here is a clear hint that Ramalingam Pillai entertained the Christian notion of the possibility of the resurrection of the dead. While Ramalingam was for burial, the members of the Theosophical Society are, I believe, in favour of cremation.

(h) There is a clear mention made here of that one thing with which Ramalingam Pillai's memory is inseparably connected in the eyes of those that know anything of him, viz., his promise to raise the dead. To speak of Ramalingam and to omit his avowed powers to raise the dead, is to describe the figure of "Polyphemus with his eye out."

I am prompted to remark that of all the Pandit's omissions in publishing a true version of Ramalingam Pillai's life this seems to be the most serious and objectionable.

(i) I cannot suppose for a moment that the Theosophical Society at all entertain the opinion that one can wholly escape paying the final debt to Nature.

(j) As the 13th sentence is not clear I may be allowed to state here what the popular notion is on the subject, viz., that the building was erected for the purpose of receiving God when he makes his advent.

You will thus note that there are several important points in connection with the life of Ramalingam Pillai, of which not the least mention is made by the Pandit in his account of the same. Far from the views of Ramalingam Pillai being "identically those of the Theosophical Society," you will observe that there is not one important point about which both parties would mutually shake hands; or one common ground except perhaps as to the obnoxious distinctions of caste in which Ramalingam Pillai was naturally much interested for this plain reason, viz., that he occupied, though by the accident of birth, the lowest round of the ladder, or, in other words, he was a Sudra. In conclusion, I shall also leave the readers "to draw their own inferences from the facts" as you have done.[2]

N. CHIDAMBARAM IYER

Trivadi, September 24, 1882.

Rejoinder of Pandit Velayudam.[3]

The Iyer says that there were numerous errors and omissions in the life of Ramalingam Pillai as sketched by the Tamil Pandit. Nowhere does the author of the criticism, N. Chidambaram Iyer, say what the error is. The criticism, seems to be full of irrelevant questions and answers.

Supposing that he means the passage "I need hardly remark that these principles are identically those of the Theosophical Society" to be an error, the meaning of the phrase "Samarasa Veda Sanmarga Sangam," as understood from the works of Ramalingam Pillai, and the primary objects of the Theosophical Society, as given in the rule book of the Society (on page 5), show to any man of ordinary common sense, how the principles of both the Societies may be considered identical.

Samarasa Veda Sanmarga Sangam is a society formed to propagate a feeling of Brotherhood and social unity among all mankind without distinction of caste or creed, as enjoined in the Vedas and Agamams, and to look after the well being and happiness of all living objects, without doing the slightest harm; knowing that the nature of the Supreme Power is to pervade all life and to inseparably connect itself with the Soul.

What N. Chidambaram Iyer means by the Question 1 cannot easily be seen.

It was written that Ramalingam Pillai said that those who are capable of being members of the Sangam exist in the North. That this statement is true, Venkatesa Iyer (the so-called chief Chela, by the critic) and the rest admit. Is it a mistake to say that Mahatmas are the only fit persons to explain and reveal the Vedas and Shastras, when once their existence is admitted?

It is nowhere pointed out in the Pandit's sketch that Ramalingam Pillai ever said that there is not a Personal God. Here may be adduced in favour of the statement "That what men call 'God' is, in fact, the principle of Universal Love," a stanza from "Thirumanthiram" by "Thirumular" one of the Sivemata Acharyas, and who lived for 3,000 years.

---

[2] Certainly they will, and perhaps some may fail to agree with our correspondent. We should say this was more than probable. – ED. T.

[3] Freely rendered into English by G Subbiah Chetty Garu, F. T. S., who speaks in the third person. – ED. T.

"The ignorant say that Love and Brahmam are different. None know how love becomes Brahmam. After knowing that love is Brahmam one becomes absorbed in love and Brahmam."

This is also shown in Ramalingam Pillai's works, viz., "Arulperumjothi Akaval," &c Nothingmore is said in the sketch about a personal God.

Question 5 – "You are not fit to become ... upon this country." (P. 224, THEOSOPHIST, July number.) N. C. might have meant to call an error. That this is a fact Venkatesa Iyer and others admit; though not in the very same words, yet in other words. Sabapathy Gurukal, who signs N. C.'s criticism also signs the certificate appended to the Tamil pamphlet published by the Pandit.

If the statement that the door was closed by the orders of Ramalingam Pillai be untrue, and that it was closed (4) four days after, without his orders, be true, could these (Venkata Iyer and others) the chief Chelas, do what was not ordered by their Guru? Let wise readers judge. If it be an error to have said that the door of the Samadhi room was opened 12 months after, when it was 30 months after, the Pandit need only remark that he was not present at Vadalur and that he only wrote what he had heard. That the remains of Ramalingam Pillai were found by the daring fellow who entered the Samadhi room, even Venkatesa Iyer himself does not believe.

It is said that the Pandit has made many omissions in his sketch of the life of Ramalingam Pillai which Chidambaram Iyer and Venkatesa Iyer hint at by a series of questions and answers. (Can omissions be considered as errors?)

As the lectures of Ramalingam Pillai were of a scientific nature, the Pandit interpreting their meaning in a scientific light, wrote his sketch. He does not, like others, give a fabulous meaning to what has been said. If this (the fabulous meaning) be the real meaning of the sayings we shall rejoice to see them fulfilled.

N. Chidambaram Iyer says, "I have the greatest respect for the Adept Brothers (Mahatmas), and for Ramalingam Pillai himself who was no doubt a great man in his own way." And yet further writes: there is not one point about which both parties could mutually shake hands as on common ground, except perhaps in the impropriety which both perceived "in the obnoxious distinction of caste in which Ramalingam Pillai was much interested for the plain reason, viz., that he occupied through the accident of birth the lowest round of the ladder or, in other words, he was a Sudra."

Not only Ramalingam Pillai and the Founders of the Theosophical Society, but also the Upanishads and the works of the Rishis named by

N. C., and those of Sankaracharya, the Guru of the present Brahmins, imply that the distinction of caste is nothing but trivial prejudice.

"O! Precious! He who has seen you is divine and finds divinity (Pasa Brahmemo) in everything he sees, such as grass, trees, &c."

Such is the meaning of a stanza of Ramalingam Pillai. But why should Venkatesa Iyer be called the Chief Chela? While there is no one to object to his being called even the Chiefest, the Pandit does not at all say, nor presume to say, that he is the only Chela of R. P.'s. It may here be asked how long it is since Venkatesa Iyer became a *Sanyasi.*

(for) T. VELAYUDAM MUDALLIAR, F. T. S.,
Tamil Pandit of Presidency College.
Madras, October 30, 1882.

EDITOR'S NOTE. – The matter must stop here; at least until we can see some better reasons than at present to continue it. The facts are all in and the reader can judge which party is nearest right.

Appendix II

Sources on the contact between J. M. Nallasvami Pillai and Vivekananda

K. Sundarama Iyer

(From: *Vedanta Kesari*, January-February 1923; reprinted in *Reminiscences of Vivekananda by his eastern and western admirers*. 4th edition. Kolkata: Advaita Ashrama, Publication Department, 2008. pp. 85–88)

Later in the same afternoon, at about 4 p. m., there came a deputation to the Swami from Tiruppattur in the Salem District, a place now transferred to the North Arcot District. The Swami was, I think, seated in the same room as before. The deputation consisted of five or six persons, all Shaivites. There was no Brahmin among them. This would be easily understood, when one knows that they seemed – at least to me – to have been prepared and sent on to meet the Swami by the then District Munsiff of the place, who was later on in the same year to become the founder and editor of the *Siddhânta- Deepikâ,* now for some years defunct, and also the founder and organizer of the movement known as the "Shaiva-Siddhânta-Mahâsabhâ", which continues still to hold a peripatetic annual gathering and has also given the inspiration for many local Shaiva Sabhas and their activities and annual festive gatherings. Mr. Nallaswami Pillai was well known to me and even very friendly. Though he was a strong advocate of the Shaiva cult and *siddhânta,* he wanted to liberalize it and propagate its tenets so as to make it acceptable to all, not only in India, but all over the world. He seemed to me – and I still think so – to have been fired by the example of the Swami and his activities and triumphal progress in America, England, India, and elsewhere. He was anxious to maintain the traditions of Shaivism, and to include the Brahmins, too, among the believers and brethren of the Shaivafaith. As the Swami was an Advaitin, the deputation from Tiruppattur was, perhaps, expressly prepared and sent to beard the lion in his den and to tackle him on some fundamental points of Advaita doctrine. The head of the deputation had a whole sheet filled with questions, and he told the Swami that he wanted answers. The Swami nodded assent, and wanted him to begin. The first question was, "How does the Unmanifested become the manifested?" The Swami's reply came on at once without a moment's hesitation, but it fell, too, like thunder from the blue vault of heaven, paralyzing its victims and stultifying their nervous system and its workings. The same question was put later at one of the Swami's question meetings (in the *shâmiâna* put up for the purpose at Castle Kernan) by a young Mâdhva Brahmin who was then, I think, a college student and is now an active member of the Madras Corporation. He, too, got the same answer, couched in the same or similar terms, and with the same stunning and electrifying effect. The Swami's reply was, "Questions of how, why, or wherefore relate to the manifested world, and not to the Unmanifested which is above all change and causation and therefore above all relation to the changing universe and our *sâmsârika* (transmigrating) life in it. The question, therefore, is not one which can be reasonably put. Put a proper question – a more rational question – and I will answer." The reply brought about an *impasse,* and his interlocutors felt that they were face to face with one who could meet and solve philosophic puzzles and queries of all kinds, a master before whom they must need bow in humility and meekness rather than launch forth in a game of dialectics. They seemed at once to have forgotten their carefully prepared and transcribed scheme and synopsis of questions in the manuscript they had brought, and suddenly, felt the wand of the magician in their front, and his enchantment was stealing over their minds and hearts with its occult power and overpowering grasp. The Swami at once realized the situation. Then followed a scene which it is not possible adequately to depict. This past master of the arts and weapons of Indian dialectics, this lion of the Vedanta with his conquering air and roar, the impetuous and rolling thunder of his voice, and his lower jaw symbolizing, as he once told me himself, his "combative temperament" all on a sudden became transformed into what seemed a long-lost comrade of one's youth or a tenderly-loved brother restored after a long separation and whole-heartedly interested in all that concerned one's welfare. The Swami began to address them in a strain and in tones captivating all his listeners and all who were present. He spoke somewhat as follows: The best way to serve and seek God is to serve the needy, to feed the hungry, to console the stricken, to help the fallen and friendless, to attend upon and serve those who are ill and require service, and so on and on. The deputation kept listening while the Swami's heart went out to them in a fervour of passionate exhortation to serve their fellow-men. It seemed as if after all they had met the one messenger of joy and peace from heaven for whom they had been searching in vain, one in whom there was no doubt or equivocation, a master who had searched their hearts and finding the void in them, had supplied the pabulum they needed, had taught them the central truth of life and of deliverance from its troubles. The shades of evening fell, they offered their homage at the feet of the saint; and as they took their departure, their countenances showed traces of a new light having touched their hearts and given them a new impulse to life and work.

K. M. Balasubramaniam

(From: K. M. Balasubramaniam, *The Life of J. M. Nallaswami Pillai.* Tiruchirapalli: Githa Press, 1965, pp. ix, 122–125)

(The description of the historic meeting between Swami Vivekananda and Mr. Nallaswami Pillai is entirely based on the faithful account of it given by the late Sri Isaana Sivaacharya Swamigal at a public meeting at Chennimalai in 1947. The Sivaacharya authenticated with his word of honour and averred that he, as a youth had had it described to him in all details by the late Mr. Nallaswami himself.)

Innumerable were the receptions that the enthusiastic public of Madras arranged in honour of the Swamiji. The glorious and eloquent addresses that the Swamiji himself delivered then are also too well known. They have become literature on Hindu Religion. In one of these meetings held in honour of Vivekananda, Mr. Nallaswami Pillai had to take part. His pre-eminent position in the religious world as a powerful exponent of Saivism could not be ignored by the people who were in charge of the Swamiji's reception. In the course of the speech extolling the services of Swami Vivekananda, Mr. Nallaswami Pillai naturally enough made references to Saint Gnanasambandar and his unrivalled services to Saivism. Of course, he also said something about his pet creed of Agamantam and the principal features thereof. The great Swamiji was very much struck with those features of Saiva Siddhantam that were in vogue in the Tamil country, It was strange that he had not heard about these things. He confessed to a sense of regret that he had not known of them before. Naturally, like a true searcher after truth that he was, the Swamiji was curious to know something more about them in detail. He cordially invited Mr. Pillai to come to him and have a talk. There took place a meeting between the two – the redoubtable champion of the Idealistic View and the resourceful advocate of Suddhādvaita Saivism.

The interesting and epoch-making talk between the pair of savants of two different sects of Hinduism took place at Mylapore to the amazement of all. To begin with, Swami Vivekananda expressed his pleasant surprise at the interesting story of St. Sambandar. Then the conversation drifted to the essential tenets of Siddhantam. Mr. Nallaswami Pillai postulated the existence of the Tripadartha i. e. Pathi, Pasu and Pāsam, which according to the Siddhantic School are the sheet-anchor of its metaphysics. "Belief in the eternal existence of these three fundamental entities constituted the bed-rock and the back-bone of Siddhanta Saivism. On the ultimate analysis of the world, said Mr. Pillai, everything in the universe, the seen and the unseen resolves itself into one of the three eternal Verities, They are God, Soul and Pasam or Bondage." Needless it is to point out that this is entirely opposed to the Vedantic doctrine of Vivekananda. There is only one thing and that is God. It is otherwise called the Self. All other things we see are nothing, mere illusion, Maya. And it is here that the difference comes in and it was on these points that Mr. Pillai dwelt in detail in order to completely clarify them. "The conception of the Monistic Maya is altogether different from the conception of Siddhantic Maya," continued Mr. J. M. N. "The former means illusion, a negation, a non-substance while the latter means a positive substance that not merely exists but is also eternal. There is such a thing as soul which is also eternal and which has a distinct existence. God is at once a separate entity and also one with souls and the universe." Of course, it is impossible for us so easily to give a detailed account of what all Mr. Nallaswami spoke on that occasion to the Swamiji. But let us only consider the fact namely that, in spite of the initial immunity of the Swamiji to any conversion, in the course of the talk he, however, saw the entire beauty of the conception. Visishtadvaitam, of course, Swami Vivekananda had known and that too very well. But Sri Kanta's commentary and the Siddhantic edifice based upon the Saiva Agamas he bad not been familiar with. When Mr. Nallaswami Pillai had spent much of his energy, intelligence and ingenuity in completely presenting to the Swamiji a comprchensive picture of Agamantam, the latter became perfectly convinced that the doctrines of Saiva Siddhantam were altogether logical and perfect. But then, he asked Mr. Nallaswami Pillai as follows:

"Would it not be a source of greater help and clarity if, instead of these three (i. e. Pathi, Pasu and Pasam) a few more verities were invented and added as the constituent elements of the universe?"[1]

Mr. Pillai: "Is it not a fact that everything has a definition based on a clear analysis of the thing?"

Swamiji: "Yes, of course"

Mr. Pillai: "The Siddhantins have by their experience postulated these three entities as fundamental and have given the definition of each one in clear and unmistakable terms. For example, God is Pure Intelligence, Love and Light Who knows everything by Himself and enables souls to know. He exists by Himself and enables all else to exist. The soul is an intelligent being no doubt but it cannot by itself and without the aid of God see or know anything. Pasam or the world cannot know anything; it is insentient. God is all-knowledge; soul is capable of knowledge but is saturated with impurity or wrapped in darkness and the world is unknowing and incapable of knowing. This unintelligent world (Pasam) is neither the All-knowing God nor the soul, which is ignorance. Each one of the three has a separate and exhaustive definition and everything we know must come under one head or the other. So far as we have been able to see, there cannot possibly be a fourth thing with a distinct definition other than these three.

"If, however, the Swamiji or some one else could kindly mention any such extra entity, we can certainly add it on to these three things we have already known."

The great Swami Vivekananda was unable to conceive of any thing that could not be possibly brought under the head of one or the other of these three entities. Hence he magnanimously confessed to his inability to see anything in addition to these three and thanked and complimented Mr. Nallaswami Pillai. And as we have already mentioned the Swamiji expressed his wish that he had known about these things earlier. Mr. Pillai, after discussing with Swamiji some other knotty problems like the origin of the universe or the cause of creation etc. and clearly explaining the answers furnished by Siddhantam to these baffling questions, sincerely thanked that High-Priest of Hinduism and took leave of him with pleasure.

Pleasure and pride Mr. Pillai must have felt in the highest degree possible. And who would have been more perfectly justified than he? The pleasure was at the fact that God Siva, the All-Love had so contrived to arrange for such an historic interview between himself and the Swamiji as would otherwise have been certainly well-nigh impossible. It is also stated that the immortal H. H. Bhaskara Sethupathi, the then Rajah of Ramnad had sponsored this interview. The pride of course, was born from the conviction his Siddhantam had wrought in the sage.!

[1] (Editor:) This passage has a parallel to a note in *Siddhanta Deepika* 1 (1897/1898) 119–120, probably written by Nallasvami:

The October number of the 'Awakened India' has a short appreciative notice of our last two issues and proceeds to say, "An another side aims at establishing the preference of Sivite Siddhanta over the Vedanta. The Vedantin welcomes all such attempts and says, 'so long as it is a mere matter of theory why assume only three padarthas, assume three hundred as well, if by that means, you can simplify the problem and put an end to all metaphysical wrangeling.[']" We appreciate no doubt the good nature which prompted the observation but we fail to see neither logic nor truth in it? All systems divide themselves into a code of practice, moral and spiritual and the exposition of a metaphysical or natural Theory as to the nature of things, and their ultimate origin or resolution.

Contributors

Gnanasigamony Aloysius is a sociologist and historian, who works as an independent scholar in New Dehli. He is the author of *Religion as Emancipatory Identity: A Buddhist Movement among the Tamils under Colonialism* (New Delhi, 1998) and *Nationalism without a Nation in India* (Delhi, 2007).

Michael Bergunder is Professor of History of Religions and Intercultural Theology at the University of Heidelberg. He has recently published *The South Indian Pentecostal Movement in the Twentieth Century* (Grand Rapids, 2008) and edited *Westliche Formen des Hinduismus in Deutschland* (Halle, 2006).

Heiko Frese is an indologist and historian, affiliated to the University of Heidelberg. He is the author of *Variationen von Wirklichkeit: das Bild Jayasthitimallas in der Bhasavamsavali* (Hamburg, 2002), and co-editor of *Text and Context in the History, Literature and Religion of Orissa* (New Delhi, 2004).

Chris Fuller is Professor of Anthropology at the London School of Economics and Political Science. His major publications include *The Renewal of the Priesthood: Modernity and Traditionalism in a South Indian Temple* (Princeton, 2003) and *The Camphor Flame: Popular Hinduism and Indian Society* (Princeton, 1992). *Haripriya Narasimhan* is Research Fellow in Anthropology at the London School of Economics.

Mary Hancock is Professor of Anthropology and History at the University of California, Santa Barbara. She is the author of *The Politics of Heritage from Madras to Chennai* (Bloomington, 2008) and *Womanhood in the Making: Domestic Ritual and Public Culture in Urban South India* (Boulder, 1999).

Andreas Nehring is Professor of Religious Studies and Intercultural Theology at the University of Erlangen-Nürnberg. He is the author of *Orientalismus und Mission: Studien zur Repräsentation der südindischen Kultur und Religion durch deutsche Missionare 1840-1945* (Wiesbaden, 2003), and co-editor of *Religious Turns–Turning Religions: Veränderte kulturelle Diskurse, neue religiöse Wissensformen* (Stuttgart, 2008).

Vakulabharanam Rajagopal is Lecturer at the Department of History, University of Hyderabad, India. He is the author of 'Fashioning Modernity in Telugu: Viresalingam and His Interventionist Strategy' in: *Studies in History* 21,1 (2005), and 'The Rhetorical Strategy of an Autobiography: Reading Satyavati's Atmacaritamu' in: *Indian Economic and Social History Review* 40,4 (2003).

Velcheru Narayana Rao is Professor Emeritus, Languages and Cultures of Asia, University of Wisconsin-Madison. He is the author of *God on the Hill: Temple Songs from Tirupati* (with David Shulman, New York, 2005), and the co-author of *Textures of Time: Writing History in South India* (Delhi, 2002).

Peter Schalk is Professor of History of Religions at Uppsala University in Sweden. His publications include *Buddhism among Tamils in Pre-Colonial Tamiḻakam and Īḻam* (Uppsala, 2002) and *God as Remover of Obstacles: A Study of Caiva Soteriology among Īḻam Tamil Refugees in Stockholm, Sweden* (Uppsala, 2004).

Ulrike Schröder is a scholar of history of religions, who currently works in the collaborative research centre 'Ritual Dynamics' at the University of Heidelberg. She is the author of *Religion, Kaste und Ritual: Christliche Mission und tamilischer Hinduismus in Südindien im 19. Jahrhundert* (Halle, 2009) and 'Hook-Swinging in South India: Negotiating the Subaltern Space within a Colonial Society' in: *Negotiating Rites*, ed. by U. Hüsken and F. Neubert (New York, 2010).

Torsten Tschacher is a south asianist and research fellow in the Cluster of Excellence 'Asia and Europe in a Global Context: Shifting Asymmetries in Cultural Flows' at Heidelberg University. He is the author of *Islam in Tamilnadu: Varia* (Halle, 2001) and 'Rational Miracles, Cultural Rituals and the Fear of Syncretism: Defending Contentious Muslim Practice among Tamil-speaking Muslims' in: *Asian Journal of Social Science* 37, 1 (2009).

Ravi Vaitheespara is Associate Professor for History at the University of Manitoba. His recent publications include *Theorizing the National Crisis: Sanmugathasan, the Left and the Ethnic Conflict in Sri Lanka* (Colombo, 2007) and 'Maraimalai Atigal and the Genealogy of the Tamilian Creed' in: *Economic and Political Weekly,* Vol. XLIV, No.14, April 4, 2009, pp. 45–51.

A. R. Venkatachalapathy is Professor of History at the Madras Institute of Development Studies, India. His recent publications include *In Those Days There Was No Coffee: Writings in Cultural History* (New Delhi, 2006) and *Muccanti ilakkiyam* (Nagercoil, 2004).

Index